Venice and the Renaissance

The MIT Press
Cambridge, Massachusetts
London, England

Venice and the Renaissance

Manfredo Tafuri

translated by
Jessica Levine

English translation © 1989 Massachusetts Institute of Technology

Originally published under the title *Venezia e il Rinascimento* © 1985 by Giulio Einaudi editore s.p.a., Turin.

This book was set in Sabon and Futura by Asco Trade Typesetting Ltd., Hong Kong, and printed and bound in the United States of America.

Library of Congress Cataloging-in-Publication Data

Tafuri, Manfredo.
   [Venezia e il Rinascimento. English]
   Venice and the Renaissance / Manfredo Tafuri; translated by
Jessica Levine.
       p.   cm.
   Translation of: Venezia e il Rinascimento.
   Bibliography: p.
   Includes index.
   ISBN 0-262-20072-4
   1. Venice (Italy)—Civilization—To 1797.   2. Renaissance—Italy—
Venice.   3. Architecture, Renaissance—Italy—Venice.   I. Title.
DG675.6.T2413   1989
945'.3107—dc19   89-2792
                                                          CIP

Contents

Introduction

Venice and the Renaissance: two antithetical abstractions, held together by an ambiguous and disjunctive *and*. At first glance, the title of this book contains something paradoxical that does not vanish even when one repeatedly brings it into focus. In fact, which Venice? The official one, of "myth" and apologies, satisfied with the fullness of her own representations, or the Venice increasingly shaken by internal conflicts, marked by anxieties that obliquely cut across classes and groups? And then, will one be talking about the Venice that has preserved as a valuable heritage the institutions and mentality of the late Middle Ages, or of the city that partakes of the new mental universes under construction? An *Idealtypus*, someone will reply, contains all antitheses tranquilly: Venice is this, and more.

An abstraction, therefore—one of those that Paul Veyne warned us against[1]—and as such it can only be used with difficulty. But the worn concept of the Renaissance is no better off. The same question imposes itself here: which Renaissance? The one conceived in macrosociological terms by Alfred Doren, Alfred von Martin, and Frederick Antal, which is by now very dated? Or the one of Roberto Lopez, who sees inconsistencies between the economic recession of the fourteenth and fifteenth centuries and culture, attempting a dialectical reading of such phenomena? Or should one speak of a "long Renaissance"—as Cantimori wished and as, in the end, Braudel maintained—or of an inflection in European history that is to be read on its own? And how does one reconcile "high" history with material history, the mystical afflatus of evangelical thought with the rebirth of Greek mathematics, the new episteme [knowledge] with the cabalistic alchemy of the Word, the long duration of the institutions with the brevity of innovations?

There is good reason to abandon the universe constructed by Michelet and Burckhardt, and to dedicate ourselves to the "particular": the Renaissance, in the end, lies only in the title of this book.[2]

Moreover, is it not possible that such difficulties are, perhaps, due to the traditional use of historical categories? Instead of characterizing the latter as "containers," wouldn't it be more productive to try to use them metaphorically? In other words: one could try to distinguish ephemeral boundary lines, or limits, in the immense collection of phenomena that have been crushed by the words Venice and Renaissance. Venice: she can be seen as the place in which antitheses have been removed, in which dialectics has no function, in which there is no contradiction between tradition and innovation, development and memory, continuity and renewal, sacred and mundane. A large part of this book demonstrates the way in which Venice tried to *endure within her origin*: Venice will become the symbol of such a resistance, when continuity in her begins to be betrayed by repetition and impotent fetishism.

Analogously, the Renaissance can be considered as the moment in modern history of *repraesentatio*. In *Holzwege* Heidegger speaks of the "era of the image of the world":[3] an era in which man carries before him "simple presence like a contrary thing," brought back to the subject, produced (pre-formed) by the subject. Heidegger sees the essence of the "modern" in the world's becoming an image and in man's becoming *subjectum*: "it is not surprising that humanism imposes itself only there, where the world has become image."[4]

To such a "construction," the architecture, cartography, the new systems of surveying, and even the new military art gave a fundamental contribution between the fifteenth and sixteenth centuries. And here again a difficult relationship with Venice stands out: the city that Jacopo de' Barbari depicted and gave one of the most complete and amazing representations is the same that adopted, from 1474 to 1808–11, uniquely descriptive cadastres. But it is also a city that gave birth to an advanced plan, like the one of Cristoforo Sabbadino (1557), and in which an entire Senate debated the features to be given to the urban center.

"Era of the image of the world": a disturbing metaphor. Implicit in it is the configuration of a destiny. If one takes Heidegger literally, one risks adopting, for the culture of the fourteenth, fifteenth, and sixteenth centuries, a prejudice that is similar to the one that is rendered overpowering by the writings of Ernst Cassirer: in the latter, the sequential development of Western philosophy is extended on an inclined plane, teleologically oriented toward a contemporary thought that proceeds through calculation and planning.[5] Whoever intends to avoid apologizing for the present and wishes to turn toward the past in order to "work with it," in order to liberate current decisions from surreptitious weights, will have to submit similar teleologies to criticism. The encounters and conflicts that took place in Venice in the fifteenth and sixteenth centuries render invisible fractures that would gradually become fatal. But as long as these conflicts remain open, a proliferation of hypotheses and endeavors can emerge from the debate: we intend to make history out of such products, granting the expectations the same rights as the resistances, delays, anachronisms.

It is inevitable, then, that our point of observation should be placed at the nodes where events, times, and mentalities intersect. It involves the reconstruction of the ways in which political decisions, religious anxieties, the arts and sciences, the *res aedificatoria* became irrevocably interwoven: especially in the case of Venice, rigidly disciplinary histories end up demonstrating their own poverty. But more than that: a history of plots requires an adequate philology, capable of setting the problem of verification astride several disciplines. For these reasons the present book does not meet the requirement of "completeness." The narration concentrates around a set of events that have been chosen based on the questions guiding our research, and inevitably leaves "blanks"—invitations for research and further verifications. Nor should it be necessary to warn the reader that our work has no connection with the sociology of art or with similar historiographical products. And it should not be necessary to recall the "fathers"—Simiand, Bloch, Febvre—to remember that history is called upon to create its own plots out of men, their interactions, and their mentalities.

An undefined history, the history of mentalities, Le Goff warned us.[6] A science based on mutability and subtlety, it can use—according to the French historian—quantitative methods developed by social psychologists, but it is mainly characterized by the emergence of a sphere removed from traditional history, as it places itself there, where the individual and the collective, the unconscious and the intentional, structure and circumstance converge.

As a collective apparatus, mentality obliquely cuts across groups and individuals, involving unreflective behaviors, ignoring oppositions and struggles. For this reason it is articulated, made plural, and above all confronted by its immediate rival: the history of ideas and conflicts.

By setting the history of a constructed environment within institutional history, religious history, and the history of mentalities, we are not necessarily turning it into an effect of "structural" causes, nor are we taking away its specificity. On the contrary, our efforts are directed toward eliminating—insofar as possible—prejudices, toward liberating the history of architecture and the city from the suffocating and provincial ghetto to which some of its scholars have tended to confine it. Moreover, visible forms—as we will amply demonstrate—carefully conceal the history of their genesis and, even more so, conceal the losing alternatives: from the archives and the testimonies of contemporaries there emerges a continuous stream of projects that together describe "other" cities, never realized but reconstructible as future objects of historical investigation. It is necessary to go beyond mere appearance and to ask these unrealized projects the reasons for their failure.

This is all the more the case for a reality like the Venetian one, which is so inflated with visual values and such a jealous custodian of its own inner tensions. And though we proudly oppose all normative history, the present work has something to offer our adopted city. The symbolic status of nondialectical Venice has been captured by Nietzsche, beyond all romanticism: "A hundred deep solitudes taken together form the city of Venice—that is her charm. An image for the men of the future."[7] It is a question of a Venice disconnected from "firm ground," resistant in austere duty, about which Massimo Cacciari has written profound pages.[8] This Venice is a problem for the "moderns." Fascinated by a crystalized continuity, which has been mistaken for banal organic unity—perhaps to be regained—they cannot tolerate the challenge that Venice hurls out to them. And they multiply their violent and faithless attempts, with sadistic traits that are barely hidden beneath the masks of phrases like "respectful project," the "past as friend," and the "new Caprice,"—masks of mummification of ephemeral revitalization.

This book has nothing to communicate to such practitioners. But for those who truly intend to try to listen, it can indicate ways to remove the obstacles that turn Venice into a problem that becomes more and more disturbing with every distortion.

The research that gave birth to this book was financed by research funds from the Ministero della Pubblica Istruzione and by the Consiglio Nazionale delle Ricerche.

The author wishes to thank all those who have helped, aided, or advised him in the course of his work: Doctor Maria Francesca Tiepolo, director of the Archivio di Stato in Venice, Professor Giandomenico Romanelli, director of the Museo Correr, Doctor Mario Piana, of the Sopraintendenza ai Beni Architettonici e Ambientali in Venice, Doctor Fernando Rigon, director of the Museo Civico in Vicenza, Professors Howard Burns, Donatella Calabi, Ennio Concina, Gaetano Cozzi, Antonio Foscari, Christoph Luitpold Frommel, Fernando Marías, Paolo Morachiello, Lionello Puppi, Carlos Sambricio, Wolfgang Wolters, Doctors Antonella Barzazi, Giovanni Battista Gleria, Antonio Manno, Stefano Maso. Special thanks, for their dedication and patience, go to the secretaries of the Dipartimento di Storia dell'Architettura in Venice, Bruna Fontanella, Laura Correggiari, and Tiziana Semenzin. What the author and his book owe Doctor Manuela Morresi—who on a practical level revised the manuscript and edited the index of names—cannot be expressed with mere thanks.

Venice and the Renaissance

Memoria et Prudentia.
Patrician Mentalities and
res aedificatoria

Writing toward the end of 1539, Nicolò Zen—the twenty-five-year-old future *Magistrato sopra i Beni Inculti* [Reclamation Commissioner], *Savio alle Acque* [Minister of the Waterways], *Provveditore alle Fortezze* [Commissioner of Fortresses], and reorganizer of the Arsenal—bitterly reflected upon the condition of the smaller Italian powers and alluded to the perils menacing the *Serenissima's* primary value, that is to say, republican liberty.[1] His essay, which was dedicated to the Venetian-Turkish war of 1537, set forth the pacificist, pro-Gritti political line taken by the Zen family. Even more so, it revealed a conception strongly rooted in the "orginal" value of commerce. Seen as the foundation of internal harmony and identified as the Republic's instrument of greatness, the exercise of commerce was for the author the ring that united domestic strategies and state politics: service rendered for the homeland was identified with private "fame and honor." The manuscript constitutes valuable testimony of a particular mentality—one that jealously guarded a tradition founded on the mythic interpretation of the lagoon's first inhabitants offered by Cassiodorus in his famous letter asking for auxiliaries for the fortress of Ravenna:

You have abundance only of fish, rich and poor live together in equality. The same food and similar houses are shared by all; wherefore they cannot envy each other's hearths, and so they are free from the vices that rule the world. All your emulation centers on the salt works; instead of ploughs and scythes you work rollers (to pack the base of salt pans) whence comes all your gain. Upon your industry all other products depend, for although there may be somebody who does not seek gold, there never yet lived the man who desires not salt, which makes every food more savory.[2]

The Zen family demonstrates their loyalty to these same values: the idealization of equality as the foundation of internal harmony, and the commercial destiny of Venice. The antimilitary attitude and the reaffirmation of the centrality of the *Stato da Mar* [Maritime State] should be read as a link between

Nicolò's essay and certain testimonials of Venetian "dissent"—for example, dating from about four decades earlier, that of Domenico Morosini[3]—in order to define a group with precise political and cultural characteristics. A struggle against the causes of the growing crisis, a revision of mental systems, and a promotion of technology and sciences are chapters of a *renovatio* to which the Zens made a determining contribution. But they did not intend to break with tradition: like most of the lagoon's patrician class, the Zens did not identify *renovatio* with the cult of pure and absolute *novitas*. Renewal, on the contrary, was a goal that could be realized through a "progression" that was also a "return": the original could guarantee, legitimize, and confirm the "new."

Nicolò Zen explores this universe of values in his reflections on the causes of the decadence of the ancients and moderns: his reflection implied a search for a collective behavior that was to be adopted in the immediate present. And here we find that, what is particularly interesting, his remarks include meticulous observations on the public functions of art and architecture. The great powers, he asserts, began "without pomp, without concern for vainglory or needless expenses": an echo of the austere ethic that Cassiodorus attributed to the first Venetians. But once these powers have grown,

When one, two, and three generations or more have passed, they fall into the same sins as those they have conquered and, as though they could no longer acquire either empire or fame, or as though they could no longer lose what they had acquired, they think only of idleness and pleasure, and then they come to value architects, songs, sounds, players, palaces, clothes, and having put arms aside, they scorn furthermore those who enjoy them, and certain other follies are valued, that are commonly called courtier's arts. But miserable is that city, that Prince who enjoys such entertainments, because he will be subjugated by vile and ignoble people, and if not briefly, then gradually, will lose his reputation, and the State in the end will remain subject to the most vile people.[4]

Behind such admonishments, there is certainly the ideal of a "mixed" State that has been constituted with the aim of political stability without conflicts. The Venetian concept of equilibrium, of harmony safeguarded from distur-bances, of "mixture" as a machine that neutralizes social dynamism, also circulates in writings of Matteo Palmieri and Guicciardini; and it contrasts with the "breaking" of all harmonious frameworks theorized by Machiavelli.[5] The classical *topos* of decadence, caused by "empire," idleness, and inequality, barely masks the faith, already compromised by facts, in a mythical concord.

One ought to study, however, the role that Nicolò Zen attributed to archi-tecture and music within the context of his reasoning: they are considered sumptuary displays harmful to the Republic, "courtier's arts" that under-mine the *virtus* and stability of the State. Looking only at this passage, one is tempted to read in it a decisive rejection of cultural "innovation." How then does one justify the Zens' adherence to Doge Andrea Gritti's program of renovation, Francesco Zen's interest in architecture, the latter's tie to Sebastiano Serlio, or the friendship that the same Nicolò would develop with Daniele Barbaro?[6]

Ennio Concina has formulated an intelligent answer to these questions.[7] He notes that when *Dell'origine de' barbariche distrussero per tutto'l mondo l'imperio di Roma* ["On the origin of the barbarians who destroyed the Roman Empire throughout the world"] was published in 1557 by Francesco Marcolini, Nicolò Zen's earlier studies became known. The work was dedicated to Daniele Barbaro, who had published his Vitruvian *Commentari* the preceding year. Developing the myth of Entinope, Zen narrated the history of the original city center ("civitas" rivoaltina). After the people's flight from Radagaiso, the mythical architect of Candia built one walled house and twenty-four houses of reeds; then, after the destruction of the settlement by fire, he built the church of San Giacomo di Rialto on the site of his own residence. For Nicolò Zen, therefore, architecture had sacred and foundational functions. But it is necessary to better understand his concept of architecture. The first resolution of the original Venetian government, proposed by Zeno Daulo, foresaw, as Zen wrote, "for greater equality and similarity . . . to leave the palaces and magnificent residences in order for the one not to overcome the other; fixing by law, that all residences should be equal, alike, of similar size and ornamentation."[8]

This was the concept that guided the design of the Palazzo Zen in Campo dei Crosechieri (fig. 3), built according to a project by Francesco Zen beginning in 1533, with Serlio's advice for the revision of the building's distribution; and the palazzo was conceived as the *speculum* of a history of the Republic seen from a familial point of view.[9] It was no accident that, in the *Origine*, Nicolò Zen concluded the above-mentioned passage by declaring that the rejection of magnificence, essential to the *libertas Reipublicae*, was "something that is still observed today."

The foundational function of architecture does not include, therefore, perilous autonomy for architecture itself: civil construction, for the mentality exemplified by Nicolò's words, is subject to the precepts of a collective ethic that aims—with a steady view to the moment of "birth"—at safeguarding and transmitting communal values. Is it perhaps necessary to emphasize the degree to which this idea, which the young Zen certainly received from his patrician education, was antithetical to the one that dominated fifteenth-century Florence and the Rome of Julius II, Leo X, and Clement VII? In Venice, *mediocritas* was proudly greeted by families who wished to display their loyalty to the Republic that had been established after the suspension of the *Maggior Consiglio* [Great Council] and the events of the fourteenth century. In Florence, the civic pride that resulted from the formation of the territorial State and the wealth distributed to parties free of family interests—given the practice of hereditary partition—provoked the immobilization of huge amounts of capital for the construction of palaces destined to consecrate the fame of individuals who were often in competition.[10] And it was certainly not in papal Rome that one might find a tradition like the Venetian one, which was meant to safeguard "equality and similarity."[11] It is clear, however, that there had been a leap, in Florence, between the traditions of the fourteenth century and those of the fifteenth. Not only was the merchant class pressured by Franciscan pauperism and the moralism that would express itself again, in the sixteenth century, in the arrows that Erasmus aimed at the architectural magnificence of Julius

II.[12] An anonymous Florentine merchant declared, "it is a bad practice to hold a rich estate and make great expenditures," while Giovanni di Pagolo Morelli made the following recommendation: "Never reveal yourself by your expenses . . . with anyone, neither with relative nor friend nor companion. . . . Do not reveal yourself with many possessions: buy what suffices for your life, do not buy estates that are too ostentatious, have them be useful and not for display."[13]

These invitations to moderation were clearly motivated by factors very different from those stated by Nicolò Zen: above all they did not bind the merchant class, which was their target, to an ethical system of a patriotic or civic nature. This may explain the weakness of the tradition they advocated. Giovanni Rucellai's *Zibaldone*—which reproduces a remark that Cicero made regarding the glory that an ancient Roman acquired by constructing a palazzo—demonstrates that new needs had been created within the Florentine patronage.[14]

Was the Venetian mentality, therefore, resisting the Renaissance? We have already suggested that, insofar as possible, it is better to leave historiographical abstractions aside. This does not prevent us from recognizing, in the patrician architecture of the fifteenth and early sixteenth centuries that chose to abandon the internationality of the *opus frangicenum* (fig. 1), a "translation," in idioms and in consolidated principles of construction, of linguistic models that were vaguely *all'antica* (inspired by ancient models). The defense of the Venetian "type" was, furthermore, often dictated by specific circumstances of building: the singular contamination between the traditional structure and the humanist-inspired detailing, which one sees in the Palazzo Zorzi in San Severo, was—though it constituted an exceptional achievement—anything but methodologically isolated.[15]

Francesco Sansovino offered a glimpse of a different conception, right in the middle of the sixteenth century, when he wrote in *Venetia città nobilissima*, "One reads that in early times, our citizens, wishing to show union and equality in all their things, built, in accordance with the Daula law, all houses of equal height. But once the riches had grown for the commerce that was always the nerve of this Republic, they went up and down according to the builders' appetite."[16] He later adds that "no matter how much the men of the past gave themselves to parsimony, they were however magnificent in the decoration of the house."[17] The *mediocritas* that Nicolò Zen recognized as a current ethical principle in 1539, was in 1581 considered an obsolete value by Jacopo Tatti's son, Francesco Sansovino. And yet, two doges of different political tendencies, Andrea Gritti and Leonardo Donà—the first in the early 1530s, the second in 1610–12—were, in the construction of their palazzi (figs. 145, 146), almost polemically faithful to that *mediocritas*. We will examine in subsequent chapters the meanings that Gritti and Donà would give to their declarations of loyalty to the patrician class's ideology of "harmonious equality." For now, the fact remains that neither accepted the exhibitionism that marked the display of the Ca' Foscari and the Ca' Loredan on the Grand Canal. And one should note that it was Andrea Gritti who encouraged architectural renewal in Venice, especially of the San Marco area. He was thus acting in exact accordance with the ideas expressed in Nicolò Zen's writings: a public, foundational function was reserved for architecture—especially, in this case, a refoundational function—while the face of the familiar palazzo was called upon to join the chorus of the urban fabric.

Let us try to articulate this analysis. After Codussi's experiments and the palazzi generically called "lombardesque" (fig. 1), the first attempt to introduce in Venice a language and type of residential construction clearly in line with Roman research of the early sixteenth century was due—as we have demonstrated elsewhere[18]—to Jacopo Sansovino, who had recently arrived in the lagoon after the Sack of Rome. We are in the last months of 1527 and in early 1528, and the client is the procurator de supra of San Marco, Vettor Grimani, who would later oversee Jacopo's major public works. The structure Sansovino devised was of great interest (fig. 2). Organized around a sequence of two communicating courtyards—a device the artist had already tested in the Palazzo Gaddi in Rome[19]—it takes advantage of the site's difficult position by making the most of a virtuosic rotation of compositional axes; moreover, a triumphal and innovative grand staircase intelligently determines the distribution of the apartments on the upper level. In addition, the entrance on the Grand Canal is ennobled by two flights of stairs that converge toward a structure with baldachin, reminiscent—from what we can deduce from the plan—of Bramante-like solutions. The project is one of Sansovino's best; nevertheless it unequivocally shows a remarkable naiveté about his patron. The architect, who had just arrived in Venice, displayed his great design virtuosity; he developed numerous "inventions"—one notices the astonishing precedent provided by the elliptical staircase that opens onto the loggia of the small garden—and demonstrated his qualities as a manipulator of space. He behaved, in other words, as though he were still in Rome, engaged in satisfying clients who were anxious for novelty and who intended to compare his achievements with those of Raphael, Antonio da Sangallo the Younger, and Giulio Romano. The palazzo designed for Vettor Grimani would never be executed. This "failed action" was undoubtedly also due to the family's own decisions, for they were advised to consider other alternatives;[20] but the *novitas* of the design, which Sansovino had so emphasized, probably had something to do with the shelving of the initiative as well. For this was a palazzo *alla romana*: it would have been an unequivocal declaration, a choice that would have once again implicitly placed in question an entire tradition—and at a time that was politically rather delicate for the *Serenissima*. The time was not yet ripe for such a departure: such a choice would have been too involving had it been taken by a family, even an eminent one. The celebration of the individual, in Venice of the fifteenth and early sixteenth centuries, was not accomplished by palazzi, but by the monumental tombs executed by Pietro and Tullio Lombardo (fig. 37), Antonio Rizzo, and Giovanni Burora. The inscription "*Non nobis Domine*" [give glory not to us]—which implied "*sed nomini tuo da gloriam*" [but to your name give glory]—placed at the base of Andrea Loredan's palazzo, expresses an *excusatio non petita* for the perpetrated sin of pride: here the exception really proves the rule.

As we shall see, before Doge Andrea Gritti and the procurators de supra would sanction Sansovino's classicism as a language capable of speaking of *Venice as a new Rome*, only the members of the Scuola della Misericordia—and in 1531–32—had the courage to accept from Sansovino a large structure *all'antica* (figs. 91–92); but they accepted it in a spirit of contradiction, with reservations and doubts that would greatly affect the work. In the 1520s, following the catastrophic events of the preceding two decades, Venice had a respite, during which she experienced numerous doubts about her own identity and attempts at technical and cultural revision. On the whole, it was not a good time for substantial *mutationi*; this was also true due to Venice's pressing daily decisions. The following episode was symptomatic: in spite of the presence in Venice of an artist like Tullio Lombardo, *proto* [foreman] Pietro Bon was engaged for a project that was meant to remodel the institutional core of the city—the Procurators' houses on Piazza San Marco—but the choice was practically dictated by the official role as *proto* held by Bon—who, beginning in 1514, gave life to the anachronistic building based on a model by Giovanni Celestro.[21]

But let us define the term "anachronism." The cautious linguistic renovation that was brought to bear upon the preexisting Procuratie was undoubtedly the sign of conservatism, considering that the building was conceived when Bramante was at the close of his career; but it assumes a historical meaning that is not insignificant in the light of the reflections we have made so far. The historical continuity of the Republic was affirmed with the houses requested by Antonio Grimani after the fire of 1512; Sanudo claimed that Grimani wanted them to be "very beautiful, to become the glory of the earth."[22] A test of the meaning of the Procuratie Vecchie, for the patrician class that was custodian of Venice's uniqueness, would take place in 1596, when—in a debate we will have to analyze closely—a minority group would, in a controversial move, propose for the Procuratie Nuove the same designs for the façade as those begun in 1514.[23]

But let us return to the dramatic years that followed the defeat of Agnadello. The *mediocritas* of the Procuratie Vecchie fell in line with the widespread conviction that the decline of Venetian power was due to moral corruption and the betrayal of her primitive ethics. In March 1512, after a previous decision (February 1510) in the Senate, the *Tre Savi sopra le pompe* [Three Magistrates for Pomp] were instituted: those legal measures dating back to 1299 that aimed at luxury and displays of riches were to be enforced once again.[24] The purpose behind such action was aimed, since 1510, at avoiding all squandering at a time when the State needed to draw upon private wealth. But there were also determining religious motives and conditions dictated by political opportunity.[25] The sumptuary expenses targeted were: clothes, feminine ornaments, feasts, and furnishings. The law went into the most minute detail, specifying types of desserts and dances that were prohibited, carefully describing the clothing and headdresses considered improper, ordering the elimination from furnishings of gold, silver, and paintings those that cost more than 150 ducats, and also prohibiting cases, combs, and mirrors with gold and silver. A real wave of moralism and austerity descended upon Venice. In the desperate days of October 1513, Doge Leonardo Loredan himself entered the controversy: to exemplify the deprecated luxury introduced in Venice, he cited the transformation of the functional spaces of the patrician palazzi into rooms for feasts and banquets.[26] The Doge did not hesitate to recite a *mea culpa*: he, too, was responsible for the abandonment of traditional customs, he too had provoked the "Lord's wrath."

One can easily distinguish in this rigorist revival the survival of ideas that would later be reflected in Nicolò Zen's critique of "courtier's arts." But the renewal of sumptuary laws also demonstrated that a strong need for pomp and ostentation had already taken root in the upper echelons of the patrician class. Marin Sanudo regularly recorded the wedding feasts that shamelessly betrayed the law of 1512: in June 1517 the wedding in the Grimani house,[27] in October 1519 the one at the Foscaris,[28] in November 1519 at the Pisanis,[29] in January 1520 the Barbarigo-Foscarini wedding.[30] And the diarist constantly noted that the feasts were meant to strike at the Magistracy for Pomp: "and every one did what he pleased and against the law, to be rid of this office, . . . a harmful thing for the earth."

The Grimani, the Foscari, the Pisani, the Foscarini families: the *Primi*, therefore, a group that was trying to concentrate power in its own hands, that had proudly ceased to recognize either primitive equality or original austerity. These families were, furthermore, tied to Rome and the Holy See, and intent on securing or sharing ecclesiastical benefits: the "Romanists" or "Papalists" were departing—in their customs, but also in economical and political ways— from *consuetudo*, and thus formed a group that in many ways will be the protagonist of our history.

Their "disobedience" of the sumptuary laws was certainly deliberate. Many felt that they might, by displaying their wealth, show that they were culturally up-to-date; their policy of patronage also introduced Tuscan and Roman experiments to the lagoon:[31] but this demonstration of awareness, which led to an increasing taste for innovations, was also used as an instrument of group and family definition, as a sign of "difference."

This was demonstrated by some of the new residences built in Venice during the sixteenth century. These examples, though few in number, have drawn numerous analyses from historians of architecture, who have, however, rarely noted that the exceptional quality of these palazzi is in itself historically telling.

One notices the following: leaving the Ca' Dolfin aside, because of its compromising nature, only two patrician buildings built in the sixteenth century dared to break the continuity of the Grand Canal with their dimensions and triumphal language. These are the Palazzo Corner, designed by Jacopo Sansovino, and the palazzo that Michele Sanmicheli began in 1556 for senator Girolamo Grimani.[32]

Let us first consider the Ca' Corner (fig. 5): this structure unfolds around a courtyard *alla romana*, extended into a structure that recalls the type with a central hall; but even more striking is the façade, which is defined by a display of classical orders on a rusticated foundation level, rich in evocations and formal "inventions." What Sansovino could not execute in 1527–28 for Vettor Grimani he could now do—in other forms—for Zorzetto Corner. Corner was faithful to the traditional attitude of his family, which had always been hostile to Doge Gritti and was proudly "papalist": the foundations of Venice's submission to Charles V were laid by Cardinal Francesco Corner, the son of the powerful Giorgio and the uncle of Zorzetto. In fact, Francesco Sansovino said that the Palazzo Corner was "most suited . . . to every cardinal's family": Andrea Corner, the brother of Zorzetto, became the bishop of Brescia in 1532 and cardinal in 1544.[33]

As for the Ca' Grimani in San Luca—there Sanmicheli used an even more archaic and resonating syntax, in spite of alterations Gian Giacomo de' Grigi made to the original project. The façade, torn open by a Vitruvian *atrium* that opens onto the Grand Canal, was proportioned on the severe model of the triumphal arch.

Neither Zorzetto Corner, nor Girolamo Grimani seemed to accept the ideology honored by Nicolò Zen and even Andrea Gritti: the conflict between mentalities was now affecting protagonists of the same social group. The fact remains that the distance that exists between these two palazzi and others like the Loredan at Campo Santo Stefano (fig. 4),[34] the Gussoni at Santa Fosca, and the Valier in Cannaregio, eloquently exemplifies the spirit that moved some members of the oldest and most powerful patrician houses to use architecture as a status symbol indicating their separateness.

Nicolò Zen surely had not reflected on an aspect of that "architecture" he opposed as a courtier's art—an aspect that was, nonetheless, worthy of his consideration. In fact, not only were forms *all' antica* in trouble in Venice; they were putting Venice herself in trouble. The *finitio*, the *concinnitas*, the autonomous "measure" of the new *res aedificatoria* were entering into a difficult—perhaps impossible—dialogue with continuity, with dissolved syntax, with the immeasurable dimension of the lagoon's urban fabric. Sansovino would learn the difficult art of mediation, but Palladio would impose (or would try to impose) his architectural microcosms upon a Venice that they literally "interrupted."

In the same Romanist and curialist surroundings, it was, however, possible to find instances of mediation and compromise. The most famous case was that of the Palazzo Grimani at Santa Maria Formosa (figs. 7–10). The Grimani brothers, Vettore and Giovanni, directed their attention to this building after Jacopo Sansovino's project for a palazzo on the fourteenth-century Ca' del Duca, which we have already discussed (fig. 2), was abandoned. One still cannot be sure who was responsible for the remodeling work ordered by Giovanni, Patriarch of Aquileia, but the overall meaning of the operation is clear.[35] First of all, the two brothers, who lived on different floors—Giovanni on the first *piano nobile*, Vettore on the second—seem to have been working in competition: Vettore built himself an independent staircase that flanked the one leading to the first *piano nobile*. Giovanni was undoubtedly the more ambitious of the two in his renovation of the palazzo: as early as the late 1530s, he had called upon Giovanni da Udine, Camillo Mantovano, and Francesco Salviati to decorate his own rooms with a particular style; after Vettore's death (1558), Giovanni, who was now the building's only proprietor, entrusted the decoration of the staircase to Federico Zuccari, then built a new, richly decorated wing, and consequently completed the courtyard, "reduced to the Roman form" (fig. 8).

Giovanni Grimani envisioned an extremely original sequence of rooms. Organized to host the family's antiquarian collections, these rooms suggest that his eccentric taste was more than experimental. The study housing the antiquities (*Studio delle antichità*) and the room dedicated to the memory of Giovanni's grandfather, Doge Antonio Grimani, exhibit vaguely Michelangelo-like details, but the overall impression is one of a montage of heterogeneous and contradictory pieces: architecture itself becomes a collector's item here. Let us consider, however, the structure covering the "Studio," for which Giovanni—according to Nicolò Stoppio—gathered advice from the best Italian architects: a pavilion vault is broken at its summit by an original lantern ending in a cross vault (fig. 10). Here, eccentricity reaches "metaphysical" heights.[36]

Let us not judge too hastily: the same Patriarch of Aquileia, Giovanni Grimani, who seemed to prefer the "abuses" was also, in the church of San Francesco della Vigna, the client of Battista Franco, Federico Zuccari, Andrea Palladio, and Tiziano Aspetti.[37] His taste thus led him to choose *novitas* for its own sake: Giovanni Grimani's figurative culture (fig. 6) helped define his personality. A member of the patrician class, he was born around 1500, became bishop of Ceneda in 1520, and Patriarch of Aquileia in 1545–46; he was accused of heresy for the first time in 1546–47 and a second time in 1560–61, acquitted in Trent on September 17, 1563, unsuccessfully aspired to the cardinalship, and from 1576 on, he was in litigation with the Venetian *Signoria* because of the feudal land of San Vito al Tagliamento.[38] Giovanni Grimani inherited from his uncle, Cardinal Domenico, neither religious commitment nor lofty humanist ethics. He was a friend of Pietro Carnesecchi and Pier Paolo Vergerio, and must have known Alessandro Caravia; but his ecclesiastical ambitions, like his attempts at patronage, were confined to the worldly sphere. And in all his operations, his primary need was to "show himself to be different" with regard to patrician *medietas*, even at the cost—as in the question of the San Vito property—of assuming a stance harmful to the Republic.

But let us consider his palazzo: here his desire to distinguish himself through a *different* artistic culture—a non-"Venetian" one—was limited to the sequence of internal spaces. Neither the incoherent courtyard (fig. 8), nor the exterior of the palazzo are characterized by the eccentric taste that is enclosed and jealously guarded in the rooms. Only the portal on Giuffa Street and the two four-light windows, or *quadrifore*, on the canal—so crudely linked to the portal below—emerge from the unassuming and traditional architectural partitions.

Here the "compromise" chosen by the Patriarch of Aquileia became evident. Unlike Zorzetto Corner and Girolamo Grimani, Giovanni made two choices at once: "equality" in the *facies* exposed to the public and city; proud subjectivism in private. He made very different choices for the church façade and the Grimani Chapel at San Francesco della Vigna: but there they were justified by his position at the heart of the Church. Nonetheless, the sequence of equal and simple chapels, which were designed by Sansovino and flank the nave, is interrupted, broken, and compromised by the *a solo* of the Grimani Chapel, with its rich coffered vault decorated by Battista Franco, the cycle of frescos by Federico Zuccari, and the statues by Tiziano Aspetti.[39] What happened here resembles what happened on the Grand Canal: the "Romanism" of one client became the occasion and stimulus to break, and call anachronistic, the ethics that even an autocrat like Andrea Gritti had respected as specific to *libertas rei publicae*.

The conflict, therefore, centered not only on form. On the one hand, there was the enshrinement of the *habitus*, of *mores*, independently of the images that authenticated them; on the other, there was the cult of a new language—clothed in Roman garments—in which one could identify a truth that implicitly annulled the very value of the *habitus*.

The debate over art and architecture—slow and suppressed, but obvious nonetheless—was, in Venice (also called the *Dominante*), part of a much broader debate over her identity and her institutions.

One ought to note one important detail. Venice was accustomed to constantly subordinating her own actions to magistracies or commissions elected on a case by case basis. The *protomagistri*, or chief magistrates, did not have exclusive control over programs; on the contrary, these were entrusted to the *Sapienza di Stato* [the Wisdom of the State], incarnated by representative patricians. *Empireia* and *scientia* were subordinated to very distinct sources: the *proti* [foremen] were barred from all fields except "experience," since the programs, which they alone interpreted, envisaged a truth fixed in a providential unworldly time of which Venice was the *imago*.

The *architectus*, the humanist who reformed the *res aedificatoria* by attributing to it the language of another truth, was not a *faber*: this idea was expressed by Leon Battista Alberti in the first pages of his treatise.[40] How then could *architecture*, a discipline that pretends to found its own programs and to *scire per causas*, begin to be a part of a universe like the Venetian one? How could the proud autonomy of such a discipline be made to harmonize with the control exerted upon it by the magistracies and commissioners? How could tradition and *novitas* be made to *speak together*, without Venice's forfeiting the fullness of the symbolic text constituted by her continuity?

The problem was not unimportant, because language *all' antica* circumscribes, confines, and divides the completed fragment, and it does this from the inside. Is this not already a "betrayal" of *tradition* and of the undefined textual chain that shapes it? There was, however, one attempt to delineate innovation and tradition in a nondialectical fashion, to hybridize these two dimensions: the Palazzo Dolfin in the Rialto area was such a "compromise." But what was one to do when the "Roman" language claimed to be absolute? The reaction to Palladio was typical: Venice could accept his language, but only by pushing its propositions out to her margins—to the Giudecca, to the island of San Giorgio, to San Francesco della Vigna, to Santa Lucia—or on the condition that these propositions be held within impermeable interiors, as they were in the Convento della Carità.

In addition, there remained the political threat of architecture in a Republic that was used to inserting every modification of the "virgin city" into an imaginary in which technology was dominated by the "prudence" of the magistrates.

The theme of *prudentia* was, in Venice, a rich one. It was prudence that guaranteed Venice's persistence *within* her origin; prudence constituted the measure of "good government," founded criteria of justice, enabled tradition to "resist" within the new, and enabled the new to live in an uninterrupted cosmic time. The reception of the *opus frangicenum* in Venice was typical of this enshrinement of *prudentia*, as were the institutional transformations of the thirteenth century and the slow but continuous transformation of Piazza San Marco, the physical site that made these institutions visible and usable.

The emblem of this "prudence" is well known: the *tricipitium*, or "three ages of man," which offers a simultaneous consideration of the past, present, and future, analyzed by Erwin Panofsky in his interpretation of the famous painting ascribed to Titian.[41] The allegorical figure (and perhaps its meanings) has undoubtedly been transformed. It was initially represented by three identical faces, as in the tympanum of the Tabernacolo della Mercanzia in Florence (fig. 93) or in the *Madonna in gloria* by Antonio da Negroponte (fig. 11). Associated with the city "of the three faces," it appears in a miniature in a thirteenth-century codex, preserved at the Biblioteca Civica in Treviso, while its meaning becomes transparent in the illustrations of the *Tractato nobilissimo de la Prudenza et Justitia* by Francesco de' Alegris, published in Venice in 1508.[42] But the *tricipitium* had also appeared in the *Hypnerotomachia Poliphili*, associated—as in the painting by Titian—with the symbol of Serapis, the heads of a dog, a lion, and a wolf,[43] reappearing on the façade of the Palazzo Vendramin at Santa Fosca (fig. 12), the Palazzo Trevisan Cappello in Canonica (fig. 13), the Palazzo dell'Odeo Cornaro in Padua, and the Zacco in the same city.

Let us pause a minute to examine the *tricipitium* of the Palazzo Vendramin (fig. 12): it is represented twice, in the bas-reliefs on the pilasters of the main portal, where—contrary to Arasse's interpretation[44]—it is already formed by the heads of an old man, a mature man, and a youth. It is associated, furthermore, with two later significant allegories: the phoenix that rises again and the pelican that offers his own blood to his offspring. The meditation on the cyclic nature of time is resolved in the *rebirth* or renaissance assured by the sacrifice of Christ: circular, classical time is composed of the linear and teleological time of Christianity. This transfer of public symbols into a private emblem is undoubtedly significant, however: the coexistence of epochs, which guarantees human justice, connects the loyalty to tradition—represented by the head of the old man turned toward the origin—with the future, the *novus*, implicitly alluding to an eternal return. But within this age, the new root is Christ—a new root made by the lagoon city, since the age of redemption is officially identified with Venetian time.[45]

The patrician family used public symbols to identify itself: this emerges forcefully from the *tricipitia* of the Palazzo Vendramin, the building in which Marcantonio Michiel saw Giorgione's *Tempest*.[46] And Salvatore Settis justly observed that for Gabriele Vendramin and Taddeo Contarini—the probable patron of the *Three Philosophers* of Vienna—"the problem of knowledge of the divine is inextricably intertwined with the precept of looking into oneself, and the one and the other irradiate with sharper and stronger authority because they have been filtered by rediscovered classicism."[47] Christian humanism confronts the flowing of time with the *eschaton*: the *prudentia* contained in the *tricipitium* partakes of a cosmic and ineffable time. So much so, in fact, that one might see in this triadic emblem an incomplete symbol: imagined in space, a fourth element—which is the presupposition of visible ones, though it cannot itself be represented—becomes necessary to complete the symbolic wheel of time. The *hidden element* is origin and purpose: it is fitting that it should have no face. As a presupposition, it cannot be represented by a symbol.

Let us keep these remarks in mind as we try to interpret Giorgione's *Three Philosophers*, starting with its most explicit meaning: the three ages of man (fig. 14). With one warning. It is not our intention to challenge Settis and Meller's interpretations of this painting:[48] we especially appreciate the method of Settis's book and its serious approach to the works in question. We are not attempting to offer an alternative reading to the one that sees in the painting the three Magi, but only wish to complete it by identifying another level of meaning.

The youth, first of all: here, unlike in traditional representations of the three ages, he is sitting on the left and gazing in that direction. His back is turned toward us and his eyes are fixed on an *origin*, a cave that he has reduced to reason, having "measured" it geometrically. The "new"—youth with its compass and square—studies, contemplates, and "measures" nature, which is represented as a source; next to him maturity—philosophy or Arab mathematics?—and the cosmic wisdom of the "old man" confirm his *ratio* on other levels. The "three philosophers" do not stand in opposition: in a silent and serious dialogue, they clearly form an indissoluble whole in which the "youth" reads the book of nature, showing that he is paying close attention to the lesson of the first word, confirmed and universalized by the "old man," the sage who is custodian of tradition.[49] All antitheses have been removed, exactly as they are in the emblem of prudence. Furthermore, that which remained *absconditus* in the symbol of the *tricipitium* is visible here: the cave as origin, presupposition, and final destination. We will not push this iconoclastic interpretation any further as we are conscious of its conjectural character. One thing, however, can be said for our reading of Giorgione's painting: it inserts the work in the historical context we have analyzed so far. The loyalty to the Daula law expressed by Nicolò Zen and the diffusion of the symbol of the *tricipitium*, as an emblem created by the Venetian patrician class, were closely linked: "prudence," in the form of a three-headed serpent, also appeared on the coins minted in 1536 by Giovanni Zacchi in honor of Andrea Gritti, confirming the degree to which the theme in question had spread among the ruling classes.

Moreover, a significant passage in Sanudo confirms the political value that the allegory of the three ages had for the Venetian patrician class. In 1525, the diarist recorded how, many years before, the Procurator Federico Corner had said to him in the Sala dei Pregadi, "Marin my son, do you see how this room is painted? It was done in the time of the Doge Pietro Gradenigo. Do you see these trees, large, medium-sized and small? Those who enter this Senate, with the duty of governing the State, are like these trees: *the small ones learn, then come those in the middle, and then the great ones*: thus are the three estates, young, middle-aged, and old: and in this way well-instituted Republics are governed."[50]

Sanudo quotes Corner's words in the context of a passionate discourse meant to compare innovations of an institutional character. The simultaneity of ages, allegorized in the "three ages," thus assumes extremely broad meanings: prudence sanctions the "harmony of mixtures," which in turn guarantees the stability of the State.

Prudentia, universal time, and *novitas* confronted with *origine*: in Venice during the fifteenth century these founding values filtered all new additions to humanistic culture: this was fully demonstrated by the languages of Pietro Lombardo, Mauro Codussi, Gentile Bellini, Carpaccio, and Giorgione.

Renovatio was thus possible; in fact, it was constantly pursued, but in the absence of "catastrophic" decisions. In return, the voice of the origin was not crystalized in a Text, did not form a binding language: in order to resonate, it confronted eras, transformed itself, only resisting unfounded innovations.

Thus, though it pretended to be rediscovering the triumphal path traced by the ancients, the *res aedificatoria* modeled on the Roman example represented, for "the younger generation," a fashion inspired by unmeasured pride, a language destined not to take root in Venice, and an unfounded will to power.

Many of the events that we will examine in subsequent chapters were marked by fractures in the ideas we have described so far. But conflicts are productive: we will try to draw out of the context of our analyses the web of contradictions and problems that Venetian reality offers European history at one of the most delicate moments of her history.

2

Republican *pietas*, Neo-Byzantinism, and Humanism. San Salvador: A Temple *in visceribus urbis*

Two themes, seemingly in contrast, constantly emerge from the historical and literary writings of the fifteenth century to support the Venetian Republic in its programs for mainland expansion. On the one hand, the liberty and the "morality" of Venice's original customs were celebrated. On the other hand—in Porcellio Romano's writings or in *Carmen* by Filippo Morandi of Rimini (1440–41)—Venice was represented as the heir to the imperial mission of Rome.[1] A strong reaffirmation of the unbroken tradition, founded on the myth of Venice's "holy origins," contrasted with the celebration of the imperial destinies of Venice as the "altera Roma."[2] The dialectic that we have tried to describe in the preceding chapter assumed particular characteristics in the fifteenth century: one of its constants, however, was the exaltation of Venice's already consolidated political system. It was no accident that Giorgio Trapezunzio had dedicated, in 1452, his own translation of Plato's *Laws* to the Venetian Senate:[3] Venice, the perfect city, in which constitutional balances seemed to realize the ancient political models, increasingly saw itself as the site of realized utopia. The concept of *renovatio*, consequently, assumed specific characteristics in Venice: the new was called upon to develop what had been present at the moment of its genesis; there was no appeal for a return to a perfection that had been destroyed by a repeated "fall." This obsessive focus on the point of origin stimulated renovations within the continuity that contained within itself its own perfection. This had a significant effect on the mentality that guided the transformations of the lagoon's appearance in the second half of the fifteenth century, especially after 1480. The neo-Byzantine revival, which John McAndrew and James Ackerman have stressed, was given a precise meaning by Lionello Puppi: in the revival of Byzantine planimetric schemes and syntactic elements in Codussi's ecclesiastical works—in the churches of Sant' Andrea alla Certosa and San Geminiano, in the façade of the Scuola Grande of San Marco—one can see the expression of a "peace party" tied to the influence of the Camaldolensian religious order and to humanistic culture, and intent on imposing on Venice signs alluding to a *renovatio Imperii christiani*.[4] This hypothesis, which relies upon significant evidence, is fascinating, notwithstanding Ackerman's observations on the conservative elements that a portion of that revival unequivocally demonstrated.[5] In any case, Cardinal Bessarione, addressing the Doge in 1468, wrote that, when the Greeks arrived in Venice from the sea, they felt as though they were entering "*quasi alterum Byzantium*": and it is evident that the gift of the Greek and Latin library to the Republic, made by Bessarione himself, was a way of solemnly entrusting Venice with the Christian and anti-Turkish mission that the Greek Cardinal had advocated with vehement dedication as early as July 1453.[6]

Even outside the Camaldolensian ambit, however, the appeal to the Byzantine repertory corresponded to Venice's need to renovate her identity by reaffirming the specific nature of her origins. Between the end of the fifteenth and the first decades of the sixteenth century, the *imago urbis* emerging from the circumscribed architectural interventions multiplying within the lagoon's urban fabric responded to a need for continuity—and this need was clearly widespread and taken into account even by the most obvious linguistic innovations. The new interventions did not subvert the urban structure, which was considered, at most, as needing works of completion, substitution, and "decor."[7] And yet, right at the beginning of the new century, a few exceptional works—among them the Fondaco dei Tedeschi [German Commodity Exchange] and the church of San Salvador—indicated that new ideas were fermenting, even within the programmatic statement. Innovation not only concerned the individual object: in different ways, it was an entire conception of the city that reverberated from these interventions, affecting the symbolic stratifications that were inherent in individual works as well as the entire range of relations they created.

Our theme clearly emerges: in which way did *novitas* penetrate Venice? What concessions did it make to traditional representations? And what was the nature of its dialogue with the structures of the collective imaginary, as well as with the urban whole?

As we will demonstrate later, the history of the new church of San Salvador was in fact intertwined with that of the Fondaco dei Tedeschi. But, for our purposes, the example we have chosen will help us explore a particularly precarious historical phase with the purpose of considering its implications: therefore, we are not interested in the church only as an object. The *event* that it represents, in fact, can be analyzed as the result of a mentality that evolved over the long period of the Venetian Middle Ages: it manifests, if not the crisis point of this long period, then certainly a point of deflection.[8] In order to respond to the many questions formulated, we will need a nontraditional philology: we must first identify the areas to be analyzed, seeking specific codes that governed Venetian religious sentiment, but also seeking the conditions that permit an encounter—or clash—between those codes and the choices manifested in the specific case. In fact, for an extreme example of neo-Byzantine revival like San Salvador, an analysis conducted on several levels of significance appears to be the only type capable of avoiding vague terms and concepts like *renovatio* or *Venetian humanism:* the programmatic contents and the superimposition of formal choices will be examined as "words" that presuppose the action of fully articulated languages, captured in a delicate moment of transition.

1. An Ideal "Refoundation": Church, Imaginary, Myth

Thus we see that a number of languages were spoken in San Salvador (figs. 15–29): we must consider each one in its specificity and study their intertwinings without trying to "balance accounts" a priori.

Let us first consider the language of the collective imaginary deposited in sacred sites. The language in question is, as we know (especially after Innocenzo Cervelli's analyses), one in which the sacred legitimizes and consecrates the deepest values of the Venetian *communitas*: an amalgam of *fides* and republican pride cements a patriotism that recognizes itself in the "divine" origin of the city.[9] Our inquiry must be oriented toward those texts and documents that reveal the meanings—with all their allegorical implications—that popular *pietas* attributed to places of faith.

One must begin with Sanudo, who tells us that San Salvador was one of seven churches that Bishop Magnus built immediately after he learned "through a revelation, how he should come to the lagoons of the islands of the Rialto, where people had started building a city on water called Venice." After San Pietro di Castello, founded by Magnus according to the instructions of the Apostle Peter, and the church of the Angelo Raffaele, situated by that angel at the other end of the city, "there appeared to him Jesus Christ, the Savior of the world, and he ordered him *etiam* in the middle of the city, that is to say of the circle where [the church] should be, that he should build a church there where he would find a red cloud, and he did so, and it was called San Salvador."[10]

The "foundation," far from being identified with a sacrilegious transgression—as it was in the legend about Rome or in the passage of *De civitate Dei* concerning the role of Cain—was assimilated into the triangulation of sacred sites, set up through divination.

And the location of the first three churches attributed to the "first bishop of Venice" was significant. At the center was San Salvador; at the two ends, the churches of San Pietro *in castro olivensi* and of the Angelo Raffaele, which were ideally located as bulwarks. Their inspirers were equally significant. Venice appeared to be defended by the Apostle Peter and the Angel Raphael; the latter, according to Sanudo, ordered Bishop Magnus to construct a church "in Osso Duro," "because he wished to be the patron of this new city";[11] but in the story, Christ's special position is made explicit by the identification of the urban core with the site dedicated to the Savior, which has precise points of correspondence in the city's mythology.[12] The legend certainly still had deep roots, especially if in 1749 Flaminio Corner could write, "And when the Venerable and Great Bishop came to this same Venice, where he had been called by the light of the Holy Spirit, on that day [it is said] the Savior of humankind showed himself to him while he was in fervent prayer and commanded that in the center of that city, where he would see a purple cloud, there should he undertake to build a Temple to Him."[13] Venice therefore guarded in her breast the sign of salvation, which had taken the shape of a church that testified to her ineffable origins.

The mixture of the sacred and the profane could no longer be explicit. An anonymous writer of the thirteenth century was quoted by Corner as saying, "The *Carvernarii* made a Church to the honor of God and the Savior; in its pavement they placed iron grids; they stand, however, above the course of the water; in this form was the church made, like the tomb of God in Jerusalem."[14]

According to this anonymous writer, then, the original church of San Salvador, with grids in the floor that allowed one to see the water underneath, reflected the model of the Holy Sepulcher in Jerusalem. The reference was significant for the history of Venice's identification with Jerusalem, as the *sigillum veritatis* and seat of Solomonic justice.[15]

This site, subject to numerous interpretations, accumulated extremely important memories for Venice's political identity: in 1177 Pope Alexander III consecrated an altar to the Savior. Later that same year (on August 29) he went on to dedicate the church in a solemn rite.[16] These were not routine events. Alexander III was in Venice, in 1177, to celebrate peace with Frederick Barbarossa, with Venice as the mediator. This work of mediation would have numerous meanings for the Republic. Venice's national thesis was sanctioned—after the historic meeting between the Pope and the Emperor Frederick—with the papal bull of 1180, which repartitioned the Aquileian jurisdiction between Grado and Aquileia. Furthermore, this work of mediation was celebrated as a sign of independence by the Papacy as well as the Empire, and would thus remain the central element of the Republic's official mythology.

Therefore, it is perhaps not coincidental that after being dedicated by Alexander III the church of San Salvador was reconstructed "in a larger and more ornate form":[17] the mixture of the sacred and the political assumed concrete form within the city.

The new church, which was completed with its bell tower in 1209, acquired further significance in 1267, when it acquired the relics of Saint Theodore.[18] Edward Muir, in an illuminating volume on civic rituals in Renaissance Venice, has studied the development of the cult of Theodore and determined its principal significance: the saint who was, according to the legend, the first patron of the Venetian *dux* was the result of the fusion of two different personalities, a soldier martyred in Amasea (whose feast day falls on November 9) and a general of Eraclea (whose feast day falls on February 7).[19] This saint, whom the tradition indicated as the patron of Venice *before* Mark, was not only a soldier, but, significantly, a Byzantine as well—Muir expresses his doubts about Antonio Niero's thesis that this legend originated during the time of the war of Chioggia (1377–81) and that the installation of the statue of Theodore next to the one of Mark, on the columns of the Molo, occurred around 1380.[20]

It is undoubtedly true that the cult of Saint Theodore was revived around the middle of the fifteenth century. In 1434, Eugene IV granted indulgences to visitors of the church of San Salvador on the feast day of Saint Theodore; on April 2, 1448, Nicholas V granted indulgences to people visiting the saint's altar; on January 3, 1449, nineteen cardinals, including Bessarione, granted further indulgences in the chapel of San Teodoro; in 1450, the Senate decided that on November 9 of every year—note the date—there should be a dogal procession in honor of Theodore, and Sanudo's *Diarii* record three processions to San Salvador between 1506 and 1530.[21] In 1552, finally, the Scuola di San Teodoro, founded as *piccola* in the thirteenth century, was elevated to *grande*.[22] Muir has suggested that the figure of the saint might have symbolized the sovereignty of Constantinople:[23] the renewal of his cult in Venice would have had—if we accept this hypothesis—the significance of a *translatio Imperii*, significantly sanctioned by the Senate with the decision of 1450. Though it is a good idea to be cautious in evaluating this cult's resumption, one ought not to forget that the dogal processions established in 1450, like the later reconstruction of the church of San Giovanni Crisostomo—among the few in the West to be dedicated to this Byzantine saint—constituted important chapters in the history of Venice's identification, in the fourteenth century, as a "second Constantinople," an alternative, therefore, to Rome. The fact remains that these dogal processions gave a new connotation to the urban route that led from Piazza San Marco to San Salvador. We will return to this observation and develop it later. In the meantime, we wish to discuss the implications that affected this building. Politics and religion were tightly intertwined in the designing of San Salvador as an "original" place, the depository of a divine will that intended to make Venice the seat of universal justice, the emblem of the *Serenissima*'s proud independence, and the "house" of the city's original patron.

The church was, however, the object of ecclesiastical conflicts: violent quarrels erupted between the friars of San Salvador and the clergy of San Bartolomeo over jurisdictional matters and conflicting interests; at the beginning of the fifteenth century, furthermore, there was a decadence of morals and customs. Beginning in 1427, the future Eugene IV, Gabriele Condulmer, began working on the religious reformation of the monastery, introducing the Lateran Regular Canons.[24] He intervened a second time in 1442, when he was Pope, assigning the church and monastery to the Augustinian Regular Canons of San Salvatore of Bologna.[25] One notices here that this religious renewal occurred at the same time as the resumption of the cult of Saint Theodore; this was not a coincidence, even though one can find initial, though vague, references to the renovation of the church in documents between 1445 and 1475.[26]

There was a close connection between the meanings assigned to San Salvador in the early Middle Ages and the fifteenth century and those surrounding its reconstruction at the very beginning of the sixteenth century. Nonetheless, as we shall attempt to demonstrate, during the beginning of the new building's construction there occurred events that led to a redefinition of its civic value, a reformulation of its program, and an exact definition of its function at the urban level. While one clearly cannot overemphasize the closeness of the relations between the new church and the other two operations conducted by Giorgio Spavento in that area—the reconstruction of the Fondaco dei Tedeschi [German Commodity Exchange] after the fire of 1505 and the restorations of the Rialto bridge—it is also true that the structure of the new Fondaco substantially changed the iconography of the Grand Canal and a section of Venice's urban core, whereas the new San Salvador was introduced into the urban fabric with a spatial arrangement that was completely new in the Venetian architecture of the early sixteenth century. The structure of the Fondaco, with its echoes of Vitruvius, and the interior of the new church redefined, in points, the heart of the lagoon city: this redefinition would have been even broader if the idea of reconstructing the Rialto bridge in stone, proposed in 1502 and then again in 1507, had been accepted.[27] These works obviously arose out of different circumstances: but they were clearly "exceptional" works, located in an extremely significant section of Venice, and they led to the acceptance of innovative languages.

In our search for further programmatic indications, we now turn to the documents that gave the go-ahead for the reconstruction of San Salvador. On May 23, 1506, the Council of Ten issued a mandate to the commissioner of the Cassa del Sal [the Salt Bank] to "compute and pay to the venerable friars of San Salvador of Venice fifty ducats for the month of April, toward the six thousand ducats spent by them in the building of the church," claiming the payment of March 31st of the same year.[28] The reconstruction of the church was thus financed—at least in its initial phase—by the State; this reveals a particular interest in the initiative—an interest that was explained in a later official document.[29] In the ratification of the financing by the three heads of the Council of Ten (May 29, 1506), it was recorded that the original church had been "designated" as the center of the city by "Our Lord Jesus Christ Savior of the world, whose will and command together rule, governor from the beginning of this our city." The reconstruction of the church was furthermore made necessary "for the enlargement of the city and the spiritual consolation of all."[30] A remembrance of the city's origins, the dedication of Venice to Christ, the sanctity of the *umbilicus urbis*, and the civic value of the reconstruction clearly emerged as complementary motives. The document becomes even more interesting when one considers the signatures of the three leaders who validated it: Bernardo Bembo, Pietro Capello, and Giorgio Emo. Bembo, the humanist—formerly connected with Lorenzo de' Medici, Marsilio Ficino, and Poliziano; a supporter, in the late fifteenth century, of an alliance between Venice and Florence; a friend of Aldus Manutius, Pomponio Leto, and Battista Mantovano; and an orator in 1505 in the service of Julius II—found himself next to an exponent of the extremist political wing, Giorgio Emo.[31] At this point one must ask whether Bembo's interest in San Salvador was of a purely bureaucratic nature, given his particular interest in architecture and the arts. In May 1483 Bembo had engaged Pietro Lombardo in the restoration of Dante's tomb in Ravenna. He possessed, certainly since before 1485, a copy of Alberti's *De re aedificatoria*, which he had obtained through Poliziano—according to Cecil Grayson's supposition.[32] As for Giorgio Emo, as the procurator of the friars of San Zanipoli, he presided—beginning in 1510—over the transformation of the Dominican church into a pantheon dedicated to the heroes of the war of Cambrai: Girolamo Mocetto's work in the window of the right transept was only one chapter in this enterprise. Furthermore, one can recognize Saint Theodore and Saint George in the two warrior saints represented by Mocetto at opposite ends of the window—a significant union, for reasons we will discuss later on.

But let us proceed with the reading of the documents. On August 7, 1507, the convent of San Salvador addressed a petition to the Doge and the Council of Ten, in order to obtain facilities for the collection of authorized credits.[33] And new motivations emerge from the context: whereas "the divine temples [are] the walls . . . and bastion of this Catholic and very Christian republic," it was recalled that the church of San Salvador was "miraculously constructed and founded by the hand of that very blessed bishop of Altinum master Sancto Magnio (Bishop Magnus) in the middle of the center of this very great city," and it was observed that the church was assiduously frequented by a mass of faithful worshipers "both nobles and popular." Reconstruction was therefore necessary "for the decoration and ornament of this famous and renowned city, since, being located in its viscera [in visceribus suis], it deserves a larger and more magnificent building to be constructed."

In visceribus urbis: the phrase reaffirms the exceptionality of an *ecclesia* destined by Christ himself to mark a focal spot in the urban space. Let us compare this praise of San Salvador in another bureaucratic text. In the section that deliberates, on February 19, 1461, the assignment of 1,000 ducats for the reconstruction of the church of San Zaccaria, it is stressed that "the temple . . . lies in the center and eye of our city," adding that it is "the first edifice belonging to the serene prince of the Venetians."[34] It is clear that in the evaluation of official acts it is necessary not to attribute anachronistic values to generic and rhetorical speeches—which were very frequent. But this cannot exempt us from asking why *these* particular speeches appeared: why these praises of the sacred buildings chosen to incarnate the *renovatio urbis* reveal motivations that are otherwise nonrealizable, especially for a time period that was so caught between contradictory motivations as was the second half of the fifteenth and the first half of the sixteenth centuries. It is also worth noting how, alongside themes that justify the civic importance of the *templa*—their mediating function between patrician *pietas* and popular *pietas*—there now appear topographical identifications referred to the human body. San Zaccaria is in the "eyes" of the city, San Salvador in its "viscera." One begins to think of an anthropological reading of Venice's urban structure, parallel or superimposed upon a phytomorphic one.

Let us turn to the document dated August 7, 1507: one cannot miss the consistency established between the traditional praise of *Venice's uniqueness*—a city, Felix Faber had written, that has "the sea for a floor, the channel for a wall, the sky for a roof, the waters of the lagoon for the pavement and the roads of the kingdom"—and the values of wall *et propugniacolo* ["and bastion"] attributed to her sacred buildings.[35] It was a matter of confirming the civil sense of Venetian religion, underlined by Cervelli: the "sense of religion and the divine from which one might ideally draw a norm for political action,"[36] of a spirituality that reflected the mental paradigms of a patrician class deeply convinced of the analogy existing between divine justice and the justice of the Republic.

Moreover, the significance of the new church was clearly expressed by

Sanudo, who recorded the following: "Today the 25th, Friday, was the day of the Annunciation of the Madonna, on which day, in 421, there began the city of Rivoalto [or Rialto, the islands now referred to as Venice] and the first stone was laid, on that day was formed the world, was crucified Our Lord Jesus Christ, according to Saint Augustin; it was in 1507 on this day that the first stone was laid for the new reconstruction of the church of San Salvador on this ground."[37]

The foundation of San Salvador was thus inserted into a divine and universal temporal rhythm: the same enigmatic time, both solemn and eternal, scanned by the birth of the world, by the Annunciation and the Crucifixion, beat again with the "divine" birth of Venice. There is sufficient evidence for one to read in the symbolic act completed with the laying of the first stone of the church a rite of refoundation that was immersed in the absolute time sanctifying the lagoon city.

But agreement on the new church was not unanimous: there were strongly diverging opinions. This is demonstrated by a document dating from April 1508, concerning a quarrel between the Redaldi brothers and the clerics; there were those who felt that the destruction of the venerable medieval building was inopportune and sacrilegious. Bernardino Redaldi and his brother declared,

And as we hold it certain that the said church was founded by the glorious Saint Magnus, it is the duty of the friars and would constitute greater devotion if the said Church were to be conserved in its ancient form, in which the holy Saint had ordained and constructed it according to divine law than to change it according to human appetite with the mutterings of the many, and, with the trappings of goodness and religion, to be concerned with what is not fitting, for the aforementioned Church is menaced by immanent ruin in some of its parts and with a small amount of money could be restored without complaint, injury or damage to its good neighbors. It is clear to the whole world which the Christian faith has brought together that since the ancient temples were largely founded by miracles, just so should the said church of San Salvador not be destroyed, but conserved and repaired, and, if it needs expansion, this should be carried out without arrogance or damage, for it is written in the law and in the evangelical disciplines: "Render unto Caesar what is Caesar's, and unto God what is God's."[38]

The testimony of the Redaldi brothers should not be taken too seriously: they stood to lose from the construction of the new San Salvador. Nevertheless, their words brought to light a conflict between diverse mentalities that is worth taking into account.

It becomes even more significant, then, that the petition of August 7, 1507, bears the signatures of twenty-eight patricians, including the prestigious names of Hieronimo Contarini q. Bertuccio, Alvise Pisani and brothers, Gabriele Barbarigo, Nicolò and Giacomo Gussoni, Giovanni Antonio Giustinian, Alvise and Hieronimo Grimani, Taddeo Contarini di Nicolò, Nicolò Zorzi, Alvise Malipiero, and Pietro Contarini. (See document 5 in the appendix.) The group supporting the building enterprise of the canons of San Salvador was certainly exceptional; it both accentuated and confirmed the complex of meanings attached to the reconstruction of the church. It was also a reflection of the particular political moment in which Venice found herself between 1506 and 1507. The compromise with Rome of 1505 had not begun to resolve the fundamental problems of the Italian territory, but had left the *Serenissima* in a position of cautious defense and Julius II in a state of unabated aggression. Already in 1504 Fra Giocondo, from Paris, had warned the Republic— through ambassador Francesco Morosini—of the movements of Julius II, the Emperor, and the French king; furthermore, at the end of 1506, Maximilian's secretary, Antonio Semen, revealed those movements of the pontiff that were meant "to unify His Majesty the Emperor with the King of France and His Holiness, which union can only take place to the detriment of your Serenity."[39]

The building of the new church of San Salvador thus coincided with a moment of uncertainty dominated by an intense and convulsive political debate; at the same time, events menacing the security of the city began to take shape. The reference to churches as the walls of "the Catholic and very Christian Republic" seemed to refer to a dramatically precarious situation.

The highest government authorities considered the church with a degree of interest that did not diminish after Agnadello. Already on April 26, 1513, Doge Leonardo Loredan intervened alongside Fra Nicolò of Bologna, the general of the congregation, recalling the financial obligations that the chapter had contracted but not yet met, in favor of "the rapid construction of our temple in the center of this our city."[40] The completion of the building was already visible, and used as a demonstration of the *Serenissima*'s *ripresa* [recovery] in spite of the continuation of the war, which resumed with the Franco-Venetian alliance of March 1513. The completion of San Salvador probably had a meaning analogous to the reconstruction of the Procuratie Vecchie and the top of the tower of San Marco (1510–14): the vitality of the Republic was demonstrated by works that unequivocally characterized the *imago urbis*. On the other hand, the widespread sense of guilt regarding moral corruption, which was seen as the cause of the decline of Venetian power, led—as we have seen—to dogal censorship against private wealth, to the resumption of the sumptuary laws, and to the institution of the Ministers for Pomp. And one notes that on March 3, 1512, the Senate, in launching this new magistracy, declared that it was urgent to "placate the anger of Our Lord." Amid such calls for a return to the purity of "orginal customs," the construction of the church continued, and Doge Loredan intervened in its favor a second time in April 1521, while Andrea Gritti would support it later, in 1524, reaffirming that it was an "ornament and convenience of the city." Gritti would speak out in its favor in extremely severe tones in 1529 and 1531 and call for the financial support that the abbey of San Michele di Candiana had promised.[41] And the fact that Gritti had a special interest in the church of San Salvador was demonstrated not only by his visit of January 7, 1529, on which occasion the location of the "choir" was discussed, but also by expressing his intention to place his own tomb there—a choice later changed in favor of the church of San Francesco della Vigna (fig. 61).[42]

The available evidence thus confirms and defines the civil aspects of a temple that was called upon to consolidate a highly symbolic place within the polymorphous fabric of the lagoon city. The problem at this point concerns the ways in which the meanings attributed to the church may have influenced architectural invention, for it was undoubtedly among the most original Venetian churches of the early sixteenth century, and, as we have already pointed out, a borderline case of the "neo-Byzantine" movement. In other words, we must explore the extent to which the collective imaginary was "translatable" into a technical and subjective language.

We undoubtedly owe the guiding idea behind the structure, which is modeled on a repetition of the quincunx scheme, to Giorgio Spavento (figs. 20, 21). The agreement of January 4, 1507, between the prior Antonio Contarini and the master masons establishes the obligation:

To build the church of this monastery, or part of the church, depending on time, with all surrounding houses, which are divided into a cloister, chapter house, sacristy, dormitory, guest house, and infirmary. . . . Likewise, to build and dig all of the foundations of the church, of the shops and the sacristy, and the chapter house attached to the church, all with external finish, building them according to the size ordered by master Giorgio Spavento and the friars. . . . Likewise, to place all the top quality stone attached to the walls in the church and in the housing and shops; all other top quality stone, including porphyry, will be installed on the outside façade of the church facing the campo*. . . . Likewise, to make the outside fascios that surround the church; Likewise, to make all the domes, large and small. . . .*[43]

Thus the program established by Spavento—the design of which had been elaborated prior to August 9, 1506[44]—included not only the church, with major and minor domes, but also the façade covered with marbles, the rental houses, the convent, the sacristy, and the new shops. It is also clear that the planimetric form of the church (figs. 19, 20), with unusual protruding transepts, goes back to the original programs. John McAndrew has dwelt on the peculiar protrusion of the transepts, unusual in church buildings of the Renaissance, and mentioned the Urbino cathedral as its precedent; and Ackerman has correctly suggested that the Latin cross plan might be an echo of the preexisting medieval structure (fig. 15).[45] Jacopo de' Barbari's map confirms Ackerman's hypothesis: in it the old San Salvador has a long nave and protruding transepts and its position is similar to that of the present church. This can be explained by the need, always strong in Venice, to reuse old foundations and lands that have settled with time: but the preexistence of the planimetric scheme is also to be interpreted as a faithfulness to a form that clearly alludes to the cross of Christ, to whom the church is ideally dedicated.

How then can one explain drawing 513 of the *Miscellanea Mappe* of the Archiviodi Stato in Venice (fig. 22), which shows the plan of a church whose left side—unlike the present one—is tangent to the Mercerie [street of shops]? One notices that on the folio the structure has only its perimeter drawn and shows three apses—of which the central one has an external niche. It has no transept, and is noticeably smaller than the one represented by de' Barbari. In the drawing—which inserts the church into its architectural context incorrectly—there appears, finally, on the side of the Mercerie, a kind of irregular platform that extends into the public space and that contains a *loggetta*, or small loggia, and another minor, unidentified element. One can cautiously advance the following hypothesis: that the church represented on the sixteenth-century folio is a rough plan of the primitive San Salvador, the remains of which probably came to light when the building was demolished in the late twelfth century.

But let us return to our analysis of the new structure (fig. 27). McAndrew has rightly observed that the church is one of the largest ecclesiastical spaces built in Venice during the Renaissance; he stresses its relationship with San Marco and the fact that work on the building began shortly after the first stone of St. Peter's in the Vatican was laid (April 18, 1506).[46] It would not be at all surprising to learn that the reconstruction of San Salvador constituted a kind of Venetian "response" to the church that Julius II wanted to build. Such a discovery would enable us to explain better the interest of the Council of Ten and of the large patrician class, the syncretic choice that was made on a formal level—the explicit and very interesting appeal to a structure, like San Marco, that contained deep political meanings inserted into a humanistic language—and the continuous appeal to the church's "centrality" in the city. And, in fact, we have in the Venetian church the reaffirmation of a *renovatio* faithful to its origins, in line with the traditional religious sentiment of the Republic, opposed to a comprehensive design aimed at affirming the Pope's supremacy over a centralized State, as well as a politically "restored" Church.[47]

The reference to San Marco may, however, have further significance. The venerable medieval church had taken the Holy Sepulcher in Jerusalem as one of its symbolic referents: according to legend, Venice, identified as the new Jerusalem, had defended herself against the Byzantine Theodore, whose relics were placed later in San Salvador. The church, located in *visceribus urbis*, was thus ideally linked, through Saint Theodore, to Saint Mark (fig. 17). The two patron saints, represented on top of the two columns of the Molo, were thus connected by the processional path that runs along the Mercerie and by the analogy between the spatial layouts of the two churches. The new San Salvador, with its repeated quincunx configuration and projecting transepts, clearly expressed (fig. 20)—with the force of an image capable of explicitly entering the popular imaginary—the union of the patron saints (fig. 16). From San Marco, via the Mercerie, to San Salvador: the explicit message of the *porta da mar* [door on the sea] formed by the two columns on the Molo, was thus projected onto the urban body.

In this way the reconstruction of San Salvador actually assumed the significance of a "refoundation." The route formed the Mercerie took on new conceptual meanings. This explains again the meaning of the churches invoked as "walls of the very Christian city": the places consecrated to the two patron saints and the streets that unite them, leading on the one side toward San

Giorgio Maggiore and on the other toward the Rialto, symbolically formed the spinal structure of the *civitas Venetiarum*.

Two drawings in the Archivio di Stato in Venice (*Miscellanea Mappe*, 468 and 463) demonstrate the care that was taken in designing the opening of the Mercerie onto Campo San Salvador. This *campo* was of considerable importance because it was the meeting point for two economically important arteries: the first led to Piazza San Marco and the second to Campo San Bartolomeo, the Rialto, the Fondaco dei Tedeschi, and San Giovanni Crisostomo. Drawing 468 (fig. 23) is an accurate survey of the last section of the Mercerie, flanking San Salvador: the only visible parts of the church are the apse emerging from the rear, the ancient *loggetta* on the eastern side, and the new, deeply inset side entrance. In all probability, the drawing documents the improvements made in the streets;[48] but one notes the oblique position, relative to the present façade of the church, of the building line facing the *campo*. This may have been the position of the church's medieval façade, given that drawing 463—which, according to a note on the reverse side, was presented to the Ufficio del Piovego on March 13, 1550—shows oblique stairs connecting the new façade to a diverging alignment. The new shops are sketched in on the left; the triangle across from the church is more difficult to interpret—Is it supposed to be a platform indicating the *raxon del monastero*?[49]

The two drawings, therefore, document the transformations that the urban surroundings underwent as a consequence of the new building, whose particular characteristics we shall now discuss.

The entire spatial organization of the church is guided by a rigid proportional system, based on the planimetric module of the minor domes (figs. 21, 26, 27). Two modules are used to determine the width of the vaulted spaces on either side of the domes of the central nave (fig. 20), four modules to the domes themselves, four more to the spaces between the walls of the transepts and the piers of the last dome. The same proportional system is projected vertically (fig. 21): the protruding structures, up to the inferior line of the architrave, contain two cubes (2 spatial modules); the larger spaces, up to the impost of the domes, are formed by another two cubes, double the size of the preceding ones. The proportions are based on simple ratios of $1:1$ and $2:1$, with a formalization of the Byzantine composition within a static type of harmony, in spite of the scheme's dynamic nature.[50] The horizontal emphasis contrasts with the vertical thrust of the domed spaces: the dialectic is resolved through a hierarchical connection of the spaces. The interior space of San Salvador can be divided into simple bodies (fig. 25); thus the church seems to present Pythagorean and Neoplatonic ideas of space that seem even more inflexible and explicit because they do not appear in the later church of San Francesco della Vigna (fig. 61).

On the other hand, the time was ripe for Venice to accept this type of mathematical and proportional rigor. It is significant that two years after the acceptance of Giorgio Spavento's model for the church of San Salvador, on August 11, 1508, Luca Pacioli delivered his famous and much acclaimed inaugural speech in the church of San Bartolomeo di Rialto—later published in his Latin edition of Euclid—which contained numerous references to a mystical mathematical system similar to the one that characterized the *dispositio harmonica* of San Salvador.[51] Moreover, Pacioli's thinking was based on the idea that knowledge mainly results from "seeing": mathematics—"very true and in the first step of certainty,"—as he says in *De divina proportione*[52]—can begin to become a part, by way of a "scientifically" shaped form, in the stage of human relationships, producing a mirror of universal harmony and justice. Furthermore, the enthusiasm with which the patrician public received the Neoplatonism of Fra Luca should be emphasized. It is not to be excluded that in Venice one could read in the symbolic and mystical meaning of the number the sublimation of many mathematical ideas.

But was Giorgio Spavento really responsible for the translation of these sublimations into architectural models? Though few doubts really persist concerning the attribution of the overall planimetric scheme, Tullio Lombardo's presence on the construction site, beginning in 1507, raises a number of questions.[53] On October 29, 1507, Tullio was nominated "architect and governor of the design and building of the façade of the new Basilica of San Salvador, until its completion," with his father, Pietro Lombardo, as consultant. However, in spite of the advice of his father there was a clause that only in the case of Pietro's death would "Tullio be considered the one and only architect." The agreements reached with the masons Antonio and Ambrogio, dated November 7, 1507, concerned "three complete pedestals, that is, base, dado, and cornice of the pedestal, and the plinth that goes; the base goes above the said cornice and below the half pilasters attached to the wall, according to the designs provided by master Tullio and master Pietro Lombardi." But in later agreements, also from 1507, "where two half-pedestals go in the beginning of the choir" and "two pedestals go in the beginning of the opening of the large chapel"; only Tullio was mentioned—Tullio who, however, seemed during this period to be providing designs under the direction of Giorgio Spavento, who was quoted again in the documents of November 1507.[54]

In March 1511—after Spavento's death and shortly after Agnadello and the treaty with the Pope—Tullio Lombardo and Fra Giacomo Martini entered into agreements with different master stonemasons for cornices, frieze, and architrave . . . according to the designs that master Tullio will provide them":[55] the building, which began from the apse, thus reached, in 1511, the height of the entablature. On March 22, 1518, Marco Tron, the procurator of the building, entered into an agreement with Father Crisogono Novello of Venice and his nephews for the mosaics of the chapel of Corpus Domini (the presbytery); its construction was financed by the patriarchal revenue.[56] From 1507, therefore, Tullio Lombardo followed the execution of Giorgio Spavento's model—as we have seen, in 1531, the year before the death of Tullio, the building was not completely finished—and starting in 1509 Tullio would be the sole protagonist on the construction site.

Both Paoletti and McAndrew have insisted upon attributing the conception of the structure to Spavento, although McAndrew has assumed that Tullio was responsible for the detailing of the orders and for the attic placed above the cornice of the Corinthian entablature, with the groups of tripartite windows.[57]

But if one accepts McAndrew's very plausible hypothesis, one cannot trace the entire proportional symphony of the interior of San Salvador to the original model. If we admit that the latter was guided by harmonious proportions and accept the hypothesis that the interpolation of the attic was Tullio's, then we must conclude that those proportions were different from those that are presently visible. Moreover, not only does the attic in the interior of San Salvador speak an erudite language, but the combination of the two orders and their detailing belong to an antiquarian culture. How much of the model approved in 1506 developed the grammar used in the structuring of the space?

In attempting to answer this question, we have found that a comparison with Spavento's existing works unquestionably attributed to him does not appear to be very useful. Neither the sacristy of San Marco nor the chapel of San Teodoro are very convincing; the facade of the Palazzo Ducale on Rio della Canonica, adjacent to the facade by Antonio Rizzo, employs a design that is severe but devoid of antiquarian references; in the Fondaco dei Tedeschi, it is hard to recognize the *proto*'s hand.[58]

Some useful indications for answering our question, however, can be found by examining a work demolished during the Napoleonic era that can be attributed to Giorgio Spavento on the basis of a document of 1490: we are referring to the church of San Nicolò di Castello (figs. 30, 31), built next to the Ospedale di Gesú Cristo, consecrated in 1503, and known to us thanks to a few survey drawings done by Antonio Visentini.[59] Located to the left of the hospital, as one can see in the plan by de' Barbari, as well as in Selva's survey,[60] the church of San Nicolò must probably have been part of a much larger welfare complex, with a single courtyard, than the one that appears in de' Barbari's plan of 1500. Brian Pullan has demonstrated that the project for the Ospedale di Gesú Cristo underwent a reduction in size between 1474—the year in which its construction was decided—and 1503;[61] the placement of the church enables us to hypothesize an initial overall plan based on two buildings with a courtyard, situated on the sides of San Nicolò and in some way connected to it. Finally, the aforementioned document of 1490 also leads us to attribute the church of San Nicolò to Spavento, for it records a payment made to Bartolomeo Gonella for the work he did as the hospital's *proto* (starting in 1483). In it, in fact, the *proto* is mentioned "in respect to the work done by master Giorgio and others of ours," whereas a later payment, registered on June 11, 1488, was made to the "account of master Giorgio di Pietro Spavento, *proto* for the remainder of the Ospedale di Gesú Cristo."[62]

Let us try to analyze the plan and the three sections of the church of San Nicolò di Castello surveyed by Visentini, keeping in mind the exterior of the church as it is portrayed in Canaletto's famous painting. A presbytery with a square plan and covered by a shallow dome is connected to a decidedly neo-Byzantine quincunx plan (fig. 31), with a dome supported by detached piers: Codussi's design for San Giovanni Crisostomo, anticipated by the spatial plan of the initial form of Sant'Andrea alla Certosa, has been enriched by an original division of the structure. The spatial rhythm adopted by San Nicolò di Castello can be simply expressed by the pattern a–B–a–B'–c: we see that a rhythmic framework has been sketched out as well as a two-part, albeit syncopated, organization of spaces. It is more difficult to establish—using only the eighteenth-century surveys—the ways in which the proportions were later modulated: according to Visentini's drawings, the domed spaces are formed by two virtual cubes (fig. 30), if one considers the central space up to the impost of the semispherical dome and the presbytery up to the summit of the shallow dome.

A number of the linguistic ingredients that characterize San Salvador had thus already been revealed in San Nicolò di Castello. In particular, the system formed by the two domes on spherical pendentives appears as an important precedent of the triadic spatiality that distinguishes the first church. This leads us to make a potentially important observation. The symbolic motivations that we have drawn out of the program for the new San Salvador were not external conditions imposed on the designers: San Nicolò di Castello demonstrated that in the Venice of the late fifteenth century the neo-Byzantine *schemata* suggested complex spatial experiments done *per architecturam*; the result achieved in San Salvador cannot be explained without referring to the modality of this experimentation within the programs that were probably recommended or imposed by the clergy—one notes, incidentally, that unlike Santa Maria Formosa and San Giovanni Crisostomo, the church of San Nicolò di Castello was new from the ground up: its neo-Byzantine character therefore has special significance.

Having analyzed the structure, we shall now examine the grammar used in San Nicolò: in the piers vertically divided by the fascias indicating the impost of the vaults and the base of the windows, it is easy to recognize a nonclassical solution—a solecism that echoes the solution Spavento adopted for the facade of the Palazzo Ducale—used as a device to avoid resolving a difficult problem. It was the same problem that Mauro Codussi had resolved in a very particular manner in Santa Maria Formosa and in San Giovanni Crisostomo: in the latter, one sees the connection formed by the piers supporting the arches of the central space. The problem was how to incorporate the height of the impost of the minor arches and the entablature that wraps around the whole interior: Codussi overcame the difficulty by laying aside classical grammar and freely placing a kind of shortened pilaster, with a pseudo-Corinthian capital, above the moldings that take the place of the capital and entablature of the lower pilaster. It was a way of asserting the grammatical freedom reaffirmed by Spavento in the rear façade of the Palazzo Ducale as well as in the church of San Nicolò di Castello: in the latter, on the contrary, Codussi's lesson became even more abstract and nonclassical.

All this was firmly rejected in San Salvador. The problem was resolved by the adoption of two different orders, complete with separate entablature (figs. 24, 28): Corinthian for the major pilasters and Ionic for the minor ones, both resting on a single pedestal. In this way, the rigidity of the spatial structure was appropriately reflected in the network of orders, and, significantly, in a canonical language that was explicitly *all'antica*. San Salvador revealed—in other words—the need to end the experiments based on unlimited deformations tions of classical elements, and represented an example of linguistic severity that was undoubtedly exceptional for Venice. Nevertheless, the Corinthian capitals still have a single band of leaves and the Ionic order is extremely rigid, whereas the architrave of the major entablature follows a typically Codussian device, derived perhaps from Veronese *exempla*—the fascias are laid out according to an oblique pattern (fig. 29).

The new application of syntactic rigor in a classical sense also prompted the superimposition of the attic above the Corinthian entablature. Together, the attic and the entablature link the polycentric spatiality of the entire interior space to a triumphal imperiousness: the formal device transforms the bodies emerging from the minor domes into four front arches reduced to baldachins.

Tullio Lombardo's language and research stand out from these innovations with authority. Tullio certainly must have subjected Spavento's solutions to careful criticism and invested the original model with a *ratio* entrusted to new proportional variations and to a rhythmic interpretation resolved through the duality of orders. Even the use of the Ionic—which was extremely rare in Venice of the late fifteenth and early sixteenth centuries—reminds us of Tullio's manner: if we accept McAndrew's well-founded attributions, the Ionic order of San Salvador can be compared with that of the church of Santa Maria Maggiore in Venice and with that of the abbatial church of Praglia (figs. 35, 36).[63]

In the end, Tullio Lombardo's work on the initial spatial idea tended to increase the coherency of the innermost harmonic values, to bring together its Byzantine qualities with an unusual syntactic and grammatical control, and to develop the "heroic" structure of the building's dimensions. When we consider that the exceptional status of the church was thus accentuated, Doge Andrea Gritti's special interest in it quickly becomes comprehensible.

McAndrew has nevertheless criticized the windows that open up in groups of three, breaking up the continuity of the attic fascia (fig. 21): in fact, a decision made around 1569, which placed lanterns on top of the three domes, corrected an error of judgment regarding the intensity of the original sources of illumination (fig. 18).[64] One must, however, observe that the windows placed under the big round occular windows, *oculi*, are of a fixed size; they seem to be an attempt to cope with a difficulty inherent in the original model. The present illumination, moreover, certainly enables one to read with absolute clarity a structure made of multiple series of spaces and volumetric structures and protrusions, but it also compromises the abstract purity of the domed structures (figs. 26, 27).

Purity and abstraction: it is at the grammatical level that these characteristics emerge in a particular way. Tullio seems to have proceeded analytically, motivated by a desire to illustrate the mechanics of architectonic reasoning. The Corinthian pilasters for example, are juxtaposed on the junction crossings between the central nave and the rectangular spaces on the sides: the vertical continuity of the projections—pilasters, entablatures, small attic pilasters, large vault moldings—is protected to the detriment of the structure of the pilasters (fig. 28). But this was exactly what the architect was striving for: a hierarchical and Albertian distinction of elements, achieved by interpreting the ancient lexicon as pure abstraction. For this reason, the major and minor pilasters look as though they had been "applied" to the building supports. By the same token, the Corinthian half pilasters that designate the limits of the minor domed spaces, are literally flattened onto the interior building surface, showing through from behind the Ionic pilasters. The agreement between the mathematical framework of the space and the building structure also points to the conceptual role given to the ornamental elements. Furthermore, the rectangular panels obsessively evident in all the vertical elements and in the undersides of the arches, accentuate the artful character of the framework itself, which has been formalized by a scholastic interpretation of the orders.

One can therefore read in the interior of San Salvador the results of a dialogue between two protagonists, but also between two generations of Venetian architecture. Tullio's "rebellion" against the paternal manner was not turned into a polemic against Spavento. That which can be attributed to Lombardo, in San Salvador, has a kind of maieutic function with respect to the architectural program established by the *proto* of the Procuratia de supra, Giorgio Spavento. It is in this sense that the church was really an extreme work in the history of Venetian culture: calmly, but firmly, it proclaimed the end of an era, translating the scheme it had derived from San Marco into spatial terms that were paradoxically antithetical to the Byzantine manner. A reticulated, mathematical, and perspective space, modularly arranged and based on the organization of the classical orders, forced the neo-Byzantine program to speak a humanistic language.

3. Venetian Humanism: the Cult of the "Word"

Tullio Lombardo's detachment from the Venetian self-satisfied hedonism of the late fifteenth century should be considered within the context of the cultural renewal that had its epicenter right in the lagoon. Vittore Branca has intelligently demonstrated that in identifying Angelo Poliziano's new literary direction, after 1479–80, it is very important to recognize his contact with the Venetian intellectual environment.[65] The Aristotelianism of Poliziano's most authoritative and faithful friend in Venice, Ermolao Barbaro, and the rigorous philology of Barbaro, Girolamo Donà, and Giorgio Merula revealed to the poet a universe different from Landino's and Ficino's: Poliziano's new philology approached the word—as Eugenio Garin has written—"with the seriousness of a rite," defending the critical claims set forward by the *studia humanitatis* against the escapism that they had expounded on the part of the Laurentian cultural circle.[66] Branca has said that it was "the taking of a stand against the hybridism of affectation and popularization, of literary and spoken languages, that characterized so many writings of the period; . . . an affirmation of the language of the true and real—from words to things, from *verba* to *res*—that was the newest and most appropriate expressive means in Poliziano's writings between the late eighties and early nineties."[67] Given the substantial identity between thought and language, the manner of expression was closely tied to strategies of thinking. "The humanism of the word" tended toward a plain and precise language, capable of renouncing the richness of both erudite and popular literature written in the vernacular, in the name of a search for clarity and universality.

The consecration of the *verbum*, accomplished by Ermolao Barbaro and Giorgio Valla's philology was—like Poliziano's—geared toward the examination of the instruments of human communication. The Venetian cultural circles of the late fifteenth century identified a new way of analyzing reality, as was demonstrated by Ermolao, whose new Aristotelianism intended to embrace syncretically language and thought, poetry and philosophy, as well as the human and natural sciences.[68]

It is impossible to transfer automatically the cultural atmosphere that characterized the philological school of Barbaro, Valla, and Donà, onto the Venetian artistic experience of the end of the century. Above all, the mechanical quality of the operation would be too obvious. Rather, one must wonder how this patrician elite—which was so interested in the authenticity of ancient texts, in their amendment, and in the comparison of codices and glosses—could have either encouraged or embraced Tullio Lombardo's "new manner," so obviously hostile to linguistic pastiche, to expressive adornment for its own sake, and to the "extraordinary" manipulation of humanistic themes.

Incidentally, the appearance of the names of Bernardo Bembo and Pietro Contarini among the supporters of the new San Salvador is a historical fact of notable interest. The first—as we have already mentioned—was one of Poliziano's intimate friends; as for Contarini, Poliziano called him "a man of refined spirit" and would remember him again in the *Epistolae* (3, 6) with great regard, along with Ermolao Barbaro. In fact, Poliziano composed a piece—a *rispetto*—that was set to music by Enrico Isaac for a theatrical performance held in the house of Pietro Contarini, "philosophus," which would later be described by Marcantonio Michiel as "famous for its ornaments of antiquities."[69]

Finally, to complete the picture, let us mention the well-founded relationship that existed between Poliziano and Fra Giocondo, whom the former described, in *Centuria secunda* (1, 77) as "the one man, I believe, above all others in questions of ancient inscriptions and monuments, not merely diligent, but even, undoubtedly, most skillful." Moreover, on the same page, Poliziano recalls that Fra Giocondo had sent, "recently," a collection of approximately 2,000 inscriptions for Lorenzo the Magnificent, which he had arranged with Alessandro Cortese's help.[70] Branca suggests that Poliziano and Fra Giocondo met either in 1484 or 1488. It is clear that Fra Giocondo was later linked to Aldus Manutius, the Venetian typographer, while Poliziano became interested in Vitruvius in the 1490s, as he himself mentions in chapter 31 (*Aquae vitruvianae*) of his *Centuria secunda*.[71]

The Venetian circle in touch with Florentine humanism and philological and antiquarian studies had thus already created, in the last decades of the fifteenth century, a *humus* capable of accepting Tullio Lombardo's rigorism as an expression congruent with its own cultural ambitions. In fact, Tullio's sculpture and architecture accepted in substance the consecration of the *verbum* dear to the Venetian philologists. At the risk of appearing hyperclassical, Pietro Lombardo's son, Tullio, attempted to purify and amend the "figurative Latin." The operation had no precedent in Venice and harmonized with Ermolao Barbaro's efforts: the common objective was the recovery of a solidly established manner of communication, one intent on a clarity of expression and a universal dialogue filled with *pietas* toward the ancient *exemplum*.

Nor should we forget, as we attempt a better definition of the culture and mentality of the Venetian humanistic circle, that Tullio Lombardo's works were mainly public (churches) or dedicated to the "triumph of Glory" (monumental tombs). Neither Bernardo Bembo, nor Ermolao Barbaro seemed interested in startling humanistic renovations of their residences. Moreover, the examples set by the Zorzi family in San Severo and by Andrea Loredan—clients for two of Codussi's significant buildings—would remain almost isolated: the palazzo of Gabriele Vendramin at Santa Fosca was built according to Lombardesque models, albeit limited and controlled ones (fig. 1).[72] In other words, already in the fifteenth century a trend was being defined, one which will be examined later: the forms *all'antica* seemed to be set aside even by those favoring cultural renewal, for those places meant to strengthen the *res publica*. In private, the ideal physical environment remained the one prescribed by tradition.

And yet, Tullio Lombardo's art did not establish a transmittable manner, nor did it create an atmosphere characterized by the Florentine study of Antiquity: isolated, Tullio would live to see himself cast aside in favor of a Tuscan-Roman master, Jacopo Sansovino. And in looking for the reasons behind this isolation, besides the climate that had existed in the years after Agnadello, we will also have to consider the scholasticism with which Tullio, in architecture, gave life to his linguistic purity: his recovery of the ancient models brought into the lagoon an abstractionism that could only be united with great difficulty to the dominant aesthetic ideas apparently sanctioned by the average taste of the Venetian public.

4. Tullio Lombardo and Fra Giocondo

Tullio Lombardo's participation in the construction of San Salvador marked a very significant step in his career. After the perspective bas-reliefs for the Scuola di San Marco, his work in the main chapel of the Duomo in Treviso, and the monument to Andrea Vendramin, Tullio's manner became more defined in the altar of the Bernabò chapel in San Giovanni Crisostomo (1501) and in the Mocenigo Monument (fig. 37).[73]

Furthermore, the attribution to Tullio of the roof cloister and the abbatial church of Praglia seems to be based on stylistic considerations (figs. 35, 36); we can add to all these achievements the consultation work he did, along with his father, for San Giorgio Maggiore (1507) and the Scuola Grande della Misericordia, as well as his work on the exterior of the Zen chapel in San Marco (around 1512–13) and in the Duomo in Belluno, and the project, since lost, for the façade of the church of Sant'Antonio di Castello in Venice (1517).[74] Tullio Lombardo proposed an Albertian type of austerity with increasingly rarified modifications: the monument to Giovanni Mocenigo (fig. 37) clearly reveals a tension toward the ancient dictates characterized by an abstract and hermetic self-restraint, different from the tension that inspired his sculpture of that period. Let us also look at the church of Praglia (figs. 35, 36). *Columnae quad-*

rangulae, with an Albertian flavor, rest on tall pedestals; their Ionic capitals are "oriented" toward the longitudinal axis of the nave, and they support a regular series of arcades. The lateral naves reflect the central one, which is covered with a barrel vault, with a dynamic succession of small domes, while the space of the presbytery is marked by an unexpected leap in scale: in the corners of the square supporting the dome, four gigantic columns, also Ionic, intersect with the minor orders, reaching the level of the upper entablature. The intersection of the columns and the piers is still automatic, and the details are schematic: the sloping fascias of the architrave and the correctness of the proportions are united with barely elaborated profiles, like the solutions for the connection of plinths and pedestals, or the latter's moldings. It is, however, difficult to relate the design of this interior to that of San Salvador, which features a more skillful use of ancient syntax. The fact remains that the church of Praglia features an attempt at a dialogue between orders of different dimensions—the uniform use of the Ionic is certainly due also to iconographic motives, given that the church was dedicated to the Virgin Mary—an experiment that went beyond Mauro Codussi's solecisms and the Venetian milieu in general.

The strict structuralism of the church of Praglia would later be reduced to schematism in the interior of the Duomo in Belluno. On the other hand, it is more difficult to judge Tullio's contribution to the interior of the Duomo in Cividale. We cannot, however, agree with Carolyn Lewis Kolb's attribution of the Villa Giustinian Roncade to Tullio Lombardo,[75] given the syntactic irresolution that characterize the building, as well as the "picturesque" interpretation of the language it adopted.

Tullio Lombardo demonstrated, therefore, a predilection for elementary rhythms and "simple" words. But what were his sources? And how did he manage to receive a message that seems to have come from contacts with non-Venetian sources?

Fra Giocondo's arrival in Venice may in fact have catalyzed latent antiquarian interests, but that does not explain Tullio's linguistic "turning point" which had already occurred at the end of the fifteenth century. Scholars have been able to identify ancient models that Tullio Lombardo used in his career as a sculptor: Wendy Stedman Sheard and Debra Pincus have insisted on the possibility that the artist came into contact with Zaccaria Barbaro, a collector of Greek pieces, as well as with Ermolao. Moreover, in describing Andrea Odoni's collection in 1532, Marcantonio Michiel noted the following: "the marble figure of a woman, entirely dressed without a head or hands, is ancient; and it used to be in Tullio Lombardo's shop, and was portrayed by him many times in his works."[76] Debra Pincus has, in addition, thrown light on Tullio's career as a restorer of ancient sculptures, insisting on Mantegna's painting and on his contact with Venetian collectors.[77] But Pincus has also been forced to admit that the way in which Tullio arrived at the results of the Vendramin Tomb poses a historical problem that is far from being solved.[78]

One should also seriously consider Stedman Sheard's hypothesis, based on a wealth of evidence, that Pietro and Tullio Lombardo knew of Bramante's works from the frescoes in the Panigarola house and in Bergamo, after the Prevedari engraving, in Santa Maria sopra San Satiro.[79] The fact that Tullio (or an associate of his) encountered, in the 1490s, the last version of Leonardo's *Last Supper* (in the bas-relief then in Santa Maria dei Miracoli, and now in the Galleria Franchetti in the Ca' d'Oro) seems, finally, to point toward a study trip taken by the artist to Milan, which might explain the Bramante-like aspect of a few of the solutions present in his works.

We have, however, more questions than answers: and this is inevitable, given the scarcity of our knowledge of the sources used in Venice and in the Veneto region in the late fifteenth century, the available archeological knowledge, and the quality and circulation of sketch books containing drawings of ancient remains. It is better, for now, to leave these questions open: it is better simply to report the existing gaps to be filled than to increase the number of unfounded hypotheses.

Given that we are forced to make judgments on the basis of only a few proven works by Tullio Lombardo, we must recognize in the church of San Salvador a syntactic coherence superior to that demonstrated in Praglia or Belluno, but of the same nature. The recovery of the Ionic order and its use as a "secondary voice" relative to the Corinthian order, the loyalty to "quadrangular columns," certainly planned by Giorgio Spavento but translated into an ancient, Ciceronian, language, the rigid canonical quality of the proportions and the profiles: these factors testify to a study of ancient sources that was at odds with the linguistic empiricism of the Venetian tradition. But Tullio's humanism—and this is an appropriate time to stress this point—revealed its limitations in the reelaboration of the *verbum* and the *exemplum*: the subtle and refined equilibriums that animate the *Adam* of the Vendramin Tomb remain for the most part extraneous to his architectonic experiments.

In San Salvador as well as in the Mocenigo Monument, in fact, it seems as though Tullio Lombardo's Latin has given up trying to become a live language. The reexhumation shows itself for what it is: a work of interpretation and study, an effort completed in order to protect the rediscovered syntax from contamination, while clearly rejecting variation and poetic licenses.

But the road to experimental research based on polycentric spatial dynamics remained open: this applied not only to Santa Giustina in Padua (figs. 39, 40), but also to the church of San Sepolcro in Piacenza by Alessio Tramello (fig. 42), and to Peruzzi's studies for San Domenico in Siena (fig. 43), and even to the later and mannered church of Sante Flora e Lucille in Arezzo by Giorgio Vasari.

We must, however, face a question that arises when we compare Fra Giocondo's well-known project for St. Peter's (UA 6r) with the structure of San Salvador (fig. 38):[80] is there a connection between these two "rereadings" of San Marco or are we dealing with completely independent ideas that are only casually related? The question is not insignificant, in light of the observations we have made on the possible connections between the Venetian church and St. Peter's. One might even propose the tantalizing hypothesis that the design of San Salvador offered something analogous to the experience that was supposed to have occurred in the Fondaco dei Tedeschi. As we already know, Pietro Contarini—son of Giovanni Alberto—affirmed, in 1517, that Fra Giocondo was responsible for the design of the Fondaco; this affirmation deserves close examination.[81]

We need to note the following: Giorgio Spavento seems to have been involved in the Fondaco as well as in San Salvador; the two instances occurred extremely close in time; both works were practically "ceded" by Spavento shortly after they began—the first to Scarpagnino, and the second to Lombardo. If Fra Giocondo had become more concretely involved in choices regarding the design of the Fondaco—choices that Contarini "revealed" as though he wished to reestablish a hidden truth—one might legitimately extend the hypothesis to the church of San Salvador. But a few problems appear here.

Contarini's testimony is not to be ignored, especially when one considers that it was given in a eulogy dedicated to Andrea Gritti, with whom Fra Giocondo had collaborated during the war to reconquer lost territory.[82] Furthermore, Contarini's speech was written in 1517: barely three years after Giocondo's failure in the competition for the reconstruction of the Rialto district.[83] Contarini seems to have carried out a historical restoration of Fra Giocondo's work in Venice, and in a persistent fashion, given that he reaffirmed the attribution of the Fondaco in two later works—which Manlio Dazzi later noted.[84]

In his *Argoa voluptas*, published in 1541, Pietro Contarini wrote,

We cross a bridge that divides the city / into twin parts: but our glance first falls on the / residence of the wealthy Germans: / the artifice of the marble walls reaches above the clouds: / the Glory of geometry.

And he reaffirmed in the first book of *Argo vulgar*, which is not dated but may have been written before the other, "Then we cross the bridge which divides the city into two parts, and first we admire the Fondaco built with three stories where the rich Germans live; the walls are of marble and their height surpasses that of the clouds—the Glory of geometry."[85]

The Senate approved the model for the Fondaco on June 19, 1505, while the latest news regarding Fra Giocondo's stay in France included a dispatch from Ambassador Francesco Morosini of November 18, 1504, which presented the architect to the Venetian Senate. An exceptional presentation: Morosini could supply precious political information about the pacts between the King of France, the Emperor Maximilian, and Julius II, including the project of excommunication concerning Venice, reported to him by Fra Giocondo. The latter, in fact, was on familiar terms in Paris with the Emperor's delegate, to whom he was giving private lessons on Vitruvius.[86] Fra Giocondo's choice was thus clear as early as November 1504. We can assume, however, that he was still in France in April 1505: Jacopo d'Atri mentioned in a letter written on April 8 that he had asked Fra Giocondo to "look for the library of the King and many others."[87] What Ciapponi has suggested is, therefore, very likely: Fra Giocondo went directly from Paris to Venice sometime during the second half of 1505 or early 1506. In addition, his petition mentions the cases of books and *inzegni* [devices] he left in France, while in the report *Intorno alla Brentella* (1507) he records how he rejected the offers that the Pope made him.[88]

If this reconstruction of facts is correct, we might think that Fra Giocondo gave Giorgio Spavento advice about the Fondaco as early as 1505, but we also must remember that he had sent the project for St. Peter's—otherwise so "Venetian"—to Rome from the lagoon.

We do know that on May 28, 1506, the Council of Ten decided the architect's *condotta* [conduct] with the award of an annual salary of 200 ducats. Fra Giocondo, when he presented himself to the *Serenissma*, demonstrated that he was fully aware of his own value, as an expert in fortresses, waterways, shores, foundations; he offered "to teach . . . to three or four or however many [men] of allegiance and nobility it may please the illustrious *signoria* to assign."[89] The deliberation of the Ten, in return, underlined the friar's great fame in repairing shores, in aquatic matters, in defending and building fortresses and citadels." One notes, furthermore, that the agreement was presented by the heads of the Council of Ten, Bernardo Bembo and Giorgio Emo: the same men who, five days before, had given the commissioner of the Salt Bank a mandate to finance the church of San Salvador. A series of coincidences begins to throw light on the relations that might have led Fra Giocondo to two such important construction sites in Venice: the Fondaco and San Salvador. The first, with its courtyard vaguely *all'antica* and the archaic Vitruvian tonality of its *dispositio*, has its counterparts in an illustration from Fra Giocondo's edition of the *De architectura* of Vitruvius printed in 1511: this makes us suspect not so much a design by Fra Giocondo but rather his consultation, which might also have been given in the first months of 1506, for the definition of a few formal elements, especially the courtyard. In that same year, moreover, Fra Giocondo wrote a report opposing Alessio Aleardi the Elder's intervention in the diversion of the Brenta,[90] while Giorgio Spavento reinforced the embankments of the Malamocco.[91]

Given the position that Fra Giocondo had attained in Venice, it is more than likely that he discussed the embankments with Spavento. The possibility that Fra Giocondo played the part of a "consultant" for the most significant buildings begun between 1506 and 1509 thus presents itself. Even if we ignore this hypothesis, we must reflect upon the following coincidence: a humanist, for whom technology and architecture were only parts of a cultural universe tending toward Antiquity, proposed to Julius II a design for St. Peter's that was interestingly modeled on San Marco in Venice (and consequently on the ancient Apostoleion of Constantinople) (fig. 38); shortly thereafter, an idea vaguely analogous to Fra Giocondo's was adopted for the church that marks the "mystical heart" of Venice. In this significant sequence of events there may be a historical problem worth investigating. But not before we take this opportunity to stress that the church of San Salvador, in comparison to the design for St. Peter's, expresses greater clarity and self-confidence, at least in its present form.

We have already warned the reader that the history of San Salvador brings together two histories that meet without canceling each other out: a history of the collective imaginary and a history of cultural innovations. And we have already extended the historical importance of the church of San Salvador, calling upon the works of Alessio Tramello, Peruzzi, and Vasari. Whence it is possible to deduce several things. The neo-Byzantinism of Fra Giocondo's design for St. Peter's demonstrates that within the ambit of humanistic culture—even as interpreted by a very particular individual, such as this Veronese architect—an interest in Byzantine spatiality, evident in San Marco, was increasing; it succeeded in harmonizing with analogous experiments that were taking place in the late fifteenth century such as in the projects of Bramante, Mauro Codussi, and Giorgio Spavento. In this disciplinary environment, Fra Giocondo's design for St. Peter's appears archaic and eclectic: Bramante's Byzantinism was aimed at searching for a spatial and structural organic unity with a coherence all its own. It is, however, significant that these examples emerging from the architectural research found their counterparts, in Venice, in the religious ambitions fed by the political trend of the early sixteenth century. It is certainly not by chance that in 1507, in Venice, the first stone was laid for a church that adopted the scheme of San Salvador reducing it "in a minor tone": this was San Fantin, based on a project by Sebastiano da Lugano and made possible by a bequest from Cardinal Giovanni Battista Zen (fig. 41).[92] Three cross vaults instead of domes and a simplified arrangement of the orders characterize this church that Scarpagnino worked on very slowly. It constituted a "reply" that abandoned Tullio Lombardo's more significant elements: the attic, the minor Ionic order, the explicit reference to San Marco. The *ecclesia* placed *in visceribus urbis* became a simple typological scheme for the minor church—the product of a long and tormented history—that faces onto Campo della Fenice.

This helps us evaluate Tullio's contribution more accurately, even with regard to a possible consultation by Fra Giocondo for the plan. All our considerations confirm that Lombardo's innovations consisted in the neo-Pythagorean and antiquarian "proportions" to which he subjected a structure whose *dispositio* had been preceded by the small church of San Nicolò di Castello and by Fra Giocondo's design for St. Peter's. The ideal chain articulated by these works, extending as far as Baldassarre Peruzzi, demonstrates how a structure that had risen to incarnate the dictates of a republican *pietas* endowed with its own consolidated tradition could become the progenitor of a typological quest with autonomous motivations.

5. San Salvador: a Typological Model?

The church of San Sepolcro in Piacenza, by Alessio Tramello, might constitute a decisive link in such a chain (fig. 42). Unfortunately, the philological research in this area cannot be considered definitive; for that reason we are obliged to accept a hypothesis—the most likely one at present—that situates its beginning around 1513. Moreover, the church, as it now stands with cross vaults above the main nave, seems more closely related to San Fantin than to San Salvador. But a drawing preserved in the archives of the church of San Vittore al Corpo, in Milan, portrays a structure with three domes, transepts with apses, and lateral chapels also enclosed with apses, that may correspond to an initial design for San Sepolcro and that seems to suggest an interpretation by Tramello of Spavento and Tullio Lombardo's work.[93]

Let us leave this question of "derivations" aside for now. The comparison of

the Piacenza church and the Venetian one throws light, instead, upon the profound differences between the cultures that gave life to the two works. San
Sepolcro, in spite of the presence of the quincunx repeated three times, and the
attic above the main order, abandoned the mathematical division and the
ancient-like aura of San Salvador: there dominates rather a taste for continuity
in the treatment of the building surfaces and for structural consistency—a taste
demonstrated by the dimensions of the piers, the apses that articulate in pairs
the boundaries between the vaulted piers, and the trabeated fascias that absorb
the capitals. Tramello ignores the erudite solutions of continuity that characterize San Salvador, in favor of variations that may be archaic—the coupling of
the partitions of the building perimeter—but are also capable of enhancing the
tectonic and material qualities of the building: the structuralism evinced here
had clearly been learned from Bramante's work in Milan.

It is likely that San Sepolcro, and not San Salvador, was a model for Baldassarre Peruzzi during the design of San Domenico in Siena. Bruno Adorni has in
fact demonstrated, on the basis of drawings UA 459, 461 and 460, that Baldassarre conceived a design for the rebuilding of the castle of Sant' Antonio in
Piacenza, for which he probably visited Piacenza.[94] Therefore, drawing UA
340 reelaborates the *type* of San Salvador and San Sepolcro, projecting on the
outside—with an astonishing and precocious spatial intuition—the last domed
interior space: the "boundary" was forced, made elastic, absorbed into the
configuration of space. But in UA 339, the sequence of domical-vaulted rooms
also foregoes supplementary spaces (fig. 43): the neo-Byzantine type is transformed into a dynamic vibration of major and minor interior spaces that cut
into the area of the transept, articulating an exceptionally bold organic
sequence.

Compared with this creative open-mindedness, the model of San Salvador
shows all the limitations connected to the historical moment in which it was
situated, while the "variations" proposed by Giorgio Vasari in the Aretine
church of Sante Flora e Lucilla attempt to "modernize" a theme now taken to
be a simple alternative to typological fossilization.[95]

It is significant that, with the exception of the minor and limited case of the
church of San Fantin, Venice would not witness the development of syntactic
research intent on "dissolving" the rigidities present in San Salvador. In the
lagoon, that church assumed a significance that surpassed its architectural substance. Paradoxically—but not excessively so—this attribution of significance
blocked elaborations that might have risked reducing its influence on a highly
figurative problem.

6. An "Introverted" Theorem

These last considerations lead us to further evaluations. In fact, the structure of
the church, though its ties to the city are deep, did not alter in the least the "late
antique" continuity of the urban fabric. Better yet: it did not even touch it. The
recessed side entrance from the Mercerie street is significant in this regard (fig.
33). The church does not reveal its own structure on the outside; it is instead
immersed in the urban *continuum* and displays an introverted character. A

building—which was, moreover, envisioned as early as 1506—surrounds the church, allowing only the left transept and a portion of the apse to emerge (fig. 34): the "popular" language that characterizes the houses with arched windows, single or paired (fig. 32), provokes symptomatic contrasts of scale wherever the structure of the church manages to show itself to the city. Nor did the program take into consideration the relationship between the church itself and the structure of the monastery, whose first cloister could, according to Moschini, be attributed to Jacopo Sansovino (figs. 19, 48).[96]

As for Sansovino, he is not mentioned in the documents pertaining to San Salvador; we cannot, however, exclude a priori the possibility that he participated, perhaps on a consultation basis, in the designing of the monastery. We know for sure only that agreements were signed on September 10, 1540, between Bernardo da Venezia, the prior of the convent, and the master masons Giovanni da Lugano and his nephew Antonio, for the construction of "the monastery of San Salvador and a few contiguous houses": the document continues, specifying that "the said masters must first tear down all old constructions and dispose of the roof tiles and carry away the stones and unhouse and dispose of the top quality stone and *gome*, and dig the foundations; . . . and then they must build the main walls as well as the supports and covering and build passageways upon the roofing, and tile the said roofing, and prepare the openings which go in the ceiling, and do all that which is needed to enclose the said construction."[97] On March 8, 1541, furthermore, Fra Leonardo da Pozzo, general of the order, and Fra Andrea Bollani, abbot of Candiano, bought from Pietro Pollani "a hundred thousand stones well baked and tempered and measured in the Trevisan manner," tiles and "small stones and bricks" for the construction of the refectory, signed by "Joanne Celestro a Syrico."[98] Construction on the minor cloister (fig. 48) began in the early 1550s, but a document dated January 20, 1563, ordered Vettore Barbon di Bernardo, merchant, "boatsman," to "carry the earth away, dig the foundations to be dug for the entire construction of the monastery, . . . for the main walls as well as the minor walls, and everything of whatever sort is required; this they must do," and to "fill in the foundations with the same earth which shall have been dug out for this foundation."[99]

The construction of the monastery must therefore be properly dated between the 1540s–60s, though the documents do not mention any models to be followed. It is, however, reasonable to think that a few of the studies for the monastery were executed during the first two decades of the century—at least we can deduce as much from some documents and a few of the drawings in the Archivio di Stato in Venice.

The drawings 463b and 463a of *Miscellanea Mappe*—which are schematic and, from a graphic point of view, rough in parts—show the eastern perimeter of the church and studies for the organization of the monastery (figs. 46, 45). In the first (fig. 46), a big rectangular cloister opens, on the north side, with surrounding cells interrupted at the point of the bell tower, while a second structure, the walls of which are not completely aligned, includes a small cloister and rooms with unknown functions. Drawing 463a seems to be a later study (fig. 45): the large cloister has been enlarged, with cells reaching the side canal; a vast arcaded gallery—its bays numbering sixteen by twelve—coordinates the whole; the small cloister, separated from the first by irregular spaces and enclosed by a structure built in the shape of an L, assumes a trapezoidal form and has a single arcade with eight bays, parallel to the side of the church. The formulation of these studies as well as their execution demonstrate remarkable ingenuity; a different hand seems to have executed a third plan (*Miscellanea Mappe*, 463c), which approaches the definitive solution, in spite of a few significant variations (fig. 47).[100] But what interests our analysis here is the continued independence of the monastery—which in the end followed the lines of the preexisting one—beginning with the church, from the first studies through its execution. The two structures are juxtaposed in a completely paratactic fashion; the church remains enclosed in its own rigorous spatial design, proud of its own completeness.[101]

The last episode that affected the San Salvador complex, testifying to another renewal of taste, was the large stuccoed vault in the refectory (fig. 52). The absence of documentary information regarding its paternity is strange when contrasted with the eloquence demonstrated by this exceptional work, which was probably designed in the 1540s. The vault, with its shallow arch and deep coffers, was built on the basis of a honeycomb with chambers of varying dimensions, which facilitated the insertion of octagonal and circular elements as well as elongated ovals. The vault clearly asserts its autonomy within the room: there is no connection between the windows and the arches on the exterior wall, while the richness of the moldings and decorations, and the union between the stucco-work and the fresco paintings in the deep coffers, turn this "geometric sky" into one of the most remarkable examples of Venetian "architectural decoration" of the fifteenth century.[102]

The comparison between the portico vaults of the Library of San Marco and the vestibule of Villa Garzoni in Pontecasale is quite relevant in this regard. Its value lies in the structure made of linked geometrical figures, a clear transfiguration of ancient models, here complicated, however, by an excessive geometric expression.

We must leave the problem of attribution unsolved for now, while we wait for the more precise analyses that will emerge when the restoration has been completed. The elements that we have noted can, instead, help us explore the mentality that silently guided the sequence of choices. Let us go over the analysis we have drawn so far. The space of the church strongly expresses a Pythagorean theorem on the divisibility of space; but it is "hidden" behind a curtain of "ordinary" buildings, for a drastic distinction has been made between the mathematical and abstract "word" of the "sacred enclosure" and the "dialect" of the merchant city. Analogously, the external appearance of the building mass facing the *campo*, the street, and the canal, is camouflaged and blends into the existing environment. The convent of San Salvador "does not speak"; it respects, scrupulously, a *mediocritas* that enables it to slip into the continuity of the urban fabric without rupturing it: even its cloisters respect this bracketing of the architectural eloquence. But here too, that which has been rejected on the outside triumphs in secret on the inside; the vault of the refectory is extremely telling in this regard.

For the Venetian mentality of the early sixteenth century this duality does not seem born of contradiction, but rather of an articulated consideration of the roles that the religious communities, schools, and patrician families felt it was their duty to assume in the *communitas*. The introversion exhibited by the church, the sacristy, and the refectory of San Salvador, is the same that characterized the Corner chapel in Santi Apostoli, Palazzo Grimani at Santa Maria Formosa, and even Palladio's monastery della Carità.[103] We realize that the use of the term "rejection" can lead to unwarranted speculations, and we do not wish to be misunderstood. What emerges from the history of San Salvador is, however, so intrinsic to the Venetian imaginary that it prevents one from taking a polemical stand.

Sacred and private sites, which are also sites of collective exchanges, belong to different symbolic universes. The confluence of these universes, when it happens, is almost always the sign of a programmatic fusion, which was what happened in Piazza San Marco, the votive churches, the Scuole Grandi, and in a few "exceptional" residential buildings. And though it may be obvious that the mimesis masking the church of San Salvador is also due to the economic needs of the convent, it is significant that the *oeconomicus* was allowed to prevail over the ambition to draw attention to the new presence of order in the city. The façade of the church mentioned in the documents of 1522 would never be executed. Had it been completed, it would have constituted a "symbol" of the renewal completed on the inside. Instead, it was set aside until Giuseppe Sardi's intervention. But the complexity of the structure of San Salvador could not have been expressed on the outside by means of a simple facade: the "architectural rationale" is contrasted with a conventional structure of behavior that imposed limitations and set specific conditions.

The symbolic universe at work in this conventional behavior and the *novitas* implicit in the rationalization of architectural space were thus deposited in distinct places: the conflict was avoided. The *mathesis* of the internal space of San Salvador, which was thus "protected" and isolated, did not assume utopian traits. The first condition for the conservation of this equilibrium was the *boundary* traced within the metaphorical enclosure of *architecture*. The Venetian suspicion of whatever might disturb the context sanctioned by tradition seemed to have prevailed once again: at the same time, "novelty," enclosed and hidden, assumed a sacred value.

The themes interwoven in the complex of San Salvador also explain the reason why the experience utilized by Venetian humanism would remain a *unicum*. Extraneous to the language that was being developed in the Roman milieu in the first years of the sixteenth century, and the product of transplantations that were safeguarding deeply rooted traditions, the church of San Salvador, in fact, could not define—in Venice—a "type." Besides, the ideal motivations that had guided the church's renovation excluded such a result. Not by chance, new "representations" of the myth of Venice were taking shape while the construction of San Salvador was being completed: and Spavento and Tullio Lombardo's church, in comparison, could only seem a work belonging to an age long gone.

Appendix to
Chapter 2

1. ASV, "Corporazioni religiose soppresse, San Salvador," b. 44, tomo 91, c. 7r.

Notto che del 1475 alcun dubio occorse delle arche della scolla de Santa Maria el qual fo chiaritto nel anno sequente nel tempo di pre priore frate Augustino di Iacobi da Bologna vicario e pre Francesco Thoaro da Eugubio i quali io conseio dei piú antichi sacerdotti insieme con el sacrestano e fratti li fu concese che poteseno posedere le loro arche pacificamente como anno fatto fino ad ora, cioè arche tre dananti la porta de magiore della chiesia sotto el portegho et quando se avesse a sgrandire la chiesia si acordino e tratano de far le loro sepolture altrove in loco da esso priore e capitollo de quel tempo a loro asignata et fo confermate tutte le sue consuetudine fatte per i tempi passatti come apar in questo medesimo libro a carta 28, le qual furono ordinate nel 1445. / Io frate matheo francese compagno de sagrestan frate Sixto de volontate del pre Priore et sagrestano scripsi de mia mano.

2. Ibid., b. 39, tomo 81. cc. 135v–36r. (29 May 1506).

Dominus noster Jesus Christus salvator mundi, cuius nutu et voluntate cuncta reguntur et gubernator a primordia huius urbis nostre, ut in medio nostri foret voluit et sua finita clementia et providentia disposuit quod templo sanctissimo suo nomini dedicatum poneretur et construeretur in illo celeberrimo loco ubi reperitur et quoniam templum ipsum ob illius vetustatem videtur minari ruinam, ita indigere restaurationem cum consequenti reformatione in ampliorem et honorificentiorem formam ob reverenter respectum nominis Salvatoris pro amplitudine civitatis et pro consolatione spirituali omnium, tam nobilium quam civium nostrorum quam alliorum frequentantium et se reducentium ad illud ad divina officia. Digni propterea sunti prior et fratres ipsius monasterii ut exaudiatur in humilima petitione eorum, quando presertim ipsi pauperes fratres pro possendo facere tantum bonum quantum est istud se spolient affictibus apotecarum et domorum que sunt contigue ecclesie, et quando maxime complurimi nobiles et cives nostri creditores in officio nostro salis eorum supplicationi pie et favorabiliter responderint ad ea propter.

Vadit pars quod autoritate huius consilii dictis priori et fratibus concedatur quo ad computum crediti diversorum millesimorum quod in officio nostro salis habituri sunt per provisores nostros salis dentur eisdem per ipsum officium singulo mense ducati sexaginta usque ad summam ducatorum sexmillium erogandorum in fabrice dicte eclesie, et vadant dicte pecunie ad computum ducatorum 1500 mensualium mercatorum.

El special messer lo provedidor alla cassa del deposito de comandamento di signori capi delo excellentissimo Conseglio di X, dia, paghi et numeri a i venerabili frati de San

Salvador di Venetia ducati 50 per il mese presente per li ducati siemillia da esser spesi in la fabricha della giesia, i quali vano a computo de ducati 1,500 mensuali di mercadanti ut in parte de dí 31 marzo 1506, dechiarando che i abino credito in l'officio del sal. Et per lo advenir darete a i venerabili frati ogni mese ducati 50 ut supra. Datum die 29 mensis mai 1506.

Bernardus Bembo doctor. ducati 50

Petrus Cappello caput consilii. X.

Georgius Hemus caput consilii. X.

3. Ibid., b. 44, tomo 91, c. 45r. (9 August 1506).

Jesus Marie filius.

Frater Seraphinus de Venetiis Canonicorum Regularium congregationis sancti Salvatoris generalis prior sed inmeritus dilecto nobis in Christo priori et conventui monasterii nostri sancti Salvatoris de Venetiis ceterisque quibuscumque hoc scire volentibus salutem in Domino. Notum facimus quod cum alios placuerit illustrissimo dui domino nostro Veneciarum ob eius magnificentiam et liberalitatem prefacto nostro monasterio sancti Salvatoris pro eius de novo construenda ecclesia, certam non exiguam peccuniarum quantitatem concedere sub certis modis et forma annuatim recipiendam ab offitio salis ad effectum huiusmodi distribuendam. Et cum per priorem huiusmodi monasterii a nobis et diffinitoribus nostri capituli qui pro expiditionem seu huiusmodi constructionis inchoationem licentia petita fuerit (ut tenebatur) cui benigne et gratiose de eius prudentia, industria et solicitudine plurimum in Domino confisi omnem nostram auctoritatem plenissime concessimus et ilariter dedimus ut ex litteris superius confectis clarissime patet. Qui ut apis argumentosa considerans quod ubi plurima sint conscilia ibi etiam salus, plures et diversos modelos a variis et peritis magistris huismodi architectorie fieri fecit. Et quia ex ipsorum inspectione unus vi pulchrior videbatur, altero in se ipso remanebat perplexus ex quem illorum pro idoniori accipere deberet penitus ignorabat et tandem sapienti usus conscilio omnes modelos prefactos ante nos ac venerabiles consocios nostros visitatores nec non nullos priores qui Venetiis tunc aderant humiliter ac devote aduxit et presentavit ut sic etiam nostro conscilio nostroque iuditio pariter et favore illius trepidatione seu titubatione vel perplexione ab eius animo penitus semotis et reiectis unus ex ipsis eligeretur qui in omnibus et per omnia elegantior videretur et ad propositum situs et loci magis indicaretur comodus et ad satisfaciendum omnibus preceteris videretur honestior.

Quibus omnibus optime visis et diligenter discussis et exsaminatis, nos generalis et visitatores prefacti, Deum solum pre occulis habentes, considerantes piam mentem ac immensam devotionem quam erga predictum monasterium seu ecclesiam, ipsum illustrissimum ducem dominum nostrum et non nulli nobiles ac populares devote gerunt, qui non cessant quotidie nos incitare ut huiusmodi expeditioni operam dare velimus quia iuxta illud et si debile principium nunc melior fortuna sequitur ellegimus ex ipsis modelis unum secundum magistri Georgii Spavento notum constructum qui preceteris nobis aparuit nobilior et ellegantior et ad propositum nostrum magis congruus, quem pro electo a nobis et acceptato volumus haberi et nullus contra eum quoquemodo vellet contra ire. His tamen pactis, modis et condicionibus, videlicet quod apotece que construi debent ex latere strate seu vie que discurrit ad sanctum Marcum non excedant in sua latitudine tres passus sive pedes quindecim liberos intra suos muros. Ecclesia vero prefacta volumus pacto aliquo excedat passus duodecim, itaque in sua latitudine infra suos muros vacua et expedita remaneat per dictos duodecim passus et non ultra lata. Quo autem ad eius longitudinem et altitudinem volumus ut sit et esse debeat secundum artem et dispositionem architectorum quam proportionaliter secundum suam latitudinem altam et longam indicabunt esse debere. Et fiat tamen una cuba super capella maiori. Rogamus itaque nos omnes in Domino ut omnem solicitudinem et diligentiam huic operi dare velitis ut iuxta pium et devotum desiderium prefacti illustrissimi duci dominii et nostrum ipsa constructio cito incipiat et quantum possibilitas subministrabit

citius finiatur. Hortamur itaque vos et precipimus ut ne dictum reiectis omnibus super-
fluis expensis sed etiam a victu et vestitu vestro in quantum humana patitur fragilitas,
necessariis abstractis, omnia que ad honorem Dei, patrie decus, et divini cultus augumentum et pulchritudinem in huiusmodi rehedificatione pertinent adhibere curetis.
Dantes tibi fratri Antonio de Venetiis priori de novo omnem nostram auctoritatem et
licentiam destruendi et in toto minandi dictam ecclesiam veterem ut novam erigere
valeas, secundum modum et ordinem superius enaratos cum plena potestate obligandi
auctoritate nostra etiam si accideret casus ut exigeretur licentia spetialis offitii nostri,
quam pro hac causa tenore presentium tibi damus et concedimus quoscumque introitus
dicti monasterii tam affictum quam camere imprestitorum Montis veteris et novi et
aliorum quorumcumque ad ipsum monasterium pertinentium quocumque nomine cen-
seantur pro inveniendis pecuniis pro dicte ecclesie celeriori constructione, ad hoc ut
illustrissimo ducali dominio omnibus nobilibus et cuncto populo citissime possit esse
satisfactum.

In quorum fidem et testimonium has presentes fieri sigillique offitii nostri iussimus
impressione muniri cum subscriptione omnium nostrorum qui in huiusmodi expedi-
tione presentes fuimus. Datum Venetiis in prefacto nostro monasterio sancti Salvatoris,
die VIIII augusti 1506.

Ego frater Seraphinus generalis qui supra confirmo omnia suprascripta,

Ego frater Petrus Michael visitator confirmo ut supra,

Ego frater Joannes Franciscus Peregrini visitatore confirmo ut supra,

Ego frater Philippus monasterii prior sancte Marie de insulis confirmo ut supra.

4. Ibid., b. 5, pergamena 48. (Papal bull by Julius II, 6 January 1507).

Dilecti filii salutem et apostolicam benedictionem. Cum, sicut nobis nuper exponi fecis-
tis ecclesia domus vestre dudum per Sanctum Magnum episcopum Adriensi cum septem
ecclesiis ex revelatione divina in civitate Venetiarum fundata ob eius vetustatem ruinam
minetur ac propterea ad dei laudem et divini cultus augumentum ecclesiam ipsam de
novo redificare et ampliare ac ad felicem statum reducere proponetis. Quod propter
domos et apothecas circum circa consistentes et Vobis victum prebentes et quas pro
amplianda dicta ecclesia demoliri oportebit non sine magnis vestris sumptibus et expensis ac interesse perfici non poterit necesseque erit ex capite et uno latere ipsius ecclesie
tollere et ex aliis addere. Nos ad ea que ad divini cultus et commoditatis vestre augumentum ac ipsius ecclesie decorem et venustatem cedere voleant favorabiliter
annuentes vestris in hac parte supplicationibus inclinati vobis quicquid ex ipsa veteri
ecclesia huic inde tam ex capite et latere quam subtus novam ecclesiam reedificando
extra remanserit illud corporibus et cineribus mortuorum in ibi sepultorum in loco
sacro repositis et superfitie terre abrasti ad prophanos usus absque alicuius conscientie
scrupulo seu ambiguitate aut sine censure seu pene incursu convertendi ac desupor in
recompensam aliarum domorum et apothecarum demolendarum. Domos et apothecas
ac alia necessaria pro laicorum habitatione ac vestris victu et sustentatione construendi
plenam et liberam auctoritate apostolica licentiam concedimus et etiam facultatem, non
obstantibus permissis ac constitutionibus et ordinationibus apostolicis, nec non domus
congregationis et ordinis predictorum iuramento confirmatione apostolica vel quavis
firmitate alia roboratis statutis et consuetudinibus privilegiis quoque et indultis apostolicis eisdem congregationi et ordini sub quibuscumque tenoribus forsan concessis et
iteratis vicique innovatis et confirmatis ceterisque contrariis quibuscumque. Datum
Bononie sub annulo piscatoris, die VI ianuarii M.D. VII. Pontificatus nostri anno
quarto.

5. Ibid., b. 39, tomo 81, cc. 134r–35v. (7 August 1507).

Serenissimo et excellentissimo Principi suoque Consilio Consilio. X.

Ali Piedi de la Sublimità Vostra reverenter et devote se supplicata per li devotissimi et
fidelissimi servitori prior et convento de San Salvador che cum sit ch'essendo li divini

templi muri et intelle et propugniacolo di questa catholica et cristianissima republica, ne li qual continue tante messe et divini offici sono celebrati et ritrovandossi fra le altre chiesie quella de li ditti supplicanti miraculosamente constructa et fondata per mano di quello sanctissimo episcopo de Altino messer Sancto Magnio nel mezo el centro di questa amplissima città sotto titullo del gloriosissimo salvator nostro messer Yehsu Xristo, nel qual continue et indefesse con nocturni et diurni, con continui et religiosissimi offici è cultivato quanto alcuno altro tempio con copiosa quantità sí de nobili immo populari che assidue la frequentano, la qual per la vetustà et antiquità sua è cosí fragile et marza che non solum li muri sono in molti lochi apperti et conquassati, ma le catene che substentano li volti sono tutte relaxate con manifesto et imminentissimo periculo et total dessolatione de cosí necessaria chiesia et forza quod Deus mertat non senzia iattura et danno grande di coloro si ritrovassero in essa.

Et havendo deliberato per obviar a tanta runia instaurarla, exornarla et amplificarla prima aciò el divino culto che in quella continue è celebrato non sia intermesso ma augumentato et non sia etiam diminuitio il frequente et devoto concorso di tanta nobillità ch'a quella quotidie conffluisse si etiam per decoro et ornamento de questa inclyta et celeberrima città, ch'essendo situata in visceribus suis merita de più amplo et magnifico hedificio esser constructa. Et havendo calculato le spexe intranno in questa sesanctissima et necessariissima opera, limitatossi il viver nostro et subtracti ala bocca, considerate le decime et gravezze supportiamo et attento presertim che per perfettione de tal opera vi è forza levar via le infermarie nostre et rehedificarle in altro loco et ruvinar etiam alcune nostre case de le qual ne trazemo non mediocre utillittà, de le qual incomodità, spexa et danno patiremo in futurum non havendo respetto. Ma solum ad honor del nostro Salvator messer Yehsu Xristo, in eius nomine inititullatu est ipsa ecclesia, et de questo felicissimo stato et comodità de tuto el popullo, et perché ritroviamo le forze nostre esser sí debille et exigue che impossibil cosa è a noi comenciar tal opera se da la clementia de la Sublimità vostra non siamo suffragati, adiuvati et subvenuti, imperhò nui prior et convento humiliter supplicamo alla Sublimità vostra et alo Excelso suo conseglio de .X. con la zonta che per suffragio de tanta spexa se degni de concederni de gratia special che per li magnifici signori proveditori al sal de li crediti che per noi per tal pia opera semo per haver de sali de diverssi milleximi che non obstante alcuna legie ne ordine in contarrio ne sia dato ducati 50 in 60 al mese fino ala summa de ducati 6,000, vogliando solum questo avantagio, che siando li nostri denari de che milleximo si voglia siino li primi datti in ogni cassa, perché tenemo certo se li mercadanti alcuna incomodità per questo haverano, per sua bontà per far questa opera pia [se contentarano: cancellato]. Aciò el nostro salvator benedetto prosperi la casa loro de bene in meglio et per esser piui la chiesia sua che nostra sarano contentissimi, et tanto piui che questo non li tarda a scoder il suo, salvo de ducati 3 e 1/3 al'ano per cento a tutti loro che sono infiniti et la Sublimità vostra non ha danno né incomodo alcuno. Aciò una chiesia intitullata al nome del nostro salvator messer Yehsu Xristo cusí celebre e necessaria non perisca con cosí manifesto periculo et oltra el divino culto possimo far una opera di sorte che meritta quel sanctissimo nome et il sitto dove è situata et sempre possiamo come indifferenter faciamo, licet indigni et peccatores, pregar et supplicar el sommo Idio per la conservatione et amplificatione di questo felicissimo stato, et per la Sublimità vostra et per coloro da li quali receveremo suffragio per construtione de ditta opera, a perpetua gloria del nostro signor messer Yehsu Xristo de cuius re aggitur et ornamento de questa amplissima città et laude de la Sublimità vostra et del suo excelso Conseglio ali piedi de li quali humiliter et prostrati si recomandamo.

Presentata coram clarissimis dominis capitibus Consilii decem sub die 7 augusti 1507. Questi sono quelli che hano sottoscripto ala presente supplica videlicet

Messer Hieronimo Contarini quondam messer Bertuci el procurator

Messer Zuane Gritti quondam messer Lucca

Messer Domenego et Anzolo Contarini

Messer Alvixe Pisani et fratelli fo de messer Zuane

Messer Cabriel Barbarigo fo de messer Antonio

Messer Nicolò e Jacomo Gussoni

Messer Zuanantonio Justinian di messer Benetto

Messer Vetor Pisani quondam messer Marin

Messer Bernardo Donado et fratelli

Messer Lorenzo Dolfin fo de messer Zuane

Messer Alvixe et Hieronimo Grimani

Messer Thadio Contarini fo de messer Nicolò

Messer Sebastian dal Pozzo

Messer Marco Gritti quondam Lucha

Messer Mathio di Priuli quondam messer Francesco

Messer Fantin Dandolo quondam messer Andrea

Messer Nicolò Zorzi quondam messer Bernardo

Messer Alvixe Malipiero quondam messer Jacomo

Messer Alvixe Juxtinian quondam messer Marco

Messer Lorenzo di Priuli quondam messer Piero procurator

Messer Cristopholo Moro quondam messer Lorenzo

Messer Zuanbattista Morexini quondam messer Carlo

Messer Constatin di Priuli

Messer Hieronimo Querini di messer Piero

Messer Piero Contarini quondam messer Zuane.

6. Ibid., b. 36, tomo 74, c. 7. (The Doge Leonardo Loredan to the general of the congregation, 26 April 1513.)

Leonardus Lauredanus Dei gratia dux Venetiarum et cetera. Reverendo domino fratri Nicolao bononiensi generali congregationis Sancti Salvatoris et visitatoribus eiusdem congregationis salutem et sincerae dilectionis affectum. Quod auxilii et favoris contulerimus et conferamus assidue constructioni celeberrimi templi vestri in medio huius urbis nostrae Salvatori nostro dicati, vos omnes testes estis locupletissimi. Id autem instaurari cupimus quale et dignitati loci in quo situm est et religioni vestrae conveniat, ad quod necesse est ut omnes illi quorum interest ad pia suffragia concurrant, que quo erunt ampliora et uberiora eo erit opus eiusmodi honorificentius et perficietur celerius.

Memores sumus reverendas paternitates vestras annis superioribus dum in monasterio Sancti Antonii capitulum vestrum celebrarent constituisse et taxasse et isti de Candiana et aliquibus aliis monasteriis portionem seu contributionem quandam huic fabricae singulis annis quoad absolveretur erogandam, quod tamen malignitate temporum ac bellorum turbinibus locum habere non potuit et ob eam rem tam laudabile et pernecessarium opus protractum fuit et adhuc protrahitur, cum universali omnium incommodo et molestia non vulgari. Quocirca decrevimus has nostras ad reverendas paternitates vestras scribere, quarum religio pietas et in nos studium est nobis apprime notum. Hortantes et rogantes velint nedum limitatam (ut supra diximus) portionem sive eius non solutum et collatum residuum inbere ut prompte et hilariter conferatur, sed etiam illam augere et ampliorem reddere aliosque addere, auxilia et suffragia collaturos. Erit hoc vestro religioso proposito consentaneum, summo Creatori et Salvatori nostro acceptum et nobis summopere gratum. Hoc etiam addito, quod sicuti nunc opportune fabrica haec et monasterium Salvatoris et indiget et exigit alienam opem, ita postmodum et poterit et aequum erit ut pariter aliis in similibus subveniat et opituletur. Datum in nostro ducali palatio, die XXVI aprilis, indictione prima. MDXIII.

7. Ibid., b. 36, tomo 74, c. 10. (Doge Gritti, 21 February 1523, m.v.).

Andreas Gritti Dei gratia dux Venetiarum et cetera. Nobilibus et sapientibus viris magistratibus huius urbis nostrae Venetiarum et tam presentibus quam futuris quibus spectat seu in futurum spectare poterit notum esse volumus qualiter vista et intesa la supplicatione del prior et convento de li venerabili frati de San Salvador de questa città nostra de Venetia exponenti che, desiderosi loro dello augmento del culto divino et decoro, ornamento et commodo de questa città nostra de Venetia predicta hano principiato et in bona parte constructo uno amplissimo tempio non perdonando a spese et fatiche cum grande interesse de diminution de afficti de case et botege vano a terra cum ruina et demolitione de una gran parte del suo monasterio et habitation de i frati, et quod peius est, perdeno lo addito per la via da terra de andar in monasterio, se dalla Serenità nostra non sono suffragati. Che ritrovandose una casa contingua a esso monasterio, che fo del quondam ser Zuan da Roma, ordinata per suo testamento sub fidei comisso, non perhò domenticandosi beneficiar essi supplicanti de parte dell' usufructi de essa casa, senza la qual li è impossibile redur a perfection cussí laudabile et magnifica opera. Et perhò supplicati alla Signoria nostra de gratia special concierderli la prefata casa per li predicti bisogni non obstante el fidei comisso, offerendosi loro supplicanti ex adverso dar et pagar ogni anno nomine livelli alli commissarii del dicto quondam Zuanne da Roma ducati Novanta .90. neti et expediti da ogni graveza et infortunio potesse intravenir alla casa predicta, iuxta la forma de uno instrumento facto cum li procuratori nostri de supra, come fornitori del testamento del dicto quondam ser Zuan da Roma et questo acciochè possano perficer dicta giesia, a decoro et commodo de tuta questa città nostra de Venetia. Et vista et presa la risposta facta per li Provedadori nostri de Commun de ordine de la Signoria nostra, sopra la dicta supplicatione habuta prima per loro sopra quella la risposta et consentimento delli prefati procuratori nostri de supra, fornitori del testamento del predicto ser Zuan da Roma, aliditi prima quelli hano o potessero haverne interesse o beneficio et oblation sive obligation de essi frati, ut in eis. Consulenti dicta gratia poter esser concessa ad loro frati, cum le condition perhò et obligation contenute nel proprio instrumento tra dicti procuratori nostri de supra et li prenominati frati facto et altre condition, oblation et obligation in quelle contenute, ut in eis. Cum li nostri Consegli minor, de Quaranta et mazor habbiamo fatto gratia ad essi venerabil frati et convento soprascripto quod fiat ut petitur et consulitur. Quare auctoritate suprascripta mandamus nobis ut suprascriptam gratiam supradictis supplicantibus observetis faciatisque ab omnibus inviolabiter observari. Facientes has nostras ad successorum memoriam ubi opus fuerit registrari. Datum in nostro ducali palatio die XXI februarii, indictione XII. M.D.XXIII.

8. Ibid., b. 36, tomo 74, c. 12. (The Doge Gritti to General Pellegrino da Bologna, 5 May 1531.)

Andreas Gritti Dei gratia dux Venetiarum et cetera. Reverendo patri fratri Peregrino de Bononia ordinis Sancti Salvatoris, generali, et eius sociis visitatoribus in capitulo generali salutem et sincerae dilectionis affectum. Scrivessemo del mese de april preterito al prossimo reverendo precessor della reverenda paternità vostra per il carico della protetione habbiamo al monasterio de Sancto Salvator de questa città, si come facessemo et l'anno preterito, acciò si facesse la debita ordinatione, in quel reverendo capitolo, per la provision pecuniaria alla fabricha della chiesa et monasterio predicto et tamen come è sucesso l'anno preterito, che niuna provisione è sta fatta, così vedemo se desistissamo da quell'officio che a nui è precipuo seguiria etiam l'anno presente, non havendo fin questo giorno habuto risposta delle ditte nostre, segno manifesto che fin hora non è sta fatta alcuna provisione, sí come etiam per bona via habiamo persentito cosí essere. Cosa che veramente n'è tanto molesta quanto piú exprimer non li possamo, et tanto maggior che siamo fatti certi in quel monasterio di Candiana fabricarsi con excessiva spesa per satisfattion particular di qualch'uno, in villa, loco non veduto da alcuno, et in questa città, nel mezo d'essa, si desiste da cosí necessaria et laudabil opera, cosa che non siamo per patir a modo alcuno. Et perché habbiamo inteso la reverenda paternità vostra con quelli reverendi visitatori esser meritatamente successa al carrico dil generalato, havendo ottimo odore all'esemplar vita et dottrina soa, li habbiamo prima voluto far queste, exhortandola et efficacemente pregandola ad esser contenta poner immediate il debito ordine in quel reverendo capitolo, che la debita et necessaria contribution dell'abatia de Candiana corri alla fabrica predicta et quel più parerà alla reverenda paternità vostra, acciò tanto più presto essa fabrica se possi redur al perfecto termine, cosa che sarà de maxima satisfation nostra et molta laude di quella, alla qual non volemo commerorar il favor prestò la Signoria nostra acciò quell'abbatia fusse concessa alla religion sua a fine et effecto che l'havesse a debitamente contribuir alla fabrica preditta, et fu favor di qualità che successe quanto si desiderava, perché ben sapemo il tutto esserli a memoria. Et perhò iterum atque iterum la pregamo a darne causa che star possamo con l'animo quieto et desister da quello che saressemo forciati operar a beneficio et perfection della fabrica preditta. La reverenda paternità vostra sarà contenta fare risposta a queste nostre, della qual staremo in expettatione, pregandola che in satisfattion nostra sia contentre, della qual staremo in expettatione, pregandola che in satisfattion nostra sia contenta ch'el presente confessor delle venerande monache osservante de San Servolo di questa costumi, continui nel carrico suo di confessarle, cosa che a nui sarà molto grata et accetta, offerendosi in cadaun tempo al beneficio dalla religion sua et in particulari alla reverenda paternità vostra. Datum in nostro ducali palatio, die V. maij indicatione quarta. M.D.XXXI.

9. Ibid., b. 25, tomo 50. (8 March 1541).

In Christi nomine amen. Anno nativitatis eiusdem e millesimo quingentesimo quadragesimo primo, indictione XIIII. Die octavo mensis martii.

Il reverendo padre messer fra Leonardo da Pozzo, general del ordine et congregatione di San Salvador, item lo reverendo padre messer fra Andrea Bollani, abbate de Candiana, facendo ambi dui per il monasterio suo di San Salvador di Venetia da una parte et il magnifico Piero Pollani fo di messer Jacomo da l'altra parte nel nome de Idio contrazeno et fano lo infrascripto mercedo, videlicet promette et se obliga ditto messer Piero Pollani dar et cusí dà e vende alli predetti padri reverendi intervenienti per ditto monacsterio di San Salvador miara cento de pietre cotte e ben sasonate et governate della mesura commune trivisana che al presente si lavora, a lire dodese de pizoli el miaro; item coppi a L. 18 el miaro, pietre pizole et tavelle a L. 8 el miaro, cioè tante quante bisognerà de queste tre sorte per la fabrica del refetorio tantummodo, non possendo dicti padri tuor da altri dicte tre sorte ultime de lavoreri per ditto refettorio salvo da lui, messer Piero Pollani dovendo darli robe bone et sufficiente come è preditto, et non essendo bone, li padri possano refudarle e tuorle da altri a dano et interesse de misser Piero, qual tuti lavori, cioè cusí li primi cento miara de pietre come li altri laori delle tre sorte predite sia obligà, et cusí promete ditto misser Piero darli condute qui in Venetia a tute sue spese in Canal Grando per mezo la casa del magnifico misser Zuan Dolfin et questo ad ogni rechiesta et beneplacito delli predetti reverendi padri, qual poi habino la spesa del descargar.

El pagamento veramente die esser in questo modo videlicet primo li predetti padri consegnano ad esso misser Piero uno suo credito de ducati 106 grossi 23 che die haver el monasterio de San Michele de Candiana dalla commissaria de misser Benetto Corner per una obligation de ducati vinti all'anno che paga ditta commissaria a dicto monasterio per fra Federigo suo fiol del ditto quondam misser Benetto, qual credito de ducati 106, grossi 23 serà finito adí 9 zugno proxime futuro prometendo dicti padri mantenir ditto credito vero et liquido et farlo commisso irrevocabile a scoder et conseguir ditto credito et disponer di quello come li parerà. Item li consignano e die far scriver ad esso misser Piero el credito che el monasterio di San Salvador si atrova al offitio di signori proveditori di Comun over sora le aque per danari per esso monasterio sborsadi per cavation de rii, qual sono ducati cinquanta in circa. Item li prometeno darli de contadi ad ogni beneplacito de esso misser Piero ducati cento cioè 200 a L. 6 s. 4 per ducato. El restante veramente del amontar di questo mercado prometeno et se obligano ditti padri dar et exbursar ad esso misser Piero. Consignata che sarà tuta la quantità delli laori soprascritti et prometeno ditti padri pagar a conto di esso misser Piero li nolli de li burchi de tempo in tempo secundo che sarà conduto li laori in questa tera, qual danari vadino a conto dil suo restante di esso misser Piero.

Actum Venetiis in studio factorie dicti monasterii sancti Salvatoris, presentibus ego r. D. Joanne Celestro a Syrico et magistro Joanne q. Antonii de Marcho de laccu Lugani murario.

10. Ibid., b. 25, tomo 50.

1563, adí 20 genaro (m.v. = 1564).

El si dechiara con il presente scrito qualmente io Don Nicolò come commesso et procurator del monastero di San Salvador son venuto d'accordo con Barba Vettore di Bernardo Mercero burchier dalle Gambarare di portar via el terreno, cavar tutte le fondamente che si caverano per tutta la fabrica del monastero in questo modo, cioè et prima che lui se obbligha portar via tutto il terreno che si caverano dalle fondamente alte, basse, strette, larghe per quel tanto che ordeneranno li mureri maestri, sí delli muri maestri come delle tramezere et di ogni qual sorte si voglia che li sarà comesso de far. Item che siamo contenti che possi avalizar et rempir li fondamenti dello istesso terreno che caverà de ditte fondamente. Et io al incontro li prometto per sua merzede di darli et pagharli lire diese cioè L. 10 el passo, se intende passo corente distesso in cima et questo con la presentia de misser Steffano murero de Marco, il quale sottoscriverà per esso Barba Vettori per non saper lui scrivere et maestro Zuane taiapietra da Lugan testimoni al presente scritto et accordo.

Io don Nicolò sopranominato ho scritto di mia man

Io Zuan taiapiera da Lugan fui presente al supraditto scripsi

Io Steffano de Marco ho sottoscritto per nome di Barbon Vettore per non sapere lui scrivere ut fui presente.

Vos enim estis templum Dei vivi. Religious Anxieties and Architecture from Venice to the Court of Marguerite de Navarre

One can hypothesize that in Venice expressions of religious sentiment also traversed a phase of uncertainty after the peace of Bologna. The circulation of Venetian religious themes tied to the *devotio moderna* was intertwined with attempts at reform that began—with mystical and eschatological traits—with the Franciscan family, the spread of the evangelical ideas of the Murano circle and of San Giorgio Maggiore, and the formation of heterodox religious groups. It is a well-known historical situation, and has been told by Aldo Stella, Paul Grendler, and Cesare Vasoli, who have approached it differently, by defining precisely the changing attitudes of the governing authorities toward the Roman Inquisition and the problem of heresy.[1]

For our part, we are faced with a historiographical problem. May we not perhaps examine other signs capable of speaking of the mental transformations—collective and subjective—that occurred during the crucial years 1530–50? In what way can the history of ecclesiastical architecture illuminate otherwise inaccessible paths? And how can we interweave the results of our inquiry into forms with what is known about the context, without giving into generalizations or setting up unverifiable relations?

We have studied elsewhere the events pertaining to the Observant Franciscans' large enterprise—the renovation of the church of San Francesco della Vigna (fig. 61)—and that analysis has already furnished us with useful information.[2] The work of Sansovino, which was supervised by Francesco Zorzi, appears to be the point of intersection between aspirations toward a *renovatio Ecclesiae* guided by irenical speculations and the political plans of Doge Andrea Gritti and his circle. But the conflicts sparked by this church do not seem any less significant. The exceptional quality of the Franciscan intervention in Venice in the first half of the sixteenth century makes it necessary for us to ask new questions that directly address the problematic dialectic between Venice and Rome and the debate on the specific forms of Venetian religious sentiment. The protagonists of this debate were: the groups that expressed, especially in the 1520s and '30s, new religious requirements; the decision-making authorities that were animated by an internal dialectic; and the interpreters of these debates—that is to say, the artists—with their doubts, their professional knowledge, and their subjective ambitions.

We will therefore adopt a particular method based on circumstantial evidence. Our approach to the interweaving briefly defined above will begin with a test case; we will then direct its results into divergent rivulets that will carry us rather far from our point of departure, with the advantage, however, of linking groups and situations that substantiate the historical construction permitted by the data thus conveyed. For our test case we have chosen the modest parish church of San Martino, designed by Jacopo Sansovino, near the Venetian Arsenal (figs. 54–60). The reasons for this choice lie in the formal simplicity of the building, whose specific meanings we must investigate.

It will, therefore, be necessary to make some preliminary remarks. It is an established fact that Jacopo Sansovino used widely differing languages, depending on the project he was working on. And it is also clear that Sansovino's stay in Venice during the middle of Doge Andrea Gritti's tenure was exceptional from a creative point of view: in his works, which were called upon to speak of the Grittian *renovatio*, he attained a level he would never reach again. In fact, after 1545, the artist seems to have entered a period of retreat, which turned into a withdrawal from contemporary debates on Italian architectural culture. Sansovino, who had broken a tradition by succeeding Pietro Bon in 1529 as *proto* of the Procuratia de supra[3] and who was the first to officially incarnate the figure of the *architectus* in Venice, seems to have slowly reentered—with few exceptions—the ranks of a completely "Venetian" professionalism. Empirical concerns and a minute official practice, more than the dignity of the *ars liberalis*, seem to have guided Sansovino's later work. And yet, these remarks do not completely explain the particularities of his ecclesiastical architecture. Of course, Sansovino was forced, in the cases of San Martino and San Giuliano, to deal with modest parishes and scarce financial means, as has been observed many times. But the case of San Francesco della Vigna was different, and in its turn had a precedent in the project for the Servite church of San Marcello al Corso in Rome.[4]

Attempting a philological analysis of the building of San Martino—which, as we shall see, contains a number of surprises—our first objective will be an inquiry into the motivations that seemed to have constantly dissuaded Sansovino, in his ecclesiastical interiors, from using a manner *all'antica* in favor of a true linguistic austerity. Our reconstruction of the original intentions relative to the church of San Martino will therefore be utilized in a manner that will permit numerous uses: to explore the aspects of Sansovino's personality that have until now remained beyond systematic inquiries, but also to set those particular choices within the context of Venetian religious anxiety. Only in a second moment will our circumstantial exploration be able to go beyond the confines imposed by our test case, in order to connect the data concerning Sansovino with findings about the individuals and influences that acted upon the artist; these included Cardinal Domenico Grimani, Lorenzo Lotto, Sebastiano Serlio, and Gasparo Contarini. The result will be parallel and strangely interwoven stories, which we will further investigate with new working hypotheses.

1. Jacopo Sansovino and the Church of San Martino in Venice

We will begin with an objective reconstruction of the architectural history of our test case (fig. 53). The church, in the first years of the sixteenth century, was a structure with three naves, oriented from east to west, with its front facing on the west side a churchyard of beaten earth bordered by the Rio di San Martino.[5] The medieval church faced onto an open space that belonged to it and was separated from the nearby churchyard by a high wall; the open space was bounded to the north by a house with three apartments for titular priests,[6] constructed—shortly before the sixteenth century—on the remains of an ancient portico that joins the church to the Romanesque bell tower standing further south.[7] A few buildings—among them the Scuola di San Martino—flank the northern nave of the church. This group of buildings formed, however, only a portion of the complex under the management of Antonio Contarini, who was named the parish priest of San Martino in 1528.[8] In fact, the church had gradually accumulated, around the land that Doge Ordelafo Falier had donated in 1107 to the Patriarch of Grado, a rather conspicuous group of properties, where it had promoted the construction of a few houses.[9]

One should also realize the importance of an agreement between the Ca' di Dio and the Church of San Martino that had been in effect since 1364 and by virtue of which the parish was in charge of worship in the chapel of the ancient hospital; also important were the relations established with the "Ospedaletto" of San Giovanni Battista and the Conservatorio delle Pizzocchere.[10] It was in this context that Antonio Contarini decided to start the reconstruction of the ancient church, the deterioration of which had been aggravated by a fire at the end of the fifteenth century. The architect who was chosen was, as we have already indicated, Jacopo Sansovino, who had, with his works begun between 1531 and 1537, emerged as the most distinguished artist working in Venice. According to Flaminio Corner, who must have had access to documents that have since disappeared, Sansovino's project was prepared in 1540;[11] on the other hand, according to a text dated September 29, 1615, only in "the year 1546 approximately, the present model having been formed and proposed . . . did they begin to cast the foundations; but, as there was very little money, the houses of the church were sold by common consensus, and the houses that are now of Ca' Mocenigo, and were sold some fields in the town of Fanzuol, below Castelfranco. . . ."[12] In fact, only on July 18, 1550—after three unsuccessful auctions—was the *vigna* transferred to Alvise and Giovanni Mocenigo for 1536 ducats.[13] And it was probably only after the purchase was completed that they went on to draw up the contract to begin construction. In fact, there is no date on the agreement "with master Hieronimo da Manerba and master Zuan Maria da Lona, masons, and associates to build the said church and make the walls according to the design made by master Jacopo Sansovino, with the methods and details instructed by him,"[14] but probably the construction did not begin in 1550 either. Only beginning in March 1553, in fact, were "the procurators of the building of the church of San Martino" active. These included Jacopo Salomon q. Lorenzo, Bernardo Giustinian q. Giovanni Francesco, Francesco Soranzo q. Giovanni Alvise, and Andrea Rizzo[15]—who on March 20 and July 14, 1553, closed a deal with two *tajapiera* [stonemason] contractors for the supply of stone materials. And the work actually began soon after that. There are documents from October and November 1553 attesting to payments for the organization of the construction site, for the execution of the new foundations, and for visits paid by the bishop and the architect; on November 23, Sansovino's model also reached San Martino.[16] The supplies of *mageri de larese* [thick wood boards], which began arriving in October and November, indicate the beginning of the new foundations. These rested on planks that distributed over the muddy terrain the weight of the structures begun that very November with reclaimed materials.

The project drawn up in the 1540s was thus set in motion only in 1553—the same year that the Senate gave Tommaso Rangone the right to build the façade of San Giuliano at his own expense, and three years before the beginning of the work on San Geminiano.[17]

The church of San Martino was, therefore, a work belonging to a climate that had little to do with the one that had stimulated Sansovino's research in the 1530s.

But the operations affected only a part of the ancient church, surely because of the scarcity of financial resources: not coincidentally, the contract with the *mureri*, or masons, stipulated that the demolition of the old building should proceed "as the need will be to make the new one." Sansovino intervened on the right side of the church, beginning with the ancient wall facing south and arranging the demolition of the priests' residences (fig. 55); the largest chapel flanked by two smaller chapels and the sacristy were built under his direction on the reclaimed grounds (fig. 60).[18] These are the same works mentioned in the arbitral decision of the technical college chaired by Sante Lombardo, on January 31, 1557 (1556 *m.v.*), regarding the parts furnished by the *tajapiera*. The document, in fact, recognizes the indebtedness of the commissioners of the church:

for the erection of the Sacristy door, the two windows of the said Sacristy, for all of the cornices and the architrave of the large chapel, for all the pilasters of the said large chapel with all of its details, for the other two pilasters of the small chapels. . . . Likewise for the two pilasters with their details and the cornice that connects the chapel inside the large chapel. Likewise for the vault, with its ocular window, which is in the said chapel and its large vault. Likewise for the ocular window which is in the other small chapel, on the fondamenta. *Likewise for the creation of some of the windows above the vault of the chapel of the chorus. Likewise for the steps measuring 44 Venetian feet.*[19]

The architect thus continued the work from a fragment, from which one may, however, deduce the entire organization of the architectural apparatus. That fragment, in fact, shaped the lateral section of a squared interior space: one only has to repeat the tripartite composition on the other sides to obtain the entire model. It is clear, however, that the sides of the interior space of the new church were as long as the width of the three naves of the ancient building, while the depth of the chapels was determined by their length (figs. 54, 55): Sansovino worked skillfully with the grid provided by preexisting structures.

Antonio Contarini, the promoter of the initiative, died in 1556,[20] during a period of economic difficulties that led to a dispute with the *tajapiera*: the stonemasons—feeling that their work was no longer guaranteed—suddenly requested a payment of what was owed them and left the construction site.[21]

Only in 1573—three years after the death of the architect—did the parish priest Daniele Crisonio warn that the wall of the façade was "old and deteriorated," but the drive opened for the new façade had meager results;[22] on March 9, 1584, a petition was presented to the *Signoria* and the Doge to obtain a portion of needed land;[23] in 1601, after damages inflicted upon the roof and the bell tower by lightning, a new petition explained that the church had "its most precarious summit held up not by firm walls but by columns and might fall at the slightest accident";[24] in 1607 Giacomo Polesan gave estimates for the interior piers, but only in 1611 was a competition announced for the completion of the structure.[25] This, as a document dated August 10, 1617, makes clear, was far from concluded on that date: the procurators of the church decided to finish the decoration of the large chapel with arches "of baked stone, carved and polished, finished over with top quality stone" and, in the same way, to prepare the external cornices.[26]

It seems that Sansovino's small church, or at least the inside, was only finished shortly before 1633: at that time Doge Francesco Erizzo constructed his own monument in the right portal (fig. 56), while in 1641–42 Domenico Bruni painted the perspective decoration of the ceiling and Giacomo Pedrali did the central panel.[27]

The construction of San Martino, therefore, proceeded by fits and starts. Its paradoxically long duration was due to a severe lack of financing: especially in the sixteenth century, the *Signoria* paid little attention to this small church situated near the Arsenal. This method of proceeding by successive additions is especially visible in the facade. For a long time thought to be a work by Sansovino, it bears traces of at least three different interventions, as our graphic schemes demonstrate (fig. 57). In all probability, the petition of 1584 had its effect, given that a tombstone still in position indicates that a provision was made in 1585 for the renovation of the school situated next to the façade, which, with its body jutting out toward the *campo*, cuts into part of the preexisting school. But the work probably came to a halt rather soon. If one carefully examines the masonry construction, one can easily see that a scant cover with two roofs defined, until circa 1611, the first level of the unfinished façade (fig. 57a).

The work done after 1611 gave the entire exterior of the church its present appearance: but a small painting that can be attributed to Giacomo Guardi (Venice, private collection) shows the church of San Martino with a simple façade, vaguely neomedieval in its starkness (fig. 57b). The painting tells the truth: the present façade—this is substantiated by a few letters written by the parish priest Angelo Bianchi in 1897 and by a booklet published on the occasion of some nineteenth-century work[28]—was executed by Federico Berchet and Domenico Rupolo (fig. 57c), who transformed the bare sixteenth-century building decoration with the addition of capitals, entablatures, lateral scroll-like forms, statues, and decorations in Istrian stone for the window. Berchet thus carried out a true "Sansovinian reinvention" on this façade. Here, too, the "restorer" of the Fondaco dei Turchi [Turkish Commodity Exchange] manipulated the original data in a way that was meant to excessively define an acritical and stylized image of "Venetianness."[29]

Only the portal, the *oculi*, and the design of the window are original; on the other hand, it is difficult to guess at Sansovino's intentions for the façade, even after one has mentally stripped the nineteenth-century front. Nor is the date of construction of the portal clear. It was probably executed after 1611, and only vaguely recalls Sansovinian solutions: it appears, however, in Visentini's *Osservazioni*, which discusses Gallaccini's treatise on the errors of architects, because of the engaged columns cut by the cornices flanking the columns.[30]

The documentation we have gathered and objectively organized enables us to reconstruct the main points of the Sansovinian model. In place of the primitive church with three naves, Sansovino arranged an interior space with a square plan, articulated upon a Greek cross design by means of additional chapels (fig. 54): this annulled the original orientation of the edifice, and shaped the structure as an autonomous object in the surrounding building fabric. Rather, the volumetric coherence of the new architectural "mechanism" rotated 90° relative to the medieval building, tends to distinguish itself from the preexisting ones (fig. 55); it presupposes, furthermore, a direct relationship with the *campo* and the *fondamenta* [a street beside a canal] that link the church itself with the "great door" of the Arsenal.

The simplicity of the design—in which fifteenth- and sixteenth-century models of centrally planned structures were subjected to an elementary type of revision—does not, therefore, prevent the new church from assuming a role in the redefinition of the urban environment where it stands. Linked to the Arsenal and to the Ca' di Dio, Sansovino's small building sets itself up as one of the limits of the *pietas* and *charitas* that formed constellations around the *città altra* [other city] of the Arsenal.[31]

We have, in addition, demonstrated that its interior, in spite of the multiple interruptions and the lengthy duration of its execution, can be judged as corresponding approximately to Sansovino's model (figs. 56, 59). The centrality of the plan flows out of the dual axiality of the structure: the portals on the *campo* and on the Rio di San Martino were planned to be equal, and Sansovino's "reductive" attitude prevents one from reading into the planimetric design a specific reference to Byzantine types.[32]

Moreover, Sansovino had already come to terms with neo-Byzantine *schemata* in the church of San Francesco della Vigna (fig. 61). In San Martino, the four triadic groupings of chapels that are situated on the sides of the central square suggest rather "crosscuts" of the apparent pyramids planned on successive levels, given, also, the austere corner solution that accentuates the effect of a simple juxtaposition of the four protruding structures. In fact, the pilasters are only placed on the sides of the large chapel and the three entry spaces: the central space is devoid of "limits," of *finitio*. As in the interior of San

Giuliano, the measurement of the spatial organization is not entrusted to the architectonic order: the interior space of San Martino and San Giuliano give up the *dignitas* of mathematical abstraction.

The built structures seem, in addition, to exclude the possibility that Sansovino ever thought of placing a dome at the center of the square space: a text from circa 1553 (doc. 1) does not mention it. The interior space of the small church—which the architect, incidentally, wished to be plastered on the outside as well as the inside—was conceived from the beginning as covered with a flat ceiling and completely unarticulated. A simple place for worship, it is notable for the solecism created by the elongated pilasters and the contracted entablature (fig. 56). A language that has given up explicit references to Antiquity, or rather, that—as in all of Sansovino's ecclesiastical architecture—is reduced to barely hinted phrases that take on almost polemically ascetic forms. And within such a formal "silence," there are allusive fragments. We are referring in particular to the two large windows that open onto the back of the large chapel. Thanks to the documentary analysis completed above, these may be considered original "pieces" by Sansovino (fig. 58). The opening in the lower structure is identical to the one—also by Sansovino—of the Badoer-Giustinian chapel in San Francesco della Vigna (fig. 61): a large semicircular arch containing an inscribed circle tangent to its top. As for the upper window, it is identical to those that Sansovino placed on the sides of the Loggetta: it was an original invention, derived—through a subtraction of elements—from a Bramante-like scheme; that is to say the double arch ornamented with roundels that first appeared in the rotunda of Santa Maria delle Grazie in Milan, and later, to crown the serliane, in the Nymphaeum of Genazzano and in drawings UA 4v and 5r, which are copies of a project for St. Peter's—the latter being a work that Sansovino had probably studied carefully.

In 1537, when Sansovino "invented" the motif as a reference to the triumphal arch in miniature formed by the Loggetta, it was undoubtedly true that it demonstrated an attitude that had something to do with the *sprezzatura* [studied carelessness] dear to Baldassare Castiglione. In San Martino, Sansovino repeated himself, adopting, in addition, a motif that had since become archaic. The appearance of the large window on the four sides of the church probably belonged to the original model: the plain volume was perforated by an element that echoed a detail used in the structure built in Piazza San Marco, capable of calling attention to itself like a complete and allusive phrase. We also find a submissive, but mainly nonclassical language for the exteriors. So much so that the medieval aspect of the façade on the *campo*, as it must have appeared before the additions made by Berchet and Rupolo, strikes us today as being more evocative than the present "Sansovinian" façade (fig. 57b). Furthermore, the same window, as it appears—with simplified stonework—on the back or—in brickwork—on the sides makes the enrichment of the one on the front even more improbable. In the end, the church is reduced to a building mass—which the plaster would have rendered abstract—perforated in order to obtain new luminous effects. And on the inside we find a triadic rhythm uniformly repeated and assembled in an elementary fashion—in such a way as not to disturb the space in a state of "repose" determined by the *empty space—*

around the central square without clearly defined corners. This specialist of "rhetoric," the same architect who had spoken with Hellenistic emphasis in the Library and with triumphal emphasis in the Palazzo Corner, spoke an "ordinary" barely whispered language in San Martino, as he had in the Ca' di Dio; the latter work was perhaps the most ostentatiously "simple" of any "architect" in Italy during the sixteenth century (fig. 67).[33]

2. Sansovino, Lorenzo Lotto, Sebastiano Serlio: a "Spiritual" Clique?

As we warned the reader at the beginning, it is this "simplicity" that becomes a specific historiographical problem. It is undoubtedly true, as we have already remarked, that Sansovino demonstrated a flexible and antidogmatic attitude toward the sixteenth-century debate on imitation and language.[34] But, even taking this into consideration, it seems excessively limited, and in the end evasive, to interpret the elementary quality of some of his Venetian buildings—from the Ca' di Dio to the interior of San Giuliano—uniquely on the basis of the shortage of funds.

Sansovino *also* acquired in Venice the mentality of the traditional *proto* who pays careful attention to the context, to the profitability of an enterprise, and to the minimal material conditions of the building: the *case da statio*, or large residence, for the Morosini family, the establishment of the shops on the Zecca bridge and of the Osteria del Pellegrino, the speculative building for the Moro family, and the Fabbriche Nuove di Rialto provide sufficient documentation for this aspect of Sansovino's career.[35] But was there not, perhaps, something particular—which we can understand with appropriate historiographical instruments—in Sansovino's constant attitude toward ecclesiastical and charitable building? One ought to note the following: with the possible exception of the church of San Giovanni dei Fiorentini in Rome—which Leo X envisioned as an object defining the "Florentine citadel"—Sansovino constantly favored an ascetic and elementary language in his church interiors and welfare complexes: San Marcello al Corso in Rome, San Francesco della Vigna, San Martino, San Giuliano, the Ca' di Dio (fig. 67), and the Ospizio degli Incurabili. Moreover, the events that surrounded the construction of San Martino demonstrated that the artist was not completely inattentive or indifferent in his attitude toward this constant. Sansovino's commitment to his design was demonstrated by the rotation of the building's axes, the recovery of some of the ancient foundations, and the attention paid to the building's volumetric effect within its context. We are, therefore, examining the reductive linguistic process evident in this church for the specific mental attitude that it indicates.

But first, one observation is called for: the works we have mentioned seem a positive response to Erasmus's criticism of the cult of Antiquity for its own sake, of the intellectual passion for the ancient world that dangerously borders on a pagan dream, of the *elegantiae* incapable of speaking Christ's name. Erasmus had treated these themes in his *Ciceronianus* of 1528, which bristles with accusations of Roman formalism. In that dialogue he thoroughly attacked the cultural fashions of Rome during the papacy of Clement VII in favor of a welding of formal research and content, the latter being of an evangelical nature. Erasmus's criticism was ideally linked to Savonarola's and Giovan Francesco Pico's: the rigorous conscience placed in question the legitimacy—for an "imitator of Christ"—of intellectual classicism for its own sake, separated from deeper instances of simple hedonism or from the cult of elegance. Sansovino probably never had any knowledge of the content of the *Ciceronianus*. Moreover, between 1528 and 1540, Erasmus could have included much of Sansovino's architecture among his negative examples of rhetorical Ciceronianism—with the exception of his churches and the works he completed after about 1545: in them, a kind of evangelical humility barred the way to the language of the *gentili* [pagans].

This comparison, however, between Erasmus and the Florentine artist is unsatisfying. It is too generic, and not sufficiently supported by known, documented accounts. We must increase—a great deal—the power of our historiographical lenses. Let us try to approach the problem from the beginning, by studying the young Sansovino's most significant contacts. We know from Vasari, as well as from recent research, that Cardinal Domenico Grimani was Sansovino's first admirer in Rome and his link with the Venetian environment.[36] Let us therefore carefully assess this exceptional prelate and humanist. Grimani, the son of Doge Antonio, came into contact with Giovanni Pico at an early age, and was so interested in Pico's learning that he acquired the Count of Mirandola's library; in 1509 he enthusiastically received Erasmus in Rome and would continue to correspond with him; he was interested in the fourteenth-century *calculatores* of Oxford, but also in Roman antiquities; he collected paintings, including Flemish ones, and was appreciated by Francesco da Diacceto for carrying on Ficino's thought; he was a friend of Adrian VI and an enemy of Leo X; finally, he was in many ways in touch with a piety and will for ecclesiastical reform close to those of the Oratorio del Divino Amore.[37] Pico's insights and Erasmus's *pax rei publicae christianae* were united, in Grimani's learning, with inquiries that brought Neoplatonism and the Hebrew cabala together. Domenico Grimani defended Giovanni Reuchlin and was in contact—also as a protector of the Observant Franciscans—with Francesco Zorzi, a friar who was a friend of a number of heterodox individuals such as Lucio Paolo Rosello and Gershom Soncino. This was the same Zorzi with whom Sansovino collaborated for the rebuilding of the church of San Francesco della Vigna, and the author of the two treatises most expressive of the spiritualism of sixteenth-century Venice.[38] Nor should we forget to mention that Grimani's religious sentiment—it was no accident that he supported the rigorist and reformist line of the Flemish Pope—echoed in some ways the *devotio moderna* of the Brothers of the Common Life and a fundamental treatise that some have attributed to Thomas a Kempis, the *De Imitatione Christi*.[39] And the centrality of Christ—the *exemplum* and reference of a direct dialogue between the interiority of the spirit and the Divinity—linked the *devotio moderna* to the evangelical tendencies that were expressed by Zorzi in a mystical and cabalistic form, and by Gasparo Contarini with more explicitly reformist intentions.

This interiorized religious sentiment was, as we know from the research done by Lucien Febvre, Hubert Jedin, and Delio Cantimori, rich in innovative ferment, intent on restoring the simplicity of the primitive *Ecclesia*, and inevitably controversial in the eyes of Rome. This fermentation had solid roots in Venice since the beginning of the sixteenth century: there emanated from the congregation of San Giorgio in Alga a spiritual afflatus that would define it as the *propago italica* of the Brothers of the Common Life.[40] On the other hand, Gasparo Contarini made a reference to the two patricians Vincenzo Querini and Tommaso Giustinian, who—unlike Contarini himself—rejected the *vita activa* when they entered the Camaldoli monastery. And they were responsible for one of the most significant documents of early Catholic reform, the *Libellus ad Leonem X*.[41]

The *Libellus*, in proclaiming the absolute necessity for a reform of the Church and of ecclesiastical customs, was not devoid of a polemic against the idea of "pagan" culture as a model of religious education. Though this fact is not to be underestimated, especially in the context of our inquiry, it would be erroneous and simplistic to consider the work an antihumanistic manifesto. Felix Gilbert, in underlining the great friendship that tied Giuliano de' Medici—the brother of Leo X—to Querini and Giustinian, has suggested that Giuliano had a direct influence on the papal bull *Apostolici Regiminis*, of December 19, 1513.[42] This is, in fact, rather probable: but it gives us a glimpse of a particular mentality of the early sixteenth century, revealing its fullness and versatility. Giuliano de' Medici was also a friend of Leonardo da Vinci's, and it was in all probability for him that Antonio da Sangallo the Younger designed the palazzo with two courtyards that would have opened onto Piazza Novona, documented by drawing UA 1259r and v (ca. 1514–15).[43] Evangelism, spiritualism, and humanism could thus still find themselves connected, in the first half of the sixteenth century: and this is evident in Domenico Grimani as well as in Giuliano de' Medici.

Significantly, Jacopo Sansovino first came into contact with Cardinal Grimani, then with Francesco Zorzi, and finally with Cardinal Francisco Quiñones.[44] But he was also linked to two artists, who were both deeply affected by the religious anxiety lurking in the hearts of the evangelicals and "spirituals" of the early sixteenth century: Lorenzo Lotto and Sebastiano Serlio. Puppi has advanced a rather probable hypothesis—that Sansovino and Lotto first met in Rome around 1509.[45] In fact, Lotto did all he could for Sansovino beginning in 1527, when the Florentine arrived in the lagoon. Their long friendship is well documented. The painter's *Libro di spese diverse* enables us to follow a few episodes in this relationship, from the convivial to the financial: it was Sansovino that Lorenzo Lotto turned to for loans in 1542 and 1545, and it was again to him that he left his famous *gioielletti* on deposit and, in 1549, six paintings "to make of them a sale and money" as a guarantee against the debt that he had previously incurred. In May 1550 Lotto finally paid off his debt to Sansovino, who returned what had been entrusted to him.[46] But after the identification of Lotto's hand in the cartoon for San Marco, which would be translated into a mosaic in the atrium of that church, it is possible to imagine that the *proto* of the Procuratia de supra intervened in a concrete fashion in favor of his friend. The well-known letter that Aretino wrote to Lotto (1548) expressed an attitude that was certainly not Sansovino's: it suggests that one should not consider the triad formed by Aretino, Titian, and Sansovino in too schematic (or mythic) a fashion. Moreover, Lotto's religious sentiment has been persuasively described in the definitive studies by Giovanni Romano, Maria Calí, Renzo Fontana, and Bernard Aikema:[47] Lotto owned a copy of Thomas a Kempis's *De Imitatione Christi*, a text that Erasmus as well as Luther reflected upon; from that treatise Lotto drew inspiration for works like the *Pietà* of Sant'Alessandro in Colonna in Bergamo, and he appears to have known such heretical and religiously restless figures as Giovan Battista Suardi, Antonio Brucioli, Alessandro Citolini, and the jeweler Bartolomeo Carpan, and it was Lotto again who, in 1540, entrusted his portraits of Martin Luther and Caterina von Bora to his nephew Mario d'Armano. Although the matter needs further documentation, we thus emerge with a picture of Lotto's religious sentiment that indicates that the painter's conscience was affected by the conflict between the new evangelical demands and the progressive inflexibility of Roman institutions.

But it happened that two characters we have already mentioned, Lotto and Citolini, appear together in a reference to Sebastiano Serlio and to another "restless" figure of the sixteenth century, Giulio Camillo Delminio: and the document attesting to their relationship is an important one, as it concerns the testament that Serlio dictated in Venice on April 1, 1528.[48] Our analysis begins to get complicated here. We are already far from our starting point. Loredana Olivato has accurately explored the cultural nexus that connected Serlio to Giulio Camillo and Citolini. But one cannot separate the cultural and religious concerns of the group: Giulio Camillo dedicated his *Discorso in materia del theatro* to Trifon Gabriele, a "Socratic" figure who was close to Gasparo Contarini; he also demonstrated that he was familiar with the *Beneficio di Cristo*, a work Marcantonio Flaminio would collaborate on in 1542. Cesare Vasoli, beginning with these facts, has suggested that a relationship may have existed between the religious sentiment of a Platonic and cabalistic origin and the circle around Pole, Flaminio, Contarini, and Gregorio Cortese.[49] Moreover, the church was considering the evangelism of the early sixteenth century with increasing suspicion; Alessandro Citolini, a close friend of Claudio Tolomei, was already professing heretical ideas in 1538.[50]

This is not all. Giulio Camillo Delminio—who has been studied too often only in relationship to his project on the theater of memory—was the author of an undoubtedly disconcerting work, *Sermoni della cena*, which bristles with obscure cabalistic themes, and must have been influenced by the works of Francesco Zorzi and the thinking of Guillaume Postel.[51] It was in his *Sermoni* that Giulio Camillo expressed a heterodox religious sentiment in striking harmony with that of the *Beneficio*: Christ, through his incarnation and sacrifice, had redeemed all sins by redeeming all worldly things, while the significance of the sacraments was reduced to the pure manifestation of the Word. Furthermore, he stressed the wait for the next total *immutazione*—another of Zorzi's themes, derived from Origen—and that the justifying "grace" is received in an esoteric *raptus*. Cesare Vasoli has properly drawn attention to Giulio Camillo's later religious works, including the *Lettera sul rivolgimento dell'huomo a Dio*, the *Trattato dell'humana deificazione*, and the *De*

Transmutatione:[52] all partake of a Platonizing, hermetic and cabalistic air, similar to that of Citolini's *Tipocosmia*.

Giulio Camillo Delminio seems to have gone through the great religious crisis of his epoch by remaining detached from the dogmatics in opposition. His "occult rhetoric" lent a certain continuity to the grafting of Platonism and the cabala on the evangelical root—see for example his interpretation of Paradise as a world of external ideas and pure "exemplars"—which makes his association with Lorenzo Lotto and Sebastiano Serlio, in 1528, even more interesting. So we must ask the following question: the biographical fact aside, are there any other elements that can lead us to imagine a "heterodox" Serlio who in some way participated in the evangelism of his universal heir and the witnesses of his testament? It is Serlio who informs us of the friendship that bound him to a later friend of Giulio Camillo's, the Bolognese Achille Bocchi.[53] Bocchi was an extremely interesting figure who stood at the center of a network of cultural relations with heterodox roots: in his own time, Delio Cantimori considered Bocchi a typical Nicodemite and gave an acute analysis of the *Symbolicarum quaestionum libri quinque*, published in 1555.[54]

Bocchi's circle, of Platonic inspiration, emphasized man's capacity to raise himself above the contingent, "to the benign breathing author of aetherial light." For our purposes, it is more significant that Bocchi was in contact with a heretic like Camillo Renato, *praeceptor, dux et informator* of the young Lelio Sozzini: Aldo Stella has authoritatively identified the influence that Bocchi and his circle exercised on the ex-Franciscan Camillo Renato who, imprisoned in Ferrara, wrote an extremely explicit defense of his own "spiritualism" in 1540.[55] Sebastiano Serlio mentions Bocchi and Alessandro Manzuoli at the end of his *Terzo Libro*, which was published in that same year. But when might a meeting between the three have taken place? One might, very cautiously, imagine a circle in Bologna that included, around 1525, Serlio and Giulio Camillo Delminio; moreover, Camillo certainly visited Bologna in 1519, 1521–23, and 1525,[56] and the architect, who in 1528 showed so much familiarity with the cabalist from Friuli, must have come into contact with him some time before that date.

A friendly relationship did, however, certainly exist between Giulio Camillo and Marcantonio Flaminio,[57] the "coauthor" of the *Beneficio di Cristo*, which contained ideas rather similar to those of Juan de Valdés. And we come full circle here: Achille Bocchi was in fact in touch with Flaminio from approximately 1515, and a significant emblem in the *Symbolicae quaestiones* is dedicated to Flaminio.[58] The emblem—elaborated by Giulio Bonasone in November 1548[59]—contains an entire program: the snakes and devils emerging from Pandora's box are linked to Rome, and offer a portrait of the corruption of the pontifical Curia presented in the illustrative verses. And, as we shall see, Serlio's writing also demonstrates his contempt for the Roman "scandal": all the elements at our disposal support the idea that the architect belonged to a circle that must have recognized itself in the religious ideas expressed in the *Beneficio di Cristo*.

Justification by faith alone, incorporation in Christ, and the value of artistic works as a simple "manifestation of faith": the Calvinist ideas and Waldensian corrections of Don Benedetto Fontanini and Marcantonio Flaminio were combined in a unique mixture that became the "manifesto" of an interiorized religion extraneous to the institutions of the Roman church.

And doubtless, since all true Christians are members of Christ, we can do neither good nor ill toward true Christians without doing good or ill toward Christ, insofar as he takes pleasure or pain in his members. Thus, since Christ is our garment of faith, we must be clothed in the love of our brothers, and the same concern we have for our body, we must have for them, as they are the true members of our body, of which Jesus Christ is the head. This is that divine love and charity which is born from unpretentious love which God inspires in his elect and which Saint Paul says works through charity.[60]

I say that whoever, by virtue of these promises of God, does not convince himself truly that God is a propitious and indulgent father, and whoever does not await with solid faith the inheritance of the heavenly kingdom, that man is not truly faithful and makes himself unworthy of God's grace. For Saint Paul says that we are the house of God so long as we keep a firm faith, glorying in hope until the end.[61]

There were, in 1543 in fact, a few trials that confirmed the existence of a specific evangelical sphere in Bologna: Ludovico Medigni, a rich weapons merchant, tried in Brescia after an escape to Bologna, declared that: ". . . in Bologna there were four thousand people who followed the faith of Christ according to the Scripture and not according to the modern priests."[62] In 1549, furthermore, the young Ulisse Aldovrandi was investigated by Girolamo Muzzarelli: Aldovrandi had studied Greek with Achille Bocchi and was tried for his correspondence with Lelio Sozzini, who had exhorted him "to follow the path of the gospel already begun."[63]

The prudence and Nicodemical beliefs of Bocchi and his friends—Alessandro Manzuoli and Claudio Lambertini, who were also friends with Camillo Renato[64]—were not very "Waldensian," but had something in common with Flaminio's attitude; the "manifesto" of the group seems to have been the *Symbolicae quaestiones*, with its theories on the art of dissimulation.

Religious dissimulation did, however, keep pace with worldly ostentation. The palazzo that was the seat of the Bocchian Academy certainly did not speak the language of modesty (figs. 64–66). Perhaps it was congruent with its owner's preference for the vernacular language. Which brings us back to Serlio.

The relationship between Achille Bocchi and Sebastiano Serlio leads us, in fact, to place in question much of what has been written on Bocchi's palazzo in Bologna. Egnazio Danti made sure that Vignola, from 1545, "constructed" the building of the Bocchian Academy "following the humor of its owner."[65] Other documents uphold the correctness of the date.[66] The efforts of modern criticism to assess Vignola's contribution, however, have not been satisfactory. After the publication by Schmidt and Lotz of two engravings representing different projects for the façade of the palazzo, from 1545 and 1555 respectively (fig. 64), a recent monograph has appeared and created some confusion—with somewhat inconsistent hypotheses—around the question of the Palazzo Bocchi as well as the young Vignola's career.[67] Let us examine these two engravings: in both of them we see an attic marked by "Venetian type" windows with a central element dominated by a serliana. In both, also, the windows of the first mezzanine are crowned with a design solution not unknown in Serlio's work. These elements, however, would not be built (fig. 65). But the origin of the two engravings may lie, in our opinion, in models that Serlio provided his friend Bocchi, perhaps before 1541. It is especially difficult to explain the form of the attic otherwise, even if one seriously considers the possibility of the client's intervention.

Bocchi's "humor" may thus have originated with a Serlian idea that was later modified and "minimized" by Barozzi. The idea that Bocchi may have at least consulted his friend, foreseeing the architectural enterprise that would take shape shortly thereafter, is congruent—at least—with what we know about the relations that linked the circle that formed around him. Besides, the heterodoxy of Bocchi's *domus virtutis* had to have an emblematic character, at least for Bocchi himself, given that two images of the palazzo appeared in his volume of 1555:[68] without forcing our historical reading, we can perceive here the path that led from religious faith to the formal universe.

3. Sebastiano Serlio and Marguerite de Navarre: antipapism, heterodoxy, and libertinism

We began with Sansovino and arrived at Serlio through their common friend Lorenzo Lotto. For now we will continue to rely upon trustworthy documents, and wait awhile before asking them to clarify that which is left unsaid.

It is quite clear that Serlio and Sansovino were on friendly terms. Both were involved in the innovative programs of Gritti's circle—which Serlio duly recorded in the dedication to his *Regole generali*[69]—even though Serlio always appeared in Venice as a consultant or scholar, rather than as an architect in the strict sense of the term.[70] From the information we have gathered so far, we thus arrive at a portrait of a group of artists and men of letters in which Jacopo Sansovino, Serlio, and Lotto were in communication with each other, and who had documented exchanges with mystics like Francesco Zorzi—one ought not to forget that Serlio was among those who signed the *memoriale* of 1535 for the church of San Francesco della Vigna—and with "irregulars" like Giulio Camillo and Citolini, not to mention Pier Paolo Vergerio, another "heretic" and a friend of Aretino as well as Sansovino. Vergerio, in fact, made a significant gesture in Venice even before he revealed his Lutheran faith: in 1528, in an oration delivered on the occasion of Marino Grimani's appointment as cardinal, he proclaimed that the most urgent undertaking of the epoch was without a doubt the reform of the Church.[71]

We must complete this picture with a few remarks on an astounding passage from Serlio's *Quinto Libro*, which has until now been underestimated by scholars—with the exception of a passing remark by Isermeyer. In the dedication of his book, Serlio wrote, "And even though the true temples are the hearts of pious Christians, which Jesus Christ our Savior inhabits through faith (as is well testified by the vessel of election Divine Paul, among all the Apostles the most distinguished preacher of our sacred religion), nonetheless material temples are necessary for the divine cult, since they stand as representations of the house of God. . . ."[72]

This was a proclamation of Pauline faith. And the reference to Saint Paul is significant, given that all the evangelicals of the sixteenth century—whether reformed or faithful to the *Ecclesia una et sancta*—reflected upon his letters. In fact, there is a passage in Luther that bears some resemblance to Serlio's: the true church—Luther wrote—is the house of man, that is to say, the site of his worldly activity.[73]

Serlio's position certainly cannot be reduced to Luther's, according to whom God himself was against the construction of churches.[74] Serlio's call for a deeply interiorized devotion is striking, however; it was in some ways controversial with regard to the theories of the Catholic contingent that wanted sacred art and architecture to be conducive to an *excitatio animi ad Deum*. Moreover, the *Quinto Libro*, published in 1547, bore a dedication that was an open "manifesto" of a religious tendency. The volume is dedicated to Marguerite de Navarre, the sister of Francis I of France, an evangelical who has been skillfully studied by Lucien Febvre, a correspondent with Bishop Briçonnet and patroness of the most restless religious souls, even after the repression of heretical tendencies begun by her brother following the *affaire des placards* of 1534.[75] And the dedication cannot have been instrumental there: by 1547 Marguerite had lost her influence and was living in retirement, dedicated to the writing of her *Heptameron*.

Serlio's brief comment on churches, rather, has its precedent in the cultural milieu of the reformers of Meaux, to whom Marguerite was indebted for much of her religious thinking in the 1520s. On September 7, 1525, the faculty of theology of Paris censored the opinions of Pierre Caroli on religious images, pomp, and traditions. Caroli had been in contact for about three years with Lefèvre d'Etaples and the Meaux circle before going to Paris, and in a hearing at his expense he was accused, among other things, of having said in a sermon delivered at St-Gervais, ". . . any place under the sky, which is God's real tabernacle, is more fitting and proper to worship God and to make sacrifices to him, specifically, to consecrate, than those made by men's hands."[76]

The theme is God's immanence in the entire universe—an idea not foreign to Marguerite, given that she had been influenced by Briçonnet. The theme of "God's tabernacle" appears here in a context different from the Erasmian one, but in remarkable agreement with the sentence that Serlio wrote much later, which was certainly the product of several strands of heterodox thinking. Furthermore, Febvre does not do justice to Marguerite's intellectual curiosity. In an undoubtedly valid volume, though uselessly polemical in its stance toward the French scholar, Gerhard Schneider has detailed the connection between Marguerite de Navarre and the two heads of what Calvin called "the fantastic and furious sect of the libertines," Quintin and Pocquet. In fact, as it appears from Calvin's polemical text, these two "libertines" were received and protected by Marguerite around 1546.[77]

We know that the "libertines" included in the term *cuider* all the sins derived from man's presumptuous reflection upon his own free will: to free oneself from *cuider* would mean to abandon oneself completely, to suppress one's conscience and return to original innocence, ignoring the differences between good and evil.[78] It was this desire to force the concept of "law" that scandalized Calvin. But it did not scandalize Marguerite: two books had been dedicated to her, Sebastiano Serlio's book on churches and Rabelais's *Tiers Livre* —which had been condemned by the Sorbonne in 1546, the year of its publication.[79]

Marguerite's exalted mysticism—which Febvre justly contrasts with the rationalism of Erasmus and Budé[80]—could thus accommodate libertine themes, as her farcical *L'Inquisiteur* makes clear.[81] The libertine rejection of private property could thus accompany—in the syncretic culture of Francis I's sister— the aspiration to free oneself from constraining law, as expressed in the utopia of the abbey of Thélème.[82] Nonetheless, Marguerite was not an Erasmian, nor was she a libertine, a Calvinist, or a Lutheran; she was instead remarkably tolerant in religious matters and remained open-minded and free of prejudice in her approach to free inquiry and innovative behavior. Thus, it is not surprising to find in the *Heptameron* a passage remarkably close to the one by Serlio quoted above. At the end of the fifty-fifth novella of the sixth day, Marguerite has Oisille say,

Indeed, I am frequently astonished . . . that they presume to be able to appease God by means of the very things, which, when He came to earth, He condemned—things such as fine buildings, gilded ornaments, decorations and paintings. But, if they had rightly understood what God has said of human offerings in a certain passage—that "the sacrifice of God is a troubled spirit: a broken and contrite heart, O God, shalt thou not despise"—and again, in another passage, what Saint Paul has said—that "ye are the temple of the living God, in which He will dwell"—if they had rightly heard these words, I say, they would have taken pains to adorn their conscience while they were yet alive. They would not have waited till a time when man can do neither good nor evil.[83]

Marguerite composed the *Heptameron* between 1540 and 1549, and the character of Oisille is known to be a reflection of her mother. Serlio owed much to Marguerite: to begin with, she had awarded him an annual pension of 100 scudi, which he began receiving on December 6, 1514.[84] But let us look at the dedication of the *Quinto Libro*. Serlio wrote that he owed it to Marguerite: "Your Majesty is not only supremely noble, and for that reason deserving the greatest work, but also the sole example of piety and true faith in this our century. . . ." Marguerite, the patroness of the libertines, was thus the only example of "piety and *true faith*." Serlio, a writer of treatises and friend to Lotto, Citolini, Giulio Camillo Delminio, Achille Bocchi, and Alessandro Manzuoli, felt the need to express a spiritual solidarity that we find rather revealing. And even the criticism—which had already been made by Erasmus and Luther—of the power politics of the Roman Church, expressed in the quoted passage, has its corresponding points in Serlio's work. In the first manuscript of the *Sesto Libro*, on the *Habitationi di tutti li gradi de gli huomini* [Habitations of all levels of men], Serlio distinguished the "noble gentleman, pacific and a lover of Justice," and the *partiale* who "participates in

Tyranny, [who], having many enemies, is hated until death, and always desiring revenge"; he then added a significant and courageous reference to the "lands of the church; where the seat and nest of partiality lies."[85] And this was not Serlio's only "anti-Romanist" statement. Again in the first version of the *Sesto Libro*, Serlio felt the need to engage in an ethical and political digression on his project for the "house of the gentleman."

Speaking now of the houses of gentlemen, I cannot avoid telling of the miseries of the lovely but, alas, divided Italy, since in many of her cities there are discords and civil wars and especially in lands and cities subordinate to the pope; these discords and wars are not without cruel murders, great fires and the ruin of houses and the dispersal of families. For this reason that gentleman who will be involved in these divisions will be in effect the Head of a region. His house must be strong in its site and in its walls; . . . this house should be situated among modest and poor people, so that its owner may make them his friends through his liberality, always giving to the poorest and treating the modest men with blandishments and hosting them at his table and favoring them in their needs. . . . But above all this the regional chief should repulse from himself ugly Avarice, because of which many heads of regions in my day have died miserably; . . . but I seek to fulfill the function of an architect and not of a chronicler, so as not to offend any criminals or their relatives living today.[86]

One rarely finds this kind of political consciousness in an architect of the sixteenth century. Serlio deplored the division of Italy, implying that the State of the Church was responsible for the "misery" of the peninsula.[87] And in discussing the "duties" of a gentleman, he wavered between a Machiavellian mentality and Erasmian precepts, resigning himself only in the end to "retire," out of prudence, to "the function of an Architect."

Serlio's antipapal position recalls the same attitude of Achille Bocchi and Marcantonio Flaminio, which we have already examined. From what we have been able to uncover, we find it impossible to dismiss the idea of Serlio's association with the religious sentiment shared by Bocchi, Manzuoli, Camillo Renato, and Giulio Camillo Delminio, and expressed by the "sweet booklet" of the *Beneficio di Cristo*. In this sense, the last lines of the first edition of Serlio's *Quinto Libro* are revealing: ". . . other things are waiting for me, perhaps in greater comfort and happier than for most men."

Once again, the ecclesiastical site is depreciated, as it had been in the dedication to Marguerite de Navarre. *Other buildings are more useful to man*: the statement is coherent with the call for interiority, the "true temple" of the "true Christian." One may, perhaps, see a sign of a new prudence—the product of the first encounters with censorship and the Inquisition in Venice—in the fact that those final lines were radically changed in the 1551 edition: "Now this is the end of the book on sacred Temples, so that I may proceed with two other books, one on all types of habitations and the other about the many accidents that frequently befall Architects."[88]

These words, however, contain no determinism: it is almost too obvious that Lotto, Serlio, and Sansovino developed and experimented with artistic languages that often contradicted each other, which is just as obvious as the fact that other artists of evangelical and "spiritual" beliefs—first among them Michelangelo—were pursuing very different paths. The models of ecclesiastical architecture that Serlio presents in his *Quinto Libro* indicate choices different from Sansovino's. Serlio's plans, based on elliptical pentagonal, composite, and extended designs, speak of a great desire for experimentation that recalls Baldassarre Peruzzi, the master whom Serlio would not forget to praise.[89] For us it has been more important instead to reconstruct the climate in which a few thinkers found themselves in the first half of the sixteenth century; and we should remember that the questions of *devotio moderna* had cast even Hugo van der Goes into a state of deep anxiety. The call for interiority, which would thwart the Church's function as mediator and guarantor, actually led to the most anguishing solitude. A direct dialogue with Christ and continuous self-analysis—in the feverish search of the symptoms of faith, the only possible justification—had as their dark side an anxiety in daily life. And the attitude of the Roman Church certainly did not contribute to pacify those souls who—like those of the artists—were not capable of resorting to the refined instruments of intellectual self-justification held by men of letters, theologians, and prelates of a "spiritual" and irenic propensity.

Insofar as Serlio was concerned, another connection with the evangelical faith can be distinguished in his constant preoccupation with finding a "manner" capable of mediating between the appeal to Antiquity and more readily understandable, "ordinary," inflections and etymons—this was exactly what Lomazzo would later reproach him for. Nor should one underestimate the significance of the fact that, unlike Leon Battista Alberti, Filarete, and Francesco di Giorgio, Serlio offered models for houses for the poor in his *Sesto Libro* (figs. 68–69). Myra Rosenfeld has seen in this concern for the lowest groups of the social pyramid a reflection of the welfare policy of the Venetian Republic;[90] but the mere fact that Serlio recorded these experiments, rationalizing them in typological *inventions*, has an historical significance that flows back into the course of our inquiry.

At the same time, Serlio seems to have reflected upon a theme that was specific to the *rhetoric* of Giulio Camillo Delminio: the use of "types" as functions of "invention"; that is to say, use taken to the limits of artifice, with the aim of reaching innovative results.[91]

The desire for innovation, on the other hand, often reached, and not only in Serlio's case, deformations and linguistic paradoxes: it was no coincidence that, within a culture influenced by the thinking of the Reformation, latent criticisms were being made of the edifice of humanistic harmonies. The matter of justification by faith rested upon the realization of the "corruption" of human nature caused by Adam's sin: for Calvin as for the *Beneficio di Cristo*, sin lay in the vain and absurd affirmation of man's autonomy in relation to his creator.

Thus man, Pico's "divine chameleon," the microcosm chosen on the "scale" [*misura*] of the cosmic order, has been soiled—according to the evangelicals—by lust and rage. But what is the role of matter and "baseness," in the knowledge of evil necessary to the "true Christian"?

The appearance of this thinking about the body, about materiality and the abnormal, which links Rabelais's prose to some of Sebastiano Serlio's *inventions*—the *ordine bestiale* [bestial order] comes to mind for all of them[92]—strikes us as congruent with the preceding remarks, even when we take into account Mikhail Bakhtin's observations.[93] And irony is grafted onto the root of this display of matter and imperfection, irony which is also present in Serlio, but expressed—and on the central theme of the architecture of humanism—by Francesco Berni, a "familiar" of Giovan Matteo Giberti and Ippolito de' Medici. Berni—who was not only a friend of Michelangelo, Sebastiano del Piombo, Francesco Maria Molza, and Pietro Carnesecchi, but also antimonkish and in touch with heretical circles in Italy—included among his *Rime* a *Capitolo dell'orinale* [Chapter of the Urinal], which begins thus:

He who has no great natural gifts / and a lot of knowledge / cannot know what the urinal is / nor how many things are inside it; / I mean, besides urine / there are nearly one hundred. . . .[94]

He continues a little further on,

And, first of all, I say it should be known / that the urinal is round / the better to hold more things: / it is made just like the world / for the fact that it has a circular shape / means that it has no ending or bottom: / everyone who knows how to build walls knows this / and every one who understands architecture / which teaches one how to measure things.

As early as the 1520s, then, the metaphor of architecture as the Platonic *imago* of the "beautiful theater of the world"—which Palladio would return to in his introduction to the *Quarto Libro*[95]—was transported by Berni's irony into "low" regions dominated by the "indescribable" excrement. The sacred—the circular form's value as *archè*—was "dirtied" by the phenomenal, by the refuse of the human body. This irony based on desecration insists on the emblematic values of Platonic and Pythagorean culture, which are made to fall into a paradoxical and spectral analysis of an object censored by "high" discursive practices.

The idealization of architecture, which had found exceptional exponents in Marsilio Ficino and Leon Battista Alberti,[96] collapsed when it came into contact with human feces. But it was often the content of the game that revealed changes in mentalities and faith. Matter, which, according to Ficino (*Commento al Convito*), was only "similar to the incorporeal Idea of artifice,"[97] upheld its own dignity in the "rustic" work interpreted by Serlio: with a desecrating spirit undoubtedly inferior to Berni's, Serlio—conscious of his own "licentiousness"—challenged an entire culture that had entrusted its own "truth" to Pythagorean "means."

And at this point we would like to recall Henry Heller's observation, recently repeated by Jane Wells, on the use of language in Marguerite de Navarre's *Heptameron*.[98] Heller maintains that Marguerite was influenced—through Bishop Briçonnet—by the mystical text of Dionysus the Aeropagite: the naming of low and sordid things, in the ambit of negative theology, was congruent with the consciousness of human abjection and of absolute divine transcendence, so that the scatological subject opened—in a mystical paradox—an evangelical message of salvation.[99]

We are exploring paths that enable us to read without naiveté the messages implicit in the *misture* [mixtures], in the deformations, and linguistic innovations proposed by Serlio, keeping in mind that our intention is not to invent fictitious parallels, but rather to reconstruct the mental surroundings in which we can relocate, in their specificity, works born of different cultural traditions. It is no coincidence that our point of departure has been the rhetoric of Giulio Camillo Delminio.

That Serlio does in fact present a problem of innovation tells us little, if we do not remember that the problem rests upon a terrain made of deformations and empirical approaches. The almost academic rigorism that emerges from Serlio's declarations of loyalty to Vitruvius—perhaps written in praise of "strict critics of license" such as Gabriele Vendramin[100]—sound like suspicious self-justification on Serlio's part.

It is undoubtedly true that Jacopo Sansovino's artistic culture was rather far from these concerns. And when we evaluate his personality, we will have to take into account aspects that may be used to challenge our hypotheses. For we cannot ignore the nature of his association with Aretino and Titian, the love affairs that Vasari mentions,[101] his taste for luxury, or the careful way he managed his many estates, perhaps through speculative practices.[102] On the other hand, there is his testament of 1568, in which he favored masters and artisans of humble origin and wrote that he wished to be buried "dressed in sack cloth," adding that "the stretcher should bear no cloth ornamentation, since I came naked into this world and I wish not to be adorned by these frail and transitory ornaments."[103] Sansovino quotes a passage from the Book of Job cited in Augustine's *Civitas Dei*: and even if the epoch was at that point dominated by Tridentine devotion, the fact remains that Sansovino developed with the evangelical Lorenzo Lotto a friendship that included reciprocal reflection upon their respective artistic languages. The triumphal centrality of Christ, in Sansovino's relief on the altar of the Sacrament in San Marco, has its equivalent in Lotto's *Cristo in gloria*, today in the Kunsthistorisches Museum of Vienna.[104]

But if Sansovino was really affected by the themes of *devotio moderna* or by the thinking of the Catholic Reformation, he probably interpreted them in a rather aristocratic but less dramatic way than Lotto did. Compared to the painter, Sansovino appears to have had—from what we can gather—a milder and more accommodating personality, though many aspects of it may still offer surprises.

4. Gasparo Contarini, Erasmus, and Alberto Pio da Carpi: a debate on *charitas* and ecclesiastical building

The path we have pursued has led us to complete a circumstantial process woven around the group formed by Sansovino, Serlio, and Lotto, in our attempt to discover how much of it remains submerged. Three "uprooted," maladjusted men, who witnessed catastrophic events and *mutationi* that must have played a role in their psychological development; and certainly, of the three, Sansovino seems the most hermetic, the least open, or perhaps simply the most "prudent." Our path has undoubtedly been insidious. We wish we had more direct testimony regarding the dramas experienced—and clearer testimony about the rifts. And yet, the mere fact of being constrained to tortuous approaches is itself a historical argument. Our artists are either silent or provide us only with clues that must be analyzed from an archeological perspective. The rivers of ink that have flowed in order to describe the "crisis" experienced by Italian men of letters and artists in the crucial 1540s and '50s have rarely taken into consideration situations that were less rending, but, for that very reason, more indicative of the widespread mental malaise that affected those who crafted with brush, chisel, and compass: a category of people whose social identity was still incompletely defined and who were especially vulnerable to disruptive pressures coming from men of letters, artisans, the laws of the Church, and the devotional literature they encountered.

We would like to know something that no document can tell us. What might Sansovino's reaction have been to the news that his friend Vergerio, bishop of Capodistria, had passed over into the camp of the Protestants? And what was the inner repercussion, for Sansovino and Titian, of the news that Paul IV's Index (1559) had condemned the complete works of their friend Pietro Aretino?[105] In the late 1540s, after the hopes raised by Francesco Donà's election to the office of Doge and the subsequent defeat of the League of Smalcalda, a whole world crumbled for the artists who had lived through the years of Doge Gritti's *renovatio*.

These points must also be kept in mind as we explore the reasons for Sansovino's withdrawal in the 1550s and '60s. And there is one other question. Sansovino abandoned the role of *architectus*, as we have already indicated, and seems to have adapted himself to that of a traditional *proto*. But that very adaptation is problematic. Even if we refrain from theorizing about Sansovino's religious thinking, his nonclassical building "without language" of later years speaks for itself, subtly and without commotion. Sansovino demonstrated that, on a subjective level, the events that occurred toward the middle of the fifteenth century left a vacuum that could not be filled, a confusion that received a spontaneous response in the form of a prudent reserve bordering on silence.

But even this reading of the facts is unsatisfactory. We began by considering a work of ecclesiastical building and by asking questions about the meaning of its simplicity, and we had linked that church to Savonarola's *simplicitas* and to concerns already present in Sansovino's work in San Marcello al Corso in Rome: the "withdrawal" we have resorted to above is a weak motive if separated from other considerations—it is, in the last analysis, deterministic. In fact, the choice of the *minus dicere* only has sense in a cultural *humus* ready for it. Once again, motivations coming from different historical contexts are interwoven.

Nonetheless: how does our analysis relate to the specific situation in Venice in the years after the institution of the *Savi sopra Eresia* [three lay members added to the Inquisition]?[106] What was the resistance, in Venice, of the civic religious sentiment that we discussed in the previous chapter?

Carlo Ginzburg and Adriano Prosperi have intelligently observed that "not only the function, but also the genesis of religious need in a society and in a determined period are extrareligious,"[107] recognizing that, during the age of humanism, function and genesis lay in the political and social crisis that overwhelmed the Italian states between the end of the fifteenth and the beginning of the sixteenth centuries. Passing from a diffused and diluted religion to a limited and concentrated one, and with the wearing out of institutional instruments of mediation—both civic and ecclesiastical—the religious demand, which socio-political catastrophes had rendered acute, was never satisfied: this is the picture that the two scholars offer of the background to the success of the *Beneficio di Cristo*.[108] Venice, in this context, constitutes "at least in appearance, the exception that proved the rule": the imperative, here, seems to have been the conservation of traditional religious structures.

How can such a reading be acceptable from our point of view? Of course, the role that had, in the fifteenth century, been typical of churches destined to unite the social body—such as San Zaccaria or Santa Maria dei Miracoli—would be handed over to the renovated San Giorgio Maggiore and the votive church of the Redentore. But how can we justify this practice of enclosing with parentheses, in the case of the "minor" churches, of courtly languages and the adoption of a significant *mediocritas*?

We must shift the focus of our attention to the context, to the shocks impressed upon the collective imaginary by ambitions that were related to the religious universe we have explored in the preceding pages. The plot is enriched by new paths, infinitely tangent with those traveled by the subjective consciousnesses of the artists.

We have, in fact, elements that can be separated from the point of view that has been adopted so far and allow us to use the "case" of the church of San Martino, with which we began, in another way. It is undoubtedly the case that Venetian religious architecture in the sixteenth century was largely congruent with the reductive and elementary program drawn up by Sansovino himself. The San Salvador of Giorgio Spavento and Tullio Lombardo was truly, as we have seen, an "extreme" case. The next era would see churches such as San Felice, San Sebastiano, Santa Maria Nova, and Santa Maria Mater Domini, which in different ways expressed a departure from the Roman experiments of Antonio da Sangallo the Younger, Raphael, and Baldassarre Peruzzi.

And when Palladio introduced in Venice an alternative language that was clearly polemical with regard to Sansovino's, the support for his work would come, not surprisingly, from the "papalist" and Romanist patrician class, as well as from scientistic circles.

Furthermore, the religious sentiment emerging from the monastery of San Giorgio in Alga determined a climate, a devotional sensibility, and a religious mentality that harmonized with some of the *topoi* belonging to Venetian politics and its myth. So much so that when Paolo Sarpi took it upon himself to defend the comprehensive structure of the reform movement, trying—as Cozzi has observed—to act upon on its most resolute sector, Calvinism, his objective would be to safeguard that which the *devotio moderna* had introduced into subjective consciousnesses—that is to say, the spiritualistic conception of the *Ecclesia* and the predominance of individual and inner religious experience.[109]

Moreover, beginning in 1516 with his *De Officio Episcopi*, Gasparo Contarini began moving toward Erasmian ideas in matters concerning public assistance and episcopal duties. The treatise was dedicated to his friend Pietro Lippomano, who had recently been named bishop of Bergamo, and reflects the inspirational lines of the pastoral work of Pietro Barozzi, who was bishop of Padua at the end of the fifteenth century, as well as the ideas of the *Libellus ad Leonem X* and the Murano group. Gasparo Contarini especially recommended assistance to the poor and touched upon the problem of the administration of episcopal wealth. By suggesting that the display of luxury was not suitable for a bishop, Contarini was implicitly accusing the magnificence cultivated by the Roman cardinals of the Church, which was shown off in the cardinals' palazzi of the late fifteenth and early sixteenth century. (The palazzo of Cardinal Alessandro Farnese was begun by Antonio da Sangallo the Younger around 1514.)

Gasparo Contarini wrote, "I believe the truth to be different from the magnificences of the bishops, first of all in that it is poor and everywhere, and it builds great hospices in which the poor may come, especially when they are sick, and there is care for nourishment and health; then, as for temples, chalices, vestments and other things pertaining to the divine cult, however much they may be esteemed, as a duty, I do not omit from among them the poor, however, ornate and magnificent these other things may be."[110]

Contarini thus prescribed a scale of priorities in which charitable duties took precedence over those related to the cult. His view certainly rested upon a tradition that had already been confirmed in the heart of the Venetian patrician class, in which the widespread structure of public welfare was used as a strategy to control poverty and alienation. But this view certainly conformed to the policies that inspired the religious sentiment of the Oratorio del Divino Amore in Rome. In any case, we find Gasparo Contarini's thoughts about the decoration of sacred sites most interesting:

First, therefore, that which is necessary to the divine cult should be close at hand, the reliquary for the poor should be paid for from the treasury; for if there is to be such indigence among the poor, it is necessary to reduce the sumptuousness that habitually pertains in the divine cult in order to care for their life; I believe, secondly, Christian piety to be the duty of the bishop, even if God must dwell in less magnificent stone temples, in order for Him to return, one must build temples to God that are not stony and unfeeling, but living and intelligent. "You are yourselves the Temple of God," he said. If such necessity does not burden him [i.e. the bishop] in this, let magnificence pay respect to God, as is seen habitually in the dignity of the city. As for the rest, truly, he pays for the poor and feels himself to be a procurator and rather a protector of the poor than a lord; if anything remains [after the assistance to the poor] it should be used to decorate the temple.[111]

The passage reaffirms the primacy of *charitas* as a Christian duty. At the same time, the text argues against the view that considers churches as the fossilizations of *pietas* or as occasions for worldly ostentation. Significantly enough, Paul's letter, which was also quoted by Serlio, is reechoed here: "*Dei enim templum vos estis.*" The *mediocritas* of the constructed *templum* represents the richness of the inner *templum*. The simple "decor" of the sacred site should attest to the fulfillment of a social practice that unifies the *res publica christiana*. This was not, therefore, a pedantic adherence to rites: there was no "wide and easy way" to reach the body of Christ, only participation, as Erasmus had proposed in his *Enchiridion Militis Christiani*. The interiorization of religious experience has as its correlative—in Erasmus as in Gasparo Contarini—the humanization of practices: and in Contarini's thinking one can certainly find the typically Venetian identification of religion and civil life.

And in fact the *Serenissima's* social policy, read next to the *mediocritas* that pervaded Venetian religious architecture, especially parochial architecture, seems on the whole to reflect Contarini's recommendations. The practice of *charitas*, rather than the magnificence of external worship, was chosen as an element of political *stabilitas*. The mechanisms of alienation found their remedies in public assistance, even though—as Giovanni Scarabello has remarked[112]—the strategies that were, in Europe, working to select the poor and create the *grand renfermement*, as posited by Foucault, did not take hold in Venice. The *simplicitas* of Venetian churches is, therefore, telling in its own way. It enunciates the supremacy of public assistance over passive worship, and of the action of institutions over the ceremonial act. Venice, as a State of divine origin dedicated to Christ, also seemed to be setting itself against Roman eloquence through this *simplicitas*. In this sense, the schematic quality of Venice's parochial churches can be read for the programmatic values it reveals: Sansovino's church of San Martino rests on the shoulders of a tradition whose determining influence cannot be denied. *Christus pauper* is contrasted with *Christus dives*. The theme assumed particular tonalities in the Anabaptist community, but also pervaded the religious sentiment of Venice and the Veneto region in general, appearing in particularly significant episodes such as the "Lando court" in Padua.[113] And although the spatial simplicity we have emphasized was often contradicted by the luxurious "furnishings" they contained, one cannot deny the specific quality of the Venetian ecclesiastical architecture of the sixteenth century—a quality that ought to be set next to the results of the debate on images and religious architecture that took place between the late '20s and the first years of the following decade.

Gasparo Contarini's theories, in fact, clashed with those of Alberto Pio da Carpi—a humanist whose work is rich in chivalrous motifs and a friend of Angelo Colocci, Johannes Goritz, and Girolamo Aleandro—who sustained an articulate polemic with Erasmus. Alberto Pio's attack was published in 1529 in Paris—where the Prince of Carpi went after the Sack of Rome. In it he accused Erasmus of corrosive skepticism, which he saw as the cause of Lutheran leprosy and of the destruction of images in Wittenberg.[114] Moreover, the Sorbonne had already accused Erasmus in 1526 for saying that it was a mortal sin to decorate churches and endow monasteries. In reality, Erasmus had, in the *Con-*

vivium religiosum, written against the vacuousness of exterior ceremonial, in a tone that bears some resemblance to Contarini's: "Hence those who adorn monasteries or churches at excessive cost, when meanwhile so many of Christ's living temples [i.e. the poor] are in danger of starving, shiver in their nakedness, and are tortured by want of necessities, seem to me almost guilty of a capital crime."

And in the famous passage against the luxury of the Carthusian monastery near Pavia, he added, ". . . And some people think it a crime to divert that money, contrary to the testator's intentions, to pious uses. They prefer to pull down what they begin rather than not to build at all."[115]

Alberto Pio's problem, regarding the criticism directed against the vacuity of ecclesiastical luxury, was how to justify the majesty of the rites and singing, and of the building and sacred furnishings. While the human mind "is enclosed in the prison of the body," Pio wrote, "and buried in its weight, it needs the instrument of the senses to ascend to sublime things." *Externa* are thus seen as means of ascent. Alberto Pio took a Neoplatonic approach in praising aesthetic experience as an instrument of detachment from the weight of matter; *honesta voluptas* was thus associated with the *gaudium* induced by aesthetic contemplation. Images are thus indispensable to devotion. Since human emotions are triggered by the senses, vision has an exciting influence on the mind and soul, and can direct them to the contemplation of divine mysteries. The contemplative value of religion releases the faithful from a direct and intimate contact with the Scriptures: Giuseppe Scavizzi has written that the Prince of Carpi "resuscitated medieval schemes with instruments updated to the level of Renaissance culture."[116] The contemplative morality defended by Alberto Pio clearly complemented prevailing theories about the concealment of the Scriptures, which need to be protected against contamination by the common people.[117] One thus obtains a dual unambiguous relationship between display and concealment. The image has social and educational aims, and reveals the divine character of the real; but the Church holds the keys to the mysteries displayed in the image.

This was the argument that Alberto Pio reaffirmed when he responded to Erasmus in 1531.[118] The discussion also covered the form of churches: a delicate argument for the defenders of the Roman theories, given that the scandal of indulgences for the building of St. Peter's had been one of the causes of the schism. And here was Alberto Pio proposing theories that contradicted both Erasmus and Contarini. The priority of *charitas* over the construction of churches was rejected without appeal: alms for the poor were to be postponed in favor of the church, which, as the place of Christ's ritual sacrifice, was an homage due to God. The entire text is inspired, moreover, by a need to defend the power politics—of which buildings and images were the means of communication—used by the Roman Church. Public assistance was pushed aside in favor of latria and Christian duty, which was to be expressed with donations to the Church. God himself had established this duty when he ordered the construction of the temple of Solomon.

Here, then, is the *exemplum* that modern churches are so far from imitating:

a temple all of gold and precious metals. Furthermore, the sacred temple is an image of the sky and of the celestial Jerusalem as it appeared to John: "Who can doubt that the decorations and treasures of sacred buildings indicate and reflect as much as possible the form of the eternal celestial temple . . . the image of which was shown and expressed at Patmos?"

The Holy Spirit, so Alberto Pio said, resides in the church.[119] Its interior should be considered as the spirit with regard to the exterior—or body—and consequently merits greater richness and special attention.

Thus the interior of churches must, for the real presence of the Holy Spirit, offer itself as an instrument of ascent: beauty becomes a vehicle to the divine, and images are seen to lead to *gaudium* and *excitatio*.

The interpretation of images as a *Biblia pauperum* and the emphasis placed on contemplation, rather than on social action, gave Erasmus the opportunity to respond, in his *Apologia* of 1531, that true latria does not consist in the construction of sumptuous churches: instead, it takes place in the depths of the Christian soul.[120] And, for Erasmus, God does not live in churches, which are places created only to worship in comfort: though of course—he continues— the church must be majestic, and he deplores those that are "similar to stables," often seen in his time.

One cannot miss the similarity that once again appears between Erasmus's theses and Contarini's. Both were concerned with stimulating a deeply anti-Roman tradition: the battle against pomp was inserted into a general vision of religion that created a connection between social duties and an active and secular morality. The interiorization of faith has tangible works as its "consequence." The cult of the visible—an expression of hierarchy—was replaced by the practice of social assistance, though the radicalism of iconoclastic Protestantism was avoided.

We do not wish, however, for our analysis of the polemics surrounding ecclesiastical luxury, to provoke any historiographical schematization. We believe we have already demonstrated that there existed, in Rome and Venice, different traditions and mentalities with regard to religious architecture. But Venice's adherence to the theories of Erasmus and Contarini is not something that can be proven: the "scandal" of the policy of pomp that was pursued by the Scuole Grandi and denounced in *Il sogno dil Caravia* does, for example, indicate tendencies to analyze in a specific fashion,[121] while one cannot forget that it was Erasmus who criticized ceremony and private ostentation in sacred places, which were anything but avoided in Venice:[122] "we see certain churches full, on the outside and on the inside, of noble insignia, clipei, helmets, lions, dragons, birds, dogs, bulls . . . vessels taken from the enemy; [and] the space occupied by the ambitious monuments of the rich."

The façades of the churches dedicated to the "glory" of private individuals and the funeral decorations that invaded Venetian churches certainly did not place themselves in the wake of Erasmus's or Contarini's thinking. In the religious sphere as well, one must recognize the existence of conflicts and articulations, which, moreover, pervaded the entire official attitude toward heterodoxy.

Contarini's acceptance of heterodox individuals is well known, as is his aversion to the preconceived intransigence of the so-called zealots. On June 12, 1537, Contarini wrote Bishop Giberti in order to defend the Benedectine Dom Marco da Cremona, who gave a public commentary of Saint Paul's letters in the Paduan monastery before many lay listeners and university students.

Since Luther has said different things regarding God's grace and free will, [the zealots] have placed themselves against anyone who preaches and teaches the greatness of grace and human infirmity; and they believe that when preachers contradict Luther they are contradicting Saints Augustine, Ambrose, Bernard and Thomas; and, in short, moved by good zeal but with a certain vehemence and passion of the soul, they don't recognize that in these contradictions they deviate from the Catholic truth and draw near to the Pelagian heresy and bring tumult among the people.[123]

We are now approaching the time of the fatal colloqium of Ratisbonne (1541) and the defeat of Italian evangelism. The appeal to interiority had not been supported by plans of institutional reform, and this absence would give rise to aristocratic attitudes, Nicodemical practices, and tragic individual drifting. When Lorenzo Lotto wrote of himself "alone, without a faithful government, and very anxious of spirit," he expressed the psychological and ethical drama that even the most "prudent" men—such as Marcantonio Flaminio and Achille Bocchi—would find it difficult to escape. And when Paolo Sarpi later planned the institution of a reformed Venetian church, he was clearly aware that only the result of a political *"mutatione"* might reintroduce Venice into the European game under a different sign—but he would dream of such a change in vain.

Let us consider once again the simple ecclesiastical building of Jacopo Sansovino. In the final analysis, it can be compared to Serlio's most "populist" experiments and to Lotto's most interiorized painting, in spite of the linguistic differences that characterize the three artists. And there can be no doubt about it: neither Sansovino nor Serlio managed to express their deepest aspirations with Lotto's tension and formal mastery. Especially in Sansovino's hands, the language of modesty became so impoverished that it began to move toward renunciation. The example of Sansovino aside, however, the shocks induced by the new religious needs of the period did not harmonize easily with the proud premises of a language *all' antica*. The equilibrium between humanism and reformist themes—which Gasparo Contarini, Michelangelo, Zwingli, Curione, and Castellione would attempt to protect in different ways[124]—resulted in an irremediable compromise favoring those experiences that saw in the "visible" less and less of a privileged instrument of knowledge.

All of this needs to be adequately historicized, however. On the one hand, we have Serlio's models, with their broad contaminations, their popularizations, and their receptivity to local dialects: they constituted an unpredictable "reduction" of the universalistic pretexts of the humanistic lesson in favor of a more comprehensible language with populist overtones. On the other hand, there are Sansovino's "renunciations": unlike Serlio's, these could not be codified, and they denounced those uncertainties that resolve themselves in obvious contradictions. The austere interior of the church of San Giuliano was challenged by the triumphalism of the façade, dedicated to the consecration of Tommaso Rangone's glory, who was formerly Domenico Grimani's doctor (in 1516).[125]

The patrons and the nature of financing conditioned the products, of course. But even the architectural "mechanism" that honored the doctor from Ravenna speaks of uncertainties that are, practically speaking, unverifiable in the works of Sansovino in the 1510s–30s. The faithful functionary, having donned the garb of the *architectus*, exhibits the residues that an empirical praxis deposited in his linguistic laboratory. With no offense intended to Gramsci's theories about the cosmopolitan and abstract role of Italian intellectuals of the Renaissance, it was the crisis—local, restricted, and difficult to communicate—of that role which, in different ways, the spiritualism of Lorenzo Lotto, the skepticism of the late Sansovino, and the empiricism of Sebastiano Serlio stated with utmost clarity.[126] And if our hypotheses on the religious roots of that crisis are at all valid, the analyses that remain to be completed will have to explore the paths opened by such attitudes within the triumphant paradigm: the "modern" paradigm of abstraction and reckoning.

Appendix to
Chapter 3

I. APSM, busta B 1–4, "Fabbrica della chiesa." (No date, but after July 1553).

El se dechiara per la presente scrittura come li reverendi misser lo piovan et preti con li clarissimi procuratori della chiesa de San Martin de Venetia sonno romasi d'accordo con maestro Hieronimo da Manerba et maestro Zuan Maria da Lona murari et compagni de far la chiesia preditta de manifattura de murer secondo il dissegno fatto per messer Jacomo Sansovin, con modi et ordeni da lui serà comandato in ditta fabricha.

Et prima che li ditti maestri siano obligadi a descoverzer et ruinar tutta la chiesa vecchia segondo farà bisogno per far la nova, mettendo coppi et legnami et tutte le robbe, qual se chaveràno de ditta chiesa in logo dove li serà consegnado obligandosse chavar tutte le muraglie che sonno nelle fondamente vecchie el descalzinar tutte le piere vecchie de ditta fabricha et fare la fondamente nove dove il sopraditto misser Jacomo ordinerà, scavando terreno et acqua delle ditte mettendo magieri in fondi et spianar tutti li ruinazzi et terreni a livello delle fondamente che i farà de novo et far tutti li muri cosí sotto terra si come sopra terra et far li pilastri con le sue lesene dentro et fora de ditta chiesa ben tiradi dretti de piera cotta, eceptuando base, capitelli, cimase, architravi et porte, le qual habbino ad esser de piera viva et le fenestre et li occhi habbino ad esser de piera cotta over de piera viva come piacerà al reverendo piovan, obligandosse li ditti maestri de smaltar et bianchisar tutte le ditte muraglie de dentro et de fuori et terrazzar dove dal ditto misser Jacomo li serà ordenato et tutte le ditte muraglie cosí sotto terra come sopra terra li sieno mesurade et redutte a muro de una piera mesurando pien et vodo, eccettuando dove caderà il passo et tutte le lesene sí dentro come de fuora li sieno mesurade et reddutte a muro d'una piera. Intendandosse che li ditti maestri siano obligadi a far tutti li sexti che bisognerà in ditta fabricha, et tutte le muraglie che farà li ditti maestri se obligano a far passa quatro e un quarto al ducato a rason de lire sie soldi quatro per ducato, obligandosse etiam li detti maestri de coprir tutta la chiesa sopra marchado senza premio alcuno et volendo tavellar il colmo de ditta chiesa il reverendo pievan et li clarissimi procuratori de ditta chiesa de darli per sua mercede ducato uno per ogni diese passa de intavelladura de ditto colmo. Et el reverendo misser lo pievan con li clarissimi procuratori siano obligadi dar alli ditti maestri tutte le robbe che farà bisogno per ditta fabricha idest come calcina, piere cotte, piere vive, legnami per far ponti et darli l'acqua posta in terra su ditta fabricha et sabioni et ogni altre robbe apertinente a ditta fabricha et dando li danari a ditti maestri de settimana in settimana secondo che lavorerano.

Dechiarando che quando non si volesse smaltar qualche parte de ditta fabricha se debbia stimar et abater del marcado sopraditto alli ditti maestri murari quanto sarà stimado montar la fattura de essa smaltadura.

2. APSM, busta B 1–4, "Rodoli," etc. (Dated on the reverse side of the sheet, 29 September 1615.)

Questa povera chiesa di S. Martino, essendo per l'antichità de tempi consumata e ridotta a pessima conditione, fu per ordine de nostri antecessori gettata a terra con disegno di reedificarla dalle fondamenta sicome anco fu fatto, impero ché l'anno 1546 in circa, essendo stato formato et proposto il presente modello [. . .] cominciarono a buttar le fondamenta, ma essendo il danaro molto poco, per comune consenso furono vendute le case della chiesa, quelle che hora sono case de Ca' Mocenigo, furono venduti alcuni campi in villa de Fanzuol, sotto Castelfranco, et tutta quella parte dove è fatto il choro, che era fondi de ragion dei preti fu assegnata alla chiesa et con quel tratto ridotta non a forma di chiesa ma ad un semplice et imperfetto imbozzo.

In progresso poi di qualche anno, concorrendo l'elemosine de fedeli si sono fabricati questi quatro pillastri che si vedono, si sono ridotte a qualche perfettione le capelle, onde per metter la chiesa a coverto, sicome da periti è stato consultato, è necessaria provisione di ducati 3627 in circa, dalla qual spesa accioché restino informate le vostre signorie illustrissime le diciamo che la lunghezza della chiesa è passa n 13 con la muraglia e larga passa n 14 con la muraglia, sono in tutto passa n 41 che saranno passa n 82. Redotte tutte le muraglie passa n 574, a ducati 3 il passo sono d. 1722.

Per il coverto tavellado cadene, braghe di ferro finito	duc. 800
Per li 4 pillastri che si hanno da far da novo tra pietre et fattura	duc. 640
Per le pietre vive per far li 3 volti	duc. 135
Per la fattura dei volti	duc. 150
Per le muraglie dei fianchi et sopra le capellette, passa n 50 a duc. 3 il passo	duc. 150
Per metter in opera li 4 pillastri con la robba	duc. 30
Somma	duc. 3627

On the reverse side of the sheet: "Scrittura letta alli procuratori della chiesa per la fabbrica." (29 September 1615.)

4

The Scuole Grandi

But I want to tell you of the many errors / of some; who dress in proud
vestments / I won't yet tell their names / They are part of the saint of the plague
/ and have done such good works at the arrogant school / Foliage, Harpies, and
so many beautiful heads / Columns carved in the newest manner / So as to
prove everyone a Master. // So that every new bench will be the real one /
Everyone wants to show himself a great inventor / Changing now this stairway, and now that / Dismantling gutters and doors / Quarreling with one
another / Saying, "so-and-so didn't know what he was doing" / And these
so-and-so's, who pretend to be so wise / Want to know everything, and don't
know anything.[1]

This was how *Il sogno dil Caravia* branded the construction projects of the
Scuola Grande di San Rocco (figs. 75–80, 86–89): pride, vanity, and cultural
whims had led to errors, superfluous expenses, ridiculous displays, and internal fits of pique. We have already mentioned how Alessandro Caravia
expressed the violent criticism that evangelical groups in Venice directed
against the luxury pursued by the Scuole, which were condemned for having
forgotten their original mission of public assistance. Caravia continues thus:

*They have spent eighty thousand ducats when six would have been enough /
The rest, that was spent in vain, / Could have been spent for the barefoot and
naked who cry, "Alas" / Each one unhealthy and hungry / I'd like to say one
word to you / I'm not surprised / that investments in the banks are now
smaller. . . . The investments in the poor are botched / In order to build, but
not out of devotion / Columns that jut onto the piazza / Changing the new
inventions each year / Spending their money on a crazy project / They should
have affection for Christ / And for love of him these ill-spent ducats / Should
clothe the naked and feed the hungry.*

Caravia was indicating that waste was the main result of the misgovernment
he was denouncing. The mass of wretched poor asking for compassion was

contrasted with the empty triumphalism exhibited by the Scuole Grandi, which were, moreover, uncertain about the direction they were taking. The Erasmian matrix of *Il sogno* is obvious, although the text contains an open appreciation of Luther.[2] A polemic against friarly hypocrisy, the idea of a religion reduced to an essential nucleus completely contained in the "pure Gospel," and the implied denial of purgatory and of the *mercati* [markets] of the Roman Church: Caravia's text orchestrates these themes into an attack that seems anything but ingenuous, especially when one considers that it was published in the fateful year of 1541.

And the Scuola di San Rocco was not the only target of Caravia's irony. Its rival, the Scuola Grande della Misericordia (figs. 91–92), was also attacked, as was the vacuity of the rivalry between the two Scuole:

They've made such a bad beginning / That, truly, the walls are bigger / Than those of the so-called "impossible" bastion / Master Guardian appeared to do great things / And he left incredible hunger / Chasing out the poor with all force / With no mercy whatsoever / To then create discord among them. // One should give the name "Counter-Misericordia" / To this school, so ill-governed, / Of the sweet pious virgin of the Val Verde / [This school] which, this way and that way, has ruined her / To satisfy their every fantasy / They want to compete with San Rocco / Whereas it would be better if their wasted money / Had given comfort to the poor.

Readers of Erasmus and Gasparo Contarini would have once again found familiar themes here. Moreover, Alessandro Caravia—who had a jewelry shop on Ruga degli Orefici, in the Rialto district—was not a completely isolated figure in Venice. Born in 1503 of simple and strict morals, and inspired by austere ethics—as his last will and testament of May 1, 1563, demonstrates— Caravia was in touch with Pietro Aretino, Giovanni Grimani, and Andrea Calmo: and he would imitate Calmo's language in a later work, the short poem "Naspo bizaro," written in 1565.[3]

Caravia, however, certainly could not—or did not want to —realize what was clear to Botero: the latter, in praising the indirect system of aid to the poor that had been organized by the Republic, immediately identified the Scuole with the State and with the maintenance of the established order.[4] As Brian Pullan has demonstrated, not only had the Scuole Grandi of Venice always been integrated into the structure of the State, but even at the end of the fifteenth century they had undergone processes that changed their original character of purely devotional confraternities.[5] The division into two orders of rich members and poor ones, the centralization of authority within the Banks, the redistribution of wealth mainly within the limits of each Scuola Grande, and the uses of capital for security investments in properties and buildings: these phenomena concerned all of the Venetian Scuole, which thus assumed limited duties regarding the control of lower groups, in the context of a policy intent on conserving the social order essential to the aristocratic Republic. Pullan has correctly read in the new forms of charitable practice introduced by the new religious movements—the Company of Divine Love, the Theatines, the Jesuits—the grounds for contrast, rather than conflict, with the social functions fulfilled by the old institutions. The assistance to permanent residents of respectable and pious behavior, which had been offered "in the bosom" of the Scuole Grandi, would at first contrast with and then complement the activity of the new orders, which extended beyond predetermined boundaries and the limits of conventional morality.

The integration of the Scuole Grandi into the State's policies did, however, continue, and in a fundamental fashion: this integration would become visible during the Interdict of 1606, when the Scuole and the new religious orders found themselves on opposite sides.[6] One can thus understand all too well the reasons opposing an evangelical like Alessandro Caravia against the Scuole that were turning into powerful financial, building, and real estate organizations. Nor should one overlook the fact that the "popular" character of the Scuole had been challenged by patrician groups who, inside the associations benefiting from financing and legacies, were organizing compliant clienteles for themselves. Officially governed by the original citizens, the Scuole were in many ways linked to the private and collective interests of the patrician class. This made the publication of *Il sogno dil Caravia* even more significant. In February 1559, speaking before the Tribunal of the Inquisition, Caravia denied ever having wanted to laugh at religion, noting, moreover, that *Il sogno* had been authorized by the Senate and the Heads of the Ten. He also referred to an argument, which had occurred before the Heads of the Ten, concerning the publication of his work: "and this litigation was brought against me by those of the Scuole Grandi, of whom I speak in this work, who did not want the work to be printed; nonetheless, they were sent away and the permit to print it was given to me."[7]

The accusations that Caravia directed against the Scuole Grandi, which he saw as lairs harboring factions, sordid alliances, and maneuvers mounted to satisfy worldly ambitions, clearly corresponded to the attitude of the Ten, who authorized *Il sogno* in 1540. Caravia thus unwittingly became an instrument of control and pressure acting, for the State, upon the major confraternities in ways we will discuss later.

Let us concentrate for now on the most apparent fact of the luxury policy stigmatized by Caravia: we are speaking of the exhibitions that were well-tolerated by the State, given that their aim was to glorify the public *charitas* in Venice through visual apotheoses. There was, incidentally, great rivalry between the Scuole: this much has become a historiographical slogan. We will have to penetrate into the recesses of these rivalries in order to single out the reasons that can be linked to the description of mentalities in transformation, the object of our interest.

But first we must ask one question: can we find any evidence, in the choices made during the architectural rebuilding of the fifteenth and sixteenth centuries, that might help us distinguish a "civic taste" from a patrician one or from the taste revealed in the architectural projects for the State? In the second half of the fifteenth century, the Scuole di San Marco and di San Giovanni Evangelista had adopted singular procedures. The first, especially under Pietro Lombardo's direction, had aimed at the exasperation of the "picturesque" (fig. 70): in spite of Codussi's later interventions and the rigor of Tullio Lombardo's perspective bas-reliefs, the Scuola di San Marco presented itself as an event rich in fabulous evocations, a triumph of visual hedonism. On the other hand, the Scuola di San Giovanni Evangelista, beginning with the construction of the remarkable external atrium opening onto the Calle del Caffettier, had showed a preference for proportion and purism, in order to later turn toward its own interior, with the masterful perspective structure of Mauro Codussi's double staircase (fig. 71).[8] The contrast, in this case, is clear. It is obvious that the Scuola di San Marco made the more "popular" choice, a choice more strongly linked to collective visual traditions, whereas the Scuola di San Giovanni Evangelista seems to have aligned itself with the most aristocratic culture of the patrician élite. And yet, the Scuola di San Giovanni Evangelista had sought to outdo the Scuola di San Marco in one particular area, by focusing on the novelty of the double set of stairs (fig. 71), preceded by the one Codussi finished in 1495 for the rival Scuola Grande. The Scuola di San Marco solicited an accumulation of themes and forms; the Scuola di San Giovanni, on the other hand, sought to be selective. In some way—but only at the beginning stages, as we shall see—this duality would also characterize the competition, in the following century, between the Scuola Grande di San Rocco and the Scuola Grande della Misericordia.

The architectural history of the Scuola di San Rocco, which has already been partially explored, holds more surprises, especially when reread in the light of our inquiry and linked to the history of the Scuola della Misericordia.[9]

There do not seem to have been any events of particular importance during the first stages of the building's construction. Perhaps one should note how the general tone of the enterprise was subdued in comparison with the undertakings of the previous century, a change that can be explained by the difficulties the Republic encountered in the first decades of the sixteenth century. Moreover, the relations between the Scuola and its first *proti* were characterized by an attitude that wavered between rigorism and distrust. The Scuola's members seem to have imposed upon master Bon, who was employed on January 11, 1517,[10] an overall project that may have been prepared before. In fact, in a document from June 3, 1524, they speak of "our mode,"[11] after lamenting that the *proto* wished to "construct our building in his way, according to some plan of his."[12] But at the same time, this model was quite far from being a complete or definitive project, given that on January 1, 1525, Zuan Celestro *toschan* received 10 ducats in payment for his work, which consisted in "designing for them the style of the portico above the canal and the entrance of the portals."[13]

Thus began a history marked by pride, clumsily concealed doubts, second thoughts, dismissals, and vindications. The project progressed in fits and starts. The experience was, as we have already suggested, conditioned by the cultural situation of the time. The architectural initiative of the Scuola was part of a reaction to the widespread dismay that followed the defeat of Agnadello and subsequent events; there were, however, still no precise choices responding to the exhaustion of the themes that had animated Venetian architecture in the last decades of the fifteenth century. The Scuola's members evidently did not have the courage to trust Tullio Lombardo's erudite language, probably because he was not familiar with local dialects. The only remaining choice was empirical, and it was invoked as a guarantee of collective identity. The initial program was anything but clear, in spite of the members' firm intention to maintain control over the initiative. Let us look at the parts that can be attributed to Bon: the completely traditional definition of the plan (fig. 77), the columns resting on octagonal pedestals in the hall on the ground floor (fig. 95), and the lower level of the façade on the *campo* and of the façade on the left side (figs. 75, 87). Elements borrowed from the Scuola di San Marco (the columns supporting a ceiling with uncovered beams) were combined with elements borrowed from the Scuola di San Giovanni Evangelista (the Codussian *bifora*, or two-light window) in an obvious attempt to create a synthesis between the rival Scuole—an attempt that outdid them both in narrative richness. The members cared little or not at all if the mullion window invented by Codussi was, by 1517, clearly anachronistic: indeed, the competition had not been engaged on the level of *inventio*. What counted was that the *bifora* in the façade carried a cornice with polychromatic marble inlays (fig. 87).

Aside from its desire to present itself as the exponent of a tradition to be preserved and enriched, the Scuola di San Rocco was not at first clear about the direction it wished to take. Its uncertainty was reflected in the entanglement of commissions and the polemic that surrounded the form of the stairs: in February 1522, the Chiefs of the Ten became interested in the matter and ordered four experts, among them Tullio Lombardo and Scarpagnino, to choose one of the models proposed by the Scuola. But the Bank remained unsatisfied and did not give the go-ahead for construction. This caused further interventions by the Heads of the Ten, in December 1522 and in 1523, when—after having pointed out the scandal that the matter was creating in the city—they ordered the Scuola to construct a staircase similar to those in the Scuola di San Marco and the Scuola di San Giovanni Evangelista.[14]

On May 20, 1524, Sante Lombardo was engaged as the new *proto*; he was confirmed on June 3, the same day that Bon was dismissed.[15] But, as we have seen, Giovanni Celestro was working there at the same time, though on January 1, 1525, he declared that he did not wish to "to help anymore under direction."[16] Nor would the fact that the notary of the Scuola was Sante's brother, Giovanni Lombardo, be of any use to the new *proto*. He would appeal to the lawyers of the Avogaria against the intrusion of the clients, and, though he had chosen the path of a friendly agreement, he too would soon be dismissed (1527).[17]

This time, however, the architect seems to have wished for his dismissal. The following words occur at the bottom of the document notifying Sante that he had been fired: "On this hour and day, as noted above, and in our establishment, master Santo Lombardo, as above, together with his father, . . . refused to be *proti* and took their leave."[18]

The job of *proto* working for a Scuola with such confused ideas was clearly not highly desirable, and rather troublesome on the construction site. The contract engaging Sante Lomardo was clear: the architect "should do nothing of his own invention on this said construction, but in everything is to consult with the guardian and the bank with our procurators who will come by from time to time."[19]

The members' attitude was typical of someone who knows what he wants but is completely unsure about how to obtain it. One must not, however, remain blocked by Caravia's moralism. One can certainly detect, behind the strict and contradictory behavior of the Scuola, an experimental spirit that had to come to terms with the conservatism that was making the entire experience schizophrenic, since the two extremes shared a common attitude. And it was this vacillating that Caravia denounced as internal and contradictory vacuousness. For us, on the other hand, that insecurity is a sign of cultural fluidity, to be read as valuable evidence of a delicate moment in which collective mental systems were once again being placed in question. Clearly, there was an anxious need for experimentation, undoubtedly disordered and incoherent, but obvious in the members' irregular progress; over and above the outcome, this observation is not useless.

One can, for example, study the procedure that was followed in the definition of the façade on the canal, which was at the time a subject of contention with master Bon (figs. 78, 80). We have seen how "the form of the portico" was determined by Celestro; it acquired new significance thanks to Sante Lombardo's work. On January 25, 1526, however, the Guardian Grande [the chief officer] demonstrated his concern about "the great expenses incurred," establishing "that on the façade of our large hall on the *rio*, no more money can be spent except to set in place the two windows which have been built . . . and the base, and no other work which requires expenditures, this because the place cannot support it."[20]

The economic factor—"in order not to throw away the money of ms. San Rocho"—was compounded by a static one: this leads us to believe that the central arch of the portico on the canal was originally open.[21] But less than three months later, on April 8, 1526, the Bank annulled its previous decision, establishing that the new Guardian Grande "might finish the right-hand façade of our large hall."[22] A façade designed and executed by Sante Lombardo, given that on May 20, 1527, it was stated that in the building "all that remains to be completed is that small right-hand façade, and its eaves," while other documents indicate that the idea for the decorative details should also be ascribed to Tullio Lombardo's son, Sante.[23]

Let us take a closer look at the façade on the canal (fig. 78). The portico—even excluding the two arches inserted into the central arch, which introduce an uncontrolled rhythmic caesura—is marked by unequal spans: the greater width of the central arch forces it to be defined with an arc of a circle, while the end openings, somewhat narrower, are coarsely resolved with arches on raised Byzantine-like piers. Furthermore, there are clear variations in proportion: the pedestals of the lateral pilasters of the portico are annoyingly out of phase with one another. But the façade above is not without originality (fig. 79): the upper *bifore* windows, which are enclosed with a triangular pediment, the small niche inserted into a triadic motif, and the upper fluted pilasters, create a visual variation that is accentuated by the reliefs of the entablatures, the continuous base of the upper order, and the figurative elements.

The compositional framework does not stiffen the design of the façade: the upper *bifore* windows are the product of Sante Lombardo's critical revision of Bon's windows, but even so they do not speak a purist's Latin. Linked by corbels to the fascia of the base, they introduce a subdued antiperspective-like language into the whole. But let us examine the central aedicule: the motif, which is repeated on the sides by niches between fluted pilasters, sets out a plastic and erudite theme and enriches the structure with atmospheric effects.

The complex history of the staircase (figs. 76, 96)—the reconstruction of which began in 1545—would later insert an important volumetric detail on the right side of the Scuola (fig. 80), accentuating the paratactic character of that part of the building.[24] But at this point we would rather turn to the façade executed by the *proto* who succeeded Sante Lombardo on October 6, 1527, that is to say Antonio Abbondi, known as Scarpagnino (figs. 75, 86, 87).[25] This new architect, who was a *proto* of the *Magistratura del Sal* [Salt Office] and had already proven himself with his work on the complex and delicate restructuring of the Rialto district, was an important technician and destined to gain great prestige in Venice: from 1506 he directed the construction of the churches of San Sebastiano and Santo Spirito, in April 1520 he did restoration work on the old Ponte di Pietra in Verona with his friend Francesco Lurano da Castellion Cremonese, and from 1522 he continued the church of San Fantin while working very hard on the rearrangement of the Palazzo Ducale.[26] Scarpagnino's appearance did not mark a new cultural phase in the architectural history of the Scuola di San Rocco, but introduced instead a variation on the evocative impressionism that had been practiced by the Scuola's first *proto*.

Furthermore, the Venetian architectural climate still had not changed: the phase of doubt and "waiting" still persisted. Jacopo Sansovino, driven by the tragedy of the Sack of Rome, did in fact arrive in the lagoon in 1527, but—as we have already remarked—his project for Vettor Grimani's palazzo would remain uncompleted and the new phase stimulated by Gritti's circle would only begin—and slowly—in the mid-thirties.

At first busy with the rebuilding of the hall on the ground floor and with the construction of the hall that would later be removed, Scarpagnino finished the construction of the Sala dell' Albergo in 1534; in the end he found himself facing the delicate question of the façade on the *campo*, which Bon had never completed (fig. 75). In an unpublished document, Cicogna maintains that Sebastiano Serlio had been commissioned for that task—information that has never been verified, even after the publication of an estimate that Serlio gave for the construction of the floor.[27] It is, however, most likely that the members disagreed over a work that had been called upon to indicate as eloquently as possible the cultural sign of the Scuola. The fact remains that on March 14, 1535, two "skilled" brothers—Alvise Noal and Costantin de Todero—were called upon to collaborate with the building's five deputies for ten years.[28] The management of the construction site thus experienced a change in direction— one that needs to be evaluated next to a tragic event: the plague of 1527–29.

The rationalization of decisions became associated with a new symbolic theme, since the Scuola's patron saint was considered a healer. The plague was a public illness, not a private one, and in Venice the protection of health was a political matter. Furthermore, as Stefania Mason Rinaldi has pointed out,[29] gratitude and signs of victory over the calamity merged—once the plague was over—in ceremonials that explicitly labeled the festivities instituted by public decree as "triumphs." But the lay confraternities—in this case, the Scuola di San Rocco—were working alongside the State: the construction work of the 1530s resounds like San Rocco's triumph over evil and a collective ex voto. In fact, on July 9, 1536, Scarpagnino's model for the façade was approved, and on June 3, 1537, an agreement was drawn up with the stonemasons Tonin Sorella and Domenego de Baldisera for the *bifore* windows of the upper floor and of the Sala dell' Albergo in the back.[30] A final phase thus began, one destined to deeply change the overall significance of the building.

In fact, Scarpagnino's new project assigned a secondary role to the parts Bon had executed (fig. 75): two orders of free-standing Corinthian columns, which defined the structure of the halls with surprising eloquence, were superimposed upon the original plan for the façade (figs. 86, 87). It was, therefore, an addition that encroached onto the *campo*: the eight large columns, exhibited as trophies, proclaimed a triumphalism that engaged the urban space before it, involving it in a new architectural narrative. It was obvious that the model of the columnar apparatus detached from the façade was to be found in the structures of ancient triumphal arches—or in those of the Nerva Forum. There was in the building of the Scuola a sudden and unexpected suggestion of Antiquity. And there was a significant—though perhaps casual—coincidence. A receipt from January 2, 1538, testifies that "they had begun to set the bases for the front façade of the Scuola of San Rocho":[31] the decision made in July 1536 was being acted upon while, in the Piazza, an equally explicit citation of the Roman triumphal arches was characterizing Sansovino's Loggetta—with the advantage, for the Scuola, of a magniloquence that the Republic's *speculum virtutis* carefully avoided.

Pietro Paoletti has suggested that Scarpagnino designed a pediment as the termination of the central intercolumniation and planned statues to stand above the projecting entablatures on the sides. This hypothesis is not essential, even if one takes into account a solution that figures in a drawing from the Venetian Archivio di Stato and probably dates from the seventeenth century (fig. 75). There remains the problem of the greater width of the central intercolumniation, which, as in the case of the façade on the canal, imposes visual devices. Scarpagnino was playing here with a variation on the model of the *bifora* window that he had invented for the upper story: the structure, which is divided by three small columns on cylindrical bases and terminates in a triangular pediment, is enriched in the central window by a fourth column, thus producing a coupled motif (fig. 88). The mental procedure followed is clear: the *bifore* windows of the upper level—which differentiate themselves almost polemically from the inferior ones by Bon, while also contrasting with those executed by Sante Lombardo in the façade on the canal—may, according to several scholars, be referring to the "heretical" game based on the doubling of the Porta Borsar in Verona and to the decorative solutions of the figures (perhaps also by Scarpagnino) in the Palazzo Contarini (fig. 78).[32] One could add to this the illustration regarding the Basilica di Fano contained in Cesare

Cesariano's edition of Vitruvius's *De architectura*, in which the coupled windows bear more of a resemblance to Lombardo's than to Scarpagnino's. What matters is that the imperiousness of the triumphal motif *all'antica* is mitigated by *bifore* windows that allude to a Roman "otherness" and are treated as nonperspective objects: the pair, placed so as to define the axis of the rooms, is, incidentally, a masterpiece of ambiguity (fig. 88).

And one may consider almost too amusing the decorative treatment that accentuates the hiatus between the apparatus formed by the eight large columns and the upper *bifore* windows. We are referring not only to the upper frieze or to the bases of the windows, but also to the corbels beneath the latter, crowned by amusing abacuses of Corinthian columns: this last motif was already present inside San Zaccaria and at the top of the *bifore* windows of Codussi's Palazzo Loredan. Was Scarpagnino simply obeying an ordinance issued in 1536 that ordered "as many ornaments as possible in praise of the Lord"?[33]

Let us take a closer look at the eight columns (fig. 87): they appear ancient only in a superficial way. The shafts of the lower order show a unique pastiche: the flutings do not respect the ancient rule and stand next to each other in the Doric manner, while the figured capitals correspond to the singular fascias interrupting the continuity of the columns. And one can clearly recognize the interwoven branches encircling the lower columns: grapevine, lemon, bay laurel, and oak. Some erudite member must have intervened to dictate the iconographic program: allegorically, the fertility of Christ's blood is associated with wealth [*aurum*], glory, and *fortitudo*. The symbolic narration spells out the triumph "sung" by the projecting columns; the carelessness with which the "Latin" language is deformed finds its compensation. This is especially clear when one considers the surprising animals that function as *griffes* in the medieval-like manner on the bases of the columns, and that—their possible allegorical meanings aside—form a kind of "popular" countermelody. Once Scarpagnino and his stonemasons had intoned a "major" tonality, they began, in a number of ways, to soften its pompousness and to return to consecrated traditions: the animal figures exhibited on the bases have a precedent in the columns standing in the atrium of San Marco.

We have considered the various Scuole Grandi in our search for traces of the mentality typical of the urban classes. We found an emulation of the patrician elites in San Giovanni Evangelista, and a hyperresolution of images in the Scuola di San Marco; in the Scuola di San Rocco the stress was laid on the need to seem up-to-date in the absence of sure points of reference but with the help of forms produced through accumulation. One must also observe the addition of the deformations of dialects and narratives that we have already mentioned: perhaps what we are looking for lies right here, in this wavering between codes of taste fixed by the patrician class and the wish to go beyond them by aiming at excess, a wish that was, however, coupled with a desire to popularize prechosen etymons.[34]

It is also clear that pompous tones were anything but congenial to Antonio Abbondi. His best work is not to be found in the ambiguous façade of San Sebastiano, but in the reserved functionalism of the Fabbriche in Rialto. The *proto's* awkwardness in the Scuola di San Rocco is clear in the building's imperfections: the columns are not positioned next to each other according to the preexisting pilasters. As a result, a crude conflict erupted between the capitals and it was necessary to cut the lower tori of the bases. Furthermore, when one examines the pedestals under the corner pilaster and column (fig. 89), one sees the obvious "junction" of the new stone parts: Scarpagnino was not only concerned about unifying the base, he freely varied the panel framing in the added pedestal.

It would not be very useful to continue to stress the way in which Scarpagnino's interpretation of classical themes was subject to solecisms: to dwell upon the evidence would be a completely academic exercise. Rather, what is striking in Antonio Abbondi's work for the Scuola di San Rocco is the calm fusion between two distinct "orders of discourse." Two languages contaminate each other here: one *all'antica*, by definition cultured and abstract, and the other a "popular language," narrative and sensualistic. The difference between erudite language and a narrative in images has disappeared. "High" speech and "low" speech lose their qualifications; they fuse together and propose a new thematic context. A triumphal epic resonates with words borrowed and deformed from a dialectal "pronunciation" that intentionally ignores stylistic hierarchies. The façade of the Scuola di San Rocco is not the only Venetian work in which a similar contamination appears; one thinks of the façade of the small courtyard dei Senatori in the Palazzo Ducale, for example. What gives significance to the elimination of a hierarchical arrangement of languages is, here, the very fact that it applies to the *facies* of a Scuola Grande, whose final form was not even desired at the beginning. For now, let us limit ourselves to observing that the theme of the triumph, expressed by the allegorical reference to the precious force of faith and the perpetuity it assures, resonates with a double meaning: it clearly celebrates the "triumph" over the plague of 1527–29, but at the same time consecrates the Scuola dedicated to the saint from Montpellier as a protagonist in the urban context.

Let us temporarily suspend the thread of this analysis and try other avenues in our attempt to recapture the mental universe of the confraternity members of San Rocco. Caravia accused the Scuola of having spent 80,000 ducats for the new building when 6,000 would have sufficed. He was undoubtedly exaggerating. But the goldsmith was certainly justified in attributing the squandering of funds to the quarrels between the different factions and the continual changes imposed upon the project. A document cited by Pullan, moreover, maintains that, between 1516 and 1564, the Scuola spent 47,000 ducats on construction, to which one must add 2,500 ducats for interior decorations: the same scholar observes that these sums, when totaled, amount more or less to what the Scuola and its commissioners distributed in charities of various kinds between 1551 and 1572.[35]

In the 1520s and '30s, revenue depended mostly upon gifts from the faithful and the devotion to the body of San Rocco: construction in those decades was largely financed by the contributions of pilgrims.[36]

The civic goals mentioned above were signs of the deep tie between the Scuola and the Republic: it was not only a matter of doing justice to Venetian *pietas*, but of demonstrating—from 1517 to 1527—the *Serenissima*'s vitality, and, in 1536–37, of collaborating on the laborious work directed by Andrea Gritti.[37] The Scuola's "squandering" needs to be evaluated within such points of reference. The role assumed by the Scuola, once it had been redirected in a political direction, offers a better explanation of the first building operations and of the sudden change introduced into Antonio Abbondi's *columnatio*.

Moreover, it has been demonstrated that, in the 1540s, Caravia's criticisms agreed with the State's interest in freezing the private capital that the State itself had often needed. In February 1543, the Council of Ten forbade banquets in the various Scuole,[38] and, significantly enough, in April 1553, the same Scuola di San Rocco engaged in a kind of self-criticism when it censored superfluous expenses and proposed the nomination of a commission of *Reformatori* when necessary:

...so many excessive expenditures are being made out of our own purse that the Majesty of God is offended, and cause for gossip is given to those watching who cannot believe that these are not the Schuola's funds and that what should be spent on the poor is being consumed in human ostentation, a thing that takes people's devotion away from the place and removes the souls of those who perhaps intend to place them [here], our Most Illustrious Leaders are constrained to take steps with our help, so that it would be better to take care of and moderate these abuses among ourselves and not let this terrible practice continue; ...and there are also things that excite envy between brothers, so that fraternal love is not maintained, as it should be.[39]

Was this an acceptance of Caravia's criticisms? In order to evaluate this document from 1533, one must keep in mind that, beginning in 1528, the Scuola di San Rocco found itself in the position of having to administer four huge estates, the revenue from which was also meant to benefit poor people not belonging to the Scuola. Between 1545 and 1589, 185 impoverished nobles received aid through the commissary of Maffeo of Bernard Donà, while in 1552 Nicolò di Antonio Moro instituted a fund to provide dowries for poor girls from families partly unconnected with the Scuola.[40] In this way, the traditional role of the Scuole Grandi—the administration of charity for its own members—was taken one step further by the Scuola di San Rocco, which was probably rather proud of its new responsibility toward the entire city.

Donà's office was also used to finance charitable housing. On February 21, 1534 *m.v.*(= 1535), a document by Antonio Abbondi was recorded regarding the houses of the Scuola di San Rocco in Santa Maria Zobenigo, according to a decision reached by the chapter [the general assembly] on January 3:[41] "and first they must make five houses of two floors that contain two residences per house, ... which makes ten houses, of which each will be divided into a bottom section and an attic section and there will be one floor for each and each will have its own well..."

The same Scarpagnino who celebrated the Scuola's splendor with a new façade was engaged by the confraternity for a charitable and speculative building. The Scuola, beginning in 1512–15 and with interventions in 1527–28 and after 1550, concerned itself with the construction of the Corte San Rocco on the island of Santa Maria Maggiore (fig. 84):[42] four blocks of houses to be conceded to poor members *amore Dei*, with types arranged in groups with two or three floors above ground (fig. 85). It was also through the Doná commissary that the Scuola came to own, at the end of 1527, a group of twelve houses in the neighborhood of San Simeone Profeta, most of which would be restructured after 1558.[43]

In 1533–35, finally, the Scuola acquired, for 1,400 ducats, "empty land, that is to say, open space" near what would become a block of the stairs actually belonging to the Scuola; but the decision to use that land to construct "new houses" was only reached in 1548.[44] A competition was announced, and the winner was Scarpagnino, who executed the four houses on the Campo di Castelforte San Rocco (figs. 81–83). They are distributed on three levels, in addition to the ground floor, and the steps cross in "the manner of Leonardo." This work is extremely interesting for a number of reasons. The theme, which was treated "in the vernacular," seems to have been more congenial to the *proto* than the rhetorical one the Scuola had desired for its own building. While founding his "popular" language on the tradition established by speculative building in Venice, Antonio Abbondi did not completely give up the attempt to qualify his intervention (fig. 81). The apartments, which were furnished with service facilities, cellars, and washrooms, are composed of a large *portego* flanked by three rooms and a kitchen; these were spacious quarters, as is indicated by the rent—between 60 and 72 ducats in 1554—and the presence of servant quarters in the attic. This housing was therefore not charitable in its aim, but speculative, and called upon to define, along with the Chiesa di San Rocco, the Scuola, and the Campo di San Rocco and of Castelforte near the San Pantalon canal, the compact presence of the "Repubblichetta" in the urban site (figs. 73, 74).

And here was Scarpagnino elaborating a project that spoke not only of pure structural consistency, as in the *amore Dei* building. On the façade facing the Campo di Castelforte (fig. 83), the two main floors are indicated through a format defined by the syncopated rhythm of the openings: one-light windows with cornices *alla veronese* flank the central bearing wall; on the sides, two three-light windows spaced out by squat Doric columns stand in an ambiguous relationship to the adjacent single-light windows, forming irregular windows with five lights that are placed in relation to the entrances on the ground floor. The rhythm of the openings does not respect the internal spacing of the rooms: it is a pure formal apparatus, turning toward the short sides and reappearing in the back, and has the function of ennobling the building's structure.

The "dialect" used by Scarpagnino is legitimized by an entire architectural tradition, which was in turn the reflection of an ideal image of the city created by one sector of the patrician class: it was a conception that tended to preserve a continuity between charitable and popular interventions and those of higher quality, a conception that paid homage to an urban compactness rich in ideal motivations. The triumphalism of the Scuola di San Rocco was certainly not in line with such a conception: we must now explore the reasons for this triumphalism, in order to explain the double-faced appearance that the members presented in the city.

Although the motif of the columns detached from the façade was treated by Scarpagnino with the solecisms we have already mentioned, there remains the problem of its conception. How did a motif characterized by ancient models reach this *proto* who was clearly devoid of antiquarian culture? One may, in an attempt to simplify the problem, think of the surveys and drawings of fantastic reconstructions—like those of the Rothschild codex in the Louvre[45] —that Scarpagnino came across. But such a reference would only shift the problem and bring in an unverifiable conjecture.

One should, however, certainly not overlook the fact that beginning on March 15, 1535, the building was supervised by Alvise Noal and Costantin de Todero, the two "skilled" brothers called upon to collaborate with the deputies. The clients may have given directions or suggestions, if not for the solution of the triumphal *columnatio*, then at least for the idea of an apparatus of columns that would stand as a specific sign of the Scuola. Let us try to examine this possibility, shifting our circumstantial method onto the building history of the Scuola that was the rival of the one we have been considering.

The Scuola della Misericordia, which was motivated by a desire to emulate the Scuole di San Marco and di San Giovanni Evangelista, decided on a new building (1498), adopting in 1507 a model by Alessandro Leopardi; but Pietro and Tullio Lombardo were elected *proti* of the building in 1509, and in 1531, after a brief interruption due to the wars, Jacopo Sansovino defeated Guglielmo de Grigi and Falconetto in a competition that was meant to replace Leopardi's project and to replace Tullio Lombardo with the new *proto* of the Procuratori de supra.[46] At first glance, the 1531 decision seems to place the Scuola della Misericordia in a vanguard position, insofar as the taste of the Venetian patronage is concerned. In fact, that decision substantiates our initial affirmation: the Scuola della Misericordia, accepting a project of "new architecture," was actually behaving, in the new cultural climate of the 1530s, analogously to the way the Scuola di San Giovanni Evangelista had behaved in the preceding century. The members of the Misericordia also gave up expressing themselves with a "popular" language; they, too, made themselves the forerunners of an aristocratic and highly selective language. Forcing the interpretation, one might say that they betrayed their "civic" matrix in their attempt to stand among the first advocates of an erudite and "Latin" architecture.

In reality, the initial choice must have been partly conditioned by pride about being the supporters of a polemical renewal in Venetian architectural taste. Neither the patrician class nor the public magistracies had ever promoted an enterprise of this kind, and the Observant Franciscans—with the intervention of the *Signoria*—would commission Sansovino with the renovation of their church only three years later.

Sansovino, who officially became the *proto* of the Scuola's building in 1532, thus found himself designing his first building of importance in the lagoons where he was able to develop, unimpeded, a language *all'antica* that resounded in the city like an explosive novelty (figs. 91–92). Sansovino assumed the traditional spatial type of the rooms of the Venetian Scuole, transforming their simple cadences into a binary rhythm of Corinthian columns projected onto the peripheral walls, turned to 90° on the shorter sides and revealed on the exterior walls (fig. 91). Moreover, the niches excavated between the engaged columns, recalling Bramante's schemes, tested the consistency of the wall, entering into a dialogue with the windows that opened onto the larger bays.

The room was in this way subjected to a rigorous design logic based on a rhythmic framework: the building explains its own coherence, presenting itself—with its exalted dimensions—as a rigorously unitary "mechanism" (fig. 94).

The members of the Misericordia seemed, in 1531–32, to be aiming at anticonformism: Sansovino's compact building was called upon to speak of a desire for cultural renewal coming from a civic group that was anticipating the patrician class, the State, and the clergy. The Scuola desired an architecture that would be heir to the Roman debate, and not a dialectal pastiche; and its author was a first-rate artist, not *faber*—however skillful—like Scarpagnino.

But subsequent events did not confirm a similar clarity of intention. The construction site experienced obstacles, changes in direction, and interruptions due to doubts and tension between the Scuola and its architect: something rather similar to what was happening on the parallel construction site of the Scuola Grande di San Rocco. Above all, Sansovino was asked—as early as 1532—to change his project and to eliminate the exterior columns in order to comply with a previous agreement made with the Moro family: the question dragged on into 1535, when Sansovino's second model was approved and the first stone was laid.[47] But, in that same year, new and singular doubts were expressed by the deputies responsible for the building. Examining Sansovino's model and the "two very beautiful ways of doing the stairs," they concluded that "these stairs should not be decided upon" until the walls had reached the second floor.[48] In 1544, when the vaulted ceiling designed by the architect was rejected, the indecision about the stairs became paradoxical: on May 25 it was decided to invite four or five, "masters, or *prothi*, beginning with Jacopo Sansovino, if possible," asking them for projects and estimates, "each one according to his architecture and good sense," relative to the stairs and the "interior as well as external decoration and the hall [albergo] above and other rooms below."[49] The tense relations between Sansovino and the Scuola had come to a head: the decision reached in 1544 had not only offended Sansovino, it had also reduced the impact of his language to that of any other *proto* in Venice. The coherence of his project was ignored. The Scuola was behaving in a traditional fashion, seeking certainties as it considered a number of solutions that were a priori comparable. If those who had been initially responsible had actually completed a precise cultural choice—as we have suggested above— that choice was soon forgotten in favor of an attitude composed of whims and suspicious conservatism. The mental route completed was the exact opposite of the one taken by the Scuola di San Rocco.

Jacopo Sansovino would not forgive the Scuola della Misericordia for its retreat.[50] But let us stop to look at one detail in the history we have just summarized: the replacement of an external structure characterized by columns with a simplified project, which in the end remained partially unexecuted. It is rather likely that drawing D. 18 of the Museo Civico in Vicenza in some way reflects one of Sansovino's projects (fig. 92). Burns has considered the drawing—a copy of the upper part exists in the R.I.B.A. (Burlington Devonshire, VIII/12)—to be a Palladian reinterpretation of Sansovino's façade: and a few details of the lower level, such as the bases in simple cylinders, or the concave moldings [*raccordi a guscia*] between the columns and the pedestals, recall the schemes of Andrea della Gondola, known as Palladio.[51] But a superimposition of the drawing upon the survey of the executed structure shows that the entire installation was Sansovino's affair, as was, surely, the motif of the large windows with small columns barely detached from the sides. Not only did the theme echo the third floor of the Library; its source was Florentine: small spiral columns and an arch decorated in a manner strikingly similar to those of the upper level of the Misericordia are to be found in the Merchandise shrine in Orsanmichele (fig. 93). Sansovino was in Venice quoting a work emblematic of early Tuscan humanism, superimposed, moreover, on a building that had become the symbol of communal charity and of the corporative structure of Florentine society: he restrained himself to updating the syntax of the fifteenth-century shrine, substituting a window for the niche that was originally meant to hold Donatello's statue. Only Sansovino could have completed such a subtle act of interpretation in Venice, and one with an autobiographical aspect: Sansovino was making—surreptitiously—a declaration of *florentinitas*. In fact, even the motif of the triangles that embrace a circle, in the last pediment, derives from Tuscan sources: the model, which was borrowed from Alberti, reflects the façades of Santa Maria Novella and Sant'-Andrea in Mantua. Sansovino would, however, never see his ambitious project—for him a source of continual frustration—completely executed.

Was Scarpagnino aware of the events surrounding the design of the Misericordia? This seems more than likely, given the contact that the *proto* of the Magistratura del Sal [Salt Office] maintained with the *proto* of the procurators of San Marco: in January 1533, Scarpagnino and Sansovino were asked to collaborate on the design of the main altar of the Scuola Grande di San Marco.[52] But, again, it is most likely that news of the difficulties surrounding the execution of the first model for the exterior of the Scuola della Misericordia must have reached the members of the Scuola di San Rocco: in fact, given the rivalry between the various Scuole, it is hard to imagine that they were not keeping tabs on each other. One item confirms our hypothesis: the sequence of dates regarding the choices made for the exterior of the Misericordia and for the façade of the Scuola di San Rocco that faces the *campo*. In July 1535, Sansovino elaborated his definitive model; a year later Antonio Abbondi's façade was approved. What was not possible for the Scuola della Misericordia became possible for the Scuola di San Rocco. In fact, the latter, in appropriating the motif that the first had been forced to abandon, defeated its rival on its own ground. And we believe it legitimate to imagine that Jacopo Sansovino provided the inspiration for the triumphal display: in doing so, we are certainly not thinking of a design idea that Sansovino might have furnished the *proto* of the Magistratura del Sal [Salt Office], but rather of evidence that some ancient model may have inspired him.

Though this hypothesis rests only on circumstantial evidence, it explains Scarpagnino's sudden design "exploit" and confirms what others have observed about the exchange of ideas and models among artists of the sixteenth century.[53] And one ought to note in this connection a later and unique coincidence. On June 21, 1545, the Guardian Grande Marcantonio Rizzo convened the chapter of the Scuola di San Rocco, which recognized the following:

"Our Schola is constructed with such beauty and quality that it is known to everyone in the present chapter, each can see this with his own eyes, but it can be said to be a yoke of lead, and to lack things, like a human body lacks some of its true members . . . and not to have the due proportions which it should have, because since it is known to everyone as a palazzo that has been constructed or built, the principal thing everyone requires is the stairway. . . ."[54]

One is necessarily struck by the parallel between the architectural histories of the Scuola di San Rocco and the Scuola della Misericordia: about a year after it had set aside Sansovino's project for the stairs of the Misericordia, the chapter of San Rocco declared that stairs play a role of primary importance in a building. As Philip Sohm has correctly remarked, the replacement of already executed stairs with a staircase with three flights did not turn the Scuola di San Rocca into an imitator of the Scuola di San Marco and the Scuola di San Giovanni Evangelista, but into a building that was introducing a new formal prototype (figs. 77, 76, 96).[55]

As is known, Scarpagnino's staircase, with its intentional magniloquence, was not deviod of errors or incoherence, especially in the upper flight of stairs and the connection of the latter with the large hall (fig. 96).[56] He was, in essence, repeating what had happened in the façade on the *campo*: the *proto* articulated the given theme with impudence, unconcerned about syntactic or grammatical rigor. Moreover, it was Jacopo Sansovino, and not Scarpagnino, who came off as the "specialist" of stairs in Venice: in his project for Vettor Grimani's palazzo on the Canal Grande (fig. 2) as well as in the Zecca, or Mint, Sansovino integrated his "inventions" into the structures, resorting to daring spatial forms such as the elliptical staircase in the Correr drawing or the diverging flights of stairs in the Zecca.[57] The offense that the Scuola della Misericordia had given Sansovino was, therefore, even more serious than might first appear. But the Scuola's indecision ought to be read for what it was: a symptom of a resistance mounted by mental systems that were not yet completely ready to place themselves in crisis. Sansovino would learn how to deal with such difficulties and would try—in the formulation of the Palazzo Dolfin, for example—to temper the rigor of the manner *all'antica*. Scarpagnino, on the other hand, had no need to lower himself to compromises. His training and his mentality were in complete agreement with the empirical taste of his patrons.

The circle of Venetian *intendenti* or "connoisseurs" must surely have considered the Scuola di San Rocco a monstrosity. Scarpagnino died in 1549; around 1547 Daniele Barbaro began his Vitruvian studies: these two dates, so close to each other, designate symbolically a cultural turning point, anticipated, though not thoroughly realized, by the works Sansovino began under Doge Gritti. Antonio Scarpagnino's dialectal accumulations and evocations, on the other hand, seem to have fully satisfied the ambitions of the Scuola di San Rocco. Formal exhibition, balanced between a visual wealth destined to strike Venice's urban classes and the absorption of vaguely "Roman" schemes, was sufficient to declare the Scuola's support of the *renovatio urbis* launched in the 1530s. There was "nominalism" in the exaltation of Scarpagninian *pastiche*: *verba* and *res* do not coincide here. We are poles apart from San Salvador's austere language. And, whereas that austere language had hidden itself from the city, this one instead had showed itself without any complex, finding it natural to exhibit itself a little later next to the houses *scritte in lengua bravea* [expressed in bold language]. Even the Scuola di San Rocco would, in Venice, remain an exception without consequences. And its *plus dicere*, compared with the *minus dicere* of Jacopo Sansovino's charitable building, revealed conflicts that belonged not only to the subjects, but also, and mainly, to structures and institutions that—drawn between divergent ambitions— were finding it difficult to isolate the reasons for their own identity.

1. ASV, "Scuola Grande di San Rocco," 2nd cons., reg. 45, c. 41r–v.
(1526) adi 8 april

Con zio sia che adi 25 zener proximo passato fossi messo una partte per el spettabile mis. bort. o de zuane de la seda fo nostro vardian grando che nela faza de la salla nostra sopra el rio non se podesse far altra spexa se non di metter in opera le finestre fate per quel luogo et bassamento come in quella per il che el nostro spetabil mis. grazioxo de andrea nostro dig.mo vardian grando se retrovi ligado et non sa quello luj abj ad exeguir perche volendo lui observar tal parte el non puol far lavorar ne serar de dredo la sala nostra come che el voler suo et de tuta la fraterna se el non fa disfar parte de quelo che e fato chossa che lui malvolentieri faria perche el suo voler sie di far far et non di far dexfar ma perche le debixognio di due cosse farne una over di andar dredo al prenzipio fato et meter in opera tutte le chosse aparechite per quel locho che sono fate le qual sara di grandissima spexa occor disfar parte di quelo che efato et portar davantij chon tutte le chosse che sono aparechiade et pero esso mis. lo vardian grando ozi afato redur la bancha et zonta et li nostri prochuratori sopra tal cossa et reduti de la bancha n. undexe et de la zonta n. nuove et de li prochuratori sopra la fabricha n. / quatro et se mete la soto schrita parte

che la parte messa per mis. bort.o de zuane antedita sia per nulla come che mai quella non fosse sta fata et che luj possi far conpir la faza de dredo de la sala nostra dita con il meter in opera tute cosse aparechiade per quel luocho et chon quelo ordene senza alchun inpedimento chon quello piu utile dela schuola nostra che lj sera posibele et cossi fo manda la parte atorno et fo prexa ala balotazion n. venti de la parte de si n. / dixdoto et de non n. do xe la bancha et zonta sopra dite.

2. Ibid., 2nd cons., b. 423. (Loose contracts.)

1525 adi 12 fevrer

El se dechiara per el prezente schrito che queli maistri che tora a far dite soto schrite fenestre sia obligadi a farle simile a quele o fato far de dentro via in chao la sala de suxo sora el portegal intendando da la parte de dentro la sopradita sia lavorada da menno stia ben e neta senza schaie intendando che da la parte de fuora la sopradita sia simile a un desegno per mi fato et mostrado a miss. el vardia et prochuratori alla fabricha de miss. san rocho et mostrado ali maistri che ano a operar intendando pero che le souaze [cornici] et inchasadure da la parte de fuora sia simile ale altre che fare per de fuora sora el rio in zima el sotoportego azervando tuti li intaii et squarizadure de diti intaii et squarizature de malmori segati qual va investidi intendando che li diti mistri sia obligati a dar chanali a chavar gripie et buzi per meter li feri et sia obligadi a lavorar su la dita opera fino la sia fenita et non posi tuor altri lavori ne lavorar zornate fuora de la dita et se altra mente farano che puosi tuor latri maistri a sue speze tuta via non li manchando piere intendando che li die uno dar li volti spontaii chome el solito

m.o marcho da cazaniga chotenta al soprascritto et compagni zoue cecho garzoto et peruzo moro et andrea de graciol semo contento al sopra scritto per el marchado che avemo fato con mis. bertolamio gardia grando per duchati sesentasie zoue duchati 66.

On the reverse side:

jesus m.a 1525 adi 25 zenero

jo piero de via de olera taiapiera per mio nome e per nome de mie chonpani m.o iachomo sidi et m.o iachomo furla et m.o domenigo da venicia e m.o bernardi da veneiza se chiamemo chontenti da far li fanesti per ducati sesanta oto zoue duc. ti 68 chome questo perzente em piero sopadito scrise de mia man piopia

1525 adi 25 zianari

mi antoninio sorela in chompagnia chon domenego de pongone franzescho suo fradelo et Sator [?] da rado et tomaso de borino semo chontenti se fazi sono fanestre 5 e in sala de suso segondo i pezi e chondizion che se chovien in questo schrito per prezio del furlan zoue duchati sesata sete.

3. Ibid., 2nd cons., b. 413. (Unnumbered loose contracts.)

1537 / adi 3 / Zugno A Vinexia

Maistro tonin Sorela e m.ro domenego de baldisera tagia piera cunpagni a cadaun de loro insolidum promete al mag.co miss. anzolo maza dignissimo vardian et a vichario deputadi sopra ala fabricha de la scuola de miss. s. rocho de far de manifacture de tagia piera de quadro fenestre n.o 7 / tre nela faza denanzi nela scuola et quatro nel albergo do nela faza denanzi et do nela faza de driedo sopra larequia [sic: reliquia] che sono intute fenestre n.o 7 / in chanpi n.o 7 / luna che sono chanpi n.o 14 lavorade dopie de drento et de fuora apiem muro sovanzade in nele faze large et le faze strete de fuora via in volto cum le menzole sovanzade de dretovia quadre fazando piane sovanzade de dreto et di fuora inlexenade cum i suoi quariseli de dreto et de fuora tonde sovanzade de soto et di sopra fin ale cholone cum le sue cholone de marmo lavorade tonde squadrizado i chapiteli sovazando labacho di sopra fazendoge el rodin dabaso angoli de volti architravi sovanzadi dananzi et le teste requadrate de sotovia cun uno rondo in mezo cun uno smuso frixi de marmo over piere sciete chornixe dreta frontizo di sopra voltado le teste el chapo del frontoza investido de marmo over de piera inchasado chome per li sopra dicti lavori ben lavoradi ale sagome li sera datto per m.ro antt.o protto chavando impiombando tuti buxi eseri etuto quelo che achadera de larte de tagia piera indicte fenestre li achadera cholone de marmo n.o 44 cun i soi fornimenti quariseli cholone capiteli chome e dicto disopra per sua manifactura die aver duc. 100 de luna che sono in tuto duc. 700 zoue duchati setezento da eser dadi de tempo intempo secundo loro andarano driedo alavorando.

a m.ro piero de lorenzo e m.ro alexandro borin per lintagii di chapiteli de le cholone fazendoli secundo la forma de li modeli et miorar queli et far de piu tuto quanto che per m.ro antt.o protto li sera hordinato die aver de manifactura de bono scudi vinticinque zoue scudi n. 25

m.ro rocho fregador die aver de manifactura del fregar dele cholone de marmo et quelle lustrar atute sue spexe de piere pomege et tripoli ben lustrade die aver per sua manifactura lire quatro de luna zoue L.4.

On the reverse side:

1537 adi 3 Zugno

fatura nea aprexentado m.ro Antt.o scarpognin nostro protto del marcado dela manifattura dele collone che sea con m.ro toni sorella taiap.a e chunpagni et de m.ro piero de lorenzo et m.ro alex.ro borin taiap.a et chom. m.o. rocho fregador.

4. Ibid., 2nd cons., b. 413 (Loose expense contract.)

1537 adi a zener

fo principiatto a metter li basamentti per la faza davantti dela schola de messer San Rocho partte chavadi de opera per inchasar le piere fine et mettarli in opera et far li pontti sula faza davantti.

(There follows a list of the days paid to the workers, up to February 17 of the same year, for a total expense of L.675 and s.13).

5. Ibid., 2nd cons., b. 413 (Unnumbered sheets.)

1546 adi 10 Zugno

Mag.co miss. Zuane dignissimo vardian de s. rocho piaque de far creditor m.o domenego de baldissera tagia piera per li sotto scritti lavori fatti per lui per la portta de lalbergo mesuradi per li s.ri deputadi sopra al render di contti zoue miss. marchant.o rizo et miss. saba de piero et miss. matio davanzo et prima mexurado la porta del albergo di sopra la qual portta sono de fora nella salla de marmo sovanzada de dentro-via de piera viva sovnzada. mexurado. nuna volta sola. marmj et piera viva ertte et sogier di sopra sono in tuto.

p.a. 35 L.6 s. 4 chome apar per el suo marchado sono	*L. 217 s. . . .*
per la manifatura de Soier da basso aredutto a pie	
quadri sono pie 42 a L. 7 a pie sono	*L. 14 s. 14*
per le do alette de dretovia de piera viva sovanzade sono piere	
a s. 32	*L. 38 s. 8*
per una pilastra de piera viva che arompette li mureri per sua	
manifatura fatta in essa pilastra	*L. 24 s. 16*
per la manifatura dela porta del albergo del vardian de matin	
da basso dachordo in ditti 23 sono	*L. 142 s. 12*
. . .	
per manifatura dele piere vive imese nel salizado del campo	
sono pezi n.o 52: foradi per meter le antinelle per le fesse a	
s. 12 luna muta	*L. 31 s. 4*
. . .	
suma L. cinquecento e cinquanta none piz. octo zoue	*L. 559 p. 8*
vista per nuj Sabba de piero	
vista per nuj Mateo davanzo	

Ant.o protto scrisse.

On the reverse side:
Conto de m.ro domenego da baldissera taiapiera
1546 adi 28 dicto aprobatto per la bancha et zontta.

6. ASGSR, r. II, c. 78-v. (See ASV, "Scuola Grande di San Rocco", 2nd cons., reg. 47, c. 80r–v).

1547 adi 15 zener in Capitolo General

Attrovandosi la schuola nostra al presente in Zecca alo 5 per cento ducati 1260 da Cavedal e dar ducati 735 per conto della Commissaria del dignissimo ser Marchio della Seda et ducati 525 per conto della Commissaria Marco Bigarelli de qual danari adi 13 del presente sono finito el mandato et per quanto se intende non voleno piú accettar danari se non alli 4 per cento, che daria de poco beneficio massime havendo la predita nostra schuola de spesa ogni anno per conto della commissaria s. Marchio sopradito duc. 45, i qual se danno a soa mogier fin che la vive vedovando per l'accordo fatto con lei, et per conto del mis. Marco Bigarelli duc. 31 s. 12, che se paga per una mansionaria et poveri 6 li qual danari sono messo in Zecca alli 7-6-5 per cento si no se trovasse da investir, ne mai fin ora è sta fatto altro, al presente essendo reduto in si poca utilità in 4 per cento non se die mancar trovandosi qui in Castel Forte el nostro Terren vacuo sopra el qual se poria far de' bone case delle qual se troveria conveniente affitto per esser in bon loco, et non cosse de non poca utile saria nel sopradito Terren far tante case quante li potesse intrar in le qual prima fosse investido li danari delle predite Commissarie, et lo restante anderà oltra li sopraditi dinari in ditta fabricha se habbia a trazer del sacco de Cavedal de monte novo quello che se retrova al presente, et che per tempo li aspetterà restando peró quanto se investirà per conto del ditto Saccho obbligato per el livello de Frati Minori, et in caso non bastasse li denari di monte novo, ch'al presente se attrova et per tempo li aspettasse se debba compir ditta Fabricha delli denari del saccho del terzo del Deposito, della qual Santa Opera ne seguirà du' beni uno de cresser l'Intrade alla Schuola della qual assai si ha bisogno, l'altro quello se spende oltra li denari de sopradite Comissarie, et quelle se trovasse in li doi Sacchi saria per reintegrar ditti sacchi, qual vano credadori de bona summa de danari de modo che in uno medesimo tempo se daria Augmento alla Schola et de le medeme spese pagar debiti de quella; et però a laude del nostro Sig. Dio e de mis. San Roccho; l'Andara Parte messa per el Mag.co mis. Venturin de varischo Vardian Grando, che per l'Autorità del presente Capitolo General li sopraditi danari saranno tratti di Zeccha delli qual se habbia a fabrichar nel ditto Terren tante case che resteno investidi tutti e lo restante delli do sacchi de monte novo et del Deposito del terzo come è ditto de sopra, le qual case se habbiano a fabrichar della sorte, et qualità parerà alla presente Bancha, et Zonta, et Deputadi sopra danari delle commissarie siano presto investidi rispetto le Gravezze che protano con loro, et lo Mag.co Vardian presente, et Deputadi alla fabricha da poi presa la presente Parte siano obligati far far li modelli, et altro più presto se pol a fine se possi dar principio per scanso delle spese che altramente desponesse de sopraditti denari de reintegrar la Commissaria delli suoi propri Beni di quanto lui spendesse contra el presente Ordine, et cussi fu mandà la parte, et fu presa.

De si   n.44   de non   n.5.

7. Ibid., 2nd cons., reg. 47, c. 104v.

[Zugno 1550] die 27 ditto

Essendo necessario per acomodar la pocha fondamenta sj atrova nela faza dele doi caxe qui in castel forte et so le chioere farsj achomodar una pocha de ttera del comun in cambio del qual se ne po dar alttrettantto in cao del campielo de ditto de castel forte

landera parte messa per el mag.co vardian grando mis. jac.o di obizi che nel presente honorando capitolo generale sia dado auttoritta a sua mag.ia ant.o vardian da matin et s. zuan in summa de lj signori .5. sopra la fabricha comprexo li do che ano compido che son mis. piero falger ett mis. venturin de varischo de potter baratar con li sopraditi piovegi et far questo cambio di tterenj per utilitta et avanzo dela schuola nostra et quanto per loro sara fatto firmo et valido come se in questo capitolo fosse sta fatto fo manda la parte et fo prexa et prexa de si balotte 42 de no 19 et fo prexa

jo jac.o di raim scrivan.

5

Science, Politics, and Architecture. Advancements and Resistance in Venice During the Sixteenth Century

The web we are about to analyze may seem artificial in the light of the preceding chapters. In Venice, politics and religion formed a unity that can be divided only with difficulty, and, as we have seen, the processes of symbolization and formalization lend themselves to different interpretations of that unity. We must, therefore, define the questions we want our historical analysis to answer. Our inquiry now turns toward those tendencies that sought changes of an institutional nature and were connected to a slow transformation of mental systems. We ought, however, to issue one warning: what happened in Venice did not have a "local" character but had a broader, European influence that needs to be taken into consideration.

Let us specify one more thing before we begin. Science and architecture: instead of science we ought to say technical practices, and *scientia* applied in architecture. As studies of Vitruvius have demonstrated, especially in the fifteenth century, the *res aedificatoria* acquired a symbolic meaning that went beyond the praxis of building: it sought to mediate between a branch of knowledge that concerned the "reasons" of the divine *harmonia mundi* and a mode of action that emphasized the human environment, with the aim of rationalizing or "restoring" the Rule. The recycling of medieval thought, with all its allegorical apparatus, led, through the tiresome recovery of ancient organicism, to a resymbolization charged with new values.

All this is part of a history that has already been explored in detail. Less studied, on the other hand, has been the link that ties *architecture* to political debate: though there are a few laudable exceptions, the tendency has been to accept unverifiable assertions that mercilessly deform the thinking and actions of the artists, patrons, and protagonists of the centers of power. We must, for this reason, base our analysis on concrete evidence. And, insofar as the Venetian context is concerned, we will not be able to find a more eloquent beginning than the one offered by a document that explicitly relates the political project to demands for urban *renovatio*: we are referring to Domenico Morosini's *De bene instituta re publica*.

1. Domenico Morosini and Francesco Patrizi of Siena: "Res Publica" and "Architecture"

Morosini's work was a unique one.[1] Begun in 1497, during a war that was fought in support of Pisa and that drained the Republic's finances, it contains a succinct polemic against expansionist politics and an explicit criticism of Venice's constitution and government. The ideal *res publica* recommended is a "State of peace" ruled by a limited circle in power: but the author, who clearly opposed the "*nobilitatis multitudo*," does privilege the "ordinary" and the "old."[2] The procurator's political treatise, which even in 1508, a year before his death, would oppose taking action against the Emperor Maximilian, remained unpublished until the twentieth century. And this is not surprising: in essence it proposes a concentration of power that would have disturbed the foundations of the Venetian institutional order while undermining the myth of the "mixed State."

It is extremely interesting that in the *De bene instituta re publica* the political proposal is translated into real urban and territorial projects: Domenico Morosini gives precise information on the forms needed to realize a new *Venetia triumphans*. First of all, an equilibrium between city and country, with a division of duties and with the aim of organizing agriculture, developing markets, and increasing manufacture, especially of luxury items; Morosini also recommends a real policy of public works that includes the reclamation of swamplands, the renewal of defensive structures, and the construction of new streets.[3] As for the city, it would have to consolidate itself and celebrate its own peaceful power with ostentatious and magnificent displays, in its public ceremonies as well as in its architecture: the beauty of the city was acknowledged as a political instrument, for it enabled the city to gain the respect and fear of the enemy. Morosini thus recommends splendor for public buildings, *decoro* or adornment for private palazzi, orderliness for the streets, the organization of monumental centers with perspective views, and the institution of a magistracy that would concern itself *ad ornatum civitatis* [with the adornment of the city]: the *virtus* of the Republic *bene instituta* was to be manifested through visible and eloquent structures.[4]

The art of architecture, of building walls, of woodwork, as well as at times that of ironwork, stonework, and others of this type are necessary arts. For, although [hiring] practitioners of these arts reduces the city's riches, the lesser of these arts serve the needs of the citizens and the greater increase the city's magnitude and beauty; it is right for a well-instituted city to have experienced architects rather than unlearned and rough ones. For it is possible to build something well or badly for the same amount of money, and that which is well-built is commended and that which is poorly built is rejected and cursed. Between the experienced architects and the unlearned ones there is only this difference, that the unlearned ones immediately come to a place where they may receive money from others, whereas the experienced ones are people who are generally summoned and who never lack recompense for their labor, and thus no reward other than that of great praise can induce them to undertake [a project]. For in the first place the building of temples and palaces and buildings is a matter involving beauty, but it also involves opinion, which is not to be underestimated by anyone since opinion helps the city avoid great dangers and expenses . . .[5]

Magnificence and *auctoritas* thus manifest themselves through the work of "skillful architects": Morosini's opinion is the opposite of the opinion that was later expressed by Nicolò Zen. The *De bene instituta re publica* also provided norms that would have greatly changed the morphology of the lagoon's urban fabric: Morosini recommended standardizing operations to introduce a new *decoro* into the city:[6]

. . . all private dwellings should extend the same distance along the streets. Those extending beyond the correct measure should be brought into uniformity with the others. Crooked streets should be straightened, narrow ones should be widened, those open spaces that give a beautiful view between the buildings in the city and that show the city's pleasantness and brilliance should be smoothed out, and should be adorned according to their settings and the houses in them. For such diligence requires no great labor and shows off the ornament and decoration of the city.[7]

These programs only partly explain the concerns that guided the patrons of Mauro Codussi, Pietro Lombardo, and Antonio Rizzo: they seem rather to have been borrowed from a culture that was aware of the revival of Vitruvian studies and perhaps mindful of Leon Battista Alberti's *De re aedificatoria*—all of which is not surprising. Morosini had been a friend of Doge Cristoforo Moro as well as of Pietro Dolfin, the Camaldolensian general who was an admirer of Codussi's and a friend of Lorenzo the Magnificent, Bernardo Rucellai,[8] and Bernardo Bembo—and we have already commented upon the latter's interest in Alberti's treatise.[9]

The *De bene instituta re publica* thus delineates programs aimed at a renewal of the urban fabric that was inspired by new humanistic studies. These programs were probably supported by the vast sector of the patrician class participating in the critical and polemical objectives that Domenico Morosini took it upon himself to describe.

It would, however, be a mistake to interpret the many-sided tendencies of the Venetian fifteenth century by dwelling only on Morosini; in fact, his work was contradicted, for example, by the humanist Lauro Quirini. The latter was a friend of Ciriaco d'Ancona and in touch with Leonardo Giustinian and Francesco Barbaro; he was also a close friend of Cardinal Bessarione, an enthusiastic researcher, translator, and copier of codices, especially of Greek ones, and the author of a collection of extremely polemical letters against Lorenzo Valla , Leonardo Bruni, and Poggio Bracciolini.[10] In the *De republica*, Quirini draws not only upon Aristotle, but also upon Plato and Cicero, in order to achieve an ideal model that is no longer Aristotelian, but based on the Roman Republic.[11] Angelo Ventura has rightly observed that Quirini's text clearly condemns tyranny: the aristocratic regime, in which a few *prudentes* are elected by the people that is to be governed, is condemned as the premise of an inevitable and rapid degeneration into oligarchy.[12] The rejection of the *paucorum sed electorum dominium* [dominion of a few but elected persons] thus leads to an ideal of liberty that may have been linked to the debate under way in Venice at the time: the *De republica* favors those who intend to reduce the Senate's powers in order to increase the political role of the Great Council and the political magistrates.

The two texts we have just considered document the existence of a conflict that had long existed at the heart of the patriciate: the tendencies they expressed would give rise to actions and choices that first came to a head during the institutional crisis of 1582–83, and later during the experience of the Interdict.

It has not, to our knowledge, been observed that the ideas circulating in the *De bene instituta re publica* have a large degree of affinity with the ideas that pervaded the texts of a unique humanist of the fifteenth century, Francesco Patrizi of Siena (1413–94). Patrizi, a friend of Panormita, Francesco Filelfo, and Battista Guarino, was intensely active in the political life of his city, and came into contact with the Florentine surroundings, with the Emperor Frederick III—whom he accompanied to Rome in 1452, on the occasion of his coronation—and with the Malatesta family in Rimini.

Involved in the conspiracy of Jacopo Piccinino, Patrizi was exiled after having been arrested and tortured, and in June 1459 he arrived in Verona, where he was warmly received by the local humanists.[13] Having entered the religious life, Patrizi became the bishop of Gaeta (March 23, 1461) and the governor of Foligno, while remaining a close friend of Pope Piccolomini, Pius II. His *De institutione rei publicae*, which he began during his exile and finished between 1465 and 1471, was published in Paris in 1494; his second treatise, the *De regno et regis institutione*, was only published after his death, in 1519, but it may have been written between 1481 and 1484. Both volumes were widely circulated, especially in France, and reveal the exchanges that took place with certain circles of the Venetian patrician class. Francesco Patrizi subordinates economic life to ethics, even discussing what sort of food is suitable for the good citizen; he also alludes to a "mixed" republican constitution, extolling—and contrasting with the instability of Siena—the example of the Venetians "whose just republic, empire, opulence, and splendid city are held to be the most brilliant not only in Italy but in the entire sphere of nations."[14] But his republic was oligarchic. Criticizing Platonic communism for the limits it imposes upon individual initiative,[15] Patrizi opposed, as Morosini did, the unstable *multitudo*. In the *De regno* he wrote: "The multitude bears similarity to the sea, which appears to be calm or stable by the force of nature. But it will be tranquil or agitated according to how the winds blow. Even so the multitudes will follow fortune, for they are stimulated by the powerful citizens or by the wind of envy."[16] Like Domenico Morosini, Patrizi preferred the "ordinary" and supported the formation of a vast real estate patrimony for the State.[17] His "well-instituted" republic would thus be oligarchic, ruled by an ethical and economic sense of labor,[18] and dedicated in equal parts to agriculture, commerce, and industry. Patrizi also saw the urban form as an expression of "good government." The city should be located in a healthy and fertile site, near the sea or a river (fig. 97): the work of the good architect, who is capable of giving eloquent form to the "wisdom" of institutions, is evoked in specific terms. Patrizi enumerates in the *De instutione rei publicae* the duties entrusted to such a "functionary of good government": he is responsible for fortifications, city gates, streets and porticos, private and public buildings, churches, theaters, and libraries.[19]

The study of Vitruvius's treatise emerges at several points in the volume (fig. 98): the need for a most skillful architect to embellish the *res publica* is derived from the *exemplum* of Alexander and Dinocrates; chapter 8 of Book 8, Vitruvius is explicitly cited with regard to city gates; in the chapter on churches a brief excursus on architectural orders is inserted.[20] Furthermore, Patrizi gives norms for urban streets, recommending—like Leon Battista Alberti—sinuous streets, while, like Domenico Morosini, he advises regularity and uniformity in private construction:

It is important that the streets to the gates not be direct, but sinuous. Among the ancients scenum *meant curved and tortuous, wherefore I believe* scena *streets to be those that bend and twist and are vulnerable to crimes.*[21]

The private buildings near streets should be uniform and built of equal dimensions if possible so that they may adorn the image of the city. Nor by any means should their length offer an impediment to other streets.[22]

The cordial relationship between Francesco Patrizi and Enea Silvio Piccolomini, Pope Pius II, may partially explain this insistence upon the role of architecture as the *ars demonstrativa* of political wisdom and institutional solidity. But it is even more significant that Patrizi was a student of Vitruvius and a friend of Fra Giocondo. In an epigram written around 1489, in fact, the bishop of Gaeta recalls the Vitruvian research of the architect and humanist from Verona,[23] thus offering us a clue we can use in interpreting those passages on the *res aedificatoria* that support his political writings. The points of contact between Domenico Morosini's *De bene instituta re publica* and the works of Francesco Patrizi of Siena are thus many. And what is most striking is the affinity between two political projects that were both intent on prefiguring aristocratic republics ruled by the "reason of the few," characterized by the ethic of work and represented by an architecture committed to consolidating and celebrating the virtues of the State. There may be no point in asking how much of an influence the *De institutione rei publica* may have had on Morosini's treatise. The latter may have read Francesco Patrizi's work, published shortly after the presumed date of the beginning of the *De bene instituta re publica*; but the historical problem cannot be reduced here to fortuitous influences. Patrizi's books actually incorporated ideas that may have been circulating in Venice even under Doge Francesco Foscari, and they testify to the circulation of the same tendencies that Morosini's text would later attempt to organize.

Furthermore, it is rather significant that one can discover in both Patrizi and Morosini a conception of architecture as the language and instrument of the solidity and harmony of the republic: the *virtus* of *architecture* is explicitly invoked by authors in touch with politicians who had perfectly understood the messages implicit in the architectural *nova ratio*.

Humanistic thinking could, moreover, trace the link between architecture and politics back to ancient sources: back to Aristotle, who in the *Politics* (1, 6) wrote that the duty of he who commands is "the same as that of the architect, *and reason is the architect*,"[24] and to Plato, who in the *Laws*(6, 20) gives prescriptions for the architecture of the city-state, recommending uniform building and supervision by the *astynómoi*.[25] And that was not all: given the value that Plato attributed to music, in relation to the laws of the State, it also became possible to see in the architectural search for perfect and "consonant" harmonies as a symbol of the perfect constitution celebrated by the Greek philosopher in the *Republic*.[26]

It is certain, however, that Nicholas V, Pius II, Sixtus IV, Lorenzo the Magnificent, and Alfonso II of Aragon, had, each in his own way, used both the *ars aedificatoria* and urban structure for political purposes:[27] in the early sixteenth century Venice had at its disposal many models to compare with its own traditions and well-articulated ways of managing power and consent, although its particular institutional structure conflicted with the autocratic meanings expressed in those models.

2. The "*Renovatio*" of Andrea Gritti: "*Auctoritas*," Applied Sciences, and Architecture

Gaetano Cozzi is to be credited for having recognized in Andrea Gritti a doge who corresponded to the prince as described by Domenico Morosini,[28] and one can easily find reasons to recognize in Gritti's cultural policy many elements that agree with the theses of the *De bene instituta re publica*.

Let us consider Gritti's policy as a whole. After the disaster of Agnadello and subsequent events, Gritti was interested in restoring the *Serenissima*'s identity and international prestige in all fields; his policy envisioned Venice as a cosmopolitan metropolis in which the resumption of commerce and culture would be founded on a process of radical renewal. Gritti's interventions led to a unifying design, an organic policy that was conducted in several sectors, under the sign of a peaceful "rebirth."[29]

Not only did artists and men of letters become involved with the renewal of the "myth of Venice"—although the doge's partiality to Adrian Willaert, Jacopo Sansovino, Francesco Zorzi, Titian, Pietro Bembo, Pietro Aretino, and Vettor Fausto were explicit in this regard. Certainly, the literary myth of Venice, which was consolidated in Savonarola's Florence in a political tone, was an essential part of the Grittian renewal—to which Gasparo Contarini would also make his contribution. Ellen Rosand has already observed that Contarini's praise of the Venetian constitution, which was acknowledged in the *De magistratibus et republica Venetorum* as the perfect model of the mixed State, went so far as to state that the government of the Republic was an echo of celestial harmonies, an idea also based on Plato's *Timaeus*:[30] it was the same myth that was first celebrated by Willaert's music, and later by the theories of Gioseffo Zarlino. But the attempt celebrated by this ideology relied upon structural factors. The policy undertaken by the group that had formed around Gritti was enacted in four fundamental sectors: *renovatio securitatis*, with the reorganization of the defenses on a territorial level, explained in the three reports presented by Francesco Maria della Rovere in 1532; *renovatio scientiae*, with support of Vettor Fausto's experiments in *architectura navalis*; *renovatio urbis*, with the works of Sansovino concentrated in the two poles of San Francesco della Vigna and Piazza San Marco; and *renovatio Iustitiae*, with an attempt to reorganize and recodify Venetian laws. These actions were not accomplished without difficulty. Gritti's projects encountered obstacles on all levels, and many of his initiatives bore no results: the innovations and authoritarianism of the doge and his allies sparked an intense conflict.

We are indebted to John Hale and Ennio Concina for their work on the program of territorial defenses that Andrea Gritti had already proposed in 1517;[31] Concina, especially, has linked Gritti's ideas on the fortifications of Brescia, Treviso, and Verona to the work of Francesco Maria della Rovere, the *rei militaris restitutor* who, on September 7, 1523, was called upon to replace the francophile Teodoro Trivulzio in the position of Governor general of the Venetian Republic's militia.

Francesco Maria was in close contact, maybe even before 1516, with Cardinal Domenico Grimani, and became friends with Bembo, Zorzi, and Giacomo and Giovanni Corner, staying in 1530 in the palazzo of San Polo. But he was also in touch with Paolo Nani and Giovanni Moro, with Giovanni Badoer, the Field Commissioner Giovanni Dolfin, and the Procurator Antonio Cappello: Della Rovere seems to have been fully integrated into Gritti's circle. And Concina demonstrates that around 1529 the Captain general of the Republic was able to outline a unified plan for the territory's defenses. The plan harmonized with Contarini's exhortations to reinforce the State's military system and with the project of *renovatio imperii*.[32]

The plan for the renewal of the defenses of the "Stato da Terra" or the mainland part of the State was detailed in reports given by Francesco Maria between July 4 and September 17, 1532, and presented by Gian Jacopo Leonardi (July 4, 1532, and September 17, 1532) and Cristoforo Cappello, who was Savio di Terraferma [Minister for War and the Mainland] and an expert in military affairs (July 22, 1532): the plan in question proposed an organic fortified system that would protect Friuli and be integrated with the intervention already begun in Verona, Legnago, and Orzinuovi, and with projects for Padua, Treviso, and Vicenza.

A review of Francesco Maria's work would not serve our purpose here. It extended to Dalmatia, and the criticisms and proposals Maria addressed to Venice prove the exceptional sharpness of his powers of analysis. Rather, it is more interesting to note that his work was based on an interpretation that envisioned the territory as an *articulated organism*, a consolidated "machine" composed of elements with specialized functions: "military science" reveals itself as capable of advancing a proposal for the territory that is the result of a knowledge based on both practice and theory, and above all capable of overcoming the traditional paratactic representation of space. The *idea of the plan* that emerges is clearly depicted, if only for a single sector of intervention. It was no accident that the Captain general of the Republic would encounter notable opposition, just as it was not surprising that a split took place between this specialist of "military practices" and the "architect" Michele Sanmicheli.

A picture thus begins to emerge, for the fortifying machine heralded by Francesco Maria and the Doge, of a *nova ratio* at the service of security: the same *ratio* that Giovan Jacopo Leonardi would discuss in his *Libro delle fortificazioni*.[33] Leonardi reminds us of Serlio, perhaps of Francesco Marcolini, and surely of Vettor Fausto: we are passing from *renovatio securitatis* to other chapter in Grittian politics, a chapter that focused upon *renovatio scientiae*.

Vettor Fausto, a humanist who, in his youth, was attracted to mathematical studies and architecture, was also a protégé of Giovanni Badoer—who encouraged him to write the *Aristotelis mechanica* that he would finish in 1516—and a friend of Bembo, Gritti, Bernardo Navagero, Pier Francesco Contarini, and Francesco Maria della Rovere. In 1526 Fausto would attempt to revivify naval design, producing his famous quinquereme for the Arsenal. The study of ancient *architectura navalis* was applied to a new mode of production, which entered into a fatal conflict with the traditional organization of the State's shipyard and with the praxis of *artifices*.[34] For Fausto, as for Francesco Maria della Rovere, the recovery of "ancient science" was not a rhetorical pretext; the philological analysis of Greek naval science led to a new organization of knowledge, aimed at a technical practice capable of influencing particularly delicate institutional ganglia. And Vettor Fausto would also encounter difficulties in his *renovatio*; it would remain experimental, and would never revolutionize the work in the State's shipyard.

It is, however, significant that during the first decade of Andrea Gritti's tenure as doge more energy was spent in the area of territorial defenses and the Arsenal than in *renovatio urbis*. And yet, Jacopo Sansovino's stay in Venice began in 1527—he became *proto* of the Procuratia de supra in 1529—and he was soon a member of the Grimani and Giustinian circle, and would ultimately form, with Pietro Aretino and Titian, an association that would soon have its own power—although he would remain tied, as we have seen, to problematic figures like Sebastiano Serlio and Lorenzo Lotto.[35] Let us reflect on this choice of Sansovino: a long tradition was broken when a *peritissimo architetto* [a most skilled architect] finally became superintendent of the public works overseen by the Procuratori de supra. On the other hand, between 1523 and the early 1530s Venetian building remained in a state of suspension: the "grand manner" was not followed by the palazzo of the Camerlenghi, the church of San Giovanni Elemosinario, or the palazzo that Gritti began to build for himself in 1525 in front of the church of San Francesco della Vigna. A program was slowly maturing; it took off after 1534–36—that is to say, after the launching of Francesco Maria della Rovere's territorial plan and after the peace of 1529 allowed the formulation of a foreign policy that promoted stability.[36]

Let us examine the sequence of decisions: in July 1531 Sansovino's model for the new Scuola della Misericordia was chosen; in August 1534, Gritti attended the laying of the foundation-stone of the church of San Francesco della Vigna; in 1535, Francesco Zorzi, procurator of the building, wrote the famous "memorial" that ratified a variation under way for the enlargement of the building: a complex question of building sites connected to construction problems thus found a solution that turned the Franciscan church into the first example of "modern" architecture in Venice, while Zorzi's hermetic and cabalistic speculation sanctioned architecture's capacity to reveal transcendent "truths"; in 1535 the Senate also approved a new magistrature that "would take care of embellishing and adapting the city"; in 1536–37, Sansovino was charged with the renovation of the area around Piazza San Marco and with the planning of the Library, the Mint, and the Loggetta. The two patricians who, according to a decision taken by the Senate in 1535,[37] had to remove the "many ugly and occupied parts that undermine the splendor of the . . . city," were not only the Venetian equivalents of the Roman *Maestri delle strade*. The decision revealed the intention to make the entire urban body conform to "reason" and *decoro*, regulating from above the conflicts between public interest and private property. These were the same conflicts that had afflicted the Chiesa degli Osservanti,[38] and that, in 1531 and 1532, had been confirmed during the improvement and enlargement of two important streets, the *salizada* of San Giovanni Crisostomo, and the alley leading to the ferry crossing of San Felice.[39] Nor would it be forgotten that the new magistracy was responding to one of the requirements state—as we have mentioned— by Domenico Morosini.

One observes, furthermore, that the two spots chosen for the urban renewal that Jacopo Sansovino's *sapientia architectonica* rendered eloquent were connected in a symbolic fashion.

On the one hand, San Francesco della Vigna: legend had it that the angel had appeared to Mark on this spot; the site was therefore linked to Saint Mark, and sacred in the *Serenissima*'s tradition. On the other hand, the Piazza: the place in which power makes itself visible, in which the angel's prophecy is realized. It was no coincidence that Andrea Gritti had chosen the site of San Francesco della Vigna for his own palazzo, nor was it coincidental that during his tenure as doge the Library was executed—with the help of Vettor Grimani—in the form of a classical basilica. The building would eventually house the library that Cardinal Bessarione had donated to the Republic—a gift overflowing with symbolic meanings.

The San Marco forum, with the Sansovinian "basilica" and the triumphal arch in the form of the Loggetta at the foot of the Campanile, explicitly spoke of Venice as a "new Rome." The lagoon city presented itself as the heir of a *virtú* the traits of which were fixed in the allegorical figures of the Loggetta itself, while its riches were contained in the *forziere* or coffers of the Zecca [Mint]; the rustication of the latter—with a motif taken from Baldassarre Peruzzi's fresco of the *Presentation of the Virgin in the Temple*—alludes to an idealized fortification. The use of metaphor is clear: the three works executed by the *proto* of the Procuratia de supra adopted different languages according to their symbolic roles. As André Chastel has rightly observed, a kind of *translatio* followed the Sack of Rome in 1527:[40] Venice, ready to accept the Roman legacy, finally acted upon some of the suggestions contained in the treatises of

Francesco Patrizi and Domenico Morosini. *Auctoritas* was expressed through an architecture *all'antica* that was called upon to speak of political stability and new aristocratic pride.

Thus Sansovino's poetics were in the 1530s closely linked to Gritti's intentions, as were Willaert's music and Vettor Fausto's *ars navalis*: the "new Venice," resurrected after the dark years of the war against the League of Cambrai, renewed its own "myth," opening itself simultaneously to new organizational structures and new cultures.

We have already had the opportunity to observe that the *renovatio urbis* was connected to a *renovatio iuris*—that is to say, to one of the sectors in which Gritti's action encountered unyielding obstacles. We are referring to the endeavor initiated in December 1531, which came to standstill in 1535–36; Cozzi has intelligently reconstructed the significance of that endeavor, which would have upset Venetian *consuetudo* in the area of law, compromised the traditional *arbitrium* conceded to the judge, and introduced a specialization that the dominating mentality considered dangerous.[41] Aspirations that remained unfulfilled emerge from the mass of initiatives undertaken by Doge Gritti. The themes of political renewal, technical and scientific knowledge, and the *urba formis* were, however, already circulating and would soon become the prerogative of specific groups. But the oligarchic ambitions described in the *De bene instituta re publica* would continue to act, becoming intertwined with those themes.

3. Oligarchs and "Romanists"

Right after Andrea Gritti's death, Marco Foscari, who was his cousin and protégé, undertook an initiative that represented the most openly oligarchic proposal in the history of Venice in the sixteenth century, and Angelo Ventura has appropriately emphasized its importance.[42] On November 17, 1539, a majority of the Council of Ten debated the idea of forming a committee of fifty members: elected by the Senate and approved by the Great Council, the committee would have had to join the Ten themselves in order to deal with problems relating to peace with the Turks. Marco Foscari—along with Marcello Gabriele and Federico Renier—proposed an amendment to that provision, which was already in itself provocative with respect to the prerogatives of the Senate and antioligarchic mood of the Great Council. The fifty—according to the amendment, which was rejected by a close vote—would have had to be elected by the Council of Ten with the ordinary "*zonta*" (an additional group of twenty men). The Great Council and the Senate would thus have been deprived of their most jealously guarded prerogatives, while—as Ventura put it—"a perhaps fatal and irreversible blow" would have been dealt to "the political rights of the patrician class."[43] Paolo Giovio testified that Marco Foscari believed that "the Republic of the nobles would soon perish because of the masses and the evil of the citizens unless it be saved through a healthy undertaking by the judgment of the few":[44] there was a direct link between Foscari's attempt—which was meant to keep the power in the hands of the Council of Ten and the additional fifty—and Domenico Morosini's theses.

In posing as the strict moralizer of public life, Marco Foscari had already demonstrated that he had a strong sense of the State's authority: his political vision clearly emerges from his report on the embassy to Florence (1527).[45] His interests, moreover, remained in the area of the important families, most of which were "Romanist": groups, therefore, that had reserved for themselves the most desirable high offices and ecclesiastical benefices, and that were connected by specific agreements and instances of reciprocal investiture.[46] On September 6, 1524, Marco Foscari received in Rome, from Cardinal Francesco Pisani, the reinvestiture of the tithes due as episcopal revenue on the land of Villa di Villa and Solesino, which had been obtained in 1482 from Marco's uncle, Piero Foscari, then bishop of Padua,[47] while the alliance with the Grimani family was assured by the marriage of Pietro, son of Marco, to Elena Grimani (August 29, 1534).

The papal nuncio, Girolamo Aleandro, had called attention to the maneuvering of the important families for ecclesiastical benefices when he wrote the following to Ambrogio Ricalcati on November 23, 1534: "Three houses, Cornara, Grimana, Pisana . . . want to enclose all the clergy into their domain."[48] Doge Gritti had also called attention to the same phenomenon when, in 1533, he declared that he felt it was not appropriate for three families to maintain a monopoly over the bishoprics on the mainland.[49]

But let there be no mistake about it: a niece of Gritti's had in 1527 married Giovanni Pisani, the son of the powerful banker Alvise and the brother of Cardinal Francesco, and we know that between Doge Gritti and the Grimani and Pisani families there was a real political alliance.[50]

The papalist and oligarchic circles at the heart of the Venetian patrician class of the sixteenth century were thus precisely drawn. We have already considered the behavior of the families that, around the middle of the sixteenth century, supported a policy of mutual agreement with the Apostolic See: the Foscari, Barbaro, Badoer, Corner, Emo, Grimani, and Pisano families formed a group that was undoubtedly diversified, but inevitably united in its antagonism—thanks also to Venetian laws that excluded from public office those patricians who were endowed with ecclesiastical benefices—against those who felt that "Romanism" might injure Venice's identity.

It was also thanks to the political tendencies of those families that the art of Michele Sanmicheli, Palladio, Giovanni da Udine, Francesco Salviati, Battista Franco, and Federico Zuccari came to the city. It was a new patronage system for Venice: but there was also the desire to demonstrate the compactness of a circle that was in various ways arrogating the direction of the State. Andrea Gritti's autocracy had fought a battle aimed at efficiency; the *Primi* or leaders, toward the middle of the century, would follow this line only partially. In fact, it so happened in Venice that impulses toward innovation intersected with a return to sumptuous displays, which were often hard to reconcile with traditional ways of judging: it was not unusual for the advocates of cultural novelty to be conservative in politics; in return, behind the obstinate will to safeguard Venice's particularity, one could often find voices advocating independence from Rome and openness toward Europe.

And one should not ignore the ambitions, sometimes limited, of the militant *giovani*, or "younger generation," their weakness over the long run, and their failures on the level of the cultural battle. There are few other cases like the Venetian one, in which the historian is forced to free himself of all traces of Manicheism, and to confront the problem of judgment in an extremely articulated way.

In reformulating this problem we ought to reconnect the patronage and triumphalistic desires of the Romanist families to the theme that Domenico Morosini's treatise helped us introduce. *Auctoritas* and *architectura*: it is obvious that the orientation of our entire reasoning is linked to an awareness of the mentality of the patronage. The artists gave *their* own meanings to the recovery of Antiquity—which was pursued in different ways by Sansovino, Sanmicheli, and Palladio—while frequently engaging in paradoxical dialogues with their patrons: the discourses diverge on nonintersecting planes and the most delicate problem is to discover their hidden lines of tangency. We will return to this question after we have dealt with themes that may at first seem unrelated. But the recomposition of the fabrics connecting mental structures cannot follow main paths, nor shall we betray our initial argument, which tended to read architecture as a larger metaphor for human knowledge, seen as the capacity to technically transform the physical environment of social life.

4. The Accademia della Fama (1557–61): Knowledge and Power in an Ambiguous Encyclopedic Association

Technology and the organization of knowledge: our new field of inquiry differs only in appearance from the one we have favored so far. The initiative we will now discuss is in fact legible in many ways within the framework we have drawn above. We are speaking of the Accademia Venetiana, also called the Accademia della Fama, which was established by Federico Badoer in 1557 and closed amid a great deal of commotion in 1561, upon orders from the Senate, which accused it of fraudulent bankruptcy.[51] But the real motives behind the elimination of the Accademia and the *damnatio memoriae* to which it would be relegated are probably more complex than one might think. Let us first consider its members. Badoer was very young when he began his political career, and his literary studies were praised by Aretino, Pietro Bembo, Claudio Tolomei, and Daniele Barbaro. Furthermore, according to Tiraboschi, he belonged to the literary circle that had formed around Domenico Venier; by 1557 Badoer had thus reached a height of prestige, having returned from an important diplomatic mission to the imperial court.[52] Other figures of importance in the Accademia Venetiana included Agostino Valier, Alvise Mocenigo, Bernardo Navagero, Francesco Barbarigo, and Jacopo Surian. It is clear, moreover, that the Accademia also put forward a decidedly religious front: its motto was *Io volo al cielo per riposarmi in Dio* [I fly to the sky to rest with God]. But it is also clear—as Rose has observed[53]—that its religious sentiment had precise political consequences. The Cardinals d'Este, Gonzaga, Ghisleri, and Carafa, sent laudatory letters to the Accademia,[54] and Pius IV's admiration is documented by a commission of ten cardinals, who were appointed in order to found in Rome an association that would emulate the one created by Federico Badoer.[55] This association would, even after the dramatic closing of the Accademia and Badoer's arrest in December 1568 (for a second trial at his expense), be able to count upon the favor of the Roman Curia and the apostolic nuncio Facchinetti.[56] In fact, the works published under the aegis of the Accademia include the oration that Cardinal Pole had addressed to Charles V in 1554, as a delegate of Julius III, and a poem by Jacopo Sadoleto, while a collection of orations was dedicated to Cardinal Alfonso Carafa.[57]

The Accademia della Fama thus reunited a group that had "Romanist" characteristics: a few of its tendencies would be reflected in a later coterie, the Noctes Vaticanae, whose meetings were also attended by Agostino Valier. Valier consented to set the initiative at the heart of the "papalist" patrician class; and our perspective would be limited if we did not pause to consider the specific meaning that this group assumed for Venice. In this connection, one cannot miss the importance of Francesco Patrizi da Cherso, a member of the Accademia Venetiana: in 1553 he had already published his *Città felice*, a hymn to a republic based on reason, in which, as is well-known, Venice's constitution is portrayed.[58] Patrizi obviously had an idealized Venice in mind. He wrote,[59] "Therefore there will be no private enmity in our city if love rules between citizens; for love is generated only toward that which is familiar. It is thus necessary for the citizens to be familiar with each other. This can happen sooner in a medium-sized and manageable crowd than in an innumerable one, and it will be even easier if the crowd is not disorganized but divided into lineages."[60]

This Venice would be governed—like Morosini's *Res publica*—by the *vecchi* or "older generation,"[61] who would fall into two distinct groups: "the one poor and servile (peasants, artisans, and merchants), the other dominant and blessed; the latter would rightly be called the citizenry, since it rules the city and has its hand in the republic's honor and preeminence."[62]

Patrizi's ideal aristocrats were as far from More's utopianism as from the edulcorated utopianism of Anton Francesco Doni, and they acquired a meaning within the intricate tendencies that Angelo Ventura has recognized in sixteenth-century Venice.[63] But the figure of Francesco Patrizi assumes special significance at the heart of our inquiry: with his exaltation of the Venetian artistocracy and his consideration of mathematics as an abstract but "infirm and imperfect" science, he joined aristocratic ambitions with the scientistic and metaphysical ones circulating at the heart of the Accademia.[64]

According to Cozzi, however, the Accademia's programs relating to law seem to have played a role that was far from innocent. In the petition addressed to the Senate in 1558, the Accademia Venetiana offered its own services for the collection and reform of the Republic's (as well as for the writing of a history of Venice)—which was exactly what Andrea Gritti had already attempted without success.[65] Cozzi has perceptively observed that one ought to see in this pretense—which was, it seems, favorably received at first[66]—a desire for reform that resembled the legislative review begun around 1531. But then one should also seriously consider Cozzi's other hypothesis, which sees in the Accademia's brief life and the hostility that the Venetian government leaders demonstrated toward it in 1561, a political stance that was as opposed to any "betrayal" of the *consuetudo veneta* in the field of law with laws of a Romanist stamp, as it was to the formation of specialized techniques of law itself.[67]

Moreover, the reform proposed by the Accademia della Fama undoubtedly affected all aspects of social life: the program it supported seemed to be shaping into a comprehensive project of "rebirth." In the *Supplica* of 1560, Federico Badoer recalled that

the academy having made a contract regarding the construction of the palace with the most serene Prince and the most illustrious Commissioners, stipulating that the academy should undertake to have a picture placed before the doors of the most Illustrious College and Senate, the Council of Ten and the Chancery, and the academy having been given the task of finding a painter, it has resolved in writing for the most beautiful invention of the greatest ornament for this, the most serene State ever created, . . . that the subject should signify the power of the State, as it reigns in a virtuous Christian manner, in security and splendor.[68]

The Accademia thus took responsibility for an iconographic program in support of the "good government" of the Republic. Federico Badoer certainly had a precise goal in mind when he asked the Procurators of San Marco, also in July of 1560, to allow him to transfer the seat of the Accademia to the vestibule of the Library of San Marco, in which Titian had painted his representation of *Wisdom*.[69] Let there be no doubt about it: the Accademia's ambition was to be recognized as the depository of "public knowledge"; and it came close to expropriating prerogatives that the entire patriciate had been guaranteed by the Venetian constitution.

But in order to reconstruct the causes of the forced closing of the Accademia Venetiana, it is necessary to examine the entire range of its often ambiguous activities. In this way we will not underestimate the economic aspects of the Accademia, carefully studied by Pagan,[70] which probably justify the suspicions held by Venetian literary circles and ultimately led to the dismissals of Luca Contile and Bernardo Tasso. The Accademia's contacts with the literary centers of Protestant Germany and the epistolary relationships with Augustan writers intertwined with the commercial activities of the Badoers, who used the Accademia for their own purposes, especially between January and June 1560.[71] And a serious step was certainly taken when a proposal was made to give the Flecamers the privilege—granted to the Accademia, in May 1560, by the Council of Ten[72]—of printing Venice's laws and decrees. The granting of this privilege ought to have settled part of the debts contracted with Germany; Pagan claims that the consequences of this incredible transaction left traces that can be found in the Acts of the Council of Ten pertaining to the legal proceedings initiated against the Accademia della Fama between 1561 and

1567—"Badoer has dealt with the Germans, for which he was again condemned by our judges appointed for this purpose."[73]

One can be sure that the Badoers and Abbot Marlopino used the prestige of the Accademia for open-minded economic transactions; but Pagan himself has had to recognize that the Accademia undertook editorial and cultural programs on a European scale and was courageously open to countries of Protestant faith.[74] A mixture of humanistic, scientific, and political objectives, rendered ambiguous by the adventurous economic management of the association, ambiguously characterized the activities of this unique Accademia—so much so, in fact, that the suspicions and provisions of the Venetian authorities become quite comprehensible.

In this connection, Lina Bolzoni's analyses have been most helpful.[75] Insisting upon the "syncretic pluralism" of the Accademia, this scholar has identified Cosimo I's Florentine Accademia as the model for the Venetian one; moreover, she points out that if Badoer hoped to create a State cultural institution, he also intended it to be planned and managed by a private circle. This could only have clashed with the way in which the *Serenissima* regulated the relations between politics and culture; we should add that if Federico Badoer's endeavor had been actuated, it would have transferred the political design implicit in Marco Foscari's endeavor into the domain of the management of knowledge. Bolzoni's reflections on the encyclopedism of the Accademia Venetiana are also valuable. The Accademia declared that it wanted nothing more than to "restore the golden age to the world":[76] an objective that was pursued through a precise classification of subject matter and an almost obsessive concern for the thoroughness and universality of materials, above all for their definitive ordering. It was an attempt to reach a "totalizing order," a project to arrange the many forms of knowledge in mental structures capable of recovering the *idea* that threatened to disappear in "scattered teachings":[77] it was no accident that Francesco Patrizi was a friend of the "divine" Giulio Camillo Delminio. The many clues provided by the *Instrumento* of 1560 and the *Somma delle Opere* confirm the congruency that existed between the Accademia's classificatory encyclopedism and the principles that Patrizi expressed—also in 1560—in his *Discorso* for the *Rime* of Luca Contile. In that work, in fact, Francesco Patrizi recognized as fundamental, for the foundation of a new rhetoric, the idea of a correspondence between the structures and development of human discourse, the structure of the cosmos, and the development of divine ideas:[78] it was a new version of the macrocosm-microcosm analogy, which had echoes in the *Discorso intorno alle cinque parti dell'oratore*, published by Paolo Manuzio in 1560, as well as in a passage of the *Instrumento* by Federico Badoer.[79] A gnosiology founded on the *topos* of *order*, image of original Truth, is thus placed at the basis of an encyclopedic idea. In itself, the attempt was not original: there may have been original elements, however, in the lines that guided research in some of the sectors of knowledge that the Accademia proposed to gather and reduce to unity. On the other hand, the very will to "reduce to order" indicates an awareness of the threat inherent in the growing specialization of knowledge: with its programs, the Accademia Venetiana was implicitly denouncing the tension between the dogma of the "unity of Truth" and the affirmation of "special knowledges," each of which was progressing toward its own autonomy.

But for the very reason that it was tending toward an *order* (or ordering) *of truth*—one observes that the Accademia offered the Procurators of San Marco, on July 12, 1560, its own collaboration for the reordering and management of the Libreria Marciana[80]—Federico Badoer's association was characterized almost too openly as a group that upheld an almost absolute hegemony over the management of Venetian culture. This was all the more so given that the Accademia was practically identified with the Badoer family: the curators of the four councils were Federico's three nephews and Abbot Marlopino, who, having become the curator of the Oratorio, was in a way adopted by the family.[81] And here is what Federico Badoer ordered, in the *Instrumento di Deputazione* of 1560, for the new iconography for the façade of his palazzo: "That my three nephews should be held and obligated . . . to redo the façade of the house, with that model which most pleases the majority, with drawings by experts, and on the two banks, as in the section of the *campo*, that they should put Saint Mark, with the crest of the Badoer and the motto of the Accademia with the sculptured name of the Accademia Venetiana."[82]

A private palazzo had been chosen to be the "universal theater" of knowledge; so far we agree with Lina Bolzoni.[83] We do not, however, agree with her attempt to link the *domus Badoera* to the sixteenth-century tendency to concentrate universal knowledge in halls and studios. Rather, Badoer's desire confirms what has already been observed about the dangerous "*mutatione*" that the Accademia tried to impose upon the management of knowledge: and the activities of the Riformatori dello Studio in Padua, which testify to the careful way in which Venice controlled the University of the *Serenissima*, have been sufficiently studied.[84]

The closing of the Accademia in 1561 was almost certainly due to the imprudent policy of identifying a family and a group with the organization of knowledge. By arrogating prerogatives that were eminently matters of state, the circle united around the Badoer family brought failure upon itself: their economic schemes and relations with the "Alemanni" or Germans provided the Senate with plausible pretexts to liquidate a group that had become suspect because it was organized in a private circle.

It is necessary, however, to explore further the Accademia Venetiana's program and to verify those aspects that were innovative within the context of the cultural climate in Venice at the time.

Paul Lawrence Rose has identified the quality and extent of scientific interests at the heart of the Accademia.[85] In a program of publications that comprised about three hundred volumes, one hundred and three were dedicated to scientific themes, with a significant prevalence of re-publication of classical texts over modern ones. Alongside the *Physics*, the texts of the atomists, the *Timaeus* translated into the vernacular, Hippocrates, Galen, Euclid, Archimedes, Pappus, Proclus, Ptolemy, Strabo, and so on up to a total of sixty-six titles, the editorial program included the *De Fluxu et Refluxu Maris* by Federico Delfino, professor of mathematics in Padua and the teacher of Bernardino Telesio, Daniele Barbaro, and Alessandro Piccolomini,[86] Boccadiferro's commentary on the *Physics*, and works by Regiomontanus, Alhazen, Nicolò Tartaglia, and Roger Bacon. The development of the natural and technical sciences was thus seen as inseparable from the "rebirth" of ancient science: the Accademia intended to publish a translation of Proclus's commentary to Euclid I, a work, as we shall see, that was fundamental for the development of the new sciences during the Renaissance and that Francesco Barozzi would begin to study in 1559.[87] And one must take into account the fact that Barozzi, a central figure in the history of sixteenth-century mathematics, was linked with Daniele Barbaro as well as Sperone Speroni; in fact, it was Speroni who, in 1564, planned the Accademia dei Gimnosofisti—an echo of the Ptolemists' Accademia della Virtú—for the discussion of Vitruvius and the pseudo-Aristotelian *Mechanics*.[88]

Furthermore, the Accademia della Fama's members included figures such as Luca Contile—who was particularly interested in mathematics—and Agostino Valier, who, in lectures that Rose suggests were given at the Accademia in 1559,[89] recognized the philosophy of nature as the epicenter of Aristotelian thinking and accepted mathematics as an integral part of philosophy.

But it is the very accomplishment achieved by this syncretic effort that ought to put us on our guard: the scientistic tendency, in the heart of the Accademia Venetiana, was accompanied by a revival of hermetic and Neoplatonic studies proposed in translations into the vernacular. The *Somma delle Opere* mentions that the Accademia was planning a translation of *Pimander* and *Asclepius*, to be accompanied by a "learned and copious commentary, from which one will be able to understand how this admirable author had approached Mosaic doctrine and wisdom: and how almost all the ancient theology of Pythagoras, Eudoxus, and the others, derived from him."[90] Furthermore, the *Somma* also speaks of a plan for a vernacular edition of Francesco Zorzi's *De harmonia mundi*, the strangest and most representative work of Venetian cabalistic thinking of Pichian and hermetic origin, published in 1525.[91] The hermetic and sapiential substance of Zorzi's text was probably its most interesting aspect: it incorporated the tradition going back to Ficino and Pico, along with that of the Aristotelian physicists, the Greek atomists, and the new scientists. The Accademia's project to elaborate scientific editions remains remarkable, however. Although it should not be overemphasized, it did indicate a tendency alive in the Venetian milieu, the initial symptoms of which had appeared evident considering the success of Luca Pacioli's lecture, and whose consequences should be carefully considered.

We have no proof that Daniele Barbaro belonged to the Accademia della Fama, but we are certain about his friendship with Federico Badoer. And the Vitruvian commentaries that the Patriarch elect of Aquileia published in 1556 were in a certain sense connected to the cultural program laid out in the Accademia's editorial prospectus:[92] they were at least congruent with it, revealing one of the goals held by the Venetian scientistic circle around the middle of the sixteenth century. In fact, it was through a reading of the two editions of Barbaro's *Commentari* (1556 and 1567), as well as through documents pertaining to Nicolò Zen and the history of the Venetian Arsenal, that Ennio Concina has skillfully reconstructed the project for "humanistic reform" undertaken by the Arsenal.[93] Barbaro wrote that a new *ratio* had been introduced into the Arsenal as a "thing born of [Nicolò Zen's] loving study and industrious judgment." He also added, in 1567, that he often went to the Arsenal with Zen "to try to lift immense weights with little effort." Zen and the Arsenal are praised in the commentary to the twelfth chapter of the fifth book of Vitruvius: the function of the *Dieci Libri* within the program of scientific rebirth that Daniele Barbaro recommended was clear.

The Arsenal was expected to oppose the corruption of natural equilibriums (fig. 105), it was to become the State's bulwark on land and sea, a "machine" capable of acting as guarantor of the Republic's defense, of stimulating commerce, and balancing the latter with the land reclamation and territorial "conquests" already under way. All of which corresponded to Nicolò Zen's interests and duties. Zen would not only oversee the *Cantiere di Stato* (State Arsenal); in 1556, he was Reclamation Commissioner and in 1557 he would become Commissioner of Fortresses; he thus became involved with the largest-scale rationalization of Venetian territory to take place during the sixteenth century.

The very new Arsenal (fig. 105)—which the Senate had, already in 1500, considered a "machine" that supplied "in large measure the conservation of our State on land as on sea"—was recognized by Barbaro as "an apparatus to acquire kingdoms, and provinces." As an urban structure, it only spoke through the technical practices that took place within it: although it was a public structure, it had no "messages" to address to the public. It was Barbaro himself who compared the *ars rhetorica*, necessary in the San Marco forum, with the silence imposed upon the Arsenal. Daniele Barbaro wrote that the Arsenal "does not have the greatness, as regards the amount of marble and the magnificence of material, that the ancients used in their buildings, but I will say that regarding everything having to do with the use and size of things dealing with the sea, it is far ahead of anything that can be seen in our day."[94]

The Arsenal was, according to a decision made in 1539 by the Council of Ten, a secret place.[95] The "military heart" of the city, it was a heterotopia, an "other city" complete unto itself. A structure that integrated residential quarters, work, and social services, the Arsenal—protected by secrecy—was not only an "enclosure" sacred to applied sciences, but also a decisive place for the verification of hypotheses regarding the imperative of *ratio* upon technology itself.

That which had been pure enunciation became concrete action in the deeds of Nicolò Zen: as Vettor Fausto had once done, Zen tried to introduce a new scientific intelligence into the management of the *Cantiere di Stato*. And this inevitably leads one to think that, at the end of the *Amadigi*, which was published by Giolito de' Ferrari in 1560, Bernardo Tasso—chancellor, if only for a few weeks, of the Accademia della Fama—was praising the principal figures of the clique guided by Federico Badoer along with the people who were more closely involved with the Accademia itself. Tasso wrote,

I notice some others in a tight group, / worthy of statues, medals and marble, / who with their sublime and bright minds, / not only in learned prose and

polished songs / but also with their prudence and valor, / raise the honor of the Queen of the Adriatic. / Mula, Mocenigo, and Navagero, and wise and learned Zeno; / Barbaro, who raising his thought / has taken care of the free country, / thinking and writing; and Agostino Valiero / with Philosophy in his breast; / and the exquisite Tiepolo the Geographer, / who knows every shape and place in the world.[96]

We can broaden our discussion with the help of what we know about a later member of the Accademia. We are referring to the Sicilian Giuseppe Moleto (1531–88), a student of Francesco Maurolico, a close friend of Nicolò Zen, and a teacher at the Studio in Padua from 1577 until his death. His manuscripts, which were left to Gian Vincenzo Pinelli and are now in the Biblioteca Ambrosiana in Milan, demonstrate an astonishing diversity of interests: Moleto's studies ranged from geography to mechanics, to optics, anemography, hydrography, mathematics, hydraulics, rotating clocks, and the science of weights.[97]

In his *Discorso*, which has never been published, Moleto discusses ancient, medieval, and contemporary mathematical principles, demonstrating his familiarity with the works of Copernicus, Stifel, and Tartaglia, as well as with the musical theories of Gioseffo Zarlino, while, in his discussion of perspective, he cites Pacioli, Leon Battista Alberti, Dürer, and Daniele Barbaro.[98] In his *Partitio mathematicarum scientarum*, also in manuscript, Moleto concerns himself with optics, scenography, and gnomology, and with "fire and bodies used for weaponry, known these days as bombards, cannons, and other machines for breaking walls, towers, etc."[99] Charles Schmitt has remarked that Moleto's treatise was pervaded by an aura of practicality.[100] This is without a doubt true, even though one must use a good degree of caution in evaluating Moleto's personality because of the eclecticism of his interests and the generic quality of his method.[101] It is, however, true that Galileo's predecessor at Padua seemed intent on verifying the possibility of a practical use of the sciences: and his manuscripts do deal with problems pertaining to scales, architecture, and fortresses. Moleto was still very young during the years he was present at the Accademia Venetiana, but it is likely that the ideas he encountered there did not influence the development of his thinking. This is demonstrated by the appearance of the names of Daniele Barbaro and Zarlino in his works: and we know that Zarlino was also a member of the Accademia.

Adriano Carugo remarked, however, in an argument with Antonio Favaro, that Moleto turned out to be a convinced Aristotelian—in 1581–82 the Sicilian would give lessons on the pseudo-Aristotelian *Mechanics*—although he considered mathematics to be a contemplative science, useful only in the pursuit of ultimate truths.[102] Many of the often discordant motifs that characterized Venetian scientism coexisted in the work of Giuseppe Moleto, whom we will have an opportunity to discuss again in connection with Jacopo Contarini.

At this point it becomes necessary to examine the significance that the recovery of ancient science had for the groups we have been discussing: we will, therefore, continue to examine the work of Daniele Barbaro, in relation to the "scientific" project it contains, as well as the perspectives it opened to the *modi nuovi* [new styles] of Palladian architecture.

5. Daniele Barbaro, Andrea Palladio, and Jacopo Contarini

The Accademia Venetiana's programs had one blind spot that did not escape its contemporaries. Referring to the *Somma delle Opere*, Natta, addressing himself to Paolo Manuzio, lamented the fact that architecture was not one of the subjects receiving attention by the Accademia's members.[103] The temptation to use that blind spot as an argument *ex silentio* is quite strong: one could in fact deduce from it that the group had little use for architecture, or at least that it held an attitude that was typical of the Venetian mistrust of anything that might threaten the *imago* of the traditional city. One might also observe that Federico Badoer, when he gave instructions for the renovation of the family palazzo, seemed completely indifferent to its architectural appearance.

And yet, the Accademia's "Romanism" and the presence there of Jacopo Sansovino's son and of Nicolò Moravio—the abbot of San Pantalon who asked Palladio to design an altar in 1555[104]—prevents us from making such hasty conclusions. All the more so, given that in 1556—Badoer's initiative was launched in 1555—the appearance of Daniele Barbaro's *Vitruvio* imposed upon the *sapientes* of Venice a new conception of the *ars aedificatoria*, a very humanistic one with a strongly scientistic aura. But the major Venetian "connoisseurs of architecture" do not seem to have adhered to the Accademia della Fama. In spite of the friendship that existed between Barbaro and Federico Badoer, the Patriarch elect of Aquileia did not number among the patricians of the association, just as Vettor Grimani (who died in 1558), Antonio Cappello, and Marc'Antonio Giustinian also did not figure there. On the one hand, this reinforces the idea that a large sector of Venetian culture mistrusted Badoer's initiative; on the other hand, this explains the external causes, at least, of the blind spot we are examining. Furthermore, in 1556–57, the architectural culture of Venice identified itself with Daniele Barbaro. At a time rather close to Palladio's failures in the competitions for the position of *proto* of the Magistracy for Salt (1554) and for the project for the Scala d'Oro (1555), it was Barbaro himself who probably directed the group that executed and decorated the Palazzo Trevisan in Murano; and it is interesting to note, in this connection, that Camillo Trevisan, the client for the aforementioned palazzo, was a teacher of jurisprudence at the Accademia della Fama.[105]

But, although it was programmatic, the Palazzo Trevisan did not present itself as a "manifesto" of the new architectural culture. The Vitruvius of 1556 did instead.

In fact, Daniele Barbaro's *Commentari* presented themselves as a *summa* of technical and scientific knowledge, even if the *episteme* that sustained them was not original (figs. 99–102): scientific *ratio* was legitimized in the commentaries by the divine harmony of the "building of this university that we call the world." Barbaro, however, demonstrated his knowledge not only of Euclid and Leon Battista Alberti, but also of Pedro de Medina's *Arte de navegación*, Dürer's texts on the compass and on proportions, Federico Commandino's commentaries on Ptolemy, Sebastian Münster's *Compositio horologiorum*, Joannes Werner's astronomical and mathematical works, and Joannes Stabius's *Horoscopio universalis*.[106]

The text written by Barbaro sings a hymn to the *virtù* of architecture that seems to refer directly to the ethics of Leon Battista Alberti. But let us compare two passages that seem alike, the first taken from the *incipit* of the *Dere aedificatoria*, and the second from Barbaro's commentary on the first book of Vitruvius:

And then [were devised] methods to conduct over surfaces subterranean waters, which are used for so many different and indispensable purposes; such as commemorative monuments, sanctuaries, temples, sacred places in general, created by the architect for religious ends or for the use of posterity. Finally, through the cutting of cliffs, the tunneling of mountains, the leveling of valleys, the containment of sea and lake waters, the emptying of swamps, the construction of ships, the rectification of the course of rivers, the excavation of the outlets of waters, the construction of bridges and ports, he not only resolved problems of temporary circumstance, but also opened the way toward every region of the earth. In this way different peoples could through exchanges partake of all that serves the improvement of health and way of life: agricultural products, perfumes, precious stones, experiences, and notions.[107]

But let us see whether we can praise Architecture, if truly, and first of all according to cognition, then according to operations, why in knowledge, and in judgment she can be justly compared with Wisdom, and with Prudence, and (why) for her actions she shines clearly as a Heroic Virtue among the arts. A wonderful thing is the power for the common good to assemble coarse men, and unite them in faith and discipline, secure and tranquil in the cities and fortresses: then with greater violence done to nature, to cut the rocks, tunnel through the mountains, fill the valleys, dry the swamps, build ships, straighten rivers, supply ports, build bridges, and overcome Nature herself, which we have vanquished by lifting immense weights, and satisfying in part the desire of eternity. . . .[108]

The two passages agree only in a superficial reading: Barbaro does away with the strict boundary that Leon Battista Alberti placed upon human inquiry.

Nature, with its own supreme equilibrium, is for Alberti opposed to the *hybris* that characterizes this "evil animal";[109] but for Daniele Barbaro, it is no longer a sure reference, an alternative to the ingrained violence of the intellect. It is true that even Barbaro speaks of the "book of nature" that ought to be imitated:[110] for him consonances and harmonies are drawn from nature,[111] and it is also through nature that one arrives "at the magnificence of building."[112] Nonetheless, the concept of nature is not univocal for him. It designates a normative principle as well as something to be used or simply to be ameliorated or overcome. He writes, "As nature therefore does some things against man's advantage and operates always in the same way, it is necessary to find some way to deal with this misfortune that might bend nature to need and to human use. This way is hidden in the help of Art, with which one conquers nature in those things in which nature conquers us."[113]

The entire discourse concerns architecture, but not the architect: it is the institution that is being examined in its full political potential. The symmetry established by Aristotle between architecture and *politia* is echoed in Barbaro's words. Reason governs civil society through custom and learned technical skills, and it keeps that society unified, defending it from the corruption caused by time. We will return to this point in our next chapter; for now we wish to underline how the concept of architecture is used metaphorically in the Vitruvian *Commentari*: Daniele Barbaro was not representing a *bene instituta res publica*, but theorizing an ideal form that would renew consolidated mental structures. The basic theme is explicit: a planning rationality—albeit founded on *principia*—is upheld.

The *machinatio* thus readies itself to shape the natural environment according to human concerns (fig. 102): the *hybris* feared by Alberti is philosophically legitimated. But the *machinatio* itself is not an object of study: it is part of architecture in that "it is alternately classified beneath two sciences, for which reason it commands respect along with natural science receiving its subject from it . . . and is placed beneath mathematics, because it receives beautiful and fine reasons and demonstrations from it, and as if the subject is mutable, and variable, as a thing of nature, so reason is firm and immutable as a thing of the intellect, nor does it change according to matter. . . ."[114]

The "certain knowledge" assured by mathematics thus connects the harmonic principles, to which "true architecture" adapts itself, in order to help transform the natural system. Thus Barbaro placed the transparent truth of mathematical knowledge at the center of his Platonic and Aristotelian reading of Vitruvius: "But the way to know the most noble Arts is this: that those, in which the Art of numbering is necessary, Geometry and the other Mathematics, all have something great, and the rest that is without these arts (as Plato says), is vile and abject like a thing born of simple imagination, false conjecture, and is experience devoid of truth."[115]

Pure technology, the *proto* who works from *Isperienza* only, the *mecanico* who "does not know the reasons," are relegated to exercising abject and vile functions. For this reason, they are destined to be dominated by the architect, or by whoever has "the truth" and understands the causes, and as such will be called upon to exercise command. Barbaro interpreted the *Nicomaean Ethics* in his own way. Aristotle had defined *sophia* as a combination of *nous* and *episteme*, considering the latter as a process of demonstration.[116] For Barbaro, "science" is "the habit of drawing conclusions according to a true and necessary acquired proof," but it is also knowing how to "conclude many things from the right principles." This definition was not alien to the methods of investigation used by the Paduan Studio. Its formulation was affected by the philosophical doubts of the author, who, on the other hand, was not unsure of himself when arguing against the simplification and fragmentation of knowledge.

Truly divine is the desire of those, who raising their minds to consider things, search for the reasons behind them, and looking as if above them and at the truth from afar, are spurred to try to look at it; on the other hand there are many, who with great praises to Heaven raise the learned and literate men, and with amazement looking at the sciences do anything instead of tiring themselves to acquire them. There are also many, who, as it may please God, know for certain that it is necessary, if one is to learn one science, to know something of all sciences, but few are interested in these other sciences and those who are students of these sciences are disdained and taken to be errant and crazy. It is a beautiful thing to be able to judge, and approve of the works of mortals, as a superior act of virtue toward an inferior one: nonetheless few take the trouble, few want to strive; or to leave the habits of laziness, and for that reason they make no judgment, and consequently do not reach the end of Architecture.[117]

Once again we can clearly see how architecture is used as a metaphor. As a discipline that validates Wisdom, it is both a special language and a place that holds together differentiated knowledges and technical skills. On the one hand, architecture is clearly called upon to reveal the concerns of divine creation, to make evident, useful, and legible the rational harmony imprinted upon the cosmos. On the other hand, it is invoked as a structure that ensures the unity of knowledge, that opposes the fragmentation of languages and techniques. For this reason, *empiria* cannot be placed at the foundation of architecture. On the contrary: *scire per causas* lends architecture an almost absolute authoritativeness in the technical as well as in the programmatic field.[118] And this authoritativeness—since it has something to do with the immutability of *principia*—excludes all "progress" that is not the result of laborious rediscovery.

Barbaro, uniting Vitruvius with the *Nicomaean Ethics* and Catholic orthodoxy,[119] defined paradigms of rationality that enabled knowledge to take action: but knowledge remained within the limits of a truth outside of history, defined by circulation of its own hypotheses. This duality explains not only the breadth of Barbaro's scientific interests—his involvement, beginning in 1545, with the Orto Botanico in Padua, or his writings on perspective and on clocks (figs. 103, 104)[120]—but also the ultimate goal of the Vitruvian *Commentari*: to subordinate technology to the absolute sovereignty of a *philosophia perennis*, the intrinsic nature of which limits its content to a metaphysically founded *truth*.

Daniele Barbaro's thought was thus dangerously poised on a ridge: it consecrated a resonant conception of knowledge and architecture; at the same time, it extolled the victory over nature of branches of knowledge that were by nature free. It is, however, necessary to set all schematism aside and to recognize—in Barbaro as in most of humanist culture—a deep alliance between *techne* and *eidos*. Technology—which appears in Baldassare Castiglione as artifice, *sprezzatura* or studied carelessness, effort turned into habit[121]— turns out not to be in opposition to ideas. On the contrary: ideas not only justify technology, but manifest themselves through it. The model and the norm are not absolute denials of experience and events: they are, rather, measures capable of dominating all becoming, transformation, and change. The force of the norm is directly proportional to the *project of controlling time* that is contained in technical practices. For this reason, experience alone does not respond to the ends which the dialectic *eidos-techne* is called upon to answer; when we let ourselves be guided by the casualness of events, experience cannot govern becoming, it is forced to give up the possibility of possessing change. We should not let ourselves be misled by the fact that the norm is the result of "discovery," of *revolutio*. For Leon Battista Alberti as for Daniele Barbaro, technical practices must incorporate the ethical dimension, and it is useful for this purpose to identify the ideal norm with Antiquity and with Nature: the "virtue" assured by architecture furnishes the latter with a *telos*, a *plan*, a *productive* dimension. Already, in the earliest phase of the modern conception of technology there was the mythical root of the presupposition that conditions the concept of "planning": the normalization of becoming—the imposition of form on the "different"—reveals teleological and utopian values.

According to Barbaro's thinking, however, the purity of the theoretical frame was combined with easily recognizable ambiguities.

It has already been observed that the Villa Barbaro in Maser was the least Palladian of Palladio's villas, and this was certainly due to his clients' interferences:[122] the theoretical rigorism of the Vitruvian *Commentari* began to fritter away as soon as the formal charms of the Roman sphere appeared upon the scene. It is not our intention, at this point, to insist upon the contradictions inherent in Barbaro's thinking. The variations in his taste may be explained by his dilettantism, while the goal of his works remained constant, especially as measured against the reactions that they provoked in Venice and the Veneto region.

The enthusiasm for Barbaro as a thinker and as a man of science, which was expressed by Sperone Speroni, Bernardino Tomitano, Paolo Paruta, Bernardo Navagero, and Anton Francesco Doni, was followed by the partial acceptance, on the part of the Romanist patrician class, of Andrea Palladio—who, according to the *Commentari* of 1556, exemplified the "virtuous architect."[123] Barbaro helped to establish a scientistic climate in Venice, rather than a precise epistemology; furthermore, the themes explored by the Patriarch elect of Aquileia fell upon a fertile soil, as is demonstrated by the writings of the mathematicians who were directly connected to him.

That is not all: at the end of Book I of his Vitruvius, Barbaro announced the forthcoming publication of Giovan Jacopo Leonardi's *Libro delle fortificazioni*, of which he published a summary. Leonardi had probably written a good part of his treatise by the end of 1553, and it has been properly remarked that parts of his text have some affinity with analogous passages of Barbaro's Vitruvius and Palladio's *Quattro Libri*. These observations lead us to a significant conclusion: the writings of Barbaro, Leonardi, and Palladio appear to have been mutually connected, integrated within the ambit of a single cultural program.[124]

The 1550s thus appear to have been characterized by the convergence of many efforts intent on modernizing the State; a technical and scientific *renovatio* was one of the means used in the process. A revealing connection emerges. Parallel to Neoaristocratic and oligarchic tendencies, a scientism was affirming itself, one that—in spite of theoretical assertions—was headed toward a specialization of knowledge. Naturally, in order to utilize this observation positively, it is necessary to be extremely cautious: undoubtedly, it was a case of simple currents, not unmarked by internal and often incoherent contradictions; it is also clear that in speaking of "programs" we are using a term that is not at all suited to the superimposition—not always conscious—of tendencies that were *also* moving along independent and autonomous lines. But in the context of our historical construction, too many threads are intertwining into the knot we have indicated above, so that we think it best to highlight it in order to investigate it further.

The fact that circle of the Corners, Pisanis, Foscaris, and the Barbaro brothers supported Palladio so tenaciously assumes new significance in the light of the observations we have just made. If one admits, in fact, that the disparate objectives pursued by this circle formed a constellation in which private interests and public interests found some sort of synthesis, it becomes necessary to attempt to recognize in the structure of the Palladian poetic motifs that were congruent with this synthesis.

From the beginning, there must have been an appreciation for composition *more mathematico*: it is, in fact, undoubtedly the case that Palladian architecture displays an *ars combinatoria* elaborated within a true "typological laboratory"; Palladio won his syntactic freedom through a philological criticism that was in line with the best humanist traditions.

For Palladio, however, the classical code was merely a "field of variations," and not a handbook of rules. As Magagnato has observed, in the *Quarto Libro* alone Palladio published two Ionic capitals different from the ones in the *Primo Libro*, twelve Corinthian capitals, and three composite ones:[125] he overcame preceptive teaching through a fundamentally historicist reading of Antiquity.[126] Rather, the *exempla* formulated the problem of the difficult relationship between the *type* and *invention*. Palladio, representing his own work synchronically in the field of private architecture, in the *Secondo Libro*, demonstrated that for him there was no "type" that was not already *inventio*, that "variation," paradoxically, does not presuppose an archetypical model, and that the art of composing is founded on an absolute control of elements— spatial nuclei, a grammar of orders, functional devices—and on a willingness for infinite research. And it is significant that Palladio made his own "inventions" precede the reconstruction of the *casa di villa degli antichi* [villa house of the ancients] according to Vitruvius. In that case, the *exemplum*, which was reduced to a schema, drew its legitimation from the "modern": the schema was in fact followed by unrealized "inventions." The norm thus becomes something purely *conceptual*. Indefinable, it lives ideally in a planned adventure that discovers the value of a serial arrangement: devoid of "models," Palladio's *ars combinatoria* criticizes the concept of the type and presents itself as an open structure, a logical concatenation of experiments on the aggregation of spaces, on the syntax of structures, and on the composition of pivotal elements, made possible thanks to grammatical purification.

For those who love traditional historiographical definitions, we can say that Palladio in this way barred all access to architectural Mannerism in the Veneto region, demonstrating at the same time that the philological use of Latin grammar does not thwart open-minded experimentalism in the least: clearly, the issue for him was an experimentalism that was the opposite of Sebastiano Serlio's. One can formulate this another way and note that Palladian architecture, standing as the greatest achievement of humanism's competition with Antiquity, presented itself not only as a "novelty" that Venice could assimilate only with difficulty, but also as a barrier against later "novelties." The *finitio* of Palladian architecture was antithetical to the uniformity of the lagoon's urban fabric—and this was particularly evident in the two projects for the Rialto bridge—but it triumphally enunciated a "conservative" theorem at the same time.

For Palladio, architecture was a "special knowledge," guaranteed by its adherence to the "specificity" of the *imago mundi*, but disconnected from any hermeticizing residue.[127] Barbaro had defined architecture's contribution to civil life: but Palladio was even more of a realist than the Patriarch elect of Aquileia, and concentrated every "rational" ambition into the architectonic microcosm. In the second half of the sixteenth century, the *harmonia* dialectically attained by Palladio's polyphonic "inventions" might have seemed a *simulacro*: that is to say, the result of a simulation extraneous to the conflictive reality in which institutions and individuals are forced to live. That harmonic ideal, inseparable from the anthropomorphic ideal, had already expressed its elevated motivations in the thinking of Giovanni Pico and Erasmus: the *concordia philosophorum et theologorum* was irenical *pax*, and the recognition of an intellectual "duty" founded on the *dignitas hominis*, a duty that was, so to speak, a utopia of reason built upon the specific duties of the *animal imperfectus* that is man, a creature destined by God to complete creation through the exercise of liberty.[128]

The *virtus* that Daniele Barbaro and Palladio claimed for architecture was the heir of such ideals, if only through Albertian mediation. Of course, in Palladio there is no trace of the overwhelming pessimism expressed by Alberti in the *Intercoenales* and the *Momus*.[129] But both Alberti and Palladio seemed conscious of the necessity, for their "finite" islands of rationality, to remain tragically isolated: the *finitio* ruthlessly delineates the universe of representation, clearly separating it from the reality of the human world of commerce.

Then Palladio's architecture appeared on the scene—especially his work of the 1560s and '70s—and it assumed a precise historical task. It created a virtual reality that contrasted with immediate reality: this is especially evident in the context of the lagoon, where Palladio's works live thanks to their "estranging" power. At the same time, these works preserve the nucleus of the humanist hypothesis in an *absolutely pure* form. The harmony of Palladian architecture thus projects itself beyond the present, drawing a horizon of meaning that goes beyond the sixteenth century, offering a further argument to those who see in the Renaissance an age that "completed itself" in the years of Voltaire and Rousseau.

In the 1550s, Palladio surely was, for Daniele Barbaro, an architect to be disconnected from the influence of Vicenza, in which Gian Giorgio Trissino had inserted him because of an intellectual mistrust of Venice. The Palladian "project" did not, however, seem at all homogeneous with that of the Patriarch elect of Aquileia.

There was a disparity between the *Vitruvius* of 1556 and Palladio's architecture. Barbaro's architecture was still "universal"; Palladio's was completely specific, but above all proudly *autonomous*. Taken in its entirety, Palladian architecture constituted a "universe" that did not refer to anything "other," that contained its own justification within itself: this was a unique experience, in the context of the second half of the sixteenth century in Italy, even though its premises extend the humanism of Alberti, Bramante, and Raphael.

Moreover, Palladio's severe archeology defined precise limits and boundaries for the discursiveness of architecture. The issue was the identification of a "logic of discourse" verified through history—the definition of a precise ambit in which a *language of certainty* could be founded. The exception—and Palladio certainly did not interpret the relation between *techne* and *episteme* in an academic fashion—was "measured" within that logic; it became comprehensible and communicable thanks to its limits, turning into a "verifiable distortion."

Palladio's Venetian patrons, who were surely aware of the architect's "Romanism," would have found it rather difficult to understand all these thoughts: Palladio repeated trips to Rome—especially the one he made in 1554, in the company of Barbaro and other Venetian patricians, which was followed by his small volume on *L'antichitá di Roma*[130]—were significant in this regard. Furthermore, Palladio incarnated for them a precise professional figure, capable of renovating the organization of the work site and of opposing the praxis of the *proti*. His *ratio* was generated by an "understanding of the reasons"—consequently, by a rhetorical support that allowed a "*legislating of programs*," a standing outside the "arts" in order to rule over them. There is good reason to see Palladio as a figure parallel to Vettor Fausto, and, as in the *architectus navalis* protected by Andrea Gritti and Francesco Maria della Rovere, a figure destined to encounter difficulties in the Venetian reality.

This was, however, a reality that nourished at its heart a circle that recognized itself in the Palladian message: in this circle there were oligarchic and Romanist groups, but also patricians intent on fostering a radical renewal of technology. These groups were not that far apart, in their intentions, from those that had supported Andrea Gritti's *renovatio*, in the 1520s and '30s. On the contrary, they were interested in completing that *renovatio*, in pushing it as far as it would go, in reacting to symptoms of political and economic decadence. The architectural interpreter of this second *renovatio* could no longer be Sansovino, who was tied to a culture pleased with archaic formulas and whose art of composition—especially in those works done after 1537— appeared completely empirical. For Daniele and Marcantonio Barbaro, as for Giovanni Grimani, who would strive for anti-Sansovinian works,[131] another kind of formal rigor was necessary, a different professional consciousness, a renewed criticism of sources, another kind of control over modes of architectural production: Palladio's architecture represented a decisive alternative to Sansovino's.

A few more remarks are called for here. During the course of the debate on the location of the Redentore church (1576), Marcantonio Barbaro defended the site of San Vidal. It was, certainly, a less costly piece of land—2,500 ducats as opposed to 3,000 for the Cappuccini land on the Giudecca—but it was also a pro-Jesuit choice: the Company of Jesus, installed in the heart of the *Serenissima*, would have been able to do its work in exceptionally favorable circumstances.[132] Not by chance, Leonardo Donà—who, once Doge, would guide the *Serenissima* during the Interdict—determined the outcome of the pro-Jesuit choice. The episode was significant: it makes clear, regarding a problem that also involves architecture, an initial contrast between the *giovani*, or "younger generation," and Marcantonio Barbaro—a contrast that holds true even when one remembers how Donà showed his appreciation for the Palladian church of San Giorgio Maggiore, when, in 1609, he ordered the demolition of the small houses that stood in the way of the view from the Palazzo Ducale and the Piazza.

The reasons why Palladio met with favor in Venice—and the limits of it—become more comprehensible when we analyze the personality of one of the patricians who was closest to that architect, and who was, in many ways, Daniele Barbaro's most interesting cultural heir. We are referring to Jacopo Contarini, whom Girolamo Porro called, when he dedicated Vincenzo Scamozzi's *Discorsi sopra le antichità di Roma* to him, "A connoisseur of all beautiful things, including architecture, painting, sculpture, and harmonic and analemmatic instruments of war . . . almost a new Archimedes . . . of such high judgment in all the sciences and arts."[133] When Palladio was in Venice, he probably stayed in Jacopo Contarini's house in San Samuele—the same house that contained the studio praised by Francesco Sansovino for its codices, books, architectural drawings (Palladio would leave his own drawings to Contarini),[134] paintings and sculptures.[135] Jacopo Contarini, in his last will and testament, would call that studio

one of the dearest things that I have had and have . . . from which have come all the honors and respect for my person, by which I mean not only where my books are, but everything that is contained in the 4 rooms of the apartments where I am ordinarily; where there are exquisite things and such that I could not believe whoever does not think well of them, and so it is for the printed books as for the handwritten ones, for the mathematical and mechanical instruments, for the marble and bronze statues, the paintings, minerals, stones, and other things, all of which I have gathered with the greatest study and effort. Nonetheless I still wish that it be conserved and increased, so that posterity may enjoy and profit from my labors.[136]

For Contarini, then, private collecting was related to public use. We know that he was in contact with Giuseppe Moleto and Guidobaldo del Monte, and that he had close friendships with Daniele Barbaro, Giulio Savorgnan, and Gian Vincenzo Pinelli—who was a patron of Veronese[137]—the Bassano family, and perhaps Palma the Younger; his interest in Francesco Bassano, especially, indicates that he was attracted by experimentation.[138]

In the manuscripts that belonged to Jacopo Contarini, especially in those of the Bodleian Library at Oxford (MS Canon. H. 145) and of the Marciana (MS It. Z 86=4817) (fig. 110),[139] we find commentaries, based on Guidobaldo del Monte, on the Mordente compass, drawings of machines that can be traced back to models by Francesco di Giorgio Martini, drawings based on Taccola's, inventions copied from the *Organa mechanica* (BMV, Ms Lat. 3048) (figs. 106–9), and from the fifteenth-century codex in the Biblioteca Nazionale in Florence (Palat. 767), which also depicts machines and devices based on those by Taccola and Martini.

Furthermore, Contarini's library included the principal scientific texts of antiquity, in addition to texts by Valturio, Regiomontanus, Peuerbach, Clavius, Egnazio Danti, Guidobaldo del Monte, Cardano, Tartaglia, Oronce Fine, Nuñez, and Barozzi, while his collection of manuscripts included the Greek texts of Hero, writings on astronomy, naval technology, drawings of fortresses, maps, and the *Prospettiva* by Blasius of Parma (fig. 111).[140]

In order to evaluate Jacopo Contarini's scientific interests on the basis of these codices, one needs to recognize that they depended upon inventories that were largely dated. For a man with Contarini's cultural background, the activities of gatherer and collector had a specific space: the machines represented in the cited codices did not contain substantial innovations and they are valuable instead as historical documents. But Jacopo Contarini's "studio" assumed a particular meaning: at least some of the objectives that the Accademia Venetiana wished to pursue were represented in the private sphere, which fulfilled duties for a State that was not interested in organizing research and was happy to leave that task entirely to the Paduan Studio.

It is necessary to explore Contarini's cultural profile further. In 1554 and in 1556 he was *Savio agli Ordini* [Minister of the waterways], and as such he must have had contacts with the Arsenal:[141] which, given his friendship with Daniele Barbaro, makes one think. Contarini, who was employed in the reorganization of military architecture and whose ideals fully agreed with Giulio Savorgnan, was steadily employed in technical problems involving the territory: in 1579, having returned from a visit with the *podestà* in Bergamo, he presented a report that proposed the building of a navigable canal between the Brembo and Bergamo, and establishing a related network of irrigating canals for commercial and agricultural purposes.[142] And it was to Jacopo Contarini that Giuseppe Moleto dedicated an unpublished text in 1581—preserved in the Ambrosiana library—on the *Facil modo di tirar le linee parallele alle vedute, di misurar le distanze et di mettere in disegno*, which is followed, in the Ambrosiana manuscript, by a *Discorso di fortificazioni di Jacopo Contarini . . . sopra dubbi proposti da Giulio Savorgnano*.[143]

Contarini was something more than a dilettante. The treatise *Di Fortificatione* that has been attributed to him—the manuscript that is preserved in the Biblioteca Estense in Modena—is a compendium that owes much to the technical innovations of Buonaiuto Lorini and Giulio Savorgnan, but also has the continuity with which Jacopo Contarini pursued his research on the improvement of the *ars fortificatoria* and its application in new contexts:[144] Contarini, who became a deputy for the defense of the Lidi [coasts] during the war against Cyprus, would have the opportunity to put his experience to the test when he confronted the difficult problem of the security of the lagoon.[145] As for Giulio Savorgnan, he had been a student of Francesco Maria I della Rovere and would later turn out to be, along with Sforza Pallavicino, a supporter of Lorini's:[146] in 1586, Savorgnan communicated to Contarini, through Buonaiuto, his own project to "adapt at small expense" the new fortress of Brescia. Giuseppe Moleto was, moreover, also in touch with the *Serenissima*'s superintendent of fortresses: a new circle was thus taking shape, whose technical and scientific interests were focused upon military arts.

This circle, one should add, made good use of correspondence to pursue scientific subjects. In the letters that Francesco Barozzi, Jacopo Contarini, Ulisse Aldovrandi, Gian Vincenzo Pinelli, and Giuseppe Moleto wrote one another constantly, one can see a new need for exchange. The dialogue, and often the polemic, revealed a need for verification and collaboration in the formulation of hypotheses; that need, which was first met by correspondence, would, a little later, be answered by the first scientific academies. An analysis of these correspondences, which have been relatively unexplored, also reveals the variety of mentalities involved.

Moleto's *Facil modo* was addressed to the "ingegneri" or engineers and contained graphic examples in the margins; only at the text did the mathematician feel the need to add a quick theoretical justification:

But I realize that I am writing to someone who understands these things much better than I do; yet all will serve to show you, most illustrious Sir, two things: the first, that I keep in mind the things that you discuss with me, and along with that you will be able to understand the desire that I have to serve you; and the second that all this discourse that I have held so far has been dictated to me by theory, and by demonstration, by means of which man may find many, and many things most useful to human life, and many ways, which among Engineers are important secrets, are trite things to the theoretical. I am speaking of the Engineers who are simple practical men.[147]

Here, then, is more evidence of the polemic that surrounded the *faber*: for Moleto the "theoretical" was not something abstract; it is valid only when it is combined with "demonstration." All of which was not sufficient for Contarini, who, writing Pinelli a letter that was not dated but must have been written after Moleto's, strongly criticizes the instrument that the latter had invented, observing; "The thought of manually doing that which the intellect considers in abstract form is impossible because the operation contains a resistance with regard to the imperfection of vision, which cannot be overcome, and since it is necessary to use something, whatever it may be, instruments are constructed anyway with the greatest possible diligence and for all that it is still not enough to work without an instrument made, fastened, and marked with diligence."[148]

Jacopo Contarini then concludes, ". . . but let me say that with my instrument all that I wish to do I will do it exactly because the instrument will be well-regulated and accurately, and that of Signor Moletti made haphazardly, and in the operation of it, in taking designs every detail that is incorrect is cause of incredible errors."[149]

Moleto's invention was condemned because it did not take into consideration the inevitable difference between the perfection of the theoretical model and the conditionings imposed by praxis and the senses.[150] This attitude was also revealed in a short work, also by Contarini, on perfect fortifications. He wrote: "All its strength (of the fortification) consists in the fosse, major and minor fortified walls, embankments, ramparts and their small passages,"[151] offering, on c. 33r, a planimetric representation of a sector of the ideal fortress (fig. 113). One ought to note the following: Filippo Pigafetta, who was a friend of Contarini and Savorgnan, left a large number of descriptions of fortified cities;[152] and, in the context of our subject, it is very interesting that Pigafetta came into contact with Guidobaldo del Monte's work through the mediation of Giulio Savorgnan.[153] It is significant, therefore, that, in the dedication of the translation of the *Mechanicorum Liber*, published in 1581, Pigafetta cites Nicolò Tartaglia, Vettor Fausto, and Daniele Barbaro as "restorers" of ancient scientific rigor.[154]

Filippo Pigafetta thus drew a clear—and eloquent—connecting thread. Daniele Barbaro, Tartaglia, and Guidobaldo del Monte were part of a tradition that originated with Leon Battista Alberti and Vettor Fausto. The scientistic tendency defended here is unequivocal, and surely reflects the ideas professed by Jacopo Contarini as well as by Giulio Savorgnan, who was celebrated as an expert student of mechanics, and an expert in fortifications: it was a line that privileged the strict association of "theory" and experience. As for Jacopo Contarini, he corresponded, on scientific matters, not only with Guidobaldo del Monte, but also with Francesco Barozzi, to whom he sent an elliptical compass designed by Giulio Thiene. Barozzi, who would illustrate the compass in the *Admirandum Illud Geometricum* (Venice, 1586) would call Contarini "another Archimedes of our age."[155] And we know that Giovan Jacopo Leonardi the Younger was educated "in mathematics and fortifications under the tutelage of Signor Guido Ubaldo de' Marchesi del Monte, count Giulio Thiene, and others."[156]

Francesco Barozzi and Jacopo Contarini clearly had different mathematical interests. Barozzi's *Opusculum*, published in Padua in 1560, includes his inaugural lecture of 1559 and two *Quaestions* regarding the application of mathematics to the sciences: it was, moreover, dedicated to Daniele Barbaro, with whom Barozzi was constantly corresponding;[157] not only Barozzi, but Giuseppe Moleto and Pietro Catena also participated in the epistemological debate that had begun in the Studio in Padua;[158] one of the specific concerns shared by Barozzi and Jacopo Contarini was an interest in the mathematical texts of Pappus—one of the Greek sources that the Accademia Venetiana intended to publish in 1558—translated into Latin by Commandino in 1574–75, but that Barozzi, in 1587–88, examined in the new codex that Contarini had sent to him for corrections.[159]

Their interest in Pappus of Alexandria is revealing. Pappus was, in fact, a fundamental author for Renaissance mathematics: his *Collectio Mathematica* contained not only an exposition of the analytic method of Archimedes, but also a treatment of the problem of the center of gravity. Guidobaldo del Monte rendered a significant homage to Pappus in the *Mechanicorum Liber*, while

Barozzi recognized that the knowledge of the center of gravity is fundamental for building both instruments of peace and instruments of war.[160] The theme of the *Opusculum* returns here (a theme that would be familiar to Galileo): Proclus had tried to reconcile Plato and Aristotle by combining the Aristotelian theory of scientific demonstration with the Platonic theory on the sublime character of mathematics.[161] The "return of Antiquity," in the context of Venetian scientism, was thus an instrument that facilitated the exploration of new cognitive statutes; it was an inquiry into the innovative possibilities of a mathematics that was removed from the realm of metaphysics and applied to natural sciences and technology. It was a tendency that boasted in Venice of a tradition going back to the fifteenth century—the tradition onto which Pietro Bembo had grafted his work: Francesco Maurolico had turned to Bembo in 1536, when he presented a project for the revival of Greek mathematics, and Bembo had extolled Fausto's quinquereme.[162] And if Barozzi's translation of the *Poliorcetica* by Hero of Byzantium seemed due to an exclusively historical curiosity, that of the *Geodesia* by the same author, and the volume *Admirandum Problema* of 1586 were dedicated to a practical use of science.[163]

Such studies quickly presented substantial problems of an epistemological nature. Barozzi, in the *Quaestio de certitudine Mathematicarum*, polemicized—to Daniele Barbaro's great satisfaction[164]—against Alessandro Piccolomini, who in the *Commentarium de certitudine Mathematicarum disciplinarum* published in Rome in 1547, had maintained that the "certainty" of mathematics does not derive from the logical power of its demonstrations, but from the abstraction of its objects instead.[165] In this way, Piccolomini had made Euclidean mathematics gnoseologically inferior to Aristotelian logic; in addition, he removed from mathematics all access to knowledge of the sensory world. This conception contained, however, something profoundly innovative. Piccolomini had, in fact, separated mathematical logic from traditional logic —a move that had been followed in Padua by Pietro Catena, who in 1556 supported the idea of a specific language for mathematics that would be autonomous with regard to Aristotelian syllogistics.[166] Francesco Barozzi reacted to Piccolomini's theses: *certitudo*, he responded, is "also" to be found in the syntactic rigor of mathematical demonstrations. And in the *De medietate*— included in the *Opusculum* dedicated to Daniele Barbaro—he maintained that mathematical objects occupy an intermediate place between divine objects and natural ones: in the end, the mathematical instrument becomes a logical system when brought into contact with cognitive processes.

It would be superfluous to emphasize that the epistemological debate, which featured Alessandro Piccolomini and Francesco Barozzi, and was followed attentively by Barbaro, formed the *humus* on which Galileo would later found his own methods of inquiry. Insofar as we are concerned, it is significant that Barozzi and Jacopo Contarini found themselves at the center of a "scientific rebirth" whose most famous patron was the Duke of Urbino, Francesco Maria II: a solid bridge linked the *Serenissima* to the milieu stimulated by the teaching of Federico Commandino—with a rather interesting historical consequence. It was Guidobaldo del Monte who recommended Galileo Galilei to Gian Vincenzo Pinelli (Galileo would obtain his chair in Padua in 1592), and Jacopo Contarini would remain in correspondence with Galileo until 1595, the year of his death.[167]

From Moleto to Galileo via Jacopo Contarini and Gian Vincenzo Pinelli, therefore: the scientific interests stimulated by Andrea Gritti, Pietro Bembo, and Giovanni Badoer, joined those of the Barbaros, of Jacopo Contarini, and Barozzi in identifying the development of mathematical and mechanical research as the instrument capable of significantly improving the quality of the *bellica disciplina* as well as of those operations that promoted the revival of the maritime State and the rational transformation of the mainland State.

The support that Pinelli and Contarini offered Galileo can thus be considered the last act in a series of debates and attempts that had featured Daniele Barbaro in the mid-1550s, and that had also included the participation of Giovan Jacopo Leonardi and Palladio. Scientific intelligence would, in reality, only affect the *Serenissima*'s institutions marginally. One should not, however, underestimate the effort made by humanistic culture, at that particular time, to place itself at the head of processes of transformation, to cross the barrier between classical philology and scientific experimentation, to define a logical frame for the problem of the verifiability of hypotheses, and to motivate the recovery of Antiquity.

But one notes a dichotomy in this area. In fact, the picture we have drawn so far appears too compact, and may create misunderstandings. The unity of knowledge defended by Daniele Barbaro, the technical practices recommended by Jacopo Contarini and Francesco Barozzi's epistemological research defined three strands of thinking, which were only superficially congruent. Barozzi's mathematics were in fact the culmination of metaphysical concerns: Barozzi intended to demonstrate the nobility of a knowledge that would lead to an understanding of speculative philosophy, given that—as he maintained in his commentary on Proclus[168]—the soul itself is endowed with a mathematical essence. And in the *Commentarium in locum Platonis obscurissimum*, published in Bologna in 1566 and dedicated to Gabriele Paleotti, the harmony unitarily connecting macrocosm and microcosm once again had mathematical characteristics.

In the thinking of Francesco Barozzi, as in that of Patrizi da Cherso, the number is not an abstract, pure, and absolute entity. On the contrary, it is the qualitative conception of mathematics that founds its discursive autonomy. And that's not all. One finds in Barozzi's work an epistemological sketch that does not exist in the work of Giuseppe Moleto or of Jacopo Contarini, with its concreteness unrelated to general visions. There is no doubt about it: the radical criticism that Gianni Micheli had made of the assimilation of Greek science by humanistic culture—a disdain for general theorizations and a fragmentation of the empirical[169]—is fully applicable to Venetian scientism. Instead of an interest in the paradigms of knowledge, there was a focus upon limited and practical themes: neither Vettor Fausto, nor Giulio Savorgnan, nor Jacopo Contarini escaped that tendency. After Daniele Barbaro, perhaps only Francesco Barozzi asked himself about *significati* [meanings]: and even he, in proposing a new attitude, held on to the Neoplatonic tradition, in order to safeguard the *harmonia mundi* and the metaphysical paradigm.

Keeping in mind these remarks, let us turn to a new problem. The friendship between Jacopo Contarini and Palladio was certainly justified by the interest that the architect's *usanza nuova* [new manner] raised among the patrician class. And yet, Palladio does not seem to have been involved in the defensive operations that interested Contarini so much. Palladio did, however, visit the Arsenal in 1560, as is testified by a letter of his dated July 31, in which he alludes to the construction of a galleon and reveals that he had designed its *fianco* [side] and *testa* [head]: it is interesting not only that Palladio entered such a jealously guarded construction area, but that the recipient of the letter was probably the Hungarian Tamás Nádasdy.[170] And a letter by Jacopo Contarini, recently discovered by Antonio Manno, reveals that Palladio was responsible for one of the Arsenal's buildings.[171] These were, however, occasional involvements, just as Palladio's involvement in military architecture was sporadic: on September 27, 1575, the Commissioners of Fortresses issued a document called a *terminazione*, which acquitted the *proto* Bortolo Luran of charges connected to work he had done on the fortifications of the Lido, after Palladio had completed an inspection of the site.[172] Which is not surprising. Palladio resembled neither Fra Giocondo nor Vettor Fausto: he was, instead, a "specialized" professional. The group we have defined was moving toward a specialization of knowledge that included a consistent use of technical skills. In the context of the mathematical and scientistic culture of the Venetian ambit, Palladio was the prototype of an artist endowed with a specific knowledge, and it is thus fitting to choose him as an *exemplum* we can contrast with the empirical praxis of the various *proti*. The battle against technological and cultural criticism focused the attention of Palladio's supporters, who could thus act for the particularity of that knowledge, for its specificity. Nor can one say that in Palladio—as in his supporters and patrons—*ratio* and "*isperienza*" were disconnected. There is no point, then, in contrasting Palladio with the figure of Nicolò Tartaglia's pupil, Giovanni Antonio Rusconi, a professionally dubious character, although he was not devoid of theoretical aspirations.[173] It was Palladio, in fact who "constructed" a verifiable architectonic language, in tune with the rigorous language that Giorgio Agricola heralded in his time for the natural sciences.[174] And in some way, Palladio's architecture was also in tune with the polemical pages by Francesco Patrizi da Cherso, who, in his *Retorica*, after praising the "divine Giulio Camillo," declared rhetoric itself to be empty and useless, annihilated by the "proud wind of reason."[175] Wherever laws are defined and order is established—in the *bene instituta* "happy city"—everything proceeds with a rigorous "dialectic": *geometricis necessitatibus*, as Garin has said.[176] Rhetoric, oratory, all those proceedings tied to the world of emotions and passions, rule instead in periods of crisis located under the sign of "license"—that is to say, whenever the people, with its "plebeian" and passionate soul, dominates. Palladio's art, even with its programmatic refusal of "abuses" and its olympian adherence to a universe guided by the "proud wind of reason," was undoubtedly the most capable of lending its own forms to the abstract "happy city" recommended by Patrizi.

One ought to realize that it was exactly because it was polemical and representative of "partisan" intentions, that Palladio's language was used to define prestigious urban margins—as was the case around San Marco—or to celebrate personal or familial events, as in the case of the facade of the church of San Francesco della Vigna. Palladio, unlike Jacopo Sansovino, would not be received in Venice as a "State architect."

The polemic between *architectus* and *proto*, between the formal language of the "scholar" and empirical teaching "*sine scientia*" would have a sequel in the final episode of the Rialto bridge. By 1587–88 the political climate had changed: in 1582–83 the victory of the *giovani* and the limitations placed upon the powers of the Council of Ten signaled a critical turning point for the "Romanist" line.[177] This did not prevent a "building expert" like Marcantonio Barbaro from still being assigned tasks of some importance; as commissioner for the bridge, Daniele's brother opposed Alvise Zorzi, and supported Vincenzo Scamozzi's project, intervening several times against Antonio da Ponte.[178] The anonymous memorial of August 1588, which may have been written by Scamozzi and was clearly influenced by Marcantonio, begins with a praise of architecture as science: "The knowledge of all sciences, faculties, and arts is born from their start and beginning to know the cause, because as Aristotle says, one sees in nature that in most things the cause can be seen from its effect." And then Vitruvius, Alberti, Pietro Cataneo, Maggi, Castriotto, Dürer, and the Sacred Scriptures are quoted.[179] In a report presented on August 29 of the same year, Marcantonio Barbaro wrote: "But that which bothers me no less is that it has become a practice in the world to make decisions with little public dignity and without the help of those who possess skill, to let the task be governed by a *proto* whose fitness for the job is not known to anyone."[180]

The *architectus* who "knows the reasons" is now Vincenzo Scamozzi, who is contrasted with Antonio da Ponte, a simple *artifex*: beyond the polemics about solutions with one or three arches, or the stability of already begun foundations, the issue was the conception of the bridge as *monumentum*, rendered accessible by an antiquarian means—Scamozzi's loggia—versus a solution that "does not speak Latin," that crowned the bridge with another emphasized and emptied-out *bottega* or shop instead of a "temple." The language of *ratio*, reduced to rhetorical speech, is contrasted with "dialect," with the *proto*'s empiricism. The victory of Antonio da Ponte and his vernacular on the occasion of the Rialto bridge was certainly not a matter of chance. Once again, however, we ought to avoid making quick judgments. Before lining Scamozzi's work up with the scientistic front whose traits we have synthesized, it would be wise to specify the results of the thinking that started with the encyclopedism of the Accademia Venetiana and the universalistic ambitions of Daniele Barbaro. And even before doing that, it will be necessary to confront an aspect of the relationship between technology and rhetoric that has been omitted so far, summoning two protagonists of the Venetian debate on the organization of the territory, on hydrography and the lagoons. We are referring to Cristoforo Sabbadino and Alvise Cornaro. We have divided and articulated our research in order to avoid an elementary reading that would see in the events of the sixteenth century a slow but sure triumphal march toward the "age of technology." But we will also use this articulation in order to evaluate the meanings that, in Venice's specific situation, can be attributed to special knowledges, at the end of the sixteenth and the beginning of the seventeenth centuries.

A Theater, "a Fountain of Sil," and "a Shapeless Little Island with a Hill": A Project by Alvise Cornaro for the Restructuring of the Bacino of San Marco

After the reflections made in the preceding chapters, it should not seem paradoxical that in the history of Venice in the early Middle Ages and of modern Venice two seemingly disparate themes—technology and the sacred character attributed to the *imago urbis*—turn out to be closely correlated. Transformation, in the "virgin city," is necessarily related to the "sacred origins" that cemented its institutions and its social structure: the various actions taken upon the stratification of the city that had welcomed the return of Solomonic Wisdom posed delicate problems of continuity and discontinuity, which were duly faced by the magistracies, the Senate, and the Council of Ten. And this brings us to another theme: that of *time*. The intricate problem that needs to be resolved, in Venice, relates to the plurality of time: how does the worldly and contingent time of technology and markets act upon the transcendent and providential time assumed as specific to the city's origin and destiny? Is the coexistence of different concepts of time—illustrated by the threefold image of "prudence"—compatible with the fractures and innovations that resulted from urban transformations? And lastly, to what degree did the cult of Venice's origins limit transformations?

We touched upon these questions when we analyzed aspects of the history of San Salvador: time dominated by inscrutable divine purpose became identified with Venetian time. The issue is a *topos* of official Venetian historiography. Venetian time—which Alberto Tenenti has intelligently discussed[1]—and the time of the merchant—which strikes throughout the entire city from the Torre dell'Orologio in the Piazza San Marco—tend toward a coexistence. Avoiding conflict, they strike in distinct but superimposable quadrants. As a result, limits —decisive ones, as we shall see—were placed upon the mercantile development in the worldly sphere, limits that also functioned, from the fourteenth century to the first half of the sixteenth, as an efficient element of internal cohesion. The private and public realms, in their differentiation as well as the identification between them presupposed by the Venetian constitution, were perfectly reflected in the unity/difference that universal time and mechanically marked time established in an urban microcosm in which the worldly and the sacred were seeking reciprocal confirmation.

We have been creating syntheses on the abstract level of diverging mentalities. Our analysis will now focus upon the way the image of time helped to define the role of technology. Our starting point, an obvious one, will be the passage that Daniele Barbaro inserted into the second edition of his commentary on Vitruvius's *De architectura* (1567): "Time, which brings every advantage and disadvantage, works in concert with two elements *to wage war against us* and do us great harm; I am speaking of the sea and the earth, one of which seems to want to recede and the other to occupy the space of this lagoon."[2]

Time, here, is no longer unitary. *Dimidiatum*, it can bring both good and evil; the latter is identified with the alteration of the natural equilibrium. Furthermore, since that equilibrium is one that was created *ab origine* [from the beginning] as deeply rooted as in Venice, there exists a time that acts in a destructive sense. From that we get the last function of technology: "to restore" corrupted naturalness. Time that destroys is not the ally—in the lagoons—of the barbarians, at least according to the interpretation of Daniele Barbaro—on the other hand, as we shall see, the "barbarians" existed for Sabbadino and for the ruling classes of Venice and the Veneto region.

Barbaro's thinking aside, there is the big problem of the struggle against *this* corrupting time. The specific function of applied sciences in this struggle and the problem of the interrelationship between the administration of hydrogeographic transformations and politics are the themes that stand out against the background of the debate that was sparked, in Venice during the sixteenth century, by problems pertaining to the organization of the lagoon. At first glance, the polemic that opposed the theses of Alvise Cornaro to those of Cristoforo Sabbadino seems to have only concerned the restructuring of waterways and the preservation of the lagoon. The conflict, rather, was between two different conceptions of territorial equilibrium, two different visions of the relationship between technical choices and political choices, and two types of economic interests.[3] And the terms of that polemic are incomprehensible unless one keeps in mind the fact that it took place between a "dilettante"—but one whose learning was nourished by frequent exchanges with philosophers and men of letters—and a *proto*, a functionary of the *Savi alle Acque* [Ministers of the Waterways] whose talent was indisputable and who had clear ideas on the need for highly specialized knowledge about hydraulics.[4] It was indirectly, moreover, that Cornaro's proposals attacked the limits deeply rooted in the functions of technology in Venice: many of Cornaro's proposals seemed to want to transgress those limits, to challenge the cautiousness of the Venetian ruling class and to lend scientific dignity to a hypothesis, prefiguration, or even utopian improvisation.

The historical failure of an organic policy for the waterways occurred against the background of this polemic. Salvatore Ciriacono has convincingly demonstrated that Venice lacked a balanced vision of the problems pertaining to the connection between the problem of preserving the lagoon and the problem of land reclamation and hydraulic operations in the territory:[5] a situation of backwardness—unlike, for example, the situation in Lombardy, which had begun developing an organic network of canals in the twelfth century—was followed by the works of the fifteenth century, which were characterized by delays, polemics, and excessive prudence. It would certainly be simplistic to see in Sabbadino—who was the heir of his father Paolo's experience—solely a spokesman for the importance of the lagoon, and in Cornaro—who seems to have picked up on ideas already expressed by Paolo Sambo[6]—a spokesman for the interest of the mainland. But it is indisputable that the terms of that polemic would have failed if the theme of the interdependence and balance of interests had already been imposed from a mainland perspective.

Venice demonstrated its desire to limit the potentialities of technology in favor of a "prudence" that favored firmly established solutions: this was amply demonstrated by the way in which Fra Giocondo's expertise in hydraulics was not fully exploited after 1560. It was against this kind of attitude that Cornaro was reacting: but this reaction was—we repeat—hampered by all his limitations as a dilettante. Moreover, he was defending particular interests, which he tried to present as general ones.

It was, therefore, no coincidence that Cornaro and Sabbadino's proposals regarding the *forma urbis* of Venice differed widely. The "naturalness" of Venice, which Sabbadino praised, did not exclude the potential enlargement of the lagoon's urban fabric. The new building grounds and the organization of building zones introduced instead, in the "plan" elaborated by Sabbadino in 1557, a rigid definition of urban boundaries (fig. 114): continuous *fondamenta* [a street beside a canal] encircled the city and a system of perimetrical canals ran along the shores, along the present Fondamenta Nuove and behind the Giudecca.[7] It has been observed that Sabbadino's new Venice grew out of itself,[8] while the Giudecca and the island of San Giorgio Maggiore ended up being more connected to the city than to the lagoon. These proposals were in many ways destined to remain the models for future developments: the final decision regarding the Fondamenta Nuove, which had been inspired by Sabbadino's plan, was reached on February 23, 1589 *m.v.*(= 1590); its supporters included Leonardo Donà and Marcantonio Barbaro (figs. 140–44, 147).[9]

We will have to return to this analysis of Sabbadino's *aricordo* [report] in relation to choices made at the end of the century. For now let us try instead to focus on the document that was presented to the *proto* of the *Magistratura alle Acque* [Ministry of the Waterways] in 1557: its most obvious characteristics aside (and they have led to talk about a prefiguration of the modern instruments of urban planning), this document can only be understood alongside Sabbadino's theories about the lagoon.[10] At the beginning, there is a mythical image of the primitive lagoon: Sabbadino describes—with the help of Strabo—a single lagoon extending from Trieste to Rimini. And the shores that separate the future *Rivoalto* from the sea do not yet constitute an alteration and betrayal of the primitive, perfect naturalness of this exceptional site. According to Sabbadino, they were the work "of the first Venetians in order to preserve nature with art."

With those words Sabbadino had already stated the function of technology: it ought to stress the work of Nature, it should not change or disturb. It is first called upon to "preserve," and then to "renew." In fact, the author was anxious to demonstrate the damage that had been done to the lagoon by both men and rivers. The former as well as the latter, he argued, had slowly reduced the expanse and depth of a lagoon that was divided into five sectors by the flow of the Po at Ficarolo (1152), with deterioration as a result: the water had become increasingly fresh and swampy, there had been changes in the fish population, the subaquatic vegetation had decayed and degenerated, while harmful deposits and amalgams had formed because of the elimination of maritime currents. Faced with this deterioration, Sabbadino could only denounce the political authorities responsible for the administration of the waterways: he exempted neither the patricians of Venice, who were bound to dilettantish and unplanned modes of procedure, nor the inexperienced experts, nor private individuals who—like Alvise Cornaro—had compromised public property with their embankments and mills on the rivers. Sabbadino wrote,

Whoever would like to document all the demolished places, the destroyed woods, the cultivated fields, and dried up canals that are between the old Brenta river and the Sille in the territory of Mestre, they will find it too lengthy to describe: let it suffice to say, that all the woods and those that were above Castelfranco, there where the Muson begins and passes until at the bottom all the cultivated lands have been ruined and made arid, and the same has happened to many fields, I say nothing of the other places on the Sille and the Piave, because that lagoon is as good as lost. . . .[11]

Was Sabbadino's vision restricted to the lagoon? Perhaps, but such an obvious criticism ignores the originality of his contribution, which seems to have mainly consisted in the expanded scale of his field of observation and prediction. The problem of the embankments—which he considered the cause of the high tide phenomenon in Venice—was linked to the problem of hygiene, which was in turn tied in with the central theme of his inquiries: intervention as "restoration."

The plan of 1557 was the natural consequence of these premises (fig. 114): the protection of the shores, the deviation of the river currents from those shores, and the removal of the obstacles that prevented sea water from entering the lagoon remained at the base of the project, which began with the necessity to excavate the port and the Grand Canal, and posed the problem of the reuse of the alluvia. Sabbadino unconsciously established a dialectic between "dirty" and "clean." The enlargements envisioned for Venice used the deposited mud as its basic material: the cleaning of the lagoon was translated into the production of new lands suitable for building.

Alvise Cornaro's proposals began with a point of view that was the complete opposite of Sabbadino's. Cornaro's reference points stood totally outside the lagoon: in fact, he envisioned a rigorous limitation of urban development, a shifting of interest onto agricultural territory, and attempts at land reclamation and hydrographic restructuring subsidized by the State. And, finally, he proposed an authentic new plan that would have affected Venice's overall image as well as the image of the Bacino of San Marco: the same area, incidentally, had already been indicated as the center of an ideal cosmography in a map by Benedetto Bordone, published in 1528.

In order to understand the meaning of this strategy it is necessary to keep in mind the meaning of Cornaro's entire plan for Venice. The "civil competition" he envisioned would have upheld the centrality of the mainland State in a territorial system that would have included subject cities as well as the *Dominante* with renovated and detailed functions. But he also had a broad economic perspective that would have affected the *Serenissima*'s destiny in a global fashion.

In order to evaluate that perspective, however, it is necessary to ignore a large part of the traditional literature that has addressed the issue of Cornaro's personality, and to reflect instead upon the well-documented new vision of Cornaro that has been proposed by Emilio Menegazzo.[12] The singular man who—after his failed attempt to be recognized as a Venetian patrician—lived in Padua "with the secret nostalgia for a lost paradise" was entrusted by the Republic with the task of neutralizing the anti-Venetian sentiments harbored by intellectuals and the nobility: the "Cornaro court," which included many proimperial elements—Falconetto and Ruzante among them—but was also frequented by the Venetian Rectors, was a symptom of that utilization.[13] Menegazzo also tells us that Cornaro, after his daughter's wedding in 1537, and the recovery of Venice as an ideal homeland, was in all respects "another man."[14]

But a violent crisis erupted in 1541. This was the conflict with the *Signoria*, which, with a sentence on November 23, 1541, imposed a cut of the embankments that Cornaro had created—in association with Agostino Coletti and Francesco Forzaté—in order to reclaim a few valleys in Santa Margherita di Calcinara. The land reclamation had affected the equilibrium of the lagoon: the embankments had subtracted an important surface from the increase of the tides. It was at that moment that the polemic with Cristoforo Sabbadino began; Sabbadino became *proto* in 1542, but in 1541 he had already interfered with the fortunes of the consortium that was placed dangerously on the margins of the lagoon.[15] Many of Alvise Cornaro's hydraulic theories seem to have been elaborated in order to defend the criteria used in that failed episode of land reclamation. The argument with Cardinal Francesco Pisani over the management of episcopal revenue in Padua, exercised after 1529 by Cornaro, led to the failure of 1541. But Menegazzo reached a drastic and determining conclusion after carefully analyzing the fiscal reports presented by Alvise Cornaro in 1514, 1518, 1544, and 1562: the extent of Cornaro's property, in spite of the way he congratulated himself for promoting land reclamation, remained substantially the same as what he had inherited from his uncle [*barba*], Alvise Anzelieri.[16] Menegazzo's research definitely invalidates the image—which had been offered earlier by Fiocco—of Cornaro as the author of an "agricultural revolution" capable of meeting "proletarian interests."[17] From circa 1545—after the deaths of Falconetto (1535) and Ruzante (1542)—Cornaro fought on two fronts: he increased the value of his own impoverished patrimony by pursuing a more rational division of land into farms, and he created an ideology—in the literary and scientific fields—that stood in place of what he had not been able to execute.[18] The stoic and epicurean ethic of the "sober life" and his love for the theater had a precise meaning in this sublimation. That ethic proposed a battle with time—the time of human life engaged in deferring death, which Cornaro "played" with when he continuously changed his own age in his writings.[19]

As for the theater, it was a world of simulations: Cornaro's entire self-conceit represented a *comédie humaine* that is more valid as a declaration of beliefs than as reliable testimony. But even these details do not tell the whole story. One still has to explain why Alvise Cornaro chose—among all possible self-images—the one of *homo faber*, victorious over nature and creator of reality (we are tempted to say *bourgeois*, but the term might be misunderstood). His technical proposals would probably not have benefited the lagoon, but he was an individual who—while seeking to turn his own particular interests into objective ones—sought ways of mediating between the needs of the mainland and those of the lagoon. The land reclamation that has so often been praised was in reality very limited, while a true interest in the populace and Erasmian visions of poverty were never parts of Cornaro's thinking.[20] But land reclamation and the accord between private interests and the interests of the State remained the cornerstones of Cornaro's ideology. We must resign ourselves to seeing him primarily as an ideologue: this shifts the orientation of our historical analysis, but does not empty the actual field of analysis of its contents.

It is on the basis of these premises that an examination of Cornaro's *aricordo*, or report, for the restructuring of the Bacino of San Marco can shed some light on a few interesting aspects of the cultural debate that took place in Venice in the sixteenth century. The work we are referring to—which can be dated to circa 1560[21]—takes on another special significance when we consider that it was preserved in a file of papers belonging to Gian Vincenzo Pinelli, whom we have already had the opportunity to mention because of the role he played in Padua at the heart of the scientism of Venice and the Veneto region.

It is also significant that Cornaro, in introducing his essay, recapitulates the proposals that he had made for the functional restructuring of Venice.

Having demonstrated the way to preserve the virginity of my dear native land and the name of Queen of the sea, which way is to preserve her port, and her lagoon, and then to protect her from a lack of bread by means of turning uncultivated places over to agriculture; and I have demonstrated the way to make her more beautiful, stronger, more secure, and to improve the good air; and I have demonstrated the way that she can go to sea always armed the way she is now, with the money, that she spends now in unnecessary expense; and furthermore I have demonstrated the way, virtuous and pleasing to God, in which her inhabitants may live long lives, and always remain healthy by avoiding overindulgence; and I have also not forgotten to demonstrate the beautiful way of building inexpensively, but buildings that will last a long time and be comfortable.

Cornaro thus expresses a real *summa* of his philosophy as an *introibo* to his new proposal: he intended in this way to demonstrate clearly how that proposal flowed from the inspiring motives of his previous positions.

The author goes on to describe his project: it consists of an extraordinary invention that would have radically redesigned the entire Bacino of San Marco, whose first element would be a civic repertory theater isolated in the lagoon (fig. 115). Cornaro was surely thinking of a theater *all'antica*, given that he spoke of a "stage setting that will always be fixed"—a *scaenae frons*, therefore—and of a "piazza that would in the middle be surrounded by steps to sit on, which would be so many in number that there would be a place for everyone"—a cavea—adding that "in that piazza the first steps would be at the height of the piazza, and eight feet from the stage at its level."

The theater he proposed had all the characteristics of a public institution; it was concerned with ethical issues and served the entire population: an educational theater, in other words, that would be humanistic in the fullest sense of the term.[22] "And the entrance would be open to all," Cornaro wrote, "which it is not now: and if one wants to enter now to see some festival by a company [*Compagni de Calza*] or to hear a comedy one cannot enter if one does not belong to the common people: something that has nothing to do with justice or honesty, but with partisanship." Envisioned as a place that might unify the urban community, Cornaro's theater extolled a program that promoted the moral value of "entertainment": as a consequence, Cornaro harshly criticized the favorite games of the common people, such as bull races, which he judged "ugly, low, and shameful."

Not coincidentally, Cornaro's theater made references to Roman *exempla*. "Of large and comfortable stones, for all those who go to such spectacles and festivals," in it "everyone would have his place and step, as though God had given it to him and nature required that everyone should enjoy it." The theater, a symbolic place that echoes the larger text of the universe,[23] becomes the gathering place of all social classes and a place of reflection and representation, above all, of the "natural and untouchable hierarchies" that govern the cosmos and the civil order based on those hierarchies.

Of "baked stone" and stucco, Cornaro's theater anticipated in many ways the Olimpico in Vicenza and probably had its cultural roots in the tradition of the Venetian *teatri del mondo* [theaters of the world], with reference, perhaps, also to the reconstruction of the Roman theater that Daniele Barbaro and Palladio proposed in 1556.[24] Cornaro, however, did more than propose a formal idea: he immediately gave recommendations for the organization of spectacles and their purpose. Thus, in the "piazza" planned for the center of the theater,

one can make bears fight with dogs; wild bulls with men and similar spectacles; but in addition one will see war being made: how it is done and made use of now in this City; that it is a very beautiful thing to see and very appreciated by foreign gentlemen; and the fighters will be armed with sallets and breastplates, and use sticks instead of swords, as they do now. . . . But furthermore, in this same piazza, one will be able to make water enter and exit easily, in order to have a fine sea fight there, as the Romans did, and it will be a fine war on water and will make men fit for combat, and for war.

The theater would thus be used to train citizens in military virtues. But it would also be a site of remembrance. Cornaro's evocation of ancient spectacles was significant, and it became even more remarkable because of the exceptional sight he envisioned for the theater: in the lagoon, between the Giudecca and the Custom House Point. In fact, Cornaro wrote,

And this edifice will be very lovely to look at and its location will be very convenient because it will be made on the bank between the Giudecca and the Custom House Point, there where the open sea comes up on the shore, coming up on the land so far that for a few hours of the day it is covered with water, and is more harmful than useful; because there will be even too much room for the water and all around that place there will be a large and beautiful embankment with steps, and banks so that one can conveniently disembark, and there will be so much space to embark, and disembark that it will not be inconvenient for the great number of boats, and this edifice will be easily seen when one is standing in the Piazza San Marco and it will be a very beautiful view and an edifice of a type that is no longer found in any other City, for where they were, they have fallen apart; even thus ruined they are beautiful to look at, and make one judge that that city was once big, and beautiful, and if, thus ruined, they are a sign of greatness, and beauty, what then will one think upon seeing it made, and made new again, when the others have been ruined.

Cornaro's interest in the theater went back to his youth, if one is to believe a passage of the Elogio. According to that text—which Menegazzo has convincingly attributed to Cornaro himself[25]—at the end of the fifteenth century,

. . . they decided to make a company, as was the custom in Venice, called a Compagnia di Calza, which was very beautiful and pleasing, and it was the first that performed comedies, which had not been the custom before in Venice, and they were performed by their members in a very pleasing fashion, and the intermezzos were similarly made by them of perfect music, beautiful and pleasing, because four of them had very beautiful voices and he [Alvise Cornaro] composed these songs and words and the comedies, which were filled with honest laughter, such that the group provided the city with lovely entertainment and pleasure for four years.[26]

Such were the beginnings of Cornaro's theatrical experience. It is clear, however, that the protection Cornaro offered Ruzante, the spectacles organized in the Paduan "court," the building of Falconetto's Loggia (1524), which was conceived as a permanent backdrop or proscenium [scena fissa], his relations with the Accademia degli Infiammati, and the theater built in Fosson at the mouth of the Po,[27] constituted so many chapters in a professional career that aimed at combining Vitruvian classicism with what Ludovico Zorzi calls the filone pratico-romanzo or practical and Romanist tradition.[28]

All this makes the proposal for a theater in the lagoon, which Cornaro formulated at a late age, even more significant. The proposal was most likely drafted in the years after Cornaro wrote the two versions of his treatise on architecture. In fact, in the first version—which Carpeggiani has tentatively dated to circa 1547[29]—Cornaro maintains that he will not write "about theaters, amphitheaters, thermae . . . because . . . these other buildings are no longer used"—a polemical statement of principle that he uses again at the beginning of his second version, which was probably written after 1556.[30] That which is considered outmoded in the *Trattato* or treatise is seen, on the contrary, in the text from circa 1560, as a fundamental element in the *abbellimento* or embellishment of Venice, indispensable to the renewal of the lagoon's cultural life. His idea, which had a very precise origin in antiquity, acquires special significance when one considers the fact that the proposed permanent theater would have placed Venice in the avant-garde in the field of performing arts. The entire history of attempts to revive ancient theater confirms this. Raphael and Sangallo's unrealized project for a theater at Villa Madama[31]—like Bertani's later court theater in Mantua (1549–51),[32] or the one designed by Vignola in the Palazzo Farnese at Piacenza—relegated antiquarian revival to the private sphere, while the structures erected in the Campidoglio in 1513,[33] those by Serlio Vicenza in 1539, and the ones built by Palladio in Vicenza in 1561–62 and in Venice in 1565 were all temporary. In Ferrara, furthermore, Pellegrino Prisciani, in the context of extremely advanced archeological research, had clearly distinguished three forms of classical proscenia and the mechanism of the *versatilis* stage backdrops; the drawings enclosed in the manuscript of the *Spectacula* of the Bibilioteca Estense di Modena (MS Lat. 466–a. 1. 6.) constitute significant attempts to restore the form of the ancient theater.[34] The hypothesis that Prisciani's studies had been conceived with the aim of building a permanent theater in masonry is certainly suggestive; but it is significant that not even the court of Ferrara felt obliged to execute what Sulpicio da Veroli, in the dedication of his edition of Vitruvius, had recommended to Cardinal Riario: the theater arranged by Ariosto in 1531 did not adhere to the principles upheld by the Vitruvian orthodoxy.[35]

The long humanistic battle for the revival of the public theaters of antiquity was significant: but equally significant were its setbacks. The spectacle tended to be confined into the artificial space of the courts, modeling itself on the needs of the courts themselves:[36] the space dedicated to the theatrical representation might accommodate the numerous interpretations of the urban space, but projected in the scenic illusion, and sublimated through the medium of perspective. The associations villa-theater and palazzo-theater, foreseen in the projects for Villa Madama and for the Palazzo Farnese at Piacenza, played upon the totalizing value that the form of the hemicycle *all'antica* introduced into these self-contained microcosms: especially in Vignola's project, it was the Bramantesque theatricality—that of the courtyard of Statues, as well as of the terminal structure of the Belvedere—that was recovered and translated into a new language. The primacy of "representation" remained. The space of social life, carefully protected in the court, already celebrated the importance of simulation with its architectural form.

It is probable, as Bruschi has remarked,[37] that the design of the so-called Coner codex for the Capitoline theater of 1513 reproduced an initial project with structures in masonry, instead of wood, like the ones later executed. This would give us the first attempted realization of a permanent theater, and one of notable historical significance given that the structure would have invaded the place assigned to the municipal powers.[38]

Alvise Cornaro, in Padua, did not reconstruct a theater *all'antica*: such an attempt would have been premature in the 1520s, and one ought to remember that a permanent cavea would have compromised the multiplicity of the Paduan "court." Furthermore, the philospher of the "sober life" seems to have considered the permanent theater as a public and urban structure par excellence. And it was such a structure that he considered in Venice, a city that did not know the evils of courts— in this connection, one recalls what Pietro Aretino wrote on the subject[39]—and that in the chorus of the theater might see a reflection of the mythical choral quality of its own ruling group.

A theater *all'antica*, rising from the water, would have also stressed the link between the specific spectacular quality of the city and antiquarian culture. Not only would the theater be the site of spectacles; it would itself become a spectacular object, while its placement in the lagoon would have endowed it with phantasmagorical and "estranging" characteristics. The evocation of the ancient theater—a metaphorical space that insists upon the principle of a "spherical vision" of the cognitive universe and that encapsulates the urban chorus—is completed *more veneto*: the edifice becomes a fantastic object, a theatrical apparition that could be appreciated *commodamente* or easily from the greater "theater" of the *Serenissima*, that is to say the Piazzetta.

It is also interesting to note that, at the time the proposal was made, the theater was in an extremely delicate situation in Venice. In 1559, Benedetto Palmio, one of the most active and authoritative members of the Company of Jesus in Venice, obtained from the heads of the Council of Ten the prohibition of "comedies that dishonestly are usually performed several times every year." Citing a letter from Father Edmondo Augerio, of January 13, 1559, Gaetano Cozzi has pointed out that the prohibition seemed to apply to carnivals only;[40] the episode did, however, signal a shift that reflected the supremacy in Venice, at that time, of conservative and devout patricians at the Apostolic See. Benedetto Palmio's request, in fact, tended to monopolize theatrical activities in Jesuit hands with a decree that must have been unpopular. Even though one cannot interpret Cornaro's theater as a direct reaction against that maneuver —given the uncertain dating of the document—the contrast between the Jesuit program and Cornaro's project is extremely clear.

One must, however, look beyond first appearances. The many difficulties that Latin and modern comedies encountered in Venice, together with the attempts to introduce a public theater, constitute a whole history—which has been explored by Giorgio Padoan.[41] The remarkable triumph of *Cherea* by Plautus and Terence, performed in the vernacular, provoked the following decision of the Council of Ten: on December 29, 1508, performances of "comedies, tragedies, and eclogues" were prohibited, especially those with a political orientation.[42] After recalling that the *Signoria* had always been responsible for "halting all those things known to be capable, in any way, of corrupting and depraving the good habits of youth," the decree of the Council of Ten went on to proclaim; "Therefore, since it comes to pass in this city, on the occasion of festivals, weddings, feasts, etc., and in homes as much as in places suited for such events, that comedies and comedic representations take place, in which many improper, lascivious, and dishonest words and deeds are spoken and shown through masked characters, and these things, which are beyond the expense of our citizens and are full of evils, may not be permitted . . . . "[43] Moralistic reasons were reinforced by the distrust of a style that had been introduced *a paucissimo tempore* and was becoming increasingly popular: Sanudo would write explicitly that Cherea "plotted to have the loggia of Rialto from the Commissioner of the Salt Office."[44]

The moralistic motive had already guided Ermolao Barbaro the Elder in 1455 in his *Orationes contra poetas*,[45] and would inspire the revival, in 1521, 1530, and 1533, of the prohibition decreed in 1508.[46] The political concern, on the other hand, slowly diminished with the increase of literary comedies that were filled with praises of Venice, expressions of reverence for the *Signoria*, and pleasing toponymic references.[47] Venetian comedy had asserted itself by extolling the abstraction of a game that was an end in itself: such was the price of a survival that had been forced to appease the suspicious attention of the institutions. Ruzante's old protector probably had a different conception of the social function of the theater: before we place Cornaro's proposal in the context of the history of Venetian performing arts, we should also evaluate it against the background of the resistance and prohibitions we have already mentioned.

In fact, in 1565 a chapter in the history of Venetian theater came to a close with the spectacle organized by the *Compagnia della Calza* of the "Accesi" [the illuminated or passionate ones] inside the "half theater of wood in the style of the Colosseum" built by Palladio.

It has been observed that the *Compagnie della Calza* were assigned a public role—which was to affirm the political presence in the city of well-defined aristocratic groups—although that role was meant to be performed under the watchful eye of the Council of Ten.[48] Nonetheless, the same year that the "Accesi" were established, that is to say in 1562, the Office of Commissioners for Pomp was reformed. It was a first indication that a decisive change was at hand. From that point on, the State would manage the policy of pomp more and more, even though it would continue to choose its "specialists"—as in the honors for Henry III—among such figures as the Barbaro brothers and Pietro Foscari. And perhaps there is some truth in the hypothesis that sees in the Republic's reappropriation of "State spectacle" a choice that should be related to Carlo Borromeo's edicts of 1565.[49]

Cornaro's project thus became part of the debate over the political role of spectacle: his insistence on the civic and moral duties of the theater and its placement at the heart of the lagoon become even more comprehensible in this context.

Let us continue our reading of Cornaro's text. Cornaro describes two more elements of his plan for the "embellishment" of the Bacino of San Marco (fig. 115) "a fountain of fresh and pure flowing water," drawn from the Sile or the Brenta, and an artificial island with a hill to be built on the *velma* or canal channel between San Giorgio and San Marco.

And this will be done with little expense, and very conveniently with the dredged soil, and mud that will be taken out of the Canals, and the hill will be planted with trees, and its streets will be made beautiful, and it will be a very beautiful place to go for amusement, and at its summit there will be a loggia open on every side and protected from the sun; and one will see this hill stand-ing in the piazza, where there will also be a fountain of fresh flowing water; and thus in one glance one will see fountain, hill, and theater, and between them many large ships, which will then be able to enter the port; and this will be a spectacle, and more beautiful, more charming, different from any other that has ever been seen, or that one will be able to see in the future in the whole world.

Two new islands, then, and a fountain: the latter, in order to be visible along with the islands, was presumably placed by Cornaro near the columns on the Molo (the quay near the Palazzo Ducale). The three elements formed, how-ever, a real visual triangle, one corner of which was placed in one of the most representative and emblematic sites of the city, while the other two stood in the water. Let us take a look at the fountain, which would have resolved a problem of Venice's that concerned Sanudo at the time. In the conclusion of his *De origine, situ et magistratibus urbis Venetae*, Sanudo wrote,

Everything is in abundance except fresh water, for Venice is on water and does not have water; there are wells in all the campi *of the neighborhoods, and in houses, but in times of drought they are consumed, and thus one sees barges full of water taken from five miles away at Lizafusina—which goes on the mainland—from the water of the Brenta with large cases that fill up the men-tioned boats, and one shouts: "Water way," and sold 8 buckets for a soldo; which in truth is laughable to be on water, and agree to buy it, and if it were possible to make fountains, I think it would never in the world be possible to equip the city of Venice.*[50]

In fact, a senatorial decree in 1425 established that the Brenta was the only suitable source of drinkable water,[51] and after 1460, with the contract and construction of the *carro* [cistern] in Lizzafusina, equipment that was excep-tionally important for the water supply was concentrated at that site. The Pesaro family focused its interest upon that equipment, and obtained the con-tract for the *carro*, the tavern, the washhouse for wool, the small canal, and the *gorne* [channels], thus impeding any measures that might have been taken to compromise its position of power.[52] We know that on August 5, 1448, the Senate elected a commission charged to examine the possibility of channeling water from the Brenta from Lizzafusina to Sant'Andrea *per conductam*; an analogous project was discussed in Pregadi on June 25, 1463, and a third motion to provide Venice with an aqueduct—which also had no result—was taken up by the Senate on January 14, 1490 *m.v.* (= 1491).[53] Sabbadino would also contribute his ideas on the subject. He recommended eliminating the embankment of Lizzafusina, in order to move the water supply installation further upstream:

Regarding the Venetian water supply I say that one can make its operation easier and more secure. One will be able to draw sweet water from Dolo with a channel and bring it to Moranzano, placing the lower end high enough so that

one can place barges beneath the ducts, so that opening by themselves, they will move quickly, and this will cut two miles off the trip and much time will be saved, rather than drawing water in Lizzafusina by hand and throwing it in ducts with conduits, would bring it here with great speed. In this way one would have easy navigation, easy drinking water, and overall the Brenta would proceed to the sea in an orderly way, as it did not do ab antico *outside the port of Brondolo.*[54]

Although Sabbadino did not have an aqueduct in mind, he attempted to solve a wide range of problems in an integrated fashion. But even the project of building the *carro* at Lizzafusina and of opening the Brenta to the movement of the sea, which was proposed again in 1561,[55] would not lead to any concrete consequence: consolidated interests opposed themselves tenaciously to any kind of change of the status quo. This did not prevent the problem of the water supply from being discussed from other points of view: in January 1546 *m.v.* (= 1547), Giovan Battista Zorzi presented a report to the Council of Ten in which the problems of the *cavation* or dredging of the canals and of the preservation of the lagoon were connected to the problem of supplying fresh water. In this document he states, "And in this way sweet water may be brought into the city and into lands under our rule in peace time at the expense of our *Signoria* with 200 water barges divided over six sectors upon the dredging of the ordained canals . . . and our purveyors of water should shift the cost to the inhabitants, beginning with the wells and especially for the fields of the parishes in peace time, in order to provide all with water in the way which best fits them."[56]

Furthermore, new projects for an aqueduct were proposed; there was one by a "German engineer," illustrated in 1554 by the ambassador Paolo Tiepolo with a letter to the Doge from Guglielmo de' Grandi (1578) and Antonio Lupicini (1582). Thus Cornaro's idea was part of a rather lively debate that was constantly entangled in difficulties that Temanza would call exquisitely political.[57] But while he considered the idea of using water from the Sile ahead of its time,[58] Cornaro once again transformed a theme of a technical nature into an object for aesthetic contemplation. He presented his fountain less as a public service than as a third *meraviglia* or wonder, a miracle of design, which would, along with the islands, make the new Bacino of San Marco "incomparable."

Let us try to compare Cornaro's plan—which remains exceptional in the context of the proposals for urban restructuring that emerged during the sixteenth century—with another plan, which he also drew up, that would have surrounded the Venetian lagoon with walls on a continuous embankment to be used for public parks and gardens (fig. 117). The idea of surrounding Venice with fortifications built in the water was certainly in line with its author's economic ideas: Cornaro saw agriculture as the salvation of the city and the State, with the consequent limitation of the role of the *Stato da mare* or maritime State, and the enclosure of the lagoon itself.

Cornaro himself linked his proposals for the Bacino of San Marco to those he had made for the entire city. In a document dating from circa 1566 (BMV,

Cod. It. 4, 172 = 5381)—which is also useful for the dating of the plan we are considering—Cornaro concludes thus:

And I remember that this city would be encircled by walls, on the embankment there would be woods, and this city would be adorned on the inside with a theater, with the fountain of Sile, as best possible, and with a shapeless little island with a hill, which, because they are beautiful things that can be made, I am certain they will be made, and I see it now, as though they had been made. Oh what a beautiful city I see, how it will be truly famous! Then its perfect air will be incorruptible and of a kind that does not exist, and there cannot be another in the world as beautiful as this one will be, and I who see it, and enjoy in my thoughts. Oh how admirably virtuous is thought, which makes us see things before they are made, and thinking of it I will enjoy it! Whence I now see that what remains of my life will be completely full of beautiful thoughts, and I will live happy and content, find myself free, as I am in everything, of my debt, which had been to be useful to my dear native city. . . .[59]

Cornaro combined his ostentatious declarations of patriotism with proud praise of his "plan's" virtues. He celebrated his programmed preview of the transformations of the physical environment as a *human* work, as *techne* or technical practices projected into the future, opposed to the traditional empiricism and "prudence" of the Venetian magistracies. Cornaro's audacious attitude reaffirmed man's capacity to intervene upon nature: this was the same spirit that animated Manetti and Bovillus's praises of *homo faber*.[60] The "plan," however, had an unequivocally playful meaning: *techne* was called upon to make a deep mark on the lagoon's appearance; but these technical skills were sublimated, which also made them different from the severe and pleasureless technology employed by Cristoforo Sabbadino.

These, then, were the limits of Alvise Cornaro's plan; we still need, however, to examine the individual proposals in relation to the mentality of the patrician class they addressed. This class had been called upon to renovate the city with extraordinary works and to promote eloquent and heroic technical feats, but it was also being recommended to them a complex series of actions that would have upset an urban order commonly felt to be the reflection of Venice's "political perfection." Moreover, one ought to keep in mind that the idea of constructing new islands within a perfectly defined Bacino or basin had already been formulated in an illustrated letter by Girolamo Fracastoro, who enthusiastically proposed the idea of transforming Venice into a new "Themestitan," isolated in a fresh water lake.[61]

It is obvious that the idea of isolating Venice in the middle of a lake was also provocatory from the point of view of Sabbadino's theses. Nonetheless, for the purposes of our analysis Fracastoro's reference to the city of Temestitan cannot be ignored: one can, in fact, deduce from the allusion a network of cultural referents not explicitly indicated by Cornaro, but that may have influenced him during the conception of his project for the Bacino of San Marco. The map of Tenochtitlàn, published in 1524 in Nuremberg, was probably a copy of the one, since lost, that Cortés enclosed with his fourth report to Charles V. Moreover, the map that was published in 1556 in the third volume of Giovanni

Battista Ramusio's *Delle navigationi et viaggi* (dedicated in fact to Fracastoro) derived from the engraving of 1524, which depicts a city located in the center of a fresh water lake, divided into islands and linked to the mainland by streets built upon embankments.[62]

The analogy between Venice and the city of the new world, established on the basis of a medieval type of iconography, was thus reinforced by Fracastoro, who in his letter imagines having the rivers run into a lagoon that has been abandoned by the sea. Furthermore, the Tenochtitlàn seen by the conquistadores had a structure that was undoubtedly similar to Venice's (figs. 116, 118): the houses have two doors, one on the street, the other on the water, while *calzadas* and *calles*, or streets, are interrupted by removable bridges, so that districts might be isolated.[63] Even more important, in the city described by Francisco Lopez de Gomara and Hernán Cortés, the water supply problem was resolved by means of an aqueduct constituted by "two pipes made of mortar," one of which was to be kept in reserve and used when the first one was being cleaned. In this way, the water reached "the heart of the city," where it was gathered in a large reservoir near the courtyard of the *gran cu* [great temple] in the *barrio* of Mexico, from whence it was then distributed by means of canoes.[64]

It is likely that Cornaro knew of this contraption, perhaps through Fracastoro. These descriptions of the new world seemed to be forming a challenge: Venice, the "city parallel" to Tenochtitlàn, also had to be provided with a network of fresh water canals. The fountain envisioned for San Marco seemed to respond to the example of the "great city of Temistian," which, in the map of 1524 as well as in those published by Bordone and Ramusio, clearly exhibit a rectilinear canalization that flows from the river into the *barrio* of Mexico (fig.116).

Thus Cornaro, in order to recommend a public work that Venice desperately needed, used its "wondrous" aspect as pretext. The consequences of this approach were not negligible: Venice was furnished with a *caput ad triangulum*, with "wonders" situated in the space opposite San Marco and convergent upon it, with scenery composed of both natural elements (the fresh water fountain, the small wooded area on the hill), artificial ones (the islands), and antiquarian ones (the theater).

There is more to be said here. The fountain brought into the city the image—dressed in rhetorical garments—of *Santa agricoltura* (the water of the Sile), while the wooded hill and the loggia open on all sides introduced an Arcadian note into the lagoon. But at the same time, the hill and the theater directed the eye from the Piazzetta toward the Bacina, almost as though counterbalancing the venerable architectural objects that crowd around San Marco. The lagoon was no longer an indifferent "empty space": it was to be considered a site "specific" to Venice, even though the fountain would assume an "alien" aspect in the context of San Marco, and the theater and hill would appear "estranged" because of their unusual placement.

Furthermore, the island with the hill and the theater did not disturb the lagoon in any way because they were placed on two *velme* or canal channels: on the contrary, the two new islands completed what nature had begun, making the most of the site as it had shaped itself over time through the hydro-geological processes. The *atteratione* [filling up] of the *velma* in the Giudecca canal had already been proposed by Nicolò Zen (1550) and had been accepted by Sabbadino, but in Alvise Cornaro's document it assumed the value of a magical metamorphosis. The operation, however, was congruent with the appeal for "naturalness" that Cornaro made in his writings on the lagoon. As for the fresh water fountain, it demonstrated one of the principles of Cornaro's hydraulics: Cornaro, in his writings, wished to keep fresh water and salt water, land and water, quite distinct by reestablishing their original separation. The entire system, therefore, appears to have been a demonstration by theatrical means of the principles that inspired Cornaro's solutions for the "preservation" of the lagoon—a system whose polemical aspects would not disappear even in the broader context of Venetian urban politics: the insistence on the public nature of the required systems recalls the continuous park that Cornaro imagined would accompany the development of the walls that would stand at four hundred paces from the city, *confianchi, bastioni et porte* [with flanks, bastions, and gates] (fig. 117).[65] Even the trees planted on the embankment were destined for the public: the new ring-like park would serve "to go for lunch, for supper, and for different walks," and would also provide a filter to renew the lagoon's air and a reserve of wood in case of siege.

The idea of furnishing Venice with walls was not only questionable on a technical level, but also undoubtedly heretical with regard to the ideal image that the city had built for itself over time. In his *De orgine urbis gentisque Venetorum historiae*, Bernardo Giustinian had written: "This peace, this security both from land and sea needs neither walls nor gates, the inaccessible marsh and unconquerable passage are the island's well-tested protection from the shore." And Sanudo had also said: "[Venice] does not have any walls around the city, nor gates to close at night, nor does it guard itself as other cities do, for fear of enemies."[66]

The waters, then, functioned as Venice's walls. This was the theme officially consecrated by the inscription Egnazio had dictated for the seat of the *Magistrato alle Acque* in the Palazzo Ducale:

The city of Venice / benefiting from divine Providence / was founded in water / surrounded by water / with water for walls. / Thus, whoever might dare / in whatever way / to bring injury to these waters / must be judged enemy of his country / and receive a punishment not less / than that meted out to one who violates his country's walls. This law has been reckoned eternal.[67]

It was not by chance, therefore, that Navagero stated, "All contemplate the admirable and most secure site of this city, whence no army, no power, no enemy may come, closed as it is from all by the sea; for it is said that this city is impregnable and that Venice can only be reached if the attackers have a fleet sufficient to come by sea."[68]

Michele Sanmicheli, finally, in drafting his plan for the defense of Venice in 1535, had excluded all conventional models of fortification: in harmony with the site and its ideal representations, Sanmicheli proposed to "make all around the swamp a very long canal with a very big rampart made of earth."[69] And

Francesco Sansovino, when he made the following statement in 1561, seemed to be responding to Cornaro's utopian and provocative plan: "As Venice is an impossibility, therefore, she came to be placed in the impossible, being founded in the sea, because in this respect she is unlike all other cities."[70] In other words: Venice, a utopia that has become a reality, has no need of utopias. On the contrary, Alvise Cornaro wanted to force the "impossibility" of Venice. A fantastic inspiration, which was in its own way the heir of the fabulous recollections of the *Hypnerotomachia Poliphili*, was guiding his proposal.

But there is another way of reading the improbable Venice surrounded by walls in water. Thus circumscribed, the city would not only be robbed of its particular image, but would also be "put in prison." Walls surround and constrict, but also make the dominant city resemble urban structures on the mainland. From every point of view, the intention that seems to have guided Cornaro in his proposals for Venice was fatally destructive: the intervention resolves itself in a reformulation that justifies the *imago* and the organism as they had been formed over time. A programmed reification, then, was the final result of the project for walls surrounded by a ring-like park and the idea of placing new islands in the Bacino of San Marco.

In fact, Sabbadino's idea of a Venice that would enlarge itself by using the *deiezioni* or detritus produced by the dredging of the reclaimed lagoon was contrary to Cornaro's proposal of a limited Venice, fixed within itself. He opposed a playful use of the mud to Sabbadino's "productive" use. And he responded to a reformulation that took complex functional requirements into account by exalting a single site, which he transformed into a scenic space.

One reads, on the other hand, the sonnet that Cristoforo Sabbadino dedicated to Venice:

You know how great your walls were,
Venice, now you see their condition;
For if you don't look to their upkeep,
You will find yourself alone and without walls.[71]

For Sabbadino, the walls of Venice were to be identified with the lagoon's hydraulic equilibrium: other artificial defenses were not necessary. And not sufficient. In his *aricordo*, or report, of 1549, Sabbadino gave a significant anthropomorphic reading of the lagoon itself:

. . . The head is the place where the shores are situated; and that part toward the sea are the arms, which give it life; and its doors are food; the legs that keep it standing safely are the canals, lakes, and receptacle of salt water situated outside the central body of that lagoon, in the canedi *[waterways] and toward the mainland. The heart is the city of Venice. The liver on the right side is the city of Chioggia. The lungs are the districts of Torcello, Mazorbo, and Burano. The veins are the canals within the central body of the lagoon. The flesh, bones, and nerves are the various foundations of this lagoon. In order for this body to stay alive, beautiful, healthy and hardy, one must preserve it in its entirety, with all its parts, interior as well as exterior, and continuously give it life, and also keep its breath clean, good, and sweet-smelling. Its food should*

really be salt sea water, which she receives every six hours, and throws back after six hours como padito, *which is the increases and decreases of the sea, which go out through the gates and enter in it.*[72]

The lagoon, therefore, was for Sabbadino an organic and dynamic whole. His anthropomorphic version, which extended to the territorial whole, contrasted forcefully with Cornaro's proposal, which envisioned a diking of the lagoon in order to separate fresh water from salt, but also to protect the reclaimed lands placed on the edge of the lagoon from damage inflicted by the *soracomuni* [high water tides].[73] Cornaro's project for the diking the lagoon thus had its rhetorical correlative in the project for the walled enclosure that would have encircled Venice. Unlike Sabbadino, Alvise Cornaro did not limit himself to enunciating hydraulic theories: he continuously felt the need to *give shape* to technical operations. In other words, for Cornaro technology did not possess its own language; in order to take on eloquent garments, it had to resort to rhetorical garments that were validated by visual poetics. The "reasons of the earth" here found a particularly obvious limit.

Cornaro's action thus turned out to be "unpolitical." Or rather, while pretending to determine very radical programs in an autonomous fashion, it compromised the dialogue with the forces appointed to care for the city. The daring project for the Bacino of San Marco was the sign of a desire for transformation that was completely different from the spirit behind Sabbadino's plans. And the question is certainly not which of the two—Sabbadino or Cornaro—was the more "modern" or farsighted. This needs to be stressed: Cornaro's humanism tended to intervene with instruments typical of a "free" and nonspecialized intellect; the *proto* acted responsibly as the technician of a magistracy keenly aware of the ruling class's changing opinions. The dialogue between Cornaro and Sabbadino thus became the model of a debate between two different kinds of "planning," in which the interpretations freed by humanistic conscience were obliged to measure their maturity and efficiency.

We are aware, however, that the phrase "humanistic conscience" constitutes a dangerous generalization. In this specific case, Cornaro's humanism needs to be defined in relation to the architectural culture it seemed to be addressing. In 1560, Palladio began his design projects in Venice, first for the Convento della Carità and the refectory of San Giorgio Maggiore, while Sansovino's Library was being decorated on the inside—although the structure was limited to sixteen bays. Michele Sanmicheli had died about a year before; Guglielmo de'Grigi also died in 1550. It was not the right time to undertake great decisive interventions for the restructuring of the *forma urbis*: until 1565–66—when the design and execution of the Palladian church of San Giorgio Maggiore began—Palladio's contribution to the city would remain hidden from the public eye.

It is obvious that Alvise Cornaro had a degree of architectural competence: his treatise, Francesco Marcolini's dedication for Serlio's *Libro*, and Serlio's own words provide proof enough of this. In fact, it has been possible to attribute to Cornaro the completion of the Odeon in Padua and the second level of the Loggia—perhaps with the assistance of his friend Andrea da Valle—and even the original idea for an exceptional work, such as the Villa dei Vescovi in Luvigliano.[74]

Let us retrace the lines of Cornaro's thinking for the Bacino: in essence, it exalted a coordinated relation of heterogeneous elements, intuitively identifying a scale of planning that went beyond the definition of any single object. This certainly was not normal architectural practice in the sixteenth century. And if we ask ourselves about the sources that Cornaro may have mentally turned to, the answer we come up with is almost too immediate: Serlio's codified scenography, which, through the instrument of perspective, tended to dominate the multiplicity of the city, the plurality of forms, and the coexistence of structures. Cornaro stresses this in his text: the new Bacino with its fantastic islands would present itself to the eye "all at once." The words used in the description of the project imply a desire to create a visual shock. The perspective from the Piazzetta would open onto a kind of *visual utopia*, which would not presuppose any social utopia at its base. Even with regard to architectural culture, therefore, Cornaro seems to have been implicitly polemical; he even attacked the limits implicit in the cult of the finished object. His dilettantism facilitated this conceptual extension, which was confined immediately thereafter to the limbo of hypothesis for its own sake.

Nonetheless, some of the elements in the plan for the Bacino of San Marco originated through an analysis of Venetian reality that was not completely superficial. The theater isolated in the water seemed an emblem for the city of Venice itself: theater and city displayed their perfection, their uniqueness. And there was a second miniature representation standing opposite it: the wooded hill crowned by a loggia. The lagoon was thus transformed into an ideal "garden." One should, in fact, not forget that the *De re rustica* by Marco Terenzio Varrone, which Cornaro was well acquainted with in the Venetian edition of 1472,[75] describes the territory of a villa traversed by a river, which has a *museum* at its upper end and an island at its lower end, where one river flows into another.

The small hill crowned by a loggia has a vague Palladian flavor, but also brings to mind a drawing in the Codex Saluzziano by Francesco di Giorgio Martini (fig. 25): at the center of a small lake, placed at the center of a *barco* [a walled park] and tangent to a small river, Francesco di Giorgio placed a hill dominated by a "block of houses from which everything might be seen and judged." He then continues: *altezza che le loge a occupare venghi* "And around this a sloping circular garden with paths following the shape of a snail shell, crisscrossed with trees and pergolas, but not at the same height as the building."[76] The mood of the description evokes Alvise Cornaro's project. But the motif of a small hill crowned by a loggia-belvedere had its roots in the garden architecture that had developed in the late 1550s: what is strange is the idea of situating that hill in the "ideal lake" of the Bacino of San Marco. And yet, Venetian painting had often represented a wooded island placed imaginarily in the Bacino: Vittore Carpaccio's *Leone di San Marco* and Sebastiano del Piombo's *Morte di Adone* provide particularly significant examples of the theme—which does not mean that Alvise Cornaro had these specific examples in mind when he wrote his *aricordo*. What we are dealing with, rather, is a chain of images that were probably connected by the typical migrations of figurative thinking.

Whether one interprets the "shapeless hill" as the sacrarium of Venus, or sees it as an allusion to Olympus, Cornaro's singular idea retains its romantic and unreal character. With his hill, Cornaro seems to be referring to a literary *topos* that, from Poliziano to Pietro Bembo and Ariosto, identified in the *hortus conclusus* an Edenic spot, a site of eternal springtime outside the flow of history. Those writers had offered a literary image of the Golden Age that was closed to the world; Cornaro's project ostentatiously brought that image into the city with an ideal recomposition of the contrast between *civitas* and nature that had been so dear to Petrarch and Alberti.[77] The new landscape he recommended was both urban and natural: the encounter gave rise to a "moralizing" scenography. The theatrical function was thus extended to the entire space of the lagoon, opening a theme that would later take shape first with the building of the Palladian churches, and later with the Chiesa della Salute. But one ought not to force the analogy: the spatial and temporal dimensions of Cornaro's Bacino seem appropriate for what he was trying to evoke.

The hostile time feared by Daniele Barbaro was ignored here. And rightfully so, given that Cornaro was one of those responsible for the corruption of the lagoon, according to Sabbadino's theses. On the other hand, another conception of time made its appearance here: an artificial time, determined by the work of transformation and exalted as such. *The project* assumes an autonomous value: significantly, Alvise Cornaro could contemplate his own prefiguration with satisfaction, and see a work complete unto itself, which did not need to be verified by reality. The projection into the future detached itself from sacred time as well as from mathematically determined time, expressing *another time* for itself. Within that time, still imprecise, technology took on fabulous semblances. The theater, the fountain, and the hill seem to come out of a fabled world, different and far away: and Cornaro's text makes them face San Marco as surreal objects, involving them in a hermetic dialogue, of which one can, however, understand the words that belong to the language of humanistic certainties as well as the new words belonging to the language of the subjective imaginary.

Appendix to
Chapter 6

Document by Alvise Cornaro on the San Marco Basin. ASV, "Savi ed Esecutori alle Acque," busta 986, filza 4, cc. 23–25.*

Havendo dimostrato il modo, che vi è per conservare la virginità a questa mia cara patria, et il nome di Reina del mare, che il mode è con conservare lo suo porto, e la sua laguna: e per ripararla poi dal mancamento di pane con lo mezo di ridurre luoghi inculti a coltura; et ho dimostrato il modo che vi è per farla molto piú bella, piú forte piú sicura, e di migliorarvi il buon' aere: et ho dimostratoli il modo, che essa ha per poter tenere in mare continovamente altretanta armata di quella c'hora tiene, con lo dinaro, che hora la spende in spesa non necessaria; et oltra li ho dimostrato il modo virtuoso e grato à Dio, che li suoi habitanti possano vivere lungamente, e sempre sani fugendo la crapula: et non ho mancato ancora dimostrarli il bel modo di fabricare con poca spesa, ma fabriche che habbiano a durare lungo tempo, e commode.

Hora dimostrerò il modo, che lo suo popolo sí il grosso come il minuto tutto potrà godere delli solazzi e belli spettacoli, che si faranno alli suoi tempi: sendo necessarij per conservatione dell'huomo, e si lasserà quello brutto, e basso, e vergognoso del toro, et in luogo suo se ne faranno de belli, et honorevoli, et che ogni sorte di popoli potrà vederli, che ognuno haverà lo suo luoco e grado, sicome gli ha dato Dio, e la natura cosí bisogna, che ognuno lo godi, e il modo sarà con fare uno theatro di pietra grande, e commodo per tutti quelli che vanno à tali spettacoli e feste: e saranno le intrate aperte a tutti, che hora non sono: e se uno vuole entrate hora a vedere qualche festa de compagni de claza, o per sentire una comedia non può entrare se non è dello populo grasso: cosa che non tiene nè del giusto nè dell'honesto: ma del partigiano. Adunque per fuggire questi errori si fara un Theatro di pietra grande, ma non di pietra da scarpello: ma di cotta, che non costerà la metà, e sarà opera durabile come di pietra da scarpello: perché la cotta hora che si ha trovato il stucco si instuccherà; e come si vede tal stucco si converte in sasso perche e fatto di sasso; e per commodità se farà in piú anni: e con questo se fara un habitatione per li signori che vengono a vedere: Questa veramente maravigliosa Città, la quale sarà publica, e commoda, sí come hora non è alcuna publica, e le compagnie di calza si potranno accomodare per fare le sue feste, e recitare le sue comedie, e tragedie: perché vi sarà la scena che starà sempre fatta, e lo luogo da recitare, e da danzare, e nella piazza che sarà nel mezo circondata da gradi per sedere, che saranno tanti in numero che ognuno haverà luogo; et in tale piazza i primi gradi

* The present transcription corrects and completes the one provided by Mangini, *I teatri di Venezia,* pp. 26–28.

saranno alti da quella, e dal suo piano da 8 piedi; et in tale piazza si potrà fare combattere orsi con cani: tori selvaggi con huomini, e simili spettacoli: ma oltra quelli si vederà fare la guerra: come hora si fa, e si usa in questa Città; che è cosa molto bella da vedere e molto appretiata da signori forestieri; e li combattenti sarano armati di celata e corsaletto; e bastone, e non con spade come hora fanno; e non si potranno ferire con far sangue ma ben saranno caricati di bastonate su li brazzi, e gambe cosa che sarà molto piacevole, e bella da vedere: ma oltra in quella medesima piazza si potrà facilissimamente far intrare l'acqua e uscire, per poter farvi uno bello navale come faceano Romani e sarà un'altra bella guerra in acqua et un fare gli huomini atti al combattere, et alla guerra, e tale edifitio sarà molto bello da vedere, e sarà in luogo molto commodo perché si farà su la velma che è tra la Zueca, e la Doana, la in quello largo atterrando tal velma, che è tanto atterrata, che poche hore del dí sta coperta di acqua, e nuoce piú che non giova: perché allora vi sarà pur troppo luogo per l'acqua et attorno tal luogo vi sarà una fondamenta larga e bella con li gradi, e rive per potere commodamente smontare e sarà tanto lo luogo da montare, e smontare: che non sarà incommodo per la gran quantità di barche, e tale edificio si vederà commodamente stando nella piazza di San Marco e sarà un bellissimo vedere et edifitio che non sarà piú in altra Città, che dove ne erano sono stati disfatti: pure cosí ruinati fanno bei vedere, e fan giudicare quella Città per città che sia stata grande, e bella, e se tali ruine sono inditio di grandezza, e bellezza, che sarà questo vedendolo fatto, e fatto di nuovo quando gli altri li ruinano; e la spesa sarà di ducati cinquantamila; et oltra tale bello edificio che molto ornerà la Città se potrà condurvi facilmente una fontana di acqua dolce viva, e pura, et in diversi luoghi di essa, oltra la piazza di S. Marco, e molto adornerà essa Città, e la farà maravigliosa, e si condurrà con poca spesa si del Sile come della Brenta togliendola all'alta; et oltra per fare che la sia la piú bella Città, e piú compiuta, che mai fusse altra né potesse essere si farà un monte sopra la velma, che è tra 'l monasterio di S. Giorgi, e S. Marco e questo se farà con poca spesa, e con gran commodità con li ruinazzi, e fanghi, che si cavano delli Canali, il qual monte se pianterà de arbori, e se vi faranno le sue belle strade, e sarà un bellissimo luogo per andarvi a solazzo, e nella sommità haverà una logia aperta da ogni banda coperta per lo sole, e tal monte si vederà stando nella piazza, nella quale vi sarà ancora una fontana di acqua dolce, e viva, e cosí ad un tratto se vederà fontana, monte, e theatro, e tra queste molte navi grosse, che alhora potranno entrare per lo porto: e questo sarà un spettacolo, et una prospettiva la piú bella, la piú vaga, la piú varia d'ogni altra, che mai s'habbia veduta, ne che si possa vedere per l avenire in tutto 'l mondo: et è ben ragionevole: non sendo stata, ne per essere mai altra Città nel mondo simile a questa, né vergine come è questa, che niun'altra è in tutto 'l mondo che sia vergine: laonde si potrà nominare allora per capo del mondo per le sue belle qualità, e fortezza che mai ne fu una simile: e queste cose io ricordo hora perché le veggo facili da poter fare, et in poco tempo et ho trovato il modo del dinaro senza interesse, ne spesa del publico, ne del privato: ma con utile de molti che accresceranno intrata come dimostro in un mio trattato delli luoghi inculti.

Renewal and Crisis. The Debate on the *imago urbis* between 1580 and the Interdict

All the themes we have been considering underwent a kind of precipitation during the last decades of the sixteenth century. Traumatic events—such as the plague of 1576–77[1]—and the urgency of choices that were creating deeper and deeper divisions—the institutional crisis of 1582–83 and the growing tensions with Rome—made a shuffling of the cards inevitable, as roles were reformulated and the relationships between powers, technical practices, and traditions were redefined. Moreover, the question of the role of knowledge underwent a decisive test, while, once the episode of the Interdict was overcome, the need for choices regarding the future of the *Serenissima* in the international sphere presented itself in a dramatic way.

It would be rather easy, but schematic, to say that the *giovani*—the anti-Romanist patriciate anxious for the Venetian system to incorporate new religious and economic currents—were responsible for the direction of the innovations that transformed the appearance of the lagoon city from circa 1580 to the first decades of the seventeenth century. What is certain is that the game that unfolded in Venice between the crisis of 1582 and the Interdict represented the litmus paper that tested the difficult relations between *novitas* and the cult of continuity, while the dramatic aspects of the battles and their results demand standards of judgment suited to the positions involved.

We need to take one step back in order to begin. The crisis of the Venetian aristocracy had become obvious—in spite of the economic vigor and artistic triumphalism of the *Serenissima*—soon after the war of Cyprus. The political price that Venice had paid on that occasion had been very high: in order to conduct that military operation, the Republic had been forced to compromise with the more reactionary elements of its patriciate and of the nobility on the mainland. Furthermore, the decline of administrative activity and the abandonment by the lagoon's aristocracy of mercantile activity went hand in hand with the Republic's renunciatory attitude in foreign politics and with its compliance toward the Holy See and Spain.

One can understand the ethical and political rigorism of the *giovani* only if one considers this weakening of customs and this renunciation, which, even if they did not concern the entire papalist and oligarchic patriciate, had a strong influence upon Venetian life in the second half of the sixteenth century.

Let us now abandon the general political picture, and shift our field of observation, in order to concentrate on the large-scale urban transformations operated by the public sector beginning in the early 1580s: that is to say, soon after the shock of the plague and during the tenure of Doge Nicolò da Ponte. For now, let us simply enumerate completed projects and unexecuted designs. In 1580 there began a series of events that would lead to the completion of the Library and the Procuratie Nuove (figs. 131, 134), thereby introducing a new and lasting iconography of the Piazza (fig. 132); around 1585–88 a hypothesis was discussed—and rejected—for a new building that would have housed a few of the functions of the Palazzo Ducale beyond the Paglia bridge; the design of the new Prisons began in 1580–81, with a resumption of construction in 1589 (fig. 119); the construction in stone of the Rialto Bridge began in 1587–88, thereby concluding a debate that had started in 1502 (fig. 127): in 1588–90 the Fondamenta Nuove were begun (figs. 140–44, 147); beginning in 1579, a series of building operations strengthened and refurnished the Arsenal. And we can add to this list a territorial work that was in some way connected to this new fervor for transformations, that is to say, the project for the city-fortress of Palmanova (1592–93) (fig. 120).

Many of these operations implied large-scale urban restructuring. The construction of the Rialto bridge was connected to the rebuilding of the zone between the Grand Canal and Campo San Bartolomeo; the Fondamenta Nuove opened up a new and unprecedented patrimony of unbuilt lands. Let there be no doubt about it: the works we have listed are interconnected, and spell out a great process of urban renewal that was supported by a precise intention. It was a process that combined incomplete and limited programs together; this is clear. There is, however, no doubt that we are dealing with a climate different from the one that had characterized the decades that followed Andrea Gritti's tenure as doge. Almost simultaneously, a complex of restructuring projects decided by various magistracies invested Venice with functionally innovative works that were completed with relative rapidity. The perplexities, the setbacks, and difficulties—often deliberately created—that had interrupted or compromised the Grittian *renovatio* now seemed abolished by a precisely elaborated intention.

But to what purpose and with what global or sectoral results? Take, for instance, the case of the Rialto Bridge. On the one hand, Marcantonio Barbaro and Vincenzo Scamozzi, on the other Alvise Zorzi and Antonio da Ponte. We have already recorded this conflict in our analysis of sixteenth-century scientism in Venice; behind the polemics over the static stability of the bridge, we have recognized the expression of a late phase of the struggle between the empirical concerns of the *proto* and the humanism of the *architectus*. But what was this humanism reduced to in the Scamozzian project with three arches? One could respond with a series of predetermined and peremptory postulates. The "natural" perfection of the round-headed arch, the indication of the bridge's axis with a temple-like loggia, the citation, in the aedicules at the base of the piers, of the Augustan bridge of Rimini—these elements that qualified Scamozzi's design (RIBA, 8/10) reduced *scientia* to norms validated by archeological knowledge and were assumed as invariants devoid of internal flexibility (fig. 122). The abstract completeness, "without time," of Scamozzi's bridge also rejected—like the Palladian projects, but without their polemical *vis* or force—all dialogue with the existing construction, nor did it permit any links with the future one, on the side of the Campo San Bartolomeo.[2]

And in the anonymous memorial of 1588, almost certainly written by Scamozzi, *scientia* itself is legitimized by authority. Cultural oppression is united with dogmatism: "According to the laws of the mathematical sciences it is said that parallel lines do not enclose any surface . . . since the Holy Scriptures say that all disjoined and divided things are consumed and resolved in nothing, because they do not have a single center and an equal foundation."[3]

Facing this *scire per auctoritatem*, which was not very Galileian, stood the *proto's "perizia"* (expertise) and adaptability. But this is not all. As Donatella Calabi has demonstrated, what was unresolvable for Scamozzi's finished project was possible for Antonio da Ponte's empirical procedure:[4] it was Da Ponte who demonstrated that he was capable of responding to the client's demands, while keeping in mind—in the first project—the decision taken on January 7, 1588, regarding the new alignment of the bridge (figs. 124–125). And a reexamination of the question, in September of the same year, would try to resolve the delicate questions imposed by the subdivision of the area on the side of the Campo San Bartolomeo.[5] The bridge and restructuring of this zone, above which stood the properties of the Patriarcato, the *Signoria*, the chapter of San Bartolomeo, and private individuals, constituted, for the *proto* and his assistants, a unique problem that could be resolved through successive adjustments and compromises. Their realism turned out to be conducive to a delicate operation of restructuring: empirical concerns, in this case, with the flexibility they entail, eliminated the severity that the refined syntaxes of Palladio and Scamozzi opposed to initiatives of economic transformation and revaluation.

The restructuring of the zone between the bridge and Campo San Bartolomeo, which was scenographically resolved by Contin on the basis of the plan minutely studied by Da Ponte, actually came out of a choice made by Alvise Zorzi (fig. 127). On August 30, 1588, Zorzi—demonstrating a concern for the reuse of urban structures that was not shared by Marcantonio Barbaro—supported with particular energy the need to proceed with the requalification of "the entire district of Cannaregio."[6] The problem was the recovery and economic revitalization of degraded urban areas; Antonio da Ponte's studies of the areas situated at the bridge's end were only partial responses to the larger problem that had been raised (fig. 123). Alvise Zorzi di Benetto thus expressed a position that was the complete opposite of Marcantonio Barbaro's,[7] and that in some aspects agreed with the position that Andrea Dolfin, Antonio Querini, Andrea Morosini, and Leonardo Donà would later take with regard to Piazza San Marco. For now it will suffice to observe that the Rialto question raises various historiographical issues. First of all, it indicates that the traditional scientistic current was drying up: the *architectura* defended by Scamozzi was shown to be evasive and incapable of dealing with the processes needed to modify the urban situation. Secondly—and this is more relevant for us at this point—in the debate held between 1588 and 1590, special attention was paid to the role played by the public sector in the restructuring of the lagoon city, which becomes all the more interesting when one considers the fact that Alvise Zorzi prefigured an intervention of vast dimensions that can be paralleled with less obvious operations such as the construction of the Fondamenta Nuove and the reshaping of Piazza San Marco.

One ought, therefore, to note the following: on the one hand, there were initiatives meant to revitalize the urban economy, restructure dilapidated zones, organize the road system and functional zones, and plan the growth of the city; on the other hand, there was an interest in the places chosen by governmental magnificence, and attempts—never realized—to reform particular institutions, such as the prisons.[8] At the same time, moreover, works were launched for the reorganization of the State arsenal (fig. 105). As Ennio Concina has demonstrated, between 1579 and 1581 the old programs for the development and rationalization of the Arsenal received new stimulus: on May 9, 1579, the Senate discussed the rebuilding of the *teza longa* [large work shops] of the Tana or the rope factory; on March 6 the question of isolating the arsenal by means of canals was raised again; in November 1580, proposals were formulated for the organization of the area that had once belonged to the monastery of the Celestia, the Isolotto, and new covered stairs.[9] Furthermore, in 1582 duties were rationally subdivided among the three Patroni and all the buildings under construction were placed under the supervision of Antonio da Ponte, who was the *proto* of the Magistracy for Salt. It is the political imprint of the entire operation that interests us here. Insisting upon the doge's mathematical and scientific interests, Concina has properly recognized in Doge Nicolò da Ponte and his entourage—the innovative member of the *giovani*—the source of this revival of the State arsenal.[10] We will eventually have to consider this phase of the Arsenal's development in relation to the organizational decline that would take place within it only a few years later. For now, we ought to note the remarkable initiative of renewal programs for functional situations and structures so distant from each other—the Piazza and the Arsenal—in the same years and under Doge Nicolò da Ponte, the patrician who opposed Roman pretensions and who directed the choices limiting the power of the Council of Ten in 1582–83.[11]

We can at this point attempt to reread all of the operations completed in the urban body of Venice beginning in the early 1580s not as an abstract summation, but as a chain of events that came out of a precise political and economic project whose specific character needs to be identified. As we have seen, the *renovatio urbis* of the end of the century focused on the eloquent sites of the institutions and on the places of technology and building speculation; in Venice especially the aspects in question were tightly interconnected. And, on a territorial level, with Palmanova, it was the security of the Republic that became eloquent, in spite of the tormented way in which the new military city came into being.[12]

The rapidity with which such operations took off and their simultaneity reveal an intention that was in some way common: the quarrels punctually broke out—as we shall see in a few particular cases—on the *method* of the work. Is it legitimate to think that in the Venice of the *giovani* there existed at least a rough design for the revival of the *Dominante*? We will try to examine the Venetian political situation in light of this question.

The protagonists of the various operations seem to have come from the ranks of the papalists as well as the *giovani*: Marcantonio Barbaro and Jacopo Foscarini—the latter especially was clearly a conservative—played determining roles in the redefinition of Piazza San Marco; Barbaro also fought Alvise Zorzi on the question of the Rialto bridge and played a particular role in the definition of Palmanova; Leonardo Donà—the leader of the *giovani* before he became the *defensor urbis* during the months of the Interdict—was present in a minority position in the debate over the Procuratie Nuove; he was also in the *zonta* [an additional council] that assisted the *Magistratura alle Acque* [Ministers of the Waterways] in the initial phase of the Fondamenta Nuove, and he participated in the decision regarding Palmanova. One may also recall that Donà had been the main person responsible for choosing the site of the Cappuccini on the Giudecca for the votive church of the Redentore: a choice that had been explicitly aimed against the Jesuits.

We cannot, at this point, avoid considering Paul Grendler's thesis on the overall significance of the jurisdictional and political disagreement that pitted the Republic against Rome in the decades preceding the Interdict of 1606–7. We should immediately say that Grendler tends to play down the oppositions between the *vecchi* and the *giovani*, [older and younger generations] or rather, he gives a reading of their differences that seems limited when compared to Gaetano Cozzi's, for example.[13] According to Grendler, Leonardo Donà's ethical rigorism was congruent with Carlo Borromeo's life principles: there was total disagreement only over the direction for the realization of Christian society.[14] Furthermore, Grendler maintains that absolutist theories exerted a fascination upon the Venetian patriciate "as it would have upon any other governing class in Europe."[15] He writes that "During the period of the Interdict, Sarpi and the theoreticians close to him deduced, from the divine origin of the State, the responsibility of governments alone in front of God."[16] Thus, the increasingly close ties with the Holy Office are for Grendler less a sign of a new, "partisan" orientation than a phenomenon emerging from a renewed awareness of the State. Grendler's thesis is to be compared with the complex debate on the models of government that took place during the Interdict as well as with the fierce contrast—justified on an evangelical level—that Giovanni Marsilio drew between hierocratic absolutism and *res publica*.[17] Absolutism, in its oligarchic forms, might have seduced those patricians siding with the Pope, and—only as an exaltation of the autonomy of the State—may have influenced those defenders of the "government of many people" who were opposing the Pope.[18] Grendler's hypothesis can, however, provide us with some helpful clues. One can add the constellation of work sites mentioned above to all the information we have on the political and social life of Venice in the 1580s: coinciding with the institutional crisis of 1582–83, but not strictly dependent upon it, the two opposing factions seemed to have been in agreement on at least one basic principle, regarding the revival of Venice on an international level. And the recovery of the sovereignty and autonomy of the State was certainly an integral part of this revival. The exaltation of the dignity of the procurators and of San Marco—the emblem of Venice's religious autonomy—coupled with the renewal of the *platea magna* or main Piazza, the strengthening of the productive capacities of the Arsenal, and the economic revitalization of the Rialto and the northern section of the city—these three initiatives can be understood perfectly within the context of such a plan. The dividing lines emerge instead, and very visibly, when we analyze the events that took place on the construction sites. The conflicts explode when we go to interpret their meaning: at the Rialto, in the Piazza, and in the Arsenal. The policy opened to Europe and to new political, religious, and economic outlets was opposed by the policy of rhetoric or of straightforward conservation proposed by Jacopo Foscarini and Marcantonio Barbaro.

Thus our program of research is mapped out for us; it will focus on three cases that were significant in different ways: the new buildings at San Marco, the project for a new dogal building facing the Bacino, and the Fondamenta Nuove.

1. The Debate on the Procuratie Nuove and the Form of the Piazza San Marco

The operation that began in 1580 (fig. 132) and that involved the Library of San Marco, the new wing of the Procuratie, and, finally, the image of the entire area around San Marco was certainly the most explicit and eloquent with regard to the program hypothesized above (figs. 128, 134–136). But it ought to be said immediately that in this case especially, the compactness of the built forms conceals the complexity and contradictions of the motivations and debates that conditioned their birth. This concealment is so complete that more than one historian has been sidetracked by it in his research: the typological structures of the Procuratie Nuove have been analyzed, as well as their variations over time, the figurative choices, and the history of a few details, [19] while attempts to read the meaning of the new piazza have been almost futile, because of the absence of adequate philological analyses. On the other hand, philology has almost never been constructed in order to respond to the questions that emerged from the surprising course of the building of the Procuratie themselves, especially in relation to the final work done on the Library and parallel to the debates over the Rialto bridge.

It will therefore be necessary to reorganize the analysis, starting not with the object but with the interplay of historical facts. The compactness of forms will be broken in light of documents that speak of the long battle that took place between parties that interpreted the *renovatio* of the *Serenissima*'s Piazza in opposing ways: as we shall see, politics entered with its own specific languages in the area of symbolic representations on an urban level. And the conflict was not of minor importance, as it concerned the *imago* that the Romanists faithful to the Curia and the fierce supporters of Venice's jurisdictional autonomy intended to give the renewed city.

In September and December 1580 two complementary decisions were taken: the first had to do with the definitive transfer of the Beccaria [meat market] from its position next to the Zecca to Santa Maria in Broglio, which permitted the enlargement of the Library that had been decided upon in 1565; the second had to do with the Procuratie (figs. 129–31).[20] In May 1581 Marcantonio Barbaro was elected commissioner for the new buildings:[21] Daniele's brother, once Palladio's supporter, thus assumed a central role. On January 15, 1581, the Procurators of San Marco formulated an initial program, after completing surveys of the entire Piazza and having discussions with the "experts." It was thus recognized that

. . . *one could do nothing better, nor more according to the true reason of architecture, than to continue the line of the building to meet the Palazzo that has already been started with so much art, and following it straight toward the* hospidaleto *extend it to the head of the piazza near the path to San Moisè, so that one sees that with much prudence, and judgment, and with the best advice, [it] was thus designed by the preceding ministers of Their Most Excellent Signorie, nor could this otherwise be brought about without great destruction of the completed portion of the piazza, where it is nearest to the church of San Marco, which should remain the most important object in the entire mass of this present deliberation.*[22]

Thus Sansovino's Library was recognized as the result of the "true reason of architecture," while it clearly emerged that an overall plan had already been *dessignato* [designed]. This may have been the one mentioned by Francesco Sansovino.

Furthermore, the entire space of the new Piazza was called upon to exalt the church of San Marco, which was, as we have seen, an emblem of the Republic's autonomy. The formal transformation was thus not supposed to attack, but to reinforce meanings that had become mythical.

On February 26, 1581, Cristoforo Sorte was paid for a survey of the site of the new building,[23] and on March 12 it was decided to begin tearing down the Ospizio Orseolo and two of the procurators' old houses.[24] On June 4, Simon Sorella, *proto* of the Procuratori de supra, was entrusted with the construction of the new Procuratie, "exactly in everything the model that will be chosen by their most excellent *Signorie*";[25] on June 6 the three procurators chosen for the buildings—Marcantonio Barbaro, Andrea Dolfin, and Federico Contarini— once again considered the need to begin demolishing the "Ospedaletto" in order to build two houses;[26] on April 5, 1582, Vincenzo Scamozzi's model was finally chosen over those by Simon Sorella and a stonemason named Francesco.[27]

Thus Scamozzi appeared on the scene, already recognized by virtue of his projects for the Rocca Pisana and the Palazzo Trissino al Duomo in Vicenza; more important, he had recently returned from a trip to Rome and supported a *res aedificatoria* founded on an undoubtedly amazing cultural background.[28] How can one explain the choice of Scamozzi for a building of such importance for Venice? Clearly, he presented himself not only as the heir of "true" Palladian architecture, but also as the holder of superior *scientia*. The favor he encountered among patricians like Marcantonio Barbaro and Jacopo Contarini is completely explainable, especially when one takes into account the letter that Girolamo Porro, the promoter of Scamozzi's *Discorsi sopra le antichità di Roma*, published in 1582 as a preface to that volume, addressing himself to Jacopo Contarini. Porro recalls that Scamozzi, as early as November 20, 1581, had composed in a few days the chapters illustrating the engravings of Battista Pittoni, specifying

. . . in addition to the work on the present discourses, he [Scamozzi] was continuously studying in order to help others not only by designing every day very beautiful buildings wherever he was asked, but also with his writing on architecture and perspective, his main professions. In one of them, which is perspective, he has composed many books adorned with many drawings, which your most illustrious Sir has seen with great pleasure and satisfaction.[29]

Jacopo Contarini—who would later take Scamozzi's side in the quarrel over San Nicolò da Tolentino[30]—was already acquainted with Scamozzi's lost treatise on perspective: there are traces of the relations that existed between the architect and Palladio's old supporters, which can be directly related to Scamozzi's victory of 1582. And, in fact, Vincenzo Scamozzi seems to have exhibited, with the volume of the *Discorsi*, his own credentials as a theoretician and a "Romanist," confirming the tendency that had been revealed by his two illustrations of the thermae of Antoninus and Diocletian (1580) and the substantial annotations of Daniele Barbaro's edition of Vitruvius.[31] Scamozzi's erudition and antiquarian theorization, his practical experience on the construction site, and the geometrical rigorism of the buildings he had already designed made him—also due to his ability to promote himself—a "natural" ally of the scientist and Romanist patrician culture.

And, as such, he was used by Marcantonio Barbaro in the transformation of the Piazza San Marco and in the case of the Rialto bridge. But let us proceed in an orderly fashion. First of all, regarding Scamozzi's first model for the Procuratie: from the 1582 estimate for the first four vaults of the new procurators' houses one can easily deduce that the project was at the time faithfully following Sansovino's Library, even in the number of stories.[32] Furthermore, the building was not supposed to begin with the Library—the site had been occupied by the Procurators' old offices, which are clearly visible in Gentile Bellini's *Processione in Piazza* (fig. 133)—but with a site adjoining the Ospizio Orseolo: as we shall soon see, moreover, the old offices were still standing in 1596 and became the subject of bitter controversy.[33]

Nonetheless, on July 11, 1584, a new contract, which had already been discussed in February, was approved, while in January of the same year Scamozzi was paid another 100 ducats for "various designs and models."[34] The documents indicate that the beginning of construction was delayed. For what reason? Did the project of 1584 still have two stories or did it already have three, as is suggested by a document of September 27, 1587? Let us carefully look at this document, for it gave rise to discussions of fundamental importance.

The most illustrious sir Marcantonio Barbaro Procurator having presented that a few of the most illustrious Procurators his colleagues doubt that raising

*the Library by another story to conform with what has already been decided
for the rest of the new buildings adjacent to it, regarding which sir Barbaro
intending that one should proceed securely, he has proposed to the most illustrious sirs Emo, Foscarini cavalier, his colleagues Contarini and Amulio, that
the said foundation should be reviewed by experienced persons; thus Simon
Sorella proto of the Procuratia was called before his most Excellent sir who
said to him that it had been agreed to excavate next to these foundations a
place which should be designated in writing.*[35]

In 1587, therefore, the Scamozzian project being used for the Procuratie
Nuove had three levels, and Marcantonio Barbaro would try to make the
Library conform to it as well.

The respect that Sansovino's work had earned in 1582 had turned into open
criticism; the object of this criticism was not only the height of the Ionic
frieze—"corrected," with obvious disdain for Jacopo's error, in the second
level of the Procuratie—but also its overall appearance (figs. 128, 134). This
criticism would lead to the controversial intervention upon the very structure
of the Library. How, when, and why was such a solution proposed?

Let us shift our analysis to the events that surrounded the continuation of
the Library. After the decision of September 1580, there is no indication of any
construction in the records of the Procuratia de supra: the entire focus seems to
have been shifted to the buildings on the Piazza, construction of which would,
moreover, remain at a standstill until 1584. On September 3, 1582, Scamozzi
was paid for "designs and models for the construction of the new buildings";
these may have also included the new section of the Library, given that estimates for the first work on it were published soon after.[36] One can, however,
deduce from the estimate for the foundations that the idea of adding another
story had not yet been suggested at that point, given that the measures prescribed were "like those done in the rest of the said building that is already
done."[37] On the other hand, by October 20, 1582, a project for a Library with
three levels must have already been completed, given that Antonio da Ponte,
Simon Sorella, and Scamozzi were asked to examine the terrain on which the
Beccheria was being constructed, "also considering that we will need if possible to make another order or story above."[38] The three agreed that the terrain
was suitable for the new foundations. But Scamozzi's written judgment, between elegant technical and antiquarian disquisitions, stands out from the
others because of its explicit reference to the "idea of your most excellent sirs
of placing the third Corinthian order above."[39]

Who was responsible for this *pensiero*? It seems more than likely that, in
October 1582, an attempt—initiated by Marcantonio Barbaro and realized by
the "virtuous architect"—was begun to restructure the entire project of the
Library and the Procuratie. Sorella's survey was, in fact, favorable but vague,
while Da Ponte completely ignored the problem of the third order.[40] Furthermore, that the new idea created doubts and embarrassment is clear from the
fact that from 1582 until September 1587 it was laid aside, in order to be
suddenly placed on the agenda once again, after it had become clear that the
problem concerned the entire group of buildings on the piazza, which were

now included in a single project. In the fall of 1587 construction on the Library had just about reached the entablature of the second order: the decision could no longer be postponed. But now Simon Sorella presented a new survey of the foundations (October 13) that was no longer favorable to a third order.[41] It has been suggested, in order to justify the *proto's* change of opinion, that Sorella was envious of Scamozzi:[42] but such *invidia*, or envy, on Sorella's part is not very credible, given the cultural distance that existed between the two men and their distinct roles. It is much more likely that in 1587 political opinion had turned against Marcantonio Barbaro. The fact remains that Scamozzi and Antonio da Marcò only presented their surveys on December 6.[43] If the first reproduced the one already formulated in 1582, the second revealed unexpectedly the reasons behind the disagreement: the construction of another story for the Library was necessary "in order to accompany the rest of the houses that are designed to continue around the Piazza." And this was not all: Antonio da Marcò, proving himself even more Scamozzian than Scamozzi himself, criticized Jacopo Sansovino's "heretical" Ionic entablature, which he indicated as the cause of the building's structural weakness, in that "building the upper part of the structure bay too heavy and wide, [and] without sufficient piers and connections, for this reason it was affected."

It was Andrea Dolfin who requested new surveys.[44] This gives us clues about the faction that opposed Barbaro and Scamozzi: we will consider it in more detail very shortly, but one must immediately reflect upon the fact that in 1596 Dolfin would ally himself with Antonio Querini and Leonardo Donà in an interesting attempt to rid the Piazza of Scamozzi's work. And Donà and Querini's position within the more radical wing of the *giovani* is already well known and does not need to be reiterated here.[45]

The opposition was for a time disguised by technical surveys. On February 2, 1587 *m.v.*(= 1588), Simon Sorella, who was increasingly siding with Marcantonio Barbaro's enemies, finally expressed the substance of the problem: ... but what matters, as I have other times humbly said, is that if the above mentioned buildings are raised with another order, the church of San Marco, the Zecca, [Mint] and other most noble buildings of the Piazza San Marco will be suffocated by such height. . . ."[46]

Scamozzi's project for the *renovatio* of the Piazza was thus blasphemous with regard to the "sacred" preexisting structures: it did not respect the decision of January 15, 1581.

At this point, the controversy involving the buildings around the Piazza became enmeshed with that of the Rialto Bridge, of which Marcantonio Barbaro became commissioner on December 10, 1587, along with Jacopo Foscarini and Alvise Zorzi di Benetto. At the Rialto, Barbaro, as we have already mentioned, encountered Zorzi's tireless opposition, and the Scamozzian project that he defended would be set aside in favor of Antonio da Ponte's project. Da Ponte himself presented a survey that opposed the alteration of the Library on April 22, 1588.[47] The issue would no longer be that of the struggle between the *architectus* and the *proto*. Sorella and Da Ponte limited themselves to technical considerations, but precise groups were forming behind the opposing opinions: Alvise Zorzi's voice was joined by those of Andrea Dolfin, Antonio Querini, and Leonardo Donà.

After a last request for surveys was submitted to the master stonemason Bortolo and to Antonio da Marcò[48]—a request that was surely made by Marcantonio Barbaro in answer to Antonio da Ponte's survey—the debate was finally closed in Pregadi on September 7, 1588. ". . . it was resolved by those present that this corner and the bays of the said new construction should be finished by our Procurators of the Church of San Marco according to the manner and height of the rest of the construction and the aforesaid Library."[49]

Marcantonio Barbaro and Scamozzi were thus defeated, at almost the same time, in the case of the Library as in the case of the Rialto. The coincidence is significant. It confirms the hypothesis of a mature stance against the ideological program that was in both instances proposed. And although one cannot confirm that Zorzi or the Procurators opposed to Barbaro were aware of it, in both cases Scamozzi's dogmatism was targeted—a dogmatism that had been inefficient in the case of the bridge and destructive in the case of the Library.

The decision of September 7, 1588, thus unblocked the deadlock that had existed in both construction sites in the Piazza. On September 10, 1589, it was made known that "the new offices of the Procuratia would soon be finished,"[50] and on July 2, 1590, the Procuratori de supra decided to install the Grimani collection "in the library and nearby school."[51]

As a consequence of the completion of the Procuratia's new offices, it was decided to proceed with the demolition of the old offices neighboring the Library on the side of the bell tower (figs. 132, 133). But now the conflict, which had been controlled, broke out: in all the subsequent events the opposing parties would confront each other with unusual clarity, so that we can document our hypotheses with the political concerns that emerged from the debate.

The argument broke out on August 16, 1590, when Andrea Dolfin attempted to stop the demolition of the old offices—an act that was clearly meant to prevent Scamozzi's project from being completed.

The offices of the new Procuratie being brought to completion, such that it would be easy to move into and inhabit them and with all floor tiles, doors, and windows already taken from the old Procuratie and installed in the new and the empty spaces remaining, it being the intention of their most illustrious sirs that the said old constructions should be destroyed, the most illustrious Procurators, six in number (the most illustrious Barbaro being absent), have decided that they should be destroyed bit by bit, that it should all be brought down from the bell tower as far as the wall of our Procuratia. . . . The most illustrious sir Andrea Dolfin ordered that the following agreement should be noted and carried out—That for reasons expressed by his most illustrious sir to his most illustrious colleagues the demolition of the construction should be suspended for now.[52]

Andrea Dolfin—who had probably tried to profit from Marcantonio Barbaro's absence—was beaten by five votes to one, but on September 17 he once again began to polemicize against Federico Contarini, the commissioner and treasurer of the Procuratia de supra. Once again, Dolfin tried to put off the demolition of the old offices of the Procuratie, "... declaring... that one must first remake houses and shops which are threatened by ruin along [the street of] Merceria in San Zulian, according to the conclusion of the assembled Procurators last October 29...."[53]

Once again Andrea Dolfin found himself in the minority. What was the reason behind this evident and repeated attempt to place in discussion the form of the Piazza San Marco—an attempt that was thinly veiled by the pretext that San Giuliano was in more urgent need of work? One can easily explain Andrea Dolfin's gesture by looking at the positions taken by the various parties six years later, in August of 1596, when the construction site of the Procuratie Nuove became the object of much more worrisome and explicit criticism.[54] The discussion—which was concluded on September 28—was in the Pregadi this time, and there were three positions: the first was taken by Jacopo Foscarini, Paolo Contarini, and Hieronimo da Mula, who were urging the continuation of Scamozzi's buildings "in the way that they were begun, and in the same form, and situated like those that one sees."[55] This position was opposed by one proposal to invalidate completely Scamozzi's design, and another proposal "of compromise." Significantly, Andrea Dolfin had now allied himself with Andrea Morosini, Antonio Querini, and Leonardo Donà. What in 1590 had simply been an isolated attempt at disruption became, in 1596, a politically defined group taking a position against Scamozzi's project. These were the *giovani*, now, who were making their opinions known to the public; the date of the new decision was significant, given that the previous year, 1595, had seen the death not only of Doge Cicogna, but also of Marcantonio Barbaro, the supporter of the "Romanist" and Scamozzian line. Also striking is Leonardo Donà's presence among Andrea Dolfin's allies. One should keep in mind the personality traits of the patrician who would, as doge, guide the *Serenissima* from 1606 to 1612: Donà operated, as magistrate, with a rigorousness that bordered on political ascesis; he avoided patronage, corruption, and cliques, abhorred pomp and luxury, and his definite anti-Romanism was combined with a deep, interiorized religious sentiment, appreciated as such by Agostino Valier.[56] He had already, in 1583, convinced the Senate to reject a proposal for an alliance proposed by the Holy See and Spain, and in 1588 he opposed the request for the creation of Venetian cardinals because he wished to avoid all dependence, in matters of interest or morality, upon Rome.[57] His position was thus opposed to that of the families tied to the Holy See, like the Barbaro, Grimani, and Corner families: Giovanni Grimani, Patriarch of Aquileia, would always consider Leonardo Donà his personal enemy.[58] And, in the *Historia delle differenze fra Paolo V e li Signori Veneziani*, Giuseppe Malatesta would write about Donà, "... with himself, never allowing himself either immodesty, or license, or any intemperance, he was always rigorous; he disdained wealth, rejected gifts, abhorred pleasures, in short, sought in austerity the praises of Cato, in poverty those of Fabricius."[59]

As for Antonio Querini, who later wrote a *Historia della scomunica*, one ought to recall the function that Morosini's *ridotto* or private salon played Interdict, placed him, along with Nicolò Contarini and Alessandro and Alvise Zorzi di Paolo, among the more important adversaries of the Church.[60]

Andrea Morosini's position, on the other hand, was more moderate: but one ought to recall the function that Morosini's *ridotto* or private salon played in a Venice that was ideologically rearming itself, and Paolo Sarpi's participation in the reunions held there is not to be underestimated either.[61]

We can thus approach the ideas of those who supported the decision opposing the Scamozzian project by looking at the document itself.

Our Procurators de supra were heard several times in our Collegio, regarding the construction of the houses, that now need to be built in the piazza for the residence of the Procurators, part of them intending to continue these houses by making them in two stories, raising them by a third over our Library that borders on the said houses, and the others saying that the said buildings should agree with the line of the Bell Tower, as it was before, with the order of the façade that are the buildings in the part of the Clock Tower, alleging that in this way it would not only afford greater comfort and number of residences, but ornament to the said piazza, and furthermore that the expense would be less than around 240 thousand ducats, and these houses would also be built in less time, as the experts have assured us, and the model of their construction presented by our most dear noble Procurators Zuanne Mocenigo, Ferigo Contarini, and Andrea Dolfin. However there will be a resolution that the Procuratori de supra should have these houses made in line with the Bell Tower, according to the above-mentioned model spending the money of their Procuratia, uniting itself with the building begun as the drawing shows, the houses of which need to be reduced to a height of two stories, and the façade similar to the part of the Clock Tower, for the ornamentation of this piazza; which also will be done with less expense and time, as our experts have faithfully sworn.[62]

Had this decision been passed, Vincenzo Scamozzi's project would have been eliminated once and for all: once again the "good sense" of the experts would have opposed the reasons of *architectura*. But the substance of the disagreement laid elsewhere. In the absence of the plan for the link with "the started building" that the document mentions, it is difficult to reconstruct the intentions of the proponents of this delicate architectural node. One thing is certain: not only was the appearance of the old buildings preferred to Vincenzo's project, but the entire structure of the piazza established by the new alignment of Procuratie and Library was placed under attack (fig. 132).

All of which makes the Sansovinian plan that Francesco Sansovino had first described in 1556, and later in *Venetia città nobilissima*, seem problematic. Jacopo's Library—according to Francesco, his son—". . . was supposed to extend the façade, not only up to the area of the *Beccaria* [toward the lagoon], but to go around the piazza, beginning from the Bell Tower, and continuing to San Geminiano, and turning toward the new houses, terminate at the Clock Tower."[63] When might such an idea have struck Sansovino or one of the Procurators? Certainly not in 1536–37, when the Library was designed, given that the Procuratie begun in 1514 were completed between 1529 and 1538. Furthermore, Francesco's words, *"cominciandosi dal Campanile"* [beginning from the Bell Tower] are not clear. What are we to understand by *circondar la piazza* [surround the piazza], a new alignment established by the side of the

Library—as the document of 1581 seems to suggest—or the older one, formed by the Procurators' offices and the Ospizio Orsoleo? In any case, the document cited above demonstrates that the idea described by Francesco Sansovino, which had long remained purely theoretical, was being heatedly discussed in a political context at the moment when it looked like it might actually be translated into reality.

The debate of 1596 reveals a few aspects of the ideologies that animated Venice at the end of the sixteenth century. The document was signed not only by Leonardo Donà, Antonio Querini, and Andrea Morosini, but by patricians who certainly did not share the political and religious attitude of the *giovani*: Giovanni Mocenigo, who informed upon Giordano Bruno to the Venetian Inquisition, and Federico Contarini, who was also involved, in January 1593, in Bruno's extradition, and who was a supporter of the Jesuits' educational program and a confidant of the Holy See.[64] Furthermore, it is interesting to note that in 1590, regarding the question of the demolition of the old offices of the Procuratia, Federico Contarini had opposed Andrea Dolfin—whose side he would take six years later—while Andrea Morosini, along with Leonardo Donà, had attempted to acquit Giordano Bruno from Giovanni Mocenigo's accusations.

The alliance that existed between members of politically opposed parties in discussions about particular matters was actually not an exceptional phenomenon in Venice. What we need to understand is the meaning of the proposed solution, evaluating the winning ideology that—for reasons that were certainly determined by chance and are today difficult to determine—won a few of its adversaries over to its side. As for the resolution that opposed Scamozzi in 1596, it seems clear to us that it was more congruent with the ethical rigorism of the *giovani* than with the antiquarian taste of Federico Contarini or with Giovanni Mocenigo's mentality. In fact, the economical aspect of the proposed solution was stressed by its proponents, while other considerations were excluded from the proposal. What is striking, in this defense of a rigoristic management of public money, is that the Procuratie Vecchie, which had come to stand for an archaic and anachronistic taste, could be considered the most suitable for the "ornamentation" of the Piazza—a phenomenon that needs to be related to the later, implicit judgment. "To accommodate" the new building "along the line of the Bell Tower" (fig. 132) meant to opt for the preservation of a space that Vincenzo Scamozzi's project altered in a decisive manner; and there was probably no intention to criticize the actual rationalization that the new sequence proposed. The worrisome issue seemed to be the alteration of one of the city's established spots—impregnated with symbolic meaning. As the custodians of a comprehensive image of Venice that referred to its most sacred origins, Andrea Dolfin's allies opted for the preservation of a space that had been determined by Sebastiano Ziani in his time, completed by an architecture that was also deeply rooted in the site.[65]

The "new" Vincenzo Scamozzi was thus condemned not only as a subverter of traditions, but *also* for the way his Romanist triumphalism conflicted with the rigoristic and antioligarchic ambitions advocated by the *giovani*.

One thus reaches a result that is paradoxical only in appearance. Those who supported a new role for Venice and were open to European influences, turned out to be opposed to the introduction of a "modern" architectural language in the Piazza. The fact that, once he became doge, Leonardo Donà showed his appreciation for the Palladian church of San Giorgio Maggiore does not contradict our observations:[66] in that case, in fact, he intervened in order to improve the visibility of an object that had been relegated to the background of the lagoon city and did not directly touch the image of the consecrated places. We should, therefore, conclude that, for the *giovani*, forms were not independent variables: the mentality that emerged refused to see architecture as an autonomous system, cut off from the systems of meaning that were the privileged centers of attention.

The fact remains that the discussion of August 1596 was very concerned with controlling the form of the city and necessarily reflected the context of the debate: the particularity of the theme necessitated a redefinition of the requests that the various political groups were addressing to the *res aedificatoria*.

Let us examine the document—which has also turned out to be a minority decision—that we have defined as a "compromise." Presented by Marino Grimani, Alvise Foscari, Vincenzo Cappello, and Nicolò Sagredo, among others, the resolution—which received 59 votes—was formulated as follows:

Being obliged to put an end to the difficulties, and diverse opinions existing among our Procurators of the church of San Marco upon the occasion of the new buildings begun for the houses of the Procurators along the Piazza San Marco, and as it is not convenient to destroy so much and such beautiful work that has already been done, however it will be resolved, that the already begun order of these houses should remain fixed, following the order of the Library so conspicuous and lovely, as one sees, let it be decided that we ought to continue this building over time in one story only, up to the end of the piazza, clearing away the part with the bricks and wood, which you now see for the construction of the second floor; in place of which the order of the Library would be continued up to the end of these buildings. Then, at the end of the piazza, next to the church of San Geminiano, there shall be made as many similar bays as appear on the side of the frezzaria, *with the same order, as the houses of that part, in order to accompany the view toward the end of this piazza for the total adornment of this Church. And thus let it be commissioned with the authority of this Council to these Procurators, who must execute it, spending the money of their Procuratia. With the street from San Moisè up to the Bell Tower of San Marco remaining open, as one sees from the model, in order to give a view of the entire piazza.*[67]

According to this alternative project, then, the determining element of the Scamozzian project—the third order—was eliminated, in favor of an immediate continuity between the Library and the Procuratie. What was the purpose of such a choice, which softened the "heroic" character of the Procuratie Nuove? Was it the result of economic considerations or of an esthetic choice? And, if it was the latter, what meaning could the loyalty to a dated building, such as the Sansovinian Library, still have?

One should perhaps seek the answer to these questions by considering as a group the solutions envisioned by the document. There was to be continuity with the Library, henceforth a "venerable object" in the Piazza, on the long side of that piazza, but also continuity with the Procuratie Vecchie on the left of San Geminiano, "for the total adornment of that church." The project was not concerned with comprehensive spatiality, except for the view from the "street from San Moisè, up to the Bell Tower." For the remaining parts, they are considered independently, concerning themselves separately with San Geminiano's coherence with its lateral wings and with the Procuratie's coherence with the Library. The paradigm that guided, in both cases, the criteria of "coherence" was continuity with an unquestionable tradition, that is to say, with what was already standing on the site. The mentality that was expressed in the resolution supported by Marino Grimani and Nicolò Sagredo was in the end not that different from the one contained in the document signed by Andrea Dolfin, Antonio Querini, and Leonardo Donà. What mattered was the congruence with established images; what was lacking was any interest in "modernizing" the San Marco area, which was assumed as a *speculum* of the Republic's constitutional continuity and fundamental values.

The conflict with the supporters of the Scamozzian project was thus inevitable. And, the deeper we delve into the inner nature of the competing attitudes, the more we are forced to recognize that it would be altogether naive to read the debate of 1596 as a collision between myopic conservatism and an opening to the "new." It would be more useful to use the available documentation to grasp the critical moment when all the contradictions of the opposing groups exploded and to review the analysis of Venetian scientism that we have already completed. It is worth noting that one of the supporters of the Scamozzian solution was Jacopo Foscarini, the patrician whom Cozzi has recognized as an exponent of the ultraconservative wing, a man who was not only faithful to Rome, but pro-Spanish as well. More recently, however, Paul Grendler has tried to refashion this judgment, observing that on various occasions Leonardo Donà ably managed to bring Jacopo Foscarini around to positions favoring the *giovani*.[68] As for the shape of Piazza San Marco, however, it is clear that in 1596 Foscarini and Donà found themselves at opposite poles. Are we to deduce from this that the former favored a line descending from the one taken by Daniele Barbaro and Jacopo Contarini? Is the support of Scamozzi's architecture, in other words, to be read as evidence of an attitude that saw in the *res aedificatoria* a metaphor for a "knowledge" reached through "heroic virtue"?

Provveditore alle artiglierie [Commissioner of artillery] in 1588–89, Jacopo Foscarini was immediately afterward, as *Provveditore all'Arsenale* [Commissioner of the Arsenal] in favor of an agreement with Spain for the trade of pepper and spices from the Orient, and it was to him that was dedicated the *Visione* of Baldissera Drachio, the unique *Capomastro* or master builder who was an apprentice to Leonardo Bressan, that is to say, a rival of Vettor Fausto.[69] The evidence we have at our disposal does not enable us to see Jacopo Foscarini as the heir of the scientist line that was dear to Gritti and the Patriarch elect of Aquileia, Daniele Barbaro: Drachio's position was anything but innovative in the field of naval technology. Furthermore, the fact that

Jacopo Foscarini might have sustained opinions similar to Leonardo Donà on particular occasions should not be overemphasized: even Doge Marino Grimani was obliged to make clear compromises with the *giovani*. It remains indisputable, though, that the pontifical nuncios included Jacopo Foscarini among the *vecchi*, papalists, and conservatives.[70]

Furthermore, Foscarini's position seemed to combine conservatism and "Romanism" without contradictions. We can thus suggest an answer to our question: Foscarini's support of Scamozzi's project was most likely due to the triumphalism that the new Piazza, enlarged, ordered, and emphasized, would have expressed.

Moreover, in considering the role that Marcantonio Barbaro and Scamozzi carried out in the debate over the Rialto Bridge, we have already recognized the sign of a deep crisis in the link between architectural humanism and technological innovation.

The argument over the form of the Piazza went beyond the concerns that were apparently at stake. It was a matter of offering an updated portrait of Venice, and the patricians who debated the problem in 1596 seemed aware of the delicacy of the question. It was the political and religious heart of the *Serenissima* that was being discussed, the *imago* of Venetian institutions. All of which may perhaps help us explain the eruption in 1596 of contradictions that had long been latent. It was in fact in the spring of 1596 that the Clementine *Indice* [Index] was published: this work, begun in 1592, aimed at filling the lacunae of the Tridentine Index, and indicated books considered "dangerous" that had appeared since 1564.[71] Using the objections raised in the Curia by Cardinal Baronio and other prelates, Paolo Paruta, who was then the Venetian ambassador to Rome, had protested against the excessive intransigence of the Index, defending implicitly the economic interests of the Venetian print shops. Paruta, who won the Senate's approval for his actions, managed to obtain from Clement VIII that the Index be revised. Nevertheless, as soon as it reached Venice, it encountered the violent protest of the booksellers: on June 14, 1596, the Senate—which was no longer inclined to follow Roman wishes—announced its rejection of Clement's Index, objecting mainly to the forced oath that the booksellers were required to take, the new authority given to ordinaries and inquisitors to issue censures, and the consignment of manuscripts to the Holy Office.[72] The reason for the new conflict between Venice and Rome is clear. For the Venetian Senate, the requirement of an oath represented an open challenge to the authority and autonomy of the State. On July 12, Leonardo Donà led the battle, with the full support of the Collegio: the Church—he maintained—was aiming to transform four or five hundred Venetians into its subjects.[73] The Republic then demanded a formal revocation, and when, on August 13, the Nuncio Anton Maria Graziani and the Patriarch Lorenzo Priuli communicated to a group of ecclesiastics that the new Index had gone into effect, recommending that confessors deny absolution to those who refused to destroy the prohibited books, the Collegio ordered the booksellers—under penalty of death—not to observe the Index.[74] On September 14, 1596, an agreement was reached. But the tension was not mitigated: the question of the Index would be one of the main factors leading to the episode of the Interdict. One week after Clement VIII leveled accusations at Ambassador Giovanni Dolfin, Leonardo Donà would respond with an apology from the Venetian state: Venice—he maintained—is a city more devout and Catholic than Rome, and the Curia has no other objective than to favor the Roman print shops, creating difficulties for the Venetian booksellers.[75]

There is an obvious coincidence between the dates of the argument over the Index and of the quarrel over the form of the Piazza. We will not, however, rush to make our conclusions. In July, in the Collegio, Doge Marino Grimani and Jacopo Foscarini also stated that they opposed the clauses of the Index and supported the State's having full authority over its citizens, although their tone was less decisive than Leonardo Donà's. But what was for Donà a chapter in a continuous and coherent battle, for the Doge and for Foscarini was only a necessary defense of the State, an episode to be concluded with a concordat.

Thus Jacopo Foscarini, Marino Grimani, Leonardo Donà, who supported three different solutions for the San Marco area, had been among the Correctors of the Ministers for Heresy and the three aspirants to the position of doge in 1595;[76] more generally, they were recognized as the three protagonists of Venetian political life at the end of the sixteenth century. Donà's anticurial radicalism and ethical rigor, Foscarini's conservatism and antiquarian culture, Grimani's Romanism inclined to compromise—the three positions would take shape, point by point, during the course of the debate of 1596 over the Procuratie Nuove.

On that occasion, the image of the State that the three were defending, each in his own way, became obvious: it was magniloquent for Foscarini, compromising for the Doge, and for Leonardo Donà it was reflected in its own traditions, which were to be used as the foundation for a radical renewal. For Donà the demand for jurisdictional autonomy signified a loyalty to Venice's "sacred origins" as well as an opposition to forms, like Scamozzi's, that were clearly *alla romana*. We have evidence of Leonardo Donà's taste, and we will have to consider it shortly: we are referring to the palazzo that he built on the Fondamenta Nuove, which reveals an ideology deeply indebted to the themes that Nicolò Zen had expressed in his own time.

In order to understand better the position of the *giovani* on the Scamozzian project, let us take at a look at the Procuratie Nuove (figs. 134, 135), imagining the Library as it would have been with the elimination of the original Sansovinian entablature but with the addition of a third order identical to the Corinthian one of the actual Procuratie. The result is a global transformation of the San Marco site; the rhetorical excess reveals that at the base of the plan there was a *hybris* imbuing the existing structure, an impelling need to display a sign of change. We have already seen the significance that the *giovani* attributed to this attitude toward change: the new buildings, adopting an oversized rhetoric, betrayed the continuity of the *imago urbis*, compromising it with "Roman" emphasis, and exhibited a magnificence that completely expressed an unequivocal need for luxury. This need was experienced especially by the patrician sector, which used the historical moment to satisfy itself with ostentatious displays rather than to undertake substantial initiatives of renewal:

and it was this exhibitionism, empty of content, that would be the target of Nicolò Contarini's criticism.

And yet, for Marcantonio Barbaro, the exaltation of dimensions in the Scamozzian model, the rhetoric deployed in the third order, where the windows are linked together in a manner that recalls Raphaelesque and Palladian schemes (fig. 135), the sculptural richness that characterizes the pediments, had probably appeared as the signs of a "true architecture" that celebrated the unity and stability of human knowledge, considered from the point of view of a proudly oligarchic mentality. Once again, the relation between Scamozzi's design in the Piazza and his design at the Rialto was confirmed. In both cases, Barbaro supported projects that broke a cultural, as well as urban, continuity. Anyone who was, in those years, ready to defend the autonomy of the Republic in a new way, would have naturally been led to consider Scamozzi's projects as inopportune attempts to compromise a tradition that was being protected as a political weapon in the literal sense. Vincenzo Scamozzi's proposals contained too much language: those who opposed this semantic excess were rejecting an architecture that was the slave of its own autonomy. Without forcing things too much, one can draw a connection between the antirhetorical rigorism of the Erasmian and evangelical groups and the traditionalist *semplicità* or simplicity that Donà and Antonio Querini desired for the Piazza: morever, the religious sentiment of these *giovani* had a lot to do with Gasparo Contarini's own religious nature.

It was compromise that made the partial realization of the new Procuratie possible. But Scamozzi's project for the bridge (fig. 122) was not the only victim of the counterattack led by the *giovani*.[77] As we will try to demonstrate, the celebratory program envisioned for the *renovatio* of the Piazza San Marco was integrated into another project, supported by Doge Pasquale Cicogna, that would soon be abandoned.

2. An Unrealized Project for a New Dogal Building along the Bacino

We will approach our next problem by shifting our analysis to a unique drawing in the Chatsworth collection that has been attributed to Scamozzi by John Harris (fig. 137), but that Howard Burns later recognized as being a Palladian project for the rebuilding of the Palazzo Ducale after the fire of 1577.[78] With its three orders—from top to bottom: Ionic, Corinthian, and Composite—the project displays dimensions that do not correspond to those of the Palazzo Ducale. Burns, also noting that it anticipated the rebuilding of the lateral façades, explains the anomaly by suggesting an initial idea that had not yet been placed in the actual site: however, according to the English scholar, the monumentality of the project, the statuary apparatus deployed on the façade, and the lion of St. Mark inserted into the central tympanum prove his suggested attribution.

Burns's observations are not lacking in intelligence and have been persuasive for subsequent scholars; Loredana Olivato, especially, accepting his hypothesis, has suggested that the drawing was seen at the time by Paolo Gualdo— who in his biography of Palladio speaks of a project by him for the Palazzo

—with Vincenzo Scamozzi: Vincenzo could in fact have come into possession of the drawing along with other Palladian drawings that he obtained through Jacopo Foscarini's inheritance.[79]

One can, however, make several important criticisms of Burns's hypothesis. The dimensions of the project, first of all. Why, in fact, should Palladio have had to delineate—or have had Francesco Zamberlan delineate for him, as Loredana Olivato suggests—a project whose length was different from the length dictated by the site? Even supposing that his was an abstract or preliminary model, he would have had no reason to alter dimensions that had been determined by foundations it would have been impossible to change. Furthermore, if one accepts the hypothesis of an initial project that was later adapted to the terrain, one would get a peculiar result: Palladio would have determined for himself an image—the specifics of which were drawn in minute detail—without considering proportions, which were treated as independent variables.

In addition, the palazzo represented in the Chatsworth drawing (fig. 137) is rigorously symmetrical relative to the axis formed by the three superimposed arches. Where in it are we to situate the Hall of the Great Council? If we follow Burns's hypothesis, we are forced to envision a room that occupied, on the inside, a height of two stories, which would give us as a consequence the falseness for the third row of windows and balconies. In actual fact, such a solution was not foreign to Palladio. It characterized the project for the Loggia of Brescia, in which other details as well recall the drawing that we are now examining: see, for example, the superimposition of an order of pilasters, against which the statues are standing, upon two orders of columns.[80] But in Brescia Palladio was working on a situation that had already largely been predetermined, one that could not have happened in Venice, where—once that idea of completely rebuilding the Palazzo Ducale had been accepted—nothing would have prevented the use of a gigantic order and of the figurative complexity dear to the late Palladio, which oddly enough the project did not use.

In reality, the Chatsworth drawing gives the impression of an idea that is reductive within the context of the syntactic complexity of the late Palladio, of a montage of Palladian elements within a structure that has little to do with the interpolations, intersections, and free linguistic innovations that characterized the works and projects of Andrea di Pietro della Gondola in the 1560s and 1570s.

Let us proceed by analyzing a few details, as they are so often revealing. The axial emphasis, created by the three triumphal arches, already provides us with elements for reflection: it is reinforced at the base by the projection of the pairs of Ionic columns but is weakened by the thinness of the cornices of the large triangular pediment above. The latter does not make a whole with the triumphal arch underneath, given that the entablature of the last order runs uninterruptedly along the entire length of the façade, while the top of the pediment itself is placed in continuity with that of the entablature. The entire apparatus is not completely congruent with Palladian syntax, and seems as extraneous as the use of columns with vertical and spiral fluting that alternate in pairs in the aedicule windows of the first floor (fig. 92). Nor can we cite the drawing in the

Museo Civico of Vicenza (D. 18), which represents the façade of the Sansovin-ian Scuola della Misericordia, in order to support the attribution to Palladio of a similar decorative device: as we have seen, it is most probable that this drawing revived and corrected Sansovino's ideas, while the spiral columns that appear in it probably originated in Florence, and not Verona (fig. 93).[81] Furthermore, the aedicule windows in the Chatsworth drawing are furnished with pedestals placed asymmetrically relative to the columns above, in order to make room within its own width for the moldings of the windows: even this solution strikes us as foreign to Palladio's linguistic universe.

One could certainly overlook many of these objections by attributing the least convincing details to the hand of Francesco Zamberlan. But a few ques-tions would still remain: one would still have to explain why Palladio had left to his collaborator the job of drawing in such a precise fashion an important project that was not, from a formal point of view, very elaborated. But does the attribution of the drafting of the drawing to Francesco Zamberlan really hold? And what reliable parameters do we have for the comparison? Let us examine the Chatsworth drawing carefully: is it not possible that the very fine and precise lines are those that Burns himself has rightly recognized as being typical of Vincenzo Scamozzi?[82] It seems that we cannot dismiss John Harris's original hypothesis so easily. The Palladian motifs—taken from the Teatro Olimpico, the project for the Loggia of Brescia, and the Palazzo Mon-tano-Barbaran in Vincenza—come together as they subordinate themselves academically to the axial motif, in the absence of any articulation or inter-penetration of virtual plans.

Ours is only a cautious hypothesis that needs to be placed in relation to the doubts expressed above regarding the destination of the project. In this con-nection, a passage from Giovanni Stringa's supplements to Francesco Sansovi-no's *Venetia città nobilissima*—which has until now not been used by historians—presents questions worthy of attention.

For this reason under him [Doge Pasquale Cicogna] the idea of redoing the Rialto Bridge in marble was discussed: whence Luigi Zorzi, Marcantonio Bar-baro, and Giacomo Foscarini, Procurators, were elected by them to take care of such a great work, it was through their great diligence that it was brought to a perfect end in less than three years, based on the model by Antonio del Ponte . . . . And they also finished that piece of the Library, which is the present site of the offices of the three Procuratie, formerly adjacent and attached to the Bell Tower, which having been torn down to the ground, were transferred to where they are now, and the piazza began to acquire that size and magnificence that one finds now. A similar resolution was also discussed in the Senate to build for a room [per stanza] and special residence of the Doge a most noble palazzo, in the exact place where at present the new prisons stand, which is the most lovely [of sites] in the entire city; but as it was not passed, they built those prisons there with a rather strong and durable structure . . . .[83]

It is interesting to note that Giovanni Stringa closely connects—as praise-worthy works of Doge Cicogna—the Rialto Bridge and the new configuration of the Piazza, while also mentioning the rejected project for a new wing detached from the Palazzo Ducale and the decisions regarding the Fondamenta Nuove and Palmanova. The unitary character of the *renovatio urbis* begun in the 1580s thus did not escape the canon of San Marco, who reveals to us how the idea of the new "special residence of the Doge" was integrated into it. This idea was not completely new: in 1483, it had been proposed by Nicolò Trevisan, Minister for War and the Mainland, and toward 1537–38 it had been taken up again by Andrea Gritti.[84] Thus, there existed a tradition of regularly thwarted efforts for the utilization of a site of notable quality: the attempt made under Doge Pasquale Cicogna was the last that tried to place a building of emblematic value in the area that was right along the Bacino of San Marco and directly connected to the Piazza and the *Palatium*. Cicogna was doge from 1585 to 1595; starting in 1574, after the fire in the Palazzo Ducale, the idea of transferring some of the prisoners beyond the canal had been discussed (but not the *presentati*, debtors, women, and those of the Ten).[85] In 1578, however, the project was still being debated, and only in 1580–81 did the construction of the new Prisons get under way (fig. 119). It is necessary, then, to relate the development of the Prisons to the idea of a new Palazzo: strictly speaking, the two projects were not mutually exclusive, given that the second could have included the first; but the facts seem to indicate that a kind of competition emerged between them.

Antonio da Ponte, in his report, examined two possible situations for the new prison facility, favoring the area that included the Osteria della Corona and the houses and shops on the Foscari and Morosini properties, as well as of the Scuola Grande di San Rocco; it was an area that went as far as the edge of the Bacino (fig. 138). The space measured 518 Venetian square feet (1,565 square meters) and was large enough to accommodate a facility with 108 prison spaces for an expense of 80,000 ducats.[86] But neither the project by Da Ponte, nor the one by Zamaria dei Piombi resolved the situation. From 1581 to 1589 no construction work was begun: beyond the Canale di Palazzo there functioned only a small block of prisons, which had been constructed since 1563. Only after yet another outbreak of typhoid fever in the Palazzo prisons, in April 1589, was the problem of the new Prisons taken up again seriously: on May 16, 1589, the Council of Ten elected the two Commissioners for the building and—having instituted a tax in case of need that affected those who had obtained curial nominations in the Dominion, as well as other special taxes—the work was ordered to begin on April 3, 1591.[87]

We can thus say that the debate over the new Palazzo, mentioned by Stringa, took place between 1585 and 1589. The new Prisons (fig. 199) exhibited Venetian Justice in front of the Bacino, in a parade that included the Granaries, the Mint, the Library, and the Palazzo Ducale; those who supported the idea of building a new dogal residence in that area were fighting for a façade on the water that would have been less functional and much more representative. Let us consider the new dogal building together with the Scamozzian projects in the Piazza San Marco: the strengthening of procuratorial dignity would have been combined with a superlative celebration of the doge's sacredness, a consecration, even, of the doge's power that had never been seen before in Venice. The idea had been advocated, anything but casually, by Andrea Gritti in his time: the raising of a building on the other side of the Paglia Bridge is perfectly consonant with an authoritarian interpretation of the doge's position. The project recorded by Stringa thus fit perfectly into the program of reaffirmation and exaltation of the State's authority that had been launched around 1580. And the reason the project was set aside is also understandable: this kind of affirmation of dogal power was probably considered with suspicion in Venice, especially by the *giovani*.

Our hypothesis can thus be expanded and better defined. The Chatsworth drawing could be a project for a new dogal palace (fig. 137), rejected in 1589 in favor of the Prisons by Antonio da Ponte (fig. 119). The failure against the *proto* of the Salt Office, in the episode of the Rialto Bridge, could thus be associated with an analogous failure in the case in question, not long after the abandonment of the Scamozzian project for a Library with three levels.

The attribution we are hypothesizing would resolve the difficulties regarding the placement of the project. This clearly had three façades: the emerging central structure was repeated on the sides, with entryways similar to the front one. One would have to think of the creation of the *fondamenta* or sea edges on the Rio di Palazzo, in order to justify the three entrances: and in order to defend Burns's attribution, one could think of a Palladian project that, obeying such a necessity, reduced the original width of the Palazzo Ducale. But was it possible in Venice to conceive of such a global rebuilding of the Palazzo, one that, moreover, did not respect the ancient foundations?

Placing the building shown in the drawing into the area that was later occupied by the Prisons, these difficulties are limited: we know the site from the survey (n. 13) contained in Cod. It. 7, 295(= 10047) of the Library of San Marco (fig. 138). We should also mention that there is actually a note appended in that codex—on the back of a drawing of the Prisons by Zamaria dei Piombi (n. 16)—that mentions Scamozzi, even though it is not possible to link it to our hypothesis: "The other designs made by Scamozzi were given by me, Giacomo Contarini, to their most Illustrious Sirs, Heads of the Council of Ten, on 8 May 1589." While the identity of these drawings remains unknown, the pairing of Contarini and Scamozzi is significant: there is much evidence to suggest that the circle of Palladio's supporters in Venezia saw in Vincenzo Scamozzi a continuator of the cultural direction of the architect who designed the Redentore.

Let us continue to hold as our hypothesis that the Chatsworth drawing (fig. 137) represents an alternative to the prison project by Da Ponte and Zamaria dei Piombi, and let us verify its congruence with Scamozzi's projects for the Library and the Procuratie. Having three stories like these last two buildings, although its layout differed in order to stress the singularity of the dogal figure, it would have formed with the redesigned Piazza and Piazzetta a relatively unified complex: the heroic and theatrical syntax of the new Piazza would have projected itself triumphally toward the mirroring water, in an ideal "exposition" of the innovative program that was being followed.

It is not necessary, however, for our purposes, to insist too much on the attribution to Scamozzi of the Chatsworth drawing. We have only expressed doubts about Burns's hypothesis, but we would be ready to review the entire question should further evidence supporting it come to light. And we ourselves have one doubt, given that the sheet—contrary to Scamozzi's practice—is not signed, while a few of its details are not characteristic of him. What we intend to underline is that, for the historical problem we are addressing, the controversy over the drawing is not of essential importance: we began with it only in order to express our doubts and to reach the heart of our problem. Which is, however, illuminated by Giovanni Stringa's testimony: the essential point is that around 1585–88, while a design emphasizing the San Marco space was maturing, a new dogal building facing the Bacino was being envisioned as an integral part of that space. And with that building, the will for triumph connected to the new political currents of the 1580s would have been made completely clear.

3. The Construction of the Fondamenta Nuove

The debates over the shape of the Piazza San Marco and the Rialto Bridge demonstrated the existence of two opposing interpretations of the urban *renovatio*: the "Romanist" triumphalism that Marcantonio Barbaro upheld for the Rialto and that Jacopo Foscarini supported for the Piazza San Marco clashed with a functionalist conception as well as with a rigorist ideology that aimed at the restoration of the "original" ethics defended by the *giovani*. It was not a matter of naive conservationism: this becomes obvious when we study a later public work initiated at the beginning of the 1590s, the building of the Fondamenta Nuove in top quality stone.

The work's antecedent laid in the already mentioned play by Cristoforo Sabbadino, which now needs to be reconsidered from a different point of view (fig. 114). Beginning with a particular problem that became urgent—the dredging of the port and the Grand Canal—Alvise Cornaro's rival, Sabbadino, had outlined in 1557 an overall plan for improvements of the urban form that was undoubtedly exceptional in the context of sixteenth-century culture.[88] For Sabbadino, it was primarily a matter of correcting the hydrodynamics of the lagoon. The city's canals would be connected to two new canals: to the north, along the future Fondamenta Nuove; to the south, behind the Giudecca. Another, peripheral canal would flow along the coasts: the job of the new waterways would be to guide the flow of the tides toward the edges, while encouraging the flow of water in the urban canals.

The dredging would furthermore be used to eliminate the inlets that compromised the equilibrium of the lagoon; the mud, transported on barges or *burchi*, would serve to correct the *guasti*, or problem areas: and here Sabbadino foresaw, with detailed calculations of the necessary surfaces and mud, new land areas behind the Giudecca, beyond San Biagio, from Santa Maria Mazor to Santa Chiara, at the tip of Cannaregio, between the Misericordia and Santa Giustina. In addition, the entire urban perimeter was made accessible with continuous *fondamenta* that were meant to determine, in an absolute fashion, the boundary between land and water, while a bridge was planned for the outlet of the Grand Canal, between Santa Chiara and Corpus Domini.

Cristoforo Sabbadino thus formulated a particular theme—the "restoration" of the silted-up canals and the elimination of the dangerous *velme* [the edges of swampy shoals]—in a comprehensive examination that amounted to a "redesigning" of the city: here technology forced its own limits and spoke a brand-new language. Moreover, the fact that in Venice the problem was felt to be of primary importance is demonstrated by the incredible number of petitions presented by private individuals interested in obtaining patents for "inventions" devised for the dredging of the lagoon: file 122 of the *fondo*, or records, of the *Savi ed Escutori alle Acque* [Ministers and Executors of the Waterways] constitute a particularly eloquent source of information in this regard. The invention of various machines was undertaken by Bernardo di Guglielmo de' Grigi, Zuan Pietro Contarini, Pietro Antonio Pillon da Lendinara, Pellegrino Trombetta, Alessandra Lionzo, Fedel Piccolomini, Girolamo Maggi, Buonaiuto Lorini, and Vincenzo Scamozzi, among others;[89] a machine by De' Grigi was adopted and would function for a long time: in 1596 Leonardo Donà, who was then *Savio alle Acque*, lent to Bernardo's heirs the sum of money needed to repair it.[90]

The "limited technical skill" of these inventors was certainly not comparable with Sabbadino's "great technical skill." His plan of 1557 contradicted tendencies inherited from the Middle Ages only methodologically (fig. 114). The new land areas allowed Venice to grow within her impassable limits, which were determined by the peripheral *fondamenta*, and presented themselves as the results of an operation that aimed to restore "sacred naturalness" to a lagoon corrupted by time. Vincenzo Fontana rightly observed that Sabbadino gave a hydrodynamic structure—*a barca*—to his Venice: the new areas of San Biagio and Cannaregio assumed a pointed form, "in imitation of nature."[91] The plan had its own coherence: the planned interventions were presented ideally as a *restauro a grande scala* [restoration on a grand scale] of the "original" conditions of the lagoon. But it is also necessary to observe that Sabbadino, in *assigning boundaries* to the city, endowed Venice with a *finitio*. Technology intervened in order to *give form*: thus, in an Aristotelian fashion, it worked to determine boundaries.

It is thus rather significant that in 1590, the vote of the *Savi ed Esecutori alle Acque* [Ministers and Executors of the Waterways] that confirmed the Collegio's decision (9 February 1587, *m.v.* = 1588) to proceed with the construction of the Fondamenta Nuove, explicitly mentions "what in this matter has been already mentioned at other times by Sabbadino, engineer of the office."[92]

It was finally decided to confront in a global fashion the problem posed by the *proto* of the *Savi alle Acque*: the decision was probably partially influenced by the plague of 1576–77, which was attentively followed, as we know, by Leonardo Donà.[93]

Sabbadino's projects were also based on precedent. On November 6, 1531, the Collegio alle Acque had remarked that "one found in this our city, Murano and various monasteries [islands] around many lands and places without pilings or any foundation, so that when these storms come, as there have been these past days, they carry away the said lands, which then fall into the bottom of the public canals and above the swamps, and by raising them cause damage and detriment to our lagoons." The Collegio, for this reason, had decided that *all those who legitimately have the said sites without piles, whoever they may be, ecclesiastics as well as laymen, before the end of the next three months must have made either foundations of stone or pilings with planks, so that the lands cannot be carried away by the waters; otherwise the said pilings are to be made by the executors for waterways, whatever the cost, and for this execution they can have the sites sold, confiscate the rents, send the debtors away, and do any other operation they want against the disobedient ones....* [94]

The execution of the Fondamenta Nuove thus takes its place in the long history of the Venetian battle against the destructive action of nature. And it is interesting to note that the decision taken so long after the plan of 1557 concerned a *bordo* or shore that was still largely undefined, from a functional as well as a physical point of view, in spite of the decision of 1546 concerning it. At the beginning of the century, charitable institutions were situated between the church of Santa Giustina and the church of San Francesco della Vigna (fig. 139): there was the Ospedale delle Boccole, the Casa delle Pizzocchere, and the Scuola di San Francesco, not to mention the houses that the Contarini family built around 1536 for the poor, in compliance—after a long argument with the Observant Franciscans—with the last will and testament of Pietro Contarini di Zuan Ruggero. [95]

Patricians were also responsible for construction in this zone: the palazzi of the Contarini and Andrea Gritti faced each other across the San Francesco Canal. Farther to the west, the large complexes of San Giovanni e Paolo and of the Scuola Grande di San Marco stood out from the urban fabric, while the Barberia delle Tole was functionally connected to the State Arsenal. Less defined from a formal point of view, at the beginning of the sixteenth century, was the northern zone of the parish of San Canciano (Biri); Concina has, however, discovered interesting architectural interventions in that area. Along the Rio dei Crosechieri—following the Rio dei Gesuiti—and facing the monastery itself, the patricians Pietro and Girolamo Polani founded, beginning around 1542, a small development of low-income housing: the houses, which have two floors above ground, are described in the *condizime di decima* [tithe report] by Cecilia Polani Gradenigo and Girolamo Polani, [96] and are placed either in series or in a regular subdivision arrangement. A second building speculation undertaking, launched by Sebastiano Malipiero (mid-sixteenth century), is located in the center of the zone, on land that had been free until then; other isolated enterprises were registered between 1541 and 1587. [97] But the undefined character of the zone was mainly due to the buildings, on frequently muddy shores, of deposits of timber that had floated downstream: these deposits alternated with occasional production sites, like the one on the Zane property, which had a wax workshop. [98]

On the whole, there was, in the urban area we are considering, a complete absence of the public sector and a confused overlapping of private initiatives: the definitive choice made in 1590 thus constituted a reversal of this trend, an incentive for rationalization and, at least to a certain degree, the beginning of a functional restructuring.

On a more detailed level, it becomes obvious that the resolutions of 1588 and 1590 brought together two different objectives: the protection of the lagoon's equilibrium and the increase of lands available for building and private speculation. Moreover, the interplay between state operations and private enterprise was typical of Venetian tradition, and went back to the early Middle Ages: one example of this is the role that decisions taken by the Senate played in maritime trade.[99] In our case, the sacrifices that the expropriation [*usurpatione*] of lands needed for building imposed upon individuals were compensated for by the stimulation of the real estate market, while the State intended to finance at least a part of the work through the auctioning of the reclaimed lands. A wise economic mechanism, guided by the magistracy of the *Savi alle Acque* [Ministers of the Waterways], was refined in order to eliminate the obstacles that might have slowed down the "restoration" of the lagoon: the urbanization of the areas contained within the Fondamenta Nuove was presented as the necessary consequence of the main operation, and not as the subject of the initiative, which, in any case, appeared to be experimental. The general problem was set forth on February 9, 1588. "This Collegio has understood the very important benefit that the lagoon will gain from the redirection of the course of the waters with foundations in stone, filling some of the creeks that are around this our city, that ordinarily cause destruction and harm to this lagoon."[100]

The solution adopted in 1590 was the first extract of an intervention of broader intention. "That for now a foundation of top quality stone should be started on the northern side, beginning with the empty land between San Francesco della Vigna and Santa Giustina, up to the garden between Ca' Grimani and Santa Caterina according to the design made by Rigetti, vice-*proto* of the office."

The request for Sabbadino's advice should be carefully evaluated. In 1557, the *proto* of the Magistracy for Waters had offered his comprehensive model for Venice as an integrated sector of a territorial restructuring and of the mainland's hydraulic network (fig. 114). Thirty-three years later, a single section was lifted from that plan, with a notable reduction of its impact on an urban level: the Fondamenta Nuove were only a fragment of the peripheral belt envisioned by Sabbadino. His general plan had value, for the Venetian patriciate, only as a hypothetical framework from which individual parts might be lifted at opportune moments: when alternative hypotheses were to be considered, the "prudence" of the ruling class advised, as was traditional, the adoption of lengthy periods of time and debates, as though such an approach might make the moment of decision "natural" and thus less traumatic.

On February 23, 1590, the Ministers and Executors of the Waterways—Marco Giustinian, Benedetto Moro, and Giovan Battista Vitturi—decided together on a *zonta*, or additional body of men, that included the prestigious figures of Marcantonio Barbaro, Zaccaria Contarini, and Leonardo Donà; the administrative body thus constituted maintained that it had taken into consideration not only Sabbadino's opinions, but also "all the old and modern depositions of the parties."

The apparition of personalities like Barbaro and Donà allows us to make further reflections on the relations that existed between technology and politics in Venice during the second half of the sixteenth century. The brother of Daniele Barbaro, a relative of Ermolao, father of Francesco the future Patriarch of Aquileia, member of a powerful "Romanist" family, Barbaro belonged—as we have already mentioned—to a political group opposed to Leonardo Donà's.

It is, moreover, likely that Donà had a special view of the new *fondamenta*. In 1610 the doge gave the go-ahead for work on his own palazzo on the *fondamenta* to whose execution he had contributed.[101]

It was one of the few patrician palaces destined for residential purposes being built in that zone (figs. 146, 145). Sober and laconic, the building—which Leonardo's nephews continued after his death (1612)—can be seen as a personality portrait of the doge, whom the auditor of the apostolic nuncio would, in 1611, see climb up on the building's wooden scaffolding in order to supervise its execution. Donà's choice of location was significant: for the family palazzo, he boldly turned toward a site that was not yet completely finished, but still in the process of being defined.

And from a formal point of view the linguistic poverty of the building is striking. In the absence of architectural orders, unrefined corner pilasters define the palazzo at the edges, while a Serlian layout is followed on the ground floor: "architecture" is not to be found in this doge's house. Andrea Gritti had already displayed *mediocritas* in private, with his palazzo at San Francesco della Vigna. But Leonardo Donà's building was, if possible, even more anonymous. Programmatically, the doge did not entrust the design to an architect, but instead to the *proto* of the Procuratori de citra, Francesco di Pietro, the author of housing projects including some *amore Dei* [for charitable purposes].[102] Leonardo Donà's ethical rigorism thus became an architectural manifesto: not only was the doge's taste made clear, but so was the loyalty to the mentality that had been expressed by Nicolò Zen, in the words we cited at the beginning of this book. The exhibition of "modesty," explicitly opposed to the wastefulness of Roman nobiliary building, was certainly a political message for Donà: Venetian *simplicitas* demonstrated its own rigor, upholding before Rome its own traditions and its own "sanctity." The Palazzo Donà confirms what we have already written about Leonardo Donà's position during the 1596 debate over the form of the Procuratie and the Piazza San Marco.

Going back to the Fondamenta Nuove, it should be pointed out that it was probably no coincidence that the go-ahead for the project was given after the death of the rivals—Sabbadino and Cornaro—who had proposed to the Republic choices that were far too radical. If Cornaro's intellectual adventures were rejected as utopian, the realistic proposals by the *proto* of the *Savi alle Acque* were broken down into small pieces, sorted out, and—with Donà's participation—subjected to a process of redefinition.

The episode of the *fondamenta*, whose phases of execution can be reconstructed on the basis of the rich documentation that has been preserved, is revealing: once begun, the operation aimed at revitalizing construction in Venice, according to a perspective that may not have been so different from the one that Alvise Zorzi followed when he proposed a restructuring of the Cannaregio district.

Let us trace in detail the sequence of the operations.

On March 3, 1592, Giacomo Campelli, a timber merchant, observing that the "admirable foundation already begun on the swamp belonging to *master* San Francesco" was being exposed to the "problem of the waters and storms," proposed an idea of his that "will remedy all damage and will maintain and preserve it without other hindrance from the waters or the lagoon": as recompense, Campelli requested three ducats a month for himself and his heirs.[103]

On June 24, 1593, it was realized that the work had been "in large part already completed," and it was decided that "the lands that are within these foundations should be sold so as to obtain the money to compensate for the ordinary expense of the said building"—this did not, however, apply to the land between San Francesco della Vigna and Santa Giustina; the areas that had previously been expropriated were to be added to the terrain that was already available for construction.[104] But an unforeseen intervention of the Ducal Councillors and the Chiefs of the Forty reduced the designated areas: the land areas to be transferred were limited to the tract between the Rio di Santa Giustina and the "calle della Cecca."[105] It is obvious that the Zecca mentioned here is not the same as the Sansovinian Zecca, or Mint, facing the Bacino of San Marco: it was in fact a secondary establishment, the area of which can be seen in a few of the subdivision drawings by Giovanni Alvise Galesi (figs. 140–42), the vice-*proto* of the Magistracy for Waters, whose eighteenth-century plan is represented in a drawing that has also been preserved in Venice's Archivio di Stato.[106]

On December 2, 1594, the sales had been completed, and it was decided to "sell the remainder of the said lands up to the Rio de San Zuane Polo to the public's greatest possible advantage."[107]

It was evidently felt that inflating the real estate market at that time would have been unwise. The problem was how to keep prices steady and high: it was decided to proceed by introducing open areas in a gradual fashion. But there were other important considerations, regarding rational urbanization: the Ministers and Executors for the Waterways were ordered to have a drawing made of the aforementioned land areas, the streets that are to be left, and the selling prices." Galesi drew up three projects for the organization of the area, from the lagoon to the monastery of San Giovanni e Paolo (ASV, Laguna 28, 29, 30)—figs. 140–42), one of which is dated December 10, 1594 (barely eight days, therefore, after the decision). All three projects present a network of streets that intersect orthogonally and contain buildable areas of differing dimensions: only the spacing of the grid changes, being tighter in drawing Laguna 30 (fig. 140), and reduced to only three *calli*, or streets, in drawing Laguna 28 (fig. 141).

As had already been the case on the island of Santa Maria Maggiore at the beginning of the century and in the small housing project executed by Polani, an urban sector was thus organized along rigid lines that ignored the organic quality of "late antique" medieval Venice: in the case of the zone along the Fondamenta Nuove, Galesi's plans seemed to follow a "colonization," which is only partly recognizable on the site today, because of the construction of the hospital and the church of San Lazzaro dei Mendicanti. Galesi also prepared the subdivision plan of the adjoining area, between the Rio di San Giovanni e Paolo and the Rio dei Crociferi (August 7, 1600), in which the basic scheme was modified to suit the requirements of the site (figs. 143–144).[108]

The public initiative undoubtedly had results. The zone was saturated; its Venetian characteristics, however, were modified only slowly. Between 1582 and 1661—the dates of two successive *redecime* [periods of rebuilding]— the functional units in the parish of San Canciano passed from 482 to 492, with a growth of 110 units, of which approximately 37 percent were comprised of new buildings on the Fondamenta Nuove.[109] Alongside the patrician investments—Donà, Ruzini, Vitturi, Badoer—there were storehouses and speculative houses, and residential buildings were built by citizens; there continued to exist, however, right through the nineteenth century, areas used as deposit sites for timber.[110] Thus the plans of the Ministers and Executors for the Waterways and the intervention on the northern edge of Venice brought only partial changes to the city's structure. But the result had been discounted by its own premises: the artificial *argine* or embankment, placed as though to signal the boundaries between Venice and the lagoon, expressed a language that, in spite of everything, did not establish cordial dialogues with either the natural universe or the urban experience. It is clear, however, that this northern border, in a zone that has been traditionally ignored by Venetian cartography (which had been more interested—for obvious reasons—in exalting the San Marco area),[111] assumed after 1590–94 a new dignity, even though it was still restricted to a symbol of *mediocritas*. We do have one significant trace of this process: in 1708, Coronelli would represent the Fondamenta Nuove in an engraving dedicated to the "Lagoon toward Murano, iced over" (fig. 147).

Thus not only Leonardo Donà's palazzo was without form, so was the exceptional operation of urbanization in the northern zone of the city. The *oeconomicus* revealed itself there in its absolute simplicity, while the programmatic interplay of public and private came to terms with a mounting crisis that was partly thwarting the objectives of the operation. We have all the elements needed in order to read the formal silence that surrounded the urbanization of the Fondamenta Nuove as the dialectical correlative of the much more eloquent—and nearly contemporary—restructuring of the Rialto bridge and the Piazza San Marco.

Between Vincenzo Scamozzi's "overloaded" language (fig. 134), the dialectic composition of Antonio da Ponte, and the restrained subdivisions of Giovanni Alvise Galesi (figs. 140–44) there came to exist—in spite of everything—a circularity, a relationship of mutual dependence. And not only because of the differentiated functions for which these works were destined, nor because they stood at the end of a long historical cycle. In fact, these works, like the others that we have connected in order to recognize in them a vast operation of urban renewal, are to be considered within their particular historical context: we do not find an expression in them of the sullen and "scandalous" autonomy of language that had been used by the protagonists of the Roman "golden age" and reaffirmed by Palladio, while the battles fought during the course of their execution acquired a significance that went beyond their limits.

4. Crisis

Alvise Zorzi's initiative for the Cannaregio district, as well as the initiative for the Fondamenta Nuove, revealed concerns about the state of the building economy. The restructuring envisioned by Zorzi was realized, however, in a limited fashion in the zone between the Rialto Bridge and Campo San Bartolomeo (figs. 126, 127); the acquisition of new buildable lands in the northern sector of the city did not promote consistent building. On the other hand, the strengthening of the Arsenal's capacity, begun under Nicolò da Ponte and continued until the end of the century,[112] was limited to a rationalization of the spatial organization, and did not affect the structural problems connected to military production. The situation of the Arsenal at the end of the sixteenth century has been described by Ennio Concina, who has pointed out its peculiar inefficiency, which coexisted with its increased level of building.

The fact is that beyond even conspicuous accomplishments, an explanation of all this is to be found in the deep crisis of political initiative and in an equally deep crisis in the management of the Arsenal as a complex. The employment of the Arsenal as a direct instrument for the revival of commerce when naval construction was reduced to an extreme, the restoration, that is to say, of functions exercised until the past seventy years, has not been taken into consideration.[113]

In fact, the Arsenal remained entangled in a technological traditionalism incapable of renovating an obviously anachronistic production. The insistence on continuing to produce galleasses and galleons for piratic war helped keep Venice out of international commerce: in early 1619 almost half of the *Serenissima*'s fleet was constituted by English and Dutch *bertoni* and galleons, and even the boats in the merchant fleet were predominantly of foreign origin.

The organizational regression of the Arsenal was questioned by the *giovani*—by Nicolò Contarini, for example;[114] but without success. Baldissera Drachio, in 1595, also wrote that "the Arsenal rambles in a thousand of its oblique and twisted actions, and in confusion and disorder because in it one does not find anyone to impose order, even partially, let alone totally, nor [does one find] anyone whose words are worthy of obedience."[115] At the end of the century, the *architectura navalis* of Vettor Fausto and the *ratio* of Nicolò Zen praised by Daniele Barbaro seemed to be on the losing side: the failure was linked to a conservatism that was flourishing not only in the State arsenal. But at this point there came into play the results of an internal political debate that had become dramatic during the Interdict, as well as the interpretation given by opposing parties of the role of sciences and technical practices.

Was this a failure, therefore, of the *giovani*? But doesn't this question imply a unified body of intentions that was in fact limited to a small group?[116]

An episode of notable historical significance may help to understand the difficulties that hindered the plans to revitalize the *Serenissima* economically and politically. In 1610 an attempt was made, to no avail, to introduce foreign citizens into the economic life of Venice by giving them equal rights.[117] The initiative was taken mainly by the Dutch. A long memorial presented by the Venetian citizen Paolo Santoni pointed out the difficult situation besetting Venetian trade and submitted a proposal for economic revitalization. By according foreigners the same civil, political, and commercial rights that the Venetians had, the renewal of commercial initiatives with the East might have been structured not as a mass of individual deals, but as the work of Companies endowed with a fixed capital, of enormous financial means and new methods of long-term negotiation. That would have entailed the adoption of a comprehensive vision of trade that was new for Venice: for the most profitable commercial sectors—silk, cotton, sugar, oil, etc.—it would have been necessary to create monopoly situations tied to the aforementioned Companies.

In the discussion in the Senate, the *giovani* upheld positions that were decidedly reformative. During the Interdict the question of Venice had assumed an international level that was shifted onto the economic level, with a lucid reading of the *Serenissima*'s commercial crisis and a precise proposal meant to overcome the crisis, changing, in part, the traditional rules of the game. It was Nicolò Donà who observed that trade with the East was no longer a Venetian prerogative, but rather an English, French, Dutch, and Florentine one: these were now the countries that furnished Germany with goods coming from Alexandria and Constantinople. He goes on to say,

And from this it follows that when the competition of foreign merchants who came to equip themselves here stops, trade stops; when trade stops, population diminishes; when there are no people, the consumption of goods ceases, and as a consequence duties diminish, public income is exhausted and does not suffice for the necessary expenses, and individual citizens no longer take good care of their goods, reducing rents on houses, if they don't stop them altogether.[118]

The commercial crisis was thus tightly linked to urban deterioration. The picture of Venice offered by Nicolò Donà permits one to read clearly the operations of renewal that had been conducted in the preceding decades in a "heroic" language. The building market, especially, seems to have been strongly penalized by a financial crisis that was creating a real threat even for the public sector. The remedy indicated was "embracing such an occasion that places first not the men of the world, but the infinite goodness of God": the Dutch proposal was tacitly greeted as a gift of Providence. It is significant that in Donà's discourse one hears echoes of the fundamental themes of Priuli's *lamento* or lamentation over the *mutatione* that had occurred in the commercial attitude of Venice. "Now things are changed, as they understand and obviously know. We lack capital, the nobility does not want to take part in commerce, everything is employed in goods and buildings, in the possession and enjoyment of the city, and to him who has an excess of money everything that could be used in trips to the East is involved in exchanges."[119]

It was the East, in fact, that "maintained the trade of wool, silk, and so many other industries." Donà adds the following: "People are coming here who offer to bring their *cavedali* [offerings] to maintain navigation, which is almost lost,

. . . persons who will increase revenues, who will maintain the arts and the people. Will your most excellent *Signorie* refuse them?"[120]

The "reformers" who supported the entry of the Dutch citizens into Venetian economic life were well-known figures of the party of the "*giovani*," who had in different ways been the protagonists of the events we have recounted in the preceding pages: Nicolò Contarini, Alvise Zorzi di Paolo, Antonio Querini, and Francesco Priuli. The group that wanted to give a new religious and political identity to Venice also went into action in the economic sector, proposing that the *Serenissima* should courageously enter the European equilibrium and form an equally courageous alliance with the Holland of the Reformation. The battle created by the Interdict continued, shifting onto a structural level: in order to realize the project advocated by the *giovani*, in fact, it was necessary to break with traditions that were deeply rooted in Venice, persisting in both the economic and the religious spheres.

Already when Portugal had offered Venice the European monopoly on the pepper trade, the Senate had rejected the deal, for fear, Nicolò Contarini would write, "that private citizens should become dependent upon foreign Princes." In reality, the Portuguese offer of 1598, like the Dutch one of 1610, compromised the traditional organization of Venetian business, which was opposed to all monopoly and based on *colleganze marittime* [maritime cooperation].[121]

The refusal of 1610 was, furthermore, partly due to the intervention of the papal nuncio, who saw in the planned economic alliance a dangerous opening to countries of the religious Reformation.[122] But the episode revealed the weakness if the *giovani*, and especially of the Sarpian group.

Nicolò Contarini, Alvise Zorzi di Paolo, Francesco Priuli, and Antonio Querini saw in the strong reaction raised against the resolution that they were defending the manifestation of a mentality that was inert, subservient, and extremely conservative. But Cozzi has observed that the acceptance of the project would not only have centralized wealth and power, but would have also shaken the governmental organization of Venice and deepened the rifts between the political and economic classes.[123]

The refusal to admit the English and Dutch "new men" into Venetian trade was certainly a way of fending off the danger of disruptions in the areas of religion and tradition: "deterioration" was in some way accepted in favor of the "conservation" of a State as it was. Was this a rejection of "modernity"? In a certain sense, it was. But one ought not to forget that, in the mental patrimony of Venice, the cult of tradition had always been considered a symbol of strength, and that—as we have seen—the *giovani* themselves were careful not to challenge it.

What connection can be drawn between this cult of tradition and the scientistic developments in the culture of the Venetian patriciate?

It has already been remarked that Pietro Duodo, Antonio Priuli, and Jacopo Contarini demonstrated an interest in Galileo that was very different from the interest the Sarpian group demonstrated in him:[124] we will only have to specify this duality, drawing it into the mainstream of our analysis. Paolo Sarpi addressed a letter to the scientist on September 2, 1602, but the two may have met before 1600, if in the summer of that year Galileo offered the Servite "an instrument without a quadrant." The subjects that tied Sarpi to Galileo are known: magnetism—the reading of Gilbert's volume, moreover, also struck another important member of the Sarpian group, the proud anti-Jesuit Zuan Francesco Sagredo[125]—and the theory of motion.[126] For both Sarpi and Sagredo the problem of motion was a main interest. As the foundation of the new science, it provoked, in the Galileian formulation, a radical epistemological leap with regard to Aristotelian physics, founding new paradigms and opening mental constructions in which acceleration and the primacy of mathematical networks were the chief elements.[127]

One could even say that Sarpi and Micanzio lacked an understanding of Galileo's astronomical research: for them, it was the theory of motion that was bound to have the greatest consequences for the "scientific revolution."

On the one hand, therefore, Galileo was asked to provide technical inventions that would be immediately efficient: with regard to these requests, it is necessary to read Galileo's work on fortresses (fig. 122),[128] Jacopo Contarini's letter on the force of oars, and the public recognition of the Republic for the telescope.[129] On the other hand, there was the Sarpian group's appreciation for the epistemological break that Galileo's research implied—a breach that they considered in tune with their religious and civil project.

As Cozzi has intelligently observed, it is clear that the Sarpian group did not understand the battle for Copernicanism that Galileo was waging at the heart of a Church they considered closed to all spiritual and cultural needs: they missed the meaning of the battle fought "in defense of the autonomy of science, for the very reason that it was fought within the Church, and because it forced it to define its position with regard to the culture that was being affirmed."[130]

In return, Galileo seems to have ignored the battle that was being waged in Venice by the *giovani* and Paolo Sarpi. Not only was there the trip to Rome in April–May 1611, the reception of Cardinal Del Monte, the friendly discussions with Bellarmino, and the conviction, nourished by Galileo at the time, of the need to take the Company of Jesus into account. Galileo, with his attempts to make the Church of Rome legitimize his own discoveries, worked tactically in favor of a scientific language with a new autonomy: but his cultural Machiavellianism refused to consider the already existing and real divisions; in some way, it was antithetical to the spirit of the paradigm he was defending. Thus, the autonomy upheld by Galileo—who was a friend of Pietro Duodo as well as Paolo Sarpi, and ready to prefer the Grand Duke of Tuscany and Florentine tranquility to the tumultuous Venetian climate of the years following the Interdict—would turn out to be a double-edged sword. Galileo certainly believed, especially in 1609–10, that his entering into a decisive alliance with the Sarpian group would not help spread his science: such an alliance would have confined him to a "factional" ghetto. But the Sarpians proved they were not provincial by their attempt to link Galileo and the "scientific revolution" to ideas they had proposed for the Republic and its European destiny; Galileo's decision to leave the Paduan Studio in 1610—which caused a temporary weakening of his relations with Sagredo and Sarpi—can therefore be read in light of the crisis that the Sarpian group experienced immediately after the Interdict.[131]

The card played by the Sarpians did not only concern Galileo. Vittorio Gabrieli has made known 75 letters that Fulgenzio Micanzio wrote between 1615 and 1628 to Sir William Cavendish—who became Lord in 1618 and second count of Devonshire in 1626—in an English version we owe to Thomas Hobbes, who was the latter's secretary.[132] It was William Cavendish who put Bacon and Micanzio in touch with each other in 1616,[133] and the Servite (who became increasingly interested in the essayist's production as the correspondence proceeded) announced in a letter (February 24, 1617) his intention to print in Italy, upon the request of friends, Bacon's *Essays*.[134] It was significant that he showed an interest in the author of the *Advancement of Learning*, which offered an example of a proud defense of lay culture against the "devout ignorance" predicated by "the zeal and jealousy of divines." For Micanzio, the *Advancement* was to be placed alongside William Gilbert's revolutionary treatise on magnetism;[135] it was, in fact, in 1617 that Sarpi wrote to Jérome Groslot de l'Isle his famous letter on the "imminent yoke around the neck of Italy":[136] science was seen as an instrument in the battle against the "superstitious . . . and the vicious who like serving in laziness better than working in freedom."

At the end of 1619, Micanzio communicated euphorically to Lord Cavendish that Bacon's work had deeply penetrated cultured society in Venice,[137] and Bacon—who between 1624 and 1625 wrote the Servite twice[138]—proved equally interesting for Fra Fulgenzio, even after the philosopher's death: the faith in the fertility of the critical spirit and of free scientific research sustained an ideal struggle that continued even after the dissolution of the "Sarpian faction" and of the hopes raised by the European participation in the episode of the Interdict.

What connections can be drawn between this interest in the epistemological fracture in process and the events of Venetian architecture that we have reexplored in the preceding pages? And, more important, is it legitimate to try to draw such connections? In our chapter on Venetian scientism of the sixteenth century, we traced a series of situations that went from the technical interests of Vettor Fausto to the thinking of Daniele Barbaro and Jacopo Contarini, to the calling of Galileo to Padua: and it had become clear that Palladian architecture was inherent to that scientistic current. But after Galileo's first definitions of his thinking and the placing in evidence of the alternative paradigms he had introduced, what remained of the humanistic interpretation of architecture as an emblem of *scientia "in primo gradu certitudinis"* [the "first degree of certitude"]? The question seems to contain the answer in itself. It is certain that a few of Galileo's friends favored Vincenzo Scamozzi: the Scamozzian projects for the Duodo at Monselice testify as much. But—as we have amply seen—this is not the point. Scamozzi's overflowing erudition modified only marginally the conceptual grid established by Palladio. Formal overdetermination may have introduced metaphysical nuances in a language that was placing its trust increasingly in atemporal abstraction; and this overdetermination, while trusting mathematically determined grids, was still coming to terms with old values, crystalized like pillars of salt. It is perhaps in this crystalization that one ought to look for Scamozzi's substantial contribution; seen from this perspective, Scamozzian abstraction seems to have foreshadowed the even more radical abstraction of Inigo Jones and the ambiguity of an international Palladianism made of emptied forms.

The fact remains that the dialogue between the sciences and architecture started becoming more rigid during the last decades of the sixteenth century. What contemporaries realized about all this is a matter that deserves a separate discussion and extended inquiries. As far as we are concerned, we could conclude abruptly with a thought about the role, by now exhausted, of architectural research as linked to a humanism of an Aristotelian and Pythagorean nature. The union between philological analysis and *invention*, and the one between the mathematic structure of space and the poetics of the *concordia discors*, appear to have been instruments that outlived themselves, until the revisions of the seventeenth and eighteenth centuries. But history does not provide us with palingenetic moments—but rather with slow-moving processes, various levels of adaptation, zones full of nuances and recurrences, and non-linear superimpositions.

We have tried to define Leonardo Donà's taste: and it appears to have been essentially conservative and "poor." And yet, that poverty, in the light of our considerations, is revealing: unconsciously, it takes its place in a history that includes Savonarolian *simplicitas*, the Erasmian disdain for the beautiful word resounding in the void, and the doubts about the values of form that tormented the heterodox individuals of the sixteenth century. With the events and choices of the first decades of the seventeenth century, Venice certainly planned its own definitive crisis: survival was preferred to adventure, and the libertinism of the Accademia degli Incogniti was the poor heir of the kinds of freedom of thought practiced by Sarpi, Micanzio, and Sagredo. Venice's legacy would be received elsewhere. But the significant elements of this legacy would be the intimate tensions, the laceration, the superimpositions of the aspirations for reform and for the return to origins in the flow of a consecrated tradition that we have tried, in our historical constructions, to capture as open problems of modern European culture.

1. Palazzo Vendramin at Santa Fosca, late 15th–early 16th centuries: façade on the canal. Photo Martinelli, Venice.

2. Jacopo Sansovino, Project for Vettor Grimani's palazzo on the Grand Canal, circa end of 1527. Venice, Library of the Museo Correr, Collezione disegni, cl. 3, f. 6038r. Photo Civico Museo Correr, Venice.

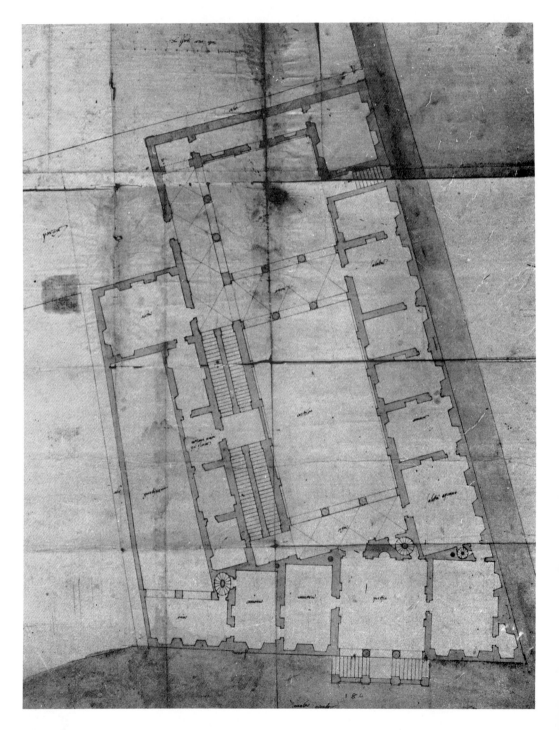

3. Palazzo Zen, circa 1533 ff.: side views on the Rio di Santa Caterina and the Campo dei Gesuiti (formerly dei Crosechieri). Photo Biggi, Venice.

4. Palazzo Loredan at Campo Santo Stefano, first half of the 16th century: façade. Ibid.

5. Jacopo Sansovino, Palazzo Corner
at San Maurizio: façade on the Grand
Canal. Ibid.

6. Jacopo Tintoretto, *Portrait of Giovanni Grimani, Patriarch of Aquileia*. Great Britain, private collection.

7–10. Palazzo Grimani at Santa Maria Formosa: façade on the canal, view of the courtyard, the "Study of antiquities," and view of the vault and of the lantern in the "Study of antiquities."

8.

9.

10.

11. Antonio da Negroponte, *Madonna in gloria* (detail), 15th century. Venice, San Francesco della Vigna. Photo Böhm, Venice.

12. Palazzo Vendramin at Santa Fosca:
tricipitium bas-relief on the pilaster placed
to the left of the main portal. Photo Biggi,
Venice.

13. Palazzo Trevisan Cappello in Canonica: *tricipitium* on the façade. Ibid.

14. Giorgione, *Three Philosophers*.
Vienna, Kunsthistorisches Museum.

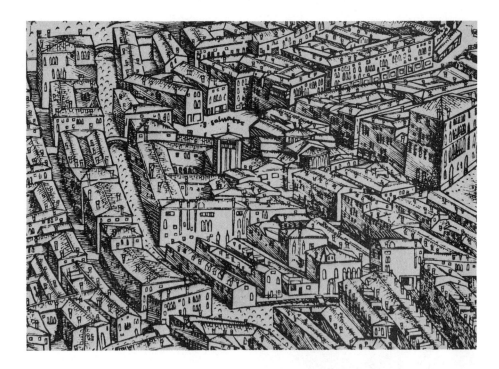

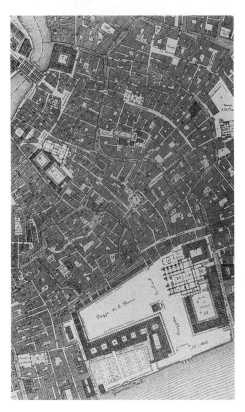

15. The church and convent of San Salvador in Jacopo de' Barbari's map (1500). Photo Biggi, Venice.

16. Bernardo and Gaetano Combatti, Map of Venice (detail), 1846. The connection between the Mercerie, San Salvador and San Marco is clearly visible. Ibid.

17. View of the church, the bell tower, and the convent of San Salvador; in the background, to the right, are the domes of San Marco. Ibid.

18. San Salvador: the domes with the lanterns added in circa 1569. Ibid.

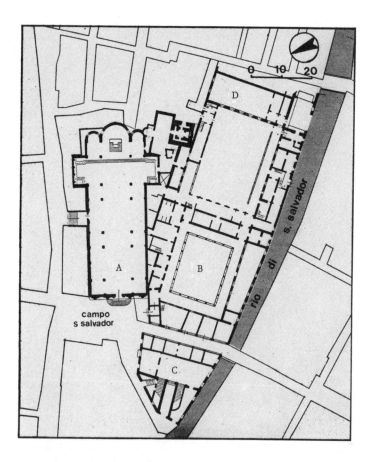

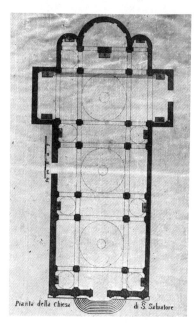

Pianta della Chiesa di S. Salvatore

19. Schematic plan of the church and convent of San Salvador: (A) church; (B) small cloister; (C) Scuola di San Tedoro; (D) refectory room.

20. Plan of San Salvador, engraving, 18th century. Venice, Archivio di Stato, *Miscellanea Mappe*, 621. Photo Archivio di Stato, Venice.

21. Longitudinal section of San Salvador, engraving. From L. Cicognara, A. Diedo, G. Selva, *Le fabbriche e i monumenti cospicui di Venezia*, vol. I, 2nd ed. (Venice, 1838), plate 96. Photo Biblioteca Marciana, Venice.

22. Survey of the primitive church of San Salvador (?), 16th century. Venice, Archivio di Stato, *Miscellanea Mappe*, 468. Photo Archivio di Stato, Venice.

23. Survey of the section of the Mercerie tangent to San Salvador, 16th century. Ibid.

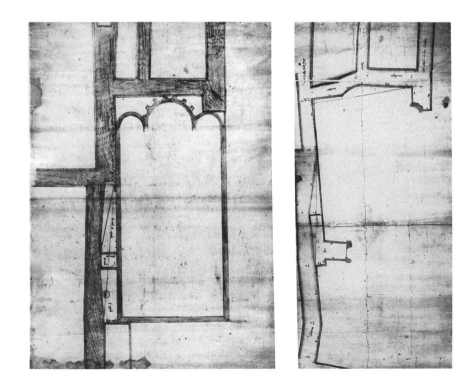

24. San Salvador: view of the interior toward the main altar. (Photo Biggi, Venice).

25. San Salvador: view of the interior
toward the entrance. (Photo E. Monti,
Rome).

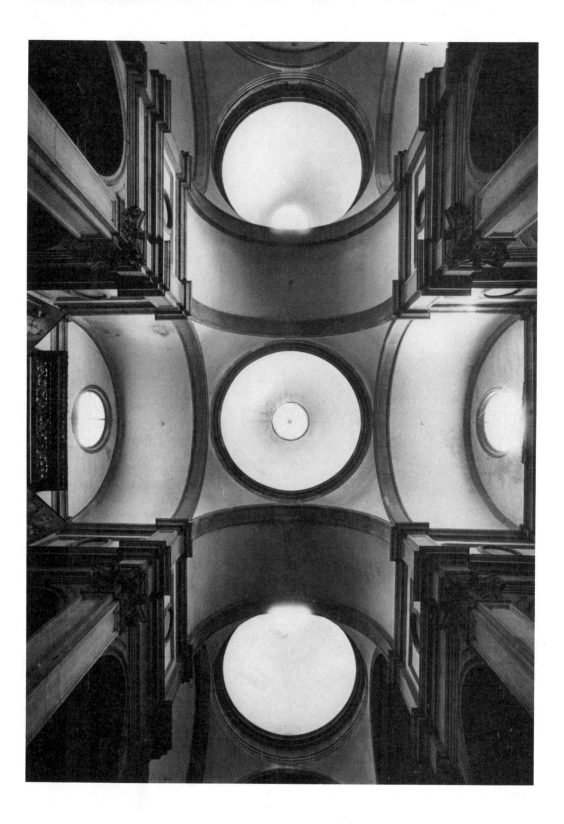

26–27. San Salvador: the domes seen from the inside, and the system of major and minor domes seen from the inside. (Photo Biggi, Venice).

28. San Salvador: detail of the interior.
Ibid.

29. Details of the order in San Salvador,
engraving. From Cicognara, Diedo, Salva,
Le fabbriche, vol. I, plate 97. Photo Biblioteca Marciana, Venice.

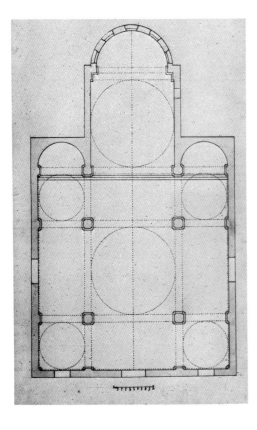

30. Antonio Visentini: longitudinal section of San Nicolò di Castello. London, Royal Institute of British Architects 133/1 and 133/3. Photo Royal Institute of British Architects, London.

31. Antonio Visentini: Plan of San Nicolò di Castello. Ibid.

32. The houses next to San Salvador: façade on the *campo*. Photo Biggi, Venice.

33–34. San Salvador: entrance to the church from the Mercerie, and view of the apse from the Merzaria del Capitello. Ibid.

35–36. Tullio Lombardo and Andrea Moroni, Abbatial church of Praglia: details of the interior. Ibid.

37. Tullio Lombardo, Monument to
Giovanni Mocenigo. Venice, Santi
Giovanni e Paolo. Photo Böhm, Venice.

38. Fra Giocondo, Design for the new St. Peter's in Rome (plan), 1505. Florence, Uffizi, Gabinetto dei Disegni e delle Stampe. Photo Soprintendenza per i Beni Artistici e Storici, Florence.

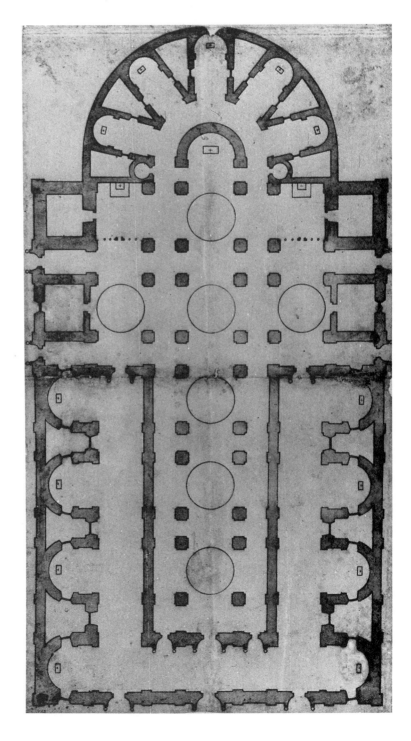

39. Plan of Santa Giustina in Padua, 16th century. Padua, Museo Civico, Raccolta iconografica padovana, 3653/XXXIX. Museum Photo, Padua.

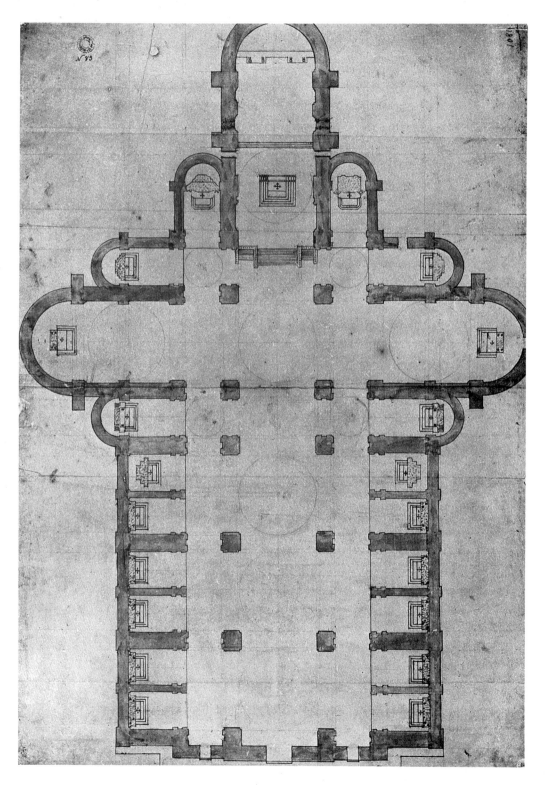

40. Andrea Moroni and Andrea da Valle
(based on a design by Matteo da Valle),
Santa Giustina in Padua: interior. Photo
E. Monti, Rome.

41. Antonio Abbondi called Lo Scarpagnino (based on a design by Sebastiano da Lugano), San Fantin: interior. Ibid.

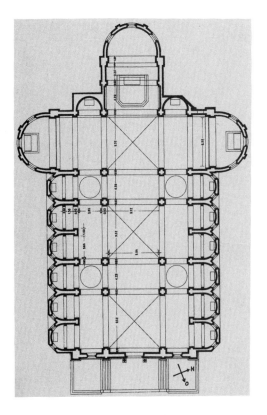

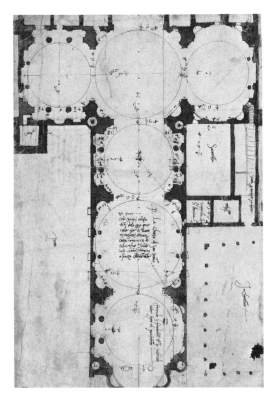

42. Alessio Tramello, San Sepolcro in Piacenza, early 16th century; plan.

43. Baldassarre Peruzzi, Study for San Domenico, in Siena. Florence, Uffizi, Gabinetto dei Disegni e delle Stampe, 339A. Photo Soprintendenza per i Beni Artistici e Storici, Florence.

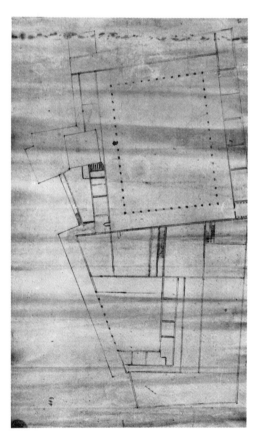

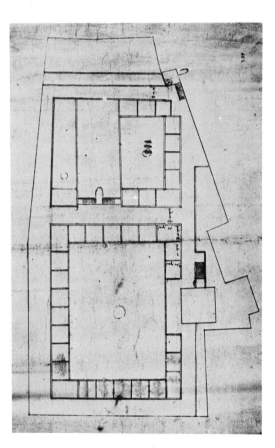

44. Study for one of the cloisters of San Salvador, 16th century. Venice, Archivio di Stato *Miscellanea Mappe*. Photo Archivio di Stato, Venice.

45–47. Study for the convent of San Salvador, 16th century. Ibid, 524, 463a, 463b, and 463c.

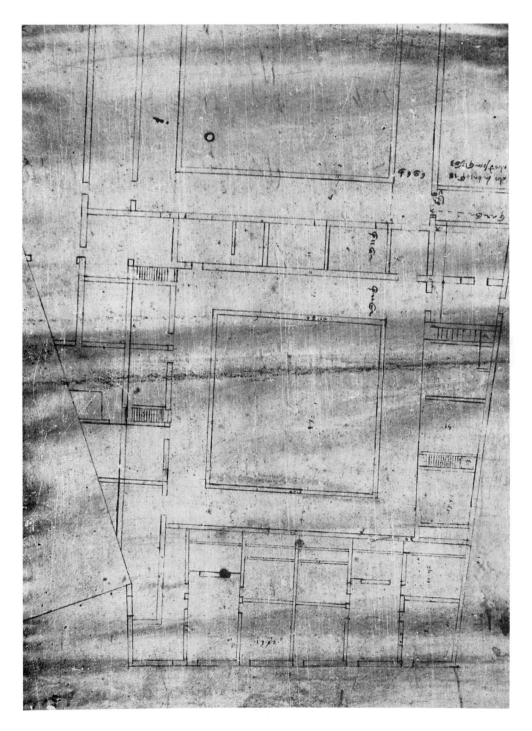

48–49. San Salvador: view of the major
and minor cloisters. Photo Biggi, Venice.

50. Convent of San Salvador: façade on
the canal. Ibid.

51. San Salvador: sacristy with frescoes
by Francesco Vecellio. Ibid.

52. Convent of San Salvador: view of the
vault in the refectory.

53. San Martino and the Ca' di Dio as they were before 1500, in the map of Jacopo de' Barbari (1500). Photo Biggi, Venice.

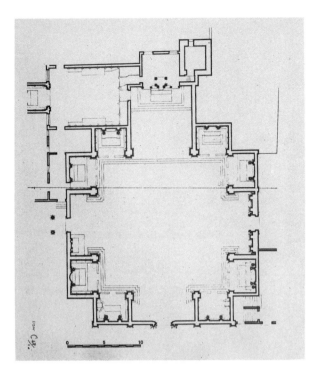

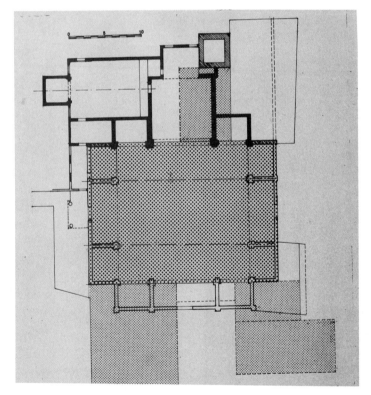

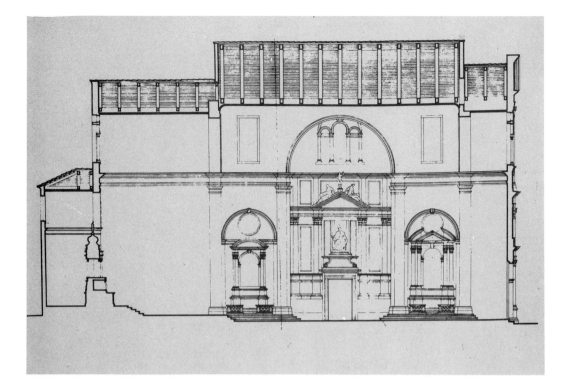

54. Jacopo Sansovino, San Martino: plan.
Venice, Archivio della Soprintendenza per
i Beni Ambientali e Architettonici, c. 48,
n. 2186. Photo Soprintendenza per i Beni
Ambientali e Architettonici, Venice.

55. The plan of the Sansovinian church of
San Martino superimposed over the
medieval church (dark mesh), and of the
preexisting, adjoining houses (light mesh).
In black, the walls executed before 1570.

56. Longitudinal section of San Martino.
Venice, Archivio della Soprintendenza per
i Beni Ambientali e Architettonici, c. 48/3,
n. 2183. In the central chapel one can see
the monument to Doge Erizzo. Photo Soprintendenza per i Beni Ambientali e
Architettonici, Venice.

a

b

c

0   5   10

57. Phases in the construction of the façade of San Martino, deduced from documents, from a picture attributed to Giacomo Guardi, and from an examination of the existing walls. From the top: (a) situation before 1611; (b) situation in the eighteenth century; (c) present façade, due to the intervention of Federico Berchet and Domenico Rupolo (1897).

58. San Martino: the apse section. Photo Biggi, Venice.

59–60. San Martino: Interior and sacristy
by Jacopo Sansovino. Ibid.

61. Jacopo Sansovino, San Francesco della Vigna, 1534ff.: view toward the Badoer-Giustiniani chapel and toward the presbytery. Photo Martinelli, Venice.

62. Lorenzo Lotto, *San Vincenzo Ferrer in gloria*, fresco transferred onto canvas, circa 1513–15. Recanati, San Domenico.

63. *Elemosina di Sant'Antonino*, circa
1540–42. Venice, Santi Giovanni e Paolo.
Photo Böhm, Venice.

64. Project for the façade of Palazzo Bocchi in Bologna, engraving, 1555.

65. Palazzo Bocchi in Bologna, 1545 ff.
Photo E. Monti, Rome.

66. Palazzo Bocchi in Bologna: portal at
the entrance. Ibid.

67. Jacopo Sansovino, Ca' di Dio, begun
in 1545: façade on the canal and on the
fondamenta. Photo Biggi, Venice.

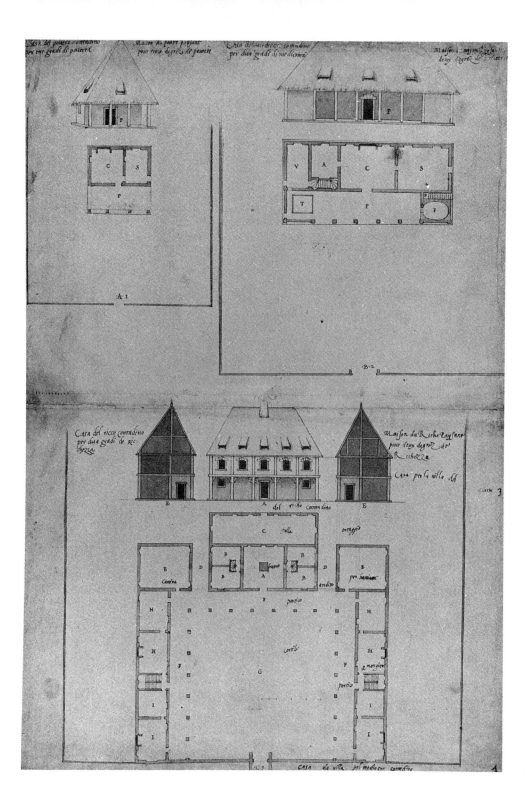

Casa del povero contadino
per vno gradi di povertà

Maison du povre paysans
pour trois degres de pouerte

Casa del minor ricco contadino
per dua gradi di mediocrita

Maison mayson de la
deux degres de pouerte

A 1

B 2

Casa del ricco contradino
per dua gradi de ric:
chezza

Maison du Riche Paysant
pour deux degrez dr
Richesza

Casa per la villa del

Cart 3

E   A del richo contradino   E

C   villa   orraggio

B   B
B   D   D   pri hecalien
Camera

A   fuoco
B   B

E   portia   andito

H   H

H   H

F   F   p mansion

G   Cortile   portia

I   I

I   I

C 3   CASA da villa   per mediocre contadino   A

68–69. Houses "of the poor farmer," the "mediocre farmer," and the "rich farmer," and four different types of houses "of the poor artisan," house of "a more comfortable artisan," house of an artisan "in the French manner." From Sebastiano Serlio, *Sesto libro inedito*. New York, Columbia University, Avery Library, c. 1r and 48r.

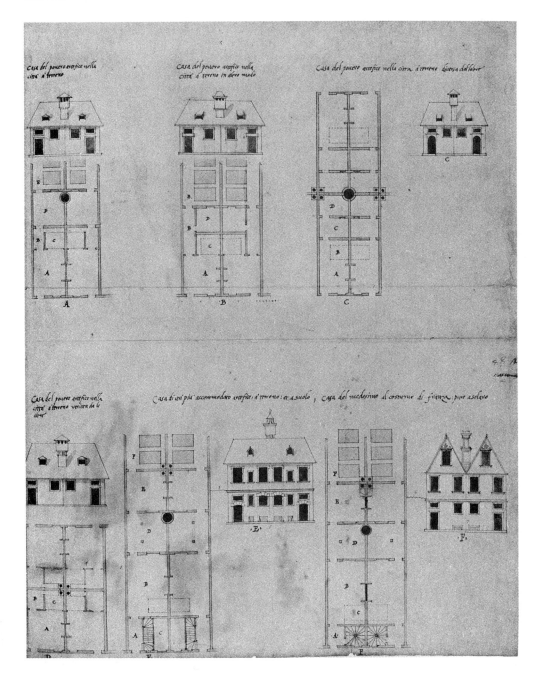

70. Pietro and Tullio Lombardo and
Mauro Codussi, Scuola Grande di San
Marco: façade on the *campo*. Photo Biggi,
Venice.

71. Mauro Codussi, Scuola Grande di San
Giovanni Evangelista: staircase. Ibid.

72. Titian, *San Rocco e storie della sua vita*, xylograph, circa 1523. London, British Museum. The xylograph was circulated as a propaganda sheet in order to collect the funds needed to continue with the construction of the Scuola di San Rocco.

73. The churches of the Frari and of San Rocco in the map of Jacopo de' Barbari (1500). On the left, one can see the area where the new Scuola Grande di San Rocco would be built.

74. Location plan of the Scuola Grande di
San Rocco (B), the church of San Rocco
(A), and the Castelforte houses (E), from a
seventeenth-century cadaster. Venice,
Archivio di Stato. Photo Archivio di Stato,
Venice.

75. Pseudo perspective view of the Scuola
Grande di San Rocco, from a seventeenth-
century cadaster. Ibid.

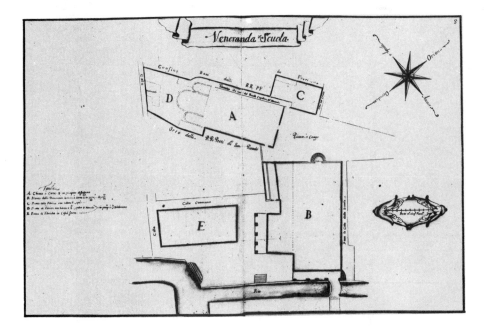

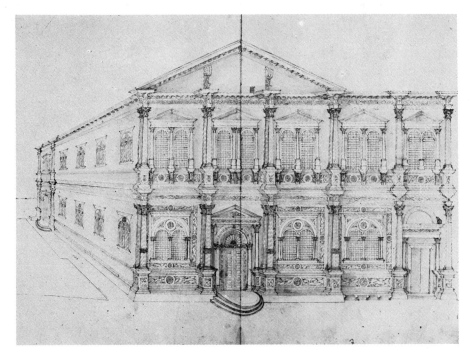

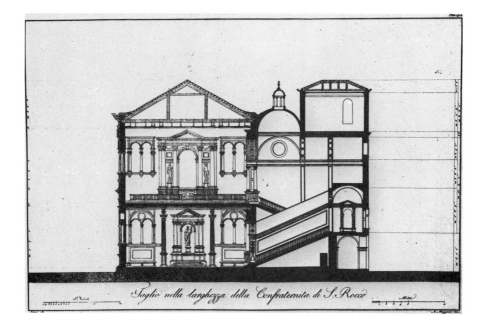

Taglio nella larghezza della Confraternita di S. Rocco

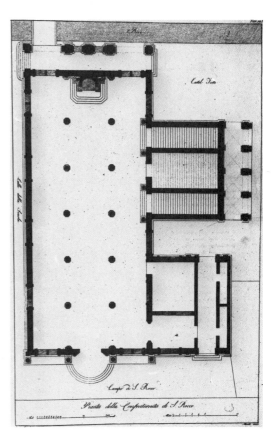

Pianta della Confraternita di S. Rocco

76–77. Cross section and ground floor plan of the Scuola Grande di San Rocco. From Cicognara, Diedo, Selva, *Le fabbriche*, vol. 2, 2nd ed. (Venice, 1840), plates 192 and 195. Photo Biggi, Venice.

78–79. Sante Lombardo, Scuola Grande di San Rocco: façade on the canal and detail of the aedicula. Photo Biggi, Venice.

80. Scuola Grande di San Rocco: connection of the body of the staircase onto the building volume facing the canal. Ibid.

81. Giorgio Fossati, Survey of the ground
floor of the Castelforte houses, cadaster
from 1770. Venice, Archivio di Stato,
Scuola Grande di San Rocco, 2ª cons.,
vol. 26, n. 22. Photo Archivio di Stato,
Venice.

82. View of the Castelforte houses and, in
the background, the church of San Rocco,
cadaster from the seventeenth century.
Ibid, 2ª cons. b. 30.

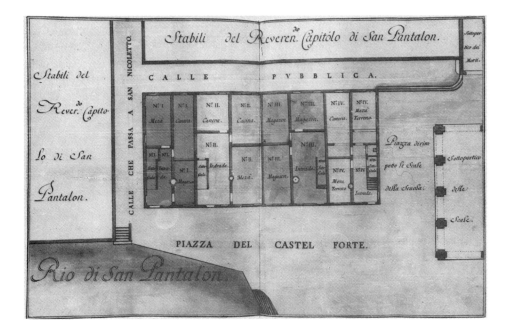

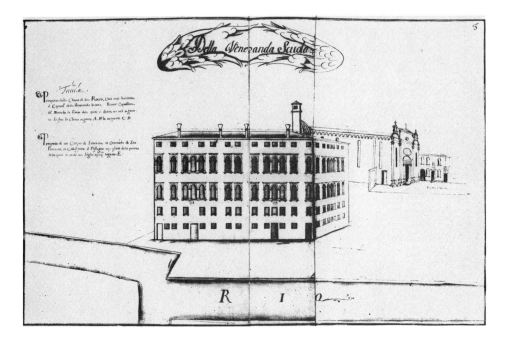

83. Antonio Abbondi called Lo Scarpagnino, Houses of Castelforte San Rocco:
façade on the canal. Photo Biggi, Venice.

84–85. Giorgio Fossati, Survey of the ground floor and interior elevation of Corte San Rocco at Santa Maria Maggiore, cadaster from 1770. Venice, Archivio di Stato, *Scuola Grande di San Rocco*, 2ª cons., vol. 26, n. 31, 42. Photo Archivio di Stato, Venice.

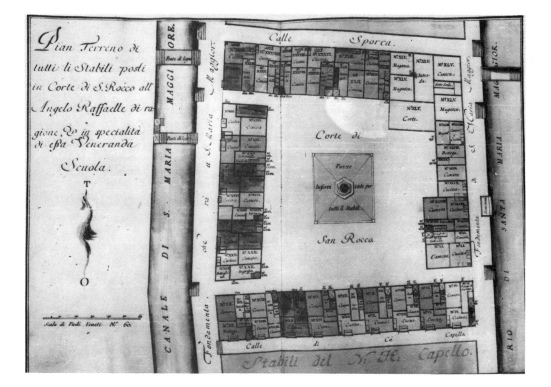

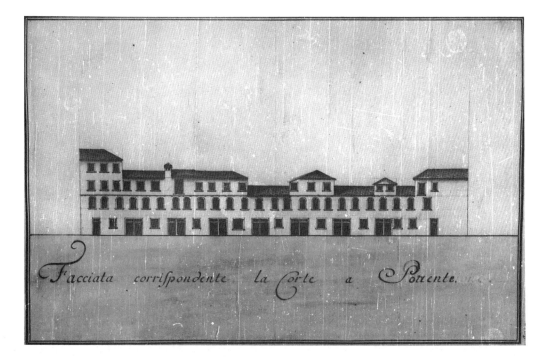

86. The Scuola Grande, in perspective, and San Rocco. Photo Biggi, Venice. Daniele Barbaro. Venice, Biblioteca Marciana, MS It 4, 37 (= 5133), f. 16r and 152 (= 5106), f. 12v. (Photo Biblioteca Marciana, Venice).

87. Pietro Bon and Antonio Abbondi
called Lo Scarpagnino, Scuola Grande di
San Rocco: façade. Ibid.

88. Antonio Abbondi called Lo Scarpagni-no, Scuola Grande di San Rocco: mullion windows on the upper level of the façade on the campo of the Scuola Grande di San Rocco. Ibid.

89. Detail of the columns superimposed
by Scarpagnino on the façade by master
Bon: note the rough junction of the bases
and the different design of the panels.
Ibid.

90. Anonymous artist of northern Italy, Triumphal arch *all'antica* with urban perspective, drawing, early, 16th century (?). Paris, Louvre, Rothschild Collection, inv. 1408 DR. Photo Réunion des Musées Nationaux, Paris.

91. Plan of the ground floor, the upper hall, and longitudinal section of the Scuola Grande della Misericordia, in a schematic survey executed by the students of the Istituto Universitario di Architettura di Venezia.

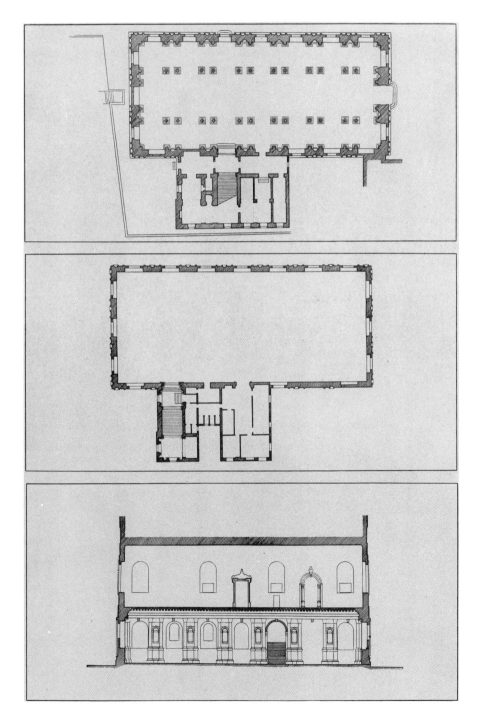

92. Andrea Palladio (after Jacopo Sansovino), Design for the façade of the Scuola
Grande della Misericordia. Vicenza,
Museo Civico D, 18r. Photo Museo Civico, Vincenza.

93. Donatelli (and Michelozzo?), Tabernacolo della Mercanzia, circa 1423. Florence, Orsanmichele, Rear façade. Photo
Archivi Alinari, Florence.

94. Jacopo Sansovino, Scuola Grande della Misericordia, 1532ff. Photo Biggi, Venice.

95. Scuola Grande di San Rocco: the hall
on the ground floor and the beginning of
the two flights of the staircase. Ibid.

96. Scuola Grande di San Rocco: the staircase by Scarpagnino seen from the intermediate landing. Ibid.

SEPTIMVS.

¶FRANCISCI PATRICII SE:
nenſis Pontificis Caietani liber Septimus, De
inſtitutione Reſp. incipit.

¶DE SITV ORBIS, ET REGIONIS, DE LOCI
oportunitate, De eligendo ſolo, agroque qui ea omnia ſuppetat, Quæ ad vi
uendum ſpeċtant, & animalia omnia, ac plantas cum plagis, regionibuſque
cœli conuenire.
¶Titulus Primus.
De ciuſſi

OCAVVS.

¶FRANCISCI PATRICII SENEN:
ſis Pontificis Caietani liber Oċtauus, De inſtitutione Reſp.
incipit.

¶ARCHITECTVM OPTIMVM AD:
hibendum eſſe cum vrbs ſtatuitur.
¶Titulus primus.
V.j.   Poſtquam

97. A city in its territory, xylograph.
From Francesco Patrizi Senese, *De institutione rei publicae* (1494), Paris 1520,
book 7, f. 102r.

98. *Il buon architetto e la città*, xylograph. From Francesco Patrizi Senese, *De
institutione*, book 8, f. 115r.

99–100. From the preparatory manuscript of the Vitruvian *Commentari* by Daniele Barbaro. Venice, Biblioteca Marciana, MS It 4, 37 (= 5133), f. 16r and 152 (= 5106), f. 12v. (Photo Biblioteca Marciana, Venice).

l'architraue ionico et i suoi membri, à questo è molto simile l'architraue corinthio, ilquale è sculpito et ha di piu ch'è tra il gocciolatoio, et il denticulo un'una uiuola tanto alto quanto è la p̃a fascia dello ar... co i suoi cauetti... le ciuciuli. et piu sotto in somma si mettano poco si aggiungono i listelli, & la ottaua par... della lor fascia, il pͦ ha i denticuli, il secondo è pirustilo.

sia la metà della colonna, et habbia lo spor
to sia la quarta parte del basso della colon
na. et così allhora larga, et longa sarà della
grossezza della colonna una uolta e mezza.
l'altezza di essa, se sira fatta al modo atti
co sia diuisa in modo, el la parte di soß.ᵃ
sia la terza parte della grossezza ella co
lonna, il restante poi al zocco si dia. Et
cetto il zocco diuidasi il restante in quat
tro parti, et facciasi il bastone per la 4.ᵗᵃ
parte, et le altre ch sono tre, siano egual-
mente diuise, una sia del bastone iferio
re, l'altra gli con i soi quadretti si dia
a i cauetti.

Ma se le base ioniche si hauerãno a far, bi
sogna in questo modo misurarle. la
longezza della base per ogni uerso sia ella
grossezza di una colonna, aggiuntaui uo
ra di essa grossezza la quarta, et l'ottaua

l'occhio.
il compartimento ella uoluta, il capitelo ha
dalla sua cima.

base.

101. Illustration from Daniele Barbaro's *I dieci Libri dell'Architettura di M. Vitruvio*, Venice 1556, p. 4.

102. Machines for the lifting of water. From Daniele Barbaro's *I dieci Libri*, book 10, p. 265.

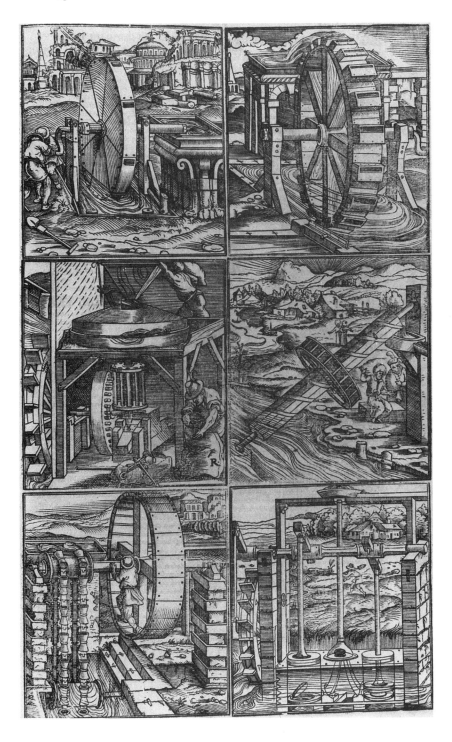

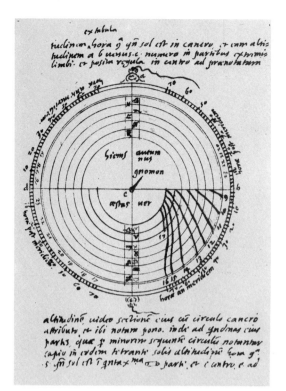

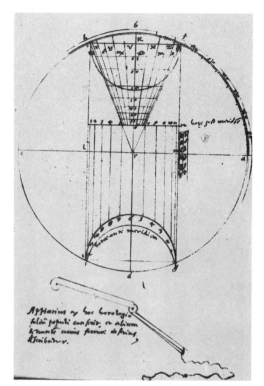

103. Calculation of the height of the sun at different hours and seasons. From the manuscript by Daniele Barbaro, *De horologiis describendis*. Venice, Biblioteca Marciana MS Lat. 8, 42 (= 3097), f. 5r and 23r. Photo Biblioteca Marciana, Venice.

104. The clock of Appiano. Ibid.

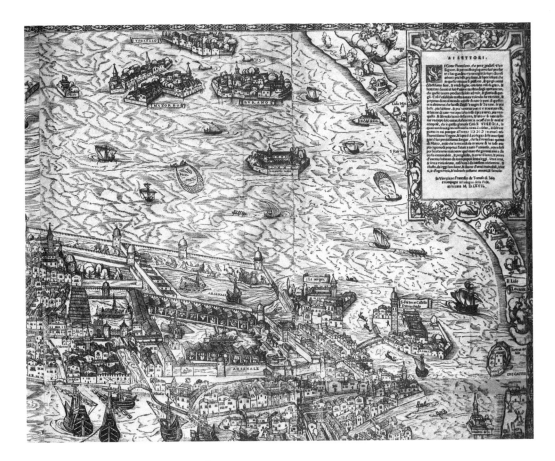

105. The Arsenal in the Great map of
Venice by Matteo Pagan (edition of Francesco Tommaso da Salò, Venice 1567).
Venice, Civico Museo Correr. Photo Civico Museo Correr, Venice.

106. Machine for the lifting and positioning of capitals. Venice, Biblioteca Marciana MS Lat. 8, 87 (= 3048), f. 2v. Photo Biblioteca Marciana, Venice.

107. Machines for the leveling of embankments, the lifting of water, and the propulsion of boats with wheels. Ibid, f. 27r.

108. Machines for the transport of heavy materials and obelisks. Ibid, f. 33r.

109. Machine for the transport and raising of columns and heavy materials. Ibid, f. 34r.

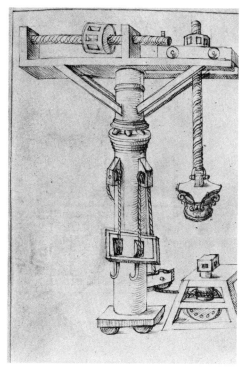

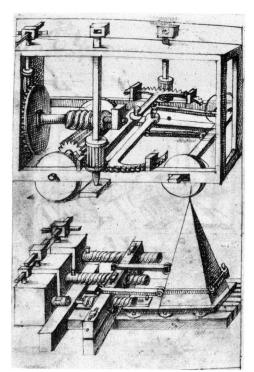

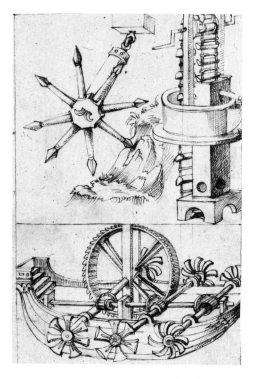

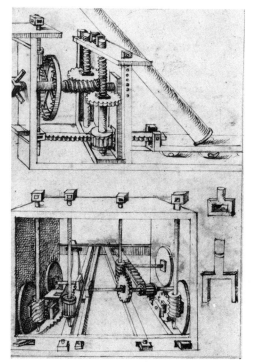

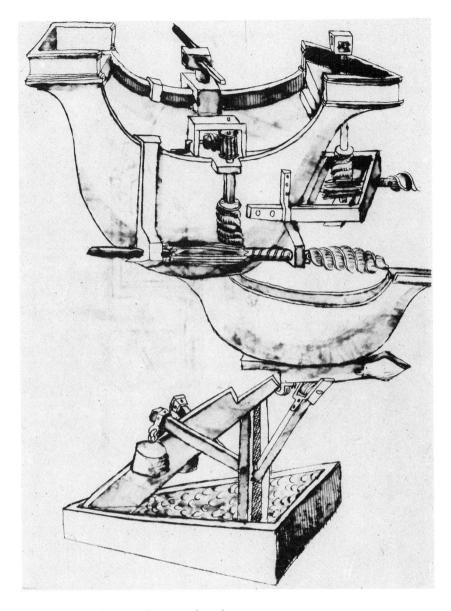

110. Mechanical devices from a codex of drawings that belonged to Jacopo Contarini. Ibid, MS It. z86 (= 4817), f. 48r.

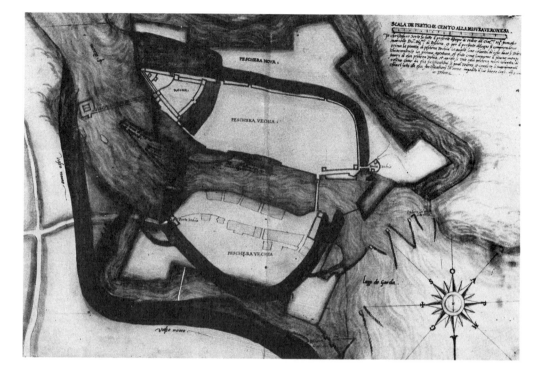

111. Cristoforo Sorte, Survey of the city of Peschiera "as ordered by the Illustrious Signor Francesco Marcello," July 3, 1571. Ibid, MS It. 6, 188 (= 10039), n. 43.

112. Illustrations of the manuscript by Galileo Galilei, *Trattato della Fortificazione*, once preserved in the library of Gian Vincenzo Pinelli. Milan, Biblioteca Ambrosiana D 296 inf., pp. 14–15. Photo Biblioteca Ambrosiana, Milan.

113. Drawing included in the *Discorso di Fortificationi di Jacopo Contarini sopra dubbi proposti da Giulio Savorgnano*. Ibid, MS A71 inf., c. 33r.

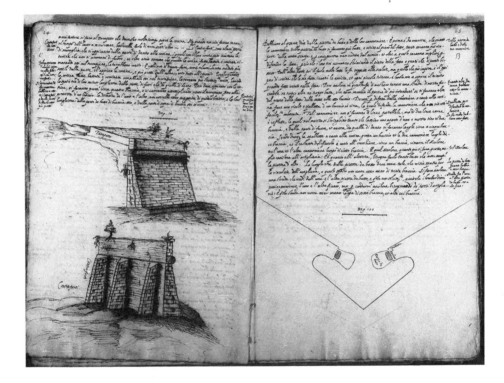

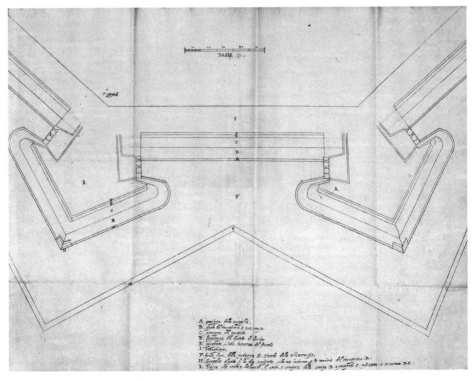

114. Cristoforo Sabbadino, Plan for the development and hydraulic organization of Venice, 1557. Venice, Archivio di Stato, *Laguna*, 14. Photo Archivio di Stato, Venice.

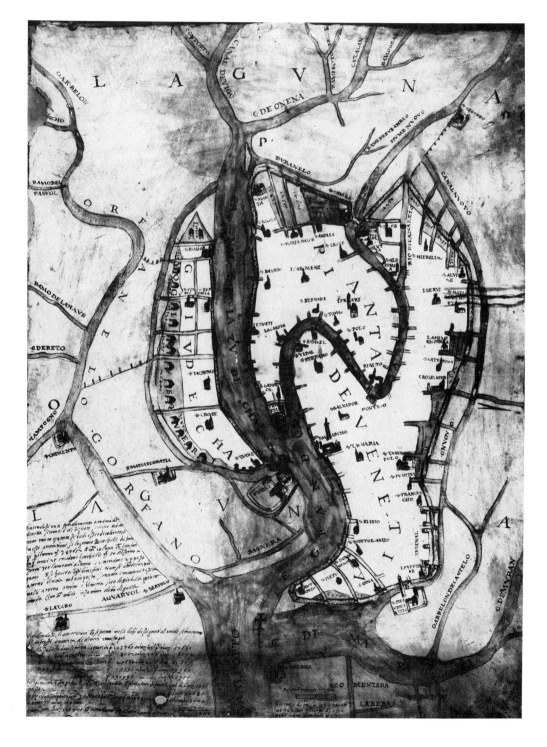

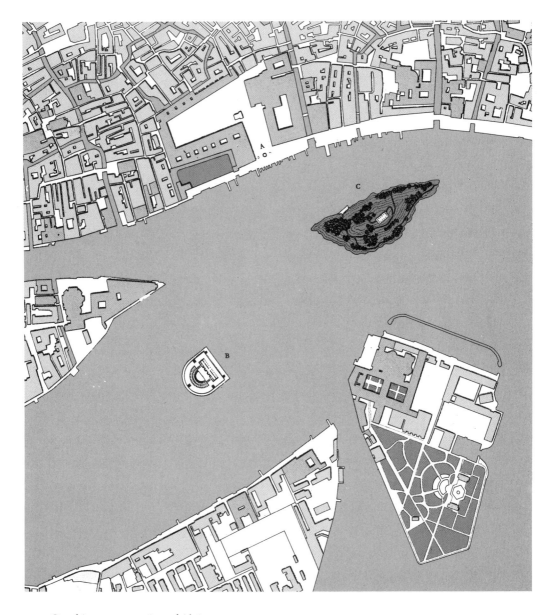

115. Graphic reconstruction of Alvise Cornaro's project for the Bacino of San Marco: (A) the fountain; (B) the theater in the water; (C) the "shapeless little hill." Drawing by Luca Ortelli.

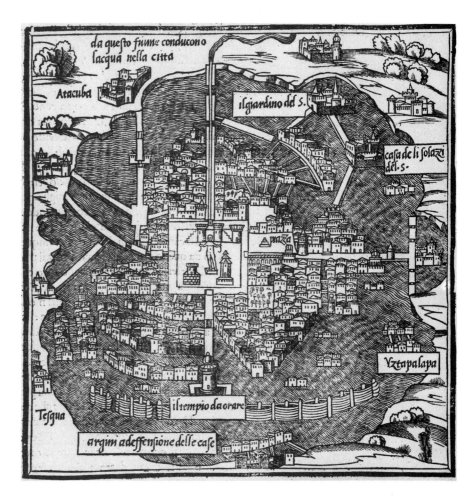

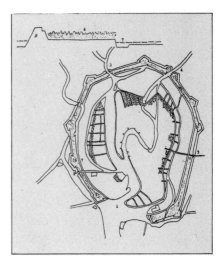

116. *La gran città di Temistian.* From Benedetto Bordone, *Isolario*, Venice 1528.

117. Reconstruction of Venice surrounded by walls in water according to Alvise Cornaro's proposal.

118. The city of Tenochtitlàn, drawing, before 1538. Florence, Biblioteca Nazionale MS Magl. 13, 18 (BR 234–36), c. 126. Photo Biblioteca Nazionale, Florence.

119. Antonio da Ponte, The Prigioni Nuove, 1589 ff.: façade toward the Bacino of San Marco. Photo Biggi, Venice.

120. Venetian artist of the second half of
the 16th century, *La fortezza di Palma tra
le città di Terraferma*. Venice, Palazzo
Ducale.

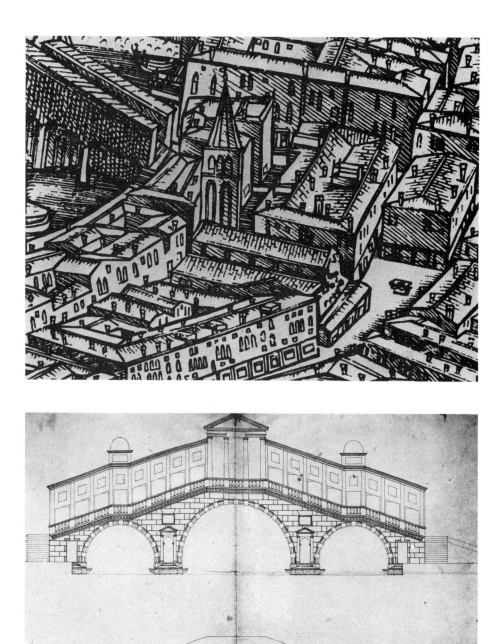

121. The urban area between Campo San
Bartolomeo and the Rialto Bridge in the
map by Jacopo de' Barbari (1500). Photo
Biggi, Venice.

122. Vincenzo Scamozzi, Design for the
Rialto Bridge. London, Royal Institute of
British Architects, VIII/10. Photo Royal
Institute of British Architects, London.

123. Guglielmo de' Grandi, Survey of the house of Zuan Francesco Lippomano, once situated between the Ramo del Fondego and the narrow *calle*. Venice, Biblioteca de Museo Correr, Miscellanea disegni. Photo Civico Museo Correr, Venice.

124. Graphic reconstruction of the urban structure between Campo San Bartolomeo and the Grand Canal before the interventions of Antonio da Ponte, with the position of the ancient wooden bridge and, in hatched outline, the initial alignment chosen by the Senate for the new bridge in stone. From D. Calabi, *La direzione del nuovo ponte di Rialto e il "negotio" degli stabili di San Bartolomeo.*

125. Graphic reconstruction of Antonio da Ponte's first project for the Rialto Bridge and for the buildings aligned with it. Ibid.

126. Graphic reconstruction of the final project for the Rialto Bridge, for the *stradone*, and for the new buildings; in hatched outline, the alignment of the second project. Ibid.

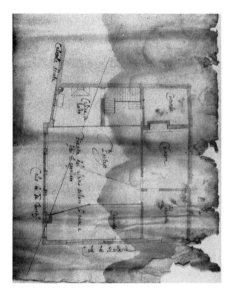

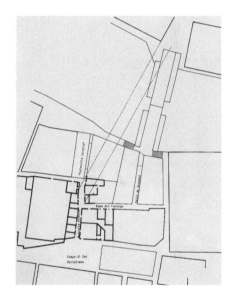

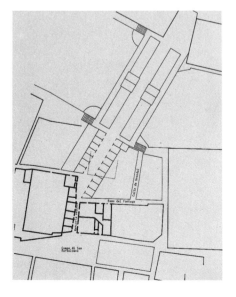

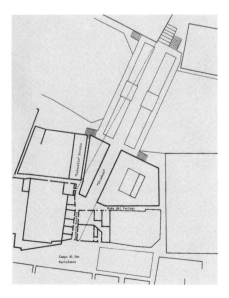

127. View of the *stradone* and the Rialto
Bridge. Photo Biggi, Venice.

128. Vincenzo Scamozzi, Project for the connection of the Procuratie Nuove onto the Sansovinian Library. Florence, Uffizi, Gabinetto dei Disegni e delle Stampe, 194A. Photo Sansoni, Florence.

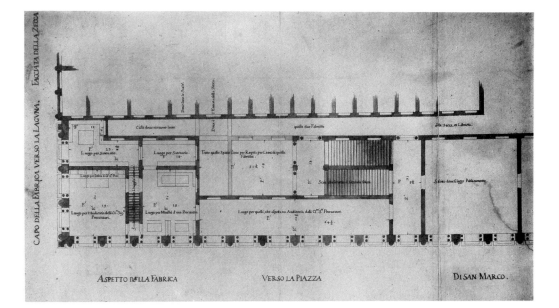

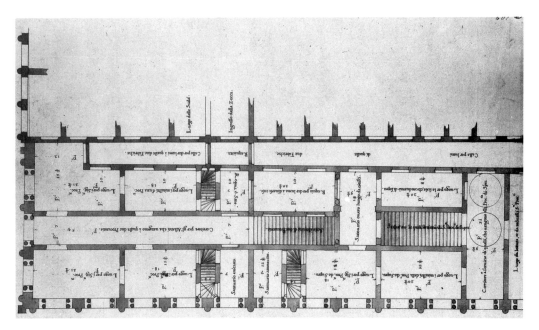

129–30. Vincenzo Scamozzi, Project for the completion of the Sansovinian Library: plan of the second floor above ground in the solutions with three and two floors. Florence, Uffizi, Gabinetto dei Disegni e delle Stampe, 193 A and 192 A. Photo Soprintendenza per i Beni Artistici e Storici, Florence.

131. The "clash" between Jacopo Sansovino's Zecca and the Library completed
by Vincenzo Scamozzi. Photo E. Monti,
Rome.

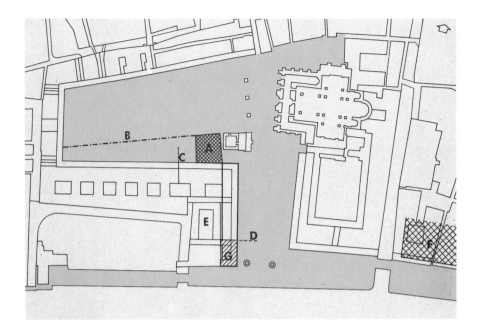

132. Location plan of Piazza San Marco, with the positions of the Procurators' old offices (A), the alignment of the Ospizio Orseolo (B), the approximate position of the new dogal residence discussed in circa 1585–89 (F), the limit of the Scamozzian intervention in the Procuratie Nuove (C), and the body of the Library executed by Vincenzo Scamozzi (G). Also indicated is the extent of the Library executed by Jacopo Sansovino (D) and the Zecca (E). (Drawing by Marta Dalle Mule).

133. Gentile Bellini, *Processione in Piazza* (detail of the old offices of the Procurators of San Marco next to the bell tower). Venice, Gallerie dell'Accademia. Photo Böhm, Venice.

134. Vincenzo Scamozzi, Procuratie
Nuove in Piazza San Marco. Photo Biggi,
Venice.

135–36. Vincenzo Scamozzi, Procuratie Nuove: detail of the third order and the first courtyard. Ibid.

137. Vincenzo Scamozzi (?), Design for the façade for the doge's new residence (?). Chatsworth, Devonshire Collection. Photo Courtauld Institute of Art, London.

138. Survey of the Palazzo Ducale and of the areas on the other side of the Rio di Palazzo, 16th century. Venice, Biblioteca Marciana, MS It. 7, 295 (= 10047) n. 13. Photo Biblioteca Marciana, Venice.

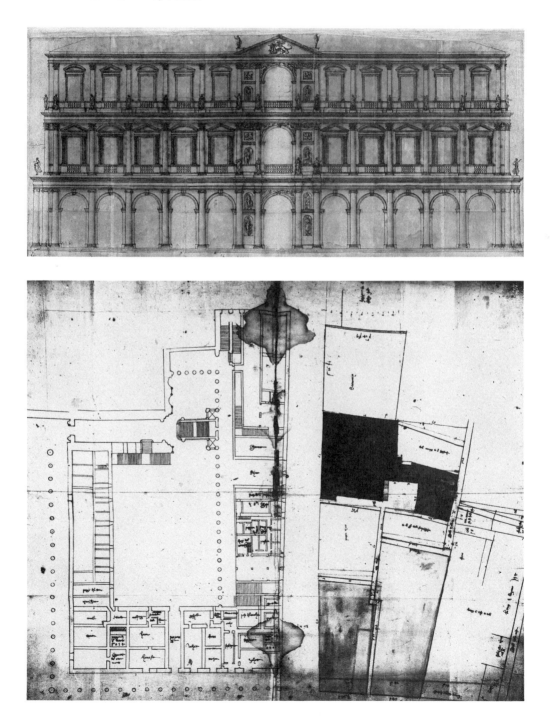

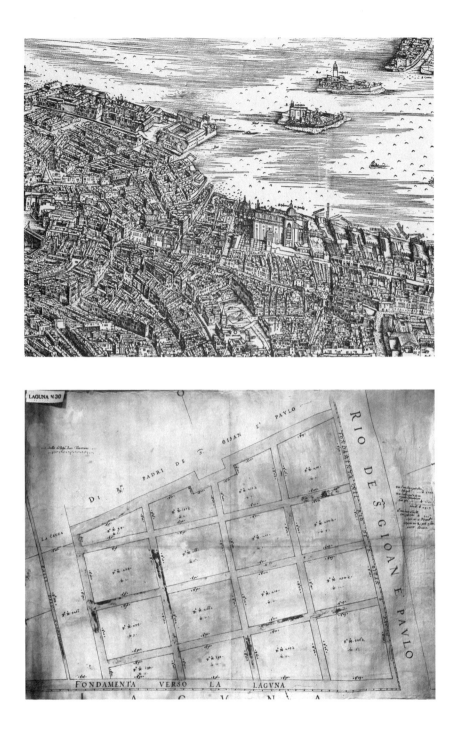

139. The zone of the Fondamenta Nuove in the map by Jacopo de' Barbari (1500). Photo Biggi, Venice.

140–42. Giovanni Alvise Galesi, Projects for the urbanization of the areas between the Rio dei Santi Giovanni e Paolo, the Zecca, and the Fondamenta Nuove, 1594. Venice, Archivio di Stato, *Laguna* 30, 28, 29. Photo Archivio di Stato, Venice.

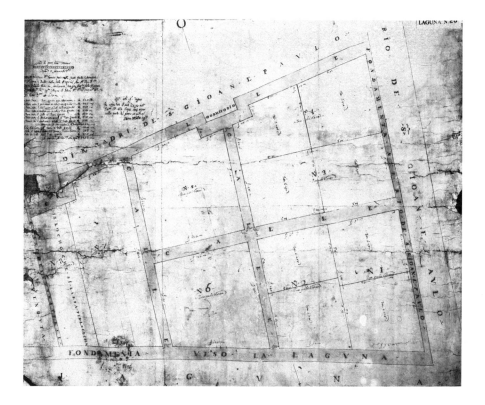

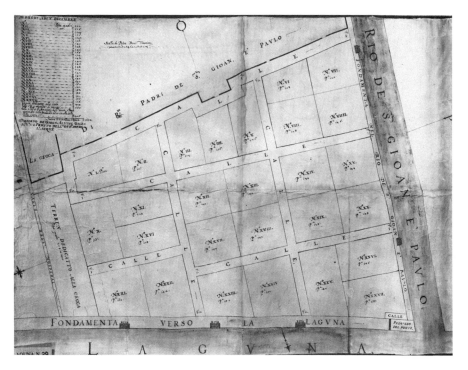

143. Giovanni Alvise Galesi: Project for the subdivision of the land between the Rio dei Crociferi and the Rio dei Santi Giovanni e Paolo, August 7, 1600. Venice, Archivio di Stato, *Laguna*, 34, 35 Photo Archivio di Stato, Venice.

144. Project for the subdivision of the land between the Rio dei Crociferi and the Rio dei Santi Giovanni e Paolo, with the names of the first buyers. Ibid.

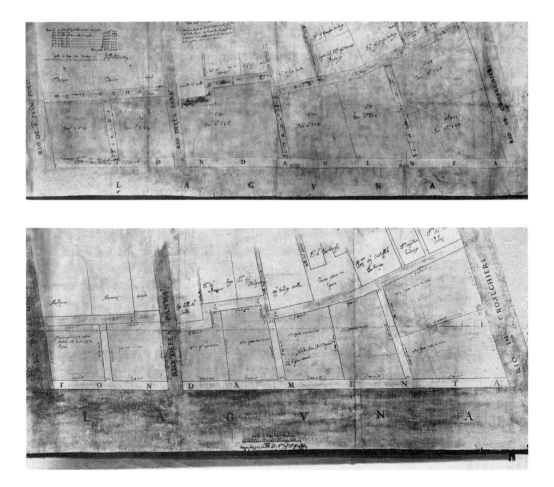

145. View of Palazzo Donà on the Fondamenta Nuove (*proto* Francesco di Pietro), 1610 ff. Photo Biggi, Venice.

146. Antonio Visentini, Survey of the plan and elevation of the palazzo of Leonardo Donà. London, British Museum, King's Library.

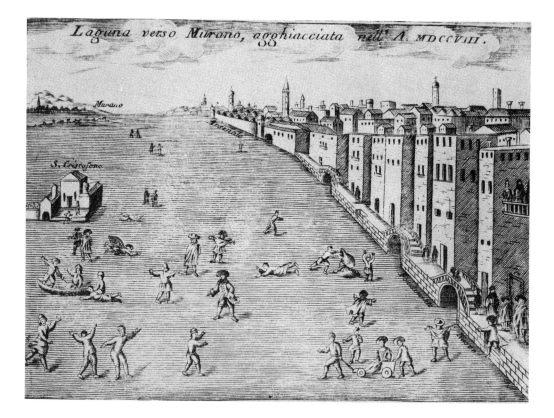

Laguna verso Murano, agghiacciata nell' A. MDCCVIII.

147. Vincenzo Coronelli, The Fondamenta Nuove, engraving, 1708.

Notes

Abbreviations

AMV   *Archivi Municipali, Venice.*

APSM   *Archivio della parrocchia di San Martino, Venice.*

ASBAA   *Archivio della Sopraintendenza ai Beni Architettonici e Ambientali, Venice.*

ASGSR   *Archivio della Scuola Grande di San Rocco, Venice.*

ASV   *Archivio di Stato, Venice.*

BAM   *Biblioteca Ambrosiana, Milan.*

BAV   *Biblioteca Apostolica Vaticana.*

BEM   *Biblioteca Estense, Modena.*

BMC   *Biblioteca del Museo Correr, Venice.*

BMV   *Biblioteca Nazionale Marciana, Venice.*

Cisa   *Centro Internazionale di Studi di Architettura Andrea Palladio.*

IUAV   *Istituto Universitario di Architettura di Venezia.*

Riba   *Royal Institute of the British Architects, London.*

UA   *Uffizi, Florence, Gabinetto disegni e stampe, Architettura.*

c.   carta *(sheet number).*

t.   tergo *(reverse side of sheet).*

b.   busta *(box file).*

f.   folio *(sheet number).*

fil.   filza *(collection of loose documents).*

fasc.   fascicolo *(booklet).*

m.v.   more veneto *(the Venetian calendar year began on March 1; therefore the first two months of the conventional calendar year maintained the date of the preceding year).*

proc.   piocesso *(series).*

reg.   registro *(bound volume).*

Introduction

1. See Paul Veyne, *Comment on écrit l'histoire.* (Paris, 1971; It. trans. Rome and Bari, 1973), in particular pp. 207ff., in which the author develops his criticism of the typical and of historical concepts.

2. The studies done on the concept of the Renaissance seem to have lost some of the interest that they had for historians like Chabod or Cantimori. See Federico Chabod, *Scritti sul Rinascimento*, 2nd ed. (Turin, 1974), which gathers essays written between 1933 and 1950, and Delio Cantimori, "Sulla storia del concetto di Rinascimento" (1955), and "La periodizzazione dell'età del Rinascimento" (1955), in id. *Storici e storia. Metodo, caratteristiche e significato del lavoro storiografico*, 2nd ed. (Turin, 1971), 414–

62 and 553–77 respectively. It is very interesting to compare the concerns underlying the essays just cited with those that emerge from the texts collected in the volume dedicated to Eugenio Garin, *Il Rinascimento. Interpretazioni e problemi* (Rome and Bari, 1979). On the history of the concept of the Renaissance, in addition to the authoritative volume by Wallace K. Ferguson. *The Renaissance in Historical Thought* (Cambridge, Mass., 1948; It. trans. Bologna, 1969), and the splendid essay by Lucien Febvre. "Comment Jules Michelet inventa la Renaissance" (1950), in id., *Pour une histoire à part entière* (Paris, 1962); It. trans. in id., *Problemi di metodo storico*, 2nd ed. (Turin, 1971), 55–65; see also Michele Ciliberto, *Il Rinascimento. Storia di un dibattito* (Florence, 1975), Cesare Vasoli, *Umanesimo e Rinascimento* (Palermo, 1976), and Peter Burke, *Culture and Society in Renaissance Italy 1420–1540* (1972); It. trans. (Turin, 1984), esp. 5–28.

3. Martin Heidegger, *Holzwege* (Frankfurt am Main, 1950); It. trans. (Florence, 1982), 71ff.

4. Ibid., 98.

5. A timely analysis of Cassirer's thought, in this sense, can be found in the recent volume by Silvia Ferretti, *Il demone della memoria. Simbolo e tempo storico in Warburg, Cassier, Panofsky* (Casale Monferrato, 1984), 82–142.

6. See Jacques Le Goff, *Le mentalità: una storia ambigua*, in the collection *Faire de l'histoire* (Paris, 1974), It. trans. (Turin, 1981), 239–58. The criticism of the history of mentalities developed by Ginzburg strikes us as productive in its attempts to extrapolate cultures and group or individual behaviors from collective structures. See Carlo Ginzburg, *Il formaggio e i vermi. Il cosmo di un mugnaio del '500* (Turin, 1976), XXII–XXIV. Ginzburg's arguments aim at discerning intersections between structures of long duration (*longue durée*) and particular mentalities or cultures, stressing the plural significance to be given to the concept of mentality. This remark is also meant to respond to the kind observations made to us by our friend Calabrese. See Omar Calabrese,

"Un armonioso conflitto," *Alfabeta* 54 (1983): 11. The reflections contained in Enrico Castelnuovo's essay, "Per una storia sociale dell'arte" (1976 and 1977), in id., *Arte, industria, rivoluzioni* (Turin, 1985), 3–64, are still useful.

7. Friedrich Nietzsche, *Aurora e scelta di frammenti postumi* (1879–1881), fragment from spring 1880, in *Opere*, ed. Giorgio Colli and Mazzino Montinari, vol. 5, tome 1 (Milan, 1964), 296.

8. See especially Massimo Cacciari, *Viaggio estivo*, in the collection *Venezia Vienna*, ed. Giandomenico Romanelli (Milan, 1983), 127ff.

Chapter 1

1. The document in question is Nicolò Zen's, *Storia della guerra veneto-turca del 1537*, BMV, MS It., cl. 7, 2053 = 7920, analyzed in Ennio Concina's essay, "Fra Oriente e Occidente: gli Zen, un palazzo e il mito di Trebisonda," in the collection *"Renovatio urbis." Venezia nell'età di Andrea Gritti (1523–1538)*, ed. Manfredo Tafuri (Rome, 1984), 265ff. (esp. 276–80). Regarding Nicolò Zen, his function at the Arsenal and his relations with Daniele Barbaro, see E. Concina's later work, *L'Arsenale della Repubblica di Venezia* (Milan, 1984), 122–24 and 146ff., and chap. 5 of this volume.

2. "Habitatoribus igitur una copia est ut solis piscibus expleantur; paupertas ibi cum divitibus sub equalitate convivit, unus cibus omnes reficit, habitacio similis universa concludit, nesciunt de penatibus invidere et, sub hac mensura degentes, evadunt vicium cui mundum constat esse obnoxium. In salinis autem exercendis tota contencio est; pro aratris, pro falcibus, cilindros volvitis; inde vobis fructus omnis enascitur, quoniam in ipsis et que non facitis posidetis; moneta illic quodammodo percutitur; victualis arti vestre omnis fluctus additus est: potest aurum aliquis querere; nemo est qui salem non desideret invenire; merito quoniam isti debet omnis cibus, quod potest esse gratissimus." Cassiodoro's text can be found in *Andrea Danduli Chronica per extensum descripta*, ed. Ester Pastorello, in *Rerum Italicarum Scriptores*, vol. 12,

pt. I (Bologna, 1938), 69–70 (the quotation is on p. 70). Also see Frederic C. Lane, *Venice, A Maritime Republic* (Baltimore, 1973), 3–4.

3. Regarding Domenico Morosini's *De bene instituta re publica*, see chap. 5 of this volume.

4. Cited in Concini, "Fra Oriente e Occidente," 280. Our emphasis.

5. In this connection, see the penetrating hypotheses contained in the volume by Roberto Esposito, *Ordine e conflitto. Machiavelli e la letteratura politica del Rinascimento italiano* (Naples, 1984), esp. on pp. 111ff. The theme of original unity compromised by *regno* and *robba* (kingdom and property) recurs in humanist literature with obvious teleological aspects. See, for example, Girolamo Savonarola's 14th sermon at Aggeo: "Thus the Church of Christ, that was founded by his apostles in poverty and in simplicity and in union and in peace . . . was totally united in one desire and *erat eis cor unum et anima una*. . . . Then that fervor and that poverty were lacking and the Church came into a temporal kingdom and property, and *tunc est factum regnum Darii*. . . ." Girolamo Savonarola, *Prediche sopra Aggeo ecc.*, ed. Luigi Firpo (Rome, 1965), 239–40. The same Savonarola, in his 13th sermon at Aggeo (ibid., 228), declared: "and I believe . . . that the Venetians' form of government is very good, and there is no shame in learning from others, because that form which was given them by God, and because they took it, there has never been civil dissension among them."

6. On the relations between Sebastiano Serlio and Franceso Zen, see Loredana Olivato, "Per il Serlio a Venezia: documenti nuovi e documenti rivisitati," *Arte Veneta* 25 (1971): 284–91, but on the implications of the Bolognese architect in Palazzo Zen, see again the cited essay by Concina.

7. Concina, "Fra Oriente e Occidente," 280–81.

8. N. Zen, *Dell'origine de' barbari che distrussero per tutto 'l mondo l'imperio di Roma, onde hebbe principio la città di Venetia libri undici* (Venice, 1557), 194–95.

9. See Olivato, "Per il Serlio"; Concina, "Fra Oriente Occidente," which sets 1526 and 1533 as the dates *post* and *ante quem* for the model of the palazzo, (p. 267).

10. On these themes see the volume by Richard A. Goldthwaite, *The Building of Renaissance Florence. An Economic and Social History* (Baltimore, 1980); It. trans. (Bologna, 1984), esp. 53–167. Though it is based on ample documentation, Goldthwaite's analysis is not persuasive when it attempts to demonstrate that the exceptional freezing of capital destined for palazzi and private chapels, in fifteenth-century Florence, had consequences for the entire economy. Furthermore, the author's underestimation of the instability of the banking and commercial sector leads him to emphasize the demands made by the new taste, which—freed from the creeping economic crisis—thus became almost mythical. And yet, Goldthwaite also remarks in passing that the Florentine economy's failure to develop was due not only to a lack of investments in systems that would break the "technological barrier," but also to the exceptional investment in building (see ibid., 79). On Goldthwaite's book, see Sergio Bertelli's critical review, which we agree with, "Un amore accecante," *L'indice*, 2, no. 3 (1985): 18–19. On the situation of Italy between the fourteenth and early seventeenth centuries, see Ruggiero Romano, *Tra due crisi: l'Italia del Rinascimento*, 4th ed. (Turin, 1977), which contains analyses that are also fertile for themes indicated here.

11. On the Roman palazzi of the early sixteenth century, see Christoph Luitpold Frommel's fundamental work, *Der römische Palastbau der Hochrenaissance*, 3 vols. (Tübingen, 1973), of which a completely revised edition, in Italian, is about to appear. Frommel offers extremely refined philological analyses as well as precise typological and functional reconstructions that allow a thorough reading of sixteenth-century residential building.

12. Poggio Bracciolini had already turned, through Pietro da Noceto, to Nicholas, in order, he maintained, "ut

cesset ad impensa aedificandi, quam, ut tecum vera loquar *omnes non culpant, sed detestantur*" (our emphasis). See Massimo Miglio, "Una vocazione in progresso: Michele Canensi biografo papale," *Studi Medievali*, ser. 3, no. 12 (1971): 463–524, reprinted in id., *Storiografia pontificia del quattrocento* (Bologna, 1975): 63–118; the quotation is on p. 105 n. 55. Pastor recalls an analogous judgment by Nicodemo Tranchedino, while the *carme* cited by Stefano Infessura hailed Sixtus IV as the "new Nero" (*Diario della città di Roma di Stefano Infessura scribasenato*, ed. Oreste Tommasini, Fonti per la Storia d'Italia, 5 [Rome, 1890], 158). The "sumptuous and excessive construction" stimulated by Julius II was violently criticized—for exquisitely political reasons—by Marcantonio Altieri, a representative of municipalist nobility: see Marcantonio Altieri, *Li Nuptiali*, ed. Enrico Narducci (Rome, 1873). For Erasmus's criticisms, see Erasmus of Rotterdam, "Sileni Alcibiadis," in *Adagia*, ed. Silvana Seidel Menchi (Turin, 1980), 96, and "Julius exclusus e coelis," in *Erasmi Opuscula*, ed. Wallace K. Ferguson (The Hague, 1933).

13. Giovanni di Pagolo Morelli, *Ricordi*, ed. Vittore Branca (Florence, 1969): 251–52. See also Goldthwaite, *The Building*; p. 118 in the It. translation.

14. See ibid.; pp. 125ff. of the It. trans.

15. See Loredana Olivato and Lionello Puppi, *Mauro Codussi* (Milan, 1977), 140–59, 183–85, and 247–54; John McAndrew, *Venetian Architecture of the Early Renaissance* (Cambridge, Mass.-London, 1980), 320–35; Ralph Lieberman, *L'Architettura del Rinascimento a Venezia 1450–1540* (Florence, 1982), entries 59 and 60. A few reflections on the typology of Venetian palazzi of the sixteenth century can be found in Hellmut Lorenz's essay, "Überlegungen zum venezianischen Palastbau der Renaissance," *Zeitschrift für Kunstgeschichte*, 93, no. 1 (1980): 33–53.

16. Francesco Sansovino, *Venetia città nobilissima e singolare* (Venice, 1581), f. 140r.

17. Ibid., f. 142r.

18. See Antonio Foscari and Manfredo Tafuri, "Un progetto irrealizzato di Jacopo Sansovino: il palazzo di Vettor Grimani sul Canal Grande," *Bollettino dei Civici Musei Veneziani*, 34, n.s., no. 1–4 (1981): 71–87. Jacopo Sansovino's project is in BMC, *Collezione disegni*, cl. 3, 6038r. The drawing had formerly been attributed to Michele Sanmicheli and Sebastiano Serlio, on the basis of incorrect or incomplete analyses. See Douglas Lewis, "Un disegno autografo del Sanmicheli e la notizia del committente del Sansovino per S. Francesco della Vigna," *Bollettino dei Civici Musei Veneziani*, 17, no. 3–4 (1972): 7–36; id., *The Drawings of Andrea Palladio* (Washington, 1981), 23–24; L. Olivato, "Sebastiano Serlio. Planimetria di un palazzo e profilo di una base di colonna," in the collection *Architettura e utopia nella Venezia del Cinquencento*, ed. L. Puppi (Milan, 1980), 175.

19. See Frommel, *Der römische Palastbau*, 1:120–22; Stefano Rezzi, "Palazzo Gaddi-Niccolini in Banchi," *Quaderni dell'Istituto di Storia dell'Architettura* ser. 27, no. 169–74 (Rome, 1982): 35–48, with interesting observations on the original polychromy of the first courtyard. On the experiences of the palazzo during the Strozzis' ownership, see Pier Nicola Pagliara, "Palazzo Niccolini in Banchi: problemi di attribuzione," *Controspazio*, 4, no. 7 (1972): 52–55.

20. See Foscari and Tafuri, "Un progetto irrealizzato," 84.

21. On the Procuratie Vecchie, see McAndrew, *Venetian Architecture*, 400–25; A. Foscari, "Il cantiere delle 'Procuratie vecchie' e Jacopo Sansovino," *Ricerche di Storia dell'Arte* 19 (1983): 61–76; Tito Talamini, "Le Procuratie Vecchie a Venezia," *Parametro*, 15, no. 129 (1984): 17–43, 61–62, 64.

22. Sanudo, *Diarii*, 15:541 (February 1513).

23. See chap. 7 of this volume.

24. On the history of the Magistratura alle Pompe, see Giulio Bistort, *Il Magistrato alle Pompe della Repubblica di Venezia. Studio storico*, R. Deputazione Veneta di Storia Patria, Miscellanea di

Storia Veneta, ser. 3, vol. 5 (Venice, 1912), esp. pp. 44ff and 239–41. After the laws of May 2, 1200, and May 22, 1344, the Great Council decided on November 17, 1476, to launch a permanent judiciary, which on February 14, 1510, was requested from the Procurators of San Marco. For the text of the 1512 law, see ASV, "Senato Terra," reg. 18, May 8, 1512, cc. 11r–14v and Sanudo, *Diarii*, 14:113–17. Also see Felix Gilbert, "Venice in the crisis of the league of Cambrai," in the collection *Renaissance Venice*, ed. John R. Hale (London, 1973), 274ff. (esp. 277–80). Regarding furnishings, the law—published on May 11, 1512, "super scallis Rivoalti"—prescribed (c. 13r): "Sia preterea prohibito decetero à Cadauno nostro Zentilhomo, e citadin in ornamento de camere dove intravegna legname, oro, e pictura, spendere piu de ducati 150. Non possino, ne debono haver, ne tenir casse dorate, cune, restelli, specchi, code, scuole e pettini, che siano ornade d'argento, oro, Recamo, ne Zoie. Ne possino haver ne tenir in Camera, in lecto linzuoli, linsoletti, intimelle, ne Cussin ornadi de seda, argento, oro, Zoie, o perle, Recamo, ne argentarie, ne haver, ni tenir al lecto alcuna Cortina, coltra, ne coperta, ne Covertor, ne tornolecto, ne altro apparato, ne ornamento in camera ne in sala, che siano facti de panno d'oro, d'argento, brocado, veludo, raso, damaschin, e talj: ma ben possino tenir li predicti ornamenti e apparati de cendado, tafta, samito, catasamito, ormexin, e zambellotto: quali perhò non habino sopra altro oro, argento, ne altro ornamento. . . . Le Anteporte, spaliere, banchali, tornolecti et altri fornimenti de panni de seda, et panni de lana intaiadi, cusidi, o incoladi, far ne usar per alcuno se possino sotto pena de ducati XXV, et perder i fornimenti a quelli dechi fusseno tal lavori, et ali Maistri che i fasseno, de ducati X, et star mesi quatro in prexon."

25. See Bistort, *Il Magistrato alle Pompe*, 51.

26. See Gilbert, "Venice in the crisis," 277; Sanudo, *Diarii*, 17:246 (25 October 1513): the Doge declared that "el nostro Signor Dio è sta corozato con nui per le

injustitie si feva a forestieri . . . per le pompe si usava in terra ferma . . . e poi in questa terra, cussí come prima ogni casa avea la soa lanziera di arme, cussí è sta disfate e poste tavole di compagni, e confessa lui Principe fo di primi che disfé la lanziera a San Canzian in la sua casa per metter la tavola di la soa festa."

27. Ibid., 24:341.

28. Ibid., 28:13.

29. Ibid., 71.

30. Ibid., 192.

31. For a general panorama, see Rodolfo Pallucchini, "Per la storia del Manierismo a Venezia," in the collection *Da Tiziano a El Greco 1540–1590*, catalogue of the exhibit (Milan, 1981), 11ff. (but for a critique of the concept of Mannerism, including notes on the Venetian milieu, see the excellent essay by Antonio Pinèlli, "La maniera: definizione di campo e modelli di lettura," in *Storia dell'Arte italiana. Cinquecento e Seicento* 6/1 [Turin, 1981]: 89–181); Gaetano Cozzi, "Politica, cultura e religione," in the collection *Cultura e società nel Rinascimento tra riforme e manierismi*, ed. Vittore Branca and Carlo Ossola (Florence, 1984), 21–42; Oliver Logan, "La committenza artistica pubblica e privata," ibid., 271–88 (which returns to themes already treated in the volume by the same author, *Culture and Society in Venice 1470–1790. The Renaissance and its Heritage* [London, 1972; It. trans. Rome, 1980]).

32. On the Ca' Corner, see Deborah Howard, *Jacopo Sansovino. Architecture and Patronage in Renaissance Venice* (New Haven and London, 1975), which dates its construction to around 1545 (but the well-known letter by Pietro Aretino to Sansovino, of November 20, 1537, speaks of the *fondamenta*, of the "splendid Cornari roofs," which would lead one to suppose a model dating from approximately that year). On the Palazzo Grimani in San Luca, see Rodolfo Gallo, "Michele Sanmicheli a Venezia," in *Michele Sanmicheli. Studi raccolti dall'Accademia di Agricoltura, Scienze e Lettere* (Verona, 1960), 97ff. (esp. 120–125); L. Puppi, *Michele Sanmicheli architetto di Verona* (Padua, 1971), 136–

42; Vincenzo Fontana, "Construire a Venezia nel Cinquecento. Progetto, materiali, cantiere e teoria in palazzo Grimani a S. Luca," *Congresso Nazionale di Storia dell'arte*. I, Rome 1978 (Rome, 1980), 41–53.

33. See Sansovino, *Venetia*, 149. The imperial ambassador to Rome found that Cardinal Francesco Corner was "well disposed in every way, especially in virtue of the fact that he is, as his father and family were before him, most favorable to the Empire; and secondarily because the actual doge [Andrea Gritti] was particularly hostile to him." Letter from Louis de Praet to Charles V, July 30, 1529, cit. in Robert Finaly, "Al servizio del Sultano: Venezia, i Turchi e il mondo Cristiano, 1523–38," *Renovatio urbis*, 109 n. 64. Giorgio Corner, the procurator who died in 1527, ordered from Falconetto the familial monuments in the transept of San Salvador in Venice, and his son Girolamo Corner, along with his brothers, made payments to the artist between 1531 and 1532. See BMC, MS P.D.C. 2384/18, cc. 54–55, and Vasari-Milanesi, *Vite*, 10 : 234. The tombs, however, would be executed at the end of the sixteenth century by Bernardo Contin. Giorgio Corner (called Zorzon) of Girolamo, son of Giorgio, was a client of Palladio's for the Villa Corner in Piombino Dese. Andrea Corner, the brother of Zorzon, was the husband of Marietta Priuli, the daughter of the sister of Cardinal Francesco Pisani, bishop of Padua from 1524 to 1555, patron of the "episcopal villa" by Luvigliano and in contact with Alvise Cornaro. See Douglas Lewis, "La datazione della villa Corner a Piombino Dese," *Bolletino del Cisa* 14 (1972): 381–93. The web of familial relations and patronage therefore confirms the existence of a precise "group" taste, confirmed by the formal homogeneity of the Palladian villas of Montagnana and Piombino Dese, also noted by Lewis.

34. See Anthony Edward Kurneta. "The Palazzo Loredan in campo Santo Stefano: counter currents in XVI century Venetian architecture" (Ph.D. diss., Boston University, 1976; Ann Arbor and London: University Microfilms International, 1980). Kurneta remarks that the palazzo detached itself—by means of its entrance hall and *portego*—from traditional typology, and he suggests that the same architect was responsible for it, the Palazzo Gonnella Valier in Cannaregio, and for the Palazzo Loredan in San Vio. The attribution of the Palazzo Loredan to Scarpagnino can perhaps still be questioned.

35. On the Palazzo Grimani at Santa Maria Formosa, see Gallo, "Michele Sanmicheli a Venezia," 125–29, 143–48, 157–58; Elena Bassi, *Palazzi di Venezia* (Venice, 1976), 228–35; Marilyn Perry, "A Renaissance Showplace of Art: the Palazzo Grimani at Santa Maria Formosa," *Apollo*, 113, no. 230 (1981): 215–21; Marina Stefani Mantovanelli, "Giovanni Grimani Patriarca di Aquileia e il suo palazzo di Venezia," *Quaderni Utinensi* 3–4 (1984): 34–54 (with insufficiently grounded hypotheses regarding its attribution).

36. The restoration of the palazzo, once completed, may be surprising. Without suggesting that our remark should pass as a hypothesis for its attribution, we should stress that the vault of the "Museo" recalls the manner of Giovanni Battista Bertani. (We are thinking of the Palatina Basilica of Santa Barbara in Mantua.) Bertani was in Venice in February 1551, in contacts, soon to be interrupted, with the Ministers for the Rialto Bridge, among whom was Vettor Grimani. See Paolo Carpeggiani, *Schede 101–104*, in Architettura e utopia, 123–24. However, the "Studio delle antichità" dates after 1568: Piovego's measurements for the building on the San Severo Canal bear the date of June 30, 1567 (ASV, "Giudici del Piovego," b. 21, fasc. 2, c. 7r). The letters from the Dutch Nicolò Stoppio, whom we have mentioned in the text, were sent to Johann Jakob Fugger on November 26 and 28, 1568. See Otto Hartig, "Die Kunsttätigkeit in München unter Wilhelm IV. und Albrecht V. (1520–1579)," *Münchner Jahrbuch der bildenden Kunst* 10 (1933): 220. Muzio Sforza, in 1588, praised Giovanni Grimani's "domus mirifica," while commenting to the latter: "tua instructione, velut optimi architecti, exaedificata." See Muzio Sforza, *Elegie*

sacre (Venice, 1588), quoted in Bassi, *Palazzi*, 231.

37. See A. Foscari and M. Tafuri, *L'armonia e i conflitti. La chiesa di San Francesco della Vigna nella Venezia del '500* (Turin, 1983), 131ff.

38. On Giovanni Grimani, the details of his lawsuit and his artistic patronage, see Giuseppe de Leva, "Giovanni Grimani Patriarca d'Acquileia, "*Atti del R. Istituo Veneto di Scienze, Lettere ed Arti*, ser. 5, 7 (1880–81), 407–54; Luigi Carcereri, *Giovanni Grimani Patriarca d'Acquileia accusato d'eresia* (Rome, 1907); Pio Paschini, "Il mecenatismo artistico del Patriarca Giovanni Grimani," in *Studi in onore di Aristide Calderini e Roberto Paribeni* (Milan, 1956), 851–62; Peter J. Laven, "The 'Causa Grimani' and its Political Overtones," *Journal of Religious History*, 4 (1966–67): 184–205; A. Foscari and M. Tafuri, "Sebastiano da Lugano, i Grimani e Jacopo Sansovino. Artisti e committenti nella chiesa di Sant'Antonio di Castello," *Arte Veneta* 36 (1982): 100–23; id., *L'armonia e i conflitti*, 131ff. Rodolfo Pallucchini has recently identified and published a portrait of Giovanni Grimani painted by Jacopo Tintoretto (fig. 6), now in an English collection. See R. Pallucchini, "Un nuovo ritratto di Jacopo Tintoretto," *Arte Veneta* 37 (1983): 184–87. Let us add, incidentally, that Pallucchini's identification has been confirmed by the eighteenth-century drawing (Museo Correr), which we published in *L'armonia e i conflitti*, fig. 85.

39. See Walter R. Rearick, "Battista Franco and the Grimani Chapel," *Saggi e Memorie di Storia dell'Arte* (1959), 107–39; Foscari and Tafuri, *L'armonia e i conflitti*, 132–49.

40. Leon Battista Alberti, *De re aedificatoria*, Incipit, edition edited by Giovanni Orlandi (Milan, 1966), 2.

41. See Erwin Panofsky and Fritz Saxl, "A Late-Antique Symbol in Works by Holbein and Titian," *The Burlington Magazine* 99 (1926), 177ff.; E. Panofsky, *Meaning in the Visual Arts. Paper in and on Art History* (New York, 1955); It. trans. (Turin, 1962), 149–68; id. *Problems in Titian, mostly Iconographic* (London, 1958), 102–08. Also see Edgar

Wind, *Pagan Mysteries in the Renaissance* (London, 1958); It. trans. (Milan, 1971), 318–20, which questions the attribution to Titian; David Rosand, *Tiziano* (New York, 1978); It. trans. (Milan, 1983), 148; Daniel Arasse, "Titien et son 'Allégorie de la Prudence': un peintre et des motifs," in the collection *Interpretazioni veneziane. Studi di Storia dell'Arte in onore di Michelangelo Muraro*, ed. David Rosand (Venice, 1984), 291–310 (a development of Panofsky's interpretation that is arbitrary in some respects). Let us mention, finally, the article by Juliano Hill-Cotton, "An Identification of Titian's 'Allegory of Prudence' and some Medici-Stuart Affinities," *Apollo* 63 (February 1956): 40–41, which maintains that it is possible to identify Cardinal Ippolito de' Medici in the traits of the young man as well as in those of the mature man. Panofsky justly rejects these hypotheses as fantastic (*Problems in Titian*, 103 n. 29). Observations on "historical time and harmonic time" in Venetian painting of the early sixteenth century can be found in the volume by Augusto Gentili, *Da Tiziano a Tiziano. Mito e allegoria nella cultura veneziano del Cinquecento* (Milan, 1980), 40–49, with analyses that are, however, based on hypotheses that do not always agree with the historical context in question.

42. On the miniature of the initial S (pt. 2, chap. 216) of codex 448 preserved in the Biblioteca Comunale in Treviso, see L. Puppi, "I tre visi di Treviso," in Id., *Verso Gerusalemme. Immagini e temi di urbanistica e di architettura simboliche* (Rome and Reggio Calabria, 1982), 3–24. On the treatise by F. de' Alegris, see Barbara Mazza, "Un tassello del 'mito' di Venezia: due cinquecentine di Francesco de' Alegris," *Antichità viva* 4–5 (1978): 53–57. The painting by Antonio da Negroponte is in the church of San Francesco della Vigna: the *tricipitium* is represented on the step right beneath the Madonna.

43. See Francesco Colonna, *Hypnerotomachia Poliphili*, critical edition edited by Giovanni Pozzi and Lucia A. Ciapponi (Padua, 1980), 1:338–41, 2:222 n.8.

44. See Arasse, "Titien," 292, which attributes to Titian the invention of the

triple figure with different ages. Arasse also recognizes the *Hypnerotomachia* as one of the first combinations of the symbol of Serapis with that of prudence (303ff.)

45. See, for example, the passage by Marin Sanudo, quoted in note 9 of chap. 2. It is, however, clear that the "Venetian time" alluded to in the text, and which we will return to in chap. 6, has nothing to do either with the time oriented principally toward the future (see Agnes Heller, *A Reneszánz Ember* (Budapest, 1967); It. trans., *L'uomo del Rinascimento* (Florence, 1977), 266ff., or with exclusively eschatological time. On the transformations of time, from the 14th to 16th centuries, see the well-known work by Jacques Le Goff, *Tempo della Chiesa e tempo del mercante* (Turin, 1977), as well as Jean-Claude Schmitt, "Il tempo come parametro e come oggetto della storia," in the collection *Le frontiere del tempo*, ed. Ruggiero Romano (Milan, 1981), 45–59, and the observations contained in Giacomo Marramao, *Potere e secolarizzazione. Le categorie del tempo* (Rome, 1983), esp. pp. XVIIff. and 5ff. The various forms of the Venetian myth, which we refer to in this chapter and in later ones, had their roots in the changed constitution of the late thirteenth century and the stabilization of the fourteenth. Nonetheless, the patricians of the fifteenth and sixteenth centuries could calmly forget the historicity of their own ideal constructions, and consider that the fundamental problem had been resolved: the completion of the Origin extends into the relativity of the process insofar as the Venetian legal system is divine and removed from nature— removed, therefore, from corruption, change, and death. The fifth book of Aristotle's *Politics* was read as a strategy of neutralization of conflict and becoming. One ought to notice, finally, that the pelican and the phoenix appear also— and with Christological meanings once again—in the decorations of a foundation in the inside of the Corner Chapel at Santi Apostoli, in the pilasters of the portal of the Scuola Grande di San Marco, and in the pilasters of the original portal of the church of San Rocco.

46. See Salvatore Settis, *La 'Tempesta' interpretata. Giorgione, i committenti, il soggetto*, 2nd ed. (Turin, 1978); id., "Giorgione e i suoi committenti," in the collection *Giorgione e l'Umanesimo veneziano*, ed. R. Pallucchini (Florence, 1981), 373–98. Also see Donata Battilotti and Maria Teresa Franco, "Regesti di committenti e dei primi collezionisti di Giorgione," *Antichità viva* 4–5 (1978): 58–86.

47. Settis, "La 'Tempesta'," 134.

48. Ibid., 19–45; Peter Meller, "I 'Tre filosofi' di Giorgione," *Giorgione e l'Umanesimo veneziano*, 227–47. Meller reads in the parchment held by the old philosopher the word *cristo* (while Settis reads *celus*) and proposes that the "philosophers' education" is the subject being represented, according to Plato's *Republic*. According to Meller, the old man is Plato himself, and the philosopher with the turban is Aristotle. The picture was seen by Marcantonio Michiel in the house of Taddeo Contarini in 1525; at that time, the latter was living at Santa Fosca, in a house of the Vendramins', as was demonstrated by the tithe presented on August 28, 1524, by Federico Vendramin and his brothers. See Battilotti and Franco, "Regesti di committenti," 60.

49. On the "book" as a metaphor for nature and on the history of that metaphor, see Hans Blumenberg, *Die Lesbarkeit der Welt* (Frankfurt am Main, 1981; It. trans., Bologna, 1984).

50. Sanudo, *Diarii*, 39:24–25. Our emphasis. Giorgione's *Three Philosophers* also seems to reflect a passage of the *Nicomachean Ethics*, in which Aristotle observes that young people were becoming geometers and mathematicians, that is to say knowledgeable, but not wise. And then he adds, "The cause is that such wisdom is concerned not only with universals, but with particulars, which become familiar from experience." And therefore experience, which is attained with age, enables one to possess the "principles of wisdom and physics." Aristotle, *Nicomachean Ethics* in *Introduction to Aristotle*, ed. Richard McKeon (New York: Random House, 1947), 433; *Etica Nicomachea*, in *Opere*, vol. 7 (Rome and Bari, 1983), 6:8:151.

Chapter 2

1. See Barbara Marx, *Venezia—altera Roma? Ipotesi sull'umanesimo veneziano*, Centro Tedesco di Studi Veneziani (German Center for Venetian Studies), Quaderni 10 (Venice, 1978). Also see Agostino Pertusi, "Gli inizi della storiografia umanistica del Quattrocento," in the collection *La storiografia veneziana fino al secolo XVI. Aspetti e problemi*, ed. A. Pertusi (Florence, 1970), 269–332.

2. Filippo Morandi sang the following praise: "Urbs Venetum salve o celsis elata triumphis / Salve, sidus Italis radians, salve altera Roma / Foelix perpetuum tellus dignissima mundi." See Marx, *Venezia*, 8.

3. See Felix Gilbert, "The Venetian Constitution in Florentine Political Thought," in *Florentine Studies*, ed. N. Rubinstein (London, 1968); It. trans. in F. Gilbert, *Machiavelli e il suo tempo* (Bologna, 1977), 115ff., esp. 121–22. See also Franco Gaeta, "Giorgio di Trebisonda, le 'Leggi' di Platone e la costituzione di Venezia," *Bullettino dell'Istituto Storico Italiano per il Medio Evo e Archivio Muratoriano* n. 82 (1970): 479–501.

4. See John McAndrew, "Sant' Andrea alla Certosa," *The Art Bulletin* 51 (1969): 15–28; James S. Ackerman, "L'architettura religiosa veneta in rapporto a quella toscana del Rinascimento," *Bollettino del Cisa* 19 (1977): 135–64; Loredana Olivato Puppi and Lionello Puppi, *Mauro Codussi* (Milan, 1977), passim. In addition, see Wladimir Timofiewitsch, "Genesi e struttura della chiesa del Rinascimento veneziano," *Bolletino del Cisa* 6, pt. 2 (1964): 271–82; Ralph Lieberman, "Venetian Church Architecture around 1500," ibid., 19 (1977): 35–48, and Anna Maria Odenthal, *Die Kirche San Giovanni Crisostomo in Venedig. Ein Beitrag zur venetianischen Sakralarchitecktur des späten 15. Jahrunderts*, Inaugural Dissertation (Bonn, 1985).

5. Ackerman, "L'architettura religiosa," 144.

6. On July 13, 1453, Bessarione wrote to Doge Foscari, outlining a program that would have directed the Republic away from its expansionist projects on the mainland and oriented it toward the reconquest of Constantinople. If Venice, acting rapidly, had won the crusade—Bessarione wrote, playing on Venice's will for power—it would have become the capital of a vast empire, inheriting the functions of ancient Byzantium. One should remember that Bessarione, who was received triumphally in Venice on July 22, 1463, worked there for seven months in order to prepare for the crusade that was canceled after the death of Pius II. See Lotte Labowsky, "Bessarione," in *Dizionario Biografico degli Italiani*, vol. 9 (Rome, 1967), 687–96; Deno John Geanakoplos, *Byzantine East and Latin West: Two Worlds of Christendom in Middle Ages and Renaissance*, 2nd ed. (Hamden, Conn., 1976), esp. 113ff. Also see Carlo Ginzburg, *Indagini su Piero* (Turin, 1981), 84–88.

7. See André Wirobisz, "L'attività edilizia nel XIV e XV secolo," *Studi Veneziani* 7 (1965): 307–43, and L. Puppi, "Venezia: architettura, città e territorio tra la fine del '400 e l'avvio del '500," in the collection *Florence and Venice: Comparisons and relations, II. Cinquecento* (Florence, 1980), 341–55.

8. On the church of San Salvador, see Francesco Sansovino, *Venetia città nobilissima e singolare* (Venice, 1581), cc. 47v–48v (the church has been ascribed entirely to Tullio Lombardo, with a model "imitated by part of half of the church of San Marco"); Flaminio Corner, *Ecclesiae Venetae antiquis monumentis*, 2 (Venice, 1749), 243–99; Tommaso Temanza, *Vite dei piú celebri architetti, e scultori veneziani* (Venice, 1778), 119–20; Giannantonio Moschini, *Guida per la città di Venezia*, 1, pt. 2 (Venice, 1815), 542–59; Leopoldo Cicognara, Antonio Diedo, Giovanni Selva, *Le fabbriche e i monumenti cospiqui di Venezia* (Venice, 1838–40), vol. 1 (ed. 1858), pp. 155 and 158 (with a supplement by Zanotto); Pietro Selvatico, *Sulla Architettura e sulla scultura in Venezia dal Medio Evo sino ai nostri giorni* (Venice, 1847), 204–5; Pietro Paoletti, *L'architettura e la scultura del Rinascimento in Venezia*, vol. 2 (Venice, 1893), 241–44; Giuseppe Tassini, *Iscrizioni della Chiesa e del convento di San*

Salvatore a Venezia (Venice, 1895);
Giulio Lorenzetti, Venezia e il suo
estuario (Rome, 1926; Trieste, 1979),
388–92; Adolfo Venturi, Storia dell'Arte
Italiana 11, pt. 1 (Milan, 1938), 852, 858;
Erich Hubala, Venedig. Reclams Kun-
stführer, Italien, II. Oberitalien Ost
(Stuttgart, 1965), 930–35; Ludwig
Heydenreich and Wolfgang Lotz,
Architecture in Italy 1400 to 1600 (Harmondsworth, 1974), 91; Umberto Franzoi and Dina Di Stefano, Le chiese di
Venezia (Venice, 1976), 353–59; Ackerman, "L'architettura religiosa veneta,"
146; Deborah Howard, The Architectural
History of Venice (London, 1980), 131–
33; J. McAndrew, Venetian Architecture
of the Early Renaissance (Cambridge,
Mass. and London, 1980), 448–60; R.
Lieberman, L'architettura del Rinascimento a Venezia 1450–1540 (Florence,
1982), 13, 19, 20, and the text of plate 42.

9. For example, Sanudo wrote that
Venice "fo comenzata a edificar . . . del
421, adí 25 Marzo in zorno di Venere cercha l'hora di nona ascendendo, come nella
figura astrologica apar, gradi 25 del segno
del Cancro. Nel qual zorno ut divinae tes-
tantur litterae fu formato il primo homo
Adam nel principio del mondo per le
mano di Dio; ancora in ditto zorno la ver-
zene Maria fo annonciata da l'angelo
Gabriel, et etiam il fiol de Dio, Christo
Giesú nel suo immaculato ventre miracu-
lose introe, et secondo l'opinione theolo-
gica fo in quel medesmo zorno da zudei
crucefisso. . . ." Marin Sanudo the Younger, De origine, situ et magistratibus urbis
Venetae, overo la città di Venetia (1493–
1530), ed. Angela Caracciolo Aricò,
(Milan, 1980), 12–13. Consequently, the
birth of Venice—and the "zorno di Venere" is a reference to her pulchritudo—
was inserted into a temporal cycle made
of holy births and a crucifixion that enabled a universal "rebirth." See also, in
this connection, Francesco De Alegris, La
summa gloria de Venezia (Venice, 1501),
which is discussed in Barbara Mazza, "Un
tassello del 'mito' di Venezia: due cinquecentine di Francesco de Alegris," Antichità viva 4–5 (1978): 53–57.

10. Sanudo, De origine, 16.

11. Ibid.

12. See note 9, above.

13. Corner, Ecclesiae Venetae, 2:244.
In a miscellaneous codex in the British
Museum Library, which Ennio Concina
has kindly brought to our attention (Ms
AddL. 12032:1, Vita del glorioso San
Magno che vienne alli 6 di Ottobre), a
writer of the early seventeenth century
once again took up the legend of Bishop
Magnus, writing that "sí che per li meriti
di lui, miracolosamente fu rivelato il modo
di edificare la città di Venetia" (c. 3r)
and that, after the apparition of Saint
Peter, there appeared to Magnus "Giesú
Cristo, il quale gli disse che egli era il Salvatore del Mondo, e comandogli che gli
fosse fatto una Chiesa in meza [sic] della
Città dove trovasse una nuvola rossa il
quale tempio insino al di che oggi si vede"
(c. 4r).

14. Corner, Ecclesiae Venetae, 2:244.

15. See, on this theme, L. Puppi, "Verso
Gerusalemme," Arte Veneta 32 (1978):
73–78, reprinted in the volume by Puppi,
Verso Gerusalemme. Immagini e temi di
urbanistica e di architettura simboliche
(Rome and Reggio Calabria, 1982), 62–
76; and also by Puppi, "Venezia come
Gerusalemme nella cultura figurativa del
Rinascimento," a conference paper on the
theme: "The Italian city in the Renaissance between utopia and reality," at
the Centro Tedesco di Studi Veneziani,
Venice, September 27–29, 1982; id.
"'Rex sum justicie.' Note per una storia
metaforica del Palazzo dei dogi," in the
collection I Dogi, ed. Gino Benzoni,
(Milan, 1982), 183–213. On the structure
of the urban imaginary in the Middle
Ages, with references also to Venetian
mythologies, see Jacques Le Goff, "L'immaginario urbano nell'Italia medievale
(secoli 5–15)," in Storia d'Italia Einaudi.
Annali 5. Il paesaggio (Turin, 1982),
5–43.

16. Corner, Ecclesiae Venetae, 2:249.

17. "Monasterio per annos duos cum
dimidio optime administrato, Martinus
[Venerio] ad meliorem vitam assumitur
anno 1182 die duodecima Novemb.
Canonicae regimen suscepit Gregorius
Floravanti, supralaudati Viviani nepos,
Juris Pontificii Doctor, qui Templum
angustum, et incendio pene combustum,

in ampliorem, ornatioremque formam a fundamentis sollicita cura renovari curavit. Id validius citiusque ut praestaret, ex Gregorii VIII sibi concessa authoritate, oeconomum ordinavit, qui Monasterii, et Ecclesiae negotia utiliter administraret" (ibid., 249). Corner continues (p. 250): "Erecto Templo ac turri campanaria perfecta, ipsaque Congregatione multis praediis adaucta, benemeritus Prior ex hac luce migravit anno Domini 1209. mense Decembris. . . ." We thus have the dates *post* and *ante quem* of the second San Salvador.

18. See ibid., 258–59, 266–68. For the miracles wrought by Saint Theodore, see ibid., 262–65.

19. See ibid., 258, and Edward Muir, *Civic Ritual in Renaissance Venice* (Princeton, N.J., 1981), pp. 92–93.

20. See Antonio Niero, "I santi patroni," in the collection *Culto dei Santi a Venezia* (Venice, 1965), 92–93, and Muir, *Civic Ritual*, 95. Furthermore, Niero remarks that the feast day decreed in 1450 seemed to compensate for Venice's renunciation of the banner of Saint Theodore, hypothesizing, about the latter, a symbolic significance of a political nature. See Niero, "I santi," 94. Gallo recalls that in the statutes of the Scuola di San Teodoro it was written that the saint was carried "per gonfaloni anni continui 361" ["banners for 361 years"], when the church of San Marco "was called the church of Saint Theodore." See Rodolfo Gallo, "La Scuola Grande di San Teodoro di Venezia," *Atti dell' Istituto Veneto di Scienze, Lettere ed Arti. Classe di Scienze morali e lettere*, vol. 120 (1961–62): 461–95 (esp. 461).

21. See Corner, *Ecclesiae Venetae*, 2, document H (September 13, 1434, indulgences granted by Eugene IV), 292–93; ibid., document N (April 2, 1448, indulgences granted by Nicholas V), 298; ibid., document O (January 3, 1449, indulgences granted by nineteen cardinals), 298–99. See also the document transcribed on p. 268: "In l'anno 1450 adí 21 del mese di Settembrio per missier Zaccaria Bembo savio del Consiglio e per missier Alluixi Stolado procurador di Sancto Marco e per sollicitudine de sier Nani da

la Colonna G. G. fo misso la parte nel Consiglio di Pregadi, e fò presa ch'al zorno de la festa di missier Sancto Theodoro si dieba gardare, e far festa solenne. Item missier lo Vescovo de Castello la facto un decreto, che al dito zorno si debia festezare e far festa solenne a la pena di scomunigazion, per le quali tutte pietose caxoni l'è sta provisto pel nostro Gastaldo e Compagni." On the processions of 1506, 1527, and 1530, see Sanudo, *Diarii* 6:496, 46:289, 53:72.

22. Corner, *Ecclesiae Venetae*, 2:269, and Brian Pullan, *Rich and Poor in Renaissance Venice* (Oxford, 1971), 34. Also see Gallo, "La Scuola Grande di San Teodoro," 469–70. Gallo has traced in great detail the history of the Scuola and documented the objections raised by the Canons of San Salvador when a new altar and a new residence were granted to the Scuola. On December 4, 1551, the Scuola finally acquired the altar to the left of the major altar, which had already been assigned to the Gritti family in 1526, along with the chapel (see p. 467). In 1555 it was generally felt to be time to build a new Scuola, and the site of Santo Stefano was considered. In January 1572 and in 1573 the monastery of San Salvador offered to the Scuola of San Teodoro a portion of the monastery, but the Scuola refused. The new Scuola, next to the church and convent of San Salvador, would be built soon thereafter, first with the assistance of Simon Sorella, and then (from 1608) with the help of Tommaso Contin, while Giuseppe Sardi and Baldassare Longhena would intervene for the main and lateral facades.

23. Muir, *Civic Ritual*, 94.

24. See Corner, *Ecclesiae Venetae*, 2:254–55.

25. Ibid., 256–57, and doc. M (June 21, 1442), 295–97. Some of the restoration work done on the monastery goes back to Eugene IV, while an epigraph of 1528, published by Corner (p. 257), states: "Quam aedem Eugenii IV. Pont. Max. liberalitate Salvatoris Canonici Reg. LXXXVI ab hinc anno adepti sunt, eamdem vetustate collabentem a fundamentis augustiore facie restituendam curarunt,

sui in Pontificem grati animi, in Deum Pietatis perpetuum monimentum 1528."

26. "Memoria come adí 27 Iugno 1445 io fratte Nicolò sagrestano da licentia del Priore del convento fece li patti con li compagni della scolla de Santa Maria, et in prima de licentia del priore le concedemo due arche sotto el portico davanti la chiesia con questa condicione, che quando noi volessemo edificare et alongare la chiesa posiamo desfare esse anche senza alcuna contradicione, con questo che noi le dobiamo dar un altro luogho dove lor possino edificar le loro arche. . . ." ASV, "Corporazioni religiose soppresse, San Salvador," b. 44, tomo. 91, c. 7r. The medieval church of San Salvador was, therefore, equipped with a portico on the front: see also document I transcribed in the appendix.

27. Giorgio Spavento had restored the wooded Rialto bridge in 1502, but in 1507, it again seemed about to collapse, and the Council of Ten considered rebuilding the bridge in wood "con le garavate di alzar in mezo," charging the Commissioners of the Salt Office with the task: as is known, the decision would have no effect. See Roberto Cessi and Annibale Alberti, *Rialto. L'isola, il ponte, il mercato* (Bologna, 1934), 171–73. In an entry dated March 4, 1502, Sanudo noted (*Diarii*, 4:241): "El ponte di Rialto che minazava ruina, *auctore* maistro Zorzi spavento fo compito de ajustar et perlongato ancora a durar cercha X anni, fin si provvedi far lo di nuovo o di legname, come è, o di piera, che costeria assai."

28. ASV, "Provveditori al Sal," b. 60, Not., c. 97r. The document specifies: "vadino dicti denari ad computo de i ducati mille e cinquecento mensuali de i mercanti, come si contien in la parte presa nel consiglio Excellentissimo di X adí 31 marzo prossimo passato." The bull of Julius II for the rebuilding of the church bears the date January 6, 1507, from Bologna. See ASV, "San Salvador," b. 5, parchment 48. (See the transcription in the appendix of the present volume, doc. 4.) Other bulls came from Leo X on January 8, 1519 (ibid., b. 5, n. 55) and from Clement VII on February 1, 1523 (ibid., b. 5, parchment 57). The latter, for the de-

molition of a house that belonged to the deceased Giovanni da Roma and was blocking the entrance to the new monastery. Regarding Andrea Gritti's concession of that house, see note 41 and doc. 7 in the appendix.

29. In 1553 the brothers of San Francesco della Vigna would record another 6,000 ducats granted to San Salvador, in their request for a sum of 2,000 ducats for the completion of the roof of their church: their petition would not be heard, and another request would result, on December 28, 1554, in only 500 ducats. See ASV, *Senato Terra*, f. 20 (petition of July 14, 1553, and November 22, 1554) and Reg. 39, cc. 199r–200v (section from December 28, 1554).

30. ASV, "San Salvador," b. 39, tomo. 81, cc. 135v–36r. See the transcription of the document in the appendix (no. 2).

31. A good biography of Bembo is in Angelo Ventura, "Bembo Bernardo," in *Dizionario Biografico degli Italiani*, vol. 8 (Rome, 1966), 103–8 (with an appendix by M. Pecoraro on humanistic activity, on pp. 108–9). Giorgio Emo, who in 1507 was commanding the Veronese, firmly defended in the Senate, along with Andrea Venier, the decision not to return the territories of Romagna to the Pope; he refused, however, the position of commissioner in charge when it was offered to him at that time. (He would, on the other hand, accept this nomination later on, in 1515.) See Emanuele Cicogna, *Delle inscrizione veneziane*, vol. 1 (Venice, 1824), 72–73. Priuli wrote in his *Diarii* (June 1509) that it was public knowledge in Venice that "Zorzi Emo not only accepted monies and gifts and was easily bribed, but managed very well for himself . . . and for him, and for Paulo Pisani the Senate had abandoned ancient wisdom and badly foreseen extreme dangers . . ." (Ibid., 356). In substance, most of the blame regarding the defeat of the armies of the League of Cambrai fell, after 1509, on Giorgio Emo. Also see Robert Finlay, *Politics in Renaissance Venice* (New Brunswick, 1980); It. trans. (Milan, 1982), 81. We are grateful for Puppi's precise reconstruction of Giorgio Emo's work in San Zanipolo. Under his gui-

dance, the transepts of the church were transformed into a mausoleum for the heroes of the Cambrai war, beginning in 1510: Nicolò Orsini di Pitigliano, Dionisio Naldi and Leonardo da Prato were celebrated in monumental tombs, thus becoming part of the official Pantheon of the Republic's praiseworthy. In 1513, Emo was one of the procurators of the convent, and in March 1515 the "plenariam potestatem edificandi dormitorium versus Muranum usque ad aquam" was conferred upon him. After the death of Giannantonio da Lodi (circa 1513), Mocetto executed the section of window in the transept on the right with the four warrior-saints: it is significant that Saint Theodore and Saint George, the patrons of Venice, were represented on the sides. Equally significant was the placement of the statue of Dionisio Naldi at the foot of the window: the church, with these sacred and secular figures, was tightly connected to the military fortunes of Venice, becoming the place of political memory and the glorification of patriotic virtues. See L. Puppi, "Il tempio e gli Eroi," in the collection *La grande vetrata di San Giovanni e Paolo* (Venice, 1982), 21–35. Also see Serena Romano, "La vetrata: i maestri e gli artefici," ibid., 51–71 (esp. 66–71).

Pietro Capello had supported the anti-Turkish alliance, concluded in 1501, between Venice, the Pope, and Hungary; he had also sustained a vigorous fiscal policy. Elected Savio di Terraferma (Minister for War and the Mainland) in 1503, Capello supported the territorial expansion of the *Serenissima* to the detriment of the collapsing Borgian *Signoria*. Having joined the Council of Ten in 1504, in May 1505 he entered the Collegio dei quindici alle Acque, as a deputy responsible for decisions about interventions regarding the course of the Brenta, and in October of the same year, he was chosen, along with Leonardo Grimani and Girolamo Diedo, to inspect the canals of Venice. At the end of 1505 he was still in the Council of Ten: on March 8, 1506, he was elected lieutenant of Friuli, but took command of the regiment only in July. In 1511 his political career was thwarted by Antonio Savorgan's entry into the imperial troups. Capello had previously defended him

against accusations of criminal abuse. See Francomario Colasanti, "Capello Pietro," in *Dizionario Biografico degli Italiani*, vol. 18 (Rome, 1975), 813–16.

32. See Cecil Grayson, "Un codice del De re aedificatoria posseduto da Bernardo Bembo," *Studi letterari*, a miscellany in honor of Emilio Santini (Padua, 1956): 181–88; idem, "Alberti, Poliziano e Bernardo Bembo," in *Il Poliziano e il suo tempo*, Acts of the fourth Convegno Internazionale di Studi sul Rinascimento, Florence, 1954 (Florence, 1957), 111–17. The manuscript is Cod. 128 of the Library of Eton College, with Bembo's coat of arms on f. 1r and a long autograph note in the margin of f. 208, with a description of a trip to Lake Nemi taken in 1489 and a praise of Cardinal Giovanni Colonna. In another context, Puppi indicated the importance of Bernardo Bembo's interest in Alberti's text, underlining the friendship that tied Bernardo to Cristoforo Landino and Pietro Dolfin. See Olivato and Puppi, *Mauro Codussi*, 22. On Bembo and the arts, also see André Chastel, *Art et Humanisme à Florence au temps de Laurent le Magnifique* (Paris, 1959); It. trans. (Turin, 1964), passim.

33. ASV, "San Salvador," b. 39, tomo. 81, cc. 134r–35v. See document 5 in the appendix.

34. Cited in Olivato and Puppi, *Mauro Codussi*, 52.

35. Alberto Tenenti has appropriately emphasized the continuity of the myth of the uniqueness of Venice connected to the ideality of the site: Venice, the impregnable "virgin" city, situated in a privileged space and the projection of a reign of celestial beatitudes into the real, is praised by Bernardo Giustinian in *De origine urbis gentisque Venetorum historiae*, with words that would be echoed, much later, in *De Magistratibus* by Gasparo Contarini and the popular publications of Francesco Sansovino. See Alberto Tenenti, "The Sense of Space and Time in the Venetian World," in *Renaissance Venice*, ed. John R. Hale (London, 1973), 17–46, reprinted in the volume, also by Tenenti, *Credenze, ideologie, libertinismi tra Medioevo ed età moderna* (Bologna, 1978), 75–118.

36. Innocenzo Cervelli, *Machiavelli e la crisi dello Stato veneziano* (Naples, 1974), 15. But see the entire chapter 1 of the volume, pp. 11–24.

37. Sanudo, *Diarii*, 53:72.

38. ASV, "San Salvador," b. 45, tomo. 95/3, cc. 15v–16r, April 14, 1508, quarrel over the placement of a pier, before the judges of the Proprio.

39. See Roberto Cessi, *Storia della Repubblica di Venezia* (Florence, 1981), 489. On the information given in 1504 by Fra Giocondo, see further on in our text.

40. ASV, "San Salvador," b. 36, tomo. 74, c. 7. See doc. 6 in the appendix.

41. Ibid., c. 8 (Leonardo Loredan "priori generali et diffinitoribus capituli generalis Canonicum Regularium Congregationis Sancti Salvatoris," April 6, 1521); ibid., c. 10 (February 21, 1523, *m.v.* = 1524, Andrea Gritti granted to the convent of San Salvador a house adjacent to the monastery, under the will of the deceased Zuan da Roma); ibid., c. 9 (Gritti to the general Fra Pellegrino da Bologna, April 9, 1529); ibid., c. 12 (May 5, 1531, Gritti to Fra Pellegrino of Bologna).

42. "A dí 7, la matina. Il Serenissimo, havendo heri posto ordine, vestito di veludo ruosa secca scuro, vene per terra con la Signoria il Collegio et zerca 20 altri patrici . . . Et prima introe in la chiexia nuova di S. Salvador a veder la fabrica. Li vene contra il zeneral di l'ordine fra Pelegrin da Bologna, qual è qui, il prior fra Piero . . . venetian et altri frati. Et era preparata la chiexia, dove si parlò del loco dove si havesse a metter il coro, per esser varie opinion, et la piú parte sente di metterlo fra le do prime capelle, et il Serenissimo et molti conseiò si mettesse fra mezo le do prime capelle. Et si dice il Serenissimo vol far far la sua arca in ditta chiexia, dove è dati li lochi za a la rezina di Cipri et al cardinal primo Corner." Sanudo, *Diarii*, 49:333, January 7, 1528 (*m.v.* = 1529). According to Lewis Kob, the "choir" that Sanudo spoke of could have been the exhibit of the organ, usually attributed to Jacopo Sansovino. See Carolyn Lewis Kolb, *The Villa Giustinian at Roncade* (New York and London, 1977), 89–91, with an analysis of the church on 86ff.

43. ASV, "San Salvador," b. 25, tomo. 92, cited in Paoletti, *L'architettura*, 2:242 n. 6, with a few errors in the transcription (*fosse* instead of *fasse*, for example). The masons were Gabriele fu Simone de Castellieri, Zorzi di Andrea from Lake Como, and Giacomo di Giovanni from Treviso. On August 27, 1506, Antonio Contarini had established the obligations "di mistro Antonio de Michelino da Ruigno, il qual se obliga di dar al ditto monasterio le infrascripte piere vive da Lemo, in le mixure qui sotto notate a posta per posta . . . cusí per le botteghe come per la ghiesia et per le caxe, le qual tute piere die dar nette de spelli et squarate et sia spontate a spexa del monestier." See ibid., 2:241 n. 6, also for the later agreements of 1506 with other stonemasons (p. 242).

44. See ASV, "San Salvador," b. 44, tomo. 91, c. 45r, of which a single sentence is cited in *Archivio Veneto* vol. 31, fasc. 62 (1886): 496, and in Paoletti, *L'architettura*, 2:241: the prior general maintained he had chosen "ex ipsis modelis unum secundum magistri Georgii Spavento notum constructum qui preceteris nobis aparuit nobilior et ellegantior et ad propositum nostrum magis congruum." A competition had, therefore, been announced for the church; Spavento's model is not described in the document we have transcribed in the appendix (n. 3), except for one detail: "fiat tamen una cuba super capella maiori." It is probable, however, that Spavento later modified the original project, on the basis of the Canons' orders. Antonio Contarini, prior of San Salvador, became the Patriarch of Venice in November 1508 and probably held a significant role in the iconographic definition of the new church of San Salvador. Sanudo writes that Contarini, having become the Patriarch, built two chapels in San Pietro di Castello, intending to furnish the church—the cathedral of Venice—with a façade. Sanudo writes (*Diarii*, 37:18): "Ha detto far dil suo una capella a San Salvador, dove si ha fato meter di sopra musaico, et fo quello che fé ruinar la ditta chiesa per rifarla, come si fa al presente." The Patriarch left 700 ducats to San Pietro di Castello and 300 ducats to San Salva-

dor: furthermore, he left his entire library to the monastery of San Salvador (ibid.).

45. See Ackerman, "L'architettura religiosa veneta," 146, and McAndrew, *Venetian Architecture*, 453.

46. Ibid., 448–55.

47. On this theme, see Paolo Prodi, *Il sovrano pontefice. Un corpo e due anime: la monarchia papale nella prima età moderna* (Bologna, 1982), esp. 92ff.

48. As of December 21, 1521, Angelo del Cortivo and Gabriele da Castello measured the "calle publica de San Salvador che discore in Marzaria . . . ad instantia dei signori frati del monastero de San Salvador et anco de poter veder per le prexenti mexure quello che el dito monastero de San Salvador ha lassato del suo al publico per el fabrichar che hano fato per le caxe che hano fato de nuovo." ASV, "San Salvador," b. 44, tomo. 91, c. 53r and v. In 1521, therefore, the houses to the left of the church were finished. The document proceeds with measurements of the street "la canton che discore in Marzaria dela dita fabricha nuova recto tramite a le caxe et botega de cha di Martini dove sta el merzer . . . fo trovada larga passa 2 et uno dedo. Item mexurada la dita calle piú oltre . . . dove xe la botega de quel de le perle, che tien per insegnia i 3 re, fo trovada passo uno, piè quattro e mezo et uno dedo." Finally, "mexurada piú oltre la dita calle suxo el canton tra la botega del marzer sale a seguir per insegno San Sebastian e quel de i pater nostri . . . reto tramete al canton de la calle de stagneri dove xe le caxe de quelli de cha Zustho dove xe la botega de la garze che tien per insegno el capello, fo trovada large passa duo pie tre et quarti tre de pe'." A document published by Moschini shows that in 1522 they were thinking of beginning the façade of the church, almost certainly on the basis of a project by Tullio Lombardo: "1522, die 8 julii. Che sia concessa a venerandi frati di S. Salvador et al p. della fabrica, che per far della fàsà della ditta chiesa possino uscir fora sopra il comun della Signora nostra sul campo de San Salvador, come appar sopra il disegno distinctamente piè tre e mezo in la cantona dela chiesa verso la speciaria, e li dicti frati al incontro relaxa del suo passa 15, pie

XI, quarti due quasi della banda del Pistor come è conveniente a sí buona opera." See Moschini, *Guida*, 1, pt. 2, 557–58. Also see ibid., 557, the document of June 13, 1522: the brothers were allowed "che per la fabrica della chiesa possino fare uno staglio su el suo campo, che sia longo passa sie e largo passa cinque, acciò li tajapiera possino lavorar sotto le pietre per ditta fabrica."

49. In drawing 463 of the *Miscellanea Mappe*, drafted for a lawsuit against the parish priest of San Luca (see the verso), the situation of the shops on Campo San Salvador is indicated as it appeared in the sixteenth century. In the notes one reads (from left to right): "frutarol per avanti la botega de le do colone de spicier"; "speciaria deli 7 zigli per avanti li Schiarelli"; "savoner de la testa del Lion d'oro"; "botega de l'aquila"; "botega olim de la X del monastero."

50. John McAndrew has given a reading of the interior of San Salvador in which he emphasizes the dynamic values and harmonious relationship between parts. See McAndrew, *Venetian Architecture*, 454.

51. On Luca Pacioli's Neoplatonism, see A. Chastel, *Marsile Ficin et l'art* (Geneva and Lille, 1954), 110ff., and Arnaldo Bruschi, "Nota introduttiva a De divina proportione," in the collection *Scritti rinascimentali di architettura* (Milan, 1978), 25–49. On the inaugural lecture of August 11, 1508, see Bruno Nardi, *La scuola di Rialto e l'Umanesimo veneziano*, ed. Vittore Branca (Florence, 1963), 113ff., and Fernando Lepori, "La scuola di Rialto dalla fondazione alla metà del Cinquecento," in the collection *Storia della cultura veneta. Dal primo Quattrocento al Concilio di Trento*, ed. Girolamo Arnaldi and Manlio Pastore Stocchi, 3/2 (Vicenza, 1980), 597–600, and n. 359. One observes that, according to what Pacioli wrote, among those present at the inaugural lecture delivered in San Bartolomeo were, in addition to Giovanni Lascaris, Giovan Battista Egnazio and "Frater Iocundus Veronensis Antiquarius," Pietro Donà, Pietro Contarini, Bernardo Bembo and "Petrus Lombardus, hi quatuor praefati Architectonica clari."

See Luca Pacioli, *Euclidis Megarensis . . . Opera*, etc. (Venice, 1509), text prefacing Book 5, f. 31r, cited in Nardi, *La scuola*, 116–17 n. 46.

52. Pacioli, *De divina proportione*, 60. The expression is the same as the one that Federico da Montefeltro used in his license to Luciano Laurana of 1468. See *Scritti rinascimentali*, 19. On the relations between applied mathematics and formal elaborations, see the hypothesis formulated in the book by Michael Baxandall, *Painting and Experience in Fifteenth Century Italy* (Oxford, 1972); Italian trans. (Turin, 1978), 85–99. As is known, however, mystical numerology—a means of raising to God—had been theorized by Saint Augustine in *De vera religione* and in *De musica*: the seven stages of mathematical raising were then reviewed by Bonaventura da Bagnoregio in his *Itinerarium mentis in Deum*, in which a passage of Boethius is also cited, from *De institutione arithmetica*, on the number of the "principal model in the mind of the Creator." The humanistic novelty thus consisted in the creation of a normative system, founded on the Ancient, capable of visualizing the mathematical symbology inherited from the Middle Ages: an operation that was anything but devoid of consequences for the secularization of the "number," even if the path taken would not be completely linear.

53. See Paoletti, *L'architettura*, 2:242–43 n. 6.

54. Ibid., 243: ". . . sono acordati cum mi Prior . . . m. ro Jacomo e Marco tajapiera per li do quariseli formiti . . . li quali vano nel principio dela Croxera signato E . . . presente m. ro Zorzi Spavento et maistro Zacharia tajapiera." Puppi has interpreted Tullio Lombardo's appearance on the work site as a sign of Spavento's expulsion, but the hypothesis is contradicted by the cited document of November 1507. In all probability, as John McAndrew supposes, Lombardo's nomination was due to the condition of Spavento's health. In the same context, Puppi accepts the hypothesis formulated by Nancy De Grummond, regarding the identification of the church with the neo-Byzantine dome that appears in the background of Giorgione's *Tempest* as Spavento's model for San Salvador. See Nancy Thomson De Grummond, "Giorgione's Tempest; the Legend of St. Theodore," *L'arte* 18–19 (1972): 5–53, and L. Puppi, "Giorgione e l'architettura," in *Giorgione e l'Umanesimo Veneziano*, ed. Ridolfo Pallucchini, vol. 1 (Florence, 1981), 358–59, reprinted in *Verso Gerusalemme*, 92–93. De Grummond's interpretation has been criticized in the volume by Salvatore Settis, *La "Tempesta" interpretata. Giorgione, i committenti, il soggetto* (Turin, 1978), 66–69.

55. See Paoletti, *L'architettura*, 2: 243 n. 6, document of March 9, 1511.

56. Ibid., note 1, documents of March 22, 1518, of July 31, 1519, and of 1523. Sanudo (*Diarii*, 29: 89, 97) testifies that part of the church was already operative by 1520 (ibid., 97: "In questo zorno si comenzò a dir messa a la capella granda nuova di San Salvador, che è una bellissima chiesia."). Sanudo also wrote, in an entry dated September 20, 1521 (ibid., 31: 438–39): "La matina fo aldito prima il prior di San Salvador contra sier Marco Trun qu. sier Antonio, intervenendo voriano tuor certi danari li frati per compir la fabricha i fanno drio la chiesa, di le botege butade zoso. Et a l'incontro sier Marco Trun voria se compisse la chiesia e loro frati desse tanti danari a la fabricha di la chiesia justa uno istrumento fato, quanti dà la Signoria ecc., i qual danari è in man di sier Hieronimo Justinian procurator, qual è procurator di la chiesia. E fo parlato *hinc inde, tamen* terminato li frati habbi danari da compir le botege."

57. See Paoletti, *L'architettura*, 2: 242; McAndrew, *Venetian Architecture*, 451, 454, 457. According to Francesco Sansovino, Temanza (*Vite*, 119) attributes the entire church, with the exception of the apse, to Tullio Lombardo, with the assistance of Giulio (whose existence Paoletti denies, pp. 241–42), and also ascribes to Tullio the monastery, which he maintains was finished by Sante Lombardo. Corner (*Ecclesiae Venetae*, 2: 265) had attributed the reconstruction of San Salvador to Giulio Lombardo instead.

58. An analysis of Giorgio Spavento's works can be found in McAndrew, *Venetian Architecture*, 426–55.

59. See ibid., 532–33; id., *Antonio Visentini. Catalogue of the Drawings of the Royal Institute of British Architects* (Farnborough, Hants, 1974), entry 133, p. 35. For the document of January 12, 1490, see Paoletti, *L'architettura*, 2:118.

60. See Giandomenico Romanelli, *Venezia Ottocento* (Rome, 1977), p. 50 and fig. 21.

61. Pullan, *Rich and Poor*, 212–15.

62. See Paoletti, *L'architettura*, 2:117. Also see A. Foscari and M. Tafuri, "Sebastiano da Lugano, i Grimani e Jacopo Sansovino, Artisti e committenti nella chiesa di Sant'Antonio di Castello," *Arte Veneta* 36 (1982): 103 and 121 n. 25.

63. See McAndrew, *Venetian Architecture*, 473–83.

64. Ibid., 457.

65. See Vittore Branca, *Poliziano e l'umanesimo della parola* (Turin, 1983), esp. chap. 1, pp. 3ff.

66. Eugenio Garin, *La cultura filosofica del Rinascimento italiano* (Florence, 1961), 340ff.

66. Branca, *Poliziano*, 21. Note that Poliziano, in chapter 90 of *Miscellaneorum Centuria prima*, asked extremely competent judges, the "quadumviri literrari," "macti prudentia, ingegno, doctrina viri, ad quorum iudicium iure sit elaborandum, qualis, puta, si líceat . . . Medices Laurentius . . . Joannes Picus . . . Hermolaus Barbarus . . . Hieronjmus Donatus." But the friendship between Bernardo Bembo, Ermolao Barbaro, Girolamo Donà and Poliziano does not need further commentary, given the mass of documents on the subject.

68. One thinks, for example, of the *Oratio ad discipulos*, with the exposition of its Aristotelian program. On Ermolao Barbaro, see V. Branca, "L'Umanesimo veneziano alla fine del Quattrocento. Ermolao Barbaro e il suo circolo," in *Storia della cultura veneta*, 3/1 (Vicenza, 1980), 123–75.

69. See Branca, *Poliziano*, 60. Poliziano's dialogue was printed by Sarpi in 1494 in *Cose vulgari del Politiano*. Pietro Contarini di Giovan Ruggero, who died in 1528, was a collector of antiquities and modern art and linked to the circle of the Crociferi and the Zens. On this subject, see Daniela Delcorno Branca, *Sulla tradizione delle Rime del Poliziano* (Florence, 1979), 27ff.; Donata Battilotti and Maria Teresa Franco, "Regesti di committenti e dei primi collezionisti di Giorgione," *Antichità viva* 4–5 (1978): 58ff. (p. 83, entry on Michele Contarini, ed. M.T. Franco); Paolo Frasson, "Contarini Pietro," in *Dizionario Biografico degli Italiani*, vol. 28 (Rome, 1983), 203–64, which quotes a historical document against Julius II composed by Contarini on the death of Pope Della Rovere. On the quarrels between Pietro Contarini and the Observant Franciscans, which involved lands destined by the former for houses for the poor of the Contarini family, see A. Foscari and M. Tafuri, *L'armonia e i conflitti. La chiesa di San Francesco della Vigna nella Venezia del '500* (Turin, 1983), 32–33.

70. See Raffaello Brenzoni, *Fra Giovanni Giocondo* (Florence, 1960), 109ff.; Lucia A. Ciapponi, "Vitruvio nel primo Umanesimo," *Italia Medievale e Umanistica* 3 (1960): 98ff.; Branca, *Poliziano*, 209 and 269–70 n. 64.

71. See Branca, *Poliziano*, 219. Poliziano, moreover, quoted in *Centuria secunda* the codex of Vitruvius that existed in Nicolò Tegrini's library, and amended—as Ermolao Barbaro had already done—Pliny's text with the help of Vitruvius's (chap. 42). Branca remarks that Poliziano carefully studied the codex that entered the Medici library in 1492 (Laurenziano Pluteo 56, 1), annotated by the humanist on cc. 86–138: Poliziano was particularly interested in the Greek epigrams that Vitruvius cited in speaking of miraculous sources and that Poliziano himself said had been reduced, in the manuscripts, to a few illegible Greek letters, but that he rediscovered in the cited codex (ibid., 209). See also Vladimír Juren, "Politien et Vitruve. (Note sur le MS. Lat. 7382 de la Bibliothèque Nationale)," *Rinascimento*, ser. 2, vol. 18 (1978): 285–92; it analyzes a Parisian

Vitruvius that was, according to the author, annotated by Poliziano between 1480 and 1489 (see p. 291).

72. See Olivato and Puppi, *Mauro Codussi*, 242, entry 10.

73. On Tullio Lombardo's work as an architect, see Camillo Semenzato, "Pietro e Tullio Lombardo architetti," *Bollettino del Cisa* 6, pt. 2 (1964): 262–70; L. Puppi, "Per Tullio Lombardo," *Arte Lombarda* 17, no. 36 (1972): 100–3 (on an altar of the church of San Francesco in Rovigo, built around 1526); McAndrew, *Venetian Architecture*, 456–83; Lewis Kolb, *The Villa Giustinian*, 75ff.; Wendy Stedman Sheard, "Sanudo's List of Notable Things in Venetian Churches and the Date of the Vendramin Tomb," *Yale Italian Studies* 1, no. 3 (1977): 219–68.

74. See Foscari and Tafuri, "Sebastiano da Lugano," 109 and 122 n. 55.

75. Lewis Kolb, *The Villa Giustinian*, passim. Particular attention should instead be paid to Tullio Lombardo's presence in Mantua: Howard Burns made a few intelligent remarks on the subject in a lecture given at the CISA of Vicenza in September 1982.

76. Marcantonio Michiel, *Notizia d' opere di disegno pubblicata e illustrata da D. Jacopo Morelli. Seconda edizione riveduta ed aumentata per cura di Gustavo Frizzoni* (Bologna, 1884), 155.

77. See especially Giovanni Mariacher, "Tullio Lombardo Studies," *The Burlington Magazine* 96 (1954), 366–74; John Pope-Hennessy, *Italian Renaissance Sculpture* (London, 1958), 111–12, 114–17, 353–55; W. Stedman Sheard, "The Tomb of Doge Andrea Vendramin in Venice by Tullio Lombardo" (Ph.D. diss., Yale University, 1971; Ann Arbor, Mich.: University Microfilms, 1971); id., "'Asa Adorna': The prehistory of the Vendramin Tomb," *Jahrbuch der Berliner Museen* 20 (1978): 117–56; Sarah Wilk, *The Sculpture of Tullio Lombardo. Studies in Sources and Meaning* (New York and London, 1978); Debra Pincus, "Tullio Lombardo as restorer of antiquities: an aspect of fifteenth-century Venetian antiquarianism," *Arte veneta* 33 (1979): 29–42; id., "An antique fragment as workshop model; classicism in the Andrea Vendramin Tomb," *The Burlington Magazine* 123, no. 939 (1981): 342–46; Bruce Boucher, "Tullio Lombardo," in *The Genius of Venice 1500–1600*, ed. Jane Martineau and Charles Hope (London, 1983), 365 (and entries on 365–67); W. Stedman Sheard, "The Birth of Classicizing Relief in Venice on the Façade of the Scuola di San Marco," in the collection *interpretazioni veneziane*, Studi di storia dell'Arte in onore di Michelangelo Muraro, ed. David Rosand, (Venice, 1984), 149–74.

78. Pincus, "Tullio Lombardo as restorer," 29ff.

79. See W. Stedman Sheard, "Bramante e il Lombardo: ipotesi su una connessione," in the collection *Venezia Milano* (Milan, 1984), 25–26. In her excellent study, Sheard also examines the contacts between Pietro Lombardo and Ambrogio Barocci, the use of perspective in the bas-reliefs of the façade of the Scuola Grande di San Marco, and Cristoforo Solari's presence in Venice in 1489, giving credit to the critical reading of the Scuola of San Marco provided by Philip Sohm, *The Scuola Grande di San Marco, 1437–1550: the Architecture of a Venetian Lay Confraternity* (New York, 1982).

80. On Fra Giocondo's project for St. Peter's, see Franz Wolff Metternich, "Der Entwurf fra Giocondos für Sankt Peter," in *Festschrift für Kurt Bauch* (n.p., 1957): 155–70.

81. Brenzoni and McAndrew have looked at Pietro Contarini di Giovanni Alberto's testimony with suspicion, although McAndrew has not entirely dismissed the possibility of a consultation with Fra Giocondo for the Fondaco dei Tedeschi. See Raffaello Brenzoni, *Fra Giocondo Veronese* (Florence, 1960), and McAndrew, *Venetian Architecture*, 435. Muraro has instead interpreted Contarini's statements in a positive fashion. See Michelangelo Muraro, "Frà Giocondo da Verona e l'arte fiorentina," in *Florence and Venice*, 337–39.

82. Pietro Contarini, son of Giovanni Alberto—not to be confused with the man of the same name, son of Giovanni Ruggero—was born in 1477, in the fami-

ly branch of San Felice. A representative of the poor nobility, he held minor positions in the magistracy, becoming on August 28, 1508, the commander of the citadel of Novgorod in Dalmatia. In 1536 he gave up the political life, and he died in 1543, two years after the publication of his *Argoa voluptas* (Venetiis: Bernardinus de Vienis). Regarding Contarini, see Giuseppe Gullino, "Contarini Pietro," in *Dizionario Biografico degli Italiani*, vol. 28 (Rome, 1983), 264–65. Both the *Argoa voluptas* and the *Argo vulgar* were dedicated to Doge Pietro Lando and describe the pleasures of the city of Argo, identified with Novgorod: in the first book, the author takes the occasion for a laudatory description of Venice, beginning with the Rialto district. *Petrus Contarenus in M. Andream Grittum panegyris*, with the first attribution of the Fondaco dei Tedeschi to Fra Giocondo, is in BMV, Cod. Lat. 14, 230 = 4736, 3rd opuscolo, 21 of the miscellany, and in Cod. Lat. 14, 246 = 4683, c. 297, vv. 186–87. On the relations between Andrea Gritti and Fra Giocondo, see Achille Olivieri, "Fra Giocondo: tecniche urbane e cultura vitruviana," in *Palladio e Verona*, ed. Paola Marini (Verona, 1980), 239–41. See also, on Fra Giocondo's role during the Wars of Cambrai, the documented essay by Angiolo Lenci, "Note e considerazioni sul ruolo di Fra Giocondo nella difesa di Padova del 1509," *Atti dell'Istituto Veneto di Scienze, Lettere ed Arti, Classe di scienze morali, lettere ed arti*, vol. 139 (1980–81): 97–108, which underlined the role of the architect in the use of water for defensive purposes, especially in Limena.

83. On the reconstruction of the Rialto district after the fire of 1514 and the reasons behind the failure of Fra Giocondo's project, see the excellent essay by Donatella Calabi and Paolo Morachiello, "Rialto 1514–1538: gli anni della ricostruzione," in the collection *"Renovatio urbis." Venezia nell'età di Andrea Gritti, 1523–1538*, ed. M. Tafuri, (Rome, 1984), 291ff.

84. Manlio Dazzi, "Sull'architetto del Fondaco dei Tedeschi," *Atti del R. Istituto Veneto di Scienze, Lettere e Arti*, vol. 99, pt. 2 (1939–40): 873–74. Also see M. Dazzi, Mario Brunetti et al., *Il Fondaco nostro dei Tedeschi* (Venice, 1941), 36.

85. *Petri Contareni, q. Domini Io. Alberti Patricii Veneti, Libro Primo. Argo Vulgar* (Venetia: for Alouise de Torris, n.d.), c. 3v.

86. For the text of Francesco Morosini's dispatch, see Brenzoni, *Fra Giocondo*, 26–29. On Fra Giocondo's familiarity with Maximilian's ambassador, see L. A. Ciapponi, "Appunti per una biografia di Giovanni Giocondo da Verona," *Italia Medievale e Umanistica* 4 (1961): 131–58.

87. See ibid., 149. On Fra Giocondo's cultural contacts in France, see V. Juren, "Fra Giovanni Giocondo et les débuts des études vitruviennes en France," *Rinascimento*, ser. 2, 14 (1974): 101–15, which details Fra Giocondo's contacts with Guillaume Budé—the recognized author of the marginalia in the *Vitruvio* of 1497, *Rés*, 5, 381, of the Bibliothèque Nationale in Paris—and Lefèvre D'Etaples. On Fra Giocondo's Vitruvianism, see, finally, entry 3.3.5 by Pier Nicola Pagliara, in Christoph L. Frommel, Stefano Ray, and M. Tafuri, *Raffaello architetto* (Milan, 1984), 426, and L.A. Ciapponi, "Fra Giocondo da Verona and his edition of Vitruvius," *Journal of the Warburg and Courtauld Institutes* 47 (1984): 72–90.

88. Ciapponi, "Appunti," 152.

89. Fra Giocondo's petition to the *Signoria* is inserted in the original minutes of the *parte* of the Council of Ten, dated May 28, 1506. ASV, "Consiglio dei Dieci," Miscellaneous Documents [*Misti*], filza 18, c. 98, published in *Laguna, lidi, fiumi. Cinque secoli di gestione delle acque*, Catalogue of the documentary exhibit of the Archivio di Stato in Venice, ed. Maria Francesca Tiepolo (Venice, 1983), 57–59.

90. Fra Giocondo's essay on the diversion of the Brenta, signed by the Savio alle Acque (Minister of the Waterways) Hieronimo Duodo, is registered, along with Aleardi's answer, in the *Libro Deposition primo*, which in 1537 the minister directed to record opinions on

the lagoon, rivers, and waters, including those before his term. ASV, "Savi ed Esecutori alle Acque," Reg. 172, "Deposition," Book 1, cc. 37v–38r. See *Laguna, lidi, fiumi*, 59, entry 109.

91. See McAndrew, *Venetian Architecture*, 427.

92. On the church of San Fantin, in addition to Paoletti and to pp. 322–25 in Franzoi and Di Stefano, *Le chiese*, see Gastone Vio, "I 'mistri' della chiesa di San Fantin in Venezia," *Arte Veneta* 31 (1977): 225–31, which identifies the church's first architect as Sebastiano Mariani da Lugano, replaced by Scarpagnino between 1516 and 1522. There remain many unanswered questions, however, regarding the works of Sebastiano da Lugano and Antonio Abbondi, which are being examined, with the help of unpublished documents, by Stefano Maso. The basilica of Santa Giustina in Padua (figs. 39, 40) also seems to have been influenced by San Salvador, but is marked by uncertain planning and evident solecisms in the treatment of the orders, due perhaps to Andrea Moroni's intervention, which began in 1532. See Erice Rigoni, *L'architetto Andrea Moroni* (Padua, 1939); Giulio Bresciani Alvarez, "La Basilica di Santa Giustina. Arte e Storia storico-costruttive," in the collection *La Basilica di Santa Giustina. Arte e Storia* (Padua, 1970), 67–165.

93. On the church of San Sepolcro, see Jürg Ganz, *Alessio Tramello. Drei Sakralbauten in Piacenza und die oberitalienische Architektur um 1500* (Frauenfeld, 1968), 37–51 (now in a very poor Italian translation, Piacenza, 1983), which reproduces a drawing from the Archivio di San Vittore al Corpo in Milan depicting three domes instead of the three cross vaults that presently cover the square spaces of the central nave. See also Bruno Adorni, "Alessio Tramello a Piacenza," in *Storia della Emilia-Romagna*, vol. 2 (Bologna, 1977), 701–3. Adorni is also working on a systematic work on Tramello.

94. B. Adorni, *L'architettura farnesiana a Piacenza 1545–1600* (Parma, 1982), 156–57 (UA 459 and 461, surveys of existing work; UA 460, remodeling design). On Peruzzi's designs for San Domenico in

Siena, see Marinella Festa Milone, "Fra sperimentalismo e utopia: il progetto di Baldassarre Peruzzi per il San Domenico di Siena," *Storia architettura*, 1 : 2–3 (1979): 51–74 (which contains many errors), and Heinrich Wurm, *Baldassarre Peruzzi Architekturzeichnungen. Tafelband* (Tübingen, 1984), 219–38. One notes, however, that drawings UA 138r, 340r, 341r, and 339r, and the cross section of the Ashmolean Museum (all with repeated domical vaults) enter into an ideal dialogue with the typology of the Duomo of Faenza, of the church of San Nicolò in Carpi, and of Peruzzi's design for the church of Sant' Agostino in Monte San Savino (UA 504r).

95. See Christian A. Isermeyer, "Le chiese del Vasari e i suoi interventi in edifici sacri medievali," *Bollettino del Cisa* 19 (1977), 281ff., esp. 291–94. As for non-Italian experiments with repeated domed spaces, let us mention those of Hernán Ruiz the Younger, culminating in the remarkable church of the Hospital de la Sangre in Seville. See Pedro Navascues Palacio, *El libro de Arquitectura de Hernán Ruiz, el joven* (Madrid, 1974). A design by Alessandro Bolzoni, inspired by Alessio Tramello's church of San Sepolcro, has been published in Adorni, *L'architettura farnesiana*, 415, and photo on 420.

96. Moschini, *Guida per la città di Venezia*, 1, pt. 2, 554. Moschini draws this information from a report on the history of the church made in 1744 by Pietro Rota, abbot of the monastery (ibid., 556).

97. ASV, "San Salvador," b. 25, tomo 50. Two master masons were paid for their work "a rasone de passa cinque et mezo per ducato," while "li volti . . . pasa due et mezo al ducato, videlicet a lire sei et soldi quattro per ducato, mesurando dicti volti in terra per longeza a la destra senza mesurar altri pedussi." The text of the agreement continues: "Item siano tenuti a smaltar tute fabriche, bianchisar et farne coprir et tuti camini sí de sotto come sopra al coperto. Ittem li prometteno dare al messe barille due de vino, videlicet queste due sopra ditto mercado et questo se intende quando lavoreranno et perche el taveler de ditte fabriche maestro Zuan sopra ditto non voria stare sopra questo

per acontentar ditti maistri, li promettemo ducati XX sopra ditto mercado a lire sei et soldi quattro per ducato. Ittem siano obligati a fare tuti li sesti anderano in ditta fabricha dandoli nui li legnami, et tutti sottoscriverano al sopra ditto scripto et presente maestro Zacaria tajapiera da Lugano et Zuane da Lugan, garzone del ditto maestro Zaccaria. Ittem, andando muro de piere piccole overo de meza piera, tuto se intende a muro de una pietra, mesurando el paso quadro el muro."

98. Ibid. See the transcription of the document in the appendix, no. 9. The appearance of a Celestro among the witnesses of the act of 1541 provokes a spontaneous search for a link with the mysterious "Zuane Celestro toschan fo de ser Andrea" mentioned in the documents of the building of the Scuola di San Rocco, and with the "toschan" who, according to Sanudo, provided a model for the Nuove Procuratie. In the document pertaining to the refectory of San Salvador, Joanne Celestro is called, however, "reverendo Domine," while "a syrico" almost certainly means "from the silk." All of which does not help us identify the witness with the Tuscan master: while waiting for new documentary evidence, we are forced to suspend our inquiry for the time being.

99. Ibid., 1563, January 20. The document is signed by Don Nicolò, the procurator of the monastery, by Giovanni da Lugano, a stonemason, and by Stefano di Marco for "Barbon Vettore," who was illiterate. See the transcription of the document in the appendix, no. 10.

100. In drawing 463c of "Miscellanea Mappe" of the ASV (fig. 47)—the upper portion of which is unfortunately missing—the minor cloister seems square, unlike the one that was executed: the structure of the southern building is consequently deeper, with corridors and service rooms—back shops?—facing the portico of the cloister itself. On the left of the folio the outline of the church is drawn with a significant variation from drawings 463b and a: the edge of the façade, which was missing in those drawings, is delineated here. Another variation relative to the executed work is the way the southern structure is grafted onto the

church. In the drawing, the short side facing the campo detaches itself a little from the alignment of the walls perpendicular to the front; in the execution, it follows the line of the side of the church, generating a trapezoidal space on the inside. The drawing is still schematic, but more professionally drawn than the previous ones. Dimensions are given for some of the spaces: the portico of the small cloister is 11.6 feet wide, as are the rooms located between the two cloisters; in the large space on the upper right is written "alto da baso p. 18 / alto de sora p. 13, 63." A later design for the convent can be found in ASV, "Miscellanea Mappe," 1007, while, in the same collection, 524 refers to the large cloister: it presents an elevation with an arched portico on columns—9 arcades—with two upper levels, marked by square windows arranged in pairs, with a cornice tangent to the arches and a second cornice with dentils that terminates the volume (fig. 44). The columns, resting on a continuous base, interrupted in the center, are rough in design and have pronounced entases; there is one refined detail, however: a pulvinated entablature between the capital and the impost of the arches. The rhythm of the arcades bears no relation to that of the windows (fig. 49). The second cloister of San Salvador was built in different forms, with a portico on three sides, and with subsequent alterations; the northern wall is solid, with elongated windows. A plan dated August 11, 1618, presented to the Ufficio del Proprio by the clergymen of San Salvador, in a case against Marzial Prezzato (ASV, "Miscellanea Mappe," 592), shows the convent's ancient cemetery, with the entrance from the Calle delle Ballotte. The outside of the convent, on the side canal (fig. 50) and the street that leads into Campo Salvador, is not without interest, in spite of the building stages and alterations: in the southern sector, on the canal, large windows reveal the structure of the refectory, while a stylistic change can be detected in the order and in the form of the windows, beginning with the corner between the canal and the street. At the conference held in Tours, July 1–10, 1981, Howard Burns presented an unpublished drawing, which he attributed to

Sebastiano Serlio, for the convent of San Salvador.

101. The sacristy (fig. 51), which stands like a hinge between the bell tower and the church, does not appear in the drawings of the ASV, *Miscellanea Mappe*, 463a and 463b. Erich Hubala and John McAndrew have attributed the design for that structure to Giorgio Spavento. See Hubala, *Venedig*, 933, McAndrew, *Venetian Architecture*, 451. However, in Girolamo Priuli's testament of 1546, which Vincenzo Mancini has kindly brought to our attention, there is a bequest of 400 ducats for the construction of the sacristy of San Salvador. ASV, "San Salvador," busta 45, tomo. 94, fasc. a, c. 20v. Girolamo Priuli di Lorenzo also left 600 ducats (ibid., c. 21r) for the construction of the "choir." Regarding the placement of the latter, see note 42. All this leaves us with a problem requiring further research, for the language of the room decorated by Francesco Vecellio clearly becomes anachronistic if we date it to the 1540s. However, the two-light windows, or *bifore*, of the sacristy exhibit variations on the Codussian model. The small lateral Ionic piers, independent of the arches that rest on backward supports, alternate with small Corinthian columns, while the corner function is resolved with a splitting of the vertical elements. In addition, the sacristy is flanked by two small domed rooms.

102. See Wolfgang Wolters, *Plastiche Deckendekorationen des Cinquecento in Venedig und im Veneto* (Berlin, 1968), 31–32. Serena Romano is writing an analytical essay on this work.

103. On Palazzo Grimani in Santa Maria Formosa, see the preceding chapter. On the monastery della Carità, see Elena Bassi, "Il Convento della Carità," *Corpus Palladianum*, 6, (Vicenza, 1971), and the corrections made by L. Puppi, *Andrea Palladio* (Milan, 1973), 2:332–36.

Chapter 3

1. See Aldo Stella, *Dall'anabattismo al socinianesimo nel Cinquecento veneto* (Padua, 1967); id., *Anabattismo e antitrinitarismo in Italia nel XVI secolo. Nuove ricerche storiche* (Padua, 1969); id.,

"Movimenti di riforma nel Veneto nel Cinque–Seicento," in the collection *Storia della cultura veneta. Il Seicento*, 4/1 (Vicenza, 1983), 1–21; id., "Tensioni religiose e movimenti di riforma (durante il dogado di Andrea Gritti)," in the collection *"Renovatio urbis." Venezia nell'età di Andrea Gritti, 1523–1538*, ed. Manfredo Tafuri, (Rome, 1984), 134–47; Carlo Ginzburg, *I costituti di don Pietro Manelfi* (Florence and Chicago, 1970); Pio Paschini, *Venezia e l'Inquisizione romana da Giulio III a Pio IV* (Padua, 1959); Franco Gaeta, *Un nunzio pontificio a Venezia nel Cinquecento. Girolamo Aleandro* (Venice and Rome, 1960); Cesare Vasoli, *Profezia e ragione. Studi sulla cultura del Cinquecento e del Seicento* (Naples, 1974); Paul F. Grendler, *The Roman Inquisition and the Venetian Press 1540–1605* (Princeton, N.J., 1977; It. trans., Rome 1983). Also see Nicholas S. Davidson, "Il Sant'Uffizio e la tutela del culto a Venezia nel '500," *Studi veneziani*, n.s., 6 (1982), (Pisa, 1983): 87–101. On the evolution of Venice's ecclesiastical structure during the sixteenth century, see the fundamental essay by Paolo Prodi, "The structure and organisation of the church in Renaissance Venice: suggestions for research," in the collection *Renaissance Venice*, ed. John R. Hale (London, 1973), 409–30. On the historical moment treated in the present chapter, see Adriano Prosperi, "Intellettuali e Chiesa all'inizio dell'età moderna," in *Storia d'Italia Einaudi. Annali 4. Intellettuli e potere*, ed. Corrado Vivanti (Turin, 1981), 161–252, with an ample bibliography in the notes. The first results of the research that led to the preparation of the present chapter were published in the essay by Antonio Foscari and M. Tafuri, "Evangelismo e architettura. Jacopo Sansovino e la chiesa di San Martino a Venezia, *Bollettino dei Civici Musei Veneziani*, n.s., 27, no. 1–4 (1982): 34–54, which we bring to the reader's attention for its documentary appendix and the photograph of the painting attributed to Giacomo Guardi, mentioned later in the text.

2. See A. Foscari and M. Tafuri, *L'armonia e i conflitti. La chiesa di San Francesco della Vigna nella Venezia del Cinquecento* (Turin, 1983).

3. That the Bon whom Sansovino succeeded in 1529 as *proto* of the Procuratia de supra was Pietro and not Bartolomeo (who had died in 1509) has been ascertained in the graduate thesis by Stefano Mariani, "Vita e opere dei proti Bon, Bartolomeo e Pietro," IUAV (1982–83), consulting professor, Donatella Calabi. Mariani has documented the existence of two men by the name of Bon, Bartolomeo (ca. 1450–1509) and Pietro (ca. 1460–1529), whom recent historiography has—erroneously—understood to be one individual. See, for example, John McAndrew, *Venetian Architecture of the Early Renaissance* (Cambridge, Mass. and London, 1980), 506–27.

4. See Foscari and Tafuri, *L'armonia e i conflitti*, passim and on pp. 107–8 n. 108, for the church of San Marcello in Rome.

5. Regarding the church of San Martino, see Flaminio Corner, *Ecclesiae Venetae antiquis monumentis*, vol. 4 (Venice, 1749), 331–38; Giulio Lorenzetti, *Itinerario sansoviniano a Venezia* (Venice, 1929), 83; Erich Hubala, *Venedig. Reclams Kunstführer Italien, II. Oberitalien Ost* (Stuttgart, 1965), 911–12; J. McAndrew, *Antonio Visentini, Catalogue of the Drawings of the R.I.B.A.* (Farnborough, Hants, 1974), 34 (entry 128); Deborah Howard, *Jacopo Sansovino. Architecture and Patronage in Renaissance Venice* (New Haven and London, 1975), 77–81; Umberto Franzoi and Dina Di Stefano, *Le chiese di Venezia* (Venice, 1976), 496–97; D. Howard, "Le chiese di Jacopo Sansovino a Venezia," *Bollettino del Cisa* 19 (1977): 57–58; Giuseppe Della Puppa, *Storia della chiesa di S. Martino "De Geminis" in Venezia*, mimeographed booklet (Venice, 1978). Della Puppa (ibid., 5ff.) writes of the church's history in the Middle Ages, recalling that our earliest information about it goes back to 932, assuming we can trust the chronicle that Domenico De Grandis maintains he saw in Nicolò Tebaldi's library; the foundation of the church ought, however, to have taken place during the first half of the eighth century. According to Antonio Niero (an oral communication), the foundation was Longobard. In 1026, however, the building was rebuilt, but in

1107 Doge Ordelafo Falier gave Giovanni Gradenigo, the Patriarch of Grado, land for a later reconstruction. The new Romanesque church was completed in 1161: its maintenance was paid for not only with the usual charitable donations, but also with the rents from the houses built on the grounds within the parish's dominion, which extended beyond the canal of Ca'di Dio and to the north, up to the area where the monastery della Celestia would be built. Della Puppa's mimeographed text is the only one interested in documenting the history of the building but it also contains many philological oversights and a number of lacunae.

6. Ibid., 18, note how at the beginning of the fourteenth century the church had in its service, in addition to the parish priest, three priests, a deacon, a subdeacon, and a few clerics (ibid., 10).

7. The portico is mentioned in a partriarchal decree of 1450 that concerns its closing at night (ibid., p. 9). It was threatened by a fire between 1450 and 1500. Looking onto the parish priest's garden, furthermore, was a rental house [*da sarzenti*] owned by the Scuola di San Giovanni Evangelista, acquired May 2, 1472 (ibid., 12).

8. See Corner, *Ecclesiae Venetae*, 4:335.

9. See Della Puppa, *Storia della chiesa*, 10–12. In 1468, the Arsenal acquired from the church, for 1,100 ducats in gold, ten small houses for the poor built according to the last will and testament of Giovanni Boso of August 13, 1316: they would eventually give way to the "*via lata et pulchra*" adjacent to the door of the Arsenal, while the parish priest of San Martino would use the proceeds from the forced sale to acquire, in 1472, a rental property belonging to the Scuola di San Giovanni Evangelista. On the "via lata," see Ennio Concina, *L'Arsenale della Repubblica di Venezia* (Milan, 1984), 68–70.

10. Della Puppa, *Storia della chiesa*, 14-16.

11. Corner, *Ecclesiae Venetae*, 4:332. Note that Antonio Contarini was the dogal canon, and thus the "minister" of the Doge's chapel: as such, he surely must

have known Sansovino personally in the preceding years.

12. APSM, busta B 1–4, "Rodoli." See doc. 2 transcribed in the appendix of the present volume.

13. See Corner, *Ecclesiae Venetae*, 4:332–33, and Della Puppa, *Storia della chiesa*, 19.

14. APSM, busta B 1–4, "Fabbrica della chiesa." See doc. 1 transcribed in the appendix.

15. Ibid. (January 31, 1556). Transcribed in the appendix of Foscari and Tafuri, *Evangelismo*, doc. 3.

16. APSM, busta B 1–4 (October 21, 1553ff.), transcribed in the appendix of Foscari and Tafuri, *Evangelismo*, doc. 2.

17. See Howard, *Jacopo Sansovino*, 81–87.

18. As was recorded in the text, already cited (doc. 2 in the appendix), of September 29, 1615.

19. APSM, busta B 1–4 (January 31, 1556).

20. See Corner, *Ecclesiae Venetae*, 4:335.

21. See, again, doc. 3 transcribed in the appendix of Foscari and Tafuri, *Evangelismo*.

22. See Della Puppa, *Storia della chiesa*, 21.

23. APSM, busta B 1–4, "Rodoli," March 9, 1584. The petition makes it clear that "fa di bisogno di destruger parte della scola di S. Martino congionta con la fassada di essa chiesa."

24. Ibid. The petition insists on the fact that San Martino was the Arsenal's church and visited by all the foreigners who came to Venice. On November 6, 1601, the College submitted the petition to the Procurators in Zecca. The bill of a mason who had redone "la fondamenta in la sua ghiesia . . . per far le arche del santissimo Sacramento" bears the date December 23, 1604. APSM, busta B 1–4, "Fabbrica della chiesa," at the date.

25. Ibid., March 1, 1607, transcribed in Foscari and Tafuri, *Evangelismo*, doc. 5; also in docs. 6 and 7.

26. See doc. 9 in Foscari and Tafuri,

Evangelismo. On September 20, 1618, however, the parish priest and his parishioners once again appealed to the *Signoria*, entreating it to provide for their "very poor church" that "had already been imperfect for a long time, not being able to celebrate decently in it the divine offices."

27. See Della Puppa, *Storia della chiesa*, 26. The church was consecrated on February 5, 1653 (*m.v.*), by Patriarch Gianfrancesco Morosini, more than a century after the beginning of the reconstruction. See Corner, *Ecclesiae Venetae*, 4:333. The documents in the busta B 1–4 of the APSM allow one to follow later operations: on August 30, 1662, the parish priest and the chapter implored Patriarch Morosini for 250 ducats for the restoration of the house "sopra la fondamenta de portoneri, l'ultima . . . quale per l'antichità è in stato ruvinoso"; September 29, 1769, is the date of the contract with the stonemason Giuseppe Fadiga for the restoration of the church floor, but on October 8, 1783, the chapter complained that the flooring itself should be "oggetto di continua mortificazione all'animo nostro . . . imperfetto da ben dieci anni . . . rozzo ed informe per difetto della necessaria lisciatura, spoglio dal piú decoroso armamento per la mancanza dei balaustri a tutte le cappelle che lo circondano e privo dell'intiero suo compimento per la necessità dei piani corrispondenti nelle cappelle medesime e singolarmente nella maggiore, destinata a Trono di Gesú Cristo sagramentato." On September 20, 1784, the chapter noted that the bells of Sant'Antonio di Castello had been acquired through a Senate action, and thanks to the intervention of the deputies responsible for the church's restoration, who had assumed the burden of the restoration of the flooring, without using any of the fund for the building of San Martino. In 1785 and 1786, contracts were drawn up with the stonemason Giovanni Battista Spiera for the banisters of the chapels, and on April 16, 1789, Spiera also signed a contract for the finishing and polishing of the floor and other finishing touches: on May 20, 1790, the public surveyor Filippo Rossi approved the executed works. The panel by Pedrali,

painted on canvas, was replaced, in the eighteenth century, by a fresco by Jacopo Guarana, who also worked on the vaults above the doors. It is interesting to note that the sixteenth- and seventeenth-century decoration of the church of San Martino—and, in particular, Bruni's rich scenography—tended to obliterate the original linguistic asceticism of Sansovino, who was thus challenged by the triumphalism of the painted interventions.

28. AMV, "Div. III, Materia Culto," antecedent 6681, letters from Don Angelo Bianchi of February 12 and March 4, 1897, with requests for financial assistance: the parish priest maintained that the work he had undertaken was considered "di ornamento della città" and "grata ai forestieri che sbarcano di rimpetto a Sua Eccellenza l'Ammiraglio che vi sta di fronte ed ai altolocati della marina che vi ripassano innanzi." See also the booklet by Marco Moro, *Cenni storici sulla chiesa di S. Martino vescovo in Venezia* (Venice, 1897), 6. Moro wrote: "Il disegno di codesta facciata ideassi dall'egregio ingegnere nob. Federico Berchet e dal distinto architetto Domenico Rupolo, che, gentilmente prestandosi, diressero i lavori con un vero intelletto di amore superiore ad ogni elogio, avendo a fedelissimo esecutore il valente impresario Sig. Antonio Pollin. Tutti e tre questi nobili corifei dell'arte e dell'intelligenza gareggiarono di zelo per la felice riuscita dell'opera che migliore effetto non poteva sortire; ed a raggiungerlo, conservando la severa antichità dell'edificio, di pietre cotte ben riquadrate a disegno, lo adornarono qua e là di marmi d'Istria finamente lavorati e scolpiti quali sono i capitelli e la croce nella sommità, con due nuove statue laterali, rappresentanti San Martino Vescovo e San Martino Papa, i cornicioni, gli architravi, e due rizzoni e il magnifico finestrone formato a sí vaghi trafori da sembrare un venusto ricamo smagliante ed una splendid gemma posta in fronte al sontuoso edifizio." Furthermore, the inscription placed between the volutes of the portal of the main façade is explicit: "Prospectus / ex novo conditus ac ornatus / a plebano Ang. Bianchi / aree proprio et fidelium / anno Dni MDCCCXCVII."

29. On Federico Berchet, an employee of the city technical office, author of the reconstruction of the Fondaco dei Turchi, of projects for the "Via Transurbana," of the central market in iron in the Rialto district and of the buildings at no. 4127 on the Riva degli Schiavoni and nn. 711–712 on the Fondamenta di San Simeone Piccolo, see Giandomenico Romanelli, *Venezia ottocento. Materiali per una storia architettonica e urbanistica della città nel secolo XIX* (Rome, 1977), passim.

30. See Antonio Visentini, *Osservazioni che servono di continuazione al trattato di Teofilo Gallaccini sopra gli errori degli architetti* (Venice, 1771), 57–58. The portal of the main façade of San Martino was also surveyed in *Admiranda Urbis Venetae*, vol. 2 (London, British Museum), 137: on the same folio, on the left, is a survey of the side portal of the church of San Francesco della Vigna. The folios of the AUV, 3:128 and 129, contain a survey of the plan of San Martino and a drawing of a façade that does not correspond to the structure of the church. McAndrew (*Antonio Visentini*, 34) has surmised that drawing 129 represents the status of the façade in the eighteenth century or a project for it, but both hypotheses are excluded by relevant documentation. The painting by Guardi mentioned in the text has been published in Foscari and Tafuri, *Evangelismo*, fig. 28.

31. See Concina, *L'Arsenale*, 84–92.

32. Deborah Howard's references to Codussian themes seem completely inappropriate (see Howard, *Jacopo Sansovino*, 78–81, and "Le Chiese," 58), and furthermore have been excluded by Ralph Lieberman's essay, "Venetian Church Architecture around 1500," *Bollettino del Cisa* 19 (1977): p. 45.

33. On the Ca' di Dio, see Howard, *Jacopo Sansovino*, 114–19; the criticism contained in James S. Ackerman, "The Geopolitics of Venetian Architecture in the Time of Titian," in the collection *Titian. His World and His Legacy*, ed. David Rosand (New York, 1982), 54; Giuseppe Maria Pilo, "Jacopo Sansovino, Baldassarre Longhena, Matteo Lucchesi, Bernardino Maccaruzzi: interventi edilizi di tre secoli alla Ca' di Dio di Venezia,"

Notizie da Palazzo Albani 8, no. 1 (1979): 100–12; Franca Semi, *Gli "Ospizi" di Venezia* (Venice, 1983), 87–95.

34. See Foscari and Tafuri, *L'armonia e i conflitti*, 69–70, 79–81.

35. On the houses for the Morosini family, see Rodolfo Gallo, "Contributi su Jacopo Sansovino," in *Saggi e Memorie di Storia dell'Arte* I (1957), 94–96; on the Moro houses, see Howard, *Jacopo Sansovino*, 146–54 (in which, however, the hypothesis about a project by Leonardo Moro, dilettante architect, lacks consistency); on the Osteria del Pellegrino, see A. Foscari, "Altre schede veneziane su Jacopo Sansovino," *Notizie da Palazzo Albani* 12, no. 1–2 (1983): 145–48. One should also note that the Moro houses are represented in the background of a painting by Francesco Guardi erroneously entitled *Giardino del palazzo Contarini dal Zaffo alla Misericordia* (Metropolitan Museum, New York), and in the watercolor drawings pertaining to it.

36. Vasari, *Vite*, eds. Licia and Carlo Ludovico Ragghianti, 4 (Milan, 1978), 546, 557. On the relations between Sansovino and Domenico Grimani, also see A. Foscari and M. Tafuri, "Sebastiano da Lugano, i Grimani e Jacopo Sansovino. Artisti e committenti nella chiesa di Sant' Antonio di Castello," *Arte Veneta* 36 (1982): 100–23.

37. On Cardinal Domenico Grimani and his relations with Giovanni Pico, Erasmus, Francesco Zorzi, Francisco Quiñones, and Sansovino, see Foscari and Tafuri, *L'armonia e i conflitti*, and the bibliography therein (esp. in nn. 91 and 92 on pp. 104–5).

38. On the relations between Francesco Zorzi, the Nicodemite Lucio Paolo Rosello, Soncino—the publisher of the *Arcana catholicae veritatis*—and Lorenzo Astemio, see Vasoli, *Profezia e ragione*, 124. Aldo Stella has also observed that in 1525 Rosello dedicated to Zorzi the *Quaestiones Joannis de Jaunduno super methaphisicam*: see Stella, *Anabattismo e antitrinitarismo*, 114, and "Movimenti di riforma," 6. Zorzi's adherence to an irenical line intent on a spiritualist and evangelical reform of the Church emerges from *De Harmonia Mundi* as well as from *Problemata*. Zorzi's influence on the thinking of Giulio Camillo Delminio and Postel is discussed in C. Vasoli, *I miti e gli astri* (Naples, 1977), 191ff.

39. On Hugo van der Goes, affiliated in 1438 with the congregation of Windesheim, which was founded by the Brothers of the Common Life, and his relations with Thomas a Kempis, see Rudolf and Margot Wittkower, *Born under Saturn* (London, 1973); Italian trans. (Turin, 1968), 123–28.

40. It may also be interesting to recall that in Venice in 1525 an anthology was published in the vernacular of texts by Luther, reprinted in 1540 and 1545. See Carlo Ginzburg and Adriano Prosperi, *Giochi di pazienza. Un seminario sul "Beneficio di Cristo"* (Turin, 1975), 131 and 204 n. 16; Silvana Seidel Menchi, "Traduzioni italiane di Lutero," *Rinascimento*, ser. 2, 17 (1977): 40ff. Regarding the circulation of Erasmus's works in Venice, see Delio Cantimori, *Erasmo e la vita morale e religiosa italiana nel secolo XVI* (1936), in id., *Umanesimo e religione nel Rinascimento* (Turin, 1975), 40ff. In 1545, a volume by Alfonso De Valdés was published in Italian, in Venice, *Dialogo en que particularmente se tratan de las cosas ocurridas en Roma el año de 1527*, in which the Sack of Rome was justified as a providential event, since the Pope had acted as a head of State instead of incarnating the evangelical spirit. See André Chastel, *Il sacco di Roma, 1527* (Turin, 1983), 18, 224. Chastel recalls the violent protest against the *Dialogo* written by Baldassare Castiglione, Apostolic Delegate to Charles V, who attempted to save the ecclesiastical institution and its symbols, though he did not deny the corruption of modern Rome (ibid, 18–19). One should also mention that the *Beneficio di Cristo* became the "arte del ben vivere" in *Della tranquilità dell'animo*, which was published in Venice in 1544 by Isabella Sforza, alias Ortensio Lando.

41. See the *Libellus ad Leonem X P. M. (1513)* in *Annales Camaldulenses*, 9 (Venice, 1773), coll. 612–719. Also see Innocenzo Cervelli, "Storiografia e problemi intorno alla vita religiosa e spirituale a Venezia nella prima metà del '500,"

Studi Veneziani 8 (1965): 447–76, and Gigliola Fragnita, "Cultura umanistica e riforma religiosa. Il "De officio boni ac probi episcopi" di Gasparo Contarini," ibid., 11 (1969), 75ff.

42. See Felix Gilbert, "Cristianesimo, Umanesimo e la bolla 'Apostolici Regiminis' del 1513," *Rivista Storica Italiana* 79, no. 4 (1967): 976–90.

43. See M. Tafuri, "'Roma instaurata.' Strategie urbane e politiche pontificie nella Roma del primo '500," in Cristoph Luitpold Frommel, Stefano Ray, M. Tafuri, *Raffaello architetto* (Milan, 1984), 59–106.

44. See Foscari and Tafuri, *L'armonia e i conflitti*, 45, and n. 127 on p. 111.

45. See L. Puppi, "Riflessioni su temi e problemi della ritrattistica del Lotto," in *Lorenzo Lotto*, Proceedings from the Convention in Asolo (1980), eds. Pietro Zampetti and Vittorio Sgarbi (Treviso, 1981), 396.

46. See Lorenzo Lotto, *Il "Libro di spese diverse" (1538–1556)*, ed. P. Zampetti (Venice-Rome, 1969), 84–85, 98–100, 114–115, 132, 223, 226. Also see Ileana Chiappini di Sorio, "Caratteri, comportamenti, religiosità di Lorenzo Lotto. Appunti e tentativo di un'analisi dei suoi scriti," *Ateneo Veneto* 170, n.s., no. 2 (1983): 207–24, which unfortunately contains less than its title promises. Interesting hypotheses about the collaboration between Lotto and Sansovino can be found in Luisa Vertova, "Lorenzo Lotto: collaborazione o rivalità fra pittura e scultura?" in *Lorenzo Lotto*, 401–14 (esp. pp. 408–10): the author, in suggesting that Lotto may have furnished Sansovino with ideas for the composition of *Cristo in gloria* and perhaps for other works, defines an exchange between the artists that deserves further examination. In the article by Francesca Cortesi Bosco, "Lorenzo Lotto dal polittico di Ponteranica alla commissione della Santa Lucia di Jesi," in the collection *Omaggio a Lorenzo Lotto*, Proceedings from the Convention in Jesi, December 4–6, 1981, monographical issue of *Notizie da Palazzo Albani* 13, no. 1 (1984): 56–80 (esp. 71–72 n. 35), L. Vertova's hypothesis is confirmed, as opposed to the idea of Sansovino's dependence on Lotto, which has recently been reaffirmed in the essay by Bruce Boucher, "Sansovino's Medici Tabernacle and Lotto's Sacramental Allegory: New Evidence of their Relationship," *Apollo* 114, no. 235 (1981): 156–61.

47. See Giovanni Romano, "La Bibbia di Lotto," *Paragibe* 317–19 (1976): 82–91; F. Cortesi Bosco, "A proposito del frontespizio di Lorenzo Lotto per la Bibbia di Antonio Brucioli," *Bergamum* 1–2 (1976): 27–42; Renzo Fontana, "'Solo, senza fidel governo et molto inquieto de la mente.' Testimonianze archivistiche su alcuni amici del Lotto processati per eresia," in *Lorenzo Lotto*, 279–97; id., "Aspetti sociali e orizzonti mentali nell' ambiente lottesco negli anni quaranta del Cinquecento," in the collection *Interpretazioni veneziane. Studi di storia dell'arte in onore di Michelangelo Muraro*, ed. David Rosand (Venice, 1984), 359–62; Maria Calí, "La 'religione' di Lorenzo Lotto," in *Lorenzo Lotto*, 243–77; id., "Ancora sulla 'religione' di Lorenzo Lotto," *Ricerche di Storia dell'Arte* 19 (1983): 37–60; id., "Tra religione e potere: il dissenso di Lorenzo Lotto," "*Renovatio urbis*," 236–62; F. Cortesi Bosco, "Il problema della posizione religiosa di Lorenzo Lotto," in *Omaggio a Lorenzo Lotto*, 81–89, which reaffirms the orthodoxy of the frescoes of Trescore, concluding, however, with a favorable judgment on a "spiritual" Lotto; Costantino Urieli, "Ancora sulla religiosità di Lorenzo Lotto," ibid., 106–7, which pointlessly defends the painter against the accusation of Lutheranism. See also Pietro Zampetti, *Lotto* (Bologna, 1983), 22–24. Ronald Steinberg has, moreover, observed that *San Vincenzo Ferre in gloria*, painted by Lotto in ca. 1513–15 (church of San Domenico in Recanati), bears similarities to Savonarola, hypothesizing that it was copied from medals (fig. 62). See Ronald M. Steinberg, *Fra Girolamo Savonarola, Florentine Art and Renaissance Historiography* (Athens, Ohio, 1977), 108. Steinberg also makes useful remarks on Savonarola's position on art and architecture. See ibid., 51ff. Also see Bernard Aikema, "Lorenzo Lotto and the 'Ospitale de San Zuane Polo,'" in *Interpretazioni veneziane*, 343–50. Interesting

reflections are also to be found in the essay by Angelo Mazza, "La pala dell' 'Elemosina di Sant'Antonino' nel dibattito cinquecentesco sul pauperismo," in *Lorenzo Lotto*, 347–64 (fig. 63). Augusto Gentili has recently attacked the hypotheses proposed by Maria Calí and this writer, in an article that touches on the limits of professional denotology: after having falsified the hypotheses of the authors chosen as antagonists—where have we ever maintained that Lotto was a Lutheran?—Gentili paradoxically arrives at conclusions that are substantially similar to ours, pretending to teach us nuances of religious history that we fortunately learned a long time ago from many other masters. One ought, however, to compare our discussion with Augusto Gentili, "Per Lorenzo Lotto e i suoi contesti storici: due episodi ri-documentati, tra polemica e progetto," *Artibus et historiae* 8 (1983): 77–93.

48. See Loredana Olivato, "Per il Serlio a Venezia: documenti nuovi e documenti rivisitati," *Arte Veneta* 25 (1971), 284–91. On Serlio's role in the development of Venetian architectural culture in the first half of the sixteenth century, see the essay by Hubertus Günther, "Studien zum venezianischen Aufenthalt des Sebastiano Serlio," *Münchner Jahrbuch der bildenden Kunst* 32 (1981): 42–94.

49. Vasoli, *I miti e gli astri*, 190ff. But also see Alessandro Pastore, *Marcantonio Flaminio. Fortune e sfortune di un chierico nell'Italia del Cinquecento* (Milan, 1981), 69–89, for the relations between Bembo, Federico Fregoso, Alessandro Manzuoli, Giulio Camillo Delminio, Achille Bocchi, Alessandro Citolini, and Agostino Steuco.

50. See Vasoli, *I miti e gli astri*, 234–37, and A. Prosperi, *Tra Evangelismo e Controriforma. G.M. Giberti* (Rome, 1969), 268–70.

51. On Postel, see the volume by William J. Bouwsma, *Concordia mundi: The Career and Thought of Guillaume Postel (1510–1581)* (Cambridge, Mass., 1957), and the bibliography cited in C. Vasoli, *La cultura delle corti* (Bologna, 1980), 215 n. 4.

52. Vasoli, *I miti e gli astri*, 197–217; id., "Uno scritto inedito di Giulio Camillo," *Rinascimento* 24 (1984): 191–224.

53. S. Serlio, *Terzo Libro dell Architettura*, 1st ed. (Venice, 1540), 2nd ed. (Venice, 1544), p. 154.

54. See D. Cantimori, "Note su alcuni aspetti della propaganda religiosa nell' Europa del Cinquecento," in *Aspets de la propagande religieuse* (Geneva, 1957), 340–51, reprinted in Cantimori, *Umanesimo e religione nel Rinascimento*, 164ff. (esp. 175–78). Carlo Ginzburg has continued Cantimori's analysis, noting that in 1538 Bocchi knew the heterodox Lisia Fileno (Camillo Renato), whose arrest he would seek to avoid two years later by offering himself as a guarantor to the Inquisitor. (Manuzuoli, too, would be a guarantor of Renato's.) Ginzburg also dwells upon a symbol of Bocchi's collection of emblems not considered by Cantimori, the 32nd (*Symbolicarum quaestionum*, 63–64), the title of which —"Sat extat ipsa veritas vana absit obstentatio"—implies an apology for silence about truth. See C. Ginzburg, *Il nicodemismo. Simulazione e dissimulazione religiosa nell'Europa del '500* (Turin, 1970), 179–81.

55. Stella, *Dall'anabattismo al socinianesimo*, 49. On Achille Bocchi and his circle, see Antonio Rotondò, "Per la storia dell'eresia a Bologna nel secolo XVI," *Rinascimento*, vol. 2 (1962), 107ff., esp. 126–29 and 132–34; id., "Bocchi Achille," in *Dizionario Biografico degli Italiani*, vol. 11 (Rome, 1969), 67–70; Pastore, *Marcantonio Flaminio*, passim; Gennaro Savarese and Andrea Gareffi, *La letteratura delle immagini nel Cinquecento* (Rome, 1980), 14–15, 27–29, and 119–26; Adalgisa Lugli, "Le 'Symbolicae quaestiones' di Achille Bocchi e la cultura dell'emblema in Emilia," in the collection *Le arti a Bologna e in Emilia dal XVI al XVII secolo*, ed. Andrea Emiliani (Bologna, 1982), 87–96.

56. See Pastore, *Marcantonio Flaminio*, 73, and n. 18 on pp. 73–74.

57. See ibid., 74ff.

58. See ibid., 23.

59. See ibid., 24. The emblem is on p. 253 of the *Symbolicarum quaestionum de universo genere, quas serio ludebat, libri quinque* (Aedibus novae Academiae Bocchianae: Bononiae, 1555); the illustrative verses are on 255–256.

60. *Trattato utilissimo del beneficio di Giesú Cristo crocifisso verso i cristiani* (1543), reprinted as an appendix to Ginzburg and Prosperi, *Giochi di pazienza*, 241.

61. Ibid., 249–50.

62. Rotondò, *Per la storia dell'eresia*, 138.

63. Ibid., 145.

64. On the relations between Achille Bocchi, Leandro Alberti, Giovanni Antonio Flaminio and Alessandro Manzuoli, see Pastore, *Marcantonio Flaminio*, 24–25, n. 39, with bibliography and information on the connections between Manzuoli, Claudio Tolomei, and the Accademia della Virtú, as well as with Gasparo Contarini. The basic text on Camillo Renato is still D. Cantimori, *Eretici italiani del Cinquecento. Ricerche storiche* 1st ed. (Florence, 1939), 2nd ed. (Florence, 1978), passim.

65. Egnazio Danti, "Vita di M. Jacopo Barozzi da Vignola, Architetto, e Prospettico eccellentissimo," preface to J. Barozzi da Vignola, *Le due regole della prospettiva* (Rome, 1583). As is known, Vasari does not comment on the Palazzo Bocchi in the notes on Vignola inserted into the life of Taddeo Zuccari.

66. See Daniela Monari, "Palazzo Bocchi, il quadro storico e l'intervento del Vignola," in *Il Carrobbio* 6 (1980), 270 n. 23, which mentions a letter by Bocchi dated August 31, 1556, in which he says that work on the *Domus Academiae* had begun eleven years before. Moreover, there is the known contract drawn up on July 28, 1545, between Bocchi and Agostino Bolognotto and Pietro da Como for the supply of masonry blocks for the sloping rusticated base and windows. But in *Graticola di Bologna*, published in 1560, Pietro Lamo says the palazzo was still not finished (ed. 1844, 33).

67. On Palazzo Bocchi, see Wolfgang Lotz, "Architecture in the Later Sixteenth Century," *College Art Journal* 17, no. 2 (1958): 129–39 (esp. 131–132); Maria Walcher Casotti, *Il Vignola* I (Trieste, 1960), 143–46; Johann Karl Schmidt, "Zu Vignolas Palazzo Bocchi in Bologna," *Mitteilungen des Kunsthistorischen Institutes in Florenz* 13, no. 1–2 (1967): 83–94 (for which the 1545 engraving was an initial project, with the intervention of the client); D. Monari, "Palazzo Bocchi e l'opera rustica secondo il Vignola," in the collection *Natura e artificio*, ed. Marcello Fagiolo (Rome, 1979), 113–28; id., "Palazzo Bocchi, il quadro storico"; Anna Maria Orazi, *Jacopo Barozzi da Vignola 1528–1550. Apprendistato di un architetto bolognese* (Rome, 1982), 229ff. This last volume represents a wasted opportunity: the author is completely unreliable because of the uncertain analytical instruments she uses. Orazi thinks that the executed palazzo corresponds to Vignola's original idea, subsequently modified in the two engravings that bore no results (ibid., 234). Walcher Casotti had previously (*Il Vignola*, 1 : 144) suspected, for stylistic reasons, that Vignola was responsible for the original project (fig. 64), and had suggested, for the engraving of 1555, the influence of Serlio or one of his students (ibid., 145). Orazi explains the late date by suggesting that the engraving made known by Lotz corresponded to a second project that reflected the one from the 1540s. Johann K. Schmidt, on the other hand, maintains that the 1555 engraving was the product of a variation of the 1545 project by Bocchi, who was defined as a dilettante in architecture. One ought to note that until now historians of architecture have underestimated the contributions coming from other historiographical areas, ignoring Bocchi's real personality or giving it deformed interpretations: Monari, for example, highlights Bocchi's Farnesian friendships, which clearly constituted a Nicodemical "cover" for him. On the other hand, he takes into account Anna Maria Orazi's inquiries into the learning of Bocchi's circle, and deduces from them, in an unfounded fashion, hypotheses about Vignola's religious sentiment. Among the elements that appear in both engravings we have mentioned, but do

not appear together in the executed work, is the flat fascia that links together the windows of the second level: one can clearly see the attention paid to formal device that Raphael introduced into the façade of Palazzo Branconio, immediately copied by Jacopo Sansovino in the façade of Palazzo Gaddi in Rome.

68. *Symbolicarum quaestionum*, 5 : 216, 230. In the two engravings the corner of Palazzo Bocchi is transformed emblematically: a cupid with a quiver restrains the head of a lion below, indicating Minerva on the left, who holds Mercury on the right. The two gods are transformed into hermae and the appearance of the palazzo—visible in the second engraving—corresponds to the building in the engravings rather than the executed one.

69. See S. Serlio, *Regole generali d'Architettura* (Venice, 1537), 3.

70. See Olivato, "Per il Serlio a Venezia."

71. See Frederic C. Church, *I riformatori italiani*, vol. 1 (Milan, 1967), 142–43. Note that Vergerio was related to Gasparo Contarini through his wife Diana, who died in 1527, and that in 1545, having been denounced for heresy and sought refuge with Cardinal Ercole Gonzaga in Mantua, he asked to be tried by Giovanni Grimani, Patriarch of Aquileia, and his immediate ecclesiastical superior. As is known, Grimani would also be tried for heresy, and absolved in Trent in 1563. See Peter J. Laven, "The 'Causa Grimani' and its Political Overtones," *Journal of Religious History* 4 (1966–67), 184–205.

72. Serlio quotes Saint Paul explicitly, Corinthians 6 : 16: "Vos enim estis templum Dei vivi, sicut dicit Deus." Serlio's religious concerns have not been addressed in the essay by Tancredi Carunchio, "I progetti serliani per edifici religiosi," *Bollettino del Cisa* 19 (1977): 179–89, which concludes by giving a distorted reading of Serlio's position. Isermeyer, whose reference to Serlio's dedication to Marguerite de Navarre we have already mentioned in the text, observes that the quoted passage of the dedication was omitted from the 1569 edition. See Christian Adolf Isermeyer, "Le chiese del Palla-

dio in rapporto al culto," *Bollettino del Cisa* 10 (1968): 48. Only after the definitive preparation of the present chapter did we learn about R. Fontana's essay, "Appunti sulle frequentazioni di Lotto con alcune cerchie riformate venete," in *Omaggio a Lorenzo Lotto*, 101–5, in which the author reaches hypotheses similar to ours, basing his argument on Serlio's dedication to Marguerite de Navarre and on his ties with the Ospedaletto dei Santi Giovanni e Paolo.

73. See Giuseppe Scavizzi, *Arte e architettura sacra. Cronache e documenti sulla controversia tra riformati e cattolici (1500–1550)* (Reggio Calabria and Rome, 1981), 47 (and references to the notes on p. 114).

74. Ibid., 114 n. 16.

75. See Lucien Febvre, "Une date: 1534. La Messe et les Placards," *Bibliothèque d'Humanisme et Renaissance* 7 (1945), now in *Au coeur religieux du XVIe siècle* (Paris, 1957); It. trans. *Studi su Riforma e Rinascimento*, (Turin, 1971), 159ff.

76. See Henry Heller, "Marguerite of Navarre and the Reformers of Meaux," *Bibliothèque d'Humanisme et Renaissance* 33 (1971): 271.

77. See Gerhard Schneider, *Der Libertin. Zur Geistes- und Sozialgeschichte des Bürgertums im 16. und 17. Jahrhundert* (Stuttgart, 1970); It. trans. (Bologna, 1974), 51ff. Note that Marguerite de Navarre had protested against Calvin because, along with her court, she felt attacked by his treatise, *Contre la secte phantastique et furieuse des Libertins, qui se nomment spirituels* (Geneva, 1545). However, the reformer Martin Butzer of Strasbourg had already warned Marguerite, in a letter written on July 5, 1538, to use prudence in dealing with the enthusiasts who, in all probability, were the libertines themselves (See Schneider, *Der Libertin*, 95). Schneider's entire volume questions the formulation of the famous essay by L. Febvre, *Amour sacré, amour profane* (Paris, 1944; It. trans., Bologna, 1980), the methodological merits of which have been correctly identified in Adriano Prosperi's "Introduzione" to the Italian edition, 7–21.

78. Calvin wrote: "For this reason, since one does not give in to illusion, according to their judgment they do not sin anymore . . . They define those who are no longer concerned with sin as new creatures, because they have freed themselves of illusions and consequently no longer have sins in them." *Ioannis Calvini Opera*, in *Corpus Reformatorum*, vol. 7, coll. 200–1, quoted in Schneider, *Der Libertin*, 71–72.

79. The dedication of Rabelais's *Tiers Livre*—strikingly close in time to Serlio's—seems to lay out and resume the concerns of Marguerite de Navarre's religious sentiment: "Abstracted soul, ravished in ecstasy, / Returned now to thy home, the Firmament, / Leaving thy body, formed in harmony, / Thy host and servant, once obedient / To thy commands in this life transient, / Wouldst thou not care to quit, just fleetingly, / Thy heavenly mansion and perpetual, / And here below for the third time to see / The jovial deeds of good Pantagruel?" See the English edition of François Rabelais's *The Histories of Gargantua and Pantagruel*, trans. J.M. Cohen (Middlesex, England: Penguin Books, 1955), 280.

80. Febvre, *Amour sacré*, 79–96.

81. See Schneider, *Der Libertin*, 96–97. In the *L'Inquisiteur*, dated 1536 by V.L. Saulnier, Marguerite appears to be not only a pantheist, but also an interpreter of the libertine concept of *cuider*. For Marguerite as for the libertines, the believer's union with God ultimately leads to an antischolastic skepticism and a distrust of reason.

82. On this theme see L. Febvre, *Le problème de l'incroyance au XVIe siècle. La religion de Rabelais* (Paris, 1942); It. trans. (Turin, 1978), 147–52, and Schneider, *Der Libertin*, 80.

83. Marguerite de Navarre, *The Heptameron*, translated with an introduction by P.A. Chilton (Middlesex, England: Penguin Books, 1984), 449–50; It. trans. (Turin, 1958), 452. Shortly before this passage, Marguerite had made Parlamente, her literary double, say: "I do not call it deranged . . . if a man distributes to the poor that which God has placed within his power. But to give away as alms what belongs to other people—I do not think that shows great wisdom. It's all too common to see the world's greatest usurers putting up ornate and impressive chapels, in the hope of appeasing God for hundreds of thousands of ducats' worth of sheer robbery by spending ten thousand ducats on a building! As if God didn't know how to count!" (*The Heptameron*, 449).

84. See William Bell Dinsmoor, "The literary remains of Sebastiano Serio," *The Art Bulletin* 25, no. 1 (1942): 73 n. 89. The salary was actually assigned to Serlio beginning January 1, 1540, even though the artist was still in Venice in December of the same year.

85. S. Serlio, *Sesto Libro, delle habitationi di tutti li gradi degli huomini* (MS of Monaco), f. 12v, in Marco Rosci, *Il trattato di architettura di Sebastiano Serlio* (Milan, n.d.), which dates this version to 1549–50, accepting the year 1546 as a limit for the first version (MS of New York). Also see Myra Nan Rosenfeld, *Sebastiano Serlio on Domestic Architecture* (Cambridge, Mass. and London, 1978), plate 14.

86. S. Serlio, *Sesto Libro*, in Rosenfeld, *Sebastiano Serlio*, plate 60.

87. In this connection, it is interesting to remember Machiavelli's words: "E la cagione che la Italia non sia in quel medesimo termine [as France and Spain], né abbia anch'ella o una repubblica o uno principe che la governi, è solamente la Chiesa: perché avendovi quella abitato e tenuto imperio temporale, e non è stata sí potente né di tanta virtú che l'abbia potuto occupare la tirannide d'Italia e farsene principe; e non è stata dall'altra parte sí debole che, per paura di non perdere il dominio delle sue cose temporali, la non abbia potuto convocare uno potente che la difenda contro a quello che in Italia fusse diventato troppo potente. . . . Non essendo adunque stata la Chiesa potente da occupare l'Italia, né avendo permesso che un altro la occupi, è stata cagione che la non è potuta venire sotto uno capo; ma è stata sotto piú principi e signori, da' quali è nata tanta disunione e tanta debolezza, che la si è condotto a essere stata preda non solamente de' barbari potenti,

ma di qualunque l'assalta." Nicolò Machiavelli, *Discorsi sopra la prima deca di Tito Livio*, vol. 1, chap. 12, in *Il Principe e i Discorsi*, 9th ed. (Milan, 1984), 165–66.

88. S. Serlio, *Quinto Libro* (ed. 1551), c. 17v.

89. See the *Sesto Libro*, text of plate 36, in Rosenfeld, *Sebastiano Serlio*, as well as what Serlio wrote in his *Terzo Libro*.

90. See Rosenfeld, *Sebastiano Serlio*, 43. Concerning the relation between evangelism and "vernacular" languages, see what Paolo Simoncelli has written, inspired by a remark of Dionisotti's: the latter is sure of a connection between "evangelism and Italian reformism on the one hand, and the new language and vernacular literature on the other." See Carlo Dionisotti, *Geografia e storia della letteratura italiana*, 3rd ed. (Turin, 1977), 233, and Paolo Simoncelli, *Evangelismo italiano del Cinquecento. Questione religiosa e nicodemismo politico* (Rome, 1979), 282ff.

91. In addition to our observations in *L'armonia e i conflitti*, 58–59 and 114–15 n. 160, see Giorgio Stabile, "Camille Giulio," in *Dizionario Biografico degli Italiani*, vol. 17 (Rome, 1974), 218–30; Lina Bolzoni, "Dall'Ariosto al Camillo al Doni. Tracce di una versione sconosciuta del 'Teatro,'" *Rinascimento*, ser. II, 22 (1982): 213–47, esp. 217–18. Also see id., "L'idea dell'eloquenza. Un' orazione inedita di Giulio Camillo," ibid., 23 (1983), 125–66; C. Vasoli, "Le teorie del Delminio e del Patrizi e i trattatisti d'arte fra '500 e '600," in the collection *Cultura e società nel Rinascimento tra riforme e manierismi*, eds. Vittore Branca and Carlo Ossola (Florence, 1984), 249–70. Also see the essay by Jean-Claude Margolin, quoted in n. 114, and the recent volume by L. Bolzoni, *Il teatro della memoria. Studi su Giulio Camillo* (Padua, 1984), in which the author gathers, with additions, her research on Delminio.

92. S. Serlio, *Libro Estraordinario* (Venice, 1566), ff. 30v–31r.

93. See Mikhail Bakhtin, *Tvorcestvo Fransua Rable i narodnaja kul'tura srednevekov'ja i Renessansa* (1965); It. trans.

L'opera di Rabelais e la cultura populare. Riso, carnevale e festa nella tradizione medievale e rinascimentale (Turin, 1979).

94. Francesco Berni, "Capitolo dell'orinale" (before August 1522), in id., *Rime*, ed. Giorgio Bárberi Squarotti, 10 (Turin, 1969), 31–33. Also see the "Capitolo dell'anguille" (ibid., 7: 20–22, also from the first half of 1522): "tutte le cose che son lunghe e tonde / hanno in se stesse piú perfezione, / che quelle ove altra forma si nasconde / Eccene in pronto la dimostrazione; / ché buchi tondi e la cerchia e l'anella / son per le cose di questa ragione" (lines 22–27). Berni's parody was here aimed at the purity of abstract forms, which he considered analogous to the purity of Petrarchan literature that he had fought against. See G. Bárberi Squarotti, "Introduzione" to Berni, *Rime*, and *Poesia italiana del Cinquecento*, ed. Giulio Ferroni (Milan, 1978), 261–63.

95. Andrea Palladio, *I Quattro Libri dell'Architettura*, 4 (Venice, 1570), prologue, p. 249 of the edition edited by Licisco Magagnato and Paola Marini (Milan, 1980).

96. See A. Chastel, *Art et Humanisme à Florence au temps de Laurent le Magnifique* (Paris, 1959); It. trans. (Turin, 1964), 139ff.

97. Ficino had written: "Se alcuno dimanda in che modo la forma del corpo possa essere simile alla forma e ragione dell'Anima e dell'Angelo, prego quel tale, che consideri lo edifizio dello Architettore. Da principio lo Architettore, la ragione e quasi Idea dell'edifizio nello animo suo, concepe: di poi fabbrica la casa (secondo che i' può) tale quale nel pensiero dispose. . . . Orsú, trai a lo edifizio la materia; e lascia sospeso lo ordine: non ti resterà di corpo materiale cosa alcuna: anzi tutto uno sarà l'ordine che venne da lo artefice, e l'ordine che nello artefice rimase." Marsilio Ficino, *In convivium Platonis sive de amore*, ed. R. Marcel, vol. 5, pt. 5 (Paris, 1956) 187–88. See Chastel, *Art et Humanisme*, 141, and *Marsile Ficin et l'art* (Geneva and Lille, 1954), 70–71. On the "rustic" that Sebastiano Serlio associated with the Tuscan order, see the essay by James S. Ackerman, "The Tuscan Rustic Order: a Study in Metaphorical

Language of Architecture," *Journal of the Society of Architectural Historians* 42, no. 1 (1983): 15–34.

98. See Heller, "Marguérite de Navarre," 273ff.; B. Jane Wells, "Folly in the 'Heptameron' of Margherite de Navarre," *Bibliothèque d'Humanisme et Renaissance* 46, no. 1 (1984): pp. 71–82. See, for the reference to the mystical thinking of the pseudo Aeropagite, Dionysus the Aeropagite, *Tutte le opere*, ed. Enzo Bellini (Milan, 1981), CH 2–5, pp. 80–89, esp. pp. 86–87 (144B–144C).

99. The system of relationships that closely united the figures of God, feces, and the soul, has been emphasized by Dominique Laporte, who distinguished in the 16th century the beginning of a discourse of the dirty and the clean that connected the 1539 edict of Francis I on hygiene in Paris with the initiatives for the purification of the language. Laporte cites the authors of the *Biblioteca scatologica* in those places where they maintain that, given the image of man as microcosm, "his evacuations are only an image of those of the big world, of the macrocosm." See Dominique Laporte, *Storia della merda* (1978); It. trans. (Milan, 1979), esp. 93–110. Interesting observations on dietetic asceticism and corporal self-auscultation by Jacopo Pontormo are in Salvatore S. Nigro, "Nota critica e filologica," in Pontormo, *Il libro mio*, ed. S. S. Nigro (Genoa, 1984), 95–116.

100. S. Serlio, *Terzo Libro*, 2nd ed. (1544), 155. "Ai lettori. / Ma se alcuno piú invaghito de le ruine de gli edifici Romani, che innamorato de la saldezza di Vitruvio, mi volesse pure in ció biasimare, piglieranno le arme per la difesa mi huomini di questa età pieni di giudicio, e de le salde dotrine del principe de l'architettura: tra quali sarà in Venetia il Magnifico Gabriel Vendramini severissimo riprenditor de le cose licentiose, M. Marcantonio Michiele consumatissimo ne le antichità, et in Bologna patria mia il Cavalier Bocchi, il giudicioso M. Alessandro Manzuolo, e Cesare Cesareano et altri, i quali con la irreprensibile dottrina di Vitruvio, e con la sana esperienza mi difenderanno."

101. Vasari wrote: "Si dilettò di vestire onoratamente, e fu sempre politissimo della persona, piacendoli tuttavia le femmine fino all'ultima sua vecchiezza: delle quali si contentava assai il ragionarne." Vasari-Milanesi, *Vite*, 7 (Florence, 1881), 509. Later Vasari adds: "Fu desideroso della gloria oltre modo; e per cagion di quella spendeva del suo proprio per altri, non senza notabil danno dé suoi discendenti, pur che restasse memoria di lui" (ibid., 511). One should, however, evaluate Vasari's words critically, taking into account the resentment they reveal, as well as Lucien Febvre's observation on the relationship between Christianity and sexual ethics in the early sixteenth century—a relationship rather different from the one that took hold after 1563. See Febvre, *Amour saré*, esp. pp. 314ff. of the It. trans. Also see Jean-Louis Flandrin, *Le Sexe et l'Occident* (Paris, 1981; It. trans. Milan, 1983), and the collection *I comportamenti sessuali. Dall'antica Roma a oggi*, special issue of *Communications*, 1982, eds. Philippe Ariès and André Béjin (Turin, 1983). Note also that Sansovino was working for the Scuola Grande di San Marco while its guardian was Mario d'Armano, the consignee of the portraits of Luther and *sua moier* and the nephew of Lorenzo Lotto, who hosted the painter in his own home in Venice. And Armano's doctor was Tommaso Rangone, who would in turn become the grand guardian of the Scuola.

102. See Foscari, "Altre schede veneziane," 149–52, which documents Sansovino's acquisition of properties and houses on July 3, 1552, in the district of San Trovaso in Venice, for the remarkable sum of 1,600 ducats (about ten yearly installments of the salary earned as *proto* of the Procuratori de supra). The wedding contract between Francesco Sansovino and Benedetta Bisocca, from January 20, 1553 (*m.v.*), mentions the houses that Jacopo Sansovino had built or "would build" at San Trovaso. On Sansovino's houses, also see D. Howard, "Jacopo Sansovino's House at San Trovaso," in *Interpretazioni veneziane*, 241–55, which uses a variety of documents and proposes an identification that needs to be examined

in the light of the papers considered by Foscari.

103. ASV, "Notarile, Testamenti, Notaio Cesare Zilioli," b. 1258, n. 452. See the transcription of this in F. Sapori, *Jacopo Tatti detto il Sansovino* (Rome, 1928), 127–30. (The passage quoted is on p. 128.)

104. See Calì, "Ancora sulla 'religione' di Lorenzo Lotto," 42–48.

105. See Grendler, *The Roman Inquisition*, 160.

106. The decree is dated April 22, 1547, and the first three members were Nicolò Tiepolo, Francesco Contarini, and Antonio Venier. On the process that led the administration of Doge Francesco Donà to institute a new magistrature, see ibid., 63–70.

107. Ginzburg and Prosperi, *Giochi di pazienza*, 186.

108. Ibid., 186–87.

109. See G. Cozzi, *Paolo Scarpi tra Venezia e l'Europa* (Turin, 1979), 132–33.

110. Gasparo Contarini, *De Officio Episcopi*, in *Opera* (Paris, 1571), quoted in Brian Pullan, *Rich and Poor in Renaissance Venice. The Social Institution of a Catholic State to 1620* (Oxford, 1971); It. trans., vol. I (Rome, 1982), 244–45.

111. Ibid., 245.

112. Giovanni Scarabello, "Strutture assistenziali a Venezia nella prima metà del '500 e avvii europei della riforma dell'assistenza," "*Renovatio urbis*," 119–33.

113. See L. Puppi, "Espiazione e charitas erasmiana in Corte Lando," *Architectura* 9 (1979): 147–69, reprinted in L. Puppi, *Verso Gerusalemme. Immagini e temi di urbanistica e di architettura simboliche* (Rome and Reggio Calabria, 1982), 120–45.

114. On the argument between Erasmus and Alberto Pio da Carpi, see Scavizzi, *Arte e architettura sacra*, 154ff. Also see Matteo Schenetti, "Il primato di Pietro in Alberto Pio III contro Erasmo da Rotterdam," in the collection *Alberto Pio III, Signore di Carpi (1475–1975)* (Modena, 1977), 67–80; Myron P. Gilmore, "Erasmus and Alberto Pio, Prince of Carpi," in *Action and Conviction in Early Modern Europe. Essays in memory of E. H. Harbson*, eds. Theodore K. Rabb and Jerrold E. Seigel (Princeton, N.J., 1969), 299–318; the collection *Società, politica e cultura a Carpi ai tempi di Alberto III Pio*, Proceedings from the Convegno Internazionale, May 1978 (Padua, 1981), esp. vol. I with essays by C. Vasoli, "Alberto Pio e la cultura del suo tempo," pp. 3–42; Jean-Claude Margolin, "Alberto Pio et les cicéroniens italiens," pp. 225–59, with an ample examination of the polemic on the *Ciceronianus* and intelligent remarks on Erasmus's position with regard to Giulio Camillo Delminio (pp. 254–58); S. Seidel Menchi, "La discussione su Erasmo nell' Italia del Cinquecento," pp. 291–382.

115. Erasmus of Rotterdam, *Convivium religiosum*, in *Opera omnia Desiderii Erasmi Roterodami*, I/3, *Colloquia* (Amsterdam, 1972), 257. "Unde mihi videntur vix excusari posse a peccato capital, qui sumptibus in modicis aut extruunt aut ornant monasteria seu templa, quum interim tot viva Christi templa fame periclitentur, nuditate horrent rerumque necessarium inopia discrucientur. . . . Et sunt qui putent esse nefas eam pecuniam in pios usus avertere praeter mentem testatoris. Maluntque demoliri, quod instaurent, quam no aedificare. Haec, quoniam insignia sunt, visum est commemorare, quanquam sunt passim in templis exempla permulta similia. Haec mihi videtur ambitio, non eleemosyna." Translated by Craig R. Thompson as "The Godly Feast," in Erasmus, *Ten Colloquies* (Indianapolis, Indiana: The Liberal Arts Press, Inc., 1957), 161–162.

116. Scavizzi, *Arte e architettura sacra*, 165.

117. Ibid., 161–64.

118. Alberto Pio da Carpi, *Tres et Viginti Libri in locos lucubrationum D. Erasmi* (Paris, 1531).

119. See Scavizzi, *Arte e architettura sacra*, 174.

120. Erasmus of Rotterdam, *Apologia adversus rhapsodias calumniosarum querimoniarum Alberti Pii* (Basel, 1531), f. 17r. Erasmus wrote: "Et templa et monasteria ditare plusquam regis opibus,

latria est? . . . Ego . . . proximi vitam necessariis et impendiis arbitror preferendum." See Scavizzi, *Arte*, 179ff.

121. See Alessandro Caravia, *Il Sogno dil Caravia* (Venice, 1541), a discussion of which can be found in chap. 4 of this volume.

122. Erasmus of Rotterdam, *Opera omnia*, 5 (Lyon, 1703–06), 1099ff. See Scavizzi, *Arte e architettura sacra*, 254–55.

123. See A. Stella, "La lettera del cardinale Contarini sulla predestinazione," *Rivista di Storia della Chiesa in Italia* 15 (1961): 412; id., *Dall'anabattismo al socinianesimo*, 29.

124. See on this subject L. Febvre, "Une question mal posée: les origines de la Réforme française et le problème des causes de la Réforme," *Revue historique* 161 (1929), reprinted in *Au coeur religieux*, It. trans. pp. 5ff.; D. Cantimori, "Umanesimo e Riforma" (1938), in *Umanesimo e religione nel Rinascimento*, 142ff.; M. Calí, *Da Michelangelo all'Escorial. Momenti del dibattito religioso nell'arte del Cinquecento* (Turin, 1980); Prosperi, "Intellettuali e Chiesa,"; Simoncelli, *Evangelismo italiano*; Chastel, *Il sacco di Roma*, 112–19.

125. See Erasmus Weddigen, "Thomas Philologus Ravennas, Gelehrter, Wohltäter und Mäzen," *Saggi e Memorie di Storia dell'Arte* 9 (1974): 24.

126. The early roots of this attitude may lie in the debate that Francis Petrarch conducted with himself, divided between Augustine and Pliny. On this theme, see the fine essay by Maurizio Bettini, "Tra Plinio e Sant'Agostino: Francesco Petrarca sulle arti figurative," in the collection *Memoria dell'antico nell'arte italiana. I. L'uso dei classici*, ed. Salvatore Settis (Turin, 1984), 221–67.

Chapter 4

1. See Alessandro Caravia, *Il sogno dil Caravia* (In Vinegia: in the houses of Giovann'Antonio di Nicolini da Sabbio, in the year of Our Lord, 1541 in the month of May). *Il sogno* is dedicated "Al molto illustre, e reverendo Signor Don

Diego Urtado de Mendoza del Consiglio della Cesarea e Catholica Maestà e suo dignissimo Oratore appresso la Serenissima, et illustrissima Signoria di Vinegia." On Alessandro Caravia and *Il sogno*, see Vittorio Rossi, "Un aneddoto della storia della Riforma a Venezia," in *Scritti varii di erudizione e di critica in onore di Rodolfo Renier* (Turin, 1912), 839–64, also in V. Rossi, *Scritti di critica letteraria. Dal Rinascimento al Risorgimento* (Florence, 1930), 191–222. See also Brian Pullan, *Rich and Poor in Renaissance Venice* (Oxford, 1971); It. trans. in *La politica sociale della Repubblica di Venezia 1500–1620*, vol. I (Rome, 1982), 130–33, 141–42; Carlo Ginzburg, *Il formaggio e i vermi. Il cosmo di un mugnaio del '500* (Turin, 1976), 28–32 and n. 28 on p. 162; Ludovico Zorzi, "Caravia Alessandro," in *Dizionario Biografica degli Italiani*, vol. 19 (Rome, 1976), 669–73. In addition to *Il sogno* of 1541 and the short poem *Naspo bizaro* of 1565, Caravia published the poem *La verra antiga de Castellani, Canaruoli e Gnatti . . . in lengua brava* (1550), which caused a trial to be brought against him in 1557–59 by the Tribunal of the Sant'Uffizio. Caravia would die in 1568. The dedication of *Il sogno* to Charles V's ambassador, Diego Hurtado de Mendoza, is also significant: K. Brandi has written that, in Don Diego, the spirit of Mercurino da Gattinara seemed to have come back to life, and the disciple of Peter the Martyr, a reader of Suetonius and a humanist, completed in Venice his chosen library, rich in codices about mechanics and scientific texts. See Karl Brandi, *Kaiser Karl V* (Munich, 1937); Ital. trans. (Turin, 1961), 489, 515, 527–28; "La biblioteca di don Diego Hurtado de Mendoza," in *Documentos para la Historia del Monasterio de San Lorenzo el Real de el Escorial*, ed. Gregorio de Andrés, vol. 7 (Madrid, 1964), 237ff. (Inventory on pp. 243–323). Don Diego was a friend to Sansovino, Pietro Aretino, and Titian, and had a Jewish lover in Venice. In a letter from Trent dated August 10, 1545, Juan Páez de Castro wrote about Diego de Mendoza: "Es gran Aristotelico y Mathematico; Latino y Griego, que non au quien se le pare. . . . Los libros que acquí ha traido son muchos, y son en tres maneras: unos de mano Griegos en gran copia, otros impressos en todas facultades, otros de los Luteranos." Cited in Luis Gil Fernández, *Panorama social del humanismo español (1500–1800)* (Madrid, 1981), 213 n. 60.

2. In *Il sogno dil Caravia*, the buffoon Taiacalze openly praises Luther: "Gli è un certo Martin Luther suscitato / che pregia poco preti, e frati manco / et è da gli Alamanni molto amato; / di chiamar il concilio mai è stanco . . . / Questo Martin per quel che si ragiona / d'ogni arte di dottrina gli è eccellente / il pur Vangel costui non abbandona / Luther de molti ha intrigato la mente." See, in this connection, Ginzburg, *Il formaggio e i vermi*, 29–30.

3. Aretino congratulated Alessandro Caravia for *Il sogno*, which he received from the goldsmith Gasparo del Toso on March 12, 1542. Caravia would then dedicate to Pietro Aretino *La verra antigua de Castellani*, adding a valuable ring to the book, which he sent in homage; this time Aretino thanked Caravia, advising him, however, to limit himself to his career as a jeweler. See Pietro Aretino, *Il secondo libro delle lettere*, ed. Fausto Nicolini (Bari, 1916), 138–39; Rossi, "Un aneddoto," 194–98; Zorzi, "Caravia," 670, 673. Alessandro Caravia frequented the shops of Gasparo and Paolo Crivelli, as one can also deduce from the statement he made before the Tribunal of the Sant'Uffizio. In this manner, Renzo Fontana has linked Caravia to the Carpan brothers, who in turn knew Lorenzo Lotto and held heterodox religious ideas, and has observed that the spread of reform ideas among the goldsmiths of the sixteenth century may be connected to the symbolic and magical significance attributed to gold and to precious stones. See Renzo Fontana, "Aspetti sociali e orizzonti mentali dell'ambiente lottesco degli anni Quaranta del Cinquecento," in the collection *Interpretazioni veneziane. Studi di Storia dell'Arte in onore di Michelangelo Muraro*, ed. David Rosand (Venice, 1984), 359–62. In the last canto of *Naspo bizaro*, Caravia wrote: "Ho visto el raro studio del Grimani Patriarca de Aquileia." In his last will and testament from 1563, see Rossi, "Un aneddoto," 216–17.

4. Giovanni Botero, *Relatione della Republica Venetiana* (Venice, 1605), ff. 107v–108.

5. See Brian Pullan, "Le Scuole Grandi e la loro opera nel quadro della Controriforma," *Studi Veneziani* 14 (1972): 83–109, and esp. the fundamental volume *Rich and Poor*. Also see, by the same author, "Poverty, Charity and the Reason of State: some Venetian Examples, "*Bollettino dell'Istituo di Storia della Società e dello Stato veneziano* 2 (1960): 17–60, and "Natura e carattere delle Scuole," in the collection *Le Scuole di Venezia*, ed. Terisio Pignatti (Milan, 1981), 9–26. On social welfare in Venice, also see Franca Semi, *Gli "ospizi" di Venezia* (Venice, 1983), and Giovanni Scarabello, "Strutture assistenziali a Venezia nella prima metà del '500 e avvii europei della riforma dell'assistenza," in the collection *"Renovatio urbis." Venezia nell'età di Andrea Gritti (1523–1538)*, ed. M. Tafuri (Rome, 1984), 119–33. On the Scuole Grandi, also see the synthesis offered in the essay by Ruggero Maschio, "Le Scuole Grandi a Venezia," in the collection *Storia della cultura veneta. Dal primo Quattrocento al Concilio di Trento*, eds. Girolamo Arnaldsi and Manlio Pastore Stocchi, 3/3 (Vicenza, 1981), 193–206.

6. See Pullan, "Le Scuole Grandi," 109; id., *La politica sociale*, 1: 60–66. One should also keep in mind that the State saw the Scuole not only as religious confraternities, but also as corporations that were not autonomous, but expected to render certain services. Beginning with the war of Ferrara, in 1482, the Republic began to ask the Scuole to supply galley men and in the course of the wars during the first three years of the sixteenth century, the State collected loans and taxes from the Scuole themselves. In October 1509, the Scuole Grandi, as well as the smaller Scuole, were subject to a general tax, and in January 1511 the four old Scuole were each forced to finance the equipment of ten boats that would service the Po. In 1514, it was established that veteran boatsmen would be assigned, through a drawing of lots, the houses *amore Dei* distributed by the Procurators of San Marco, by the Scuole, the Ospedali, and the

Commissarie; in 1527, the Senate gathered compulsory loans from the Scuole, in exchange for titles from the Monte di Sussidio; from 1537 on, they regularly asked the Scuole to offer incentives for service in the navy. See ibid., 161ff.

7. Ibid., 131.

8. See, in this connection, Loredana Olivato Puppi and Lionello Puppi, *Mauro Codussi* (Milan, 1977), 61–110, 196–203, and 218–21; Philip L. Sohm, "The Staircases of the Venetian Scuole Grandi and Mauro Coducci," *Architectura* 8, no. 2 (1978): 125–49; John McAndrew, *Venetian Architecture of the Early Renaissance* (Cambridge, Mass. and London, 1980), 144–49, 183–93, 358–77; Ralph Lieberman, *L'architettura del Rinascimento a Venezia 1450–1540* (Florence, 1982), entries 66, 67, 81; P. Sohm, *The Scuola Grande di San Marco, 1437–1550: The Architecture of a Lay Confraternity* (New York and London, 1982). The current attribution of the external atrium of the Scuola di San Giovanni Evangelista to Pietro Lombardo should, however, be carefully revised. (A discussion of this point is in the already mentioned volume by McAndrew.) The work has Codussian characteristics though a few of the details are somewhat naive. The windows that open onto empty space, which McAndrew does not care for, recur in a work of Codussi's, that is to say the inside of the church of Santa Maria Formosa. In concluding his analysis of the façade of the Scuola di San Marco, McAndrew, having stigmatized the formal intemperance solicited by the "little-littered" governors, adds that they "may have been more like the nouveaux-riches Milanese, unable to resist what their money could buy. The taste is that of old Hollywood . . . or the Moscow subway stations" (McAndrew, *Venetian Architecture*, 191). Philip Sohm, whose work is rather valuable, has tried to challenge the traditional opinion that the Scuola di San Marco is a decorative and "picturesque" work.

9. On the Scuola di San Rocco, see Giambattista Soravia, *La chiese di Venezia*, vol. 3 (Venice, 1824), passim; Leopoldo Cicognara, Antonio Diedo, Giannantonio Selva, *Le fabbriche e i monumenti cospicui di Venezia*, vol. 2, 2nd ed. (Venice, 1840), 63–70; Anonymous, *Memorie storico-artistiche sull'Arci-confraternita di San Rocco* (Venice, 1846); Giuseppe Nicoletti, *Illustrazione della Chiesa e Scuola di San Rocco in Venezia* (Venice, 1885); Pietro Paoletti, *L'architettura e la scultura del Rinascimento in Venezia*, 2 (Venice, 1893), 289–90, passim; Alfonso Bisacco, *La Scuola Grande di San Rocco* (Venice, 1931); Adolfo Venturi, *Storia dell'Arte Italiana, 11/I, Architettura del Cinquecento* (Milan, 1938), 826–30; Alessandro Mazzucato, *La Scuola Grande e la Chiesa di S. Rocco in Venezia* (Venice, 1953); Ludwig H. Heydenreich and Wolfgang Lotz, *Architecture in Italy 1400–1600* (Harmondsworth, 1974), 317; Sohm, "The Staircases" (on the Scuola di San Rocco, 142ff.); McAndrew, *Venetian Architecture*, 519–24; Claudio Mignozzi, "Scuola di San Rocco," in *Le Scuole di Venezia*, 152–62; Lieberman, *L'architettura del Rinascimento*, entries 86–89. We have not been able to consult Raban Von Der Malsburg, *Die Architektur der Scuola Grande di San Rocco in Venedig* (Heidelberg, 1976), cited by Sohm ("The Staircases") in n. 35 on p. 142.

10. See Soravia, *Le chiese*, 299–300, doc. EE, from January 11, 1516 (*m.v.*). Most of the documents quoted or transcribed by Soravia and Paoletti have been rechecked in the ASV original; the documents for which previous transcriptions are not quoted have not yet been published.

11. Ibid., doc. HH, p. 303.

12. Ibid., doc. GG. p. 302, documenting master Bon's dismissal, June 3, 1524. Furthermore, a later document from 1524 states that the measurement of the stones Bon had had cut for the portico on the canal did not correspond to what had been ordered. "Et questo el seva per che el volea non se correspondesse alla faza davanti et per voler far andar le scale segondo la sua opinion e *modelo novamente per luj fatto contra li modellj della scuola* e contra il voler de chj ha il governo de tal cose" (our emphasis). ASV,

"Scuola Grande di San Rocco," 2nd cons., reg. 600, c. 5r, transcribed in Sohm, "The Staircases," doc. 9, p. 149. In the same document, on cc. 11v–12r, there is written: "m°. bon dicha che questo modello e misure de zuan cellestro non corrisponde a quelle lha dato ali vinti savij. . . ." Philip Sohm reads the term "modello" incorrectly, claiming that Celestro was the only author of models for the Scuola (p. 143).

13. See doc. 156 in Paoletti, *L'architettura*, 2, Miscellanea. On December 21, 1524, another document speaks of the quarrels that occurred between Celestro and Bon, who were both present on the construction site: ". . . perché ele onesto che tutte lj fatige siano remuneratj e cognosendo ser zuan Zelestro se ano adoperato con grande aflizion in la fabricha nostra e ne a ineliminato dj molti erorj i qualj cauxavano in esa fabricha in el ttempo che m.ro bon erano nostro protto con el qual era in qualche contenzione e per aver arechade in molte cose che ne son stato dj uttele e onore che al ditto sier Zuan si datto de benj dela schola nostra per resto de tutto quelj per noi ha fatto e di quelo che luj sie adoperato fin questo di prexente ducati 10 a raxon di L. 6 s. 4 per ducato. . ."

14. See Sohm, "The Staircases," 142–43, and doc. 8, p. 149, regarding the intervention of the Chiefs of the Ten (March 26, 1523).

15. See Soravia, *Le chiese*, doc. 2, p. 303 (ASV, "Scuola Grande di San Rocco," 2nd cons., reg. 45, c. 30v). Dated January 29, 1524 (*m.v.*) a document maintains that Marco Dandolo, *cavaliere*, had given the Scuola two columns for the main façade (to be placed next to a portal?) The same document suggests that Pietro Spavento was the carpenter for the beams of the room, and that Andrea and Antonio Buora supplied the "*piere vive*," or high quality stone. See ASGSR, "Registro delle parti trascritte dalli libri A e B (1488–1542)," cc. 99v–100r. Also see Paoletti, *L'architettura*, doc. 158.

16. Ibid., doc. 156, January 1, 1525.

17. See Soravia, *Le chiese*, doc. KK, pp. 304–5, "1527 adi 20 Mazo" (ASV,

"Scuola Grande di San Rocco," 2nd cons., reg. 45, c. 52r).

18. Ibid.

19. Soravia, *Le chiese*, doc. 2, p. 303 (ASV, "Scuola Grande di San Rocco," 2nd cons., reg. 45, c. 30v).

20. Ibid., 2nd cons., reg. 45, c. 40r. "Adi ditto (1525, adi 25 Zenaro, *m.v.*). Anchora mete parte el ditto ms. lo vardian grando chonsiderando le spexe grandissime che se a et havevano in el sucesso di el tempo p. la fabricha nostra che sono, e serano senza fine che in la faza della sala nostra sopra el rio / che non se possi far altra spexa se non di el meter in opera le finestre n° doi che sono sta fate et aparechiade per quel locho et el bassamento et non altra opera che porti spexa et questo perche el loco non porta et per non buttar via li danari di ms. san rocho et cossí fo mandà la parte attorno, et fo prexa fo alla ballottation balotte n. / ventido / dela parte—de si, no. 18 et de non, no. 4." Also see ASGSR, reg. I, c. 106r and v.

21. The transformation of the central arch on the canal probably goes back to work done by the master builder Venturino di Ettore in 1534, as Paoletti has suggested. See Paoletti, *L'architettura*, 2:289.

22. ASV, "Scuola Grande di San Rocco," 2nd cons., reg. 45, c. 41r and v.

23. Soravia, *Le chiese*, op. cit., doc. KK. Also see ASV, "Scuola Grande di San Rocco," 2nd cons., b. 423, various receipts: "1526 adi 25 avosto. m. o. ant. o sorela e chompagni afinito el suo mercato dela fenestra quale inopera everso el squero alai el nichio vedeti quelo lui abuto et datili suo resto. Santo lombardo proto scrisse." July 4, 1526, master Zuanantonio da Carona worked on "suo merchado de architrave va sora el rio datili a bon conto duc. do / Santo lombardo scrisse." In October 1526, Sante Lombardo approved receipts of payments to Piero Dolera and associates for the cornice and the heads that went on the frieze, while on December 30 the same foreman signed a receipt for another eight heads, for 13 and 1/2 ducats, to "m.o. Silvestro," who also executed (February 24, 1526)

various capitals. Finally, a document dated June 26, 1526, confirms that Sante Lombardo was the author of the back of the Scuola: "M.o. zuanantonio da charona e chompagni a fato merchato investir li malmori in neli squanzi grandi sora rio sono tre chanpi do de si liga le fanestere e laltro liga lornamento de mezo che a un nichio et dieno star dale bande diti malmori quali sono grechi de la cholona qual o fato seghar a Vizenza et dieno refilar in suzo li diti et per testa et die chavar li buzi in le tavole et inpiombarli et li soi arpezi de rame et dar zozo ale chase dove tochara li malmori da drio . . ./ Santo lombardo proto scrisse."

24. Work was done on the original stairs in the early '30s, and Scarpagnino signed receipts "per la manifattura de le fanestre de le schale" in 1553. ASV, "Scuola Grande di San Rocco," 2nd cons., b. 418, various receipts.

25. See Soravia, *Le chiese*, doc. LL, pp. 306–7. See ASV, "Scuola Grande di San Rocco," 2nd cons., reg. 45, c. 56v.

26. No one has attempted yet a monographical treatment of the work of Antonio Abbondi, known as Scarpagnino. The contribution of Giovanni Mariacher is unsatisfactory, "Abbondi Antonio," in *Dizionario Biografico degli Italiani*, vol. I (Rome, 1960), 40–42. Stefano Maso's graduate thesis, which he discussed with this writer, marks a good beginning for work on the Salt foreman [*proto del Sol*].

27. BMC, Cod. Cicogna, 2626, 3. On Sebastiano Serlio's skill, see Wladimir Timofiewitsch, "Ein Gutachten Sebastiano Serlios für die Scuola di San Rocco," *Arte Veneta* 17 (1963), 158–60, with an undated transcription of the document.

28. ASV, "Scuola Grande di San Marco," 2nd cons., reg. 46, c. 28. "1535, 14 Marzo / Ancora mette parte lo ex.te dottor ms aurelio superchio che essendo le cosse de la fabrica nostra de le piu inportante che abiamo e che porta cussi longeza de tempo per la grandeza sua e da proveder che se elegano doi huomeni pratichi i quali insieme chon li cinque deputadi a questa abiano a proveder a tuto quello che se convien per condur afin questa degna hopera comenzata li qualli dui eletti

abiano a durar ani diexe per comodita de essa fabrica azio sempre restino persone informate de quello bixogna in ditta fabrica et fu prexa et fo alla balotacion de la banca n. 13 de la zonta n. 8 de la parte de si n. 21 de non–I quali dui eletti insieme con li altri deputadi a ditta fabrica siano obligati venir con la opinion sua et proponerla nel albergo con el nostro mag.co vardian et banca et li dodexe agionti. / rimaxe questi / lo ex.te dottor ms alvise noal / ms costantin de todero / uno di dodexe / ms donado dala chiave careter."

29. Stefania Mason, "Le immagini della peste nella cultura figurativa veneziana," in the collection *Venezia e la Peste 1348–1797* (Venice, 1980), 218.

30. ASV, "Scuola Grande di San Rocco," reg. 46, c. 41r, July 9, 1536 ("Parte di elezer uno modelo p. la faza davanti"), partially transcribed in Paoletti, *L'architettura*, doc. 165; ASV, "Scuola Grande di San Rocco," 2nd cons., b. 413, cc. unnumbered, 1537, "adi 3 Zugno" (agreement with masters Tonin Sorella and Domenego de Baldisera). See the transcription of this document in the appendix. In 1535, the Scuola di San Rocco bought eight columns that had once belonged to the church of Santa Maria Nuova, which had unexpectedly collapsed on July 16 of the same year, in exchange for 15 ducats and the promise of alms. ASV, "Scuola Grande di San Rocco," 2nd cons., reg. 46, cc. 40v–41. The motif of the free-standing column had already appeared in Venice, in the works of Mauro Codussi and in funereal monuments, but the colonnade of the Scuola di San Rocco seems to have been derived from other models.

31. Ibid., 2nd cons., b. 413, receipts from various expenses, "1537 adi 2 zener" (*m.v.*), with a list of the days paid to workers, up to February 17.

32. Paoletti, *L'architettura*, 290; Howard, *The Architectural History*, 135; Mignozzi, "Scuola," 161.

33. ASV, "Scuola Grande di San Rocco," 2nd cons., reg. 46, c. 41r.

34. It is known that the citizens of Venice did not constitute a homogenous group, but were also organized in a hierarchy, in

which the upper level consisted of an elite of professionals born in families that had resided in the city for many generations and that had never done manual work or exercised any of the *artes mechanicae*. As for the Scuola di San Rocco, in 1489, when it asked to be numbered among the Scuole Grandi, it ran into difficulties because it had been founded by "mercadanti et etiam altri i quali non sono exorti in questa prefata cita, ma habitanti con le loro done proprie e filioli con tuta la loro facultà" (Pullan, *La politica sociale*, 1:123). The offices were theoretically reserved for a group of citizens constituted by landowners, professionals, and merchants. As for the members of the Scuola di San Rocco, between 1490 and approximately 1540, they were mostly textile workers, including tailors and retailers (450, 25%), followed by workers in the food sector (135, 7.5%) and employees involved in luxury items, books, arts, and music (92, 5.1%). The lowest percentage applies to state professionals and employees (13, 0.7%). See the table found in the *Mariegola* of the Scuola, ibid., 1:107. One should also remember that those in positions of responsibility in the Scuole were expected to reproduce the Republic's methods of governments within the confraternities, and to be willing to justify the search for a cultural line capable of satisfying some of the needs of intermediary groups.

35. Ibid., 1:141. Regarding the expenses for the building and decoration of the Scuola, also see Soravia, *Le chiese*, 313–13, and Nicoletti, *Illustrazione*, 58–59.

36. Pullan, *La politica sociale*, 179. Furthermore, one ought to mention the xylography that has been attributed to Titian since the eighteenth century and that represents *San Rocco e storie della sua vita* (fig. 72) (London, British Museum, inv. 1860–4–14–140), circulated as a propaganda leaflet designed to raise funds for the construction work of the Scuola di San Rocco. In the box represented at the bottom of the page, in fact, is written "Limosina / per la fa / brica." According to the Tietzes (1938), and to Muraro and Rosand, the xylography goes back to ca. 1523; according to Pallucchini, it dates

from much later. See Michelangelo Muraro and David Rosand, *Tiziano e la silografia veneziana del Cinquecento*, catalogue of the exhibit (Vicenza, 1976), 88; S. Mason Rinaldi, entry a14, in *Venezia e la Peste*, 241.

37. See M. Tafuri, "'Renovatio urbis Venetiarum': il problema storiografico," "*Renovatio urbis*," 9ff.

38. Pullan, *La politica sociale*, 1:138.

39. Ibid.

40. Ibid., 97.

41. ASV, "Scuola Grande di San Rocco," 2nd cons., reg. 46, c. 27r, transcribed in Paoletti, *L'architettura*, 2, doc. 163.

42. See Giorgio Gianighian and Paola Pavanini, "I terreni nuovi de Santa Maria Mazor," in the collection *Dietro i palazzi. Tre secoli di architettura minore a Venezia 1492–1803*, eds. G. Gianighian and P. Pavanini (Venice, 1984), 45ff. The island of Santa Maria Maggiore was used—after the initial acquisition by Alvise Pisani q. Giovanni in 1497—for real estate speculation and welfare building: in addition to the Corte San Rocco, there was the Corte delle Procuratie, built over subsequent periods, also with the work of Jacopo Sansovino, and the twenty-four houses of the Scuola di San Marco. In 1512 the Scuola di San Rocco bought a plot of land for 832 ducats. On charitable building, also see B. Pullan, "Abitazioni al servizio dei poveri nella Repubblica di Venezia," in *Dietro i palazzi*, 39–44, and P. Pavanini, "Abitazioni popolari e borghesi nella Venezia cinquecentesca," *Studi Veneziani*, n.s., 5 (1981): 63–126.

43. See Pavanini, "Abitazioni popolari," 113ff.; *Dietro i palazzi*, 93–95. The new houses built after 1559 by the stonemason Francesco da Fermo were rented for prices rather higher than the preexisting ones: from 24 to 32 ducats, compared to 6 for the previous ones. There was an obvious change in the renters: from the humble wage earner to the small tradesman or independent craftsman.

44. See Pavanini, "Abitazioni popolari," 76ff.; *Dietro i palazzi*, 80–83, and ASV,"Scuola Grande di San Rocco," 2nd cons., reg. 46, c. 4v (May 2, 1533), and reg. 47, c. 80r and v (January 15, 1547

m.v.). See ibid., c. 90 (May 24, 1548), for the competition that Scarpagnino won.

45. See especially the drawing Inv. 1408 DR (fig. 91). An analytical study of that important codex might be particularly fruitful for later research in the area of Lombard and Venetian architecture of the early sixteenth century.

46. On the architectural history of the Scuola Grande della Misericordia, see Deborah Howard, *Jacopo Sansovino. Architecture and Patronage in Renaissance Venice* (New Haven and London, 1975), 99–112.

47. ASV, *Scuola Grande della Misericordia*, b. 166, Notatorio 2, c. 255b (September 4, 1532), c. 285a and b (April 26, 1535), c. 286a (June 4, 1535).

48. Ibid., c. 286a (July 4, 1535).

49. Ibid., c. 410a and b (May 25, 1544).

50. See Howard, *Jacopo Sansovino*, 108. The definitive model of the staircase, prepared by Francesco Smeraldi known as Frachao, was only chosen on May 14, 1587. See ASV, "Scuola Grande della Misericordia," b. 167, Notatorio 4, c. 274b.

51. The drawing D. 18 in the Museo Civico of Vicenza has been attributed to Palladio by Magrini and Adolfo Venturi: Magrini has also attributed the drawing of the statues and decorations to Paolo Veronese, while Giangiorgio Zorzi, who maintains that the drawing was executed after 1570, the year of Sansovino's death, refuses to believe that Palladio executed it, though it may have been done under his direction. See Antonio Magrini, *Memorie intorno la vita e le opere di Andrea Palladio* (Padua, 1845), 301–3; Venturi, *Storia dell'Arte*, 11/3, 116–17; Roberto Pane, *Andrea Palladio* (Turin, 1961), 311–12 (which expresses serious doubts about Palladio's having done the drawing, noting that only the lower sheet—different from the upper one also in its taste for chiaroscuro—is close to Palladio's style); Giovanni Mariacher, *Il Sansovino* (Milan, 1962), 106–7; Wolfgang Lotz, "The Roman Legacy in Jacopo Sansovino's Venetian Buildings," *Journal of the Society of Architectural Historians* 20, no. 1 (1963), reprinted in id., *Studies in Italian Renais-*

sance Architecture, 2nd ed. (Cambridge, Mass. and London, 1981), 143, which maintains that the drawing was faithful to Sansovino's project; Giangiorgio Zorzi, *Le chiese e i ponti di Andrea Palladio* (Vicenza, 1967), 173–74; Howard Burns, "I disegni di Palladio," *Bollettino del Cisa* 15 (1973): 180; id., "I disegni," in *Palladio*, catalogue of the exhibit (Milan, 1973), 152–53 (which does not agree with the hypothesis that the drawing was a copy of an original one by Sansovino); id., "Project for the façade of the Scuola Grande della Misericordia, Venice," in *Andrea Palladio 1508–80. The Portico and the Farmyard*, ed. H. Burns, in collaboration with Lynda Fairbairn and Bruce Boucher (London, 1975), 154–55; Douglas Lewis, *The Drawings of Andrea Palladio* (Washington, 1981), 182. Note that in the drawing of the R.I.B.A. the bases of the minor columns were varied with regard to the Vicenza folio. It seems reasonable to hypothesize that the latter was a copy of Sansovino's project interpreted in a few details by Palladio, while doubts remain about the dating of the two sheets that compose drawing D. 18 of Vicenza and on their purpose.

52. See Paoletti, *L'architettura*, 2:107, document from January 19, 1533. Philip Sohm maintains that the executed altar is not the one mentioned in the document from January 1533, and he attributes the work to Alessandro Vittoria, who would have designed it around 1562, when Tommaso Rangone was Guardian Grande of the Scuola San Marco. We believe that this hypothesis requires further investigation. See Sohm, *The Scuola Grande di San Marco*, 227–39. Sohm's hypothesis seems, however, to be contradicted by a document from March 19, 1550, which he himself published (ibid., 293, doc. 120), in which funds were appropriated to "prinzipiar et seguir el sofittado de la capel sopra laltar grando de la scuola nostra."

53. We refer the reader to the collaboration between Lorenzo Lotto and Sansovino hypothesized by Vertova, regarding which see chap. 3 of this volume.

54. ASV, "Scuola Grande di San Rocco," 2nd cons., reg. 47, c. 39, transcribed in

Soravia, *Le chiese*, 310–11, and in Paoletti, *L'architettura*, 2, doc. 166, but with an incorrect date (1544).

55. See Sohm, "The Staircases," 146–47, which stresses the election of Francesco Donà, a member of the Scuola di San Rocco, as doge: Donà decided to visit the Scuola every year on the occasion of the feast day of San Rocco, which Sohm relates to the architectural and decorative program.

56. See Lieberman, *L'architettura del Rinascimento a Venezia*, entry 89.

57. See A. Foscari and M. Tafuri, "Un progetto irrealizzato di Jacopo Sansovino: il palazzo di Vettor Grimani sul Canal Grande," *Bollettino dei Civici Musei Veneziani*, n.s., 26, no. 1–4 (1981): 71–87.

Chapter 5

1. See Domenico Morosini, *De bene instituta re publica*, ed. Claudio Finzi (Milan, 1969), a discussion of which can be found in the fundamental essay by Gaetano Cozzi, "Domenico Morosini e il 'De bene instituta re publica," *Studi Veneziani* 12 (1970): 405–58. Also see Leopold Von Ranke, "Venedig in sechzehnten Jahrhundert," *Sämtliche Werche* 42 (Leipzig, 1878), 3–133; It. trans. *Venezia nel Cinquecento*, with an introductory essay by Ugo Tucci (Rome, 1974), 114–17. In addition, Corrado Vivanti, "Pace e libertà in un'opera id Domenico Morosini," *Rivista Storica Italiana* 84, no. 3 (1972): 617–24; Innocenzo Cervelli, *Machiavelli e la crisi dello Stato veneziano* (Naples, 1974), 293ff.; Angelo Ventura, "Scrittori politici e scritture di governo," in the collection *Storia della cultura veneta. Dal Primo Quattrocento al Concilio di Trento*, eds. Girolamo Arnaldi and Manlio Pastore Stocchi, 3/3 (Vicenza, 1981), 521–22, 530–31, 546–48.

2. See Cozzi, "Domenico Morosini," 423–25.

3. Morosini, *De bene instituta*, 172–73, 201–3, 214.

4. Ibid., 80–83, 98–99, 134–35.

5. Ibid., p. 83.

6. Note, however, that remarkable attempts at urban and architectural standardization had been made in Florence in the fourteenth century, especially with the widening of the Via dei Calzaiuoli. See Richard A. Goldthwaite, *The Building of Renaissance Florence. An Economic and Social History* (Bologna, 1980); It. trans. (Bologna, 1984), 25–27.

7. Morosini, *De bene instituta*, 134–35.

8. See Finzi, "Introduzione," to Morosini, *De bene instituta*, 7–8, and Felix Gilbert, "The Venetian Constitution in Florentine Political Thought," in *Florentine Studies*, ed. Nicolai Rubinstein (London, 1968); It. trans. in F. Gilbert, *Machiavelli e il suo tempo* (Bologna, 1977), 115ff., esp. 127–28.

9. See chapter 2 of this volume.

10. See the collection *Lauro Quirini umanista*, ed. Vittore Branca (Florence, 1977); Agostino Pertusi, "L'umanesimo greco dalla fine del secolo XIV agli inizi del secolo 16," in *Storia della culture veneta*, 3/1 (Vicenza, 1980), 246–49; Giuliano Lucchetta, "L'oriente mediterraneo nella cultura di Venezia tra il Quattro e il Cinquecento," ibid., 3 : 2: 380–82.; Ventura, "Scrittori politici," 527–29, 537–41; Franco Gaeta, "L'idea di Venezia," in *Storia della cultura veneta*, 3/3, pp. 579–83.

11. See Venture, "Scrittori politici," 539.

12. Ibid., 540. Also see Gaeta, "L'idea di Venezia," 581–83.

13. See Felice Battaglia, *Enea Silvio Piccolomini e Francesco Patrizi, due politici senesi del Quattrocento* (Siena, 1936), 75ff., and Leslie F. Smith, "A Notice of the Epigrammata of Francesco Patrizi, Bishop of Gaeta," *Studies in the Renaissance* 15 (1968): 92–143. Jacopo Piccinino acted against Siena in the interest of Alfonso il Magnanimo. Francesco Patrizi managed to escape the death penalty thanks to the intervention of Francesco Filelfo, Nicodemo Tranchedino, and Enea Silvio Piccolomini; he had met the latter for the first time when he was studying at the University of Siena. See ibid., 93. On Patrizi of Siena also see Rino Avesani, *Epaeneticorum ad Pium II pont. Max. Libri V* in the collection *Enea Silvio Picco-*

lomini papa Pio II. Atti del Convegno per il quinto centenario della morte e altri scritti, ed. Domenico Maffei, 28–30, 62–63.

14. Francesco Patrizi Senese, *De institutione rei publicae libri 9* (Paris, 1494), l. 2, t. 4, f. 25v of the 1520 edition.

15. Ibid., l. 3, t. 6, f. 43v.

16. F. Patrizi, *De regno et regis institutione* (Paris, 1519), l. 7, 3, f. 310r.

17. Patrizi, *De institutione*, op. cit., l. 4, t. 1, f. 15r and v.

18. Patrizi, *De regno*, l.9, 3 ,10.

19. Patrizi, *De institutione*, l. 8.

20. Ibid., l. 8, t. 16, *De aedibus sacris*. On f. 124r Patrizi enumerates the architectural orders, reducing them to three in this sequence: Doric, Corinthian, Ionic.

21. Ibid., l. 8, t. 8, f. 119v

22. Ibid., t. 11, f. 121v.

23. See Smith, "A Notice," 103–4, 120. Also see Vladimír Juřen, "Fra Giocondo et le début des études vitruviennes en France," *Rinascimento*, ser. 2, 14 (1974), 111 n. 4. Let us transcribe the epigram from the Smith edition (poem 248, p. 120): "Ad Iucundum Antiquarium / Ad architectum F. Iucundum / Scrutaris veteres artes monumentaque patrum / Scripta notis priscis quae siluere diu. / Te modo in Oenotriam misit Verona peritum / Dogmate Vitruvii Dinocratisque metris. / Alter Alexandri permensus moenia clarus / Extitit ast alter vestra theatra dedit. / Nomen ab Eugania dulce est sed dulcius illud / Quod tibi dat virtus Pieridumque labor. / Dicat Iucundum licet, Antiquarius esto / Iudice Patricio. Vir venerande, vale."

24. Aristotle, *La Politica*, 10th ed. (Rome and Bari, 1982), 45, our emphasis. But also see the *Etica Nicomachea* I, 1, 2; 6, 8, in *Opere*, vol. 7 (Rome and Bari, 1983), 3–4, 140.

25. Plato, *Leggi*, in *Opere complete*, vol. 7, 2nd ed. (Rome and Bari, 1979), 208–9.

26. Plato, *La Repubblica*, in *Opere*, vol. 6, 2nd ed. (Rome and Bari, 1983), 3: 110–115, 4: 136–137. "The leaders of the State should insist on this principle, if they wish to avoid its being destroyed without their knowledge and to safeguard

it in every circumstance: they should not introduce anything new in gymnastics or in music that might violate the norm. . . . One ought to keep oneself from modifications that involve the action of a new kind of music, because one risks compromising the whole. One never introduces changes in the modes of music without introducing changes in the more important laws of the state: thus says Damon and I am convinced of this also."

27. On the architectonic operations of Nicholas V, see Carroll William Westfall, *In This Most Perfect Paradise. Alberti, Nicholas V and the Invention of Conscious Urban Planning in Rome 1447–1455* (Pennsylvania State Univ. Press, 1974; It. trans. Rome, 1984), whose hypotheses have been discussed at length in M. Tafuri, "'Cives esse non licere.' La Roma di Nicolò V e Leon Battista Alberti: elementi per una revisione storiografica," introduction to the Italian translation, pp. 13–39. On Rome under Pius II, see Christoph Luitpold Frommel, "Francesco del Borgo Architekt Pius'II. und Pauls II. 1, Der Petersplatz und weitere römische Bauten Pius'II. Piccolomini," *Römisches Jahrbuch für Kunstgeschichte* 20 (1983): 107–57. Rome under Sixtus IV has been the subject of valuable analyses by the association "Rome nel Rinascimento," chaired by Massimo Miglio, for the seminar held at Castel Sant'Angelo in October 1984 (Papers now forthcoming). On Lorenzo the Magnificent, architecture and urban management, see Mario Martelli, "I pensieri architettonici del Magnifico," *Commentari* 17, no. 1–3 (1966): 107–11; Philip Ellis Foster, *A Study of Lorenzo de Medici's Villa at Poggio a Caiano* (New York and London, 1978); Caroline Elam, "Lorenzo de' Medici and the Urban Development of Renaissance Florence," *Art History* 1, no. 1 (1978): 43–66; Piero Morselli and Gino Corti, *La chiesa di Santa Maria delle Carceri in Prato. Contributo di Lorenzo de' Medici e Giuliano da Sangallo alla progettazione* (Florence, 1982). On the Naples of Alfonso II the volume by George L. Hersey is still fundamental, *Alfonso II and the Artistic Renewal of Naples 1485–1495* (New Haven and London, 1969), but also see Roberto Pane, *Il Rinascimento nell'Italia meri-

dionale, 2 vols. (Milan, 1975 and 1977).
On the urban policies of Julius II and Leo
X, see M. Tafuri, "'Roma instaurata.'
Strategie urbane e politiche pontificie nella Roma del primo '500," in C. L. Frommel, Stefano Ray and M. Tafuri, *Raffaello
architetto* (Milan, 1984), 59–106.

28. Cozzi, "Domenico Morosini," 451.

29. On Gritti's "Roman" attitude and
the effect that the war against the League
of Cambrai had on the split between the
older patrician families and the minor or
"younger" ones, see F. Gilbert, "Venice in
the crisis of the league of Cambrai," in the
collection *Renaissance Venice,* ed. John R.
Hale, 2nd ed. (London, 1974), 274–92. A
reconstruction of the urban policy conducted by Andrea Gritti when he was
doge can be found in the stimulating, but
debatable, essay by Achille Olivieri,
"Capitale mercantile e committenza nella
Venezia del Sansovino," *Critica storica*
15, no. 4 (1978): 44–77. Also see the *Vita
di Andrea Gritti doge di Venezia tradotta
del latino in volgare* (1686), BMC, MS
Gradenigo-Dolfin 50; Robert Finlay, *Politics in Renaissance Venice* (London,
1980), 158–61 and passim; the collection
*"Renovatio urbis." Venezia nell'età di
Andrea Gritti (1523–1538),* ed. M.
Tafuri (Rome, 1984).

30. See Ellen Rosand, "Music in the
Myth of Venice," *Renaissance Quarterly*
30, no. 4 (1977), 511–37; It. trans. in
"Renovatio urbis," 167–86. The volume
by Gasparo Contarini, *De magistratibus
et republica Venetorum,* was first published in Paris in 1543, but had been
written—and the date is significant for
our analysis—in 1523–24, that is to say
at the beginning of Andrea Gritti's tenure
as doge, and was subsequently rewritten.
See F. Gilbert, "The Date of Composition
of Contarini's and Giannotti's Books on
Venice," *Studies in the Renaissance* 14
(1967): 172–85, and Lester J. Libby Jr.,
"Venetian History and Political Thought
after 1509," ibid., 20 (1973): 7–45. Also
see Cervelli, *Machiavelli e la crisi dello
Stato veneziano,* 293ff., 307ff., and
Myron Gilmore, "Myth and reality in
Venetian political theory," *Renaissance
Venice,* 431–44. On Gasparo Contarini
and the "myth of Venice," see Ventura,

"Scrittori politici," 549–53, and Gaeta,
"L'idea di Venezia," 632–41. Ventura
and Gaeta criticize the way Gilbert has reconstructed the relationship that existed
between Contarini and More. Underlining
the conservative character of Contarini's
utopianism and the sublimation of oligarchic tendencies contained in the *De magistratibus* (p. 550), Ventura defines the
encounter between Gasparo Contarini
and More as "symbolic." Also see Finlay,
Politics, 27–37.

31. See J. R. Hale, "Industria del libro e
cultura militare a Venezia nel Rinascimento," in *Storia della cultura veneta,*
3 : 2: 245–88; Ennio Concina, *La macchina territoriale. La progettazione della
difesa nel Cinquecento veneto* (Rome and
Bari, 1983), 5ff.

32. See ibid., 15ff.

33. See Giovan Giacomo Leonardi, *Libro
delle fortificazioni dei nostri tempi,* with
an introduction, transcription, and notes
by Tommaso Scalesse, in *Quaderni dell'Istituto di Storia dell'Architettura,*
Faculty of Architecture, University of
Rome, ser. 20–21, no. 115–126. But on
Leonardi's work, see Concina again, *La
macchina territoriale,* which provides a
substantial rectification of Scalesse's
interpretations.

34. See *Victoris Fausti Orationes quinque* (Venice, 1551); Alberto Tenenti, *Cristoforo da Canal. La marine vènitienne
avant Lépante* (Paris, 1963), 29ff.;
Frederic C. Lane, *Navires et constructeurs
à Venise pendant la Renaissance* (Paris,
1965), 59–65; E. Concina, "Dal 'tempo
del mercante' al 'Piazzale dell'Impero.'
L'Arsenale di Venezia," in *Progetto Venezia,* catalogue of the exhibit (Venice,
1980), 60–63; id., "L'Arsenale, una fabbrica ininterrotta," in the collection
*Architettura e utopia nella Venezia del
Cinquecento,* ed. L. Puppi (Milan, 1984),
103–6; Concina, *L'Arsenale della Repubblica de Venezia* (Milan, 1984), 108ff. On
October 16, 1518, the Senate elected Vettor Fausto to the chair of Greek at the
Scuola di San Marco, after the chair had
been empty for two years because of Marco Musuro's departure for Rome and subsequent death. See Fernando Lepori, "La
Scuola di Rialto dalla fondazione alla

metà del Cinquecento," in *Storia della cultura veneta*, 3:2: 603 and n. 384.

35. On the corpus of Jacopo Sansovino's work, see Giovanni Mariacher, *Il Sansovino* (Milan, 1962); Wolfgang Lotz, "The Roman Legacy in Sansovino's Venetian Buildings," *Journal of the Society of Architectural Historians* 22, no. 1 (1963): 3–12; Deborah Howard, *Jacopo Sansovino. Architecture and Patronage in Renaissance Venice* (New Haven and London, 1975). One ought to note that Gritti's choice of Sansovino—which was mediated by Domenico Grimani in 1523—was justified also by technical motives. It is, however, necessary to destroy the myth of Sansovino's technological inexperience. Vasari cites the restoration, technically daring, of the Palazzo Marin Tiepolo alla Misericordia, while Francesco Sansovino, also mentioning the work done on the subfoundation of the abovementioned palazzo, praised the restorations that his father had done of San Marco, stressing that for such an endeavor there had "never been found someone with enough spirit to put his hand to it." The restoration of the "cuba di mezzo" that, collapsing, was dragging "tutte l'altre dietro" ["all the others behind"], was completed by Jacopo—according to Francesco Sansovino—"con molto honor suo e con gran piacer del senato e d'universale, essendo per avanti tenuta per cosa disperata affatto da ogniuno il poterla o mantenere, o acconciare," Francesco Sansovino, *Venetia città nobilissima e singolare* (Venice, 1581), f. 144r. In the codex of Benedetto and Lorenza della Volpaia preserved in the Biblioteca Marciana of Venice (Cod. It. 4, 41 = 5363), Jacopo Sansovino is quoted twice, on c. 4v (receipt for plaster) and on c. 79r (a well for drawing water "in monte cavallo nel giardino del cardinale di Spagna," of "m. Guglielmo deglio oriuoli e di Jacopo de Sansovino.") Let us mention, incidentally, that in the same codex, on c. 56r is the drawing of "Sega de m° Andrea de Monte Sansavino fecie in Portogallo per segare il quadro de diaspro per farne colonnette": an indirect proof, therefore, of the trip Andrea Sansovino made to Portugal.

36. A complete analysis of the experience can be found in A. Foscari and M. Tafuri, *L'armonia e i conflitti. La chiesa di San Francesco della Vigna nella Venezia del '500* (Turin, 1983).

37. ASV, "Senato Terra," reg. 28, p. 66, September 2, 1535, transcribed in Giangiorgio Zorzi, *Le chiese e i ponti di Andrea Palladio* (Vicenza, 1967), 247.

38. ASV, "Notarile, testamenti, atti Bianco," b. 127, n. 731, July 30, 1527. Also see Sanudo, *Diarii*, 55: 676, and ASV, "S. Francesco della Vigna," b. 2, pt. 1, pp. 670–83; b. 5, pt. 2, pp. 199–203; b. 5, pt. 1, pp. 209–28; "Giudici del Piovego, Misure," b. 24, c. 54v, for the events concerning the houses for the "poveri Contarini."

39. ASV, "Senato Terra," reg. 26, pp. 222–23, February 3, 1531 (*m.v.* = 1532); Sanudo, *Diarii*, 55: 433; 57: 274–75.

40. André Chastel, *Il Sacco di Roma 1527* (Turin, 1983), 161–62. On Venice as the "new Rome," also see. D. S. Chambers, *The Imperial Age of Venice 1380–1580* (London, 1970).

41. G. Cozzi, "La political del diritto nella Repubblica di Venezia," in the collection *Stato, società e giustizia nella Republica veneta (sec. 15–18)*, ed. G. Cozzi (Rome, 1980), 122–37, reprinted in G. Cozzi, *Repubblica di Venezia e stati italiani. Politica e giustizia dal secolo 16 al secolo 18* (Turin, 1982), 217ff., esp. 293ff.

42. See A. Ventura, "Introduzione" to *Relazioni degli Ambasciatori Veneti al Senato* (Rome Bari, 1980), especially pp. XLIII–XLVI and XLVIII–LII.

43. Ibid., p. L.

44. Pauli Iovii, *Historiae sui temporis*, 2 (Lutetiae Parisiorum, 1554), ff. 236r–37v. Ventura ("Introduzione," LXXI n. 80) calls attention to the fact that before the first edition of that book came out (September 1552), Paolo Giovio had been requested "di passar con silenzio le laudi date e scritte a onore del prudentissimo messer Marco Foscari viniziano."

45. See "Relazion fatta per Marco Foscari nell'Eccellentissimo Conseglio di Pregadi della Legazion de Fiorenza, con qualche cosa adiuncta da lui nel scrivere

essa Legazione, 1527," in *Relazioni degli Ambasciatori Veneti*, 1: 89–184, regarding this see Ventura, "Introduzione," XLVIII–LVI.

46. For example, in the consistory of January 19, 1530, after the report by Cardinal Alessandro Farnese, Clement VII awarded Cardinals Marino Grimani and Francesco Corner ecclesiastical benefits of up to 5,000 ducats in revenue to be received by both: these were archiepiscopal, episcopal, and papal benefices, each one less than 200 ducats in revenue, providing they were on Venetian territory and according to papal designation. See Pio Paschini, "Il cardinale Marino Grimani nella diocesi di Concordia," *Memorie storiche forogiuliesi* 37 (1941): 71–88. On the "Papalists," see Brian Pullan, "Occupations and investments of the Venetian nobility," In *Renaissance Venice*, 397–400, and G. Cozzi, "Politica, cultura e religione," in the collection *Cultura e società nel Rinascimento fra riforme e manierismi*, eds. Vittore Branca and Carlo Ossola (Florence, 1984), 21–42.

47. See Ventura, "Introduzione," XLV–XLVI.

48. *Nunziature di Venezia* (March 12, 1533–March 14, 1535), 1, ed. Franco Gaeta (Rome, 1958), 301.

49. Sanudo, *Diarii*, 58: 465, July 22, 1533: "Veneno sier Vetor Grimani procurator, fradelo dil reverendissimo cardinal et sier Zuan Corner qu. sier Zorzi el cavalier procurator, dicendo per la bola hanno li reverendissimi Cornaro et Grimani di haver vescovadi per ducati 5000 nel Dominio, da esser partidi fra loro, et havendo havuto il Cornaro il vescovado di Brexa e il possesso, essendo vacà questo di Concordia, l'hanno spiritualmente za anni 4, rechiedendo sia messo la parte in Pregadi de darli il possesso; al qual il Serenissimo disse non sentiva questo, et che tre caxade in questa tera voriano tutti li vescovadi, il che non sente et vol contradirla."

50. See Finlay, *Politics*, 150.

51. On the Accademia Venetiana, also called the Accademia della Fama, see Domenico Maria Pellegrini, "Breve dissertatione previa al sommario della accademia veneta della Fama," *Giornale dell'Italiana Letteratura*, vol. 22 (1808): 3–20, followed by the "Sommario," on pp. 20–32, 113–28, 193–212, and 23: 49–68; Emanuele Antonio Cicogna, *Delle Inscrizione veneziane*, 2 (Venice, 1827), 138; 3 (Venice, 1830), 50–55; Giuseppe Bianchini, *Un'accademia veneziana del secolo 16* (Venice, 1895); Michele Maylender, *Storia delle accademie d'Italia*, vol. 5 (Bologna, 1930), 436–43; Aldo Stella, "Badoer Federico," in *Dizionario Biografico degli Italiani*, vol. 5 (Rome, 1963), 106–8; Paul Lawrence Rose, "The Accademia Venetiana. Science and Culture in Renaissance Venice," *Studi Veneziani* 11 (1969): 191–242; Pietro Pagan, "Sulla Accademia 'Venetiana' o della 'Fama,'" *Atti dell'Istituto Veneto di Scienze, Lettere ed Arti. Classe di scienze morali, lettere ed arti*, vol. 132 (1973–74): 359–92; Gino Benzoni, *Gli affanni della cultura. Intellettuali e potere nell'Italia della Controriforma e barocca* (Milan, 1978), 194–95; G. Cozzi, *La politica del diritto nella Repubblica di Venezia*, 143–45; id., *Repubblica di Venezia*, 311–13; Lina Bolzoni, "L'Accademia Veneziana: splendore e decadenza di una utopia enciclopedica," in the collection *Università, Accademie e Società scientifiche in Italia e in Germania dal Cinquecento al Settecento*, eds. Laetitia Boehm and Ezio Raimondi (Bologna, 1981), 117–67; Cesare Vasoli, "Le Accademie fra Cinquecento e Seicento e il loro ruolo nella storia della tradizione enciclopedica," ibid., 81ff., esp. 100–6. Also see L. Bolzoni, *Il teatro della memoria. Studi su Giulio Camillo* (Padua, 1984), 60–63, for Orazio Toscanella's relations with the Accademia della Fama.

52. Id., "L'Accademia Veneziana," 118–20.

53. Rose, "The Accademia Venetiana," 193.

54. Ibid., pp. 207–8.

55. See the "Supplica" that Federico Badoer addressed to the Procuratori di San Marco (1560), in ASV, "Procuratia de supra, Atti," reg. 120, published in Rose, "The Accademia Venetiana," 228–33 (esp. 233).

56. Stella, "Badoer Federico," 107.

57. See Bolzoni, "L'Accademia Venetiana," 132. The author takes the publication of Pole's oration and Sadoleto's poem as her starting point and then goes on to identify a link between the Accademia and a few of the most prestigious exponents of the Catholic Reformation, observing, furthermore, that Paolo Manuzio was a friend of Ludovico Beccadelli, Marcantonio Flaminio, and Pietro Carnesecchi.

58. One ought to note, however, that Francesco Patrizi contributed to the *damnatio memoriae* of the Accademia della Fama by not mentioning it in the autobiographical profile that he sent to Baccio Valori on January 12, 1587 (see Francesco Patrizi da Cherso, *Lettere ed appunti inediti*, ed. Danilo Aguzzi Barbagli (Florence, 1975), 45 ff.). In 1557, Patrizi "impetrò [in Rome] un beneficio assai buono," which was however disputed by an uncle, so that he appealed to the "Conte di Zaffo." Francesco Patrizi would later demonstrate technical interests, defending the Ferrarese cause in the case of the regimen of the lower Po river and the alterations of the hydraulic equilibrium in the region of Ferrara. In this he agreed with Silvio Belli, who had been appropriately called upon in 1573, and with Francesco Paciotto. See Patrizi's "Opuscoli tecnici," in the volume of *Lettere*, 191 ff. Patrizi's intellectual open-mindedness was evinced by the cordial relations he had with Teodoro Zwinger's circle in Basel, beginning in his period in Ferrara.

59. F. Patrizi, *La città felice* (Venice, 1553), reprinted in *Scrittori politici del '500 e del '600*, ed. Bruno Widmar (Milan, 1964), 72–73.

60. Patrizi wrote in *La città felice*, 74: "Per non avere, adunque da temere de i romori e de' sollevamenti popolari, sia in potere di ogni cittagino il regnare, over governare la città; che quello è veramente il vero cittadino, il quale partecipa de gli onori, e dell'amministrazioni pubbliche. Ma perché tutti cittadini ad un tempo medesimo in degnità non posson esser collocati, è conveniente che ciò facciano a vicenda, e l'un dopo l'altro sagliano al magistrato. E perché la salute della repubblica tutta da i governatori depende, e con

la prudenza loro si salva, però bisogna che coloro, che hanno ad avere il governo della città, sieno de' piu prudenti e de' piu savi."

61. Ibid., 75.

62. Ibid., 81.

63. A. Ventura, *Nobiltà e popolo nella società veneta del' 400 e del '500* (Bari, 1964).

64. Eugenio Garin has analyzed the dialogues *Della retorica* published by Francesco Patrizi in Venice in 1562, drawing attention to the double nature that they attribute to mathematics: on the one hand mathematics is seen as the source of sure knowledge, in that it is extrinsic and formal, on the other hand, it is incapable of penetrating into the substance of things. "Mathematics, while it is in knowledge alone, is pure science, but put to work and accompanied by matter it becomes art, such that it draws a good deal of imperfection out of that company." The universe, for Patrizi, is the language of God, it is "discourse," and men possessed its code "in the first antiquity of the world"; they had the "internal science of worldly things" and their original—and innocent—science had operative virtues. But after harmonic unity was broken, because of Assyrian pride and the wrath of Saturn, the rule of Jupiter provoked cataclysms and terror. Mystery took the place of primitive clarity: human societies were cemented by fear. Whence scarcity, struggles, and the race to accumulate resources. Garin concludes, "The human city, the *unhappy* city, is made of fear, structured by fear, dominated by the ignorance that is also the daughter of fear." Numbers, in this context, remain the substantial principles of the whole, but mathematics cannot clarify the enigma that surrounds the essence of that whole. See Eugenio Garin, "Aneddoti di storia della cultura del Cinquecento. I. Note alla 'Retorica' di Francesco Patrizi da Cherso," in *Umanesimo e Rinascimento: Studi offerti a Paul Oskar Kristeller* (Florence, 1980), 155–64.

65. Rose, "The Accademia Venetiana," 209 and n. 86.

66. See the "Supplica" by Federico Badoer, 229–30.

67. Cozzi, *Repubblica di Venezia*, 311–13.

68. "Supplica" by Federico Badoer, also see Rose, *The Accademia Venetiana*, 230.

69. See Harold E. Wethey, *The Paintings of Titian* (London, 1975), 204–5.

70. Pagan, "Sulla Accademia 'Venetiana,'" passim.

71. Ibid., 373.

72. Ibid., 380–81.

73. Ibid., 385.

74. Pagan published in the appendix of the cited essay, the "Riposta / degli studiosi / delle buone Arti, che sono in Germania, / All'Accademia Venetiana / nell' anno 1559" (pp. 386–92). The "studiosi," or scholars, of Augusta remained perplexed by this offer coming from a Catholic country, and engaged themselves in a long deprecation of censors and inquisitors. They wrote: "Laone pare che le letere, le quali hora ci avete scritto, piú tosto ci annoncino una guerra, che pace e intera amicitia, e preghiam Dio, che cosí non sia" (p. 388). Then they add: "La conclusion è che se vorrete inviarci libri d'altre scienze, noi gl'haremo cari, ma sarebe bene, che die Teologici nuovi, che debbon esser censurati da coteste maschere cappucciate, non ne pigliaste affanno." The letter is anonymous, but Pier Paolo Vergerio, who visited Friuli in 1558 and later saw all the books that he carried with him confiscated, has often been named the author.

75. Bolzoni, "L'Accademia Veneziana," passim.

76. Cited in Rose, "The Accademia Veneziana," 228.

77. Bolzoni, "L'Accademia Veneziana," 143.

78. Ibid., 140. Also see, by L. Bolzoni, *L'universo dei poemi possibili. Studi su Francesco Patrizi da Cherso* (Rome, 1980), which details the relations between Patrizi and the Accademia Venetiana (23–26), and mentions the short poem "Il Badoaro" (23). It also analyzes with remarkable acumen the motifs of Patrizi's *Poetica*.

79. See Paolo Manuzio, "Discorso intorno alle cinque parti dell'oratore," in *Lettere volgari* (Venice, 1560), pp. 38–39. In this work, Paolo Manuzio underlines the importance of the *dispositio* in an oration, exalting *order* as an element that is human par excellence, derived from the original order of God: "Dio creò l'huomo, sí come creò il mondo; e sí come prima il mondo con meravigliosa temperatura creò, cosí dapoi, osservando il medesimo ordiner, creò l'huomo: accioché l'huomo al mondo, et il mondo all'huomo si rassomigliasse, e l'huomo e l'altro rassomigliassero a lui." As for Federico Badoer, he wrote in the *Instrumento di deputatione* of 1560: "Ho fondato essa Academia alla similitudine del corpo humano, il quale essendo fatto alla similitudine di Dio, conseguentemente ho giudicato non poter ricevere esse perfettion maggiore. . . . "

80. See Rose, "The Accademia Venetiana," 231.

81. Bolzoni, "L'Accademia Veneziana," 149.

82. "Instrumento di deputazione di Federico Badoer," December 30, 1560, quoted in Bolzoni, "L'Accademia Veneziana," 149.

83. Ibid. The scholar also cites in this connection the dedication of the *De legato pontifico* to Bishop Antonio Perenoto, the adviser of the Spanish king: "Eius . . . domus facta est iampridem eruditorum omnium, qui ubique terrarum sunt, commune atque in primis nobile domicilium."

84. See François Dupuigrenet Desroussilles, "L'università di Padova dal 1405 al Concilio di Trento," in *Storia della cultura veneta*, 3 : 2: 607–47.

85. Rose, "The Accademia Venetiana," 196–205.

86. Federico Delfino (1477–1547) taught at the Studio in Padua from 1521 to 1547, and was a close friend of Pietro Bembo, who welcomed him in his home over many years. See P. L. Rose, "Professors of Mathematics at Padua University 1521–1588," *Physics* 17, no. 3–4 (1975), which also contains interesting information on Delfino, Pietro Catena, Francesco Barozzi, and Giuseppe Moleto.

87. Rose observes that the Accademia Venetiana's *Somma delle Opere* (1558) announced the publication of the "Quat-

tro libri di Proclo sopra Euclide, nuovamente tradotti," whereas a document of the ASV ("Riformatori dello studio di Padova," buste 284–86, "Licenze per stampa," n. 259) contains the approval of Francesco Barozzi's translation by Ettore Ausonio, a mathematician connected to the Accademia Venetiana. Rose remarks that the translation announced by the Accademia could not have been Barozzi's, but must have been a Latin one dating from 1539 and edited by the Venetian Bartolomeo Zamberti (Monaco, Staatsbibliothek, MS Lat. 6). See P. L. Rose, "A Venetian Patron and Mathematician of the Sixteenth Century: Francesco Barozzi (1537–1604) in *Studi Veneziani*, n.s., 1(1977): 119–78, esp. p. 120 n. 23. Rose also proposes that a direct relationship existed between Francesco Barozzi and the Accademia Venetiana (ibid., 149).

88. Sperone Speroni, *Opere*, 3 (Venice, 1740), 456–60.

89. Rose, "The Accademia Venetiana," 198.

90. *Somma delle opere che in tutte le scienze et arti più nobili et in varie lingue ha da mandare in luce l'Accademia Venetiana*, in the Accademia Venetiana (1558), 10.

91. On the figure of Francesco Zorzi, see C. Vasoli, *Profezia e ragione, Studi sulla cultura del Cinquecento e del Seicento* (Naples, 1974), 131–403; Foscari and Tafuri, *L'armonia e i conflitti*, with a bibliography in n. 5, pp. 91–92; William Melczer, "Ermetismo e cabala cristiana nel pensiero di Francesco Zorzi," in "*Renovatio urbis*," 148–63.

92. See Daniele Barbaro, *I dieci Libri dell'Architettura tradutti et commentati* (Venice, 1556), of which one can see the preparatory codices in BMV, Cod. It. 4, 152 = 5106, and 37 = 5133 (figs. 99–100). On Barbaro, see Pio Paschini, "Gli scritti religiosi di Daniele Barbaro," *Rivista di Storia della Chiesa in Italia* 5 (1951): 340ff.; Peter J. Laven, "Daniele Barbaro, patriarch elect of Aquileia, with special reference to his circle of scholars and to his literary achievement" (Ph. D. Thesis, University of London, 1957); P. Paschini, "Daniele Barbaro, letterato e prelato

veneziano del Cinquecento," *Rivista di Storia della Chiesa in Italia* 16 (1962): 73–107; Giuseppe Alberigo, "Barbaro Daniele," in *Dizionario Biografico degli Italiani*, vol. 6 (Rome, 1964), 89–95; Erik Forssman, "Palladio e Daniele Barbaro," *Bollettino del Cisa* 8, pt. 2 (1966): 68–81; Alan Haynes, "Daniele Barbaro: a Venetian Patron," *History Today* 25, no. 12 (1975): 818–25; Laura Marcucci, "Regesto cronologico e critico delle edizioni, delle traduzioni e delle ricerche più importanti sul trattato latino 'De Architettura libri 10' di Marco Vitruvio Pollione,' *Studi e documenti di architettura* 8 (1978): 58–62, 66–68; Bruce Boucher, "The last will of Daniele Barbaro," *Journal of the Warburg and Courtauld Institutes* 42 (1979): 277–82; L. Puppi, "La teoria artistica del Cinquecento," in *Storia della cultura veneta*, 3:3: 134–86; Giuseppe Barbieri, "La natura discendente: Daniele Barbaro, Andrea Palladio e l'arte della memoria," in the collection *Palladio e Venezia*, ed. L. Puppi (Florence, 1982), 29–54 (very debatable); Margherita Azzi Visentini, *L'Orto Botanico di Padova e il giardino del Rinascimento* (Milan, 1984), 149ff. (chap. 4, "Daniele Barbaro e il giardino del Rinascimento"); Alessandro Biral and Paolo Morachiello, *Immagini dell'ingegnere tra Quattro e Settecento* (Milan, 1985), 33–36, 142–145. Also see the volume by Fernando Marías and Agustín Bustamante, *Las ideas artisticas de El Greco* (Madrid, 1981), which analyzes El Greco's notes on Barbaro's 1556 edition of Vitruvius (Bibl. Nac. de Madrid, R 33475). On the *Storia Veneta* by Barbaro, who presented himself in 1560 before the Council of Ten to obtain the role of "public historiographer," See G. Cozzi, "Cultura, politica e religione nella 'pubblica storiografia' veneziana del '500," *Bollettino dell'Istituto di Storia della Società e dello Stato Veneziano* 5–6 (1963–64): 215–94. Daniele Barbaro, Ermolao's grandnephew, was born on February 8, 1514, the son of Francesco di Daniele and Elena Pisani, who was the daughter of the banker Alvise and Cecilia Giustinian. The Barbaro family's church was San Francesco della Vigna, in the cemetery of which Daniele would want to be buried. Marcantonio Barbaro, the brother of Daniele, would have four children by Giustina Giustinian, one of whom, Francesco, would become Patriarch of Aquileia, while another, Alvise, would marry one of Jacopo Foscarini's daughters. On Marcantonio, see Charles Yriarte, *La Vie d'un patricien de Venise au seizième siècle* (Paris, 1874); Franco Gaeta, "Barbaro Marcantonio," in *Dizionario Biografico degli Italiani*, vol. 6 (Rome, 1964), 110–12. The Barbaro brothers thus stood, socially, among the *Primi*, [older generation] and had close ties with the Pisani, Giustinian, Foscarini, and Grimani families. Sperone Speroni and Daniele Barbaro were, moreover, friends of Bernardo Navagero: the three belonged to the chosen circle of Pier Francesco Contarini, who was Vettor Fausto's patron. See Laven, "Daniele Barbaro," 1–10, 29, which cites two documents that allow us to reconstruct Daniele Barbaro's library: a list of texts, most of them Greek, in BAV, MS Vat. Lat. 7246 and an eighteenth-century catalogue in BMC, Cod. Cicogna 2273. Daniele graduated from Padua in 1540 and was the cofounder of the Accademia degli Infiammati; in 1541 he was in Bologna with Cardinal Alessandro Farnese; in 1545 he supervised the Paduan Orto dei Semplici; subsequently, he was the Provveditor di Commun in Venice. In 1549 he was nominated ambassador to England, and in 1550 Giovanni Grimani designated him Patriarch elect of Aquileia. Both Giovanni Grimani and Daniele Barbaro appear in the dialogues of Paolo Paruta, *Della prefettione della Vita Politica* (Venice, 1579), the former defending the ideal of the *vita contemplativa* and the latter the ideal of the *vita activa*. On the relations between Daniele Barbaro and Federico Badoer, see Laven, "Daniele Barbaro," 43–44, 57.

93. Concina, "Dal 'tempo del mercante,'" 60–63; id., "L'Arsenale, una fabbrica ininterrotta," 104–6; ide., *L' Arsenale della Repubblica*, 135 ff., which explains that the "mirabile ordine" ["admirable order"] celebrated by Daniele Barbaro and executed by the Capitoli of 1545 consisted in a complete revision of the modes of equipping the battle units, based on a numbering system that would function in concordance with the rapid assembly of the accessories.

94. Barbaro, *I dieci Libri*, 5: 163.

95. See Concina, *L'Arsenale della Repubblica*, 98.

96. Bernardo Tasso, *Amadigi*, 3rd ed. (Venice, 1581), canto C, pp. 721–22. One ought, however, to remember that neither Barbaro nor Zen (who, given the context, must have been Nicolò) appeared in the *Instrumento di deputazione del 30 dicembre 1560* (see Pellegrini, *Sommario*, 23: 61 ff.). The list does, however, include the names of Marino Grimani (not the cardinal of the same name, who had already died: perhaps this was the future doge), Agostino Fregoso, Antonio da Lezze, Marco Morosini, Agostino Valier, Luca Contile, Francesco Barbarigo, Giovanni Badoer, Alvise Mocenigo, Jacopo Surian, Ettore Ausonio, Francesco Tiepolo, Andrea Gabriel, Giuseppe Moleto, Alessandro and Alvise Zorzi, Giuseppe Zarlino, Alessandro Contarini, Fausto da Longiano, Paolo Ramusio, the "pievano di S. Pantalon" [parish priest of San Pantalon], etc. Bernardo Tasso (p. 67) is mentioned as "cancelliere," or chancellor. Bernardo Tasso had received from the Accademia, while he was still in Pesaro, an offer to publish the *Amadigi*, under Paolo Manuzio's supervision. Having refused that offer, the poet had Giolito publish the volume in September 1560. In February 1560, Tasso broke with the Accademia, writing in a letter: "Io mi son licenziato dall'Accademia e mi voglio licenziare di questa casa, perché la vicinità causa che il Clarissimo mi dà alcuna volta piú fastidio che io non vorrei." Quoted in Edward Williamson, *Bernardo Tasso* (Rome, 1951), 139, and n. 32. (But see also pp. 113 ff. for his contacts with Sperone Speroni and Tasso's sojourn in Venice.) In the fifth book of Bernardo Tasso's *Rime*, also published in 1560 by Giolito de' Ferrari, a few were dedicated *Agli Accademici Venetiani* (p. 62), to Luca Contile (p. 63), to Federico Badoer (p. 65), and to the abbot Marlopino (pp. 65–66). Also see the work "Mentre io polisco, e tergo," vv. 11–17. But, to return to the passage of the *Amadij* cited in the text, the presence of Barbaro's and

Zen's names alongside those of the protagonists of the Accademia Venetiana is symptomatic: the friendship between Barbaro and Federico Badoer can lead us to suggest an influence, at least, of the first upon the circle directed by the second. As for Palladio, one ought to note that he was directly connected to at least three members of the Accademia Venetiana: the priest of San Pantalon, Nicolò Moravio (see below, note 104), Fausto da Longiano, who in 1556 transmitted a letter from Anastasio Monticolo containing greetings from Jacopo Valvasone and Floriano Antonini—see Tommaso Temanza, *Vita dei più celebri architetti* (Venice, 1778), ed. L. Grassi (Milan, 1966), 297—to Alvise Mocenigo. According to Howard Burns, Palladio executed the monument to Alvise Mocenigo and his wife that stands in the Chiesa dei Santi Giovanni e Paolo, according to a project from circa 1574. See Howard Burns, "Le opere minori di Palladio," *Bollettino del Cisa* 21 (1979): 23–24.

97. Regarding Giuseppe Moleto, see Antonio Favaro, "Le matematiche nello studio di Padova dal principio del secolo 14 alla fine del secolo 16," in *Nuovi Saggi della R. Accademia di Scienze, Lettere ed Arti in Padova*, vol. 9, pt. 1 (Padua, 1880), 64–66, 85–95; id., "Amici e corrispondenti di Galileo Galilei. 40. Giuseppe Moletti," in *Atti del R. Istituto Veneto di Scienze, Lettere ed Arti*, vol. 77, pt. 2 (1917–18), 47–118; Rose, "Professors of Mathematics at Padua University," 303. Charles B. Schmitt, "Filosofia e scienza nelle Università italiane del 16 secolo," in *Il Rinascimento. Interpretazione e problemi*, studies in honor of E. Garin (Rome and Bari, 1979), 384–86; Adriano Carugo, "L'insegnamento della matematica all'Università di Padova prima e dopo Galileo," in *Storia della cultura veneta. Il Seicento*, 4/2 (Vicenza, 1984), 151ff., esp. 170–83. Giuseppe Moleto, born in Messina in 1531 and died in Padua in 1588, published a "Discorso universale" in the appendix of the *Geografia* of Ptolemy edited by Girolamo Ruscelli (Venice, 1561). In 1562 Moleto was denounced, along with Giovanni Michele Bruto, before the Tribunale del Sant'Uffizio. See Aldo Stella, *Dall'anabattismo al socinianesimo nel Cinquescento veneto* (Padua, 1967), 139. The *Efemeridi*, calculated for 1563–80, date from 1563; Moleto became professor of mathematics in the studio of Padua in 1577, after having broken his commitment to the Duke of Mantua. In Padua he became a friend of Gian Vincenzo Pinelli: in his last will and testament of May 15, 1570, he entrusted the sale of his library to Pinelli (see doc. 3, on pp. 102–4, in Favaro, "Amici e corrispondenti di Galileo"). One of his students in Padua was Paolo Gualdo, the author of the lives of Andrea Palladio and Pinelli. His manuscripts would enter Pinelli's library and then be transferred to the Ambrosiana in Milan, thanks to the acquisition of Cardinal Federico Borromeo. The manuscripts—listed by Favaro (ibid., 86ff.)—include the "Facil modo di tirar le linee parallele alle vedute, di misurar le distanze et di mettere in disegno. Scritto da Giuseppe Moleto al Cl. mo Sog.r Giacomo Contarini in data di Padova, 25 giugno 1581" (BAM, A71 inf., cc. 24ff.), and a letter to Giulio Savorgnan. Also interesting is MS S100 sup., which contains papers entitled: "il 17 settembre 1575 di fortificazione. Di G. Moleto memorie in materia di artiglieria." In addition to Moleto's ties with Pinelli, Contarini, and Giulio Savorgnan, one ought to note his friendship with Caterino di Nicolò Zen, indicated by the dedication of the commentaries to the 6th and 7th books of Ptolemy's *Geografia* and by his last will of September 9, 1587: "Item lasso all'Ill.re Sig.re Vincenzo Pinelli la mia prospettiva di Tolomeo scritta a pena et in bergamina in quarto. Anchora la sfera di Scrobosco in lingua Portoghese . . . oltre a ciò lasso a S.S. la mia Artigliaria di bronzo che è sopra le mie scancie de libri . . . . Item lasso all'Ill.mo Catarin Zeno mio amico e Sig.re il mio Teatro del mondo colorito che mi fu lassato dal Sig.r Nicolò di primo che sia in glora." See Favaro, "Amici e corrispondenti di Galileo," doc. 19, pp. 115–16. Giuseppe Moleto was thus a friend of Nicolò Zen's: information that confirms the compactness of the scientistic group adherent or close to the Accademia della Fama. In 1587, Moleto, judging a text by the young Galileo, called

him "buono e esercitato Geometra" (ibid., 92).

98. "Discorso di M. Gioseppe Moleto mathematico nel quale egli mostra che cosa sia matematica, quante sien le parti di quella, quali sienoi et come sono insieme ordinate," BAM, S103 sup., cc. 122r–75r, dated 1573–75 in Carugo, "L'insegnamento della matematica," 178.

99. BAM, R94 sup., c. 184.

100. Schmitt, "Filosofie e scienza," 385. Moleto, in a passage quoted by Schmitt (*Discorso*, c. 127r), wrote: "Et chi non sa che nell'aritmetica di Fra Luca [Pacioli] edd'altri tutte le cose che si trattano si possono con due fini trattare e maneggiare, l'uno de' quali è nel considerare la forza, et al potenza, et insieme la proportione di quei numeri che si trattano, et l'altro è di accomodare quei numeri al negotio.... " But note also the end of the treatise: "Da tutto questo discorso si può vedere da sé senza che io mi affatichi a mostrarlo quanto e quale n'à l'utile, che dalle mathematiche si può in ogni tempo et in ogni luogo cavare et quanto a ciascuna qualità di persone si convengano et particolarmente a principi" (ibid., c. 175r).

101. Charles Schmitt writes that Moleto cannot be recognized as one of the most original or able mathematicians of the sixteenth century, adding, however, that from his case we can draw the conclusion "that the Paduan mathematical tradition was ample and not in the least confined to the rather restricted current of texts indicated by official statutes." Schmitt, "Filosofia e scienza," 386.

102. Carugo, "L'insegnamento della matematica," 181–83.

103. See Rose, "The Accademia Venetiana," 203 n. 62. Francesco Sansovino did, however, belong to the Accademia della Fama; he dedicated the *Ordine de Cavalieri del Tosone. Nell'Accademia Venetiana 1557* to Don Francesco de' Medici, signing it "Accademico Venetiano." See Cicogna, *Delle Inscrizioni veneziane*, 4 (Venice, 1834), 52. After the events of 1561, Sansovino would no longer mention the Accademia in his writings. Jacopo's son, Francesco, had already participated in another Venetian Accademia, the Accademia Pellegrina, which Anton Francesco Doni mentioned in the *Marmi*, along with Ludovico Dolce, Francesco Coccio, Giason de Nores, and Ercole Bentivoglio: in 1552, Jacopo Nardi, Bernardo Daniello, Titian, Tintoretto, and Cecchino Salviati would join the Accademia, which had been founded in 1549. Francesco Marcolini, who employed Doni as his secretary, was the printer of the Accademia Pellegrina, which was sponsored by Domenico and Cipriano Morosini, and by members of the Cornaro, Contarini, and Martinengo families. See Giovanni Aquilecchia, "Pietro Aretino e altri poligrafi a Venezia," in the collection *Storia della cultura veneta. Dal primo Quattrocento al Concilio di Trento*, 3:2: 95.

104. See A. Foscari, "Un altare di Palladio nella vecchia chiesa di San Pantalon (1555)," in *Architettura e utopia*, 255–56; id., "Palladio a San Pantalon," in *Palladio e Venezia*, 89–93.

105. See Maylender, *Storia delle Accademie*, 5: 440, 442.

106. See Paolo Rossi, *I filosofi e le macchine (1400–1700)*, 2nd ed. (Milan, 1976), 26, 66–67; Laven, "Daniele Barbaro," 1: 180.

107. Leon Battista Alberti, *De re aedifcatoria*, Incipit, edited and translated by Giovanni Orlandi, vol. 1 (Milan, 1966), 8–9.

108. Barbaro, *I dieci Libri*, 1. 1: 15.

109. Eugenio Garin has recognized in Alberti's condemnation of man, whom he calls a "very ferocious" ("efferatissimo") enemy of nature, a refutation of Cicero, which was largely used by Giannozzo Manetti. This refutation was accomplished through references to such medieval texts as Alain de Lille's *De planctu naturae*. See Eugenio Garin, *Rinascite e rivoluzioni. Movimenti culturali dal 14 al 18 secolo*, 2nd ed. (Rome and Bari, 1976), 148ff. On Alberti's opposition to "innovations," see L. B. Alberti, *Theogenius*, in *Opere volgari*, ed. Cecil Grayson, 2 (Bari, 1968), esp. pp. 61, 92. Also see Rosario Contarino, "Il bestiario umanistico di L. B. Alberti," introduction

to L.B. Alberti, *Apologhi ed elogi*, ed. R. Contarino (Genoa, 1984), 15–40. As Contarino demonstrates, Alberti's position toward the investigation of nature—negative when it alters the order of things—derives from Pliny's "physics," which deems foolish all incursions into "elsewhere."

110. Barbaro, *I dieci Libri*, 1. 4: 104.

111. Ibid., 1. 5: 144–45.

112. Ibid., 1. 4: 105.

113. Ibid., 1. 10: 254.

114. Ibid.

115. Ibid, "Proemio," 7. The condémnation of action undertaken only for practical reasons is similar to the one that Barbaro directs against painters in his introduction to *Pratica della Perspettiva* (Venice, 1569): "I Pittori de i nostri tempi altrimenti celebri, e di gran nome, si lasciano condurre da una semplice pratica, e nelle tavole loro non dimostrano sopra questa parte cosa degna di molta commendatione, e nelle carte in iscritto niuno precetto si vede dato da loro." Barbaro declares instead his debt toward Giovanni Zamberto, Federico Commandino and (on p. 192) Baldassarre Lanci. The treatise on perspective is dedicated to Matteo Macigni, a friend of Barbaro's since the time they studied mathematics together; however, the volume remained a practical manual used by artists, more than a theoretical text.

116. Aristotle, *Etica Nicomachea*, in *Opere*, vol. 7 (Rome and Bari, 1983), 6: 3: 142–43, 6: 6, 7: 146–49.

117. Barbaro, *I dieci Libri*, "Proemio," 8.

118. "Not only would every ulterior real modification of machines, techniques, or arts, the development of their *istoría*, happen in opposition to the authoritative discourse of architecture and separate itself from it, but the very theoretical foundation of cognitive systems corresponding to the predominant arts would have to subtract itself from its excessively reductive tyranny, and it was the very logic of the *Commentari* that furnished the arguments for such an emancipation." Biral and Morachiello, *Immagini dell'ingegnere*, 36.

119. On Barbaro's religious position, see Paschini, "Gli scritti religiosi," and Laven, "Daniele Barbaro," 1: 122ff. Laven examines the theological letters that Barbaro sent to his aunt Cornelia, a sister in the convent of Santa Chiara in Murana, from September 25, 1549, to December 1, 1550, during his ambassadorship in England, and observes that Barbaro was clearly influenced by Saint Bonaventure's *Breviloquium*. In his second letter (October 29, 1549), Daniele Barbaro proposed a simple, rational, and well-ordered theology, with a mental attitude recalling the one that emerges from his *Retorica* and the Vitruvian *Commentari*. See Laven, "Daniele Barbaro," 1: 124. Barbaro had great respect for Gasparo Contarini and his work. Probably during his visit to Rome in 1556, Cardinal Sirleto encouraged Daniele Barbaro to translate into Latin an ancient manuscript of Greek commentaries on the Psalms. See D. Barbaro, *Aurea in quinquaginta Davidicos Psalmos Doctorum Graecorum Catena* (Venice, 1569), dedicated to Pius V and directed to comfort, with the authority of the ancient fathers, the souls perturbed by the ideas of Protestant Reformation.

120. Daniele Barbaro's manuscript, "De horologiis describendis," is in BMV, MS Lat., cl. 8, 42 = 3097 (figs. 103, 104). On Barbaro's work for the Orto Botanico of Padua, see Azzi Visentini, *L'Orto Botanico*, passim, which does, however, unjustly underestimate Andrea Moroni's work (see pp. 149–51) and emphasizes the symbolic meanings of the simple geometric outline with references that are often inadequate (pp. 33ff.).

121. Interesting remarks on the subject can be found in Roberto Esposito's book, *Ordine e conflitto. Machiavelli e la letteratura politica del Rinascimento italiano* (Naples, 1984), chap. 3, pp. 75ff.

122. See Richard Cocke, "Veronese and Daniele Barbaro: the Decoration of Villa Maser," *Journal of the Warburg and Courtauld Institutes* 35 (1972): 226–46; Norbert Huse, "Palladio und die Villa Barbaro in Maser: Bemerkungen zum Probleme der Authorschaft," *Arte Veneta* 28 (1974): 106–22; Robert Smith, "A

Matter of Choice: Veronese, Palladio and Barbaro," ibid., 31 (1977): 60–71; L. Puppi, "Per Paolo Veronese architetto. Un documento inedito, una figura e uno strano silenzio di Palladio," *Palladio* 3, no., 1–4 (1980): 53–76; Visentini, *L'Orto Botanico*, 180ff.; D. Battilotti, "Villa Barbaro a Maser: un difficile cantiere," *Storia dell'arte* 53 (1985): 33–48.

123. "... ne i dissegni de le figure importanti ho usato l'opera di M. Andrea Palladio Vicentino Architetto, il quale ha con incredibile profitto tra quanti ho consciuto... acquistato la vera Architettura, non solo intendendo le belle, e sottili ragioni di essa, ma anco ponendola in opera si ne i sottilissimi, e vaghi disegni dei piante, di gli alzati, e dei profili, come nelo esequire e far molti superbi Edificij ne la patria sua, e altrove, che contendono con gli antichi, danno lume a moderni, e daran meraviglia a quelli che verranno." Barbaro, *I dieci Libri*, 1.1: 39 bis.

124. Concina, *La macchina territoriale*, 47ff.

125. Licisco Magagnato, *Introduzione* to Andrea Palladio, *I Quattro Libri dell'Architettura* (Venice, 1570), eds. L. Maganato and Paola Marini (Milan, 1980), p. XXIII.

126. See in this connection Heinz Spielmann, *Andrea Palladio und die Antike. Untersuchung und Katalog der Zeichnungen aus seinem Nachlass* (Munich and Berlin, 1966); E. Forssman, "Palladio e l'antichità," in *Palladio*, catalogue of the exhibit (Milan, 1973), 17–26; Magagnato, *Introduzione*; Howard Burns, "Le antichità di Verona e l'architettura del Rinascimento," in the collection *Palladio e Verona*, ed. P. Marini, catalogue of the exhibit directed by L. Magagnato, (Venice, 1980), 103–20.

127. In this connection, Marcello Fagiolo's hypotheses are completely gratuitous. He inserts Palladio into a context of generic hermeticism, without taking into account the effective components of Palladio's learning, and bases his argument on doubtful evidence, such as the inscriptions placed on the façade of the church of San Francesco della Vigna, or the plan of Villa Barbaro in Maser as it appears in the *Quattro Libri*. See Marcel-

lo Fagiolo, "Palladio e il significato dell'architettura," and id., "Contributo all'interpretazione dell'ermetismo in Palladio," *Bolletino del Cisa* 14 (1972): 27–41, 357–80. Moreover, this reading contradicts the one, which is certainly more acceptable, that Fagiolo proposed in "Le facciate palladiane: la progettazione come proiezione sul piano di spazi dietro spazi," *Bollettino del Cisa* 20 (1978): 47–70. Also to be rejected are Andrè Corboz's remarks in "Procedimenti dell'urbanistica palladiana," ibid., 14 (1972): 235–50, which implicitly attributes to Palladio a responsibility for the choice of his building sites that has no basis in historical reality.

128. See André Chastel, *Art et humanisme à Florence au temps de Laurent le Magnifique* (Paris, 1959); It. trans. (Turin, 1964), passim; Eugenio Garin, "Giovanni Pico della Mirandola," in *Ritratti di umanisti* (Florence, 1967), 185ff.; the collection *L'opera e il pensiero di Pico della Mirandola nella storia dell'Umanesimo*, 2 vols. (Florence, 1965); Giovanni di Napoli, *G. Pico della Mirandola e la problematica dottrinale del suo tempo* (Rome, 1965); Henri de Lubac, *Pic de la Mirandole* (Paris, 1974; It. trans., Milan, 1977). On Erasmus's thinking in connection to the text, see Silvana Seider Menchi, *Introduzione* to Erasmus of Rotterdam, *Adagia. Sei saggi politici in forma di proverbi* (Turin, 1980). We cannot debate here the thesis developed in the recent volume by William G. Craven, *Giovanni Pico della Mirandola. Symbol of his Age. Modern Interpretations of a Renaissance Philosopher* (Geneva, 1981; It. trans., Bologna, 1984), which, in spite of its many definitions and lively objections, offers a reductive image of Pico, and does not explain the interest that his contemporaries had in his thinking.

129. See Alberto Tenenti, "Il 'Momus' nell'opera di Leon Battista Alberti," *Il pensiero politico* 7, no. 3 (1974): 321–33 (in French), reprinted in id., *Credenze, ideologie, libertinismi tra Medioevo ed Età Moderna* (Bologna, 1978), 137–54; Garin, *Rinascite e rivoluzioni*, 131ff. Lorenza Aluffi Begliomini, "Note sull'opera dell' Alberti: il 'Momus' e il 'De re

aedificatoria,'" *Rinascimento*, ser. 2, 12 (1972): 267–83.

130. A Palladio, *L'antichità di Roma . . . racolta brevemente*, Vicenzino Lucrino (Rome, 1554), regarding which see L. Puppi, *Andrea Palladio*, 2 (Milan, 1973), 443.

131. Giovanni Grimani, who in circa 1564 commissioned Palladio with the façade of San Francesco della Vigna, had already participated, on January 2, 1551, in the chapter of the cathedral of Padua in which Michelangelo replaced Sansovino as the designer of the choir. See the collection *Michelangelo Buonarroti nel Veneto*, ed. Paolo Carpeggiani (Padua, 1975), 13–15. Also see Giulio Bresciani Alvarez, "Alvise Cornaro e la fabbrica del Duomo di Padova," in the collection *Alvise Cornaro e il suo tempo*, ed. L. Puppi (Padua, 1980), 58–62.

132. Antonio Foscari has suggested that drawings R.I.B.A. 14/13, 14, 15, 16 relate to Palladio's projects for the Redentore at San Vidal. See A. Foscari, "Per Palladio: note sul Redentore a San Vidal e sulle Zitelle," *Antichità viva* 3(1975): 44ff. Howard Burns has, however, related these drawings to projects for the Redentore with a central plan on the Giudecca, on the basis of a persuasive dimensional analysis. See H. Burns, "Projects for the church of the Redentore, Venice," in the collection *Andrea Palladio. 1508–1580. The Portico and the Farmyard*, ed. H. Burns (London, 1975), 146–47. As for Palladio's relationship with the "Romanist" patriciate, one notes that the architect's first patrons in Venice included the Patriarch Vincenzo Diedo, who entrusted Palladio—under a guarantee from Daniele and Marcantonio Barbaro—with the project for the façade of the church of San Pietro di Castello: as is known, Palladio's plan would not be executed. See Puppi, *Palladio*, 2: 321–23. Diedo was harshly attacked in the Senate, in July 1559, by Giovanni di Bernardo Donà, a man—according to the papal nuncio—"ordinarily opposed to churchmen." Giovanni Donà denounced the Patriarch for not having paid 2,000 ducats in taxes to the Republic and for his life of luxury, calling him "hippocrito"; in a later speech, Donà called Vincenzo Diedo a "lupo rapace" ["rapacious wolf"]. See Paul F. Grendler, "The 'Tre Savi sopra Eresia' 1547–1605: a prosopographical study," *Studi veneziani*, n. s., 3 (1979), 320 n. 55.

133. Girolamo Porro, "Dedica," in Vincenzo Scamozzi, *Discorsi sopra le antichità di Roma* (Venice, 1582).

134. See L. Puppi, "La vera nascita di Andrea Palladio e la 'vita' scritta de Paolo Gualdo," in the collection *Vicenza illustrata*, ed. Neri Pozza (Vicenza, 1976), 222–25 (with a biography written by Gualdo on pp. 224–25). It was Gualdo who indicated the existence of drawings for a Palladian *Quinto Libro* that never appeared; they remained in the possession of Jacopo Contarini: the corpus was then passed to the Dal Peder, acquired in 1817 by Gaetano Pinali and in 1838 left to the city of Vicenza (where it is now in the Museo Civico), with the exception of three drawings—lost during the last war—that Pinali gave Verona.

135. Jacopo Contarini—Francesco Sansovino wrote (*Venetia città nobilissima*, 138r)—"con spesa indicibile ha posto insieme quasi tutte le historie stampate e le scritte a penna, non pure universali, ma particolari delle città, con diversi altri librie in gran copia nelle scienze. Co quali sono accompagnati disegni, stromenti mathematici, et altre cose di mano dei piú chiari artefici nella pittura, nella scoltura e nell'architettura, che habbia havuto l'età nostra. I quali tutti egli ha sempre, come amante de i virtuosi, favoriti e accarezzati."

136. ASV, "Notarile Testamenti, notaio Galeazzo Sacco," b, 1194, prot. 5 cc. 2–4, partially transcribed in *Testimonianze veneziane di interesse palladiano*, ed. Maria Francesca Tiepolo (Venice, 1980), 19.

137. Gian Vincenzo Pinelli, who lived in Padua in a house of Leonardo Mocenigo's that had been restored by Palladio (see *Testimonianze veneziane*, 41, entry 82, and Douglas Lewis, *The Drawings of Andrea Palladio* (Washington, 1981), 60, 99), constituted a notorious point of reference for intellectuals in Padua in the sixteenth century and was closely linked to

Jacopo Contarini, Moleto, and Galileo. Born in Naples of Genoese descent, he arrived in Padua in 1558 (and would die there in 1601): his friends included Cardinal Federico Borromeo, Ulisse Aldovrandi, Francesco Patrizi da Cherso, and Giovanni and Ippolito Aldobrandini. On Pinelli see Paolo Gualdo, *Vita Ioanni Vicentii patricii genuensis* (Augustae Vindelicorum, 1607); Adolfo Rivolta, *Une grande bibliofilo del secolo XVI. Contributo allo studio della biblioteca di Gian Vincenzo Pinelli* (Monza, 1914); Rita Calderini de Marchi, *Jacopo Corbinelli et les érudits français d'après la corrispondance inédite Corbinelli-Pinelli (1556–1587)* (Milan, 1914); A. Rivolta, *Catalogo dei codici pinelliani all'Ambrosiana* (Milan, 1933)—but regarding Pinelli's codices, also see P. O. Kristeller's *Iter Italicum*. On the correspondence with Francesco Patrizi, see Patrizi, *Lettere ed opuscoli inediti*, 6–7, and passim.

138. On Jacopo Contarini, born in Cyprus on July 24, 1536, and deceased on October 4, 1595, see G. Zorzi, *Le opere pubbliche e i palazzi privati di Andrea Palladio* (Vicenza, 1965), 132–33; Oliver Logan, *Culture and Society in Venice 1470–1790. The Renaissance and its Heritage* (London, 1972); It. trans. (Rome, 1980), 229–32, 257–58, 266–71, 425. See also P. L. Rose, *The Italian Renaissance of Mathematics. Studies on Humanists and Mathematicians from Petrarch to Galileo* (Geneva, 1975), 233ff.; id., "Jacomo Contarini (1536–1595), a Venetian Patron and Collector of Mathematical Instruments and Books," *Physis* 18, no. 2(1976): 117–30; *Testimonianze veneziane*, entries 20–22, 26, 209; H. Burns, "Andrea Palladio, Jacopo Contarini e le fortezze," lecture given at the seminary of the CISA, Vicenza, August 1984 (forthcoming); *Storici e politici veneti del Cinquecento e del Seicento*, eds. Gino Benzoni and Tiziano Zanato (Milan and Naples, 1982), 502. On Contarini's impressive collection, which went to the Great Council in 1713, see Carlo Ridolfi, *Le meraviglie dell'arte* (Venice, 1648). In 1574, Jacopo Contarini was one of three patricians responsible for the organization of festivities for Henry III's visit, for which Palladio designed a loggia and a triumphal arch near San Nicolò al Lido. After the burning of the Palazzo Ducale in 1577, he worked with Giacomo Marcello and the Camaldolensian monk Girolamo Bardi in order to draw up a program for the decoration of the rooms of the Great Council and the Scrutinio, as well as for the statues in the Antepregadi. Achille Olivieri has recently tried to link Jacopo Contarini's scientific interests to the heretical ideas of Odoardo Thiene, inappropriately using the trial for heresy undergone by Francesco Contarini—Francesco was a nephew of the bastard born to Cardinal Gasparo—and a letter sent from Stefano di Giacomo Angarano to Contarini in 1580. (Olivieri, furthermore, is mistaken in attributing the letter to Contarini.) See A. Olivieri, *Palladio, le corti e le famiglie. Simulazione e morte nella cultura architettonica del '500* (Vicenza, 1981), 52–54. There is no doubt that an inquiry into Jacopo Contarini's religious sentiment could be relevant, but the traces Olivieri has pursued strike us as marginal. Rather, one ought to note that Jacopo Contarini's brother, Giovanni Battista, was a pious man, who professed chastity and recited the canonical hours: after having participated in the last session of the Council of Trent, Giovanni Battista would work for the foundation of a diocesan seminary and encountered the opposition of the Venetian clergy and the ducal seminary. It was on account of these difficulties that Jacopo Contarini's brother fell back on the idea of founding the first nucleus of a seminary in the Ospedaletto: in 1575 he employed Palladio for an altar there. See Giuseppe Ellero, "Interventi di Palladio sui luoghi pii. L'Ospedaletto," in *Palladio e Venezia*, 121–32. For his actions in the area of charity and social welfare, Giovanni Battista Contarini, during the plague, was called "pater pauperum." In addition, we draw attention to his ties with the Patriarch and with another important figure in the Venetian welfare scene, Andriana Contarini, the widow of Vincenzo Contarini, brother of Cardinal Gasparo.

139. See *Firenze e la Toscana dei Medici nell'Europa del Cinquecento. La Rinascita della scienza*, catalogue of the exhibit

(Florence, 1980), 160–61, entries 4.25, 4.26.

140. See Rose, "Jacomo Contarini," 121.

141. See Concina, "L'Arsenale, una fabbrica ininterrotta," 106.

142. See G. Cozzi, "La strada di San Marco ed un progetto di canale navigabile tra Adige e Adda," *Archivio Storico Lombardo* ser. 8, vol. 7, 84 (1957): 114–48, esp. 116–17.

143. BAM, MS A71 inf., on cc. 24ff. the "Facil modo" by Moleto; on cc. 30r ff. the *Discorso* by Jacopo Contarini. According to M. G. Sandri, Giulio Savorgnan's "doubts," which Contarini referred to, had to do with Palmanova. See Maria Grazia Sandri, "Nuovi contributi: lettera-testamento di Giulio Savorgnan al Doge," in the collection *Palmanova* (Istituto per l'Enciclopedia del Friuli Venezia Giulia, 1982), 236 n. 15.

144. The unpublished manuscript "Di Fortificatione" is in BEM, MS Gamma v. 4. 1 (9): in it, the author—whom Rose has recognized as Jacopo Contarini—exploits the teachings of Giulio Savorgnan and Buonaiuto Lorini (see especially c. 11r) and cites Palladio as the authority on construction problems (foundations, trusses, iron, see c. 18r). In BMV there are two codices containing designs for fortifications belonging to Jacopo Contarini: MS It., cl. 6, 188 = 10039 and 189 = 10031 (fig. 111).

145. See Antonio Manno, *Le mura di Venezia e la fortezza di San Nicolò al Lido*, forthcoming from the CISA.

146. On the relations between Giulio Savorgnan, Buonaiuto Lorini, Sforza Pallavicino, and Jacopo Contarini, see id., *Buonaiuto Lorini e la scienza delle fortificazioni*, forthcoming, with references to the preceding bibliography and rich, previously unpublished documentation.

147. Moleto, "Facil modo di tirar le linee," c. 27r. Moleto continues (c. 27r and v): "Ma di tutto à bocca poiché col aiuto di Dio sarò costí fra due settimane al piú. V. S. Il.ma mi fará favore singulare di rimandarmi questa lettera: accioché con questo principio posa un dí andar piú oltre; et a cose che a V. S. Il.ma non saranno discare. Conche a V. S. Il.ma bacio la mano et priego da Dio prosperità perpetua. Da Padova il 25 di Giugno del 1581."

148. BAM, MS A71 inf., c. 23r.

149. Ibid., c. 23v.

150. Giuseppe Moleto had, however, collaborated with Contarini on other occasions. In 1579 Moleto wrote G. Vincenzo Pinelli from Venice: ". . . Ho dato ad intendere a M. Gerardo l'instrumento del Contarini, mi dice che non solo ne farà che mostrino minuti, ma anco secondi, et in diversi modi, di modo che quando vorremo sbizzarrirci havermo il modo, ma aspetto che possi havere uno che lavori di ottone a farci l'instrumento da poterci metter dentro le rotule . . . " (BAM, MS S105 sup., c. 38r). It is worth noting that the epicenter of Venetian scientific correspondence was Pinelli, who was on cordial terms with Botero (see the *carme* that Botero sent Pinelli in MS. S93 sup. and the sonnet and other writings of Botero addressed to Pinelli from Milan in 1586, in MS S105 sup.). In MS A71 inf., c. 1r and v, there is a letter from Moleto to Pinelli (February 5, 1566) with a criticism of a work by Sepulveda on shadows in gnomons; on c. 2r and v Moleto compares his own Ptolemy in the vernacular with Ruscelli's, which he strongly criticized; on June 20, 1571, Moleto returned to Ptolemy to discuss the term *chorographia* (S105 sup., c. 27r and v); while many letters, written between 1579 and 1581, informed his friend of events related to the appearance of Moleto's new volume, published in Venice upon the order of the Council of Ten (S105 sup., cc. 31r; 35r; 49r; 51r and v; 53r). In his letter of January 14, 1580 (c. 51r and v), Moleto writes that "Le lettere delle SS.VV. non potranno se non essere grande scudo al libro et a quello che le dimostrazioni matematiche si fanno la strada per loro, è vero, ma tuttavia si troverà degli huomeni che contra a quelle ardiscono di dire et molto." Also in MS 105 sup., c. 33r and v, is a letter from Moleto to Pinelli, dated November 9, 1579, with news on the volumes regarding wind instruments written—according to a testimonial from Zarlino to Moleto—by Silvestro dal Fondaco, in addition to news on the *Musica ridotta alle moderna pratica*, published in Rome, in 1555, by

Nicola Vicentino. On a few of Pinelli's *Considerazioni* regarding the organization of cities, see M. G. Sandri "Schemi di conoscenza della città europea di G. V. Pinelli," a contribution to the *Seminario di storiografia urbana*, February 1982, published by the University of Milan.

151. Contarini, *Discorso di fortificazione*, c. 30r.

152. Puppi mentions the *Relatione dell' assedio di Parigi* by Fillippo Pigafetta (Rome, 1591) and reports in manuscript form on English fortresses, on the port of Livorno, on the fortresses of Candia, and on Swedish ports, in addition to a short treatise on ancient and modern fosse, BAM, S98 sup., Q122 sup., and R123 sup. See L. Puppi, *Scrittori vicentini d'architettura del secolo XVI* (Vicenza, 1973), 71 n. 234. Puppi also cautiously suggests that Pigafetta—proposing Valerio Chiericati as an alternative—was the source of the album containing drawings of fortified cities (which are actually very ingenuous and full of fantastic elements), preserved in the Biblioteca Bertoliana in Vicenza, G.3. 10.2 (Arte B283), dated 1582 on cc. 44 and 55, and signed by a "Marcus Verriccius Venetus" (c. 55). Filippo Pigafetta was a cousin of Valerio Chiericati and in 1553, when he was not much more than twenty years old, he embraced a career in the military, fighting for the Carafa in 1556, then in Paris (1561) and at Lepanto. Once again in Paris in 1566, he often visited the Studio: his many trips in Italy, Europe, and the Near East, undertaken as a military expert and political adviser to various Italian princes, alternated with an intense writing career. Pigafetta wrote an enormous quantity of political and military reports and he translated, in addition to the *Mechanicorum Liber*, many classics of military art. A friend of Sperone Speroni, he corresponded closely with Gian Vincenzo Pinelli, and in 1585, along with the Venetian ambassadors who were paying homage to Sixtus V, he visited Giulio Savorgnan's house in Venice; in 1592 he joined the service of the grand duke of Tuscany, Ferdinando de' Medici. On Filippo Pigafetta, see Giuliano Lucchetta, "Viaggiatori, geografi e racconti di viaggio dell'età barocca," in *Storia della cultur veneta. Il Seicento*, 4 : 2 : 201ff., esp. 203–15, with the preceding bibliography.

153. On Giulio Savorgnan's military expertise, see A. Carugo, "Gli obelischi e le macchine nel Rinascimento," in Domenico Fontana, *Della trasportazione dell' obelisco vaticano* [1590] (Milan, 1978), pp. XXXIX ff. Carugo transcribed and commented upon a letter from Savorgnan to Pigafetta, who had gone to Rome to observe the transport of the obelisk. Also see Manno, *Buonaiuto Lorini*.

154. See Guidobaldo del Monte, *Mechanicorum Liber* (Pesaro, 1577); It. trans., *Le mechaniche* (Venice, 1581). See also Rose, *The Italian Renaissance of Mathematics*, 230. On the significance of Guidobaldo del Monte's work and Pigafetta's translation, also see Luigi Spezzaferro, "La cultura del cardinal del Monte e il primo tempo di Caravaggio," *Storia dell'Arte* 9–10 (1971): 57–92.

155. See Rose, *Jacopo Contarini*, 124.

156. BMC, MS P. D. C 951, "Milizia navale e terrestre," n. 19: "Servizi militari del Co. Cap° Gio. Giacomo Leonardi da Pesaro." See Concina, *La macchina territoriale*, 80.

157. On Barozzi, see B. Boncompagni, "Intorno alla vita e ai lavori di Francesco Barozzi," *Bullettino di Bibliografia e di Storia delle Scienze Matematiche e Fisiche* 16 (1884): 795–848; "Barozzi Francesco," in *Dizionario Biografico degli Italiani*, vol. 6 (Rome, 1964), 495–99, but especially the very well documented essay by Rose, "A Venetian Patron and Mathematician of the Sixteenth Century," and the one, also excellent, by Carugo, 'L'insegnamento della metamatica," 153ff. (on Alessandro Piccolomini, see pp. 151–53). Barbaro sent the Latin edition of his Vitruvius to Barozzi (letter from Venice dated July 28, 1567), asking him to examine it and correct any errors; on August 22 of the same year Barozzi answered: "A lli 14 agosto mi fu data di V.S. Rev.ma insieme col suo bellissimo Vitruvio latino, il quale m'è stato carissimo si per le cose maravigliose che in se contiene, come per esser venuto dalle honoratissime mani di V.S. Rev.ma, alla qual'io porto tanta affetione per le varie virtú sue, che invero non

mi poteva capitare il piú caro e precioso dono. Io dunque lo vederò e rivederlò et non mi sentireò di veder et goder si belle et honorate fatiche di V.S. Rev.ma dalla qual reputo esser offeso quando mi scrive che al mio ritornar le potrò dire il mio parere, et correggere i suoi errori. Il mio parer è questo che havendo io già veduto quello che la fece stampar la prima volta, mi ha parso tanto perfetto che credo huomo del mondo non gli potrà mai opporre in cosa alcuna; et son certo che anchor questo ultimo sia molto piú perfetto et piú abondante di quello" (see Rose, "A Venetian Patron," 162). The work of Barozzi's that is dedicated to Daniele Barbaro bears the title *Opusculum: in quo una Oratio et duo Quaestiones, altera de Certitudine et altera De Medietate Mathematicarum continentur* (Padua, 1560). See Giulio Cesare Giacobbe, "Francesco Barozzi e la 'Quaestio de certitudine Mathematicarum," *Physis* 14, no. 4 (1972): 357–74. In 1561 Barozzi, who was from Candia, was one of the founders of the Accademia dei Vivi in Crete, and in 1565—66 he was in Bologna studying Greek manuscripts— especially Proclus and Hero of Byzantium—in the San Salvatore library, and became the friend of Gabriele Paleotti, Ulisse Aldovrandi, and Federico Commandino. After having passed about twenty years in Crete, Barozzi—who had returned to Venice to publish the *Cosmographia*, in which he confuses Sacrobosco's *Sphaera* and the *Admirandum Problema* (1585–86)—was arrested in 1587 by the Venetian Inquisition and accused of necromancy: see the text of the sentence in Boncompagni, "Intorno alla vita ed ai lavori di Francesco Barozzi," 837–47. In 1588, however, Barozzi was free and once again in Crete. Barozzi had translated for Jacopo Foscarini, the General Commissioner of Candia, the *Vaticinia Leonis* from a Greek codex acquired from Foscarini himself (Bodleian, MS, Barocci 170), becoming interested in the symbolism of hieroglyphics. Jacopo Contarini also acquired a codex of the *Vaticinia* (from the sixteenth century: BMV, MS Graecus 7, 3 = 546). See Rose, "A Venetian Patron," 144–45. Francesco Barozzi addressed about thirty letters, preserved in Paris, to Jacopo Contarini, Jacopo Foscarini, Cardinal Paleotti, Giuseppe Moleto, Ulisse Aldovrandi, and Paolo Sarpi.

158. On the mathematic circle in Padua, see Carugo, "L'insegnamento della matematica." One should also consider the hypothesis contained in the volume by Francesco Romano, *Studi e ricerche sul neoplatonismo* (Naples, 1983), 89–96, on the influence that the Platonic Averrosists of Padua—the so-called *"simpliciani"*— exerted upon the new methodology of Jacopo Zabarella and on the new physical and mathematical sciences. According to Romano, Marco Antonio de' Passerio, known as Il Genua, the teacher of Zabarella, contributed to liberating Aristotelianism from ilomorphism, "che inficiava di metafisica la philosophia naturalis." Genua's commentary on Aristotle's *De Anima* was published in Venice in 1576.

159. Commandino's translation appeared posthumously in 1588. On Barozzi's translation and the codex acquired by Jacopo Contarini, see Rose, "A Venetian Patron," 128–35.

160. Francesco Barozzi, *Admirandum Illud Geometricum Problema, Tredecim Modis Demostratum* (Venice, 1586), dedication p. 10. In this volume, Barozzi describes an instrument for drawing conic sections, resembling the "perfect" compass of the Arabs; he also gives a way of constructing the asymptotes of hyperboles, and constructed a couple of hyperboles with the same asymptotes and some curve of a superior degree with an asymptote. The volume, like much of Barozzi's research, documents a phase in the development of Renaissance ideas on problems of an infinitesimal nature.

161. See *Procli Diadochi Lycii . . . In Primum Euclidis Elementorum Commentariorum ad Universam Mathematicam Disciplinam . . . a Francesco Barocio expurgati* (Padua, 1560). The translation of Proclus's commentary on Euclid was a fundamental work for the development of Renaissance mathematics and was united, in its objectives, with the *Quaestio de Medietate Mathematicarum*, which, according to Rose, preceded Jacopo Mazzoni in its demonstration that Aristotle and Plato agreed in their opinion that

mathematics was important for science. (See Rose, "A Venetian Patron," 124.)

162. See M. Tafuri, "'Renovatio urbis Venetiarum': il problema storiografico," in "Renovatio urbis," 22, 25, and 49 n. 68.

163. Hero of Byzantium's *Poliorcetica* and *Dioptra* (tenth century) were translated by Barozzi under the title *Heronis Mechanici Liber De Machinis Bellicis, necnon Liber De Geodesia* (Venice, 1572).

164. See the letter preserved in the Bibliothèque Nationale in Paris, MS Lat. 7218, cc. 5–6, cited in Rose, "A Venetian Patron," 122–23.

165. See Giacobbe, "Francesco Barozzi."

166. Pietro Catena, *Universa loca in logicam Aristotelis in mathematicas disciplinas* (Venice, 1556). Catena, who died in 1576, gave lectures on the *Mechanics* in Padua, which were attended by Guidobaldo del Monte and Bernardino Baldi. See Rose, "Professors of Mathematics," 302.

167. See id., "The Accademia Venetiana," 225. On Galileo's contacts with Tartaglia, Guidobaldo del Monte, and Paolo Sarpi, also see Ludovico Geymonat, *Galileo Galilei* (Turin, 1957), 26–47. Benedetto Zorzi wrote to Baccio Valori: "Del Galileo intesi dal S. or Pinelli, et ho piacere che all'huomo si sia aperta la strada di mostrare in publico Studio sua dotrina. Qui dubito che la chatedra per questo'anno ancora sarà vuota, mancando massimamente questo soggetto del quale il Cl. mo Contarini et io tenivimo vivo il nome nella memoria de chi governa lo Studio; nel quale io per me vorrei vedere ed introdurre la lettura di Plantone . . . ." Cited in G. Cozzi, *Paolo Sarpi tra Venezia e l'Europa* (Turin, 1979), 148–49. On December 22, 1592, Jacopo Contarini wrote Galileo a letter congratulating him on the occasion of his inaugural lecture in Padua. See Carugo, "L'insegnamento della matematica," 186.

168. See ibid., 157.

169. Gianni Micheli, "L'assimilazione della scienza greca," in *Storia d'Italia Enaudi. Annali 3. Scienza tecnica nella cultura e nella società dal Rinascimento*

ad oggi, ed. G. Micheli (Turin, 1980), 201–57.

170. Puppi, *Andrea Palladio*, 2: 332.

171. Jacopo Contarini's letter is dated October 1st, 1573. See A. Manno, "Un magazzino di Andrea Palladio nell'Arsenale di Venezia," *Casabella* 49, no. 514 (1985): 30–33, although we do not agree with the author's analysis.

172. ASV, "Provveditori alle Fortezze," b. 20, reg. "Terminazioni" 1543–1593, c. 108r and v, transcribed in *Testimonianze veneziane*, 76–77 (entry 209). It is interesting to note that the document speaks of "misurationi dall'error da lui [Bortolo Luran] preso" affirmed by "li magnifici messer Andrea Bernardo e Giacomo Contarini esecutori delle fortificationi sopraditte et come appar nel libro delli mercati dell' officio a carta 49, che vi è notato il laudo dato da messer Andrea Palladio et da maistro Andrea Lion a maistro Antonio et Gasparo Tagliapietra . . . ." Palladio, moreover, was in Chioggia in 1574, perhaps for an arbitration on fortifications. See L. Puppi, "Professione e professionalità in Palladio," *Il Veltro* 23, no. 5–6 (1979): 564. One should not forget Palladio's theoretical interest in Polybius and Caesar, regarding which see the essay by J.R. Hale, "Andrea Palladio, Polybius and Julius Caesar," *Journal of the Warburg and Courtauld Institutes* 40 (1977): 240–55. Also see Burns, "Andrea Palladio, Jacopo Contarini." According to Corboz, finally, Palladio contributed to the plan of Hochelega that appeared in the third volume of *Delle Navigationi et Viaggi*, published in 1556 in Venice, ed. G.B. Ramusio. See A. Corboz, "Una città sognata. (Daniele Barbaro, Andrea Palladio e la pianta di Hochelaga, oggi Montreal)," *Palladio e Venezia*, 81–87.

173. Such a contrast appears in the essay by Vincenzo Fontana, "'Arte' e 'Isperienza' nei trattati d'Architettura Veneziani del Cinquecento," *Architectura* 8, no. 1 (1978): 49–72. On Rusconi see the graduate thesis (unpublished) by Maurizio Piasentini, "Un architetto dimenticato del secolo XVI: Giovannantonio Rusconi" (Istituto Universitario di Architettura di Venezia, 1978–79), with much unpub-

lished material, and Anna Bedon, "Il 'Vitruvio' di Giovan Antonio Rusconi," *Ricerche di Storia dell'Arte* 19 (1983): 85–90, which establishes that 1552 was the year Rusconi completed his translation of Vitruvius and emphasizes the affinity between the engravings in Rusconi's volume and those contained in Ovid's *Transformationi* translated by Ludovico Dolce and published by Giolito de' Ferrari in Venice in 1553. According to Anna Bedon, the codex preserved in the Marciana (Cod. It. 4 149 = 5105), whose two types of filigree guarantees its Venetian origin and 1552 as data post quem, can be attributed to Rusconi, on the basis of a calligraphic comparison. On the codex, which reproduces drawings from antiquity from other manuscript sources, also see L. Olivato, "Due codici 'veneti' cinquecenteschi d'architettura," *Arte Veneta* 32 (1978): 153–60; id., "Trattati inediti o poco noti di prospettiva e di architettura nelle bibioteche del Veneto," in the collection *La prospettiva rinascimentale. Codificazioni e trasgressioni* (Florence, 1980), 539–46. On the productive process of Palladian construction, see the excellent essay by L. Puppi, "Palladio in cantiere," *Bollettino del Cisa* 20 (1978): 157–69 (and, with bibliographical references, in *Il Veltro* 23, no. 5–6 [1979]: 559–73). Also see Mario Zocconi, "Il Palladio nel processo produttivo del Cinquecento veneto," *Bollettino del Cisa* 20 (1978): 171–202.

174. See Rossi, *I filosofi*, 54.

175. See F. Patrizi, *Della retorica dieci dialoghi* (Venice, 1562), partly preceded by *Le rime di Messer Luca Contile, divise in tre parti, con discorsi et argomenti di M. Francesco Patritio* (Venice, 1560), cc. 23r ff. This precedent is worth stressing because it refers us—also because of Luca Contile's mediation—to the years of the Accademia Venetiana. We are following here the interpretation of rhetoric that Patrizi gave Garin, in a polemic with the essay by Benedetto Croce, "Francesco Patrizio e la critica della retorica" (1903) in *Problemi di estetica e contributi alla storia dell'estetica italiana*, 2nd ed. (Bari, 1923), 229–310. See E. Garin, "Discussioni sulla retorica," in idem *Medioevo e*

Rinascimento. Studi e ricerche (Rome and Bari, 1980), 117ff.

176. Garin, "Discussioni Sulla retorica," 138.

177. In this connection see Aldo Stella, "La regolazione delle pubbliche entrate e la crisi politica veneziana del 1582," in *Miscellanea in onore di Roberto Cessi*, 2 (Rome, 1958), 157ff.; G. Cozzi, *Il doge Nicolò Contarini. Ricerche sul patriziato veneziano agli inizi del Seicento* (Venice and Rome, 1958), 2ff.; William J. Bouwsma, *Venice and the Defense of Republican Liberty. Renaissance Values in the Age of the Counter Reformation* (Berkeley and Los Angeles, 1968); It. trans. (Bologna, 1977), 119ff. See also Martin John Clement Lowry, "The Reform of the Council of Ten, 1582–83: an Unsettled Problem?" *Studi Veneziani* 13 (1971): 275–310 (which tends to minimize the scope of the "crisis"); Frederic C. Lane, *Venice. A Maritime Republic* (Baltimore, 1973), It. trans. (Turin, 1978), 450ff.; G. Benzoni, *Venezia nell'età della Controriforma* (Milan, 1973), 50ff.; Cozzi, *Repubblica Venezia*, 173, and n. 77, which criticizes Lowry's conclusions.

178. See Roberto Cessi and Annibale Alberti, *Rialto. L'isola, il ponte, il mercato* (Bologna, 1934), 191ff., and Ruggero Maschio, "Rialto," in *Architettura e utopia*, 119ff. Also see later in this volume, chap. 7.

179. See the transcription of the document in Cessi and Alberti, *Rialto*, 390–92.

180. Ibid., 411–14. One notes that Antonio da Ponte had challenged Palladio's assertion that the walls of the Sala dello Scrutinio were dangerous after the fire in the Palazzo Ducale of December 20, 1577.

Chapter 6

1. See Alberto Tenenti, "The Sense of Space and Time in the Venetian World of the Fifteenth and Sixteenth Centuries," in *Renaissance Venice*, ed. John R. Hale (London, 1973), 17–46, now in A. Tenenti, *Credenze, ideologie, libertinismi tra Medioevo ed Età Moderna* (Bologna, 1978), 75–118.

2. Daniele Barbaro, *I dieci libri dell'architettura di M. Vitruvio tradotti e commentati* (Venice, 1567), 270–71.

3. See Cristoforo Sabbadino, *Discorsi sopra la laguna*, in *Antichi scrittori d'idraulica veneta*, ed. Roberto Cessi, vol. 2, pt. 1 (Venice, 1930); Alvise Cornaro and C. Sabbadino, *Scritture sopra la laguna*, ibid., vol. 2, pt. 2 (Venice, 1941); *La difesa idraulic della laguna veneta nel secolo XVI, Relazioni dei periti*, eds. R. Cessi and N. Spada (Venice, 1952); Salvatore Ciriacono, "Scrittori d'idraulica e politica delle acque," In the collection *Storia della cultura veneta. Dal primo Quattrocento al Concilio di Trento*, eds. Girolamo Arnaldi and Manlio Pastore Stocchi, 3/2 (Vicenza, 1980), 491–512; Emilio Menegazzo, "Alvise Cornaro: un veneziano del Cinquecento nella terraferma padovana," ibid., 513–38; Paolo Morachiello, "Alvise Cornaro e Cristoforo Sabbadino: un dialogo sulle tecniche e sulla natura," in the collection, *Alvise Cornaro e il suo tempo*, catalogue of the exhibit, ed. Lionello Puppi (Padua, 1980), 130–35; Vincenzo Fontana, "Alvise Cornaro e la terra," ibid., 120–28; id., "Venezia e la laguna nel Cinquecento," *Casabella* 45, no. 465 (1981): 12–15; Sergio Escobar, "Il controllo delle acque: problemi tecnici e interessi economici," in *Storia d'Italia Einaudi. Annali 3*, ed. Gianni Micheli (Turin, 1980), 85ff. (esp., "Il controllo delle acque a Venezia nel '500," pp. 104ff.). Also see Barbara Mazza, "Politica lagunare di Venezia nel Cinquecento e interventi sul territorio: note di cartografia," in the collection *Architettura e utopia nella Venezia del Cinquecento*, ed. L. Puppi (Milan, 1980), 130–33 and entries on 134–43.

4. On the specialized nature of Sabbadino's capacities and on the novelty of his contribution in this area, see the important observations contained in Escobar's essay, "Il controllo delle acque," 131–36. Cristoforo Sabbadino distinguished his own knowledge of hydraulics from the knowledge held by the *inzegnere*, or engineers, and from the fresh water hydraulic technicians, the empirical technicians, and the architects. He wrote: "Vedessi pure che l'architettura, la scultura, la pittura e le altre arti manuali (ancor che le escano da bonissimi intelletti) non s'acordano cum il cresser e calar delle acque, e meno cum il navicar, pescar e conoscer le cose bisognose per conservar questa laguna; e questo si prova, si vede, ma non si crede, et a questi tali s'é data maggior fede e più credito, che ad uno che sia natto, nudrito et arlevato in l'acqua salsa, e che si mova cum le raggioni delle acque cum la cognition delli lochi e con la esperienza delle cose passate per lui vedute e praticate." Sabbadino, *Discorsi sopra la laguna*, 48.

5. Ciriacono, "Scrittori d'idraulica," 492ff.

6. Ibid., 503.

7. ASV, "Savi ed Esecutori alle Acque," Laguna 14. See *Architettura e utopia*, 137, entry 133.

8. Ibid.

9. See chapter 7 of this volume.

10. See v. Fontana, entry 137, in *Architettura e utopia*, 138–39.

11. Ibid. Also see Cornaro and Sabbadino, *Scritture sopra la laguna*, 88ff.

12. Menegazzo, "Alvise Cornaro," passim.

13. Sanudo, *Diarii*, 57 : 549. Menegazzo ("Alvise Cornaro," 528) adds that even the commission, entrusted to Falconetto, of building the gates of San Giovanni and Savonarola in Padua, as well as other public works in the city, was seen as a circumspect motion on the part of the *Signoria*, which suggests that Cornaro did some mediating. In this way—he remarks (ibid., note 57)—it is not necessary to refer to the "exemplary reform" by Falconetto that has been hypothesized by Carpeggiani. See Paolo Carpeggiani, "G. M. Falconetto. Temi ed eventi di una nuova architettura civile," in the collection *padova. Case e palazzi* (Vicenza, 1977), 71–99, esp. 95.

14. Menegazzo, "Alvise Cornaro," 529.

15. C. Sabbadino, *Deposizione circa gli argini Corner e Molin* (October 19, 1541), in Cornaro and Sabbadino, *Scritture sopra la laguna*, 83–87; Ciriacono, "Scrittori d'idraulica," 511.

16. Menegazzo, "Alvise Cornaro," 530–31.

17. See Giuseppe Fiocco, *Alvise Cornaro, il suo tempo e le sue opere* (Vicenza, 1965), 91, 94–95, and Menegazzo, "Alvise Cornaro," 536–37, that makes the observation that the 25,000 peasants who were occupied in land reclamation projects, mentioned by Fiocco, were not involved in any of the operations executed by Cornaro, but with those ordered by the Reclamation Commission, whose institution Cornaro attributes, although gratuitously, to his own *aricordi*, or report. On the institution of the Magistratura ai beni inculti [Magistracy for Land Reclamation], see Ivone Cacciavillani, *Le veneziane sul territorio 1471–1789. Boschi, fiumi, bonifiche e irrigazioni* (Padua, 1984), 123ff., 217–25.

18. Menegazzo, "Alvise Cornaro," 536.

19. See E. Menegazzo, "Altre osservazioni intorno alla vita e all'ambiente del Ruzante e di Alvise Cornaro," *Italia Medioevale e Umanistica* 9 (1966): p. 263; id., "Alvise Cornaro," 514. Cornaro said he was fifty-six years old in 1540, fifty-eight in 1542, seventy in 1551, seventy-four in 1552, seventy-five in 1554, seventy-three in 1555, eighty in 1557, eighty-five in 1559 and 1560, and ninety-five in 1565. In evaluating these inconsistencies one must, however, keep in mind what Febvre has said about the widespread ignorance that many people had about their exact birth date in the sixteenth century—an ignorance that Febvre has closely related to an age that was still dominated by a "more or less" vision of things. See Lucien Febvre, *Le problème de l'incroyance au XVIe siècle. La religion de Rabelais* (Paris, 1942); It. trans. (Turin, 1978), esp. 377–78.

20. See Menegazzo, "Alvise Cornaro," 537–38, which recalls, in order to challenge a reading of Cornaro as philanthropist, a passage of the *Vita sobria* that addresses the question of diet: ". . . E quel vecchio che per povertà non può havere di quelli [brodi, minestre di carne, polli, pernici, tordi, pesci, carni di vitello, capretto o castrato] può conservarsi con il pane, panatella ed ovo; ed invero non può amanchar al povero, se esso non è mendico, e, come si suol dire, furfante: e di questi non si debbe pensare, perché sono perve-

nuti a questo per sua dapocaggine, e stano meglio morti che vivi, perché abrutano il mondo. . . . "

21. ASV, "Savi ed Esecutoria alle Acque," b. 986, f. 4, cc. 23–25 (see the transcription in the appendix). See Nicola Mangini, *I teatri di Venezia* (Milan, 1974), 26–28. Lina Padoan Urban, "Gli spettacoli urbani e l'utopia," in *Architettura e utopia*, 145–46, 157–59; *Testimonianze veneziane di interesse palladiano*, catalogue of the documentary exhibition, ed. Maria Francesca Tiepolo (Venice, 1980), 14–15, entry 8. Ludovico Zorzi has proposed, cautiously however, that the "cittadella dello spettacolo" that Cornaro envisioned in the Bacino of San Marco dates back to the years when Sperone Speroni's ideas prevailed in the Accademia degli Infiammati in Padua: in 1546 Doni promoted the Florentine edition of the *Canace*, but the problem of the recovery of tragedy had been raised in 1524 by Gian Giorgio Trissino, with the first edition of the *Sofonisba*. Zorzi observed that the late date proposed by Mangini becomes questionable when one remembers that some of Cornaro's writings on the lagoon date back to 1540–41. This is true, but it is necessary to remember that Alvise Cornaro mentioned his project for the Bacino of San Marco in a work dating from circa 1566, as part of an organic plan for the new organization of Venice. Furthermore, one ought to consider the beginning of the work itself, which seems to suggest a preparation later than the one hypothesized by Zorzi. See Ludovico Zorzi, "Tra Ruzante e Vitruvio," in *Alvise Cornaro e il suo tempo*, 103 and 104 n. 9. A brief but very debatable reading of Cornaro's project can be found in the volume by Giovanna Curcio and Mario Manieri Elia, *Storia e uso dei modelli architettonici* (Rome and Bari, 1982), 289. Also see Giorgio Bellavitis and Giandomenico Romanelli, *Venezia* (Rome and Bari, 1985), 94.

22. The invitation to build a permanent theater seemed to echo the one that Sulpicio da Veroli addressed to Raffaele Riario in the dedication of his edition of Vitruvius's *De architectura*. After having recalled the cardinal's merits in the revival

of ancient spectacles, Sulpicio wrote: "Illud unum igitur superest, ut mediocrem locum ex Victruvii institutione constituas, in quo iuventus tibi deditissima ad maiorum se imitationem in recitandis poematis fabulisque actitandis in deorum honorem festis diebus exerceat, honestisque spectaculis et moneat populum et exilaret." Furthermore, he adds later on, the Rome that was refurbished by Sixtus IV and Innocent VIII asked to be completed by a theater, which was seen as essential to civic "virtue": "Quae cum ita sint quid aliud novi huic est saeculo reliquum? nisi ut aut fontes inducantur, aut theatrum aedificetur? Fontes vel tu postea, vel quivis alius cum multa utilitate gratiaque inducet. Nunc theatrum quin vel instaures vel novum construas cave ne differas, ne tantam expectationem et spem eludere videaris." It is interesting that Sulpicio da Veroli—like Alvise Cornaro later on, who perhaps was thinking of the petition that the *pomponiani* addressed to Riario—also united *fontes* and *theatrum* in indicating the public works he considered urgent for the city. On the *pomponiani* and classical spectacle, see Fabrizio Cruciani, *Teatro nel Rinascimento. Roma 1450–1550* (Rome, 1983), 219–27. (For Sulpicio's text, ibid., 224–25.)

23. On this subject, see Giuseppe Barbieri, " 'Co 'l giuditio e con la mente esperta': l'architettura e il testo," in the collection *Andrea Palladio. Il testo, l'immagine, la città,* catalogue of the exhibit, ed. L. Puppi (Milan, 1980), 17–26.

24. In some way, the theater that Cornaro envisioned for the Bacino of San Marco constituted a "consolidation" of the floating theaters of the world that were in use in Venice, an antecedent of which seems to have been the one constructed on May 27, 1493, in honor of Beatrice d'Este. A true "theatro largo e comodo," placed on two barges, appeared on July 17, 1530: the "macchina" crossed Venice and stopped on the shores of the Giudecca, where a *momaria* [a masked festival] was presented that had the theme of "uno mondo in forma di sphera, una città in forma di Veniexia, et il ninferno" (Sanudo, *Diarii*, 53:361). As one can see, the analogy between world, city, and

theater is transparent here. In 1542, Tiziano Minio would build a round theater for the Compagnia dei Sempiterni, always with the objective of representing the "macchina del mondo." See L. Padoan Urban, "Teatri e 'teatri del mondo' nella Venezia del Cinquecento," in *Arte Veneta* 20 (1966): 137–46; id., "Le feste sull'acqua a Venezia nel secolo XVI e il potere politico," in the collection *Il teatro italiano del Rinascimento*, ed. Maristella de Panizza Lorch (Milan, 1980), 483–505.

25. See Menegazzo, "Altre osservazioni intorno alla vita e all'ambiente del Ruzante e di Alvise Cornaro," 252–63.

26. "Elogio di Alvise Cornaro," in Alvise Cornaro, *Scritti sull'architettura*, ed. Paolo Carpeggiani (Padua, 1980), 71. Carpeggiani observes, questioning Menegazzo's interpretation ("Altre osservazioni," 258–59), that Cornaro did not maintain he had founded the Compagnia della Calza, but only that he had managed the activities of one of them, expressing some doubt about the fact that the one Cornaro belonged to was really "la prima che recitasse comedie" ["the first that performed comedies"] (Cornaro, *Scritti*, 71 n. 24).

27. See Fiocco, *Alvise Cornaro*, 58. In his self-praise, Alvise Cornaro mentions a theater that he had built in the territory of Loreo: ". . . finita la chacia, facea metere ad ordine una comedia, la quale se recitava nel suo teatro, che havea fabricato ad immitatione deli antichi, che il luogo de la sena lo face di pietra perpetuo, et l'altra parte, dove stavano li auditori, lo facea di tavole da potersi poi levare. Et tute le comedie reusivano benissimo, perché havea apreso di sé in casa sua huomeni molto ati al recitare, come fu quel famoso Ruzante." See E. Menegazzo, "Tre scritti di Alvise Cornaro," in the collection *Tra latino e volgare. Per Carlo Dionisotti* 2 (Padua, 1974), 610. Ruzante's *Dialogo facetissimo*, also known under the title of *Menego,* was performed in January 1529 "alla caccia" in Fosson, and therefore in the above-mentioned Loreo. See Giorgio Padoan, *La commedia rinascimentale veneta* (Venezia, 1982), 102 n. 79.

28. Zorzi, "Tra Ruzante e Vitruvio," 94. Also see the useful synthesis in id., "I

luoghi e le forme dello spettacolo," in L. Zorzi, Giuliano Innamorati and Siro Ferrone, *Il teatro del Cinquecento* (Florence, 1982), 5ff.

29. Paolo Carpeggiani, "Elogio dell'Empiria. Alvise Cornaro scrittore di architettura," in Cornaro, *Scritti*, 32.

30. Ibid., 19.

31. See Christoph Luitpold Frommel, "Raffaello e il teatro di Leone X," *Bollettino del Cisa* 16 (1974): 173–87; id., "Villa Madama," in C. L. Frommel, Stefano Ray, and M. Tafuri, *Raffaello architetto* (Milan, 1984), 311ff.

32. See P. Carpeggiani, "Teatri e apparati scenici alla corte dei Gonzaga tra Cinquecento e Seicento," *Bollettino del Cisa* 17 (1975): 101–18.

33. On the Palazzo Farnese in Piacenza see Bruno Adorni, *L'Architettura farnesiana a Piacenza 1545–1600* (Parma, 1982), 177ff. On the Capitoline theater, see F. Cruciani, *Il teatro del Campidoglio e le feste romane del 1513* (Milan, 1968); Arnaldo Bruschi, "Il teatro capitolino del 1513," *Bollettino del Cisa* 16 (1974): 189–218; Cruciani, *Teatro nel Rinascimento*, 406–34.

34. On Prisciani, see Aby Warburg, *Arte italiana e astrologia internazionale nel palazzo Schifanoja in Ferrara* (1912), reprinted in *La rinascita del paganesimo antico* (Florence,1966), esp. 264ff.; Antonio Rotondó, "Pellegrino Prisciani," *Rinascimento* 11, no. 1 (1960): 69–110; Agne Beijer, "An Early 16th Century Scenic Design in the National Museum, Stockholm, and its Historical Background," *Theatre Research* 4, no. 2 (1962): 85–155; Eugenio Battisti, "Il manoscritto sugli 'spettacoli' di Pellegrino Prisciano," *Necropoli* 8 (1970): 47–54; Robert Klein, *La forme et l'intelligible* (Paris, 1970); It. trans. (Turin, 1975) 326–28. See also Ferruccio Marotti, *Lo spettacolo dall'Umanesimo al Manierismo* (Milan, 1974), 53–77 (which continues the essay of Cesare Molinari, "Il teatro nella tradizione vitruviana: da Leon Battista Alberti a Daniele Barbaro" in *Biblioteca teatrale* 1 [1971]: 35–38]; Elena Povoledo, "La sala teatrale a Ferrara: da Pellegrino Prisciani a Ludovico Ariosto,"

Bollettino del Cisa 16 (1974): 105–38; id., "Origini e aspetti della scenografia in Italia," in Nino Pirrotta, *Li due Orfei. Da Poliziano a Monteverdi* (Turin, 1975), 368–69 and note on p. 371; L. Zorzi, *Il teatro e la città. Saggi sulla scena italiana*, 2nd ed. (Turin, 1977), 11–15 and passim.

35. See Klein, *La forme et l'intelligible*, 326.

36. See Giulio Ferroni, *Il testo e la scena. Saggi sul teatro del Cinquecento* (Rome, 1980), esp. chap. 1, "Percorsi della scena cortigiana," pp. 9–41.

37. A. Bruschi, "Ricostruzione e nota critica sull'architettura del teatro capitolino," in Cruciani, *Il teatro del Campidoglio*, 141–42.

38. See M. Tafuri, " 'Roma instaurata.' Strategie urbane e politiche pontificie nella Roma del primo '500," in Frommel, Ray, and Tafuri, *Raffaello architetto*, 78–79.

39. See Amedeo Quondam, "La scena della menzogna. Corte e cortigiano nel 'Ragionamento' di Peitro Aretino," *Psicon* 8–9 (1976): 4–23.

40. See Gaetano Cozzi, *Paolo Sarpi tra Venezia e l'Europa* (Turin, 1979), 141–42 and note 15. Cozzi has also observed that only in 1607, after the controversy of the Interdict and the expulsion of the Jesuits, was it possible for the normal performances of comedies to resume. Also see id., "Appunti sul teatro e i teatri a Venezia agli inizi del Seicento," *Bollettino dell'Istituto di Storia della Società e dello Stato veneziano* 1 (1959): 187–92. In that article, Cozzi cites an anti-Venetian treatise by Antonio Persio, published in 1607, in the midst of the polemic over the Interdict, which speaks of an "edificio di gran spesa a guisa di anfiteatro" and of lascivious comedies that provoked criticism from the Jesuits: according to Persio, the theater was burned and the comedies were once again prohibited. In 1577, furthermore, Zaccaria Contarini convinced the Senate to maintain a decree of expulsion for the "istrioni," and in 1581 Agostino Barbarigo persuaded the Council of Ten to prohibit comedies altogether. In addition, Cozzi observes that the "vecchi"

patricians and papalists also attacked theatrical representations.

41. See G. Padoan, *La commedia*, 20–23, 38–40, 62, 113–114, 140–43.

42. See Sanudo, *Diarii*, 7 : 701.

43. ASV, "Misti," reg. 32, c. 55v. See Giulio Bistort, *Il Magistrato alle Pompe nella Repubblica di Venezia. Studio storico* (Venice, 1912), 226, and Padoan, *La commedia*, 39n. 59.

44. Sanudo, *Diarii*, 7 : 701.

45. Ermolao Barbaro il Vecchio, *Orationes contra poetas. Epistolae*. ed. G. Ronconi (Florence, 1972), esp. 91–94.

46. See Padoan, *La commedia*, 113–14 and note 90, and p. 141 n. 11. The prohibition of 1533 found its excuse in a performance held for the marriage of Francesco Diedo. Sanudo called it "piacevole" ["pleasing"] (*Diarii*, 58 : 387). But the Council of Ten wrote that, on the contrary, in the above-mentioned "comedia over egloga . . . se interserivano parole tanto obsene et dishoneste, che pervenuta tal cosa a le orechie de li provvedadori nostri sopra le pompe come diligentissimi et che abhoriscono le spurcicie che sono stà dicte, et portali de ciò querella hano formato processo . . . " In February 1537, however, the Council of Ten also allowed the performance of two comedies: "l'una alla Zudheca et l'altra in questa città, per quanto dicono tute honeste et però meritando [i gentilhuomini e i virtuosi richiedenti] in ciò essere satisfacti, l'anderà parte che per auttorità di questo Consiglio sia permesso che recitar possano dicte do comedie tutavia da esser prima vedute et facte correger per li capi di questo Conseglio che in quelle non resti alcuna parola manco che onesta." ASV, "Consiglio dei Dieci, Parti Comuni," reg. 11, c. 194v. Padoan (*La commedia*, 142) observed that in 1537 Stefano Magno, who was a lover of theatrical texts, was Commissioner for Pomp.

47. See ibid., 209.

48. See Antonio Foscari, "Ricerche sugli 'Accesi' e su 'questo benedetto theatro' costruito da Palladio in Venezia nel 1565," *Notizie da Palazzo Albani* 8, no. 1 (1979): 68–83; Padoan, *La commedia*, 214–15; L. Padoan Urban, "Feste ufficiali e trattenimenti privati," in the collection *Storia della cultura veneta. Il Seicento* 4/1 (Vicenza, 1983), 595.

49. Foscari, "Ricerche," 83.

50. Marin Sanudo il Giovane, *De origine, situ et magistratibus urbis Venetae. ovvero La città di Venezia (1493–1530)*, critical edition edited by Angela Caracciolo Aricò (Milan, 1980), 37–38 (c. 18r and v of the original).

51. For a complete history of the water supply of Venice, see the excellent volume by Massimo Costantini, *L'acqua di Venezia. L'approvigionamento idrico della Serenissima* (Venice, 1984), which uses a vast inventory of unpublished documents in a critical manner. On the senatorial decree of 1425, see ibid., 29.

52. See ibid., 31–32, 52.

53. Ibid., 37–42. The transformation of the Brenta from a rushing river into a navigable canal, sanctioned in 1507 with the dam at Dolo, began in 1501 with the deviation canal of San Bruson-Conche–Canale di Montalbano. On October 11, 1505, the Collegio dei Savi ed Esecutori alle Acque approved a *parte* [portion] that planned the enlargement of the San Bruson deviation canal, the support of the Brenta above Moranzano, and the opening of the Lizza dike: as has been documented by Costantini (pp. 46ff.), this project would have to overcome notable political difficulties before it might be slowly executed—with modifications—partly in the sixteenth, partly in the seventeenth centuries.

54. Sabbadino, *Discorsi sopra la laguna*, 66–67.

55. See Costantini, *L'acqua di Venezia*, 55–59.

56. ASV, "Savi ed Esecutori alle acque," f. 122. "1546, Zener. Arichordo de io Zuan Batista de Zorzi. Dato in execution de la mia parte prexa nel excellentissimo Consiglio de Dieci." The document continues as follows: "Essendo tenuti gli habitanti per le ditte aque a loro condute ogni anno contribuir ala Signoria nostra, per occorrer ale cavation de canali, lagune, forteze et altre spexe de benefitio universale, ducati uno per el suo pozo essendo persone nobili, ducati uno e mezo

et similiter per li pozi che si fabricherano, da esser pagati a l'officio nostro sopra le aque ogni mexe de zener, principiandosi dal primo zener 1546, soto pena a cadaun de pagar altretanto de piui. Et de presente siano tenuti li piovani andar cum uno de li executori nostri sopra le aque, ogniun per la sua contrada et anotar de habitation in habitation sopra uno alfabeto li pozi et li suoi possessori azò in uno istante veder si possino quanto numero i sono et etiam cum presteza veder si possino do quelli el suo pagamento."

57. On the aqueduct projects mentioned in the text and on Temanza's judgment, see Costantini, *L'acqua di Venezia,* 103–4.

58. The idea of using water from the Sile would in fact become popular in the second half of the eighteenth century. See ibid., 104–5.

59. Cornaro–Sabbadino, *Scritture sopra la laguna,* 69. Also see Fiocco, *Alvise Cornaro,* 145ff.

60. See Federico Chabod, *Scrittii sul Rinascimento,* 2nd ed. (Turin, 1974), 49–50.

61. *Lettera di Girolamo Fracastoro sulle Lagune di Venezia* (to Alvise Cornaro), published by S. Stratico, Alvisopoli (Venice, 1815), 9–10.

62. G. B. Ramusio, *Delle navigationi et viaggi* 3 (Venice, 1556)..Also see the map of Temistitian in B. Bordone, *Isolario* 1 (Venice, 1528) c. 10r. See ibid., c. 8v, for the description of the city and its aqueducts (fig. 116).

63. See Mario Sartor, *La città e la conquista. Mappe e documenti sulla trasformazione urbane e territoriale dell'America centrale del '500* (Reggio Calabria and Rome, 1981), 28.

64. Ibid., 28–29.

65. A. Cornaro, "Scrittura sopra la regolazione dei porti" in ASV, "Savi ed Esecutori alle Acque," b. 986, "Piú scritture di Alvise Cornaro. Scrittura terza." See Cornaro and Sabbadino, *Scritture sopra la laguna,* 58, and *Architettura e utopia,* 140–41, entry 140.

66. Sanudo, *De origine,* 20 (c. 8r).

67. See *Laguna, lidi, fiumi. Cinque secoli di gestione delle acque,* catalogue of the documentary exhibit of the Archivio di Stato in Venice, ed. Maria Francesca Tiepolo (Venice, 1983), 17, entry 4.

68. *Oratio in funere Leonardi Lauretani (1521, Die 25 Junii)* in Andreae Naugerii, *opera omnia* (Patavii, 1718), 36. Also see what Gasparo Contarini said: "At venetiarum situs divino potius quodam consilio, quam humana industria praeter fidem eorum omnium qui eam civitatem non videre, et ab omni hostili impetu terra marique tutissimus est" in G. Contarini, *De magistratibus et republica Venetorum* (Parisiis, 1543), 2. Doni also wrote: "Siamo liberi come la Città, e la nostra stanza dell'Accademia è cinta dal mare Adriatico e non ha tante muraglie che la serrino." Anton Francesco Doni, *La Zucca* (Venice, 1565), book no. 2, p. 2. As for Alvise Cornaro, he called the lagoon "sante mura" and "meraviglioso Lago," "sempre vigilantissimo Custode dell'immaculata verginità di questa sacrosanta figliuola di Dio: e custode sí perfetto, che in lei non vi debba mai lasciar penetrare pur gli terrori e spaventi, Noncij della guerra. . . . " (A. Cornaro, *Trattato di aqcue* (Padua, 1560), c. 3r). Note that Plato, in *The Laws* (6, 20) had recommended a city without walls. See Plato, *Opere complete,* vol. 7, 2nd ed. (Rome and Bari, 1979), 208–9.

69. See L. Puppi, *Michele Sanmicheli architetto di Verona* (Padua, 1971), 73–74; Ennio Concina, *Chioggia. Saggio di storia urbanistica dalla fondazione al 1870* (Treviso, 1977), 92–95; id., *La macchina territoriale. La progettazione della difesa nel Veneto del Cinquecento* (Rome and Bari, 1983), 66ff., 111–18.

70. Francesco Sansovino, *Delle cose notabili che sono a Venezia* (Venice, 1561), c. Iv. But also see A. Guisconi (F. Sansovino), *Tutte le cose notabili e belle che sono in Venezia* (Venice, 1556), p. 3. As Doglio has remarked, Francesco Sansovino mentions here the legendary words of Mariano Sozzini to the Pope. See Maria Luisa Doglia, "La letteratura ufficiale e l'oratoria politica," in *Storia della cultura veneta. Il Seicento* 4 : 1 : 166. Cornaro also wrote, in his *Scrittura in difesa della laguna e del porto,* dated February, 7, 1565:

"Neppur la potente Romana, se ben fu capo del mondo, non si poté conservare, che si sarebbe conservata se in luogo di mura fosse stata cinta da una laguna, come è questa, perché questa è la vera fortezza essendo di acqua, che è ellemento eterno e incorrottibile, sí come le mura sono di materia frale e corrottibile. Oh glorioso e grande Iddio e signor Gesú Christo, quanto ti siam noi tenuti, che ci hai fatto nascere in una città libera e vergine, se bene è attempata, et in città inexpugnabile." See Fiocco, *Alvise Cornaro*, 136. Cornaro seems to be paying homage to traditional Venetian mythology here by contradicting the proposals that he had made in *Scrittura sopra la regolazione dei porti*, (reprinted in Fiocco, *Alvise Cornaro,* 141ff.).

71. Cited in Escobar, "Il controllo delle acque," 104.

72. C. Sabbadino, *Opinion o modo di salvar la laguna* (1549), in id., *Discorsi sopra la laguna*, 138.

73. See Escobar, "Il controllo delle acque," 137. Sabbadino was opposed to Cornaro's idea of restricting the lagoon within precise and fixed limits, writing:" . . . e io dico de sí, perché il ruinar delle mura di Venetia altro non è che amonir la laguna, e sia in qual parte si voglia di quella, però che tante occupano la laguna cento burchielle di terreno, gettate tra il porto di Malamocco e quel di Chiggia, quanto appresso di Venetia" (Sabbadino, *Discorsi sopra la laguna*, 26). Sabbadino, responding to Cornaro further on, offers a precise theoretical model for the lagoon, from which follows the harmfulness of the embankment that his antagonist was proposing. Sabbadino wrote (ibid., 122): "Egli chiama e intende laguna quanto si vede di acqua salsa scoperta fuori degli canedi, et io chiamo et intendo laguna tanto quanto l'acqua, che viene dal mare, ascende e puol ascender con le sue crescentie e comune e soracomune. . . . Hor volendo lui quella parte, ch'egli intende laguna, conservar, consiglia che 'l si faci l'arzere e canali soprascriti. Dico io ch'egli propone non solo cosa dificilissima e quasi impossibile a farsi, ma cosa dannosissima quando la si facesse." On theoretical problems of hydraulics in the debate between Sabbadino and Cornaro, see Escobar, "Il controlle delle acque," 139ff.

74. See Gunter Schweikhart, "Studien zum Werk des Giovanni Maria Falconetto," *Bollettino del Museo Civici di Padova 57* (1968): 17–67; Giulio Bresciani Alvarez, "Le fabbriche di Alvise Cornaro," in *Alvise Cornaro e il suo tempo*, 36–57; id., "Alvise Cornaro e la fabbrica del Duomo di Padova," ibid., 58–62; G. Schweikhart, "La cultura archeologica di Alvise Cornaro," ibid., 64–71; also see Carpeggiani, "G. M. Falconetto. Temi ed eventi."

75. See Fritz Eugen Keller, "Alvise Cornaro zitiert die Villa des Marcus Terentio Varro in Cassino," in *L'Arte* 14 (1971): 29–53, and Schweikhart, "La cultura archeologica di Alvise Cornaro."

76. Francesco di Giorgio, Codice Torinese Saluzziano, 148, f. 25. See Francesco Di Giorgio Martini, d*Trattati di architettura, ingegneria arte militare*, ed. Corrado Maltese, vol. 1 (Milan, 1967), illustration 45 and pp. 107–8.

77. Leon Battista Alberti, *I libri della famiglia*, eds. Ruggiero Romano and Alberto Tenenti, 2nd ed. (Turin, 1972), esp. 243–45, which points out that the contrast between the idealization of the villa and the "fury" of the city tends to cancel itself out in the *De re aedificatoria*; see the edition edited by Giovanni Orlandi (Milan, 1966), 2: 793. On this theme, see the essay by Gianni Venturi, "'Picta poesis': ricerche sulla poesia e il giardino dalle origini al Seicento," in *Storia d'Italia Eniaudi. Annali 5. Il paesaggio*, ed. Cesare De Seta (Turin, 1982), 665ff.

After the publication of the first edition of the present book I became aware of the very well-documented volume by Emilio Lippi, *Cornariana. Studi su Alvise Cornaro* (Padua, 1983), which on pp. 51–92 discusses the redaction dates of the *Trattato di architettura*, with more precise information of Carpeggiani's hypotheses. Lippi, in his essay "Una lettera di Alvise Cornaro al Fracastoro," in *Studi offerti a Gianfranco Contini dagli allievi pisani* (Florence, 1984), 141–59, publishes a letter from Cornaro to Fracastoro (1550), which confirms the dating given in the present chapter. In that letter, in fact, Cornaro opposes his friend's idea, which was to create new islands (pp. 158–59). Lippi observes (p. 159 n. 43) that Fracastoro also anticipated the idea of bringing an aqueduct of fresh water to Venice.

We would like to add to the bibliography on Prisciani in note 34 the essay by Giuliana Ferrari, "Il manoscritto 'spectacula' di Pellegrino Prisciani," in *La corte e lo spazio: Ferrara estense* 4, eds. Giuseppe Papagno e Amedeo Quondam (Rome, 1982), 431–49.

Chapter 7

1. As Paolo Preto has demonstrated, the plague of 1576–77 had important political consequences in Venice. On the one hand, it helped strengthen the role of the Council of Ten and the centralizing and oligarchic tendencies; on the other hand, it led to the maturation of the *giovani*. See Paolo Preto, *Peste e società a Venezia nel 1576* (Vicenza, 1978), 144–51. Pullan has observed, furthermore, that the temporary demographic block created by the plague led to a prolonged economic recession, also because of the additional factors of crisis and stagnation that appeared in the last decades of the century. See Brian Pullan, "Wage-Earners and the Venetian Economy 1550–1630," *The Economic History Review* series 2, 16 (1964): 407–26, reprinted in *Crisis and Change in the Venetian Economy in the Sixteenth and Seventeenth Centuries*, ed. B. Pullan (London, 1968), 146–74. See also, in this connection, Preto, *Peste*, 131ff. In some way, the large urban projects to which we are dedicating this chapter seem to constitute a reaction to the plague of 1576–77 as well as an attempt to respond to the crisis it produced. On the plague in Venice also see the collection, *Venezia e la Peste 1348–1797*, catalogue of the exhibit (Venice, 1979), and P. Preto, "La società veneta e le grandi epidemie di peste," in *Storia della cultura veneta. Il Seicento* 4/2 (Vicenza, 1984), 377–406.

2. Regarding Vincenzo Scamozzi's project, see, in addition to the texts by Cessi and Alberti and Ruggero Maschio, cited in this book in note 178 of chapter 5, the entry . . . 224 in *Andrea Palladio, 1508–1580. The Portico and the Farmyard*, ed.

Howard Burns, in collaboration with Lynda Fairbairn and Bruce Boucher (London, 1975), 126–28, and Douglas Lewis, *The Drawings of Andrea Palladio* (Washington, 1980), 208–209.

3. See doc. 21, in Roberto Cessi and Annibale Alberti, *Rialto. L'isola, il ponte, il mercato* (Bologna, 1934), 391.

4. See Donatella Calabi, "La direzione del nuovo ponte di Rialto e il 'negotio' degli stabili di San Bartolomeo," *Bollettino dei Civici Musei Veneziani*, n. s., 27, no. 1–4 (1982): 55–66. On Antonio da Ponte, see the unpublished graduate thesis, under the direction of Paolo Morachiello by Brigida Balboni and Paola Martinelli, "Antonio da Ponte proto al Sal: 'L'acconciar' e le nuove 'fabbriche.' Ponte di Rialto e Prigioni," (IUAV, Dipartimento di Storia dell'Architettura, 1982–83), with a wealth of unpublished documentation.

5. See Calabi, "La direzione del nuovo ponte," 60ff.

6. Ibid., 61.

7. Alvise Zorzi di Benetto (1515–93), who is not to be confused with Alvise Zorzi di Paolo, who died in 1616 and supported the anti-Roman cause, was surely the commissioner who opposed Marcantonio Barbaro and Scamozzi's project, as Calabi and Morachiello have observed on the basis of well-founded evidence. See D. Calabi and P. Morachiello, "Rialto: 'sacrario' da conservare o da rinnovare?" in Lionello Puppi and Giandomenico Romanelli, eds., *Le Venezie possibili. Da Palladio a Le Corbusier*, catalogue of the exhibit (Milan, 1984), 54ff. Alvise di Benetto was Provveditore Generale [General Commissioner] in Corfu in 1571 and captain in Padua; on February 5, 1591 *m.v.* (= 1592), he was elected Procuratore de ultra. In 1579, the nuncio Alberto Bolognetti described him as a "senatore di grandissima autorità e molto favorevole alle cose della Chiesa"; in 1588 Alvise spoke in favor of the request submitted by nine cardinals to Sixtus V, maintaining that the patricians could easily serve two masters. However, as Paul Grendler has noted, in 1586 and in 1587 he joined Leonardo Donà against the Pope, in a matter pertaining to ecclesiastical benefices that in-

volved the patriarch Giovanni Trevisan: one notes that on that occasion Leonardo Donà condemned the power and wealth of the clergy as being dangerous to the freedom of the Republic. See P. F. Grendler, "The 'Tre Savi sopra Eresia' 1547–1605; a prosopographical study," *Studi veneziani*, n. s., 3 (1979): 321–22, n.56. Alvise Zorzi di Paolo was cited instead, along with Nicolò Contarini, Antonio Querini, and Alessandro Zorzi, as a dangerous adversary of the Church in *Relatione dello Stato, costumi, disordini et remedii di Venetia* (BMC, Cod. Cicogna 2989–90), which may have been written by a cleric at the end of the Interdict. See G. Cozzi, *Il doge Nicolò Contarini, Ricerche sul patriziato veneziano agli inizi del Seicento* (Venice and Rome, 1958), 71 n. 1. Also see pp. 103–4 and 108 for the role that Zorzi played within the Sarpian group and during the discussions of 1607: on this last occasion, he found himself taking the same side as Antonio Querini and Nicolò Contarini against the conciliatory hypothesis suddenly proposed by Leonardo Donà.

It is interesting to note that, also in the case of the Rialto bridge, Leonardo Donà expressed a position that contrasted with that of Marcantonio Barbaro. In fact Alvise Michiel reports that, on January 2, 1587 (*m.v.*), after a report of the commissioners for the bridge, in Pregadi, "questo contradisse m. Lunardo Donado dicendo, che dovevano prima dare informatione al Cons.o questo fú in sostanza, poi parlò tanto fuori del Cons.o che stancò tutti girando tutte le cose del Mondo, il pericolo, che havevano de una guerra; che bisognava sparagnare il danaro *accennando il fare il Ponte di legno, overo acconciar questo al meglio si poteva*, rispose m. Marc'Antonio Barbaro dando conto di quanta spesa, e del modo che si farà assai particolarmente, si che il Cons.o restò soddisfatto; rispose m. Alberto Badoer K.r circa le cose de Donado, replicò m. Giacomo Foscarini K. Proveditor . . . si che si stette sino alle 6 hore. . . ." (Our emphasis.) Following the results of the vote, which favored Barbaro and Foscarini, Michiel adds: "Nota che fu grandissimo rumore non volendosi udire quelli, che impugnavana il Ponte, et il Donado, et il

Badoer erano in tanta colera che rabiavano." Alvise Michiel, *Diarij delle cose della Repubblica di Venetia degli anni 1587–88*, in BMC, Cod. Cicogna 2556, 1587, January 2. Thus for Leonardo Donà the optimal *imago* for the Rialto bridge was also the one handed down by tradition.

8. See Giovanni Scarabello, *Carcerati e carceri a Venezia nell'età moderna* (Rome, 1979). Scarabello rightly remarks that the construction of the Prigioni Nuove (fig. 119), while constituting "il coronamento del processo di stutturazione delle istituzioni carcerarie veneziane" did not inaugurate a new governmental policy for the prisons in Venice, remaining within an institution that distrusted centralized organs and that saw in each individual negotiation an element that strengthened and further unified the State. See pp. 28, 80–86. On the new prisons also see Umberto Franzoi, *Le prigioni della Repubblica di Venezia* (Venice, 1966); id., "Le Prigioni," in the collection *Piazza San Marco. L'architettura, la storia e le funzioni* (Padua, 1970), 173–75; Balboni and Martinelli, *Antonio da Ponte*.

9. See Ennio Concina, *L'Arsenale della Repubblica di Venezia* (Milan, 1984), 154ff.

10. Ibid., 158.

11. See Cozzi, *Il doge Nicolò Contarini*, 3ff., and P. F. Grendler, *The Roman Inquisition and the Venetian Press, 1540–1605* (Princeton, N.J., 1977; It. trans. Rome, 1983), 74, 133, 244, 287.

12. On the complex events of Palmanova the essay by Horst de la Croix remains fundamental, "Palmanova: a Study in Sixteenth Century Urbanism," *Saggi e memorie di Storia dell'Arte 5* (1966): 23–41. Also see Loredana Olivato, "Contributo alla genesi progettuale di Palmanova: il ruolo di Giulio Savorgnan," *Memorie storiche forogiuliesi 56* (1976): 93–110, and the collection *Palmanova*, 3 vols. (Istituto per l'Enciclopedia del Friuli Venezia Giulia, 1982). New documentary material has been revealed in John Bury's paper, "Nuove informazioni su Palmanova in uno scritto inedito di architettura militare dell'epoca," given at the Seminario Internazionale, *L'Architettura mili-*

tare veneta del Cinquecento (CISA: Venice, August 29, 1984).

13. See Grendler, *The Roman Inquisition*; Cozzi, *Il doge Nicolò Contarini*; id., *Paolo Sarpi tra Venezia e l'Europa* (Turin, 1979). Also see id., "Books and Society," *Journal of Modern History* 51 (1979): 86–98, which reviews Grendler's volume (90–96) and contains criticisms we find valid.

14. Grendler, *The Roman Inquisition*, 290–91.

15. Ibid., 291.

16. Ibid.

17. See William J. Bouwsma, *Venice and the Defense of Republican Liberty. Renaissance Values in the Age of Counter Reformation* (Berkeley and Los Angeles, 1968); It. trans. (Bologna, 1977), 349–51. Bellarmino wrote: "Se Christo instituí dal principio la Chiesa in forma di Republica, ha errato la Chiesa, che lassata la forma data da Dio, si è mutata in Monarchia. Se la Monarchia è meglio che la Repubblica, et però si è fatta mutatione, dunque, ha errato Christo in dargli la forma di Republica. . . . Se Christo è Re, il Papa Suo Vicario generale, dunque la Chiesa non si governa a modo di Republica ma a modo di Regno. . . ." Roberto Bellarmino, *Riposta alla difesa delle otto proposizioni di Giovan Marsilio Napolitano* (Rome, 1606), 165. Giovanni Marsilio, who wrote in defense of Venice, answered that the Church had degenerated from the primitive republican form into a princedom, while Venice had maintained her original perfection. He observes: ". . . gli Editti che uscirono nella primitiva Chiesa à nome di Republica, hora si fanno à nome d'uno solo, il che se significa mutatione, dicalo lo istesso Signore, che lo nega." Giovanni Marsilio, *Difesa a favore dell'otto propositioni* (Venice, 1606). An alternative to Bouwsma's interpretation of the contrast between Venice and Rome is offered in the essay by A. D. Wright, "The Venetian View of Church and State: Catholic Erastianism?" *Studi secenteschi* 19 (1978): 75–106. Bouwsma's book has been criticized rather severely, and with well-founded arguments, by Renzo Pecchioli, in *Studi veneziani* 13 (1971): 693–708.

18. The pontifical nuncio wrote in 1583, with obvious vexation: "In tanta confusione delle cose [Venezia ha adottato il suo nuovo ordinamento] ch'il Senato intenda successivamente tutti li negotii che passano giornalmente con Principi et che col voto di piú di duecento teste, che sono di questo corpo, si rispondi et deliberi quanto occorrerà onde s'aspetta di sentir molte impertinenze et infiniti disgusti, oltre ad una tediosa longhezza che si vedrà nelle espeditioni, essendosi non solo abolita tutta l'auttorità del Consiglio di X, ma limitata in gran parte quella del Collegio." See Bouwsma, *Venice and the Defense*, 187. On the influence that Bodin's ideas exerted upon Paolo Sarpi and on the conception of the State that the latter held, see the stimulating volume by David Wooton, *Paolo Sarpi between Renaissance and Enlightenment* (Cambridge and London, 1983), which contains hypotheses different from Bouwsma's.

19. On Scamozzi's Procuratie Nuove, see especially Vincenzo Scamozzi, *L'Idea dell'architettura universale* (Venice, 1615), pt. I. Book I, chap. 15, p. 52; Book 3, chap. 6, p. 243, chap. 18, pp. 302–3, chap. 20, p. 314; pt. 2, Book 6, chap 7, p. 20; Filippo Scolari, *Della vita e delle opere dell'architetto Vincenzo Scamozzi* (Treviso, 1837), 29–31; Giuseppe Cadorin, *Pareri di XV Architetti e notizie storiche intorno al Palazzo Ducale di Venezia* (Venice, 1858), 173–81; Franco Barbieri, *Vincenzo Scamozzi* (Vicenza, 1952), 101, 128–29, 154–55; Wladimir Timofiewitsch, "Ein Beitrag zur Baugeschichte der 'Procuratie Nuove,'" in *Arte Veneta* 18 (1964): 147–51; Tito Talamini, "Le Procuratie Nuove," in *Piazza San Marco*, 177–84; Giovanni Battista Gleria, "Vincenzo Scamozzi e Venezia," unpublished graduate thesis under the direction of M. Tafuri (IUAV, Dip. di Storia, 1981–82), 74–201. As an example of a gratuitous and unverified interpretation, see Enrico Guidoni and Angela Marino, *Storia dell'urbanistica. Il Cinquecento* (Rome and Bari, 1982), 248–49.

20. ASV, "Senato Terra," fil. 81, September 27, 1580; ibid., December 10, 1580. See Pietro Selvatico, *Sulla architettura e sulla scultura in Venezia dal Medio Evo*

sino ai nostri giorni (Venice, 1847), 345ff., and ASV, "Procuratia de supra," b. 65, proc. 142, c. 11r and v. On the decision of 1565 regarding the Library, see Deborah Howard, "Two notes on Jacopo Sansovino," *Architectura* 2 (1974): 137ff. In 1562 the requirement that the Procurators live in their houses on the Piazza was reaffirmed. See ASV, "Procuratia de supra," b. 65, proc. 142, cc. 7r and 8r.

21. Ibid., reg. 135, c. 41v (30 May 1581).

22. Ibid., cc. 24v–25v (January 15, 1580, *m.v.*), published in Selvatico, *Sulla architettura*, 345–46 (our emphasis).

23. ASV, "Procuratia de supra," reg. 135, cc. 29v–30r.

24. Ibid., cc. 32v–33r.

25. Ibid., c. 43v.

26. Ibid. See Selvatico, *Sulla architettura*, 346–47.

27. ASV, *Procuratia de supra*, reg. 136, c. 5v (April 5, 1582).

28. On Vincenzo Scamozzi's culture, especially the period of his youth, see V. Scamozzi, *Taccuino di viaggio da Parigi a Venezia (14 marzo–11 maggio 1600)*, ed. Franco Barbieri (Venice and Rome, 1959); Carmine Jannaco, "Barocco e razionalismo nel trattato di architettura di Vincenzo Scamozzi," *Studi secenteschi* 2 (1961): 47–60; L. Puppi, "Vincenzo Scamozzi trattatista nell'ambito della problematica del Manierismo," *Bolletino del Cisa* 9 (1967): 310–29; id., "Sulle relazioni culturali di Vincenzo Scamozzi," *Ateneo Veneto* 7, no. 1–2 (1969): 49–66; id., *Scrittori vicentini d'architettura del secolo XVI* (Vicenza, 1973), 73–76, 97–105 (*Discorso intorno alle parti dell'architettura* by Scamozzi, already published in *Tutte le opere di architettura* by Serlio, Venice 1600); C. Jannaco, "I 'Discorsi sopra l'Antichità di Roma' di Vincenzo Scamozzi," *Studi secenteschi* 17 (1976): 97–100; Angelo Fabrizi, "Vincenzo Scamozzi e gli scrittori antichi. (Studio sui Sommari inediti)," ibid., 101–52.

29. See Girolamo Porro, "Lettera a Jacopo Contarini" (November 20, 1581), preface to V. Scamozzi, *Discorsi sopra l'Antichità di Roma* (Venice, 1582), regarding which see Jannaca, "I 'Discorsi.'"

30. ASV, "S. Nicola da Tolentino," b. 20, mazzo 9, proc. 340, cc. 9r–12r.

31. We are referring to Scamozzi's annotations to *I dieci libri dell'architettura di M. Vitruvio tradotti e commentati da Mons. Daniele Barbaro* (Venice, 1567), in the copy preserved in the BAV, Cicogn. 4, 718, regarding which see Leopoldo Cicognara, *Catalogo ragionato dei libri d'arte e di antichità posseduti dal conte Cicognara*, vol. I (Pisa, 1821), 133. Scamozzi's annotations prove how vast his erudition was as a young architect, with references to Aristotle's *Physics*, Averroes, Plutarch, Herodotus, Pliny, Leon Battista Alberti, Pausani, Bertani, Serlio, Guido Polluce's *Dizionario*, Titus Livy, Dürer, Hero of Alexandria, and Buteone. The notes on Barbaro were linked to the birth of Scamozzi's grandiose project to organize organically in an enormous *schedario* the historical, technical, philosophical, and literary sources with which the architect from Vincenza expected to legitimate his own *scientia*. See, in this connection, Fabrizi, "Vincenzo Scamozzi," which analyses the codex in the BMV, Cod. It. cl. 4, 28 = 5602, with Scamozzi's *Sommari* of 1586, used in the *Idea*.

32. ASV, "Procuratia de supra," reg. 136, c. 40r. ". . . Li clarissimi signori Procuratori de Supra della chiesa de San Marco danno al pubblico incanto a chi offerirà a far per minor pretio l'infrascritto lavoro per la fabrica si fa da far da novo delle case di signori Procuratori giusta la forma della Libraria, il conduttor che torra a far la sudetta sarà obligato a fare ditta faziata di fattura di piera viva giusta la forma et misura, et con quelle istesse sagome che è la sopradetta facciata, et porticale, et le boteghe sotto di detto portichale, sino sotto al peduzo di volto, qual faziata anderà fino alla ultima cornice si come sono la sudeta . . ." On September 3, 1582, Vincenzo Scamozzi was paid 50 ducats for having "fatto diversi dissegni et modelli nella materia del fabricarsi le fabriche nuove delli Clarissimi Signori Procuratori" (ibid., reg. 136, c. 34r). Immediately after the estimates were published for the "restante delle fondamente della Libraria che si ha da far dove era la Beccaria

vechia" (ibid., c. 34v), in order to "far la riva sul Canal Grande per mezo la Cecha dove era la Beccaria vechia" (ibid., c. 36r), for the "fondamenta per le due case delli clarissimi signori Procuratori quale si hanno da far da novo qual fo ordinata dal proto" (ibid., c. 37v).

33. On June 6, 1581, it was decided in Procuratia that the three men elected to supervise the new buildings–Marcantonio Barbaro, Federico Contarini, and Andrea Dolfin–"habbino a trattar il concambio col prior dell'hospetaletto, et ridurlo alla conclusione" (ibid., reg. 135, c. 43v). On the same day, the three elected procurators "hanno poste se per le cause ben considerate da tutte sue signorie eccellentissime si dè gettar giú tanto spatio delle fabriche vechie comenzando dall'hospedaletto . . ." (ibid., c. 44r): they decided to begin with only two houses. In the expert report of December 6, 1587, Scamozzi maintained that the new construction site of the Procuratie was linked to the "tre archi vechi" of Sansovino's Library, with a projected extension of ten arches (ibid., b. 65, proc. 142, c. 30r): since the contract of September 1582 concerned four bays, the last six probably corresponded, at least in part, to the ancient offices of the Procuratia.

34. Ibid., reg. 136, c. 104v (January 15, 1583, *m.v.*), payment to Scamozzi; ibid., reg. 137, c. 13r (July 11, 1584), approval of the "mercato della fabriche delle case" for Martin di Rigotti stonemason, which was decided on February 17, 1583 (*m.v.*). In order to place Scamozzi exactly in the ambit of the Venetian patriciate, one ought to note that the architect returned to Rome in 1585, following the ambassadors who had been invited for Sixtus V's election to the papacy: those involved were Marcantonio Barbaro, Jacopo Foscarini, Marino Grimani, and Francesco Donà. See Scamozzi, *L'Idea*, pt. I, Book 2, chap. 5, p. 113, and Sansovino and Stringa, *Venetia città nobilissima* (Venice, 1604), c. 416r. Also see the letter from Scamozzi to the Duke of Urbino, dated May 13, 1585, published in Puppi, "Sulle relazioni culturali," 64–65.

35. ASV, "Procuratia de supra," reg. 137, c. 118r. Our emphasis.

36. See above, note 32.

37. ASV, "Procuratia de supra," reg. 136, c. 34v.

38. Ibid., b. 65, proc. 142, c. 21r.

39. Ibid., c. 22r and v (October 23, 1582).

40. Ibid., c. 23r (report by Simon Sorella); c. 24r (report by Antonio da Ponte).

41. Ibid., b. 65, c. 28r (October 13, 1587).

42. Talamini, "Le Procuratie Nuove," 177.

43. ASV, "Procuratia de supra," b. 65, proc. 142, cc. 30r–31r (report by Vincenzo Scamozzi, December 6, 1587); c. 32r and v (report by Antonio da Marcò).

44. Ibid., reg. 137, c. 122r (December 6, 1587).

45. Andrea Dolfin q. Zuanne (1540–1602) became Procurator of San Marco in 1573, at the age of 33, after having paid 20,000 ducats to the treasury. In 1600 he would once again find himself opposing Jacopo Foscarini and the *papalino* group that defended an attempt made by Florentine merchants to sell to the Venetian Mint currency of copper mixed with silver, paid off by the pontificate and acquired by them. See Cozzi, *Il doge Nicolò Contarini*, 353 and 354 n. 1. Nonetheless, we do not have sufficient evidence to place him, in 1596, alongside the *giovani*, given, also, the curialist tendencies of the Dolfin family. His opposition to Scamozzi might have been due to immediate causes that were taken advantage of by Leonardo Donà and his friends.

46. ASV, "Procuratia de supra," b. 65, proc. 142, c. 36v.

47. Ibid., b. 65, c. 42r and v. Antonio da Ponte, after having maintained that "le fondamenta sono picholle, con poca scharpa, e che a un tanto cargo non potrà resister," adds: "cercha il cavar il cornison di opera dicho che vi serà qualche dano per molti arpessi che vi son impiombatti, ma pur si cavarà usandoli quella diligentia farrà bisogno a una tal opera, visto queste difficultà e quelle per me considerate per non incorer in questi errori, io non lasseria altrimenti essa fabrica, ma seguitaria l'ordene come si atrova. . . ."

The expert report was presented to Andrea Dolfin: see the rough draft on cc. 43r–44r.

48. Ibid., c. 45r (April 23, 1588).

49. Ibid., b. 65, c. 46r (September 7, 1588). Wladimir Timofiewitsch has recognized in drawing UA 193 (fig. 129) a plan by Scamozzi that presents an internal structuring of the new Library building that corresponds to a project with three levels, and in drawing UA 192 (fig. 130) a plan close to the one actually executed. See W. Timofiewitsch, "Zwei Zeichnungen Vincenzo Scamozzis für die Raumaufteilung der Libreria Sansovinos," *Mitteilungen des Kunsthistorischen Institutes in Florenz* 10, fasc. 3 (1962): 209–16.

50. ASV, "Procuratia de supra," reg. 137, c. 179v.

51. Ibid., reg. 138, c. 19r.

52. Ibid., reg. 138, c. 20r. Our emphasis.

53. Ibid., b. 65, proc. 142, c. 49r (September 17, 1590, in the Minor Council).

54. ASV, "Senato Terra," reg. 66, c. 89v. "Adí 28 agosto 1596. Passando fra li Procuratori nostri della chiesa di San Marco a quali è commessa la fabrica delle nuove case sopra la piazza nostra, diverse opinioni importanti intorno di essa, le quali prima che si vadi piú inanti con detta fabrica, o nell'uno o nell'altro modo, è necessario che per publico servitio quelle siano viste, et diligentemente considerate, il che far anco quanto prima, acciò col mettersi tempo di mezo non vengano le fabriche fin hora fatte a ricever nocumento, però / l'anderà parte che nel termine di giorni dieci, debbano li savii nostri di Collegio e li Procuratori sopradetti, li quali per questa occasione possono venir uniti o separati, con le loro opinioni a questo Consiglio, per metter quelle parti, che loro paressero necessarie per il finimento di esse case, dovendo etiam nel termine predetto, cosí uniti come separati, far far quelli dissegni et modelli, a uno o pià periti, che giudicheranno necessarii per compita instruttione di questo Consiglio. De parte 138—de no 12—n.s. 6."

55. Ibid., reg. 66, c. 115v. This was the winning resolution. On May 15, 1598, it was pointed out that "si ritruova la prima presa della fabrica di piazza delle case nuove per li SS.ri Proc.ri esser cosí prossima alla fine" (see Timofiewitsch, "Ein Beitrag," 149), and in a later document dated August 10, 1599, published in full by Timofiewitsch (ibid., 150), Girolamo Campagna, Tiziano Aspetti, Virgilio Rubini, Andrea Dell'Aquila, and Girolamo Paliari were commissioned to do the statues for the part of the façade that had been executed. Drawing 5448 of the Louvre, by Scamozzi, is dated 1596.

56. On Leonardo Donà, in addition to Cozzi, *Il doge Nicolò Contarini*, see Federico Seneca, *Il doge Leonardo Donà: la sua vita e la sua preparazione politica prima del dogado* (Padua, 1959); Bouwsma, *Venice*, passim; James C. Davis, *A Venetian Family and its Fortune, 1500–1900. The Donà and the Conservation of their Wealth* (Philadelphia, 1975; It. trans. Rome, 1980), 65ff.; G. Cozzi, *Paolo Sarpi tra Venezia e l'Europa* (Turin, 1979), passim. On Donà's work as procurator, see Mario Brunetti, "Il Diario di Leonardo Donà procuratore di S. Marco de citra (1591–1605)," *Archivio Veneto*, series 5, 21, no. 41–42 (1937): 101–23. On the relations between Leonardo Donà and Nicolò Contarini, see Cozzi, *Il doge Nicolò Contarini*. On Contarini, see also id., "Contarini Nicolò," in *Dizionario Biografico degli Italiani*, vol. 28 (Rome, 1983), 247–55, which contains information about the cited volume, and June Salmons, "An unpublished account of the end of Este rule in Ferrara: Nicolò Contarini's 'Istorie veneziane' and events in Ferrara 1597–1598," in the collection *Il Rinascimento a Ferrara e i suoi orizzonti europei*, eds. J. Salmons and Walter Moretti (Cardiff and Ravenna, 1984), 123–144.

57. Cozzi, *Il doge Nicolò Contarini*, 37–38; Grendler, *The Roman Inquisition*, 57–58.

58. The bond between Marcantonio Barbaro and Giovanni Grimani is, moreover, eloquently commemorated in the medal mentioned by Cicogna—Emmanuele Antonio Cicogna, *Delle Inscrizioni veneziane* 2 (Venice, 1827), 365—the two sides of which bear the inscriptions: "MARCANTONIUS BARBARO AEDI-

FICATOR" and "JOHANNES GRIM. PATR. AQU. BEN." The title of *aedificator*, applied to Barbaro, is significant. Aldo Manuzio the Younger dedicated to Barbaro one of his *Quesiti*—*De Tunica Romanorum*, praising the patrician for being more concerned about the health of the Republic than about the health of his own person. See Cicogna, *Delle Inscrizioni*, 367.

59. BMV, Ms It., cl. 7, 529b = 1817, c. 15, cited in Cozzi, *Il doge Nicolò Contarini*, 39.

60. See the *Relatione dello Stato, costumi, disordini et remedii de Venetia*. On Antonio Querini, also see *Storici e politici veneti del Cinquecento e del Seicento*, eds. Gino Benzoni and Tiziano Zanato (Milan and Naples, 1982), 645–55.

61. See Cozzi, *Paolo Sarpi*, 137–38, 154, 247; id., *Il doge Nicolò Contarini*, 50 (Fulgenzio Micanzio on the "ridotto Morosini"). Also see id., "Books and Society," 95–96, in which the condemnation of Andrea Morosini's book, *Historia della Repubblica de Venezia* by the Congregazione dell'Indice (December 12, 1624) sounds very much like an a posteriori condemnation of the author's conduct. On Andrea Morosini's moderate position, see the Introduction to *Storici e politici veneti*, XXXV–XXXIX.

62. ASV, "Senato Terra," reg. 66, cc. 115v–16r. Signed by L. Donà, A. Querini, and A. Morosini.

63. See Francesco Sansovino, *Venetia città nobilissima* (Venice, 1581), c. 112v. Also see *Tutte le cose notabili e belle che sono in Venetia* (Venice, 1556), published by Sansovino under the pseudonym of Anselmo Guisconi (reprinted on the occasion of the Piamonte-Gei wedding, Venice, 1861).

64. See, for Giovanni Mocenigo, Cozzi, *Paolo Sarpi*, 142, and Francis A. Yates, *Giordano Bruno and the Hermetic Tradition* (London, 1964); It. trans., 2nd ed. (Rome and Bari, 1981), 370ff. In Nicolò Contarini's *Historie Venetiane* (tome 2, pp. 346–47), cited in Cozzi, *Il doge Nicolò Contarini*, 77, there is the following passage on Federico Contarini, which refers to the latter's intervention in the discussion on the sumptuary laws: "Pur si svegliò Federico Contarini, il quale al tempo della guerra turchesca, con denari si fece crear procuratore, che in altra cosa poco s'impediva et era per le sue qualità inferiore all'invidia. . . ." Also see Grendler, *The Roman Inquisition*, 303; G. Cozzi, "Federico Contarini: un antiquario veneziano tra Rinascimento e Controriforma," *Bollettino dell'Istituto di Storia della Società e dello Stato veneziano* 3 (1961): 190–220; Maria Teresa Cipollato, "L'eredità di Federico Contarini: gli inventari della collezione e degli oggetti domestici," ibid., 221–53; G. Cozzi, "Contarini Federico," in *Dizionario Biografico degli Italiani*, 28: 158–60. Cozzi not only highlights the many contacts that Federico Contarini had with the Jesuit circle in Venice, but also analyzes the patrician's career as magistrato alle pompe [magistrate for pomp]: in 1599 Contarini drew attention to himself as a censor of luxury and pomp, and he seems to have supported sobriety even in his last will and testament of March 6, 1609. However, in private, the new Cato ridiculed by Nicolò Contarini did indulge in displays of wealth, especially with his collection of ancient pieces. It was Federico Contarini, in fact, who was charged with the organization of the Museo Grimani (November 4, 1599), which would involve him in disputes and accusations. Honest but "facilone," ill with remorseful moralism: this is the final portrait of Federico Contarini that we get from Cozzi. See Cozzi, "Federico Contarini," 220. Also see Grendler, "The 'Tre Savi sopra eresia,'" 329 n. 79. Federico Contarini's adherence to the anti-Scamozzian resolution should probably be interpreted within the context of the moralism we have referred to, which was very different from the ethical rigor that characterized the political lives of Leonardo Donà and Nicolò Contarini.

65. On the ideal position of the *giovani* with regard to the Venetian past, which was very different from the position held by the patricians who were content with the myth of Venice, see G. Cozzi, "Politica, culture e religione," in the collection *Cultura e società nel Rinascimento tra riforme e manierismi*, eds. Vittore Branca and Carlo Ossola (Florence,

1984), 21–42, esp. 33–35. Also see Gino Benzoni, *Venezia nell'età della Controriforma* (Milan, 1973).

66. In this connection see Norbert Huse, "Palladio am Canale Grande," *Staedel Jahrbuch* 7 (1979): 91. Leonardo Donà would, in fact, be buried in San Giorgio Maggiore.

67. ASV, "Senato Terra," reg. 66, c. 115r (September 28, 1596).

68. Grendler, *The Roman Inquisition*, op. cit., p. 287 and 308 n. 5. Also see id., "The 'Tre Savi sopra Eresia,'" 331–32, with information on Jacopo Foscarini's political career and economic situation. Also see Cozzi, *Il doge Nicolò Contarini*, 12 n. 1; 38, 86 and 95 n. 1. Cozzi also remarks that in 1604 Jacopo Foscarini ardently supported the reopening of the Jesuit schools. See id., *Paolo Sarpi*, 148 n. 24.

69. Concina, *L'Arsenale*, 169.

70. Grendler, *The Roman Inquisition*, 287.

71. Ibid., 362ff.

72. Ibid., 366.

73. Ibid., 367–68.

74. Ibid., 368.

75. Ibid., 377

76. Ibid., 302.

77. Analyzing the episode of the Church of Celestia, Giambattista Gleria demonstrated that Vincenzo Scamozzi, after having begun the building in circa 1582 according to a model with a central plan, maintained good relations with the nuns until 1584–85: in 1595, moreover, the Scamozzian church was defined, in a document relating to the quarrel between the Theatines and the architect, as a "mostro dell'architettura, et un corpo senza capo" [a "monster of architecture, and a body without a head"] (see R. Gallo, "Vincenzo Scamozzi e la chiesa di S. Nicolò da Tolentino di Venezia," in *Atti dell'Istituto Veneto di Scienze, Lettere e Arti*, tome 117 [1958–59], p. 121, doc. 3). The building by Scamozzi was demolished in early 1605, and Gleria has related that event to the political crisis that involved the patricians who supported Scamozzi. See Giovanni Battista Gleria,

"Il progetto scamozziano per la chiesa della Celestia a Venezia," *Ricerche di Storia dell'arte* 21 (1983): 97–109. Another episode exemplifying Scamozzi's misfortunes in Venice was the competition for the position of *proto* of the Magistratura del Sal [Magistracy for Salt], which was announced on April 14, 1597: on April 28 of the same year Antonio Contin was the winner, prevailing over Vincenzo Scamozzi, the carpenters Bortolo q. Alessandro and Iseppo Felici q. Vincenzo, and over Francesco di Bernardin called Il Fracao. See Giambattista Lorenzi, *Monumenti per servire alla storia del Palazzo Ducale di Venezia* (Venice, 1868), doc. 1074, p. 553. Scamozzi's failure thus repeated Palladio's lack of success in the competition held 43 years before for the same post; Scamozzi thus saw himself passed over for a relative of the hated Antonio da Ponte.

78. See John Harris, "Three Unrecorded Palladio Designs from Inigo Jones's Collection," *The Burlington Magazine* 113 (1971): 34 n. 3; H. Burns, "Project for the reconstruction of the Palazzo Ducale," in *Andrea Palladio, 1508–1580. The Portico*, 158–60 (entry 279). According to Burns (ibid., 159), the project had a façade of 190 feet, as opposed to the 225 of the Palazzo Ducale on the side of the Piazzetta and the 219 1/2 of the same Palazzo on the side of the Bacino. Furthermore, its height measured 70 feet, against the Palazzo's 74. Burns also mentions that Palladio, in his report after the fire of 1577, speaks of 17 bays, while the Chatsworth drawing only shows 11 arches.

79. See Loredana Olivato, entry 74, in the collection *Architettura e utopia nella Venezia del'500*, ed. L. Puppi (Milan, 1980), 102. Also see Donata Battilotti, "Palladio a Venezia. Regesti per un itinerario," in the collection *Palladio e Venezia*, ed. L. Puppi (Florence, 1982), 208, and Lewis, *The Drawings*, 204–5, who observes that the information about the drawing had already been contained in Antonio Magrini, *Memorie intorno la vita e le opere di Andrea Palladio* (Padua, 1845), 309–12. Norbert Huse has expressed doubts about Burns's attribution of the Chatsworth drawing. See Huse,

"Palladio am Canale Grande," 98–99 n. 154. One notes that the commission for the restoration of the Palazzo was formed by Jacopo Foscarini, Piero Foscari, and Girolamo Priuli (January 19 and 20, 1578). See Giangiorgio Zorzi, *Le opere pubbliche e i palazzi privati di Andrea Palladio* (Vicenza, 1964), 153. On Palladio's relations, see ibid., 151ff.

80. See ibid., 90–109; L. Puppi, *Andrea Palladio* 2 (Milan, 1973), 347–48; H. Burns, entry 425–27, in *Andrea Palladio, 1508–1580. The Portico*, 238–41.

81. See Chapter 4 in this volume.

82. See H. Burns, "Suggerimenti per l'identificazione di alcuni progetti e schizzi palladiani," *Bollettino del Cisa* 21 (1979): 114–15.

83. Sansovino and Stringa, *Venetia città nobilissima*, 415r and v.

84. See Sanudo, "Vita dei Dogi," in Lorenzi, *Monumenti*, doc. 198, pp. 92–93; D. Malipiero, "Annali veneti dall' anno 1457 al 1500," eds. F. Longo and A. Sagredo, *Archivio Storico Italiano* 7, no. 2 (1844): 674; N. Barbarigo, *Vita di Andrea Gritti doge di Venezia*, a translation of the sixteenth-century Latin original (Venice, 1793), 103–4.

85. See Franzoi, *Le prigioni*, doc. 32, p. VIII; Scarabello, *Carcerati*, 71. Note, however, that the Council of Ten, with a decision taken on March 31, 1563, had ordered the evacuation of the house of the children of Zuan della Vedova beyond the Rio di Palazzo, and the execution of one or two models of prisons: on July 14, 1563, Giovanni Antonio Rusconi's model was approved, and on June 30, 1564, the above-mentioned house was demolished, but in 1566 nothing had been built yet. In 1568, the Council of Ten ordered the construction of two secure and secret prisons according to Antonio da Ponte's design. See Lorenzi, *Monumenti*, doc. 669–74, 688, 741, 749; Franzoi, *Le prigioni*, doc. 28, pp. VI–VII.

86. BMV, Cod. It., cl. 7, 295 = 10047. See Scarabello, *Carcerati*, 73.

87. Ibid., 77, Antonio da Ponte was paid 3 ducats on October 6, 1595, for models, and on December 2 of the same year 10 ducats for having checked the estimates for the stonemasonry. ASV, "Provveditori al Sal," b. 414, at the indicated dates. In the same box file [busta] there are other payments made to Da Ponte between 1594 and 1596.

88. See Eugenia Bevilacqua, "La cartografia storica della laguna di Venezia," in *Mostra storica della laguna veneta* (Venice, 1970), 146. Vincenzo Fontana, entry 133, in *Architettura e utopia*, 137; id., "Venezia e la laguna nel Cinquecento," *Casabella* 45, no. 465 (1981): 12–15. On the Magistratura alle Acque [magistracy of the waterways], see *Mostra storica della laguna veneta*, and *Laguna, lidi, fiumi. Cinque secoli di gestione delle acque*, catalog of the documentary exhibit, ed. Maria Francesco Tiepolo (Venice, 1983).

89. ASV, "Savi ed Esecutori delle Acque," f. 122, examined only in part by Vincenzo Fontana in *Architettura e utopia*, entry 143, pp. 142–43. In addition to the petitions listed by Fontana, the file contains those of Pietro Antonio Pillon da Lendinara (March 9, 1547), who proposes "un edifficio" in order to "cavar canalli, laguna et altri luoghi che bisognarà, con prestezza, facilità et poca spessa," as well as petitions by the following individuals: "Fiorio quondam Zan de Fioco e Agostino q. Zuan Gratia cyrugico"; Pellegrino Trombetta, who promised "uno edificio" that he maintained would be able to "cavar burchielle 200 al dì vel circa"; Giovanni Alberto de Paulo (October 9, 1546); Alessandro Lionzo (November 3, 1546); Marcantonio da Conte (November 27, 1546); Benedetto Poscantino (December 2, 1546); Zorzi Capobianco da Schio, who offered a "modo di cavar terreno sopra aqua et sotto aqua cum poca spesa et gran prestezza," with four men a day and a hundred boats; and—in a work signed by Sabbadino, who was writing for the illiterate Guglielmo—Guglielmo del Monte, who offered an invention to "solevar aqua in alto et condur quella dove farà di bisogno" and to "far lavorar sotto aqua in grandissimo fondi di questo mare di Venetia et altrove et per questi canali homeni con martelli, pichi, manare, trivelle et altre sorte de instrumenti . . . et far levar

ogni grandissimo peso che fosse nel fondo sopra aqua facilissimamente." Also interesting are Tiberio Zorzi's proposal to "seccar ogni acqua di questa città con lo inzegno di una palificata da me trovata," and the proposals by Zuan Maria da Parma, Giovan Battista Zorzi (January 1546, *m.v.* = 1547). Drawing f. 122/1 was presented, as indicated on the back, by the doctor Fedel Piccolomini, on February 16, 1564 *m.v.* (= 1565) and is accompanied by a long explanatory note: "Le prime cinque figure . . . sono sotto uno solo instrumento detto sione le quali doppo il primo moto datoli operano per sé et si conservano ne l'opera . . . et si possono fare di grandezza inestimabile." Figures 6 and 7 represented cases for the instruments 8–12. Drawings f. 122/2 and 3 are also by Piccolomini and are accompanied by some text dated March 14, 1565, in which the author explains that he presented figures 14–28 after the Senate made a decision in his favor on February 3, 1564, *m.v.* (= 1565). Piccolomini is also responsible for the "edifitio per alzar aqua" dated February 1, *m.v.* (= 1565), drawings f. 122/4 and 5. Later *ingegni*, mechanisms or machines, for the preservation of the lagoons are recorded in *Laguna, lidi, fiumi*: August 9, 1571, the estimation of a new machine for the dredging of the lagoon given by the steward Baldissera Crachio and eleven experts in the art of *marangoni* [woodworking] of the Arsenal (p. 67, entry 133); 1589, petition by Ippolito Mariano in favor of a new machine with perpetual movement to be used in stagnant water (p. 68, entry 135); 1604, Vincenzo Scamozzi's petition for *raccordi*, or reports, regarding the protection of the lagoon, ports, and neighboring mainland (pp. 68–69, entry 137); October 30, 1607, proposal by G. Alvise Galesi for the dredging of the Grand Canal and other canals and for the draining of the muds (p. 103, entry 150). In May 1531, Marin Sanudo noted: "Fu leto uno aricordo dato per un frate di San Francesco conventual, zercha cavar i rii de questa città, vol stroppar la bocha di rii et far cresser l'aqua grande lí dentro, et quando va zoso aprir la bocha, e con maze e legni travasar il fango, dice sarà portà via, il dove non si sa. Fu preso, fare ex-

perientia in una velma, donarli ducati 10 e farli dar una camera nel monastero dei Frari." Sanudo, *Diarii*, 54 : 442. We ought to mention, in addition, the report presented on January 20, 1535, by Michele Sanmicheli on the defensive situation of Venice, in which the master emphasized the hygiene of the canals and the absolute necessity of eliminating burials. See, in this connection, L. Puppi, *Michele Sanmicheli architetto di Verona* (Padua, 1971), 73–74. Note, however, that in his report Sanmicheli reveals a decided opposition to technological invention, and writes in connection to the dredging of the lagoon: "io laudo sopra tutto il divertir de tutti i fiumi et farli andar in mar lontan . . . e . . . tenir cavado con la zappa et badil, *ché altri ingegni sono chimere. La zappa et badil è la vita di queste paludi.*" On Sanmicheli's position within the debate that separated Francesco Maria della Rovere from Vincenzo Cappello—the two generals "da Terra" and "da Mar"— see the important volume by E. Concina, *La macchina territoriale. La progettazione della difesa nel Cinquecento veneto* (Rome and Bari, 1983), passim, but especially chap. 2.

90. See Fontana, *Architettura e utopia*, entry 143, p. 142.

91. Ibid., entry 133, the date 1589 established by Fontana for the decision on the Fondamenta Nuove has been corrected here taking into account the Venetian calendar.

92. ASV, "Savi ed Esecutori alle Acque," reg. 347, cc. 4v–5r. Information on the Fondamenta Nuove (begun on February 22, 1589, *m.v.*, and a tax of 2 lire for every boat unloaded within the "palade delle Sacche da atterrarsi da San Francesco fino alla Misericordia," March 1, 1592), can be found in Giulio Rompiasio, *Metodo in pratica di sommario, o sia compilazione delle leggi, terminazioni ed ordini appartenenti agl'Illustrissimi ed Eccellentissimi Collegio, e Magistrato delle Acque* (Venice, 1771), 186 and 224. Cristofor Tentori cites a decision taken by the Senate in 1546 for the creation of fondamenta from Santa Giustina to Sant' Alvise: the zone, however, would be definitively organized after 1509, in spite

of numerous projects and sporadic interventions. See Cristoforo Tentori, *Della legislazione veneziana sulla preservazione della laguna. Dissertazione storico-filosofico-critica* (Venice, 1792), 142–43. Tentori also cites the decision of June 27, 1569, which instructed the magistrato alle Acque to build foundations in stone in all the open spots of the city (p. 143), the resolution by which the Senate gave the Ministers and Executors for Waterways, on January 9, 1587, permission to spend 1,000 ducats of the Decime delle Miniere in order to construct foundations in stone at the "bersaglio di S. Alvise" (p. 144), and the decision taken in the *Collegio* on February 9, 1587, regarding the *zonta* that had been asked, along with the Ministers and Executors for the Waterways, to study the problem of filling in the noxious creeks and the creation of foundations in stone in the six districts (p. 144). Also see Giorgio Bellavitis and Giandomenico Romanelli, *Venezia* (Rome and Bari, 1985), p. 89, figs. 56 and 57 on p. 88), which publishes a few projects for the filling in of the creek by the Misericordia.

93. See Preto, *Peste e società*, 74.

94. ASV, "Savi ed Esecutori alle Acque," reg. 333, Liber Partium 2, c. 9v. See *Laguna, lidi, fiumi*, 99, entry 143.

95. See A. Foscari and M. Tafuri, *L'armonia e i conflitti. La chiesa di San Francesco della Vigna nella Venezia del Cinquecento* (Turin, 1983), 32–33, and note 117 on pp. 108–9.

96. E. Concina, *Structure urbaine et fonction des bâtiments du XVIe au XIXe siècle. Une recherche à Venise* (Venice: Unesco–Save Venice Inc., 1982), 71.

97. Ibid. On Titian's house in Biri Grande, see Jürgen Schulz, *Houses of Titian, Aretino, and Sansovino*, in the collection, *Titian. His World and His Legacy*, ed. David Rosand (New York, 1982), 79–82.

98. See Concina, *Structure urbaine*, 74 and fig. 25 on p. 73 (schematic survey of the island of the Crosechieri, 1556, BMC).

99. See, in this connection, the fundamental volume by Frederic C. Lane, *I mercanti di Venezia* (Turin, 1982), esp. 41ff. and 237ff.

100. ASV, "Savi ed Esecutori alle Acque," reg. 346, c. 91r. For the transcription of documents quoted here, see M. Tafuri, "Documenti sulle Fondamenta Nuove," *Architettura, storia e documenti* 1 (1985): 79–95.

101. See Elena Bassi, *Palazzi di Venezia* (Venice, 1976), 500–2. Girolamo Righetti gives an example of Leonardo Donà's administrative diligence in the evaluation that he wrote about his commission, on the advantages of the Fondamenta Nuove. BMC, "Donà delle Rose," b. 457, n. 31: "1598, Calculo di Hier .mo Righeti perito dell'off.o alle aque della spesa si farebbe sulle fondamenta da S.ta Giustina sin alla Sacca della Misericordia. / Venezia. Spese per la fabrica delle fondamenta nuove. Per obedir a quanto da la v. Ill.ma Signoria è stà comesso a m. Girolemo righetti suo humilissimo servitor, ch'io li dia il conto distinto, et particolar della longhezza della fondamenta principiando dal rio de s.ta Giustina sino alla sacca della Misericordia secondo la deliberazion fatta da essa insieme con li Ill.mi suoi coleghi; ch'io li dia anco il conto quanta quantità de teren sarà serado nelle sacche (atterandosi però anco la sacca de S. Zanepolo, la qual quantunque nel mio dissegno si aperta laudo però essere ben che sia ateratta, la causa è perché sarà de maggior uttile et ornamento alla cità, et anco perché è per mezo il Monasterio dei Fratti) che insieme anco li dichi la spesa che anderà a far la ditta fondamenta et li Ponti che vanno congionti con essa; la quantità delle burchiele di fango, che si alogheranno nelle ditte sacche alciandosi però con la fondamenta piedi 3 sopra il correr de l'acqua, et anco l'utile che si caverà dale dette burchiele che discargheranno sul detto loco, et quanta utilità si caverà dalli terenni dentro esse sacche non computando la larghezza della fondamenta qual sarà piedi 15. / Riverentimente li dico, che la Fondamenta che anderà da rio de S.ta Giustina sino al rio de S. Zanepolo sarà passa n° 250. / Il Rio è largo passa 10. / Dal Rio da S. Zanepolo sino al Rio della panà sarà passa n° 39. / Il Rio è largo passa 5. / Dal Rio della panà sino al Rio d'i

Crosichieri sarà passa n° 102. / Il Rio è largo passa 9. / Dal Rio di Crosichieri sino alla sacca della Misericordia sarà passa n° 158 che summano de longhezza passa n° 549. / La fondamenta, che và per traverso nelli rij, qual và à congiongersi con le fabriche sarà passa n° 156. / che summano in tutto de fondamenta passa circa n° 705. / à ragion de ducati 30 il passo, seben ho detto nella mia deposition, che si saria fatta per ducati 25 il passo, et ciò dissi rispetto à quella che ha da andar da la Misericordia sino al Bressaglio di S.to Alvise nella qual li anderà manco spesa cioè ducati 20 circa il passo per esser luoco in gran parte atterado havendosi fatto quella del Bressaglio per ducati 22 il passo. / però al far li detti li anderanno ducati 21150. / Li tre ponti che anderanno congionti con la ditta fondamenta monta ducati 500. / che summa in tutto trà la Fondamenta, et li Ponti ducati 21650. / La quantità de teren che và seratto dentro le sacche principiando dal Rio de S.ta Giustina sino alla sacca della Misericordia sonno passa quari n° 10845. à ragion de ducati tre il passo si caverà ducati 32235. / Le burchiele de fanghi, et ruvinazzi, che si logheranno in esse sacche à burchiele doi per passo quaro sarano burchiele n° 21690. avanciando s. 30 per burchiela saranno ducati 5247. / L'utile che si caverà sarà in summa ducati trentasettemille settecento, e ottanta doi circa val ducati 37782. / Et oltra la sopra detta spesa si avancierà ducati seddecimille cento e trentasei circa val ducati 16137."

102. Cicogna, citing the *Memorie* by Leonardo Donà, made it known that the doge bought the land on October 14, 1609. Donà wrote the following in Cicogna's transcription: "Et faccio memoria come fu datto principio a quella fabbrica li cui fondamenti sono stati tutti palificati alli 16 gennaro 1609 [= 1610] secondo il nostro stile di Venetia, e la prima pietra dopo haver principiato at cavare et palificare fu posta alli 24 di marzo 1610 vigilia dell'Annunciatione della Beatisssima Vergine giorno natale della nostra città. Et il coperto fu finito a mezzo il corrente mese di ottobre 1611." (E. Cicogna, *Delle Inscrizioni veneziane* 4 [Venice, 1834], 433.) Cicogna also transcribed from a codex he owned: "Dicono, che sempre

contendeva con suo fratello havendo esso dose fabricata una casa grande et molto comoda su le fondamenta nove al ponte de Crosechieri, nella quale haveva speso grandissima quantità di danari . . . perché suo fratello le rimpruoverava che con quei danari spesi haverebbe comprato il piú bel Palazzo di Venetia, et nel piú bel sito che non era quella casa, *quale non haveva forma di palazzo*" (ibid. 420–21 n. 2, our emphasis). From Donà's *Memorie* one gathers that Francesco di Pietro was the *proto* of the building (ibid., 433). On the career of Francesco di Pietro, *proto* of the Procuratori de citra and author of the houses on the Calle degli Armeni, at San Zulian, see *Dietro i palazzi. Tre secoli di architettura minore a Venezia 1492–1803*, eds. Giorgio Gianighian and Paola Pavanini (Venice, 1984), 122–23 and 155–57.

103. ASV, "Savi ed Esecutori alle Acque," f. 122, 1592, 3 March.

104. Ibid., reg. 347, c. 23r.

105. Ibid.

106. ASV, "Provveditori alla Zecca," f. 1217. The drawing bears the date April 8, 1756.

107. ASV, "Savi ed Esecutori alle Acque," reg. 347, c. 30v.

108. Ibid., Laguna 34 and 35. See Concina, *Structure urbaine*, figs. 26 and 27 on pp. 75–76.

109. Ibid., 74.

110. Ibid., 79.

111. With regard to this question, see the remarks contained in the article by Giandomenico Romanelli, "'Venetia tra l'oscurità degl'inchiostri.' Cinque secoli di cartografia," in *Venezia, piane e vedute*, catalogue of the exhibit of the map collection of the Museo Correr (Venice, 1982), 5–6. There are interesting remarks on the relations between cartography and the collective imaginary in Venice in the essay by Giuliana Mazzi, "La cartografia per il mito: le immagini di Venezia nel Cinquecento," in *Architettura e utopia*, 50–56. The question could be reopened taking into account the methodological contribution made in Jacques Le Goff's essay, "L'immaginario urbano nell'Italia medievale (secoli V–XV)," in *Storia d'Ita-*

lia Einaudi. *Annali 5. Il paesaggio*, ed.
Cesare De Seta (Turin, 1982), 5–43.

112. Concina, *L'Arsenale*, 158ff.

113. Ibid., 171.

114. Ibid., 172.

115. Ibid., 174–75.

116. See Bouwsma, *Venice and the Defense*, 379ff.; Cozzi, *Paolo Sarpi*; G. and Luisa Cozzi, "Paolo Sarpi," in *Storia della cultura veneta. Il Seicento*, 4 : 2 : 1–36. Also see Cozzi, *Il doge Nicolò Contarini*, 105–15, for the discussion of 1606 in which Leonardo Donà upheld positions of "prudence," supported by Pietro Duodo and Andrea Morosini, and Alvise Zorzi di Paolo, Antonio Querini, and Nicolò Contarini took positions of intransigence (esp. 108).

117. See ibid., 139–47; Domenico Sella, *Commercio e industria a Venezia nel secolo XVII* (Venice and Rome, 1961), 38–40. On the economic situation in Venice during the period, see the collection *Decadenza economica veneziana nel secolo XVII* (Venice and Rome, 1961); Ruggiero Romano, *Tra due crisi: l'Italia del Rinascimento* (Turin, 1971), 187ff.; Ugo Tucci, *Mercanti, navi, monete nel Cinquecento veneziano* (Bologna, 1981); Fernand Braudel, *Civiltà e imperi del Mediterraneo nell'età di Filippo II* (Paris, 1949 and 1966), It. trans., vol 1, 4th ed. (Turin, 1982) 417–21 and passim.

118. Cited in Samuele Romanin, *Storia documentaria di Venezia*, vol. 7, 2nd ed. (Venice, 1914), 531.

119. Ibid., 532–33.

120. Ibid., 533.

121. See Lane, *I mercanti di Venezia*, 205ff.

122. The pontifical nuncio wrote to Cardinal Borghese (July 31, 1610, Archivio Segr. Vat., "Nunziatura Venezia," f. 40b): "Altri senatori che si reputano di miglior mente sono contrarij et allegano il rispetto della religione, vedendosi che con questa libertà così grande della navigazione si aprirà la strada agli Inglesi et Fiamenghi di venire qua in maggior numero et metter casa; tal che succederà all'ultimo quasi una libertà di coscienza in gran parte degli habitanti di Venezia." Cited in Cozzi, *Il doge Nicolò Contarini*, 144.

123. Ibid., 146–47.

124. Id., "Paolo Sarpi," 175 n. 87.

125. Ibid., 161–62.

126. Ibid., 163–65. Fulgenzio Micanzio, answering in 1611 a letter that the scientist had sent to Sarpi, wrote: "Io non mi posso satiare di essaltar l'inventore di questo strumento, che qua nelle nostre parti è stata V.S., a cui assolutamente si deve la lode d'haverci dato con arte certa il miglioramento, e da cui, in cosí honorato ocio, si deve aspettare la perfettione; come in altra scientia, tanto rara quanto incognita, si promettiamo di vedere, con stupore universale e sua comendatione, il tutto apparer insieme et inventato e perfetto: dico del moto, alla cui speculatione Dio e la natura l'ha fatta; et il bene comune mi sforza, come tante volte in raggionamenti cosí anco per lettere, dargline questo motto, sicuro che, come sino a questa età il mondo non l'ha saputo, se lei non ci mette la sua fortunata mano, possi stare altro tanto tempo senza uscire delle tenebre o mosso e starsene quasi moto immobile sena vita, che da lei aspetta." Galilei, *Opere*, eds. Antonio Favaro and Isidoro Del Lungo, vol. 11 (Florence, 1929–39), 57–58. Also see the letter from Sagredo to Galileo of March 8, 1619, ibid., 12 : 445. On Sarpi, see the important essay by Libero Sosio, "I 'Pensieri' di Paolo Sarpi sul moto," *Studi Veneziani* 13 (1971): 315–92.

127. On this theme see Alexandre Koyrè, *Galilée et la révolution scientifique du XVIIᵉ siècle* (Paris, 1955); id. "Le 'De motu gravium' de Galilée. De l'expérience imaginaire et de son abus," *Revue d'histoire des Sciences et de leur application* 13 (1960): 197ff., reprinted in *Études d'histoire de la pensée scientifique* (Paris, 1966), 202–49; Ludovico Geymonat, *Galileo Galilei* (Turin, 1957); Thomas S. Kuhn, "Una funzione degli esperimenti mentali," in *L'aventure de la science. Mélanges Alexandre Koyré*, vol. 2 (Paris, 1964), 307–34, reprinted in *Scientific Revolutions*, ed. Ian Hacking (Oxford, 1981), It. trans. (Rome and Bari, 1984), 13–45 (a particularly important essay, for its interpretation of Galileo's search for

alternatives to the paradigms of Aristotelian physics, and as a theoretical text of the new epistemology); Enrico Bellone, *Il sogno di Galileo. Oggetti e immagini della ragione* (Bologna, 1980). Bellone's essay develops a few of the hypotheses introduced by Koyré in his interpretation of Galileian thought. Contemporary with it is the essay by Gianni Micheli, "L'assimilazione della scienza greca," in *Storia d'Italia Einaudi. Annali 3. Scienza e tecnica nella cultura e nella società dal Rinascimento a oggi,* ed. G. Micheli (Turin, 1980), 201–57 (pp. 242ff. are on Galileo), which introduces a very different reading of Galileo and Italian scientific thought about him. Denying that there exists a "strong" theoretical nucleus in Galileo, Micheli sees in Galileian thought a conglomeration of abstractions born of particular facts: Galileo's principles would thus have resulted from a fragmented and unarticulated search without comprehensive models. One should, however, observe, that Micheli's statement, regarding the particular value that Galileo's contemporaries attributed to the "new way of observing," is partially contradicted by the Sarpian groups continued interest in the theory of motion, which functioned as a paradigm for the new parameters assumed there.

128. Pastore Stocchi has observed that Galileo's many manuscripts written in the vernacular on military architecture, astronomy, and mechanics (now in vol. 2 of the *Opere*) were compiled by the scientist in the course of the private lessons he gave in his own residence to members of the patriciate. See Manlio Pastore Stocchi, "Il periodo veneto di Galileo Galilei," in *Storia della cultura veneta. Il Seicento,* (Vicenza, 1984), 4:2:47. Galileo's works on fortifications have been analyzed by Francesco Paolo Fiore in "La città progressiva e il suo disegno," in the collection *La città come forma simbolica* (Rome, 1973), 237–41.

129. The first public demonstration of the Galileian telescope took place on August 21, 1609, and it was presented to Doge Leonardo Donà on August 25. The three reformers of the Studio of Padua who proposed to the Senate that an exceptional tribute of honor and gratitude should be paid to Galileo were Antonio Priuli, Marcantonio Memmo, and Andrea Morosini; the first two belonged to the conservative faction as did Pietro Duodo, one of Galileo's admirers who may have inspired the decision. See Cozzi, "Paolo Sarpi," 181–82.

130. Ibid., 219.

131. In this connection, see Pastore Stocchi, "Il periodo veneto di Galileo Galilei," 37–66.

132. Vittorio Gabrieli, "Bacone, la Riforma e Roma nella versione hobbesiana d'un carteggio di Fulgenzio Micanzio," *English Miscellany* 8 (1957): 195–250. The letters, translated by Hobbes, are in London, British Museum, Add. As. 11309.

133. Gabrieli, "Bacone," 203–4.

134. Ibid., 205–6. Micanzio's problem was that he had to decide whether to publish Bacon's *Essays* in Venice, where they would inevitably be massacred by the censor, or to have them translated in England in order then to obtain copies through the English ambassador to the Republic. In 1618, however, an Italian translation of the volume was published in London under the title of *Saggi Morali,* along with the short treatise *Della Sapienza degli Antichi,* ed. Toby Matthew, by the printer John Bill—the same John Bill who in 1619 would publish Paolo Sarpi's *Istoria.* Fra Fulgenzia, in a letter dated February 24, 1617 (Gabrieli, "Bacone," 207), had expressed the desire that the translator of the *Essays* should be Marco Antonio De Dominis, formerly archbishop of Spalato and apostate, who had fled to London two months before and who in 1622 would return to Rome in order to die in prison there in 1624.

135. Ibid., 209

136. *Lettere di Fra Paolo Sarpi,* ed. F. L. Polidori, vol. 2 (Florence, 1863), 429, letter of April 11, 1617.

137. In the translation of Thomas Hobbes, Micanzio writes: "My lord Chanceller's Essays are spread through all the cities hereabout into the hands of all the professors of learning and are in marvellous reputation. And I have distributed

among there my own copies . . . This I may say, that they are all bound up with gilded leaves, the hap and honour only of that book and they carry it ever about them." Gabrieli, "Bacone," 211.

138. Ibid., 216. In one of the last letters to Sir William Cavendish, from around 1626, Micanzio inserts a funeral oration of Bacon, who had died on April 9 of that year. Micanzio would write about 150 letters to Galileo between 1630 and 1644, demonstrating a new shift in interest toward Galileo after Bacon's death. On the political and cultural relations between Venice and England, also see Enrico de Mas, *Sovranità politica e unità cristiana nel Seicento anglo-veneto* (Ravenna, 1975); Francesco De Paola, Vanini e il primo Seicento anglo-veneto (Cutrofiano, 1979); E. De Mas, *L'attesa del secolo aureo (1603–1625)* (Florence, 1982).

Glossary

The Government of the Venetian Republic

The following list of Venetian government bodies and offices is provided merely as a limited description of a few terms that the reader may find unfamiliar in the book. These brief definitions are not intended to be exhaustive, nor do they explain the historical transformations of these organs of government, but are presented in order to provide a basic knowledge of their function in the decision-making procedures during the fifteenth and sixteenth centuries. For more detailed information, one may refer to the specific texts mentioned by the author in the endnotes.

Avogaria or the *Avvogadori di Comun* These *Avvogadori* or State judicial officials had the general duty of prosecuting all cases involving the interests of the Republic. Moreover, they were charged with ensuring that the decisions of the Great Council, the Senate, and the Council of Ten were in accordance with the laws, and for overseeing the observance of treaties, the collection of fines, and the legality of commercial and private legal affairs.

Collegio The Collegio was responsible for various daily official duties, which included receiving reports from officials, meeting with foreign envoys, and deciding the principal agenda for the Senate meetings. The Collegio had to review all mat-

ters before they could be presented to the Senate. It was composed of the Doge; the three groups of *Savi* or Ministers (*Savi Grandi* or Chief Ministers, *Savi di Terraferma* or Ministers of War and the Mainland, and *Savi ai Ordini* or Ministers of the Marine); and the *Signoria*. When they all met together they were called the *Pieno Collegio* or Full College.

Consiglieri ducali (Ducal or Dogal Council) One of the principal administrative bodies, composed of six Councillors representing each one of the city districts or *sestieri*.

Consiglio dei Dieci (Council of Ten) This *Consiglio* or Council was responsible for the most crucial matters of foreign affairs and of finance. The Senate decided every year on its membership. The Doge and the Dogal Councillors (*Consiglieri ducali*) attended the meetings of the Council of Ten, together with one of the three *Avvogadori*. Three *Capi* or Chiefs of the Ten were elected by the Council and functioned as the top administrators.

Consiglio dei Pregadi (Senate) Originally it consisted of sixty men elected from the Great Council. The *Consiglio dei Pregadi* was later enlarged to about 300 men, including nearly all important officials, and performed the main deliberative functions of the Republic. The meetings of the Senate were presided over by the *Signoria*, and the *Savi Grandi*, or Chief Ministers, assisted in directing the agenda. In the official documents of the Senate and other administrative bodies Venice was referred to as *La Dominante*.

Doge The Doge was surrounded by advisory councils that both assisted him in his functions and prevented him from attempting to form a monarchic rule. Nevertheless, he was the symbol of the unity and authority of the Venetian Republic. He was also at the center of the routine practical problems involving foreign policy and the supervision of administrative affairs. The Doge was elected to his post for life from the ranks of the Great Council through an extremely complicated voting procedure.

Maggior Consiglio (Great Council) The large oligarchic body that was composed of all the noble families of the Republic. It elected all magistrates charged with executing the affairs of the State and had the final word in settling unresolved issues.

Magistratura alle Acque See *Savi alle Acque*.

Magistratura or *Provveditori del Sal* (Salt Office) The Salt Office managed the money collected from the revenue of the salt tax, which was then appropriated by the Senate for construction projects.

Procuratori di San Marco (Procurators of San Marco) The office of Procurator of San Marco was originally established to oversee the financial and administrative requirements of the church of San Marco. For the patrician class the position of Procurator was second in prestige only to that of the Doge, and it was the only other office that carried life tenure. The Procuracy was divided into various divisions, the most important of which was the *Procuratia de supra* responsible for the church and for the property in Piazza San Marco and the surrounding area.

Proto The position is best defined as the masterbuilder, foreman, or superintendent of buildings; nevertheless, the title carried various other responsibilities, including the maintenance and management of the buildings, surrounding properties, and other various possessions administered by the government authority making the appointment.

Provveditori alle Fortezze (Commissioners of Fortresses) Special magistracy in charge of defense matters.

Provveditori dei Beni Inculti (Reclamation Commissioners) The members of a Commission in charge of organizing public and private irrigation and drainage projects.

Provveditori del Sal See *Magistratura del Sal*.

Provveditori in Campo (Field Commissioners) Venetian nobles who acted as the advisors and supervisors of the *condottieri*, mercenary captains, who were under contract to the Republic.

Quarantia (Council of Forty) It formed the top judicial authority and at the same time was responsible for preparing legislation concerning financial matters. Three *Capi*, or Heads of the Forty, were elected to be its presiding officials.

Rettori (Venetian Rectors) Venetian noblemen who were the Republic's chief executives in the subject cities.

Savi or *Magistratura alle Acque* (Ministers of the Waterways) They were in charge of dealing with all hydraulic problems, specifically policing the use of Venice's canals and regulating the rivers that flowed into the lagoon.

Savi Grandi or *Savi del Consiglio* (Chief Ministers) The Senate created this administrative body to assist the *Signoria* in preparing its agenda, formulating resolutions, and overseeing their execution. They formed a sort of Council of Ministers together with the *Savi*, or Ministers (*ai Ordine* and *di Terraferma*), and the *Signoria*.

Savi ai Ordini (Ministers of the Marine) Were concerned with maritime commerce, the navy, and overseas colonies.

Savi di Terraferma (Ministers for War and the Mainland) They were responsible for military conduct along with the *Savi Grandi*.

Senato See *Consiglio dei Pregadi*.

Signoria The Doge, the Dogal Councillors (*Consiglieri ducali*), and the *Capi*, or Heads of the Forty, constituted what was called the *Signoria*; in a limited sense, they were the principal government authority.

In conclusion, it is important to mention that the actual government leaders of the *Serenissima*—the adjective commonly used by Venice when referring to itself, literally meaning the most serene—were the men holding the positions of Doge, *Consiglieri ducali* (Dogal Councillors), *Savi Grandi*, and the *Capi dei Dieci* (Chiefs of the Ten). The next most important group of officials was composed of the rest of the *Consiglio dei Dieci*, the *Savi Grandi*, the three *Capi* or Heads of the Forty, and the three *Avvogadori*.

Venetian Terms

This brief list of additional terms, which occasionally appear in the book, includes nongovernment organizations, place names, and other miscellaneous expressions.

Bacino of San Marco The body of water between the Piazzetta San Marco and the Lido into which the Grand Canal empties.

Compagnie delle calze Groups of Venetian nobility that established festive organizations. Each group distinguished itself by the fancy stockings or *calze* that they wore.

More Venete (*m.v.*) The Venetian calendar year began on March 1, and therefore the first two months of the conventional calendar maintained the date of the preceding year. For example: January 1579 *m.v.* = January 1580.

Rivoalto It was the largest of the original cluster of islands now called Venice. *Rivoalto*, meaning high bank, would later be named Rialto.

Miscellaneous Venetian terms **C**alle is a street or lane; **C**ampo indicates a city square that was originally unpaved; **F**ondamenta is a street along a canal, generally very wide; **M**erceria is a street with shops—the **M**ercerie was a series of streets connecting Rialto and San Marco; **R**amo is a secondary alley; **R**iva is a street flanking the water; **R**io is a canal; **R**io terra refers to a canal filled in to make a street; **R**uga is a shopping street; **S**alizzada is a paved alley.

Special Words

Some readers may take exception to the Latin words and terms that have been preserved in the present English edition of this book. It was decided to maintain these expressions in their original form not only because they represent an integral part of the numerous historical references presented by the author but also because it would be impossible to give a satisfactory definition to these words and their usage in each particular case. One example of this is the repeated use of the word *renovatio*. A simple translation as *renewal* or *renovation* would only serve as a superficial approximation of a term that the author has painstakingly defined in each specific context.

There are, moreover, a few expressions in Italian that have not been translated for similar reasons: *all'antica*, *alla romana*, and *alla veronese*. Although it is not possible to provide a single satisfactory meaning for each term, the basic significance can be expressed in the following manner: *based on ancient*, *Roman*, or *Veronese models*.

Finally, there are a few Italian words repeatedly used by the author that do not have English equivalents that capture the nuance of their meanings. The Italian word *mentalità* is one of these. Whereas the English word *mentality* denotes "a mode of thought," the basic meaning of *mentalità* is "a way of interpreting reality or of reasoning." Recent historiographical studies—for example, those of Jacques Le Goff mentioned by the author—may be examined for a further understanding of the use of this term. Another Italian word, *tecnica*, is also sometimes very difficult to translate, and only occasionally would the English word *technique* be appropriately used. More than just "the rules or methods of execution or application of any skilled activity"—the knowledge of which is generally acquired by training—*tecnica* also denotes "any human activity itself that employs practical or scientific skills." The principle used for this translation, both in this case and in other instances, has been to give the meaning that seems most appropriate in each specific context rather than retain the same word throughout.

Index

Cacciari, Massimo, xi

Caesar, Gaius Julius, 256n

Calabi, Donatello, xii, 163

Calí, Maria, 61, 224n

Calmo, Andrea, 82

Calvin, John, 65–66, 68, 226–227n

Camillo, Giulio, 61, 64, 136

Campagna, Girolamo, 270n

Campelli, Giacomo, 189

Canaletto (Antonio Canal), 28

Cantimori, Delio, ix, 59, 62

Capello, Pietro, 20, 209n

Capobianco, Zorzi, da Schio, 273n

Cappello, Antonio, 109

Cappello, Cristoforo, 109

Cappello, Vincenzo, 175, 274n

Carafa, Alfonso (cardinal), 115

Caravia, Alessandro, 9, 81–83, 86, 91, 231–232n

Cardano, Girolamo, 131

Carnesecchi, Pietro, 9, 69, 243n

Caroli, Pierre, 65

Carpaccio, Vittore, 13, 157

Carpan, Bartolomeo, 61

Carpan, brothers, 232n

Carpeggiani, Paolo, 146, 264n

Carugo, Adriano, 121

Cassiodorus, 1–2

Cassirer, Ernst, x, 198n

Castellione, Sebastiano, 77

Castiglione, Baldassare, 57, 125, 222n

Castriotto, Jacomo, 137

Cataneo, Pietro, 137

Catena, Pietro, 133–134, 244n, 256n

Cavendish, William, 195, 279n

Celestro, Giovanni, 6, 85–86

Celestro, Zuan (Zuane, Joanne), 84, 217n, 234n

Cervelli, Innocenzo, 17, 21

Cesariano, Cesare, 89

Charles V (emperor), 8, 115, 152, 202n, 231n

Chastel, André, 111

Cherea (Francesco Nobili), 149

Chiericati, Valerio, 254n

Ciapponi, Lucia, 36

Cicero, Marcus Tullius, 4, 105, 248n

Cicogna, Emmanuele Antonio, 270n

Cicogna, Pasquale (doge), 172, 179, 181–182

Ciriacono, Salvatore, 140

Citolini, Alessandro, 61, 62, 64, 66, 224n

Clavius (Christopher Clau), 131

Clement VII (pope), 3, 58, 242n

Clement VIII (pope), 177–178

Coccio, Francesco, 248n

Codussi, Mauro, 5, 13, 15, 28–30, 33–34, 38, 83–85, 105, 221n, 233n, 235n

Colocci, Angelo, 74

Colonna, Giovanni (cardinal), 209n

Commandino, Federico, 122, 133–134, 249n, 255n

Concina, Ennio, xii, 3, 109, 119, 164, 186, 191, 206n

Condulmer, Gabriele. *See* Eugene IV

Contarini, Alessandro, 246n

Contarini, Andriana, 252n

Contarini, Antonio, 24, 53, 55, 210n, 219n

Contarini, family, 186, 213n, 248n

Contarini, Federico, 167, 171, 173–174, 269n, 271n

Contarini, Francesco, 230n, 252n

Contarini, Gasparo, 52, 59–61, 70, 73–77, 82, 108–109, 179, 209n, 225–226n, 230n, 240n, 249n, 252n, 263n

Contarini, Giacomo, 183

Contarini, Giovanni Battista, 252n

Contarini, Hieronimo, q. Bertuccio, 22

Contarini, Jacopo, 121–122, 130–136, 167–169, 193–195, 251–253n, 255–256n

Contarini, Nicolò, 172, 179, 191, 193, 266n, 270–271n, 277n

Contarini, Paolo, 172

Contarini, Pier Francesco, 110, 246n

Contarini, Pietro (di Giovanni Alberto), 22, 31, 35, 36, 211n, 214–215n

Contarini, Pietro di Zuan (Giovan) Ruggero, 186, 213–214n

Contarini, Taddeo, 11, 22, 204n

Contarini, Vincenzo, 252n

Contarini, Zaccaria, 187, 261n

Contarini, Zuan Pietro, 185

Contile, Luca, 116–117, 119, 246n, 257n

Contin, Antonio, 163, 272n

Nádasdy, Tamás, 136
Naldi, Dionisio, 209n
Nani, Paolo, 109
Nardi, Jacopo, 248n
Natta, 122
Navagero, Bernardo, 110, 114, 121, 126, 154, 246n
Nicholas V (pope), 18, 108, 199n, 239n
Nicolò of Bologna, Fra, 23
Niero, Antonio, 18, 219n
Nietzsche, Friedrich, xi
Noal, Alvise, 87, 93
Novello, Crisogono, 27

Odoni, Andrea, 34
Olivato, Loredana, 61, 179
Origen of Alexandria, 61
Orsini, Nicolò di Pitigliano, 209n
Ovid (Publius Ovidius Naso), 257n

Pacioli, Luca, 26–27, 119, 121, 211n
Paciotto, Francesco, 243n
Páez de Castro, Juan, 231n
Pagan, Pietro, 116–117
Paleotti, Gabriele, 135, 255n
Paliari, Girolamo, 270n
Palladio, Andrea, 8–10, 42, 69, 95, 113–114, 122, 126–130, 135–137, 145, 147, 149, 156, 163, 167–168, 179–181, 183, 190, 195, 202n, 237n, 247n, 250–253n, 256–257n, 272n
Pallavicino, Pietro Sforza, 132, 253n
Palma, Jacopo, the Younger, 130
Palmieri, Matteo, 2
Palmio, Benedetto, 148
Pandoan, Giorgio, 148
Panofsky, Erwin, 11, 203n
Panormita (Antonio Beccadelli), 106
Paoletti, Pietro, 27, 88, 233n
Pappus, 118, 133
Paruta, Paolo, 126, 177, 246n
Patrizi, Francesco (of Siena), 104, 106–107, 112, 238n, 243–244n
Patrizi, Francesco, da Cherso, 115, 117, 135–136, 252n, 257n
Paul IV (pope), 71
Pausani, 268n
Pedrali, Giacomo, 55, 221n

Perenoto, Antonio (bishop), 244n
Persio, Antonio, 261n
Peruzzi, Baldassarre, 35, 37, 38–39, 68, 72, 111, 216n
Pesaro, family, 150
Petrarch, Francis, 158, 231n
Peuerbach, Georg, 131
Piana, Mario, xii
Piccinino, Jacopo, 106, 239n
Piccolomini, Alessandro, 118, 134, 254n
Piccolomini, Enea Silvio. See Pius II
Piccolomini, Fedel, 185, 274n
Pico, Giovanni Francesco, 59, 68, 119, 127, 222n, 250n
Pigafetta, Filippo, 133, 254n
Pillon, Pietro Antonio, da Lendinara, 185
Pinali, Gaetano, 251n, 273n
Pincus, Debra, 34
Pinelli, Gian Vincenzo, 121, 130, 132, 134–135, 144, 247n, 251–254n
Pio da Carpi, Alberto, 70, 74–76, 230n
Pisani, Alvise, 22, 113, 236n
Pisani, Elena, 245n
Pisani, family, 7, 113, 127, 246n
Pisani, Francesco (cardinal), 113, 143, 202n
Pisani, Giovanni, 113
Pisani, Paulo, 208n
Pittoni, Battista, 168
Pius II (pope) (Enea Silvio Piccolini), 106–108, 205n, 238–239n
Pius IV (pope), 115
Pius V (pope), 249
Plato, 15, 105, 108, 124, 134, 204n, 239n, 255n, 263n
Plautus, Titus Maccius, 148
Pliny (Gaius Plinius Secundus), 213n, 231n, 249n, 268n
Plutarch, 268n
Pocquet, Antoine, 65
Polani, Girolamo, 186, 189
Polani, Pietro, 186, 189
Pole, Reginald (cardinal), 61, 115, 243n
Polesan, Giacomo, 55
Poliziano (Agnolo Ambrogini), 20, 158, 213–214n
Pollani, Pietro, 40
Polluce, Guido, 268n

DATE DUE